VOID

Library of
Davidson College

ESSAYS ON LAND, WATER
AND THE LAW IN CALIFORNIA

This is a volume in the
Arno Press collection
THE DEVELOPMENT OF PUBLIC LAND LAW IN THE UNITED STATES

Advisory Editor
Stuart Bruchey

Research Associate
Eleanor Bruchey

Editorial Board
Marion Clawson
Paul W. Gates

*See last pages of this volume
for a complete list of titles.*

ESSAYS ON LAND, WATER AND THE LAW IN CALIFORNIA

Paul S. Taylor

With an Introduction by the Author
and a Foreword by Paul W. Gates

ARNO PRESS
A New York Times Company
New York • 1979

Editorial Supervision: ANDREA HICKS

Reprint Edition 1979 by Arno Press Inc.

Arrangement and compilation copyright 1979 by Arno Press Inc.

Foreword Copyright © 1979 by Paul W. Gates

Introduction Copyright 1979 by Paul Schuster Taylor

THE DEVELOPMENT OF PUBLIC LAND LAW
IN THE UNITED STATES
ISBN for complete set: 0-405-11363-3
See last pages of this volume for titles.

Manufactured in the United States of America

Library of Congress Cataloging in Publication Data

Taylor, Paul Schuster, 1895-
    Essays on land, water, and the law in California.

  (The Development of public land law in the United States)
    1. Reclamation of land--Law and legislation--California. 2. Water-rights--California. 3. California--Public lands. 4. Reclamation of land--Law and legislation--United States. I. Title. II. Series.
KFC803.T37   346'.794'04691   78-7083
ISBN 0-405-11394-3

ACKNOWLEDGMENTS

"Excess Land Law: Execution of a Public Policy" was reprinted by permission of The Yale Law Journal Company and Fred B. Rothman & Company from *The Yale Law Journal*, Vol. 64, pp. 477-514.

"Destruction of Federal Reclamation Policy?", Copyright 1957 by the Board of Trustees of the Leland Stanford Junior University, was reprinted by permission of *The Stanford Law Review* and Fred B. Rothman & Co.

"Excess Land Law on the Kern?", "The Excess Land Law: Pressure vs. Principle," "Excess Land Law: Calculated Circumvention," and "Mexican Migration and the 160-Acre Water Limitation," Copyright © 1958, 1959, 1964, 1975 by California Law Review, Inc., were reprinted by permission of *California Law Review* and Fred B. Rothman & Co.

"The Excess Land Law: Legislative Erosion of Public Policy" was reprinted by permission of *University of Colorado Law Review*.

"The Excess Land Law: A Note on Pressure vs. Principle in the Courts," "Central Valley Project," and "The 160-Acre Water Limitation and the Water Resources Commission" were reprinted by permission of the University of Utah, Copyright Holder.

"Excess Land Law: Secretary's Decision?" was reprinted by permission of the Regents of the University of California.

"Water, Land, and Environment, Imperial Valley" was reprinted by permission of *Natural Resources Journal*.

"Public Policy and the Shaping of Rural Society" was reprinted by permission of *South Dakota Law Review* and Dennis & Co., Inc.

"California Water Project" was reprinted by permission of *Ecology Law Quarterly*.

"Reclamation and Exploitation" was reprinted by permission of *Sierra Club Bulletin*.

Walter Goldschmidt's Baptism by Fire" was reprinted by permission of the Regents of the University of California.

"Whose Dam is Pine Flat?" was reprinted by permission of John W. Dodds.

CONTENTS

THE EXCESS LAND LAW: Execution of a Public Policy (Reprinted from *The Yale Law Journal*, Vol. 64, No. 4), New Haven, Ct., February, 1955

DESTRUCTION OF FEDERAL RECLAMATION POLICY? The Ivanhoe Case (Reprinted from *Stanford Law Review*, Vol. 10), Stanford, Ca., December, 1957

EXCESS LAND LAW ON THE KERN? (Reprinted from *California Law Review*, Vol. 46, No. 2), Berkeley, Ca., May, 1958

THE EXCESS LAND LAW: Legislative Erosion of Public Policy (Reprinted from *Rocky Mountain Law Review*, Vol. 30, No. 1), Boulder, Colorado, 1958

THE EXCESS LAND LAW: Pressure vs. Principle (Reprinted from *California Law Review*, Vol. 47), Berkeley, Ca., 1959

THE EXCESS LAND LAW: A Note on Pressure vs. Principle in the Courts (Reprinted from *Western Political Quarterly*, Vol. 12), Salt Lake City, Utah, 1959

EXCESS LAND LAW: Secretary's Decision? A Study in Administration of Federal-State Relations (Reprinted from *UCLA Law Review*, Vol. 9, No. 1), Los Angeles, Ca., January, 1962

EXCESS LAND LAW: Calculated Circumvention (Reprinted from *California Law Review*, Vol. 52), Berkeley, Ca., 1964

WATER, LAND, AND ENVIRONMENT, IMPERIAL VALLEY: Law Caught in the Winds of Politics (Reprinted from *Natural Resources Journal*, Vol. 13, No. 1), Albuquerque, N.M., January, 1973

MEXICAN MIGRATION AND THE 160-ACRE WATER LIMITATION (Reprinted from *California Law Review*, Vol. 63), Berkeley, Ca., 1975

PUBLIC POLICY AND THE SHAPING OF RURAL SOCIETY (Reprinted from *South Dakota Law Review*, Vol. 20), Vermillion, S.D., 1975

CALIFORNIA WATER PROJECT: Law and Politics (Reprinted from *Ecology Law Quarterly*, Vol. 5, No. 1), Berkeley, Ca., 1975

CENTRAL VALLEY PROJECT: Water and Land (Reprinted from *The Western Political Quarterly*, Vol. 2), Salt Lake City, Utah, 1949

THE 160-ACRE WATER LIMITATION AND THE WATER RESOURCES COMMISSION (Reprinted from *The Western Political Quarterly*, Vol. 3), Salt Lake City, Utah, 1950

WHOSE DAM IS PINE FLAT? (Reprinted from *The Pacific Spectator*, Vol. 8), 1954

RECLAMATION AND EXPLOITATION (Reprinted from *Sierra Club Bulletin*, Vol. 59), San Francisco, Ca., February, 1974

WALTER GOLDSCHMIDT'S BAPTISM BY FIRE: Central Valley Water Politics (Reprinted from *Anthropology UCLA*, Vol. 8), Los Angeles, Ca., 1976

FOREWORD

I have known Paul Taylor through an intermittent correspondence and a number of exciting meetings with him during the last 24 years, in which he has needled me to be more active in urging colleagues, associates and members of Congress to take a stand in behalf of the enforcement of the excess lands provision of the reclamation laws of the United States and alerted me to the corrupting influence of the utility, banking, real estate and water interests in California. But more, I have come to know the depth of his humanitarian feelings, his concern for the health of minorities and the underprivileged. The classic treatment of the devastating effects on workers in the southern cotton fields of the great depression of the thirties that led to the swift elimination of share-croppers and their desperate search for homes and jobs was presented in pictures and simple prose by Dorothea Lange and Paul Taylor in 1939 in *An American Exodus: A Record of Human Erosion in the Thirties*. Rarely have photographs and simple words so admirably documented a tragic story. It was the culmination of work Taylor had done on migratory labor and problems relating to minority groups that had been published between 1928-1934. His *Mexican Labor in the United States,* which has been called by a recent authority "an invaluable storehouse of information on ... Mexican migrant labor," and his *An American Frontier: Nueces County, Texas* led to his being called upon for surveys and studies by the Federal Emergency Relief Administration, the Social Security Board, the famous La Follette committee investigating *Violations of Free Speech and Rights of Labor*, the latter with special reference to California, and by the equally well-known and much quoted *Temporary National Economic Committee Investigation of Concentration of Economic Power*. Paul Taylor's ability to get to the heart of a question, to marshall the facts, and to draw conclusions clearly based on the most careful and detailed examination made him a most valuable public servant, very different from the conventional picture of the scholar removed from public issues and isolated in his ivory tower. The extent of his investigations is truly amazing. They carried him to Cuba, Haiti, India, Pakistan, Vietnam, the Philippines, Korea, Japan, Indonesia, Egypt, Iran, Mexico, Ecuador, Venezuela, Panama, Jamaica and Columbia, where he surveyed the impact of land, water and population problems on peoples of these developing countries. Not only was he rendering valuable services to these countries but he must have been enriching his teaching by sharing with his students at Berkeley many of his experiences.

Paul Taylor's testimony frequently given before congressional committees and his many contacts with people in related fields of endeavor made him a well-known and highly respected scholar and one not at all hesitant to advance his views even though they might not be favorably regarded by powerful interests in California. The tenacity with which he pursued his independent course, the courage he displayed, and the fervor of his convictions have been constantly demonstrated and deeply admired.

Along the way Paul Taylor became deeply disturbed by the efforts of large land and water owners in California, as well as in other western states, to prevent the enforcement of the 160-acre excess land limitation in the Federal reclamation laws. Where farmers' organizations like the Grange had stood strongly for the single family farm, owner-operated, and had believed with Liberty Hyde Bailey that agriculture was a way of life, some, like the American Farm Bureau, stressed only the business aspects of farming. In California the Farm Bureau was to line up with the reactionary forces fighting the battle of the great landowners against those favoring improvement in the lot of migratory workers. More immediately, they opposed the implementation of the excess lands provision and sought in every possible way to assure that federally provided water of the Central Valley Project should be available to owners of thousands of acres of rich land; thus giving them a rich gratuity at government expense and making a mockery of the principal purpose for which the Reclamation Act of 1902 had been adopted, viz., the creation of small family farms. With business interests—land, utility, banking and transportation—lined up with the Farm Bureau, and with leaders of both major parties abjectly following or afraid to give public support to the enforcement of the excess lands provision, there seemed at times little possibility that the advocates of the family farm could get government to reform. But Paul Taylor was not one to take this nullification of Federal law for the benefit of a small group of great landowners and corporations.

In 1949 his "Central Valley Project: Water and Land" was published in *The Western Political Quarterly*, in which he reviewed the history of irrigation in California and the West, showed how the Army Engineers had horned in on federal irrigation development in

California to the advantage of large land owners and described other efforts in Congress to break down the fundamental objective of the reclamation legislation. He followed this up with a second article in the same journal in 1959, in which he showed the various ways administrators within the Department of the Interior and the Bureau of Reclamation were permitting the breakdown of enforcement of the excess lands provision. Then followed closely reasoned articles in law journals with meaningful titles that are included in this volume. These illustrate well the struggle he and others working with and through him were carrying on in behalf of the enforcement of the law. These essays reveal a penetrating insight into complex legal and engineering problems and clearly show how powerful economic interests have succeeded in subverting and to a very considerable degree setting aside a carefully drafted policy that is still prescribed in the statute books. As an example of how well Paul Taylor succeeded in setting forth his analysis, the United States Supreme Court cited "Excess Land Law; Execution of a Public Policy" in its landmark 8-0 decision upholding the validity of the 160-acre limitation law (Ivanhoe vs. McCracken, 1958).

Meantime, Paul Taylor was working with representatives of organizations that believed that farming is something more than inputs and production: the Grange, the AFL-CIO, Veterans of Foreign Wars, the Catholic Rural Life Conference. These and other church groups tried to exert pressure on Congress, on the state legislature and on the news media in behalf of the enforcement of the excess lands provision. Time after time Paul Taylor marshalled support before Senate and House Committees and himself testified in detail about the breakdown of enforcement. His trenchant writings and his testimony laid bare the illegalities that had been permitted, but by the sixties he was fighting an enormously powerful combination of economic interests who were benefitting from the "Calculated Circumvention."

The election of Jimmy Carter as President and his appointment of Cecil D. Andrus as Secretary of the Interior has brought about a major change in the attitude of the Federal Goverment toward the 160-acre limitation of the Reclamation Act. There has also been an equally important change toward expending huge sums of money for projects of the Bureau of Reclamation and the Corps of Engineers under the guise of aiding irrigation or providing flood control but equally for the benefit of the construction industry, and which, if carried out, would involve enormous additional subsidies to agribusiness at public expense. It is useful to see in Taylor's articles how a measure that on its face was designed to make possible irrigation of land in small farms became a means by which great agribusiness organizations have expanded their ownership of land

and their political influence. It is too early to predict what the changes in policy will result in, but the move from bureaucratic domination of policy may well be regarded as a great step toward a better America.

Paul Taylor set an example for scholars to have the courage of their convictions, to delve deeply into major social and economic questions, to present their facts no matter how unpopular this may make them with self-serving politicians who play the game of greedy economic interests attempting to monopolize natural resources made valuable at public expense.

Ithaca, New York Paul W. Gates

INTRODUCTION

> Woe unto them that join house to house, that lay field to field, till there be no place, that they may be placed alone in the midst of the earth!
> Isaiah 5:8

> No right to the use of water for land in private ownership shall be sold for a tract exceeding 160 acres to any one landowner, and no such sale shall be made to any landowner unless he be a bona fide resident on such land, or occupant thereof residing in the neighborhood of said land.
> National Reclamation Act. 1902

> The (Central Valley) project was designed to benefit people, not land.
> United States Supreme Court. 1958

Search for a congenial or at least tolerable relation between man and land has gone on throughout recorded time, for that relation largely shapes the relationship of man to man. Societies can become homogeneous or polarized, depending mainly on whether landownership is distributed widely among the many, or concentrated in the hands of the few. Throughout time, wide distribution has brought stability, while sustained concentration has jeopardized the peace and fed the forces of revolt and revolution. Our twentieth century is no exception. On the contrary, it has witnessed the largest and most pervasive revolutions of all history in Europe, in Latin America, and in Asia.

America faced the issue as early as the third decade of the eighteenth century. The founders of Georgia, the thirteenth British colony on the Atlantic coast, rejected the large plantation system manned by negro labor, already predominant in neighboring Virginia and South Carolina. Within two decades, however, those men who wanted to become Georgia planters suceeded in terminating the original 500-acre limitation on size of landholding and its companion, the ban on Afrtican labor.

A century later Civil War split North against South, dividing the country roughly between resident working farmers and planters, either residents or absentees. Pointing to the plantation system's labor aspect in his Second Inaugural, President Abraham Lincoln said, "All knew that this interest was somehow the cause of the war." Taking advantage of the wartime absence from Washington of the southern planters' spokesmen, Congress passed and President Lincoln signed the Homestead Act into law in 1862. Thus, as pioneers moved westward across the Middle West, the nation made a clear choice in favor of actual settlers working their own land over planters.

Forty years later, in 1902, as landseekers moved farther and farther westward into arid and semiarid country, Theodore Roosevelt, another Republican president, signed the National Reclamation Act. Its purpose was to extend the homestead principles while bringing to each resident farmer the water needed on his land.

The papers reproduced in this collection are from a series on the operations of the National Reclamation Act. The earliest appeared in *Yale Law Journal* in 1955, and three years later was cited by the U.S. Supreme Court when unanimously upholding the Act's constitutionality. The last and most recent article appeared in 1976 in *Anthropology UCLA*. It traces the experiences from the forties to the seventies of a distinguished anthropologist who studied two contrasting California communities on the ground to document the impact of concentrated and distributed landownership, respectively.

My own concern with the Reclamation Act began in 1943, when invited to become consultant in the office of the Secretary of the Interior. Within a few months a drive began to exempt the Central Valley (California) Project from the excess land provisions of the law.

In March 1944, Congressman Alfred J. Elliott of Kern and Tulare counties where large landholdings are common, succeeded in about twenty minutes on the floor of the House and without previous hearings in attaching a rider to the Rivers and Harbors bill exempting Central Valley Project from the excess land law. Next, California's Senator Sheridan Downey, contrary to a plank in his Democratic Party platform, undertook to persuade the Senate to approve the exemption. In due course he played a leading role in hearings on the exemption held in both Washington and California. In spite of aroused labor, farmer and church social action groups, he was almost successful. Finally Senator Robert M. LaFollette, Jr., of Wisconsin, blocked him, promising to deliver a three-hour speech against Senator Downey if he should bring the bill to the floor of the Senate. Faced with that threat the entire "gravy train" Rivers and Harbors bill to which the exemption was attached failed of to pass without coming to a vote. Shortly after the opening of the next session the bill passed, minus the rider.

In the 80th Congress in 1947 Senator Downey resumed his battle. Seeking to mobilize more support, the bill was enlarged to exempt three projects, one each in California, Colorado and Texas. The Senate Committee took over 1300 pages of testimony. A book was printed bearing Senator Downey's name entitled "They Would Rule The Valley," but the bill died in Committee.

As a further tactic, opponents of the law inserted a provision in an appropriations bill requiring that the Commissioner of Reclamation and his Regional Directors be engineers. This cut Commissioner Michael Straus and Regional Director Richard L. Boke from the payroll. Both men had stood fast for preservation of the law, but neither was an engineer. The reelection of President Harry Truman in 1948 resulted in restoration of the two men to the payroll and for the time being brought the drive for exemption to a standstill.

The political response in California was marked. Senator Downey did not even run for renomination by his party in 1950. Instead, he accepted defeat in advance at the hands of Congresswoman Helen Gahagan Douglas, who led the opposition to him on the excess land issue. She won the Democratic nomination, but lost the final election to Republican Congressman Richard Nixon, who quietly let it be known in Imperial Valley where landholdings were large, that he was against the excess land law. The outbreak of war in Korea overshadowed reclamation as an issue in the final election.

The election of Dwight Eisenhower in 1952 ended for a long time the presidential support of the excess land law given it during the administrations of FDR and Harry Truman. Sensing the change, I terminated my consultantship in the Bureau of Reclamation, changing my position from one on the inside looking out, to one on the outside looking in. So to express my concerns I turned to writing articles, mostly in law journals, seeking at critical junctures to expose the continuing threat to the excess land law and to make visible the need for public support and the place to make it effective.

The present book is not a single, integrated historical treatise on reclamation law. Instead, it is a series of thirteen articles spread over twenty-two years, each focused on a particular attack or tactic threatening the law at the time. This has some disadvantage from necessary repetition of the law's history and background. On the other hand, it has the advantage of presenting a series of battlegrounds, each written at a time of white heat and designed to reveal the situation as under a magnifying glass.

The history of the excess land law in the political arena can be viewed as a case study of the processes by which public policy may be established, altered, or destroyed as it comes under scrutiny in each of the three branches of our government, viz., legislative, executive, and judicial. Unless all three branches support the law in which policy is embodied, the policy can die.

The executive branch of the government has the duty to carry out the policy enacted into law by the executive branch. This it frequently has not done. Reclamation law, for example, requires that the receiver of water shall be a "bona fide resident" on the land irrigated or in the neighborhood. The Bureau of Reclamation ceased enforcement of residency by rulings made in 1916 and 1917. Congress apparently was not of the same mind. In 1917 it acted as if the law was still effective by suspending the unenforced law for the duration of World War I. This it repeated in 1940 to cover World War II then in early prospect. Again in 1947 Senators from three states led by Senator Downey tried to wipe the unenforced residence requirement from the statute books. Thus Congress acted as if residency were a valid law throughout; the executive branch as if it were not.

The judicial branch has moved very slowly to uphold the excess land provision of reclamation law. For one thing, the executive branch has been slow to bring charges of nonenforcement before the courts. In 1944, for example, Congress applied reclamation law to irrigation water from Army-built dams. Delivery of water to Tulare Lake lands began in 1954 with extensive nonobservance of the excess land law. Not until 1977, thirty-three years after passage of the law and twenty-three years after beginning delivery of water, did the case initiated by the government receive the Supreme Court's final word that the excess land does apply to Army-built dams. It did this by letting stand an earlier decision to the same effect by the Ninth Circuit Court of Appeals. The Circuit Court, in arriving at its conclusion cited six of the articles in the present collection.

The story of man's relation to land is already long, but one can be sure that it is not ended.

Paul Schuster Taylor

THE EXCESS LAND LAW

Execution of a Public Policy

THE YALE LAW JOURNAL

VOLUME 64   FEBRUARY, 1955   NUMBER 4

THE EXCESS LAND LAW: EXECUTION OF A PUBLIC POLICY

PAUL S. TAYLOR[†]

I

LAND, WATER, LANGUAGE

"Monopoly of land need not be feared. The question for legislators to solve is to devise some practical means by which water rights may be distributed among individual farmers and water monopolies prevented."

—Major J. W. Powell [1]

A GREAT confusion pervades discussion of the excess land law and threatens disaster to public policy regarding disposing of public domain. Congress has declared this policy to be the widespread distribution of benefits, and the curbing of monopoly and speculation, whether the domain is in form of land, water, or both. The excess land provision of the National Reclamation Act of 1902 is a means of attaining these ends in the public disposal of water.

General and legal acceptance have joined to confer authority upon either of two descriptive titles—"excess land law" or "160-acre limitation"—both of them equally deceptive. The law is not really a *land* law, and it places no limitation whatsoever upon the *acreage* a man may own. The restraint is neither upon acreage of land nor upon water, but upon the *individual*. No individual is entitled to receive more than an equitable share of the water distributed under reclamation law. The maximum *individual* share is set at an amount of water necessary to irrigate 160 acres of land.

Among the sources of this confusion of language, two are "accidents"—one physical, the other historical. The first is the unequal geographical distribution of water. Water and land are two halves of a productive whole everywhere. East of the one hundredth meridian nature has joined them, and any description or analysis of agricultural land can assume water. West of the hundredth meridian water and land are separate. Man-made works—reservoirs and canals—are required to join them. Water and land, therefore, must be treated separately, whether as physical entities, objects of private ownership, or the concern of public policy. Water cannot be assumed as the natural, inevitable

---

[†]Professor of Economics, University of California; consultant to the Office of the Secretary of the Interior and the Bureau of Reclamation successively between 1943 and 1952. Beverly Starika assisted in preparation of this paper. On October 26, 1954, the editors of the YALE LAW JOURNAL sent a copy of this article as originally drafted to Secretary of the Interior Douglas McKay.

1. POWELL, REPORT ON THE LANDS OF THE ARID REGION OF THE UNITED STATES 41 (2d ed. 1879).

and permanent adjunct of land. *Land* ownership does not equal *water* ownership west of the hundredth meridian.

The second source of confusion is an historical accident. Policy was debated and formulated in the nineteenth century when settlement was still east of the hundredth meridian, and water was not a concern. The great legislative landmarks in the nation's policy favoring actual settlers are land laws—the Preemption Act of 1841 [2] and the Homestead Act of 1862.[3] After these acts were passed, settlement crossed the hundredth meridian, and water became the primary concern. General policy was not altered with the movement to the arid belt, but the techniques and devices for implementing it had to change. The artificial union of land and water required more complex thought and language than was necessary where land and water are joined naturally. The means of applying public policy to water had to be declared separately, spelled out in new terms. Chief among the new techniques was the excess land law.

It took something of a mental wrench to turn American lawmakers and administrators from land policy to water policy. The natural tendency was to carry over the language of earlier land problems to the more complex problems of water. A result of this inertia has been confusion in thought as well as in language west of the hundredth meridian, where thinking in terms of land policy overemphasizes land and underemphasizes water. Some persons have found it advantageous to exploit the confusion. Those who achieved what Major Powell called "monopoly of land" utilize this habit of thinking in terms of *land* policy to confuse the public, to suggest that private landowners have a moral claim to water in proportion to their landholdings whatever their size, and to defeat the efforts of legislators who seek equitable distribution of water among individuals. Even administrators do not find it easy to remember that the essential question is not, who owns the land, but who gets the water.

The fact of importance above all others in federal reclamation is that the landowner calls upon the government to provide him with water. It is for Congress representing the general interest, and not for the landowner, to say upon what terms, in what amount, and in accord with what policy the public will supply water. This is a first principle inherent in a relationship between the public that gives and an individual who receives. The concern of the law is to distribute water equitably among individual landowners, not—except below 160 acres—in proportion to their holdings of land. This principle is accepted without question by most landholders seeking water under reclamation law; the few who object usually are holders of excess land.[4]

The Issue

"If we had a right to dispose of the land—not absolute but on condition that certain requisites are complied with, doing that in the interest of the democracy as a whole, we have a right to dispose of the land with a proviso

---

2. 5 Stat. 453 (1841).
3. 12 Stat. 392 (1862).
4. *I.e.*, those whose holdings exceed 160 acres.

as to the use of the water running over it, designed to secure that use for the people as a whole and to prevent it from ever being absorbed by a small monopoly."

—Theodore Roosevelt [5]

On May 12, 1903, President Theodore Roosevelt addressed the students of Stanford University on conservation. After noting that the early land laws had been "twisted into an improper use, so that . . . they tend to create a class of men who . . . obtain large tracts of soil for speculative purposes, or to rent out to others," he charged the students to take leadership in "securing the right use of the waters, and of seeing to it that our land policy is not twisted from its original purpose, but is perpetuated . . . to turn the public domain into farms each to be the property of the man who actually tills it and makes his home on it."[6] He put his finger upon the crucial weakness, saying that "good laws alone will not secure good administration," and adding, two days later in San Francisco, that "no public man worth his salt will be other than glad to be held accountable" by private citizens.[7]

Less than a year earlier President Roosevelt had signed the National Reclamation Bill to accomplish the very objectives he described at Stanford. "If it was not for the national irrigation act, we would be about past the time when Uncle Sam could give every man a farm."[8] Under that law the federal government undertook to prepare arid lands for settlement by constructing reservoirs and canals. In order to bring the price within reach of settlers it advanced the cost of construction free of interest, the capital alone to be repaid, and that only after a period of years. Public lands so irrigated were to be distributed in small units to actual settlers under the homestead laws, and private lands were to receive water in limited quantities. The urge was strong to repair the damages of "laws twisted into an improper use," to curb land monopoly, and to favor the homemakers. The chief provisions of the law —construction by public enterprise, waiver of interest, settlement on public land under the homestead laws, limitation of private landowners' right to water—singly and in combination had the same purpose. Of all these devices the "excess land law," or "acreage limitation," has become the most famous— mainly because of the strenuous, protracted, and pervasive efforts by the large landholders it was designed to control, to overthrow and escape it.

Today, fifty years after President Theodore Roosevelt enunicated the policy of the excess land law during his visit to California, Secretary Douglas McKay has brought that policy to the edge of destruction in administering reclamation law on the Kings River and Tulare Lake. Secretary McKay has left excess landholders the choice, either to dispose of their excess holdings in accordance

---

5. Roosevelt, *Conservation*, 7 TRANSACTIONS OF THE COMMONWEALTH CLUB OF CALIFORNIA 107 (1912).
6. CALIFORNIA ADDRESSES BY PRESIDENT ROOSEVELT 72, 73 (1903).
7. *Id.* at 121.
8. *Id.* at 72.

with the law, or to obtain relief from the excess land law at once and permanently, by prepaying construction charges of Pine Flat dam in a lump sum. The Secretary opened the second alternative when he authorized the Bureau of Reclamation on November 9, 1953, to negotiate the Kings River and Tulare Lake Project on the basis that "the repayment contract will provide for repayment of the irrigation allocation in 40 years without interest, with the option on the part of the water users organizations to make a lump sum payment in advance and that the excess land laws become inoperative upon payment in full of the $14,250,000."[9]

If the excess landholders should elect to make a lump-sum payment, and the Secretary should hold to his present view, then the opportunity for homemaking which President Roosevelt expected to flow from the law will shrivel. Plainly, the Secretary's action raises fundamental questions of policy and principle. Can he be right, that the reclamation law places the opportunity for the "makers of homes" at the mercy of the preferences, financial capacity, and ultimate decision of private excess landholders? Or did Congress assert its preference for the homemaker over the excess landholder? Is the purpose of reclamation law fulfilled when the government has recouped its financial outlay in construction in the same manner as a private construction contractor? Or does public policy transcend the fiscal arrangement between government and water user?

The Secretary's action involves not only principle, but material stakes as well. Bringing water to land increases its value substantially. In the Tulare Lake area, nine excess landholders owned 109,019 acres in 1947, the smallest of these holdings being 7,209 acres and the largest 19,317 acres.[10] The Tulare Lake Basin Water Storage District, consisting of 300 square miles with scarcely a home upon it, is held ninety percent "in excess"—in 1947 twenty-five corporations owned nearly fifty-five percent of the area, 102 individuals held another thirty-five percent and the remaining ten percent was owned by 635 individuals in tracts under 160 acres."[11] Thus, the Secretary has

---

9. Letter from Secretary of the Interior Douglas McKay to C.J. Haggerty, Secretary of the California State Federation of Labor, dated March 2, 1954 [hereinafter cited as McKay-Haggerty Letter]. Copies of all letters and memoranda cited herein are on file in the University of California Library. See also *Kings River Questions Answered*, Western Water News, July 1954, pp. 1-2.
Apparently directors of Kings River Conservation District signed a contract in November 1954, allowing water users "to escape" the excess land law, "subject to approval by the interior department." Sacramento Bee, Nov. 19, 1954, p. 2, col. 8. See also San Francisco Chronicle, Nov. 9, 1954, p. 8, cols. 5-7.

10. DOWNEY, THEY WOULD RULE THE VALLEY 164 (1947), presenting statistics recast from testimony of Paul H. Johnstone, in *Hearings before Subcommittee of the Senate Committee on Public Lands on S. 912*, 80th Cong., 1st Sess. 864 (1947). Whether these nine holdings lie entirely within the Tulare Lake Basin Water Storage District is not stated.

11. Letter from Commissioner of Reclamation Michael W. Straus to Senator Paul H. Douglas, dated Feb. 2, 1949, p. 2.

left to a few excess landholders the power to decide whether between 900 and 1,000 "makers of homes" will be able to obtain quarter-section farms.[12]

The Secretary has stated that he feels "constrained to follow" the administrative steps he authorized for Kings River and Tulare Lake Project "after very thorough consideration."[13] But the history of excess land law will show that he has misinterpreted it and that the accumulated effect of his erroneous interpretation, plus his own decision to permit prepayment, is the complete subversion of the law.

ENACTMENT

> *"The greatest interest in the Reclamation Act centers around the fact that it is clearly a conscious and salutary step in the direction of a national policy of conservation. It was passed soon after the conservation principles were first prominently expounded, and embodies unmistakeably the essence of those principles as applied to the use of water on the western arid lands. The purpose of the act is broad and fundamental, providing for the use of natural resources, a wide diffusion in ownership, and in consequence an opportunity to a large number of people."*
> —Benjamin Horace Hibbard [14]

Passage of the National Reclamation Act in 1902 was the culmination of long years of study and a decade or more of popular education and agitation. Organized efforts of citizens to inaugurate a plan for irrigating the arid lands of the West had been launched in 1891 when the first Irrigation Congress met in Salt Lake City.[15] A series of annual congresses had followed in various cities, including one as far east as Chicago in 1900. By 1902 a solid western bipartisan congressional bloc known as the Committee of Seventeen had been formed to promote reclamation. A new President of the United States, the first to know the needs of the arid West personally, had entered office and was giving the movement support. Congressional committees had been at work, and on February 6th of that year, a co-sponsor, Senator Hansbrough of North Dakota, introduced the reclamation bill in the Senate: "Mr. President, the purpose of this measure is to assist in providing homes for the rapidly increasing population of the country."[16]

---

12. Pine Flat dam alone fails to provide sufficient dependable irrigation water for family farms in the Tulare Lake Basin Water Storage District, and sufficient "flood control" for a portion of the Tulare Lake area. But other projects, either in progress or planned, can remedy both situations, making the area suitable for family farms. See, *e.g.*, S. Doc. No. 113, 81st Cong., 1st Sess. 132 (1949); CALIF. DEP'T PUB. WORKS, DIV. WATER RES., SAN JOAQUIN RIVER BASIN, 1931, Bull. No. 29, pp. 483, 496 (1934).

13. McKay-Haggerty Letter.

14. HIBBARD, A HISTORY OF THE PUBLIC LAND POLICIES 443 (1924).

15. See OFFICIAL REPORT OF THE IRRIGATION CONGRESS (1891). See also Taylor, *Central Valley Project: Water and Land*, 2 WESTERN POL. Q. 238 (1949), and *The 160-Acre Water Limitation and the Water Resources Commission*, 3 WESTERN POL. Q. 435-50 (1950).

16. 35 CONG. REC. 1383 (1902).

The bill was in the hands of a generation of men thoroughly familiar with the rapid agglomeration of western landholdings during the nineteenth century under defective statutes and loose administration by the General Land Office. In 1885, its Commissioner, William A. J. Sparks, lent his official voice to those of numerous others, before and since, that have told the story:

> "I found that the magnificent estate of the nation in its public lands had been to a wide extent wasted under defective and improvident laws and through a laxity of public administration astonishing in a business sense if not culpable in recklessness of official responsibility. [T]he land department has been very largely conducted to the advantage of speculation and monopoly, private and corporate, rather than in the public interest .... It seems that the prevailing idea running through this office and those subordinate to it was that the government had no distinctive rights to be considered and no special interests to protect .... I am satisfied that thousands of claims without foundation in law or equity, involving millions of acres of public land, have been annually passed to patent upon the single proposition that nobody but the government had any *adverse* interest."[17]

Paul Wallace Gates has set down the historian's corroborating verdict on the fate of the Homestead Act of 1862:

> "The land reformers reckoned too lightly ... with the astuteness of the speculators who in the past had either succeeded in emasculating laws inimical to their interests or had actually flouted such laws in the very faces of the officials appointed to administer them .... The administration of the law, both in Washington and in the field, was frequently in the hands of persons unsympathetic to its principle, and Western interests, though lauding the act, were ever ready to pervert it."[18]

From the first Irrigation Congress until after passage of the Act of 1902, the proceedings were punctuated with references to land monopoly from the nineteenth century back to the fall of Rome and the dangers of permitting monopoly of either water or land in the arid West. As far as the record shows, no one disagreed with this thesis. Many gave it vocal support. At the very first Irrigation Congress at Salt Lake City, a warning against land monopoly was combined with an appeal for irrigation: "The tendency of the great West ... is the accumulation of vast estates in land. The object of good government is to stop this in so far as it can and to give ... the poor man a chance to own ten, twenty, forty, sixty or a hundred acres if it is in his power to cultivate it ...."[19]

The proceedings of the irrigation congress for the decade disclose repetitious insistence, explicitly as well as implicitly, that preventive measures against water monopoly must be effective *permanently*. Thus Delegate Blowers of

---

17. ANN. REP. COMM'R GEN. LAND OFFICE 3-4 (1885) (emphasis in original).
18. Gates, *The Homestead Law in an Incongruous Land System*, 41 AM. HIST. REV., 655-56 (1936).
19. Statement of Morris Estee (Calif.), OFFICIAL REPORT OF THE IRRIGATION CONGRESS 26 (1891).

California told the 1893 Irrigation Congress, "I am not working for the purpose of keeping this in the possession of any one corporation, or any one people. I want the whole people, from now on—from generation to generation—to own that water—own that power."[20] Col. Hinton of New York said at the same congress: "we want to make that water *forever* what it is in law, in jurisprudence, in history . . . the public property of the people, to be . . . transferred, *under proper regulations*, to 'beneficial uses' for the people who own the land."[21] And a year later Governor Waite of Colorado expressed his doubt that the provisions of the homestead law could preserve the lands from monopoly and suggested that ultimate title be retained in the nation or state.[22] The same type of permanently effective legal measures was advocated to prevent monopoly of grass. George H. Maxwell, the "Father of Reclamation," received applause from the Irrigation Congress of 1896 when he said that arid pasture lands for sheep "should be kept *forever* as the common heritage of the people, never to be sold but to be leased only to actual settlers living upon the adjoining farms . . . ."[23]

Delegates at the last Irrigation Congress prior to passage of the National Reclamation Act regarded past land legislation as a guide to what ought to be avoided and sought to find fresh measures offering greater prospect of permanent effectiveness. Frederick H. Newell, later chief of the Reclamation Service, stressed the need for new methods: "it is impossible to trust to speculative enterprise, because of the fact that profits can not be made in the construction of a work unless the population becomes tenants of a great land-owning monopoly."[24] A delegate from Montana voiced fears that after the Government had borne all the expenses of construction, the water would inure to the profit of a few. He recommended a resolution that water conserved by the Government should "*always and forever* be under the control and distribution of the United States Government."[25] To quiet these fears, George H. Maxwell explained that the original resolution of the congress secured the end desired by the delegate from Montana in a different way:

> "[The resolution provides that] the water of all streams should *forever remain subject to public control*, and the right to the use of water for irrigation should *inhere in the land* irrigated. That means, no man can own the right for speculative purposes, and beneficial use should be the

---

20. OFFICIAL REPORT OF THE INTERNATIONAL IRRIGATION CONGRESS 27 (1893).
21. *Id.* at 83 (emphasis added).
22. OFFICIAL PROCEEDINGS OF 3RD NATIONAL IRRIGATION CONGRESS 11 (1894). Occasionally difference of opinion was expressed over whether 40 acres, say, or 160 acres was the proper size tract to be permitted. Senator Boyd of Colorado was virtually unique in expressing the view that with farm machinery a tract of three or four hundred acres was reasonable. *Id.* at 70.
23. OFFICIAL REPORT OF 5TH NATIONAL IRRIGATION CONGRESS 41 (1896) (emphasis added).
24. PROCEEDINGS OF 9TH ANNUAL SESSION OF NATIONAL IRRIGATION CONGRESS 230 (1900). See also statement of Delegate Newlands, *id.* at 116.
25. *Id.* at 303-04 (emphasis added).

basis and measure—that means to the extent you use the water beneficially, is all that you can have, and the limit to the right.

"Now there you have the fundamental principle upon which you can build irrigation institutions in these western states that will *endure as long as the human race occupies* them and *water monopoly will be an impossibility* . . . . I do not want anybody to go away from this congress with the idea that this subject has not been considered *and the solution of it found.*"[26]

The sponsors of the reclamation bill in the fifty-seventh Congress adhered closely to the objectives described in the proceedings of the irrigation congress during the prior decade. They presented their measure as one drawn with unusual care to prevent monopoly of water on reclaimed public lands and to break up existing monopoly on private land by denying water to it. Their look was a long one, to the past and to the future. Their goal was an enduring solution to an age-old problem of concentrated holdings, not a quick thrust at a current evil. And they believed they had found the solution: "It is a step in advance of any legislation we have ever had in guarding *against the possibility of* speculative landholdings and in providing for small farms and homes on the public land, while it will also compel the division into small holdings of any large areas . . . in private ownership which may be irrigated under its provisions."[27] Congressman Newlands said, "Lord Macauley said we never would experience the test of our institutions until our public domain was exhausted and an increased population engaged in a contest for the ownership of land. That will be the test *of the future*, and the very purpose of this bill is *to guard against land monopoly and to hold* this land in small tracts . . . to give to each man only the amount of land that will be necessary for the support of a family . . . ."[28]

The draftsmen of the reclamation bill employed at least five distinctive devices aimed at prevention of monopoly. First was the use of public enterprise to supplement private enterprise in irrigation development. While showing

---

26. *Id.* at 304 (emphasis added). In laying this cornerstone of anti-monopoly policy, Maxwell wanted to avoid federal interference with vested water rights under state law. His language was followed closely in § 8 of the Act of 1902, 32 STAT. 390, as amended 43 U.S.C. § 372 (1952), which forbids federal interference with vested water rights, and makes the right to water acquired under the act "appurtenant to the land irrigated." In 1901, the well-known anti-monopolist Congressman Newlands introduced a bill in Congress providing "That the right to the use of water shall be perpetually appurtenant to the land irrigated . . . ." SMYTHE, THE CONQUEST OF ARID AMERICA 344 (rev. ed. 1905). It is indeed strange that a few years later Will R. King, Counsel of the new Reclamation Service, seized upon the device of making water rights appurtenant to the land as an authorization for weakening the excess land provision to the point of its virtual destruction. See text at notes 74-80 *infra*.

27. Congressman Frank Mondell (Wyo.), 35 CONG. REC. 6677 (1902) (emphasis added). To the same effect with a challenge to any one to draft a bill providing more effective protection against monopolization, see statements of Senator W.A. Clark (Wyo.), *id.* at 2222-23, 2224.

28. *Id.* at 6734 (emphasis added).

energy in completing less costly projects, private enterprise had exhibited a reluctance to undertake the larger ones. The sponsors of the bill might have suggested giving large blocks of public land to corporations, enabling them to recoup the cost of constructing irrigation works by lease or sale of the land. Congress had used that method to get railroads built, but was not prepared to repeat it to promote irrigation. The House Committee on the reclamation bill rejected the use of land grants specifically because the sacrifice of "our time-honored policy of inviting and encouraging small individual land holdings" was too "stupendous a price" for irrigation development.[29] Instead public enterprise was to be financed by a reclamation fund consisting of revenues from the sale of public lands in the western states.[30] This fund was to recover project construction costs from the benefiting water users in annual installments, not exceeding ten, without interest.[31] In this way the fund would revolve and provide continually for new projects.

A second measure to prevent monopolization and assure occupation of irrigated lands by actual settlers was a ban on the commutation provisions of the homestead law when applied to reclamation projects.[32] The commutation privilege offered a cash alternative to the requirement of personal inhabitancy of a claim. In practice it resulted in the barter of public policy favoring actual settlers for the monopolists' ready cash. Congress, fully aware of this, forbade commutation on reclamation projects in 1902.[33]

As a third step toward encouragement of settlers and discouragement of speculators and monopolists, the sponsors of reclamation stiffened the inhabitancy requirements of the earlier homestead law. They prescribed that an entryman must be either a "bona fide resident on such land, or occupant thereof residing in the neighborhood . . ." and must reclaim for agricultural purposes

---

29. H.R. REP. No. 794, 57th Cong., 1st Sess. 3 (1902).

30. Section 1, Act of June 17, 1902, 32 STAT. 388, as amended, 43 U.S.C. § 391 (1952).

31. Section 4, 32 STAT. 389 (1902), 43 U.S.C. § 419 (1952). The longer the repayment period, of course, the greater the sudsidy to the water user. The original 10-year period has been extended. Assuming an interest rate of 3% and a 10-year development period in which no payments are made, a 40-year interest-free repayment period represents a 57% subsidy, and a 50-year period 62%. ACREAGE LIMITATION IN THE CENTRAL VALLEY, A REPORT ON PROBLEM 19, CENTRAL VALLEY PROJECT STUDIES 29 (Sept. 25, 1944).

32. Section 3, 32 STAT. 388 (1902), as amended, 43 U.S.C. §§ 416, 432, 434 (1952). George H. Maxwell had proposed abolition of the commutation privilege on *all* public lands to the eleventh Irrigation Congress in 1903. OFFICIAL PROCEEDINGS OF 11TH NATIONAL IRRIGATION CONGRESS 77 (1904). The repeal of the commutation clause had been recommended by the General Land Office as early as 1883. ANN. REP. COMM'R GEN. LAND OFFICE 7 (1883). See also Gates, *The Homestead Law in an Incongruous Land System*, 41 AM. HIST. REV. 655, 656 (1936).

33. Secretary McKay's offer to accept cash prepayment on Kings River and Tulare Lake Project resembles commutation closely, including its devastating effect on antimonopoly policy.

at least one-half of the total irrigable area of the entry.[34] Furthermore, their bill authorized the Secretary of the Interior to lower the maximum area per entry to the acreage "reasonably required for the support of a family . . ."[35] They recognized that the traditional quarter-section granted in the humid belt was often too large for a family farm on irrigated land.

The sponsors' fourth anti-monopoly and anti-speculation provision was that water rights shall be "appurtenant to the land irrigated and beneficial use shall be the basis, the measure, and the limit of the right."[36] Early irrigationists had been greatly dissatisfied with dependence on others in control of their water supply, and regarded tying water and land together in common ownership as among the surest of anti-monopoly devices.[37]

The sponsors' fifth measure against monopoly, the one that has become most famous of all, was the "excess land" provision. It prescribed that "no right to the use of water for land in private ownership shall be sold for a tract exceeding 160 acres to any one landowner . . . and no such right shall permanently attach until all payments therefor are made."[38] This law neither confiscates land nor limits the amount of land an individual may own. It merely places a limit on the amount of land owned by any *individual* which may receive *water* from a federal reclamation project. The principle upon which it rests is that no individual should obtain more public water than his equitable share. It is unfortunate that the complexity of language required to translate this simple principle into the specifics of acre-feet of water, land and individuals owning land, invites unintentional confusion and facilitates the spread of misconceptions by special interests.

---

34. Section 5, 32 STAT. 389 (1902), 43 U.S.C. §§ 381, 392, 431, 439, 476 (1952).
35. Section 4, 32 STAT. 389 (1902), 43 U.S.C. § 419 (1952).
36. Section 8, 32 STAT. 390 (1902), 43 U.S.C. § 372 (1952).
37. George H. Maxwell told the Irrigation Congress in 1900: "It simply means that water shall not be a mere personal commodity to be bought or sold like milk or beer." PROCEEDINGS OF 9TH ANNUAL SESSION OF NATIONAL IRRIGATION CONGRESS 99 (1900). He presented his thesis to the Irrigation Congress again in 1903 saying, "Speculation and monopoly in these lands *or in the water* must be rigidly guarded against. The irrigated lands must be subdivided into small farms. The ownership of land and water must be united. Speculation in water as a commodity must be made impossible. Floating water rights must be done away with and beneficial use must be the limit of all rights to water." OFFICIAL PROCEEDINGS OF 11TH NATIONAL IRRIGATION CONGRESS 78 (1904) (emphasis added).
38. Section 5, 32 STAT. 389 (1902), 43 U.S.C. §§ 381, 392, 431, 439, 476 (1952). Misconceptions as to the true nature of this law are so pervasive and persistently repeated that a regional counsel of the Bureau of Reclamation in Sacramento made this unofficial clarification: "All three terms ['160-acre limitation,' 'acreage limitation,' 'excess-land limitation'] are unrealistic in that they seem to imply that the law has said something about how much land one may *own*. The limitation neither legally nor factually is one on the ownership of land—it rather is one on the amount of the owned land which may *receive water from a federal reclamation project.*" Graham, *The Central Valley Project: Resource Development of a Natural Basin*, 38 CALIF. L. REV. 588, 604 (1950) (emphasis in original). The author finds it difficult, as does Graham, to use precise descriptive language each time he refers to the excess land limitation.

The bill passed both houses of Congress after much debate, without amendment. The only opposition was in the House, where the bill carried by 146 to 55.[39]

Reclamation law, however, is more than the single enactment of 1902 and in order to test the validity of Secretary McKay's present interpretation of the excess land law, it is necessary to examine two of the early legislative additions to the original Act. The first relevant modification was the Warren Act of 1911.[40] By enlarging the scope of the excess land law, it furnishes additional evidence of the intention of Congress to erect an enduring barrier against water monopoly. In 1902 Congress had applied the excess land law to "new" water developed by a federal reclamation project. The Warren Act expanded the provision to cover water already in private ownership when "impounded, stored or carried" by federal reclamation works.

Congress made a second important addition to the excess land law with the Act of August 9, 1912. Whether this amendment is to stand as a strong reaffirmation of what the original sponsors of reclamation thought they were doing to prevent monopoly permanently, or whether it is to be the vehicle for monopolization depends largely on whether the Secretary of the Interior adheres to his present interpretation of the proviso in section 3 of that act. It reads as follows:

> "*Provided*, That no person shall at any one time or in any manner . . . acquire, own, or hold irrigable land for which entry or water right application shall have been made . . . before final payment in full of all installments of building and betterment charges shall have been made on account of such land in excess of one farm unit as fixed by the Secretary of the Interior, as the limit of area per entry of public land or per single ownership of private land for which a water right may be purchased respectively, *nor in any case in excess of one hundred and sixty acres*, nor shall water be furnished . . . nor a water right sold or recognized for such excess; but any such excess land acquired at any time in good faith by descent, by will, or by foreclosure of any lien may be held for two years and no longer after its acquisition; and every excess holding prohibited as aforesaid shall be forfeited to the United States . . . and this proviso shall be recited in every patent and water-right certificate issued by the United States under the provisions of this act."[41]

The italicized phrase has been the center of controversy over the interpretation of this proviso. Is it overriding, so that in no case whatsoever shall a person "acquire, own, or hold irrigable land" in excess of 160 acres? Or does it modify only the clause beginning with "before," so that in no case shall a person own in excess of 160 acres of irrigable land "before final payment in full of all installments" of building charges for that excess? Because of this controversy and because the latter interpretation is the basis of Secretary

---

39. 35 Cong. Rec. 6778. Eighteen answered "present," 132 not voting.
40. Act of Feb. 21, 1911, 36 Stat. 925, 43 U.S.C. § 524 (1952).
41. 37 Stat. 266 (1912), 43 U.S.C. §§ 543, 544 (1952) (emphasis added).

McKay's offer to excess landholders at Kings River and Tulare Lake Project to permit them to pay cash rather than dispose of excess land, the legislative history of the Act of August 9, 1912 deserves examination at least equally with that of the original Act of 1902.

The Act of 1912 began as two similar bills, one introduced in each house, the avowed purpose of which was to give settlers on public land in reclamation projects an earlier title, permitting earlier mortgaging or disposition of a portion of the land, while protecting the government's financial interest by a lien on the land and appurtenant water rights.[42] The Senate bill passed first and went to the House where sharp opposition developed. With fore-knowledge of the objections to come, "a perfected substitute" was held in readiness to be offered in lieu of the Senate bill. But two members of the House objected at once that a bill so far-reaching in potential effect ought to be sent back to committee for thorough consideration. Both professed a primary interest in the original purpose of reclamation law—to promote settlement by homemakers. Congressman John J. Fitzgerald of New York implied that the public interest in obtaining actual settlers was endangered by the bill: "Some persons other than those representing those desiring to get these lands wish to have an opportunity at least to examine the legislation . . . ."[43]

The second opponent of the substitute bill, Congressman John E. Raker of California, objected strenuously that it would undo the work of the original reclamation law by permitting monopolization of farms on reclamation projects. The intention of the reclamation law was "that each man should have a homestead, and that he should not barter or sell it." Because a tract could be sold or mortgaged under the bill, "anyone owning a dozen other tracts might bid in that tract," and might come eventually to own "all the homes under that project . . . and therefore control the dam."[44] When he was asked whether under the existing excess land law, land and water holdings could not be accumulated "in regard to *private lands,* and . . . with *entrymen who have complied with the law,*" Raker replied, "it could *not* be done under the present law."[45] He proceeded to emphasize the importance of the antimonopoly features of the original reclamation law. "I admit under the general

---

42. S. 5545 & H.R. 23242, 62d Cong., 2d Sess. (1912). The report of the House Committee on Irrigation of Arid Lands on S. 5545 as it came from the Senate, stated its ostensible purposes as follows: "As the law now stands, a patent can not be issued to homesteaders under reclamation projects until full and final payment is made to the Government for the amount due for the water right . . . which may be . . . from 10 to 20 years from the date of the original entry . . . . If this act shall become a law, it will give the settler an opportunity to mortgage his land or to sell a part of it and much more readily pay the Government." H.R. REP. No. 867, 62d Cong., 2d Sess. 2, 4 (1912). Also see statement of Congressman Taylor (Colo.), reporting for the Committee. 48 CONG. REC. 9083 (1912).

43. *Ibid.*

44. *Id.* at 9083, 9038, Raker was apprehensive that defaulted titles might also be gathered up to concentrate landholdings. See *id.* at 9082.

45. *Id.* at 9038 (emphasis added).

law one man can buy as much land with his money as will enable him to monopolize the community, and this reclamation bill [law] was to prevent that very thing."[46] The bill was sent back to committee and two weeks later the committee reported a substitute bill which the House adopted without a dissenting voice.[47]

This new bill was the first to mention the excess land provision in the proviso, and except for the ambiguous "before" clause, the proviso is a clear expansion of the excess land law. It spelled out some new restrictions on acquisition of additional land or water prior to final payment of construction charges. It added to the prohibition against "sale" of water in excess of 160 acres, a provision that such a water right would not be "recognized," nor would the water be "furnished" to the excess. It prescribed that the text of the proviso should be recited "in every patent and water-right certificate issued" under the act.

Nothing in the legislative history of the Act of August 9, 1912, suggests that Congress intended to weaken excess land law. Under the charge that it might do so, the first draft of the bill was rejected. Congressman Raker, the man whose criticism was responsible for this rejection had been a public supporter of the excess land provision at least as early as 1905.[48] In his remarks on the 1912 reclamation bill he interpreted the original excess land law strictly, maintaining that the limitation continued to apply *after* the conditions of the law had been complied with. He was a member of the House Committee to which the bill was recommitted. He was present on the floor of the House on the day the revised bill passed without dissenting voice.[49] It seems fair to deduce that Congressman Raker's views of the intent and meaning of the excess land provision were embodied in the proviso to section 3 of the Act of August 9, 1912.[50]

II

INTERPRETATION

" *'Magnificent,' said the two officials already duped. 'Just look, Your Majesty, what colors! What a design!' They pointed to the empty looms, each supposing that the others could see the stuff.*

" *'What's this?' thought the Emperor. 'I can't see anything. This is terrible! Am I a fool? Am I unfit to be the Emperor? What a thing to happen to me of all people!—Oh! it's very pretty,' he said. 'It has my highest*

---

46. *Ibid.*
47. *Id.* at 9822.
48. In that year he helped to defeat an attempt to persuade the National Irrigation Congress to oppose the excess land law. OFFICIAL PROCEEDINGS OF 13TH NATIONAL IRRIGATION CONGRESS 60-62 (1905).
49. 48 CONG. REC. 9822; 9847 (1912).
50. Yet this proviso is now recited by the Secretary of the Interior to support the view that Congress intended the limitation on furnishing water to private lands to be ephemeral in its operation, terminating entirely upon final payment of construction charges.

> *approval.' And he nodded approbation at the empty loom. Nothing could make him say that he couldn't see anything.*
>
> *"His whole retinue stared and stared. One saw no more than another, but they all joined the Emperor in exclaiming, 'Oh! It's very pretty,' and they advised him to wear clothes made of this wonderful cloth especially for the great procession he was soon to lead!"*
>
> Hans Christian Andersen [51]

In the course of administering the excess land law a question of interpretation has arisen as crucially important to the effectiveness of reclamation law as was the commutation privilege to the effectiveness of homestead law. The question is whether completion of full and final payment of the construction charges allocated to a private landowner receiving reclamation project water renders the excess land provision inoperative. The question finds its source in the ambiguous language of the 1912 proviso to the excess land provision. Ordinarily, administrators, like judges, look to legislative history when unclear language obfuscates congressional policy. Yet nothing in the public record indicates that the Interior Department ever has thought such examination necessary to ascertain the meaning of the excess land law. This assumption of clarity in the language of the statute is extraordinary in the face of two flatly contradictory official interpretations by Interior itself.

The first occasion for answering the question came not long after the Act of August 9, 1912 added the proviso on the excess land law. Settlers on early reclamation projects began to seek permission to transfer their public land farm-units or to acquire water rights for private land, and confronted the Interior Department with the necessity of interpreting the proviso. In making these early decisions the Department said, in essence, that the reclamation law was intended to erect *permanent* limitations on an individual's share of project water.

The first case to receive Departmental review was *Amaziah Johnson*,[52] an application of two settlers on a reclamation project, each of whom had "made proof" on a farm-unit of public land, one desiring to sell his farm-unit and water right to the other. The would-be seller had 56 irrigable acres, the buyer 69.95 irrigable acres. Although the total irrigable acreage of the two tracts combined was less than 160 acres, the Department held that before the transfer would be permitted, it was necessary under the proviso to pay in full all installments due on the water right for the tract purchased or sold. Having passed on the particular application before it, the opinion declared a general interpretation of the proviso: even after all installments had been paid "the water rights purchased for the lands in excess of one unit shall be limited to a supply sufficient for one hundred and sixty acres."[53] In stating this rule

---

51. ANDERSON, THE COMPLETE ANDERSON 81 (Hersholt ed. 1949).
52. 42 L.D. 542 (1913). Decisions of the Department of the Interior relating to public lands are referred to as Land Decisions, and are cited herein as L.D.
53. Amaziah Johnson, 42 L.D. 542, 543 (1913).

the Department distinguished carefully between government regulation of the amount of privately owned *land* transferred, a power it disclaimed, and permanent limitation of the amount of *water* allowed to any individual from a reclamation project, a power it asserted.

The second case, *Keebaugh and Cook*,[54] was a decision upon an application by two holders of farm-units for which water rights had not been paid up, to obtain a water right for additional private land they already owned jointly. The Department rejected the application on the ground that a person could not obtain water rights for a farm-unit of public land and a tract of privately owned land, unless he had paid all installments for the private land, "not exceeding 160 acres." It declared itself in no doubt as to the meaning of the proviso: "The language on this point *is susceptible of but one construction,* namely, that the same person or association of persons can, *prior* to the time all charges have been paid, hold but one farm unit of public land and acquire a water right therefor unless the water rights for the additional lands are paid for in full, *and then not to exceed water rights for 160 acres* for such excess."[55] It construed the words in the proviso—"nor in any case in excess of one hundred sixty acres, nor shall water be furnished . . . nor a water right sold or recognized for such excess . . . ."—to require observance of the excess land provision *whether the financial obligation to the government for construction had been met fully or not.*

Notwithstanding these two decisions, the Department reversed itself eight months later. In his *Instructions*,[56] Chief Counsel of the Reclamation Service Will R. King overruled the interpretation sanctioned in *Johnson* and in *Keebaugh* and held that the excess land law does permit "the furnishing of water for land on which *payment in full has been made* of building and betterment charges *even when more than 160 acres* of such land is owned by one person . . . ."[57] The Department had ruled that the effect on the excess land provision of completing payment was nil; King said it was fatal. The Department had been confident that the language of the statute was "susceptible of but one construction"; King said that construction lacked support of "a plain intent expressed in the law." First Assistant Secretary A. A. Jones, who had approved *Johnson* and *Keebaugh*, made a personal about-face to give official approval to King's ruling. There departmental approval has rested.

King's opinion has enjoyed the intermittent genuflections of legal and lay students ever since, but apparently neither they nor the Interior Department have ever thought its foundations worthy of fresh inspection. The first reitera-

---

54. 42 L.D. 543 (1913).

55. Keebaugh & Cook, 42 L.D. 543, 545 (1913) ("prior" italicized in original; remaining emphasis added).

56. 43 L.D. 339 (1914). The *Instructions* approved the denial of the applications in *Johnson* and *Keebaugh* made before charges had been paid in full, but disapproved their interpretation that final payment had no effect on the excess land provision.

57. Instructions, 43 L.D. 339, 341 (1914) (emphasis added).

tion of King's ruling came six years after its issuance, in 1920, when Secretary John Barton Payne restated Department policy by a barren citation to King.[58]

Twenty-three years later, in 1943, a legislative analyst of the Bureau of Agricultural Economics, reviewing the history of the excess land provision, devoted a short paragraph to the effect of King's ruling.[59] He recited the opinions in *Johnson* and *Keebaugh*. But under the authority of King's *Instructions*, he concluded that no limitation is imposed after all charges have been paid, and found no occasion to examine the basis of King's opinion.

In March of 1944, experts in the Bureau of Agricultural Economics prepared a report on economic aspects of excess land problems. Relying on the Bureau's legislative analysis of the previous year, they were critical of Congress because "no provision was made *for the continuing control* of size of land holdings."[60] This led them to speculate whether Congress anticipated additional controls to maintain small holdings, but it did not generate sufficient curiosity to produce an investigation of the legal soundness of King's *Instructions*, or to suggest that perhaps the *Instructions* was the real target of their attack and not the Acts of Congress.

King's *Instructions* was mentioned again, in August 1945, in a memorandum of the Interior Department Solicitor dealing with the effects of community property law on the excess land provision. It recited the *Instructions* in a footnote, without inquiry.[61]

The next year, 1946, in a survey of excess landholdings the Bureau of Reclamation went beyond merely citing King as precedent. It gave support to King's *Instructions* with its own interpretation of the 1912 proviso: "It is apparent, however, that the quoted proviso is qualified by the phrase 'before final payment in full of all installments of building and betterment charges.' "[62]

---

58. "The Secretary has decided that the area which may be held by any one landowner after the construction charges have been fully paid may exceed 160 acres. (43 L.D. 339-341)." Instructions, 47 L.D. 417, 418 (1920).

59. Wertheimer, *Legislative and Administrative History of Acreage Limitations and Control of Speculation on Federal Reclamation Projects* 19, in ACREAGE LIMITATION IN THE CENTRAL VALLEY, A REPORT ON PROBLEM 19, CENTRAL VALLEY PROJECT STUDIES (1943).

60. *Acreage Limitation and Excess Land Problems, Central Valley Project* 33, in ACREAGE LIMITATION IN THE CENTRAL VALLEY, A REPORT ON PROBLEM 19, CENTRAL VALLEY PROJECT STUDIES (1944) (emphasis added).

Two months later an Assistant Commissioner of Reclamation apparently relied on King when he informed the owner of "a family-sized" farm of 42,000 acres who was testifying in favor of exempting Central Valley Project from the excess land law that "nowhere does this limitation apply after the project is paid for . . . ." William E. Warne, in *Hearings before Subcommittee of the Senate Commerce Committee on H.R. 3961*, 78th Cong., 2d Sess. 698, 702-03 (1944).

61. Fowler Harper, Solicitor, Memorandum for the Commissioner, Bureau of Reclamation, No. M-34172, n.4, Aug. 21, 1945, printed in Answering Brief of People of California & Water Project Authority of California, pp. 140-46, Ivanhoe Irrigation Dist. v. All Parties & Persons, No. 39627, Super. Ct. Tulare County, filed Nov. 16, 1951.

62. U.S. DEPARTMENT OF THE INTERIOR, BUREAU OF RECLAMATION, LANDOWNERSHIP SURVEY ON FEDERAL RECLAMATION PROJECTS 40 (1946). The writer does not regard this

No reasoning was offered to justify why "it is apparent," and, like its predecessors, the statement can be regarded as hardly more than an official echo of King.

The very next year the Bureau of Reclamation made a formal inquiry reaching to the heart of the issue: the relation, if any, between final payment of construction charges and the excess land provision. The timing of the inquiry is noteworthy. The year 1947 marked the second phase of a great effort to persuade Congress to exempt Central Valley Project from the excess land provision. In the lull that followed extensive and acrimonious congressional hearings on the exemption bill, the Commissioner of the hard-pressed Bureau of Reclamation formally requested the Department Solicitor to answer this question: "Does the payment in full of construction charges against 'excess lands' free such lands of the acreage limitations of the reclamation laws . . . ?"[63] The Commissioner divided his question into three parts, one relating to each type of legal authorization under which individuals could obtain irrigation water: (a) lands covered by water-right applications; (b) lands receiving water under joint liability contracts with public water districts; and (c) lands receiving water under the Warren Act.

Two aspects of Associate Solicitor Felix Cohen's answer were very familiar: King was cited as authority; the answer made no fresh examination of the legal soundness of the 1914 *Instructions*. He said simply: "As to part (a) of your question, pertinent references are to Section 3 of the Act of August 9, 1912 (37 Stat. 265, 266), and to instructions approved by the Department on July 22, 1914 (43 L.D. 339)."[64] He quoted the proviso in section 3 immediately, verbatim, and *in toto*, without attempt at construction of its language. Then without pause he summarized King's *Instructions* and proceeded to his own conclusion at once, without argument or suggestion of a doubt: "payment in full of the charges . . . removes the lands for which the water right is acquired from the operation of the acreage restrictions."[65] Once again King's *Instructions* was acknowledged as authoritative.

Cohen's answer to part (b) of the Commissioner's question was the same as his answer to part (a). Relying on the proviso, he held that whether the payment of construction charges was under a water right application or a joint-liability contract, the excess-land rule was the same.[66]

---

interpretation as "apparent." See language of the proviso in text at note 41 *supra*. And *Johnson* and *Keebaugh* reached a contrary interpretation.

63. Memorandum of Commissioner of Reclamation, Sept. 19, 1947, quoted in Felix S. Cohen, Associate Solicitor, Memorandum to Commissioner, Bureau of Reclamation, No. M-35004, Oct. 22, 1947, p. 1, entitled, Program of the Bureau for Action Consistent with the Acreage Limitations of the Federal Reclamation Laws [hereinafter cited as Cohen Opinion].

64. Cohen Opinion, p. 1. It was not conducive to clear interpretation of a law imposing a limitation upon *individual shares of water*, that the Commisioner's question and the Associate Solicitor's answer spoke of the law as a limitation upon *lands*.

65. *Id.* at 1, 2.

66. *Id.* at 2-5.

Cohen's answer to the final part of the Commissioner's question produces such extraordinary consequences that one wonders how he avoided questioning the foundation of his position. The answer to part (c) of the question, he said, would depend in each case upon how the landowner's Warren Act contract provided for payment of construction charges, *i.e.*, whether by full payment in annual installments, or by inclusion of construction charges in a permanent "annual carriage charge." In the latter event the excess land provision could never be extinguished, said Cohen, because the contract provides no means for making "full payment."[67]

The upshot of Cohen's reasoning is its implication that Congress intended that the duration of its limitation upon an individual's right to receive water stored or carried by a federal reclamation project should depend entirely on an administrative decision whether he was to pay for the service by a permanent annual charge or whether he should pay it off in installments. There is not the slightest evidence that in choosing one arrangement or the other either the Interior Department or water users ever had an inkling that freedom from the excess land provision was at stake. Nor was Cohen disturbed by a thought that he had created a reductio ad absurdum which brought into question the reliability of King's interpretation of the law.

Cohen's opinion is the latest authoritative legal statement of the Department's interpretation of reclamation law, but since, like all the other intervening statements, it represents no critical review of the validity of King's position, any fresh examination of Department policy must focus on the King opinion itself, and upon the statutes it construed. The validity of Cohen's opinion requires no separate inquiry, for it stands on King's *Instructions*.

In 1951 and 1954 King's interpretation received mention again. His *Instructions* was unargued, unexplained, un-cited, but his view was accepted and Cohen's opinion relied on by an excess landholder attempting to destroy the "9(e)" type of water contract which provides him with *lower rates* than would be possible under the older-type forty installment contract.[68] Under section 9(e) of the Reclamation Project Act of 1939,[69] Congress authorized a contract for the benefit of water users, small and large alike, similar to the arrangement for annual charges for water storage and carriage under the Warren Act. As Cohen pointed out, that type of contract fixed no date when construction charges would be fully paid, and consequently, under King's

---

67. *Id.* at 5. Cohen acknowledges that "there is no indication that Congress intended to distinguish" between Warren Act and other projects as to the effect of final payment of construction charges, and "neither is there any apparent basis for a distinction of this nature." *Ibid.*

68. See Answering Brief of People of California & Water Project Authority of California, *supra* note 61, at 8-9; Joint Reply Brief of Appellants, pp. 11-12, 16, Ivanhoe Irrigation Dist. v. All Parties and Persons, L.A. No. 23043, Cal. Sup. Ct., filed Aug. 2, 1954. Also see *California Water Policy Fundamentals*, 25 TRANSACTIONS OF THE COMMONWEALTH CLUB OF CALIFORNIA 141 (Nov. 28, 1949). Section 9(e) contracts provide lower annual rates by lengthening the period of repayment.

69. 53 STAT. 1196 (1939), as amended, 43 U.S.C. § 61 (1952).

Instructions, failed to provide excess landholders with a technique for terminating the excess land provision. The Attorney General of California, while defending the right of an irrigation district to make 9(e) contracts with the United States under federal reclamation law, relied on King's interpretation in 1951 and 1954. He was unconcerned with King's legal soundness; so long as Interior accepted King's *Instructions* it sufficed to explain the difference between the excess landholders' "ostensible" and "real" objections to 9(e) contracts.[70] Counsel for the landholders similarly accepted King's interpretation in 1954.[71]

Thus King's ruling of 1914 furnished motive in 1954 for litigation to invalidate a type of contract that Congress approved for the purpose of providing all landowners on reclamation projects with lower water rates. If successful in making their escape from the excess land law, excess landholders will raise the cost of water to smaller landowners. There is no evidence that Congress intended to create this anomaly; it is only King's *Instructions* that does this. Its validity can no longer go unchallenged without risking havoc in the nation's water policy.

KING, 1914

"Congress . . . has shown clearly that the excess-land provisions are the heart of the reclamation law."

—Fowler Harper [72]

The chief counsel of the Reclamation Service, Will R. King, persuaded the First Assistant Secretary of the Interior in 1914 to reverse his original decision that the limitation on an individual's right to receive water from a federal reclamation project is not terminated by full and final payment of construction charges. Forty years later the present Secretary of the Interior not only accepts King, but offers to go even beyond him by declaring that prepayment nullifies the limitation *ab initio*. With no more exception than proves the rule, none of the officials who have relied upon or referred to the *Instructions* during the past forty years has ever recited or quoted the reasoning.[73]

---

70. The excess landholder's principal ostensible objection to the 9(e) contract was that it failed to guarantee him a perpetual water right. Following Cohen, the Attorney-General argued that his real objection to a contract that gave him lower water rates was that the 9(e) contract provides excess landholders no way to terminate the excess land provision by payment of construction charges. See Joint Reply Brief of Appellants, *supra* note 68, at pp. 4, 7.

71. See Reply Brief of Respondent McCracken, p. 64, Ivanhoe Irrigation Dist. v. All Parties & Persons, L.A. No. 23043, Cal. Sup. Ct., filed June 1954.

72. Fowler Harper, Solicitor, Memorandum No. M-33902, May 31, 1945, p. 4, entitled, Applicability of the Excess-Land Provisions of the Federal Reclamation Law to the Boulder Canyon Project Act, printed in Answering Brief of People of California & Water Project Authority of California, *supra* note 61, at pp. 147-62.

73. Associate Solicitor Cohen did quote brief excerpts from King's *Instructions* holding that to limit appurtenant water rights after all charges had been paid would be radical departure from all the public land laws. Cohen Opinion, p. 5.

To support his conclusion that Congress could not have intended to prohibit purchase of paid-up water rights for more than 160 acres, King looked, not to the legislative history of reclamation law, but to the provision of previous land laws. He concluded that permanently limiting an individual to a 160-acre water right was too "radical" a change from past land policy without ever considering that in passing new *water* legislation Congress might have been eager to avoid the pitfalls of prior *land* legislation. Because, in seeking out congressional intent, King failed to see what Congress said it was doing, his conclusions convey an impression of dogmatism rather than conviction. His reasoning falls roughly into five arguments.

King's first argument is an inference. It is not explicitly articulated, but this appears to be a fair interpretation: since the proviso in section 3, added by the Act of 1912, contains an express prohibition against receiving water for excess lands *before* payment, the absence of an explicit prohibition *after* payment indicates that Congress did not intend the prohibition to apply *after* payment in full. King here relied on the specific words of prohibition "before final payment in full" appearing in the proviso. Yet he interpreted the 1902

It may be helpful to the discussion below to quote at length from King: "[If the clauses in the proviso, 'nor in any case in excess of 160 acres,' 'nor shall water be furnished under said acts nor water right sold or recognized for such excess,' are] construed as applying to the lands for which water right has been paid in full it has the effect of a provision by Congress limiting water rights for private land holdings, after full payment, to water rights for 160 acres.... Such a limitation is a *radical departure from all the public land laws*, as apparently *there never has been any intent by Congress* to limit the amount of land which a man may own after having complied in full with the provisions of the law in order to acquire the title, and *as the water right becomes on final payment an appurtenance to the land the same rule governs.*

"It would seem that a construction of a statute constituting *so wide a departure from the previous conditions regarding the rights of individuals* should not be adopted *in the absence of a plain intent expressed in the law*, as it would not only render the law subject to question on the ground of *constitutionality*, but would also introduce *an entirely new system of land ownership in reclamation projects* not applicable to any other public lands....

"On the other hand, there is a *rational* interpretation of this language that is in full harmony *with prior legislation and the evident intent of the reclamation law*, namely, that a person who holds a farm unit shall not be permitted, before full payment has been made on the appurtenant water right, to acquire other lands with appurtenant water rights unless the water right charges on the latter have been fully paid; similarly that a person may hold private lands with appurtenant water rights up to the limit of single ownership fixed for the project in one or more parcels before full payment of the water right charge, but may not acquire other lands with appurtenant water rights unless the water right charges thereon have been paid in full. Furthermore, that the limit of area of the farm units and of single private land holdings to which water rights are appurtenant (and as to which water right has not been paid in full) shall in no case exceed 160 acres.

"[The proviso permits] the furnishing of water for land on which payment in full has been made of building and betterment charges even when more than 160 acres of such land is owned by one person . . . ." Instructions, 43 L.D. 340-41 (1914) (emphasis added).

Act the same way, even though it contained no such specific language as the proviso.

King's second argument was founded on two "facts," one of them statutory, the other historical. The statutory fact was that Congress, in section 8 of the Reclamation Act of 1902 had made the water right an appurtenance to the land upon final payment.[74] The historical fact was that Congress had never placed a limit in prior land laws on "the amount of land which a man may own after having complied in full with the provisions of the law in order to acquire the title . . . ."[75] He concluded that "the same rule governs" water once it attaches to land, so that there was no limitation on appurtenant water to which a landowner had obtained title by compliance with the law.

Reclamation law does indeed make "the right to the use of water . . . appurtenant to the land irrigated,"[76] but it does not follow that all conditions attached to water ownership disappear once it becomes appurtenant. The very section that makes the right to the use of water appurtenant to land, plainly imposes a limitation which survives final payment: "beneficial use shall be the basis, the measure, and the limit of the right."[77] Appurtenance does not equate water ownership with land ownership, but even if it did, conditions limiting an owner's use of land to which he holds fee title are well known to the law, whether written in the deed or imposed by ordinance or statute.

Legislative history of the reclamation law shows that appurtenance was not intended to vest as an unconditional property right. Congressman Mondell said: "The settler or landowner who complies with all the conditions of the act secures a *perpetual right* to the use of a sufficient amount of water to irrigate his land, *but this right lapses* if he fails to put the water to beneficial use and only extends to the use of the water on and *for the tract* originally irrigated. These most important provisions of the law prevent all the evils which come from recognizing a property right in water with power to sell and dispose of the same elsewhere *and for other purposes* than originally intended . . . ."[78] King, the interpreter, argued that the act of becoming appurtenant extinguished all conditions attached to the water including acreage limitation; Mondell, the legislator, argued that appurtenance itself was contingent.

King's historical fact that prior land legislation furnishes no precedent for a permanent water limitation is an historical error. On March 2, 1889, Congress amended the homestead law to permit entrymen who had complied with the law and made final proof for less than 160 acres, to make further entry, but only on so much land as would bring the total lands entered to 160 acres.[79]

---

74. 32 STAT. 390 (1902), 43 U.S.C. § 372 (1952).
75. Instructions, 43 L.D. 339, 340 (1914).
76. 32 STAT. 390 (1902), 43 U.S.C. § 372 (1952).
77. *Ibid.*
78. 35 CONG. REC. 6679 (1902) (emphasis added). See also remarks of Congressmen Mondell, Tongue, and Ray in text at notes 85-88 *infra*.
79. 25 STAT. 854-55 (1889).

Thus, Congress had established a limitation on entrymen on public land, effective after compliance in full with the conditions prescribed to obtain title. And in the Warren Act of 1911 Congress imposed the excess land law on water to which private landowners already held full title.[80]

King's third argument was that the Department's original construction was so "wide" and "radical"[81] a departure "from the previous conditions regarding the rights of individuals" that Congress could not have intended it. In fact, Congress gave every indication that it intended a wide departure from prior legislation.[82] Furthermore, it is hard to see how a law infringes upon individual rights when the individual "owners of private lands are not required to subject such lands to the operation of the reclamation law or to take water therefor."[83]

King's fourth point was that imposing acreage limitation after payment was "subject to question on the ground of constitutionality." Perhaps by this he meant that Congress would not have risked raising a constitutional question in addition to the other obstacles he saw. Or possibly King meant to rest his case again on his erroneous belief that Congress had never limited the amount of land which a man may own after he had complied with the law—implying that such a limitation would be unconstitutional. But the excess land law does not "limit the amount of land which a man may own"; it limits only the amount of water an individual may receive from a federal reclamation project.[84]

The issue of constitutionality was debated when the original reclamation bill was passed in 1902. The sponsors of reclamation were clear in their own minds that Congress had power to set up a permanently effective limitation. Congressman Mondell said that Congress had the right to grant public lands, *"with or without stipulation as to their use and final disposition."*[85] And Congressman Tongue of Oregon, relying on *Gibson v. Chouteau*,[86] advanced the unrestricted powers of the Government to attach permanent conditions to grants of the public domain, either in the individual patent or by general legislation.[87]

---

80. See text at note 40 *supra*.
81. There is nothing to indicate that King, in 1914, meant "radical" in the modern sense of communistic. But the charge of "communism" did crop up temporarily in 1944 during the unsuccessful effort of Congressman Alfred J. Elliott to exempt Central Valley Project in California from the excess land provision. See San Francisco Call-Bulletin, June 1, 1944, p. 1; Superior California Register, June 11, 1944. In the Irrigation Congress the charge of "communistic" had been met by supporters of public reclamation. See OFFICIAL REPORT OF THE INTERNATIONAL IRRIGATION CONGRESS 81 (1893).
82. See text at notes 27-50 *supra*.
83. C.M. Kirkpatrick, 42 L.D. 547, 549 (1913).
84. Graham, *The Central Valley Project: Resource Development of a Natural Basin*, 38 CALIF. L. REV. 588, 603-04 (1950).
85. 35 CONG. REC. 6680 (1902) (emphasis added).
86. 13 Wall. (80 U.S.) 92 (1871). Tongue also cited KINNEY, IRRIGATION § 147 (1894), and POMEROY, RIPARIAN RIGHTS § 32 (1893).
87. 35 CONG. REC. App. p. 646 (1902).

An opponent of the bill argued that the United States, as an owner of real estate can impose no "restrictions running with and connected with the enjoyment of such land that are not subject to the laws of the State in which the land is situated . . . ."[88] With the issue of constitutionality placed squarely before it, Congress decided nevertheless to proceed with the bill, confident that the objections were without merit.

In raising questions of constitutionality, King's *Instructions* appears to have overlooked *Burley v. United States*,[89] decided four years earlier, in which the Ninth Circuit upheld the constitutionality of reclamation law. The court quoted the excess land provision in section 5 of the Act of 1902 in support of its reasoning.[90]

King's fifth argument against construing the excess land law as surviving full and final payment "in the absence of a plain intent expressed in the law," was that it would "introduce an entirely new system of land ownership in reclamation projects not applicable to any other public lands or any other lands acquired from the United States." It is doubtful that Congress would have been affected by such an argument, especially with its 1889 amendment to the Homestead Act[91] as precedent. It is an ironical commentary on the argument that Cohen, following the logic of King's interpretation, produced two systems of land ownership within the reclamation system itself, when he concluded that the effective duration of the excess land law under the Warren Act of 1911 depends (under King's *Instructions*) on whether the administrative arrangement for repayment of construction charges is made on the basis of installments or annual carrying charges.[92]

Now let us turn to the language of reclamation law. Section 5 of the Act of 1902 provides that "*No right* to the *use* of water for land in private ownership shall be sold for a tract exceeding 160 acres to any one landowner . . . and no such right shall permanently attach until all payments therefor are made."[93] The Warren Act of 1911 states in section 1 that water stored or carried in federal projects "*shall not be used* otherwise than as prescribed by law as to lands held in private ownership."[94] The law referred to is section 5 of the original Act of 1902. Section 1 of the Warren Act adds to the original limitation on the sale of water rights a prohibition against using water in violation

---

88. Statement of Congressman George Ray (N.Y.), 35 Cong. Rec. 6696 (1902). Ray argued also that the irrigation of public lands for sale to private owners promoted neither the general welfare nor interstate or foreign commerce. *Id.* at 6686. The House minority report on the bill denied the power of Congress to make water rights appurtenant to land. King, in his *Instructions*, accepted the constitutionality of the federal power to irrigate land and make water an appurtenance.
89. 179 Fed. 1 (1910).
90. Burley v. United States, 179 Fed. 1, 7-8 (1910).
91. See text at note 79 *supra*.
92. Cohen Opinion, p. 5.
93. 32 Stat. 389 (1902), as amended, 43 U.S.C. § 419 (1952) (emphasis added).
94. 36 Stat. 925 (1911), 43 U.S.C. § 523 (1952) (emphasis added).

of the excess land law. Section 2 of the later Act provides that "water *shall not be furnished* from [any federal project] to any one landowner in excess of an amount sufficient to irrigate one hundred and sixty acres."[95] This is an independent restatement of a limitation on the water an individual landowner may receive. It is unmistakably timeless and of general application.

The Act of August 9, 1912, broadens the incidence of the excess land prohibition to include not only seller and user of water rights but also the purchaser. The proviso in section 3 forbids anyone to "acquire, own, or hold irrigable land" under reclamation law in excess amounts and states that no water shall be "furnished," "nor a water right sold or *recognized* for such excess."[96]

The crux of the language is the meaning of the phrase in the proviso, "nor in any case in excess of one hundred and sixty acres." King said it is not overriding, but is qualified by the earlier phrase "before final payment in full of all installments of building and betterment charges."[97] But the "nor in any case" phrase can be read at least as easily to be overriding, as the original Departmental interpretations in *Johnson* and *Keebaugh* testify. Nor need the matter rest there. The Act of 1902 restricts entry to "tracts of not . . . more than 160 acres,"[98] and limits water rights sold to private landowners to the same maximum.[99] Since the upper limit already was established in the 1902 law, the phrase "nor in any case in excess of one hundred and sixty acres" if interpreted as qualified by the phrase "before final payment in full of all installments," would be tautological. It is more reasonable to assume that Congress meant "nor in *any* case" to be taken at face value, as an overriding limitation on water before and after final payment. And under this interpretation, later clauses in the proviso became less strained. The drastic penalty of forfeiture of excess lands acquired in good faith but held longer than two years is unreasonably severe if it could be avoided by repayment of charges. Congress had required repayment of all charges within ten years. Thus recitation of the proviso in every patent and water right certificate is hardly necessary if the restrictions would terminate within ten years, but it is a more than reasonable precaution to assure actual notice of permanent restrictions to transferees.

Although *Keebaugh* found the law "susceptible of but one interpretation," King is not without ground in pointing to a lack of clarity. But the *Instructions* is wrong in insisting that only a "plain intent *expressed in the law*,"[100] can be used to resolve the ambiguity. King may have employed the proper English rule for construing statutes, but not the American, under which reliance is

---

95. 36 STAT. 926 (1911), 43 U.S.C. § 524 (1952) (emphasis added).
96. 37 STAT. 266 (1912), 43 U.S.C. §§ 543, 544 (1952) (emphasis added). See full text of the proviso in text at note 41 *supra*.
97. *Ibid.*
98. 32 STAT. 388 (1902), as amended, 43 U.S.C. § 391 (1952).
99. 32 STAT. 389 (1902), 43 U.S.C. § 419 (1952).
100. Instructions, 43 L.D. 339 (1914).

made on external aids.[101] The original reclamation law set the maximum period for repayment at ten years.[102] Sponsors of the bill estimated that construction charges might be as low as $10 or even $5 per acre,[103] and that farm-units would be far less than 160 acres, probably as low as 40 acres. The total charge they foresaw was an amount that might easily be paid off in less than ten years. It places a strain on credulity to reconcile a protection lasting at most for ten years with the fulsome promise of the sponsors of the reclamation bill that they were providing an enduring protection against monopoly.

It is difficult to find reasonable ground either in the law or its legislative history to explain why administrators have accepted King's *Instructions*, apparently without question. The explanation seems to lie elsewhere.

III

Pressure

"In future as in earlier irrigation enterprises, large holdings will give most vexation .... In the future it will be even more necessary to insist that large holdings shall not receive water from government supplies, unless divided into farm units of proper size, and offered to intending purchasers at reasonable terms."

—John A. Widtsoe [104]

Foundations of the drive to escape the excess land law were laid in the half century before its enactment while national land policy was breaking down in the West, notably in the Central Valley of California.[105] During this period farsighted men acquired huge tracts that they turned into large-scale agricultural or livestock enterprises operating on short water supplies;[106] great mineral deposits frequently underlie these same tracts.[107] Such landholders do not welcome a national policy of distributing water that invites redistribution of

---

101. See Frankfurter, *Some Reflections on the Reading of Statutes*, 47 Colum. L. Rev. 540, 544 (1947).

102. 32 Stat. 389 (1902).

103. 35 Cong. Rec. 1384, 6681, 6766 (1902); *id.*, app., p. 256. The fact that soon after passage of the law costs were discovered to be a good deal higher is irrelevant in seeking the sponsors' intent.

104. Widtsoe, Success on Irrigation Projects 113 (1928).

105. See, *e.g.*, Gates, *The Homestead Law in an Incongruous Land System*, 41 Am. Hist. Rev. 655, 668 *et seq.* (1936); Cooper, Land, Water and Settlement in Kern County, California: 1850-1890 (unpublished thesis in University of California library, 1953).

106. See, *e.g.*, testimony of S.T. Harding, in *Hearings before Subcommittee of the Senate Committee on Irrigation and Reclamation on S. Res. 295*, 78th Cong., 2d Sess. 360 (1944); Downey, They Would Rule the Valley 171-81 (1947); testimony of George L. Henderson, in *Hearings before House Flood Control Committee on H.R. 4485*, 78th Cong., 2d Sess. 751-63 (1944).

107. See, *e.g.*, testimony of Senator Sheridan Downey, in *Hearings before Subcommittee of the Senate Commerce Committee on H.R. 3961*, 78th Cong., 2d Sess. 770 (1944); testimony of Paul H. Johnstone, in *Hearings before Subcommittee of the Senate Committee on Public Lands on S. 912*, 80th Cong., 1st Sess. 864 (1947).

land. At times a strong alliance develops between them and large organizations of other kinds, each opposed to reclamation law for its own reasons.[108] The history of this drive is a case study in the observation of William Ewart Gladstone that "Property is vigilant, active, sleepless; if ever it seems to slumber, be sure that one eye is open."[109]

Opposition to the excess land law moves to two main directions, attack on the law itself and pressure on administrators to weaken enforcement. The former tactic is preferred, for congressional exemptions are final, if they can be won. The effort to obtain outright exemptions is likely, however, to arouse popular and effective resistance in Congress. But, of the alternative, a spokesman for large landholdings candidly explained that in some cases nonenforcement "would not be a safe solution.... Landowners could not rely on continued future nonenforcement."[110] The twin campaigns against the law and its administration have proceeded simultaneously with fluctuating intensity.

Both sponsors and opponents of the original reclamation bill in 1902 joined in arguing against monopoly, sponsors saying federal reclamation would prevent it, and opponents claiming reclamation would benefit it. This unity of purpose, however, did not go very deep. Attack on the excess land law began in the 1905 meeting of the National Irrigation Congress when large landholders sought to obtain a resolution against it from the fathers of reclamation. The attempt was defeated by voice vote "amid great applause,"[111] and open attack on the law was not resumed until 1938. Then three projects were exempted within space of a few years, on the claim that special circumstances took them out of the class to which the excess land law was intended to apply.[112]

The most recent efforts to eliminate the excess land law, made in 1944 and 1947, produced the greatest congressional debates on reclamation since 1902, and defeat for the attackers. The first was the Elliott rider to the Rivers and Harbors Bill, seeking exemption of Central Valley Project.[113] The second effort followed in the 80th Congress, six senators sponsoring a bill to exempt

---

108. The provision of reclamation law which gives public agencies preference in disposing of electrical power from reclamation projects is a counterpart of the excess land law and evokes resistance from private power interests. Reclamation Project Act of Aug. 4, 1939, § 9(c), 53 STAT. 1195, as amended, 43 U.S.C. § 485 L(c) (1952).

109. MORLEY, 3 LIFE OF WILLIAM EWART GLADSTONE 469 (1903).

110. Testimony of S.T. Harding, in *Hearings on S. Res. 295, supra* note 106, at 363.

111. Testimony of Secretary of the Interior J.A. Krug, in *Hearings on S. 912, supra* note 107, at 991-92; OFFICIAL PROCEEDINGS OF 13TH NATIONAL IRRIGATION CONGRESS 60-63 (1905).

112. Wertheimer, *supra* note 59, at 38 *et seq.*; testimony of James G. Patton, in *Hearings on S. 912, supra* note 107, at 623-28; letter from Louis T. Robinson to Congressman Alfred J. Elliott, dated March 19, 1947, in *id.* at 1169-72. Another exemption of this type for Santa Maria project, California, passed in the 83d Congress. With previous House approval it went through the Senate after debate by 45-17. 100 Cong. Rec. 1101-07, A858-59, A863-66 (daily ed. Feb. 2, 1954); *id.* at 14286-88, 14290-304 (daily ed. Aug. 18, 1954).

113. Section 4, H.R. 3961, 78th Cong., 2d Sess. (1944).

projects in California, Colorado, and Texas. The hearings, marked by acrimonious passages between Senator Downey, chief protagonist of the bill, and officials of the Bureau of Reclamation, ran for nearly a month and are recorded in more than 1300 pages.[114] The bill died in committee.

The benefits of administrative nonenforcement were realized by opponents of the excess land law on some older projects such as Salt River Valley, Arizona, and the Imperial Valley Division of the All-American Canal.[115] Once nonenforcement had been achieved, they advertised it repeatedly as a sort of "precedent," arguing from it that there should be no law at all.[116]

Even the strong and sympathetic administrator is more or less vulnerable to the kind of pressure brought to bear by opponents of the anti-monopoly, anti-speculation features of reclamation law. Reclamation administrators need visible, substantial, and persistent support for their projects. Citizens whose primary interest is in widespread distribution of benefits and the general principles of water resource development seldom provide such support. They have exerted intense influence at times such as the campaign for reclamation law in 1902, and the defense of the excess land law in 1944 and 1947, but obstacles as simple as the cost of travel from western states to the national capital impede their consistent support. Such obstacles are far less deterring to those expecting substantial financial gains from projects. They provide steady, vigorous support for undertaking particular projects, but on these very projects they expend an equal effort to eliminate the excess land law or to weaken its enforcement.

Not only can excess landholders give or withhold valued support to reclamation administrators; they can also transfer it to a competing agency of water resource development. The principal competitor is the Army Engineers, to whose projects the excess land law did not apply until 1944. By the late 1930's, officials in the Bureau of Reclamation were uneasy that this difference in law might, under the influence of excess landholders in Central Valley, cause them to lose construction of important reservoirs there. Reclamation officials are reported to have intimated that the excess land law need not be taken seriously in the Central Valley.[117] But when these hints failed to

---

114. *Hearings on S. 912, supra* note 107.

115. See PENDLETON, HISTORY OF LABOR IN ARIZONA IRRIGATED AGRICULTURE, 34 *et seq.* (unpublished thesis in University of California library, 1950); Taylor, *The 160-Acre Water Limitation and the Water Resources Commission*, 3 WESTERN POL. Q. 435 (1950).

116. See, *e.g.*, testimony of Northcutt Ely, in *Hearings on H.R. 3961, supra* note 107, at 631-32; Curran, *The 160-Acre Limitation Law: Application to Private Land Will Prove Futile*, Western Construction News, Aug. 1948, p. 107; Williams, *The Vanishing American*, ADDRESS BEFORE CONVENTION OF CALIF. IRRIGATION DISTRICTS ASS'N 22 (Nov. 12, 1953).

117. See Testimony of Roland Curran, in *Hearings on H.R. 3961, supra* note 107, at 665-66, and in *Hearings on S. 912, supra* note 107, at 1310; testimony of Edward Hyatt, California State Engineer, in *Hearings on S. Res. 295, supra* note 106, at 27; testimony of Russell Giffen, in *Hearings before Subcommittee of U.S. Senate Military*

materialize, and new reclamation officials said in 1943 that they would enforce the law, Kings and Kern River projects were transferred by Congress to the Army Engineers, partly under spur of Tulare Lake Basin Water Storage District where excess landholdings predominate.[118] In acceding to pressure to assign Kings and Kern River projects to the Army Engineers, Congress did not yield entirely to large landholding interests. For the first time it inserted reclamation law, with its excess land provision, into flood control law. Thus, the Bureau was denied opportunity to construct and operate important reservoirs, and was given the troublesome responsiblity of 'enforcing the excess land law against strong resistance.

Tactics of personal harrassment of administrators began to be employed publicly. Congressman Elliott, author of the exemption rider of 1944, referred to employees of the Interior Department as "some 'dillywhackers' down here who have done everything they could do to keep the Corps of Army Engineers from doing any work."[119] The rising pitch of bitterness against administrators defending the excess land law in 1947 appears from the following examination by Senator Downey of Economist Paul H. Johnstone of the Bureau: "Are you not here, Mr. Johnstone, rather as a propagandist of the most extreme kind, rather than an economist?"[120]

In August 1947, after the Senate Public Lands Committee failed to report his bill, Senator Downey asked the Civil Service Commission to examine the professional qualifications of Richard L. Boke, Regional Director of Reclamation in the Central Valley area, who had been making strong defense of the

---

Affairs Committee, San Francisco, California, April 7, 1944, p. 93 (Mimeo.). An occasional note of pique was entered in the record against administrators who had held out prospects that turned out to be false. Giffen, a large landholder, said: "It seems to me that the Bureau was completely in bad faith in taking that $25,000 [contribution toward cost of a water survey], knowing that they were going to support as vigorously as they have the 160-acre limitation . . . ."

118. See, *e.g.*, resolution of Tulare Lake Basin Water Storage District, March 14, 1940, in *Hearings before House Flood Control Committee on H.R. 9640*, 76th Cong., 3d Sess. 552-54 (1940); testimony of Charles L. Kaupke, in *Hearings before House Flood Control Committee on H.R. 4911*, 77th Cong., 1st Sess. 181 (1941). Kaupke testified, "[We] prefer the project as reported by the Corps of Engineers . . . . [R]ather than accept the provisions of the Bureau project, we would forego a project on Kings River." Physical aspects of the two proposed projects were almost identical. On May 7, 1945, the president of Tulare Lake Basin Water Storage District wrote: "Over the several past years we have been required to incur much expense in order to assist preventing this project from being undertaken by the Bureau of Reclamation." Letter from Louis T. Robinson to Senator Carl Hayden, in *Hearings before Subcommittee of Senate Appropriations Committee on H.R. 3024*, 79th Cong., 1st Sess. 991 (1945).

119. *Hearings before Subcommittee of the Senate Commerce Committee on H.R. 4485*, 78th Cong., 2d Sess. 284 (1944).

120. *Hearings before Subcommittee of the Senate Committee on Public Lands on S. 912*, 80th Cong., 1st Sess. 904 (1947); see *id.* at 104. Senator Watkins inquired of Commissioner Straus whether he considered opposing a change in the law part of his duty. *Id.* at 123-24. Senator Downey stated that "a large part of the time of several hundred men in the Bureau" had been spent lobbying and propagandizing. *Id.* at 124-25.

excess land law. Boke was then beginning a difficult campaign against resistance, ultimately successful, to obtain water contracts containing the excess land provision as required by law. By mid-September the Commissioner of Reclamation, Michael W. Straus, also came under attack. The San Francisco News reported that "Within the last two weeks two efforts have been made to organize an appeal to President Truman to remove top officials of the Bureau of Reclamation. Foes of public transmission lines and acreage limitation have apparently jointed forces in a new drive . . . aimed at officials who enforce existing law on these two matters."[121]

The pressure on these officials culminated in a rider attached to the Interior Appropriations Bill for 1949 requiring that holders of top posts must be engineers, or go unpaid.[122] Neither Straus nor Boke met this qualification. President Truman, who signed the bill on June 29, 1948, expressed regret that he could not single out these "arbitrary qualifications" for veto: "This rider is designed to effect the removal of two men . . . who have supported the public power policy of the Government and the 160-acre law which assures that the Western lands reclaimed at public expense shall be used for the development of family size farms. [Its result will be] . . . to serve the purposes of special interests desirous of monopolizing the rich farm lands of the West and intent upon stopping the construction of transmission lines for the delivery of power from Federal dams. These same interests tried first to get the law changed but failed, and having failed then sought to get the management changed."[123] Straus and Boke remained in office for five months without pay, which only a new Congress elected in 1948 restored.

During this period of extreme pressure on both the law and its administrators the props supporting enforcement were weakened. Without arguing that these moves were made step by step in direct response to pressure, it nevertheless seems relevant to chronicle some of them. As early as December 1946, during the lull between the congressional battles of 1944 and 1947, Commissioner of Reclamation Straus officially called attention of his Regional Directors to the necessity for bringing about compliance with the excess land law.[124] On September 19, 1947, while the opening guns were being fired in the fight to remove top Bureau officials, the Commissioner formally asked the Solicitor of the Interior Department if full and final payment of construction charges against excess lands frees such lands of the acreage limitations. Cohen answered in late October, and on December 16, 1947, the Commissioner informed his regional directors that payment of charges does free excess lands,

---

121. Ruth Finney, San Francisco News, Sept. 25, 1947, p. 18, cols. 6, 7.
122. 62 STAT. 1126 (1948).
123. Text of the President's statement appears in mimeo. release. 94 CONG. REC. 9368 (1948).
124. Michael Straus, Commissioner of Reclamation, to Regional and Branch Directors, Administrative Letter No. 303, Dec. 16, 1947, p. 1, entitled, Program of the Bureau for Action Consistent with the Acreage Limitations of the Federal Reclamation Laws [hereinafter cited as *Admin. Letter 303*].

and that where payment of charges is not "an available solution" officials should press for reasonably prompt arrangements with water users for disposal of excess landholdings.[125] Not a line in the excess land statute had been changed, but the king-pin of its enforcement was quietly removed.

IV

ACTION

"So off went the Emperor in procession under his splendid canopy. Everyone in the streets and the windows said, 'Oh how fine are the Emperor's new clothes! Don't they fit him to perfection? And see his long train!' Nobody would confess that he couldn't see anything, for that would prove him either unfit for his position, or a fool. No costume the Emperor had worn before was ever such a complete success.

" 'But he hasn't got anything on,' a little child said.

" 'Did you ever hear such innocent prattle?' said its father. And one person whispered to another what the child had said, 'He hasn't anything on. A child says he hasn't anything on.'

" ' But he hasn't got anything on!' the whole town cried out at last.

"The Emperor shivered, for he suspected they were right. But he thought, 'This procession has got to go on.' So he walked more proudly than ever, as his noblemen held high the train that wasn't there at all."

—Hans Christian Andersen [126]

King's *Instructions* of 1914 lay dormant for decades, occasionally receiving an uncritical reference or a rare and brief official recitation.[127] A good indication that the *Instructions* was not used as basis for action in the first thirty-three years after its approval by the Department is the fact that the Commissioner of Reclamation found it necessary to ask the Department Solicitor in 1947 if payment of construction charges "frees" excess lands of the excess land law. This was the very question to which King had given an emphatic yes in 1914. On December 16, 1947, the Commissioner of Reclamation issued Administrative Letter 303 on the subject of a program "for action consistent with the acreage limitations." Referring to his letter of a year earlier on the "necessity of bringing about compliance with the acreage limitations," he informed his regional directors of Cohen's conclusion that payment does "free" excess lands and spoke of payment of charges as "an available solution to the excess land problem . . . ." The old solutions, the actual disposal of excess lands as a condition precedent to receiving water from a federal reclamation project, or the signing of a recordable contract to make such disposal, were still acceptable. Water users' organizations expressing a genuine "desire fully to cooperate with the Bureau to bring about full compliance" with acreage limitation were to choose from among these three alternatives.[128] Less than a year later Supple-

---

125. *Admin. Letter 303*, p. 1.
126. ANDERSON, THE COMPLETE ANDERSON 83 (Hersholt ed. 1949).
127. See text at notes 58-71 *supra*.
128. *Admin. Letter 303*, pp. 1, 2.

ment No. 1 to Administrative Letter 303 advised regional directors that under Cohen's opinion individual landowners as well as water users' organizations could "free the land of the acreage limitation" by paying charges in full.[129]

While this program for "compliance" on the basis of Cohen's opinion was taking shape, eight Democratic California Congressmen wrote President Truman of their apprehension that Administrative Letter 303 might open the way to the evasion of the excess land law and frustrate the intention of Congress.[130] Secretary of the Interior Oscar L. Chapman expressed his gratitude for their "vigorous endorsement" of the law "as an important means of encouraging family size farms."[131] He assured them that "in the entire State of California no situation exists on a Federal Reclamation project where Administrative Letter 303 has been applied or is being considered."[132]

Secretary Chapman indicated that the purpose of Administrative Letter 303 was to secure compliance on projects begun prior to the Act of May 25, 1926 on which "significant non-compliance" existed. That act had inaugurated the procedure of permitting excess landholders to enter recordable contracts to dispose of excess holdings, instead of requiring actual disposal prior to receiving water. The Bureau's Landownership Survey in 1946 had revealed "a high degree of landowner compliance" on projects begun since 1926 where "individual recordable contracts" were used. The Secretary said that Administrative Letter 303 had been applied on at least three pre-1926 projects, and that these three had "eliminated non-compliance through either the execution of recordable contracts, disposal of excess lands to qualified owners, or through the payment in full of the construction obligation in strict accord with the Reclamation laws as determined by the Associate Solicitor . . . ."[133] This evidently dates initial administrative action in reliance on the doctrine King announced in 1914, as occurring in 1950 or early 1951.[134]

More than a year after the Secretary's letter to the eight Democratic California Congressmen, he reassured a citizen of California that Administrative Letter 303 had not been applied in California and was not "considered for

---

129. Kenneth Markwell, Acting Commissioner, to Regional and Branch Directors, *Admin. Letter 303*, Supp. No. 1, Sept. 24, 1948, with attachment #1, a letter from Clifford Fix, Chief Counsel, to Commissioner, Sept. 3, 1948, entitled Excess Land Enforcement Program—Salt River and Yuma Projects. The letter indicated ways of identifying an individual excess landholder's proportionate share of charges against his district.

130. Letter from John F. Shelley, Frank R. Havenner, Clinton D. McKinnon, Clyde Doyle, Harry R. Sheppard, Cecil R. King, Chet Holifield, and George P. Miller to President Harry S. Truman, dated Feb. 19, 1951.

131. Letter from Secretary of the Interior Oscar L. Chapman to Congressman John F. Shelley, dated March 29, 1951.

132. *Ibid.*

133. *Ibid.* The degree to which one alternative or another was used was not stated.

134. See Congressman Jackson's 1949 attack on Central Arizona Project, quoting from the Los Angeles Mirror for July 9: "Some 55 percent of these 260,000 acres are owned by only 420 men. So what their scheme amounts to is simply subsidizing 420 wealthy landowners to the tune of more than $500,000 apiece." 95 CONG. REC. A4668 (1949).

application."[135] Kings River and Tulare Lake Project had been the subject of public protest by the Veterans of Foreign Wars after news reports that lump-sum payment on Pine Flat would void the 160-acre rule.[136] Chapman stated: "Negotiations will proceed only on the basis of compliance with the provisions of the reclamation laws prescribing limitations on the acreage of land . . . ."[137]

Yet four months later, and only two weeks prior to the national election that shifted control of the executive and legislative branches of the Government from one party to the other, the local district manager of reclamation in the Kings River and Tulare Lake Project area informed the Kings River Conservation District in the course of negotiations for a repayment contract that, although the landowners could not "wish" excess land law "off the books," the lump-sum payment contract furnished by the Bureau "would remove the excess land restrictions."[138] Negotiations between the Bureau of Reclamation and Kings River water users were ended for the time, however, until resumed by the new national administration.

Meanwhile in the weeks remaining to him, the outgoing Secretary responded to fresh protests made to President Truman against Administrative Letter 303. He informed the President that at no time had he "concurred in a general policy that lump-sum or accelerated payments would be an acceptable alternative to the application of the excess lands limitation."[139] And he described Bureau policy as "to do no more than deal with some situations of long standing," without explaining why "situations of long standing" were an exception to "general policy." Early in 1952 the Commissioner of Reclamation had told Chapman that approval of Cohen's opinion in 1947 by the then Secretary had "formalized" Department policy on the "lump-sum settlement" procedure.[140] About the same time he wrote the President, the Secretary informed the Commissioner that Cohen's opinion carried no Departmental approval because it contained no "policy pronouncement" and had not been submitted for approval.[141]

---

135. Letter from Secretary Oscar Chapman to Correll M. Julian, dated June 23, 1952 [hereinafter cited as Chapman-Julian Letter]. See also correspondence, and statement by Senator Paul H. Douglas, 98 CONG. REC. 9178-82 (1952).

136. Statement by M.C. Hermann, Quartermaster-adjutant, Department of California, Veterans of Foreign Wars of the United States, 97 CONG. REC. A6351 (1951).

137. Chapman-Julian Letter.

138. Letter from Jack W. Rodner to Kings River Conservation District, dated Oct. 21, 1952, pp. 1-2.

139. Oscar L. Chapman, Secretary of the Interior, Memorandum to the President, Dec. 24, 1952, entitled, Letter from James G. Patton on Acreage Limitation in Federal Reclamation Policy.

140. Michael W. Straus, Commissioner, Memorandum to the Secretary of the Interior, Jan. 18, 1952, entitled, Kings River Contract Negotiations.

141. Oscar L. Chapman, Secretary of the Interior, Memorandum to the Commissioner of Reclamation, undated (circa Dec. 24, 1952). On more than one occasion Chapman had written approvingly of the application of Cohen's interpretation to certain

Pursuant to his "policy statements," Secretary Chapman instructed the Commissioner in late 1952 to refuse to accept any lump-sum or accelerated payment of construction charges which would, under Cohen's opinion and Administrative Letter 303, free the land from acreage limitation, and to refrain from negotiating new contracts which would permit lump-sum or accelerated payment. He specifically forbade negotiation of a King's River contract that would permit repayment of construction charges "in less than a pay-out period computed by the methods regularly used by the Bureau of Reclamation."[142] Thus Secretary Chapman left office denying departmental approval to Cohen's opinion, and laying down a departmental policy against its use on Kings River and most if not all projects in the future.

The excess land law never has been an open issue between political parties, for no platform ever contained a plank against it. But as early as the national campaign of 1948 close observers believed that division was evident beneath the surface. In a list of five "tangible gains" powerful men in the Republican party would "expect a Republican Administration to deliver," Marquis Childs included repeal of acreage limitation in Central Valley, which then "could be taken as a precedent for breaking down" the provision elsewhere.[143] Candidate Thomas E. Dewey did not mention the issue publicly, but there is more than a hint of his attitude in his Seattle speech: "It will not be necessary for the Congress to force your next administration to appoint able and qualified men to the Bureau of Reclamation . . . ."[144] To those with knowledge of the attack on Straus and Boke, the opposing stands of candidates Dewey and Truman had been made clear, but the voters in general received no elucidation that enforcement of the excess land law was at stake. The national campaign of 1952 did no more than the campaign of 1948 to bring the excess land issue to the surface. However, less than a year after entering office, on November 9, 1953, Secretary of the Interior McKay authorized negotiation of a repayment contract on Kings River and Tulare Lake Project to include lump-sum prepayment at the option of water users, the payment to render the excess land law inoperative.[145]

It is appropriate to review the legal supports that McKay mobilizes for his action. He relies primarily on precedent, beginning with the Cohen opinion: "This ruling was rested on a provision that goes back a long way in reclamation law and is found in Section 3 of the Act of August 9, 1912 . . . ."[146] He quotes a large portion of the proviso in section 3, but makes no mention of King's *Instructions* of 1914, the only reported legal opinion in the history of the Department that offers reasoning in support of the interpretation of the proviso which he now accepts

---

situations of long standing. The Cohen Opinion was rendered while Secretary J.A. Krug was in office; it bears no signature indicating Departmental approval.

142. *Ibid.*
143. Childs, San Francisco News, Sept. 9, 1948, p. 21, cols. 1-3.
144. San Francisco Chronicle, Sept. 28, 1948, p. 16, cols. 4-5.
145. The text of McKay's authorization appears in text at note 9 *supra*.
146. McKay-Haggerty Letter, *supra* note 9.

The Secretary also stated that in view of the action taken "directly or indirectly in reliance" on Cohen's opinion of 1947, "the Department is constrained to follow the precedents already set . . . ." The elapsed period on which the Secretary is depending is six years at the outside. How much action intervened is not wholly clear. Administrative Letter 303 and its supplements were applied apparently for the first time around 1950 or 1951. Secretary McKay stated only that "a number" of contracts had been executed by his predecessors providing that payment of construction charges relieved lands of acreage limitations, and that such contracts with the Pathfinder Irrigation District, the Gering and Fort Laramie Irrigation District, and the Goshen Irrigation District had obtained the approval of Congress.[147]

McKay did add a note of proper caution against construing congressional approval as constituting ratification of Department policy under Cohen's opinion and Administrative Letter 303: "It should be noted, however, that the principal reason for the submission of these contracts to the Congress was the *solution of the repayment problem*."[148] When the three contracts named by the Secretary were under consideration in Senate and House committee hearings, a fourth contract was also considered involving the Northport Irrigation District. None of the three contracts named by the Secretary as precedent was printed with the hearings. The text of the Northport contract, which contains no clause that payment of charges relieves lands of the excess land provision, was the only one reproduced. The excess land issue was not discussed before the committees, in House or Senate committee reports, or on the floor of either House.[149]

The Secretary relied also on the uniqueness of the Kings River and Tulare Lake Project:

> "The Kings River area is serviced by an irrigation system which was privately developed and financed, and operated long before the Kings River Project, and there will be no Federal investment in works below Pine Flat Dam. The benefit which the water users will derive from

---

147. McKay-Haggerty Letter. The contracts were approved by the Act of July 17, 1952, 66 Stat. 754 (1952), pursuant to § 7(a) of the Reclamation Project Act of 1939, 53 Stat. 1192, as amended, 43 U.S.C. § 485f (1952). Assistant Secretary of the Interior Fred G. Aandahl wrote: "on December 12, 1952 . . . the then Under Secretary of the Interior executed 31 contracts with water users' organizations in the Minidoka and Palisades Projects, in Idaho. All of these contracts contain provisions [for] employment of the lump-sum approach to repayment, with the consequent inapplicability of the acreage limitation . . . ." Letter from Fred G. Aandahl to C.J. Haggerty, dated Aug. 6, 1954. Apparently these contracts were not submitted to Congress. The Assistant Secretary did not say whether they offered excess landholders the option of prepayment.

148. McKay-Haggerty Letter (emphasis added).

149. *Hearing before the Senate Committee on Interior and Insular Affairs on S. 2720*, 82d Cong., 2d Sess. (1952); *Hearings before Subcommittee of House Committee on Interior and Insular Affairs on H.R. 6723*, 82d Cong., 2d Sess. (1952); H.R. Rep. No. 2150, 82d Cong., 2d Sess. (1952); S. Rep. No. 1809, 82d Cong., 2d Sess. (1952); 98 Cong. Rec. 8917, 8930-31, 9066-67 (1952). Northport contract was not approved by Congress because the district opposed it.

the operation of the project, which is one principally for flood control, will be the storage of certain waters behind Pine Flat Dam and their release into the river as may permit their most effective use in the completed system."[150]

This statement boils down to four points. The first is that the irrigation system was privately developed, financed, and operated long before there was a federal project. This is irrelevant, and the Secretary does not dispute that reclamation law applies to Kings River and Tulare Lake Project the same as to any other. Congress was fully informed of that Project's uniqueness when it applied reclamation law to it. The sponsor of the Flood Control Bill covering Kings and Kern River Projects stated: "No project in this bill which may include irrigation features is exempted from the reclamation laws."[151]

The Secretary's second point is that "there will be no Federal investment in works below Pine Flat Dam." The Secretary is obviously in no position to give such assurance for the future. Tulare Lake interests have had plans for more flood control works ever since 1917,[152] and they might be as successful in the future as they have been in the past. In addition McKay overlooks investment by the Army Engineers in flood control measures of great, if not exclusive value to irrigators of Tulare Lake bed. The total expended by the Army Engineers from 1933 to 1949 was close to two million dollars.[153] All these expenditures were borne by the federal government and were not reimbursable by the beneficiaries.

The Secretary's third point is that the project is "principally for flood control." It is hard to know what he means by this, or what relevance the argument has. It is true that the project was authorized by Congress in the Flood Control Act of 1944, but reclamation law was specifically applied to the project by section 8 of that act.[154] The project was included in the flood control bill in part upon representations by the Army Engineers that the ratio of benefits of flood control to irrigation was 1.19 to 1. In 1948 the Engineers, having won authorization over the Bureau, and with construction of the project "well under way," recalculated and produced a revised estimate favoring irrigation over flood control by 1.59 to 1.[155]

---

150. McKay-Haggerty Letter.
151. 90 CONG. REC. 9264 (1944).
152. CALIF. DEP'T PUB. WORKS, DIV. WATER RES., SAN JOAQUIN RIVER BASIN, 1931, BULL. No. 29, p. 483 (1934).
153. From 1933 to 1939, $357,000 was expended by Army Engineers on minor flood-control measures. H.R. Doc. No. 630, 76th Cong., 3d Sess. 6 (1940). In 1943, $250,000 was spent on permanent control works for diverting flood waters. Between June 30, 1943, and late 1948, $1,480,551 was expended by the Army Engineers on Tulare Lake and the streams flowing into it, and an additional $52,000 was spent during the fiscal year 1949. Letter from Lt. Colonel Ellsworth I. Davis, for Sacramento District Engineer, to Paul S. Taylor, dated Oct. 15, 1948.
154. 58 STAT. 891 (1944), as amended, 43 U.S.C. § 390 (1952).
155. THE KINGS RIVER PROJECT IN THE BASIN OF THE GREAT CENTRAL VALLEY—A CASE STUDY, TASK FORCE REPORT ON NATURAL RESOURCES (Appendix L), Jan. 1949, pp. 178-79.

The Secretary's fourth point is that the water users' only benefit "will be the storage of certain waters behind Pine Flat Dam and their release . . . as may permit their most effective use." The Warren Act of 1911 appears to have had such a project especially in mind when it applied reclamation law to the service of waters "impounded" or "stored" for appropriate release later.[156] On few projects, it would seem from the record, was Congress so determined that reclamation law ought to be applied.[157]

One point remains, unmentioned by the Secretary. Congress gave special authorization that repayment on Kings River and Tulare Lake Project might be "either in lump sum or annual installments, for conservation storage when used."[158] Thus, it is within the Secretary's power to accept lump sum prepayment. However, it would place an unbearable strain on credulity to believe that in 1944, after King's *Instructions* had lain all but dormant for thirty years, Congress was cognizant of the interpretation that Associate Solicitor Cohen declared three years later. Still less could Congress have foreseen the application of Cohen's opinion to prepayment, as proposed by Secretary McKay.

V

WATER POLICY OR COLLATERAL SECURITY?

> "The effect of all system is apt to be petrifaction of the subject systematized. Legal science is not exempt from this tendency. Legal systems have their periods in which system decays into technicality, in which a scientific jurisprudence becomes a mechanical jurisprudence . . . . Conceptions are fixed. The premises are no longer to be examined. Everything is reduced to simple deduction from them. Principles cease to have importance. The law becomes a body of rules."
> —Roscoe Pound [159]

The roots of United States land policy reach into colonial times. The Legislature of Virginia abolished entail in 1776, curbing the right of individuals to hold landed estates intact by binding the next generation. This proposal, in the words of its sponsor Thomas Jefferson, "was deemed essential to a well-ordered republic." Its purpose was "to annul . . . privilege, and instead of an aristocracy of wealth, of more harm and danger, than benefit, to society, to make an opening for the aristocracy of virtue and talent, which nature has wisely provided for the direction of the interests of Society, and scattered with equal hand through all its conditions . . . ."[160] Jefferson's view became accepted national policy as statute after statute adopted, broadened, and inscribed it into provisions for disposing of the public domain. The fruit of this policy is better balanced communities and less class distinction.[161]

---

156. 36 STAT. 925 (1911), 43 U.S.C. § 523 (1952).
157. Few projects have been presented so fully to Congress as this one. There were hearings in the House on three House Bills and in the Senate on two House Bills and a Senate Resolution.
158. Section 10, 58 STAT. 901 (1944).
159. Pound, *Liberty of Contract*, 18 YALE L.J. 462 (1909).
160. FOLEY (ED.), THE JEFFERSONIAN CYCLOPEDIA 307, no. 2704 (1900).
161. The Senate Small Business Committee, seeking to ascertain the effect of great

The Virginia Legislature's action was a pure expression of social policy, but when this policy was applied to the disposition of the public domain, a financial transaction appeared. At first, in conferring title to cheap land, the financial aspect was slight, but this increased with development of the arid West when the Government expected settlers to repay costs of water development. Still anti-monopoly policy came first, and never was used as collateral to secure the financial obligation. Failure to achieve the policy goals was regarded as perversion of the statutes.

It is perfectly clear that Congress viewed reclamation law as a water policy measure. Congress knew that the problem of securing repayment could be lifted from Government shoulders by allowing monopoly of land and water, but rejected monopoly because "no one contemplates paying so stupendous a price as this for irrigation development."[162] There is no evidence that Congress intended to offer water users an option to keep or dispose of excess landholdings.[163] On the contrary, when Congress spoke on the subject, it denied the option specifically; in 1902 it forbade "commutation" of the residence requirement by cash payment, and in 1939 it created section 9(e) contracts which no administrator interprets as affording an option.[164] Congress has shown repeatedly that finance is secondary by its willingness to make repayment easier for water users at financial sacrifice to the government.

The action of Secretary McKay authorizing his negotiators on Kings River and Tulare Lake Project to accept prepayment in lieu of requiring disposal of excess lands treats the excess land law as an expendable curb on water monpoly and speculation, a lash on the end of a whip to secure repayment from excess landholders. He is apparently untroubled that his interpretation makes the Government seem more concerned over securing repayment from one class of water users than another. He maintains that "the Department is constrained to follow the precedents already set, unless they should clearly be demonstrated to be wrong . . . ."[165] Secretary McKay's immediate predecessor refused to approve what McKay suggests he is helpless to prevent. No Secre-

---

landholdings in twentieth century rural society, made a comparative study of two towns in the Central Valley of California. Indices such as distribution of occupation and income, volume and distribution of trade, richness of civic organizations, and community services demonstrate the striking differences between Arvin and Dinuba, surrounded by large and small farms, respectively. SMALL BUSINESS AND THE COMMUNITY: A STUDY IN CENTRAL VALLEY OF CALIFORNIA ON EFFECTS OF SCALE OF FARM OPERATIONS, *Senate Committee Print No. 13*, 79th Cong., 2d Sess. (1946).

162. H.R. REP. No. 794, 66th Cong., 2d Sess. 3 (1920). Because maximum repayment charges do not approach the expenditure of the Government, even the fiscal aspects of reclamation demand that benefiting land be divided into small portions, so that no individual receives more than an equitable share of the public bounty. See Note, *Acreage Limitation: Policy Considerations*, 38 CALIF. L. REV. 728, 731 (1950).

163. Sometimes it is intimated that the subsidy of interest-free money is the *raison d'être* for the excess land law. This is only another facet of the fallacy that the excess land law is essentially a collateral device to assure repayment by excess landholders.

164. 53 STAT. 1196 (1939), as amended, 43 U.S.C. § 485h (1952).

165. McKay-Haggerty Letter.

tary is bound by precedents he finds shoddy. The Secretary of the Interior in 1913 reversed a ruling permitting corporations to obtain water rights because the intent of Congress was that reclaimed lands should be "the homes of families."[166] Even if the Secretary feels constrained to follow the Cohen-King opinion and Department practice under Administrative Letter 303 holding that full and final payment of charges terminates the excess land provision, no statute requires him to accept prepayment,[167] and no precedent dictates that landholders shall not first have disposed of their excess, or contracted to do so. The Secretary is expressing his own view of desirable national policy.

Secretary McKay's present action, still revocable, shatters the excess land law already weakened by the corrosion caused by external pressures upon administrators, by their own unsympathetic attitude toward the law and by their preoccupation with technicalities. If Secretary McKay's authorization of November 9, 1953, expresses the will of Congress and represents application of the excess land law, words have been emptied of their meaning.

Roscoe Pound regretted that in substituting technicalities for a concern with premises, the courts had "wrought an injury" to themselves and "to the public regard for law."[168] It is as necessary to maintain public confidence in the integrity of public administration as in that of the judicial process. Senator Paul H. Douglas has explained the especial importance of administering reclamation law properly on Kings River and Tulare Lake Project: "The great landowners of the Kings River and Tulare Lake area apparently have not hesitated to seek public appropriations for their own benefit while deferring and possibly defying compliance with a law they should be proud to support. The President, on the other hand, has wisely declared maintenance of the family farm to be our national policy at home and abroad. Land reform has become one of our main instruments for stopping the spread of international communism and maintaining our national security . . . . Whatever we do on Kings River, therefore, will be subjected to the most searching examination of all who realize that our policy must now meet the test in our own country, as well as in foreign lands."[169]

It is hazardous to confuse collateral with policy, the pocketbook of a law with its heart, to forget to examine premises, to lose principle in a body of rules.

---

166. Instructions, 42 L.D. 250 (1913).
167. 58 STAT. 901 (1944).
168. Pound, *supra* note 159, at 487.
169. Letter to Secretary of the Interior Oscar Chapman, dated April 29, 1952, printed in 98 CONG. REC. 9181 (1952). A recent statement from India suggests a confidence in United States reclamation law reminiscent of that of the original American sponsors: "We are all glad that a number of irrigation projects are being undertaken by the present Government. But, are the same evils of land purchase speculation, rack-renting, money-lending, profiteering in trade to be repeated here too? . . . . Here is a chance for the present Government. Let them study the reclamation and irrigation laws of the U.S.A. in this respect." Sivaswamy, *The Demands of the Cultivating Tenant and Labourer*, in LEGISLATIVE PROTECTION FOR THE CULTIVATING TENANT AND LABOURER, PROCEEDINGS OF THE CONFERENCE OF AGRICULTURAL WORKERS' UNIONS 11-12 (1947).

DESTRUCTION OF
FEDERAL RECLAMATION POLICY?

Destruction of Federal Reclamation Policy? The *Ivanhoe* Case

PAUL S. TAYLOR*

I. WATER FOR 160 ACRES

No right to the use of water for land in private ownership shall be sold for a tract exceeding 160 acres to any one landowner . . . .
NATIONAL RECLAMATION ACT, 1902[1]

In 1902 Congress, urged by the unanimous congressional delegations of western states, created federal machinery—administrative, technical, and financial—to bring water to western land through reclamation law. In the fifty-five years of federal reclamation Congress has spent around three and one-half billion dollars to develop water supplies,[2] including more than $400 million for Central Valley Project in California alone.[3]

Reclamation law offers each landowner water for up to 160 acres of his land. Seeking to distribute scarce and costly waters equitably, Congress set this amount as the maximum individual share. This is the famous excess land provision, or 160-acre water limitation. It neither limits the amount of land one may own, nor

---

* Professor of Economics, University of California; Consultant to the Office of the Secretary of the Interior and the Bureau of Reclamation successively between 1943 and 1952. Beverly Starika and Klaus Loewald assisted ably in preparation of this article.

1. 32 STAT. 388 (1902), 43 U.S.C. § 431 (1952). The ceiling figure of 160 acres was set in 1902 as a liberal upper limit on an irrigated family-size farm. The question sometimes is raised whether 160 acres is not an anachronism today. Actually, the average acreage of irrigated land in 84,502 farms in California in 1955 was 83.4 acres, or only about one-half the statutory figure. The average selling value of 160 acres of irrigated land in Tulare County in 1945 was $85,760. *Hearings Before the Subcommittee of the Senate Committee on Public Lands on S. 912*, 80th Cong., 1st Sess. at 861 (1947). These data suggest that 160 acres still are sufficient to support a family properly. If land is so poor that 160 acres is insufficient for this purpose, it is a question whether public funds ought to be expended at all to water it. Besides, the limit has already been doubled in California by a questionable interpretation to allow 320 acres to man and wife.

Against possible economies of larger scale operations, which are smaller than many persons suppose and sometimes the result of Government assistance, must be set the differences in quality of communities founded on large-scale and on family-size farms, respectively. See J. KARL LEE, ECONOMIES OF SCALE OF FARMING IN THE SOUTHERN SAN JOAQUIN VALLEY 1-5, United States Dept. of Agriculture, Bureau of Agricultural Economics (1946); Note 38 CALIF. L. REV. 728 (1950). See also note 129 *infra*. The essence of the excess land provision is not a particular acreage figure but a principle: equitable distribution of opportunity and public subsidies. If ever it is determined that 160 acres (or 320) is too low, or too high, Congress can change the number or permit flexibility without abandoning the principle.

2. SECRETARY OF THE INTERIOR ANN. REP. 49 (1956).

3. U.S. BUREAU OF RECLAMATION ANN. REP. ON CENTRAL VALLEY PROJECT 27 (1956).

interferes with rights to water from sources other than a federal reclamation project. It offers to owners of more than 160 acres, at their own election, the opportunity to obtain water temporarily for their additional (or "excess") lands, on the condition that they agree to sell the excess at a price appraised "without reference to the proposed construction of the irrigation works."[4] The duration of the opportunity for temporary use of additional water is not fixed by law, but may be a decade or more; the opportunity, therefore, may prove exceedingly valuable.

Large landowners object to the excess land provision because this opportunity for additional water is not permanent, and because the law denies them the incremental values to their excess lands created by federal reclamation. This, indeed, is the issue, and it is fundamental. Congress says that reclaimed water and the incremental values it creates shall be distributed *equitably among people*. Large landholders want distribution of water and incremental values *according to ownership of property in land*.

This conflict over policy and economic interest has disturbed for generations the efforts of government, federal and state, to arrive at and establish a sound principle for water development. The battle has gone back and forth among courts, legislatures, and administrators, and from local irrigation districts to the national Congress. This Article deals with the most recent phase of the conflict as it proceeds through the California courts on the way to the Supreme Court of the United States.

II. Trusteeship

> It is . . . concluded that the title to the unappropriated domestic waters of the state is in the State of California in trust for the use and benefit of the beneficiaries of that trust; that the trust character of that title is anchored in the state by constitutional provisions, by statutes enacted in furtherance thereof, and by the decisional law of the state; that the beneficiaries of that trust are the water users of the state who in a general sense constitute all of the people of the state; that the beneficiaries of the trust relationship whose rights are here under consideration are those present or prospective users who individually or in properly classified

---

4. Omnibus Adjustment Act of 1926, 44 STAT. 649, as amended, 43 U.S.C. § 423e (Supp. IV, 1957). Central Valley contracts between the United States and irrigation districts usually provide for three appraisers, one appointed by the district within which the excess land is located, one by the Secretary of the Interior, and the third by the other two.

The administrative rule for water delivery stated in the text applies to Central Valley Project of California. A stricter rule has usually been employed elsewhere. Ivanhoe Irr. Dist. v. All Parties, 47 Cal.2d 597, 635–36, 306 P.2d 824, 847, *appeal docketed*, 25 U.S.L. WEEK 3343 (U.S. May 13, 1957) (No. 993).

groups bring themselves within the orbit of the state law under which they may be in a position to demand benefits without discrimination, and that within that category are the landowners of the District. It is they who are in position to avail themselves of the right to beneficial use of the waters to be purveyed and to demand indiscriminate service. There is nothing in the foregoing declaration which interjects anything new into the water law of the state.

IVANHOE IRR. DIST. v. ALL PARTIES, 1957[5]

On January 24, 1957, in *Ivanhoe Irr. Dist. v. All Parties*, the Supreme Court of California decided, four to three, that inclusion of the provisions of the excess land law in repayment contracts between California irrigation districts and the United States for federal construction of irrigation works violates the constitution of California.[6] In finding this historic provision invalid, the majority of the California Supreme Court asserted a series of propositions.

First, it held that water users of the state who are or may become entitled to water under the state law, hold equitable title to the "unappropriated domestic waters of the state."[7] Second, it asserted that landowners who are "present and potential" users of water have, as one of the incidents of ownership, an "inchoate right" or private "property right" in these unappropriated waters.[8] Third, it held that the state—and likewise the United States when it "steps into the shoes of the state" by acquiring its water rights for project purposes—holds title to unappropriated waters not as a proprietor but merely as a trustee for "the real owners."[9] Fourth, California, as trustee, is "answerable to the courts, in the exercise of their traditional powers in equity for the proper discharge of [its] stewardship" for "the beneficiaries of the trust," *i.e.*, the "landowners and water users" who are "present and potential water users."[10] The United States, standing in the state's shoes, must be taken to bear the same burden. Fifth, since the relation

---

5. 47 Cal.2d 597, 627, 306 P.2d 824, 841 (1957).
6. *Ibid.* Simultaneously, by the same divided vote, the court decided Albonico v. Madera Irr. Dist., 47 Cal.2d 695, 306 P.2d 894, *appeal docketed*, 25 U.S.L. WEEK 3343 (U.S. May 13, 1957) (No. 995), Madera Irr. Dist. v. All Persons, 47 Cal.2d 681, 306 P.2d 886, *appeal docketed*, 25 U.S.L. WEEK 3343 (U.S. May 13, 1957) (No. 994), and Santa Barbara County Water Agency v. All Persons, 47 Cal.2d 699, 306 P.2d 875, *appeal docketed*, 25 U.S.L. WEEK 3343 (U.S. May 13, 1957) (No. 996). All rested primarily on the court's view, elaborated in the Ivanhoe case, of the invalidity of the excess land provision.
7. Ivanhoe Irr. Dist. v. All Parties, 47 Cal.2d 597, 627, 306 P.2d 824, 841 (1957).
8. *Id.* at 626, 635, 306 P.2d at 841, 846.
9. *Id.* at 626, 628, 306 P.2d at 841, 842.
10. *Id.* at 625, 626, 306 P.2d at 840, 841.

between the United States and the "real owners" is that of trustee and "beneficiary," the court can ignore consideration of the power of the United States to determine public policy and deal only with its power as trustee "to deprive beneficiaries of the trust, namely, the water users of the state . . . of a property right thereunder or of an inchoate right to the use of water . . . ."[11] Sixth, Congress having accepted in California the status of trustee by specifically deferring to state law "relating to the control, appropriation, use, or distribution of water used in irrigation, or any vested right acquired thereunder,"[12] the requirement of reclamation law[13] that contracts with water users shall include the excess land provision is not "applicable" and "cannot be legally justified."[14]

The preceding propositions, embodying the majority's conclusion that the federal excess land law is invalid in California, depend on the validity of the trust theory.[15]

In deference to the American axiom that law rests on precedent, the *Ivanhoe* majority says its trust theory "interjects" nothing "new into the water law of the state," is "but a recognition and re-declaration of existing fundamental concepts . . . ," and is anchored in constitution, statutes, and decisions of the state.[16] Despite this disclaimer of novelty, diligent search discloses no precedent.

The majority does not specify in which constitutional provision trusteeship of water for the benefit of landowners is "anchored," nor is any discernible. Neither the original California Constitution of 1849 nor the present one dating from 1879 says that the State is trustee of water for the benefit of landowners or, indeed, for anyone. Article XIV deals with water and water rights. Section 1 declares that the use of all appropriated water is "a public use, and subject to regulation and control of the state," but regulation and control are not trusteeship. Section 2 deals with water rates only, and is irrelevant. Section 3, adopted in 1928 and referred to in the majority opinion, forbids waste of water and sets "reasonable and beneficial use" as conservation criteria limit-

---

11. *Id.* at 635, 306 P.2d at 846.
12. *Id.* at 639, 306 P.2d at 849, quoting 32 STAT. 390 (1902), 43 U.S.C. § 383 (1952). See text at notes 34–44 *infra*.
13. Section 46, Omnibus Adjustment Act of 1926, 44 STAT. 649, as amended, 43 U.S.C. § 423e (Supp. IV, 1957).
14. Ivanhoe Irr. Dist. v. All Parties, 47 Cal.2d 597, 639, 306 P.2d 824, 849 (1957).
15. See pp. 77–78 *supra*.
16. Ivanhoe Irr. Dist. v. All Parties, 47 Cal.2d 597, 627, 306 P.2d 824, 841 (1957).

ing riparian rights to water. There are no other sections in Article XIV.

A search of the statutes cited and quoted by the majority is equally fruitless. These statutes provide for public regulation of the use of water in the interest of the people, but, like the text of the constitution, they place no limit on the state's title to water.[17] The dissenting opinion by Chief Justice Gibson, concurred in by Justice Traynor, appears fully justified in stating flatly: "The fact is that no declaration of trust is intended . . . by these general provisions enunciating water policy . . . , and they are in no way inconsistent with the existence of full title to water rights in the state or in private persons."[18]

The majority cites five California decisions in support of its conclusion that "the state as an entity is the holder of the legal title as trustee for the benefit of the people of the state, all of whom in the last analysis, are the water users of the state."[19] But examination of these cases yields no more authority in decisional law than did search of the constitution and statutes. All five cases are concerned with the nature and functions of *irrigation districts*; none of them deals with the nature of the *state's* title to water. Irrigation districts are agencies of the state, created and governed by its statutes, but they are not the state. There seems to be no escape from the conclusion that the cases relied on by the majority as precedent fail because they are not in point.[20]

Although the California irrigation district decisions cited by the majority cannot be accepted as conferring the authority of precedent on the theory of state trusteeship of water, they may

---

17. CAL. STAT. 1913, p. 1018; CAL. WATER CODE, §§ 102, 104, 105, 1052 (1956).
18. Ivanhoe Irr. Dist. v. All Parties, 47 Cal.2d 597, 655, 306 P.2d 824, 859 (1957) (dissenting opinion).
19. *Id.* at 625–26, 306 P.2d at 840. These are Hall v. Superior Court, 198 Cal. 373, 245 Pac. 814 (1926); Tulare Irr. Dist. v. Collins, 154 Cal. 440, 97 Pac. 1124 (1908); Merchants Nat'l Bank v. Escondido Irr. Dist., 144 Cal. 329, 77 Pac. 937 (1904); Allen v. Hussey, 101 Cal. App.2d 457, 225 P.2d 674 (2d Dist. 1950); Lindsay-Strathmore Irr. Dist. v. Wutchumna Water Co., 111 Cal. App. 688, 296 Pac. 933 (4th Dist. 1931). See also Ivanhoe Irr. Dist. v. All Parties, 47 Cal.2d 597, 670, 306 P.2d 824, 868 (1957) (dissenting opinion).
20. See Ivanhoe Irr. Dist. v. All Parties, 47 Cal.2d 597, 656, 306 P.2d 824, 859 (1957) (dissenting opinion). One of the cases cited by the *Ivanhoe* majority uses language that appears to conflict with the trust theory: "An irrigation district is an agency of the state and its functions are exclusively governmental. It owns no lands in a proprietary sense; its property is owned by the state . . . ." Allen v. Hussey, 101 Cal. App.2d 457, 467, 225 P.2d 674, 680 (2d Dist. 1950), cited in Ivanhoe Irr. Dist. v. All Parties, *supra* at 625, 306 P.2d at 840. This language is a close paraphrase of a 1939 decision in which Justice Shenk, author of the *Ivanhoe* majority opinion, concurred. Anderson-Cottonwood Irr. Dist. v. Klukkert, 13 Cal.2d 191, 197, 88 P.2d 685, 689 (1939).

furnish the idea. In one of them the court, speaking of relationships *within irrigation districts*, said:

> [T]he beneficiaries of the trust—who, upon familiar equitable principles, are to be regarded as the owners of the property—are the landowners in the district with whose funds the property has been acquired ... and in whom, indeed, is vested by the express provisions of the statute, in each, the right to the several use of a definite proportion of the water of the district, and in all, in common, the equitable ownership of its water-rights, reservoirs, ditches, and property generally, as the means of supplying water .... Such rights as these cannot be distinguished in any way from other private rights, and therefore clearly come within the protection of the provision of section 13 of article I of the state constitution—that "no person shall be ... deprived of ... property without due process of law,"—and of the similar provision of section 1 of the fourteenth amendment to the constitution of the United States.[21]

The majority, immediately upon quoting this description of the trust relationship within *districts*, abruptly asserts an identical trust relationship between the state and its landowners. The argument, it seems, is by analogy; the sole connection is one word: "*Likewise* the state is not the owner of the domestic water of the state in the sense that it has absolute power and dominion over it to the exclusion of the rights of those who have beneficial interest therein. The title is an equitable one residing in the water users of the state."[22]

Assertion of analogy is not proof. To hold that because the state legislature creates an irrigation district in the image of a trustee for its landowners, the state itself is cast in the same image, is to argue that a limitation imposed by the creator upon the creature inheres therefore in the creator. This is a *non sequitur*. No other tangible source, much less support, of the trust theory of the *Ivanhoe* majority appears in the constitution, a statute, or the decision.[23]

Having identified the state as a trustee, the majority establishes

---

21. Merchants Nat'l Bank v. Escondido Irr. Dist., 144 Cal. 329, 334, 77 Pac. 937, 939 (1904).
22. Ivanhoe Irr. Dist. v. All Parties, 47 Cal.2d 597, 625, 306 P.2d 824, 840 (1957). [Emphasis added.]
23. The *Ivanhoe* majority notes that the briefs of all parties accept the trust theory. It says: "There is no disagreement on the part of any party appearing as to the correctness of the judgment of the trial court that the title to and control over the unappropriated domestic waters of the state are vested in the state in trust for the water users of the state." *Id*. at 613, 306 P.2d at 833. The original demurrer and answer attacked the excess land law and referred to the state and United States as trustees for landowners. It was filed by an attorney general whose successor withdrew the original answer and filed an amended answer, defending the excess land law but retaining passages from an earlier brief referring to trusteeship, *id*. at 608–9, 306 P.2d at 830, but not the trust theory as defined by the *Ivanhoe* majority. The United States was not a party to the *Ivanhoe* case.

the beneficiaries of the trust as already noted. To begin with, they are "the people" or the "water users of the state," for the majority equates these, saying the state is trustee "for the benefit of the people of the state, all of whom in the last analysis, are the water users of the state."[24] There is a substantial difference between the inclusiveness of the "last analysis," however, and the exclusiveness of those actually becoming beneficiaries with legal right to enforce a trust. The majority limits the latter to those who "bring themselves within the orbit of the state law under which they may be in position to demand benefits without discrimination, and . . . within that category are the landowners of the district."[25] Thus the majority begins its concept of trusteeship with all the people and ends with none but property owners of irrigable land, narrowing but claiming always to equate.

The very insistence of the majority on identifying a *private proprietor of unappropriated waters* capable of enforcing a trust is suspect, since it further reveals the novelty of the trust theory. To find a private proprietor requires upsetting well established doctrine on the peculiar nature of ownership of water as differentiated from ownership of land. A distinguished California specialist in water law, pointing out this distinction,[26] has cited a California decision which declares:

> The title or interest that one may acquire in the waters of a stream *is entirely different* to that which may be acquired in lands. Running water, so long as it continues to flow in its natural course, *is not and cannot be the subject of private ownership* . . . . This interest is *dependent upon user* and *it may be lost* when the owner ceases to make avail of the same . . . .
>
> . . . .
>
> . . . . It is the use of the water merely to which they may acquire an interest and not to the water itself.[27] [Emphasis added.]

Appropriation, by customary California law, marks the *beginning* of a right to water, *use* is its basis, and *disuse* is its end. The *Ivanhoe* case changes this. It asserts an inchoate private title to water "which has not heretofore been subjected to beneficial use except as contemplated by acquisition, by appropriation or other-

---

24. Ivanhoe Irr. Dist. v. All Parties, 47 Cal.2d 597, 625, 306 P.2d 824, 840 (1957). Apparently landowners are the only people within this important category.
25. *Id.* at 627, 306 P.2d at 841.
26. Wiel, *Fifty Years of Water Law*, 50 HARV. L. REV. 252, 273 (1936).
27. Big Rock Mutual Water Co. v. Valyermo Ranch Co., 78 Cal. App. 266, 274, 276, 248 Pac. 264, 267, 268 (1st Dist. 1926).

wise on the part of the State of California and the United States."[28] The majority has distorted the doctrine of appropriation beyond recognition; use or nonuse are rendered irrelevant.

As with the concept of trusteeship,[29] and in the absence of precedent, it may be possible here to identify the source of the new idea on private property in water by noting resemblance. The bases of riparian rights and of appropriative rights to water are fundamentally opposed, the former resting on ownership of land and the latter on use of water.[30] The majority, in covering unappropriated waters with a property right based on land ownership, employs a concept of property-in-water-based-on-landownership, modeled evidently on the riparian doctrine. But no riparian rights are directly involved in the *Ivanhoe* case.[31] Defendants' lands are 100 miles distant from the river that is the source of their water.[32] Before all California lands are supplied with water, it might be necessary to go even to the Columbia River in another state and to the ocean. It seems unlikely that by any stretch California land ownership could confer a property right in waters from either of these sources.

The *Ivanhoe* majority is confronted with the fact that it is invalidating a federal statute in face of a federal constitutional provision that the Constitution and laws of the United States are "the supreme Law of the Land; and the Judges in every State shall be bound thereby, any Thing in the Constitution or Laws of any State

---

28. Ivanhoe Irr. Dist. v. All Parties, 47 Cal.2d 597, 623, 306 P.2d 824, 839 (1957). The court declares a private title to unused water and simultaneously says that "the real basis, measure and limit of the appropriative right is the actual beneficial use of the water," and quotes from the state water code the words "when the appropriator . . . ceases to use it . . . the right ceases." Madera Irr. Dist. v. All Persons, 47 Cal.2d 681, 690–91, 306 P.2d 886, 892 (1957), decided the same day as *Ivanhoe*, by the same majority. Any substantive distinction between "title" and "appropriative right" to water appears insufficient to remove the evident inconsistency between discarding use and relying upon it. The court in *Ivanhoe* appears to reject use as a basis. See p. 82 *supra*. Acceptance of the opposite interpretation, suggested by the quotation from the *Madera* case, would undermine the trust theory by its inconsistency. The reader who has followed this far will have recognized that the majority opinion in *Ivanhoe* is extraordinary.

29. See text at notes 21–22 *supra*.

30. Riparian rights to water are "a part and parcel of the land itself," a "property right" which is "vested in the riparian owner and as such . . . protected by the state and federal Constitutions" and not to be "impaired without due process of law and without just compensation." Ivanhoe Irr. Dist. v. All Parties, 47 Cal.2d 597, 621, 306 P.2d 824, 838 (1957).

31. *Id.* at 623, 306 P.2d at 839. Besides, the United States acquired water rights by purchase, of which it became owner, not trustee. Justice Carter points out in his dissenting opinion that seventy-five percent of the drainage basin of Trinity Project, authorized by Congress for inclusion in Central Valley Project, is owned by the United States. *Id.* at 677, 306 P.2d at 872–73 (dissenting opinion). Trusteeship does not apply to these waters.

32. *Id.* at 658, 306 P.2d at 861 (dissenting opinion by Gibson, C.J., and Traynor, J.).

to the Contrary notwithstanding."[33] It seeks a way around federal supremacy by arguing that Congress, in enacting reclamation law, has wholly and intentionally relinquished jurisdiction over federally reclaimed waters to the states, even to nullifying the excess land law if this is found to conflict with state law. Thus the federal government, states the California majority, "both by legislation and court decision has recognized that the law of this state is determinative of rights to water in this state."[34]

To support its conclusion, the majority opinion relies first on section 8 of the Act of 1902 which provides

> that nothing in this Act shall be construed as affecting or intended to affect or to in any way interfere with the laws of any State or Territory relating to the control, appropriation, use, or distribution of water used in irrigation, or any vested right acquired thereunder, and the Secretary of the Interior, in carrying out the provisions of this Act, shall proceed in conformity with such laws, and nothing herein shall in any way affect any right of any State or of the Federal Government or of any landowner, appropriator, or user of water in, to, or from any interstate stream or of waters thereof: *Provided*, That the right to the use of water acquired under the provisions of this Act shall be appurtenant to the land irrigated, and beneficial use shall be the basis, the measure, and the limit of the right.[35]

The proviso in the very section 8 quoted by the majority to prove its contention that Congress has deferred wholly to the state in fact proves the opposite. In the proviso Congress specifically excludes its requirement that *"use* shall be the basis, the measure, and the limit" of water rights from any deferral to, or noninterference with, state law.[36] The *Ivanhoe* majority destroys *use* as the basis, measure, and limit, and is in no position to claim the sanction of Congress for what Congress expressly rejects.

The majority's claim to federal acquiescence rests on faulty reasoning. When Congress passed the Act of 1902,[37] it passed sections 5 and 8 simultaneously, the former carrying the excess land provision.[38] The majority of the California court preferred the general statement of intention to the specific declaration to the contrary. This implies that the advocates of the 1902 reclamation

---
33. U.S. CONST. art. VI, cl. 2.
34. Ivanhoe Irr. Dist. v. All Parties, 47 Cal.2d 597, 628. 306 P.2d 824, 842 (1957).
35. 32 STAT. 390 (1902), 43 U.S.C. §§ 383, 372 (1952), quoted in Ivanhoe Irr. Dist. v. All Parties, 47 Cal.2d 597, 627, 306 P.2d 824, 842 (1957).
36. 32 STAT. 390 (1902), 43 U.S.C. § 372 (1952). [Emphasis added.] See text at notes 26-28 *supra*.
37. 32 STAT. 388 (1902), 43 U.S.C. §§ 431-49 (1952).
38. 32 STAT. 389 (1902), 43 U.S.C. § 431 (1952).

bill either did not know what they were doing, or were insincere in giving the most extraordinary, voluminous, specific, and repeated assurances, including references to section 5, in committee and on the floor of Congress, that reclamation was for the many, not for the few.[39]

The *Ivanhoe* majority seeks to buttress its view by quoting from the United States Supreme Court in *United States v. Gerlach Live Stock Co.*:[40] "the Federal Reclamation Act defers" to Article XIV, section 1, of the California constitution.[41] But this section makes no reference either to water rights or to trusteeship; it merely authorizes state control of water appropriated for sale, rental, or distribution. The United States Supreme Court does not say, either in the *Gerlach* case or elsewhere, that because of section 8 of the federal reclamation law, every other provision of reclamation law yields to inconsistent state law.[42] Indeed, it has said the contrary on another occasion: "We do not suggest that where Congress has provided a system of regulation for federal projects it must give way before an inconsistent state system."[43]

The *Ivanhoe* majority, ready to argue that Congress has yielded wholly to the states where laws relating to water are in conflict, passes lightly over the fact that the California Legislature has specifically authorized districts of the state to enter into contracts with the United States under federal reclamation law to obtain water.[44]

The California majority appears unaware that as recently as 1953 the supreme court of another state wrestled with the constitutionality of the excess land provision and upheld it by a divided vote, two to one. The Chief Justice of the New Mexico Supreme Court, writing a partial dissent, said:

---

39. 35 Cong. Rec. 6770 (1902). See also Taylor, *The Excess Land Law: Execution of a Public Policy*, 64 Yale L.J. 477, 482–87 (1955).
40. 339 U.S. 725, 20 A.L.R.2d 633 (1950).
41. *Id.* at 751, 20 A.L.R.2d at 650, quoted in Ivanhoe Irr. Dist. v. All Parties, 47 Cal.2d 597, 628, 306 P.2d 824, 842 (1957).
42. What the *Gerlach* case decided is that if property rights recognized by state law are taken by the United States, the owner is entitled to compensation. United States v. Gerlach Live Stock Co., 339 U.S. 725, 20 A.L.R.2d 633 (1950).
43. Nebraska v. Wyoming, 325 U.S. 589, 615 (1945).
44. Cal. Water Code §§ 23175–23302 (1956). Section 23197 states: "[A] contract . . . may include provision for . . . delivery and distribution of water for the land in the district under the relevant acts of Congress and the rules and regulations established thereunder." If the majority had covered this point, probably it would have said, as it did in rejecting another state law, that the Legislature "could not have confirmed the 160-acre limitation for the obvious reason that the Legislature could not have . . . constitutionally authorized it." Ivanhoe Irr. Dist. v. All Parties, 47 Cal.2d 597, 645, 306 P.2d 824, 853 (1957). This begs the question.

It is interesting to note that although the excess acreage limitation, in one form or another, has been part of the Federal Reclamation Law for more than 50 years, not a single case in an appellate court can be cited holding it invalid, or subject to constitutional barriers invoked against it.[45]

The California majority missed not only the New Mexico opinion but a number of others that preceded it. It cites page forty-seven of a government study of landownership on reclamation projects for its own purposes, but apparently fails to see five cases on page forty-five of the same document that support the right to assess benefited owners of excess lands within the district notwithstanding denial of water under the excess land provision.[46]

Failing to see opposed authorities, the California majority quotes extensively from remarks made by the Wyoming Supreme Court in 1952, sharing its own repugnance to the excess land law. The Wyoming court was careful to warn that its views on this subject lack the force of law since they were "unnecessary" to arriving at its decision.[46a]

Unable to ground its own views on solid precedent, excluding all reference to contrary opinion, grasping at favorable but insubstantial dictum, the California majority implies that it is the opposite view that suffers from an absence of recognized legal foundation. With a sweeping gesture it conveys an impression that the excess land law is virtually, if not wholly, without judicial support:

> Notwithstanding the fact that the 160-acre limitation has been a part of the Reclamation Law for more than 50 years, a diligent search has failed to disclose that the imposition of the limitation has been approved

---

45. Middle Rio Grande Water Users Ass'n v. Middle Rio Grande Conservancy Dist., 57 N.M. 287, 309, 258 P.2d 391, 405 (1953). See also text at notes 57–62 *infra*.

46. Ivanhoe Irr. Dist. v. All Parties, 47 Cal.2d 597, 636, 306 P.2d 824, 847 (1957). The study is U.S. BUREAU OF RECLAMATION, LANDOWNERSHIP SURVEY ON FEDERAL RECLAMATION PROJECTS (1946). Cases cited on page forty-five are Shoshone Irr. Dist. v. Lincoln Land Co., 51 F.2d 128 (D. Wyo. 1930); Saylor v. Gray, 41 Ariz. 558, 20 P.2d 441 (1933); Nampa & Meridian Irr. Dist. v. Petrie, 28 Idaho 227, 153 Pac. 425 (1915); Klamath County v. Colonial Realty Co., 139 Ore. 311, 7 P.2d 976 (1932); *In re* Goshen Irr. Dist., 42 Wyo. 229, 293 Pac. 373 (1930). With minor variations the question in these cases was the right of districts (or a water users' association) to assess owners of excess holdings actually benefited by irrigation water from the project, notwithstanding denial of water to excess acreage in accordance with the provisions of reclamation law. These courts uniformly upheld the right to assess for benefit, notwithstanding. In Nampa & Meridian Irr. Dist. v. Petrie, *supra*, two judges said: "There can be no doubt that Congress has the power to restrict the right to the use of water furnished from government projects to 160 acres standing in the name of an individual . . . ." Nampa & Meridian Irr. Dist. v. Petrie, *supra* at 241, 153 Pac. at 430. One justice agreed with the decision but objected to the preceding statement. *Id.* at 243, 153 Pac. at 430. See also Burley v. United States, 179 Fed. 1, 7–8 (9th Cir. 1910).

46a. Owl Creek Irr. Dist. v. Bryson, 71 Wyo. 30, 61, 68–69, 253 P.2d 867, 879, 882 (1953). The California Supreme Court cited and quoted this case. Ivanhoe Irr. Dist. v. All Parties, 47 Cal.2d 597, 637, 306 P.2d 824, 848 (1957).

by any court of last resort, either state or federal, in a situation where the federal government had no interest in the lands to be irrigated and possessed only a trustee's interest in the waters to be applied.[47]

The impression created by the statement is wholly contrived. By attaching state trusteeship (as well as absence of federal interest in lands to be irrigated) as a precondition, the court effectively excludes any possibility of discovering precedent favoring the excess land provision, not because none exists, but because no court of last resort except the Supreme Court of California in the present case has ever enunciated the trust theory.

This circularity, that so effectively insulates the majority from discovering views that challenge its own, exemplifies a peculiar quality that, permeating the majority's reasoning and vain search for support, is a hallmark of fatal unsoundness.

III. Class Legislation

As to the acreage limitation of the contract, it is therefore concluded that the extent of the right of an owner of real property to the use and enjoyment of his property right, including the water right which may be attached thereto, cannot be constitutionally limited *on the sole basis of the amount of property he owns*. This is especially true with reference to *property of the same kind* and similarly situated. If there are any exceptions to the rule which should be applied, they have not been pointed out, nor, on reflection, are they apparent. In other words there appears to be no basis founded in reason or authority why the owner of a property right which is or may be appurtenant to all of his land suitable for irrigation can be limited in the enjoyment of that right to 160 acres of his larger holdings. The same right should attach to his lands in excess of 160 acres and to the excess lands of all those similarly situated. Thus to deprive members of the same class of their rights clearly results in an unlawful discrimination . . . not 'founded upon some natural or intrinsic or constitutional distinction.' If a constitutionally authorized preferment may be extended only to owners of 160 acres of land or less the question might well be asked whether a like preferment might not be extended only to owners of more than 160 acres. The suggestion of either preferment under the long and well established rule governing classification is enough to demonstrate its impropriety.

Ivanhoe Irr. Dist. v. All Parties, 1957[48]

---

47. *Id*. at 637, 306 P.2d at 848. An opposite impression, as the New Mexico court recognized, would be closer to the truth. Middle Rio Grande Water Users Ass'n v. Middle Rio Grande Conservancy Dist., 57 N.M. 287, 258 P.2d 391 (1953). The reference to absence of "federal interest in the lands to be irrigated" is of course irrelevant to applicability of the excess land law. The language of the provision makes it clear on the face that it applies only to private lands, and United States v. Gerlach Live Stock Co., 339 U.S. 725, 20 A.L.R.2d 633 (1950), further suggests that federal reclamation law applies in the absence of federal ownership, as in Central Valley.

48. 47 Cal.2d 597, 637–38, 306 P.2d 824, 848 (1957). [Emphasis added.]

The *Ivanhoe* majority finds that the federal excess land law, in refusing water to lands exceeding 160 acres in individual ownership except upon compliance with reclamation law, is class legislation, and therefore unconstitutional. It deprives the owners of that which the majority declares to be a property right, viz., water they have never used. Whether unused water in running streams is properly regarded in law as private property has been discussed and answered in the negative. It remains to be considered, granting for the sake of argument that unused water can be treated as a private property right, whether, in order to accomplish the purpose of the law, a separation of landowners into those owning less than 160 acres and those owning more is class legislation.[49]

The *Ivanhoe* majority cites the requirement of the state Water Code that irrigation districts shall distribute water "ratably to each landowner"[50] to support its view that water should be distributed according to ownership of property without regard to the amount owned by an individual. This section of the code, however, was enacted before the federal government offered to bring more water to districts than they were able to obtain by themselves. Presumably, it applied to water obtained by the district without special conditions attached. After Congress made new sources for financing water development available, the California Legislature specifically authorized districts to obtain it by contract *under the conditions established by federal reclamation law.*[51] The *Ivanhoe* majority supports the authorization of contracts, so far as a relationship of "debtor and creditor" is concerned, but withholds approval of the right of the Legislature to accept the federal requirement that excess lands be denied a permanent water right.

The majority states that classification on the basis of property, especially of the same kind and similarly situated, lacks foundation in "some natural, or intrinsic or constitutional distinction."[52] It will suffice to discuss the latter aspect only, viz., whether it is a "constitutional distinction."

In declaring the law as it sees it, the majority passes over the

---

49. Riparian rights confer a property right to unused water, but these are not involved in the *Ivanhoe* case. Ivanhoe Irr. Dist. v. All Parties, 47 Cal.2d 597, 621, 623, 306 P.2d 824, 838–39 (1957).

50. CAL. WATER CODE § 22250 (1956); Ivanhoe Irr. Dist. v. All Parties, 47 Cal.2d 597, 636, 306 P.2d 824, 847 (1957).

51. CAL. WATER CODE, §§ 23175–23302 (1956). California courts have already validated a score of these contracts and even the author of the *Ivanhoe* majority opinion, if press reports are to be believed, seems disinclined to disturb these validations. San Francisco Chronicle, Jan. 25, 1957, p. 1, col. 4.

52. Ivanhoe Irr. Dist. v. All Parties, 47 Cal.2d 597, 638, 306 P.2d 824, 848 (1957).

fact that legislatures, including the California Legislature, frequently employ the amount of property an individual owns as a basis of classification. The California constitution exempts property of veterans from taxation to the amount of $1,000, provided neither the veteran nor his wife owns property valued at $5,000 or more.[53] This classification furnishes the basis for an even sharper restriction of those with the larger amount of property than the excess land law as it is applied in Central Valley, for the California Constitution denies any tax exemption at all to veterans owning property valued at more than $5,000, while the federal excess land law allows water for 160 acres regardless of amount of land owned. The California Constitution places a ceiling of 320 acres on grants of public land to individuals, to discourage land monopoly.[54] California statutes exempt homesteads from execution or forced sale to the value of either $12,500 or $5,000, depending on whether the head of the family or another person applies for the exemption.[55] In order to assure wide distribution to those in need of the benefits of public housing programs, and of aid to the aged, blind, or children, California statutes establish similar property classifications of eligibility.[56] Such classifications, made for effectuating the purposes of the statutes, do not differ essentially from the property classification used in reclamation law.

The United States Supreme Court has given its approval to classification on the basis of *amount of property owned*, appropriate to the aim of Congress to prevent excessive accumulation of land. On March 3, 1887, Congress placed a limitation of 5,000 acres on corporate landownership in territories.[57] On May 1, 1900, it passed the Organic Act for Puerto Rico by joint resolution, declaring that "every corporation hereafter authorized to engage in agriculture shall by its charter be restricted to the ownership and control of not to exceed five hundred acres of land . . . ."[58] Thirty-

---

53. CAL. CONST. art. XVII, § 1¼ (1955).
54. "Lands belonging to this State, which are suitable for cultivation, shall be granted only to actual settlers, and in quantities not exceeding three hundred and twenty acres to each settler, under such conditions as shall be prescribed by law."
CAL. CONST. art. XVIII, § 3 (1955).
55. CAL. CIV. CODE §§ 1240, 1260 (1954). For other property-value classifications for exemption from execution and attachment, see CAL. CODE CIV. PROC. §§ 690–690.25 (1955).
56. *E.g.*, CAL. HEALTH & SAFETY CODE § 34322(a) (1956); CAL. WEL. & INST. CODE §§ 1520–1521.5, 2025, 2163–65d, 3047–49 (1956).
57. Act. of March 3, 1887, c. 340, 24 STAT. 476, 477.
58. Act of May 1, 1900, § 3, 31 STAT. 716. Congress retained the provision against "vigorous attempts to modify it," Puerto Rico v. Rubert Hermanos, Inc., 309 U.S. 543, 548 (1940), and continued it in 1917. 39 STAT. 964 (1917), 48 U.S.C. § 752 (1952).

eight years later the Puerto Rico Supreme Court described the purpose of the act:

> To prevent the development of an agrarian monopoly which would own and control the best lands of this small and densely populated Island and which might eventually convert the Island into a large sugar factory, served by a half-slave proletariat and to encourage the division of lands into small tracts, owned, controlled and cultivated by their owners . . . .[59]

The Supreme Court of Puerto Rico disposed of the argument that the acreage limitation was discriminatory in an earlier case:

> [T]he Joint Resolution of Congress of May 1, 1900, is neither discriminatory nor arbitrary in itself, or to any extent rendering the same unconstitutional . . . . Corporations may be restricted by a constitution. We fail to see, especially in an agricultural community, that a limitation as to the number of acres that may be controlled by a corporation engaged in agriculture, for the prevention of an agricultural monopoly, constitutes an unjust discrimination.[60]

The *Ivanhoe* majority, speaking evidently of land law in continental United States, says:

> It is common knowledge that after the title passed to the buyer, the land then was subject to resale to grantees either private or corporate within the ordinary channels of purchase and sale in the field of private property acquisition and ownership. The buyer was then in position to sell to whom he pleased, or accumulate properties similarly purchased by others so that his total acreage might far exceed the original statutory acreage limitation.[61]

Of course this description does not fit the 500-acre limitation on corporation ownership in Puerto Rico enacted by Congressional joint resolution of 1900, the congressional 5000-acre limitation on landownership by corporations in unincorporated territories, or the 160-acre water limitation of the National Reclamation Act of 1902, the last-named at issue here.

The United States Supreme Court upheld the 500-acre limitation in Puerto Rico in 1940 against argument that the Congressional resolution failed because it provided no specific remedy for

---

59. People v. Rubert Hermanos, Inc., 53 P.R. 741, 750 (1938). "The continuous violation of the prohibitory statute during a number of years cannot be invoked by the violator as the basis or source of its alleged right to continue *ad perpetuam* in the ownership and control of lands in excess of the amount permitted by the statute." *Id.* at 759.
60. People v. Fajardo Sugar Co., 50 P.R. 156, 172–73 (1936).
61. Ivanhoe Irr. Dist. v. All Parties, 47 Cal.2d 597, 634, 306 P.2d 824, 846 (1957).

enforcement.[62] Having before it a limitation stricter than the excess land provisions of federal reclamation law and a lower court decision citing the 5000-acre limitation in territories as precedent, both applying to property of the same kind and similarly situated, the Supreme Court of the United States gave its approval. No financial transaction between government and landowners, carrying subsidies to the latter, was involved.

The United States Supreme Court has in dictum justified federal undertaking of reclamation under the general welfare powers of government.[63] The Court of Appeals for the Ninth Circuit, in upholding federal reclamation of *private* lands against argument denying this to be a proper public purpose, quoted the excess land provisions in section 5 of the Act of 1902 and immediately added: "The act clearly provides for the irrigation of private lands *under the conditions specified* . . . ."[64] In neither of these decisions is there any hint that the excess land law ought to be excluded from the public purpose that underlies reclamation law, or that it ought to be treated as deprivation of private property; the implication of *Burley v. United States*[65] plainly is to the contrary.

In order to escape from the protective mantle of the general welfare powers cast over the shoulders of Central Valley reclamation by the United States Supreme Court, the majority resorts as usual to its own trust theory: the issue is not the general powers of the Government but deprivation of property.[66] In this vein the majority declares:

> But we are not here dealing with social objectives as such. We are here concerned with the question of the extent of power, dominion and control which the United States as a trustee may exercise to deprive beneficiaries of the trust, namely, the water users of the state and particu-

---

62. Justice Frankfurter, delivering the opinion of the Court, said: "Surely Congress meant its action to have significance beyond mere empty words. To treat the absence of a specific remedy for violation of the restriction as an implied bar against local enforcement measures is to impute to Congress a dog-in-the-manger attitude bordering on disingenuousness. We refuse to believe that Congress was bent on the elaborate futility of a *brutum fulmen*." Puerto Rico v. Rubert Hermanos, Inc., 309 U.S. 543, 548 (1940). The 5,000-acre land limitation in territories was enacted in 1887. Act of March 3, 1887, c. 340, 24 STAT. 476.
63. *Dictum,* United States v. Gerlach Live Stock Co., 339 U.S. 725, 738, 20 A.L.R.2d 633, 643–44 (1950).
64. Burley v. United States, 179 Fed. 1, 8 (9th Cir. 1910). [Emphasis added.]
65. *Ibid.*
66. Creating a diversion is a method well known to the military, to parents, to children, and, if Charles Dickens is to be believed, to scamps. It has appropriate uses, but these need to be evaluated carefully.

larly those in the plaintiff district, of a property right thereunder or of an inchoate right to the use of water within the district.[67]

Of course, the United States is not delivering water to anyone through Central Valley reclamation except to "the water users of the state." The only question at issue is how much water any individual shall be permitted to receive.

The *Ivanhoe* majority, as has been indicated, surrounds itself with a tissue of unsupported doctrine so that at every point one seeks to penetrate, he meets again the same novel doctrine barring the way, stated and restated but never proved. There is need to pierce this tissue by facing the realities of reclamation law.

Reclamation *creates* property values; that is one of its chief purposes. Between 1941 and the first half of 1946 the difference in average selling price between irrigated and nonirrigated land rose from $160 to $477 per acre, in Tulare County in the Central Valley of California.[68] On the basis of this range of differentials, diminished by an estimated cost of, say, $60 per acre for leveling land, a full reclamation project water supply creates incremental values of between $16,000 and $41,280 for 160 acres, the amount for which federal water is permitted to an individual, even though he may be an excess landowner. For man and wife these minimum and maximum estimates can be doubled, viz., $32,000 and $82,560. The *Ivanhoe* majority turns this about: the excess above incremental values of $32,000 and $82,560 is "property" of which the excess landholder is being "deprived."

Again, reclamation law for $3.50 an acre-foot brings water to private landholders along Friant-Kern canal in Central Valley that would cost them $14.00 if they had to obtain it without the subsidies and other benefits of reclamation law.[69] The differential between what the United States charges water users under reclamation law and what they would have to pay without its help (rounded for convenience to $10 per acre-foot) means an *annual* saving of $1,600 to landowners with 160 acres using *only one acre-*

---

67. Ivanhoe Irr. Dist. v. All Parties, 47 Cal.2d 597, 635, 306 P.2d 824, 846 (1957).
68. Testimony of Paul H. Johnstone, U.S. Bureau of Reclamation economist, before the *Hearings, supra* note 1, at 831, 861, 943. Johnstone estimated conservatively an incremental value of $200 per acre. A more recent estimate is higher, the difference between $150 and $800 an acre produced at a cost of $350, or $300 per acre net increment. Part of the $350 per acre cost is for well digging that would be unnecessary in a reclamation project. Donald K. White, Financial Editor, *Barony in Valley Is "Precision" Farmer,* San Francisco Examiner, June 14, 1957, § 2, p. 4, col. 1.
69. *Hearings, supra* note 1, at 869.

foot of supplemental water. Federal reclamation brings an *annual* saving of $4,000 to the same landowner using a full water supply of two and one-half acre-feet.[70] Assuming man and wife owning 160 acres each, these estimated savings to private landowners from federal reclamation become doubled, i.e., $3,200 and $8,000 annually. They mean the difference between getting water and not getting it.

Someone must pay the costs private landowners are not asked to repay under reclamation law. Data helpful in estimating who provides this financial assistance, and about how much, are spread on the public record. Federal taxpayers provide about thirteen percent of Central Valley costs outright, nonreimbursable to the public treasury. California power users are allocated thirty-three percent of reimbursable project costs, but they repay seventy-two percent of these costs. Municipal and industrial water users are allocated three percent and repay ten percent. Irrigators—the private landowners, practically speaking—are allocated sixty-three percent of reimbursable project costs and are expected to pay *only seventeen percent.*[71] Waiver of interest to irrigators as provided in reclamation law is another element of subsidy to them, equal to about one-half. Taking a total view of the process of federal reclamation, its costs, and the position landowners would be in without it, it strains credulity to suppose that in bringing water to them, federal reclamation deprives them of their property.[72] The conclusion of the *Ivanhoe* majority is tantamount to denying the public any opportunity to make great and necessary internal improvements except on the large landowners' terms.[73] Dean Roscoe

---

70. "Saving" is used in the sense of receiving more than the landowner is asked by the federal government to pay for, measured by the cost differential. Of course the differential is so great that private landowners do not undertake reclamation of their own lands. It is the reason western interests persuaded Congress to pass the original Reclamation Act in 1902, and the reason why they have frequently sought appropriations since.

71. See Note, 38 CALIF. L. REV. 728, 730–32 (1950), citing H.R. Doc. No. 146, 80th Cong., 1st Sess. 23 (1947). Federal taxpayers advance money to pay irrigation costs but require no interest from water users on unrepaid balances. Assuming an interest rate of three percent, a ten-year development period, and forty-year repayment period, this represents a fifty-seven percent subsidy.

72. This, however, is apparently the view taken by the majority of the California Supreme Court. Ivanhoe Irr. Dist. v. All Parties, 47 Cal.2d 597, 63?–48, 306 P.2d 824, 846–48 (1957). In an address at Lindsay California, on Oct. 7, 1948, Secretary of the Interior J. A. Krug said: "In all its history—covering more than forty years *under the basic reclamation law and including the 160-acre provision—Federal Reclamation has enhanced and extended water rights. It has never taken them away,* unless by purchase or exchange for specific project purposes. Reclamation always has increased wealth. It never has lessened property values." [Emphasis added.]

73. Looked at another way, it suggests the outmoded but formerly legally recognized practice of getting another to pay one's debts by willing them as a legacy. The majority

Pound's classic criticism of an attitude prevalent among courts nearly fifty years ago toward "liberty of contract," now largely outmoded, appears relevant:

> The absolute certainty which is one of our legal ideals, an ideal responsible for much that is irritatingly mechanical in our legal system, is demanded chiefly to protect property .... A ... result is to exaggerate private right at the expense of public interest.[74]

The view of the *Ivanhoe* majority that the excess land provision deprives the beneficiaries of federal reclamation of their property is matched by its view that it is class legislation. A glance at facts on the public record reveals the conditions of landownership with which reclamation law seeks to deal.

The California State Engineer reported that twenty-nine percent of the total area in Fresno County "which can receive service from the Central Valley project" was in holdings exceeding 160 acres in 1946. Comparable figures for Kern, Kings, Madera, and Tulare Counties were fifty, fifty-six, forty and twenty-two percent, respectively. In the entire five-county area, 35.6 percent was in excess holdings.[75] A substantial part of the area in excess holdings is irrigated at present, but this does not imply that more water may not be needed to supplement insufficient supplies, to replace failing supplies, or to improve seasonal distribution by regulation. The difficulties of determining in advance the precise extent to which excess landowners may require and receive water under reclamation law need not conceal the fact that substantial excess holdings are in potential need of more water; the excess land owners are sufficiently concerned over possible application of the excess land

---

insists that a repayment contract between the United States and an irrigation district is properly viewed as a mere instrument for adjusting a creditor-debtor relationship, not for achieving policy. Ivanhoe Irr. Dist. v. All Parties, 47 Cal.2d 597, 629–31, 306 P.2d 824, 843–44 (1957). This is to stress unreality again. The contract is not even a full record of the financial transaction. It omits all the subsidies to irrigators provided them by reclamation. Congress has chosen to make contracts the vehicle of enforcing policy; the majority denies it this power.

74. Pound, *Liberty of Contract*, 18 YALE L.J. 454, 461 (1909).

75. *Hearings, supra* note 1, at 45 (Edward Hyatt). Senator Downey cites Bureau of Reclamation figures indicating twenty-three percent of land is in excess holdings "in Central Valley Project." DOWNEY, THEY WOULD RULE THE VALLEY 253 (1947). He also classifies the data on "known ownerships of 5,000 acres or more in probably present and future San Joaquin Valley service areas in Central Valley Project" presented earlier by the Bureau of Reclamation. *Id.* at 164; *Hearings, supra* note 1, at 864. Senator Downey questioned whether seventy percent or more of these lands would ever get water "from any Reclamation Bureau project." See note 78 *infra*. Whatever the exact figures on excess landholdings requiring water under reclamation law may turn out to be, however, the concentration of ownership is substantial in amount and proportion to total irrigable area by any available estimate.

provision to resist it strongly. With this caution against interpreting published data as the *literal measure* of benefit from public water development, it is appropriate to point out that an extraordinary concentration of ownership exists in the southern San Joaquin Valley, of a kind that has influenced Congress to insist on the excess land provision.[76]

In 1947 the Bureau of Reclamation told Congress that thirty-four corporations and individuals in the "probable present and future San Joaquin Valley service areas of Central Valley Project" owned close to three-quarters of a million acres.[77] No individual holding among these was less than 5,000 acres, the largest was 231,000 acres, and they averaged 22,000 acres each. Another Bureau tabulation of 1,159,410 acres of "large land holdings" in three irrigable Central Valley areas, overlapping the preceding, classified lands by type of ownership. It showed that "land and development companies, banks, etc." owned 331,013 acres, "oil companies" 214,624 acres, "partnerships and estates" 101,907 acres, "individual and community property holdings of 1000 acres or more" 227,137 acres, "processors of farm products" 32,227 acres, "railroads" 43,648 acres, "corporation farms" 133,617 acres, and "other companies" 75,237 acres.[78]

The clear vision of the *Ivanhoe* majority seems reserved for the expectations of private landowners with more than 160 acres each,[79]

---

76. *Hearings, supra* note 1 at 40–45; *id.* at 831–911 (Paul H. Johnstone, Bureau of Reclamation economist); *id.* at 965–74 (S. A. Kerr, Bureau of Reclamation planning engineer); DOWNEY, THEY WOULD RULE THE VALLEY 163–81 (1947).

77. *Hearings, supra* note 1, at 864.

78. *Ibid.* Former Senator Downey said: "I am able to make this categorical statement about it: 50 percent to 60 percent of the total acreage already has adequate water and will never need, want or get any supply from any Reclamation Bureau project; 20 percent to 30 percent of the total is submarginal land, so alkaline, rough or otherwise unsuitable that it can never be irrigated. Most of the remaining area not in one of these two classes is being presently developed for petroleum purposes or acquired and held for future oil development." DOWNEY, THEY WOULD RULE THE VALLEY 164–65 (1947). Senator Downey, carefully specifying "from any Reclamation Bureau project," achieved accuracy while obscuring the essential truth; he could not have said that this area will never need or want additional water "*with public assistance.*" For example, the Southern Pacific Company, as reported in the press in 1956, said it owned about 150,000 acres it was holding for long-range purposes, and would welcome federal aid to bring water under "reasonable and bearable" conditions, *i.e.*, not under the standard excess land provisions. Sacramento Bee, Oct. 17, 1956.

79. "The appraised value must be fixed as of the time of the execution of the recordable agreement and the appraisal cannot take into consideration any increase in the value of the land resulting from the supply of water to the land, or from any other normal increase in value such as might result from an increase in population, an extraordinary increase in the productivity of the land or perchance the discovery of oil or other valuable substances beneath the land." Ivanhoe Irr. Dist. v. All Parties, 47 Cal.2d 597, 635, 306 P.2d 824, 847 (1957). Nor, of course, can it consider the conservatively estimated $200 average increment in value created by public expenditure to bring water to private lands. The incremental value from bringing a full supply of water to land, computed on this basis,

which it erects into constitutionally protected property rights—expectations that are not ordinarily fulfilled except with remarkably generous aid from taxpayers, power users, and others as provided in reclamation law.

In 1877, when agglomeration of landholdings in the Valley was in full swing, a Central Valley newspaper published at the seat of a branch General Land Office expressed these views:

> [N]o one would believe that shrewd, calculating businessmen would invest their money on the strength of land rising in value while unimproved, for even the farmer himself has to abandon it who endeavors to add to its value without water. At the same time purchasers are not lacking who would add it to their already extensive dry domain and the people, in the next legislature, will find themselves confronted by an array of force and talent to secure to capital the ownership of the water as well as of the land, and the people will at last have it to pay for ....[80]

The editor of the newspaper had the advantage of seeing at first hand the realities and problems, first of acquiring land, next of acquiring water and uniting it to land. The *Ivanhoe* opinion, by invalidating the excess land law in the name of the constitution, brings nearer the validation of the editor's prophecy.

IV. POLICY

> From the Middle Ages to the present days sovereigns and parliaments have considered it their duty to protect their subjects and citizens against attempts by large combinations of capital to monopolize the lands adapted to agriculture, which are the basic source of wealth of any community. Numerous are the statutes and precedents which might be cited in support of the validity and wisdom of legislation enacted for the purpose of enforcing such an agrarian policy. The Statutes of Mortmain in England and the legislation of Spain might be cited as precedents. The Congress of the United States, in order to protect the people of the unincorporated Territories, enacted laws prohibiting the holding of lands by corporations in excess of 5,000 acres, even though some of those Territories had areas of 100,000 and 200,000 square miles.
>
> SUPREME COURT OF PUERTO RICO, 1938[81]

---

would amount to $1 million on 5,000 acres, and $4.4 million on 22,000 acres, the average size in the group. Of course, there is no way to determine precisely how much water these lands need in addition to what they, or some of them, have, or how much they actually will get from a federal project. The high concentration of ownership implies a high concentration of potential incremental values that it is the purpose of reclamation law to distribute widely.

80. Visalia Delta, May 5, 1877, p. 2, col. 3.
81. People v. Rubert Hermanos, Inc., 53 P.R. 741, 751 (1938), decision upheld, 309 U.S. 543 (1940). The acreage limitation on corporate ownership in territories was established by Act of Mar. 3, 1887, c. 340, § 3, 24 STAT. 477.

The California Supreme Court sought a public water policy in 1886 to "secure the greatest good to the greatest number."[82] In its quest for "the principles of 'public policy' which are of themselves of paramount authority and demand that the law shall be so declared,"[83] the court said:

> [I]t does not require a prophetic vision to anticipate . . . a monopoly of all the waters of the state by comparatively few individuals, . . . controlling aggregated capital, who could either apply the water to purposes useful to themselves, or sell it to those *from whom they had taken it away*, as well as to others.[84]

In 1957 a majority of the same court no longer was in search of policy. The present decision is made to turn on *property*; *public policy* becomes irrelevant, not to be shaped by debate in court, legislature, or Congress.[35]

A sound legal principle serves not only to decide a present situation, but also to guide future action. The *Ivanhoe* majority offers as a principle a trust theory that provides questionable guidance.

If, as owners of unused water, landowners can go into court to protect their property, allocation of water becomes virtually impossible. As dissenting Justice Carter points out:

> Under the foregoing line of reasoning no vested right may ever be acquired by any individual or group of individuals to appropriate and use a given quantity of water for a beneficial purpose even though they have complied with all the provisions of the statutory law of this state, as the state would have no power to grant a specific right to any individual unless every other individual who may have a use for water has received his share.[86]

Perhaps shrinking from the chaos following logically from substitution of *ownership independent of use* for *appropriation founded on use*,[87] the majority step by step reduced the scope of the

---

82. Lux v. Haggin, 69 Cal. 255, 308–9, 10 Pac. 674, 702 (1886).
83. *Id.* at 309, 10 Pac. at 703.
84. *Id.* at 309–10, 10 Pac. at 703. The reach of this early court exceeded its grasp. As related by the *Ivanhoe* majority, the riparian doctrine of 1886 proved unsatisfactory and was changed by constitutional amendment in 1928. Ivanhoe Irr. Dist. v. All Parties, 47 Cal.2d 597, 621–23, 306 P.2d 824, 837–39 (1957).
85. Social objectives "were well within the power and control of the federal government as the *owner of the lands* to be granted . . . ." Since the court, however, chooses to rest decision on the question whether "the United States as trustee" is depriving "beneficiaries of the trust" of "a property right thereunder," it finds it unnecessary to deal "with social objectives as such." *Id.* at 635, 306 P.2d at 846. [Emphasis added.]
86. *Id.* at 667, 306 P.2d at 867.
87. *Id.* at 667–69, 306 P.2d at 867–68; see text at notes 31–36 *supra*. The dissenting opinion by Gibson, C. J., and Traynor, J., states that "the ramifications of the trust theory as applied by the majority are infinite, technical and unpredictable . . . ." *Id.* at 657, 306 P.2d at 860.

property right of the "real owners" in their water. They cannot go into court to enforce the trust to get the right to use their water, but must go through the familiar statutory process of appropriation to obtain it.[88] The trust, according to the court, does not insure the receipt of water by helping a landowner excluded from a district to get it;[89] nor will it protect him from assessment by a district if he is within it, even if it is physically impossible to serve him with water.[90]

Again, although calling landowners the "real owners" of unappropriated water, the *Ivanhoe* majority abruptly denies them the right to the accounting in the courts to which logic would entitle them for the use of their private property to generate electrical energy.[91] Has the majority exposed the state's taxpayers, and perhaps power companies as well, to suits from landowners, the "real owners" of the water? Will this distinction by the majority hold, or is it mere dictum?

What remains of a theory of private property from which its authors flee when confronted with its implications? The only point to which the majority surely holds fast is that the excess land law is unconstitutional. The majority has not stated a sound principle, furnishing a generalized and continuing support and a basis from which to reason. It has simply—possibly solely—invalidated a specific law.

Actual effects of the *Ivanhoe* decision presently discernible confirm this impression derived from internal analysis: The majority states no principle of general service to water development in California. Some of these effects may be summarized briefly:

1) Within a week the California District Securities Commission refused to validate any further contracts containing the excess land provision although the districts can only get water by means of these contracts.[92]

---

88. *Id.* at 625, 306 P.2d at 840; the majority speaks of "compliance" with the provisions of the water code prescribing how, by appropriation, "the right to use the water may be acquired . . ." is necessary, "but always consistent with the trust relationship . . . ." *Ibid.*

89. Madera Irr. Dist. v. All Persons, 47 Cal.2d 681, 691–92, 306 P.2d 886, 892–93 (1957). See Petition for Rehearing of the Appellant, the State of California, Ivanhoe Irr. Dist. v. All Parties, in the Supreme Court of the State of California, L.A. No. 23043, pp. 12, 13.

90. Santa Barbara County Water Agency v. All Persons, 47 Cal.2d 699, 711–13, 306 P.2d 875, 883–84 (1957).

91. Ivanhoe Irr. Dist. v. All Parties, 47 Cal.2d 597, 628, 629, 306 P.2d 824, 842–43 (1957).

92. San Francisco Examiner, Jan. 31, 1957, p. 6, col. 3; San Francisco Chronicle, Jan. 31, 1957, p. 14, col. 4. See also "This World," San Francisco Chronicle, Feb. 3, 1957, p. 2; Sacramento Bee, Jan. 28, 1957.

2) The *Ivanhoe* decision produces a practical absurdity of substantial proportions. The United States is now servicing twenty-one California districts under validated water contracts that include the excess land provision. Future contracts are forbidden to carry the provision. Thus, the *Ivanhoe* opinion offers for coexistence in the same state, and even on the same project, two inconsistent sets of contracts, one of them valid, the other invalid but validated.[93]

3) The *Ivanhoe* decision raises at least a doubt whether, *in the absence of a provision* to protect the reclamation purpose of encouraging home-making by limiting private receipt of water, the use of federal funds and powers to reclaim *private* lands, as in Central Valley, is constitutional.[94]

4) The *Ivanhoe* decision, denying validity of so-called "9e"[95] contracts on essentially the same grounds that underlie the remainder of the opinion, places the Secretary of the Interior in a position where he must raise water rates. Congress authorized "9e" contracts to make lower annual water rates possible by extending the period of interest-free repayment indefinitely. The *Ivanhoe* opinion denies this benefit in the future to California water users while permitting it to those covered under contracts previously validated.[96]

5) The *Ivanhoe* decision threatens to bring congressional aid for water development in California to a standstill. The six Congressmen representing areas served by Central Valley Project have stated that "Congress, in our opinion, will not permit the unearned enrichment of large landowners at the Federal treasury which can occur without an acreage limitation."[97] The Secretary of the Interior, in administrative charge of federal reclamation, has stated:

---

93. The press reported: "In explaining this position to reporters, Justice Shenk said the case will not affect any Central Valley Project developments nor will it affect any prior agreements." San Francisco Chronicle, Jan. 25, 1957, p. 6, col. 1. Apparently no mention was made of the possible effect of renegotiation of any prior agreements, which might occur for any of a number of reasons. See note 51 *supra*.

94. See Burley v. United States, 179 Fed. 1, 8–10 (9th Cir. 1910).

95. The term "9e" contracts refers to contracts made pursuant to § 9e of the Reclamation Project Act of 1939, 53 STAT. 1196, 43 U.S.C. 485e (1952). They are discussed in Ivanhoe Irr. Dist. v. All Parties, 47 Cal.2d 597, 659–62, 306 P.2d 824, 861–63 (1957) (dissenting opinion).

96. Ivanhoe Irr. Dist. v. All Parties, 47 Cal.2d 597, 639–44, 306 P.2d 824, 849–52 (1957); *id.* at 659, 306 P.2d at 861 (dissenting opinion). It, of course, does not affect the financial advantage of "9e" contracts to water users in other states.

97. Letter from Congressmen Clair Engle, George P. Weller, John E. Moss, Harlan Hagen, B. F. Sisk, J. J. McFall to Attorney General Edmund G. Brown, Feb. 4, 1957, in Petition for Rehearing of the Appellant, the State of California, Ivanhoe Irr. Dist. v. All Parties, in the Supreme Court of the State of California, L.A. No. 23043, app., pp. i, ii. See the dissenting opinion referred to in this letter in Ivanhoe Irr. Dist. v. All Parties, 47 Cal.2d 597, 658 n.3, 306 P.2d 824, 861 n.3 (1957); see also text at notes 56–59.

Excepting the validated contracts, I believe it . . . proper to observe in this regard that if the decision stands there would exist grave doubt whether any existing water user organization in California has the power to meet the requirements of the Federal reclamation laws for irrigation service and facilities.[98]

It would be sufficient under ordinary circumstances to close discussion of the opinion of the majority at this point after having searched the precedents relied on, subjected its reasoning at critical points to analysis, examined the practical effects of the decision, and produced unimpeachable contrary authority. But *Ivanhoe* is no ordinary case; it ranks with the great efforts of the California Supreme Court in *Lux v. Haggin*[99] and *Herminghaus v. Southern California Edison Co.*[100] to lay down principles of water development for the state. A constitutional amendment proved necessary in the public interest to trim from the riparian doctrine of the earlier cases what the United States Supreme Court called its "canine element."[101] Likewise, if the trust theory of ownership of unappropriated water is not to stand, only a constitutional amendment or a reversal by the United States Supreme Court can effect the change.

Comment remains to be made on two additional aspects of the opinion. First, as reflection or cause of its decision, or perhaps both, the *Ivanhoe* majority dismisses the history of relations between the State of California and the United States over construction of Central Valley Project as a "problem . . . simply . . . of *money*."[102]

Financial inability of the State of California to proceed with construction did indeed precede federal construction of Central Valley Project, but the prospect of federal help "in accord with the federal reclamation policies and precedents" was held out in 1933 as inducement to vote for a State Central Valley Act, including a bond issue.[103] California Congressmen and the authorized spokes-

---

98. Letter from Secretary Fred A. Seaton to Congressman Clair Engle, Chairman, House Committee on Interior and Insular Affairs, Feb. 16, 1957.
99. 69 Cal. 255, 10 Pac. 674 (1886).
100. 200 Cal. 81, 252 Pac. 607 (1926), *cert. dismissed*, 275 U.S. 486 (1927).
101. The "canine element" was the power to assert a right to the full flow of a stream "no matter how unreasonable." United States v. Gerlach Live Stock Co., 339 U.S. 725, 751, 20 A.L.R.2d 633, 650 (1950) (Justice Jackson); Ivanhoe Irr. Dist. v. All Parties, 47 Cal.2d 597, 622, 306 P.2d 824, 838 (1957).
102. *Id*. at 615, 306 P.2d at 834. This view carries over to the majority's insistence that the contract between California irrigation districts and the United States is one of securing repayment of money owed, a "debtor and creditor" relationship and no more. *Id*. at 629–31, 306 P.2d at 843–44.
103. Press Release for July 7, 1933, in STATE WATER PLAN MANUAL FOR SPEAKERS IN SUPPORT OF CENTRAL VALLEY PROJECT ACT, SPECIAL ELECTION, December 19, 1933.

man for the State Water Project Authority acquiesced in, when they did not assert the advantages of, federal reclamation.[104] Both Houses of the Legislature memorialized Congress to authorize construction and appropriate money to be repaid "in accordance with reclamation law."[105] There was no mystery or mere chance in the manner in which the excess land provision came to be applied in Central Valley; it was the generation-old, normal concomitant of federal participation in water development, and was made a part of the contract of repayment by an act of Congress.[106] The electors of Ivanhoe Irrigation District approved the contract by a vote of 218 to 33.

A second comment relates to monopoly of water and land as a public issue, discussion of which the *Ivanhoe* majority excludes as irrelevant.[107] A glance at the record of history confirms that it is a great issue of policy to be disregarded at peril, and, as the Puerto Rican Supreme Court reminds us, this has been so from the Middle Ages.[108] It is so in California: its constitution bears at least two marks testifying to this truth.[109]

The Legislature of California has concerned itself with the issue of land or water monopoly intermittently from the nineteenth century to its most recent session.[110]

Congress, following the example of the Virginia Colonial Legislature that abolished entailed estates in 1776,[111] spent a large part of the nineteenth century debating and deciding on a policy of

---

104. *Hearings Before the Subcommittee on Appropriations of the House Committee on the Interior Dept. Appropriation Bill for 1938*, 75th Cong., 1st Sess., pt. 2, at 1579, 1580 (1937) (Congressman Clarence D. Lea of California); *id.* at 1591 (Congressman F. H. Buck of California and Edward Hyatt, State Engineer and Executive Officer of the State Water Project Authority).

105. 80 Cong. Rec. 8413 (1936); Cal. S. Jour. 13-14 (51st Extraordinary Sess. 1936); Cal. Assembly Jour. 35-37 (51st Extraordinary Sess. 1936).

106. 44 Stat. 649 (1926), 43 U.S.C. § 423e (1952).

107. Ivanhoe Irr. Dist. v. All Parties, 47 Cal.2d 597, 635-36, 306 P.2d 824, 846 (1957)

108. People v. Rubert Hermanos, Inc., 53 P.R. 741, 750-51 (1938). See also Isaiah 5:8; Cambridge Ancient History, vol. IX, cc. I, II, "Tiberius Gracchus," "Gaius Gracchus" (Hugh Last 1932); Rostovtzeff, The Social and Economic History of the Roman Empire 186 (1926) (comment on Pliny's famous statement "latifundia perdidere Italiam").

109. Cal. Const. art. XVII, § 3, limiting public land grants to 320 acres, and art. XIV, § 3, limiting the riparian doctrine of the state supreme court. The former is not mentioned in *Ivanhoe*; the majority itself tells the latter but is uninfluenced. Ivanhoe Irr. Dist. v. All Parties, 47 Cal.2d 597, 622-23, 306 P.2d 824, 838-39 (1957).

110. See Cal. Legislature, *Report of the Swamp Land Investigating Committee*, 20th Sess. (1874); mentioned in the San Francisco Chronicle, Sept. 17, 1877, p. 3; Sacramento Bee, Jan. 23, 1957, p. 1.

111. 1 Revised Code of the Laws of Virginia 368 (1819).

wide distribution of landownership.[112] Faced in 1902 with monopolization of arid western lands by the few, a result in part of evasion and maladministration of the laws, it rejected large land grants, modeled on those given to railroads, as a means to develop water resources,[113] and tightened land as well as water policy by prohibiting commutation (money in lieu of personal inhabitancy).[114] The principle of policy on which Congress rests reclamation law was stated clearly in 1902 by the House committee on the bill:

> If we were willing to abandon our time-honored policy of inviting and encouraging small individual land holdings, and were prepared to turn over all of the public lands under a large irrigation system to the control of a single individual or a corporation, we could undoubtedly secure the construction of extensive works which can not be profitably constructed by private enterprise under present conditions, but no one contemplates paying so stupendous a price as this for irrigation development.[115]

Congress has stood by its policy ever since. It renewed its approval of reclamation law, including the excess land provision, in 1906, 1910, 1911, 1912, 1914, 1916, 1924, 1926, 1937, 1938, 1940, and 1943.[116] Determined efforts were made to lift the excess land limitation from Central Valley Project in 1944 and again in 1947. The first was not only defeated, but Congress showed its confidence in

---

112. *E.g.*, "Thus, in the period from 1786 to 1820, the price had fallen from $2 to $1.25 per acre cash, and the quantity which might be sold was reduced from whole townships and eight sections to sections (640 acres), half-sections (320 acres), quarter-sections (160 acres), and half-quarter-sections (80 acres), thus fostering small holdings at a low price, with deed in fee from the Government." THOMAS DONALDSON, PUBLIC DOMAIN, ITS HISTORY, WITH STATISTICS, Misc. Doc. No. 45, 47th Cong., 2d Sess. 205 (1884); see also the chapter "The Pre-Emption Acts." *id.* at 214–16; CONGRESSIONAL GLOBE, 32d Cong., 2d Sess., app. 199–207 (1853); *id.*, 34th Cong., 1st Sess., app. 1155–60 (1856); *id.*, 35th Cong., 1st Sess. 2239–72 *passim*, 2303–8, 2424 (1858); *id.*, 36th Cong., 1st Sess. 1506–12, 1526–39, 1551–56, 1629–37, 1649–62 (1860); *id.*, 40th Cong., 2d Sess. 2380–87 (1868).

113. Congressman G. W. Ray of New York led the attack on the reclamation bill, even with the excess land provision in it, as a "scheme" of the great railroad interests. "The land-grant railroads are behind this scheme and the real beneficiaries. These roads run through these arid lands and semiarid regions, and they own vast tracts of these lands. The construction of these irrigation works and reservoirs at the public expense will inure to their benefit, for it will bring their lands into the market at twenty times their present value. In our judgment the Congress of the United States will be false to its trust if it sanctions a scheme the benefits of which are largely, at least, to be reaped by these railroad corporations." 35 CONG. REC. 6694 (1902). See also Sacramento Bee, Oct. 17, 1956, p. A2. Ivanhoe Irr. Dist. v. All Parties, 47 Cal.2d 597, 634–35, 306 P.2d 824, 845–46 (1957).

114. 32 STAT. 389 (1902), as amended, 43 U.S.C. § 432 (1952). See also Taylor, *The Excess Land Law: Execution of a Public Policy*, 64 YALE L.J. 477, 485 (1955).

115. House Committee on Irrigation of Arid Lands, *Reclamation of Arid Lands*, H.R. REP. No. 1468, 57th Cong., 1st Sess. 3 (1902).

116. U.S. BUREAU OF RECLAMATION, REPORT ON LANDOWNERSHIP SURVEY ON FEDERAL RECLAMATION PROJECTS 53–54 (1946).

the excess land law by writing it into the Flood Control Act[117] as well; this act extended its coverage to irrigation uses of water from works constructed anywhere in the United States by the Army Engineers.[118] The second attempt left behind it a 1300-page record of committee hearings;[119] the Senate Public Lands Committee never reported the bill.

The hearings held on these occasions brought together an impressive array of spokesmen for citizens' groups in support of the excess land provision, including representatives of two of the three leading farm organizations, the leading labor and veteran organizations, and a number of church organizations of various denominations.[120] The other leading farm organization and a number of water users and other groups opposed the excess land law.[121] In all American history, colonial as well as national, few subjects have aroused citizens more than the formulation of policy for distributing land or water.[121a]

---

117. 58 STAT. 891 (1944), 43 U.S.C. § 390 (1952).
118. *Ibid.*
119. *Hearings Before Subcommittee of the Senate Committee on Public Lands, on S. 912,* 80th Cong., 1st Sess. (1947).
120. *Id.* at 495 (American Legion); *id.* at 482 (American Veterans' Committee); *id.* at 493 (Disabled American Veterans); *id.* at 533 (Congregational Christian Church); *id.* at 529 (Bay Area Jewish Forum); *id.* at 458 (National Grange); *id.* at 620 (National Farmers Union); *id.* at 574 (AFL); *id.* at 478 (VFW); *id.* at 496 (National Catholic Rural Life Conference); *Hearings Before the Subcommittee of the Senate Committee on Irrigation and Reclamation, on S. Res. 295,* 78th Cong., 2d Sess. at 265 (1944) (Pine Flat Water Users Ass'n); *Hearings Before the House Committee on Public Lands, on H.R. Res. 93,* 80th Cong., 1st Sess., No. 27 at 17 (1948) (General Assembly of the Presbyterian Church).
121. *Hearings, supra* note 119, at 674, 1261 (Irrigation Dist. Ass'n of California); *id.* at 173 (Kings River Water Ass'n); *id.* at 1310 (Central Valley Project Ass'n); *Hearings Before the Subcommittee of the Senate Committee on Commerce, on H.R. 3961,* 78th Cong., 2d Sess., pt. 5 at 652 (1944) (Central Valley Water Users Ass'n); *id.* at 709 (American Farm Bureau Federation).
121a. The following will serve as examples. COMMISSIONER OF THE GENERAL LAND OFFICE ANN. REP. 3, 4 (1885); 35 CONG. REC. 6668–6778 (1902); U.S. BUREAU OF RECLAMATION, REPORT ON LANDOWNERSHIP SURVEY ON FEDERAL RECLAMATION PROJECTS 61–98 (1946) (historical background of reclamation law and policy with respect to excess land limitation); RECORD OF PROCEEDINGS OF THE STATE IRRIGATION CONVENTION (1886); DEBATES AND PROCEEDINGS OF THE CONSTITUTIONAL CONVENTION OF THE STATE OF CALIFORNIA, vol. I at 100 (1878); vol. II, *id.* at 738, 1136; vol. III, *id.* at 1153, 1403; CHRISTMAN, TIN HORNS AND CALICO (1945); COOPER, LAND, WATER, AND SETTLEMENT IN KERN COUNTY, CALIFORNIA, 1850–1890 (unpublished thesis in Bancroft Library, Berkeley, California 1954; FARNAM, CHAPTERS IN THE HISTORY OF SOCIAL LEGISLATION IN THE UNITED STATES TO 1860, "Land Policy, 1784–1862" at 127 (1938).
In 1905 Senator Francis G. Newlands, co-author of the Reclamation Act of 1902, said:

"And so the wide policy of the National Government in this Act has been to encourage home-building and to destroy land monopoly; not only to prevent the monopoly of public land, but to break up the existing land monopolies throughout the arid regions. (Applause.) Here let me say that in my own opinion California has no greater curse than these large landed estates. (Applause.)"

Address by Senator Newlands, SACRAMENTO VALLEY DEVELOPMENT ASSOCIATION BULLETIN No. 23 at 15 (Irrigation Series no. 1, October 1, 1905).

"The conclusion is inescapable; the Di Giorgio Fruit Corporation, like the Kern

Legislation embodying policy has not been the product of the pressures of contending interests and groups alone. Decision has been illuminated by repeated and intensive investigations of land and water policy that are part of a long public record, Californian as well as national.[122] A few examples, in addition to numerous Congressional committee hearings and reports,[123] will suffice to indicate the range and scope of these investigations. A joint committee of the California Legislature reported on swamp and overflow land and land monopoly in 1874.[124] The Secretary of the Interior sent an investigator to California to study the acquisition of large holdings of desert lands in 1877.[125] The United States Commission on Public Lands reported in 1905 that

> your Commission has had inquires made as to how a number of estates, selected haphazard, have been acquired. Almost without exception collusion or evasion of the letter and spirit of the land laws was involved. It is not necessarily to be inferred that the present owners of these estates were dishonest, but the fact remains that their holdings were acquired or consolidated by practices which can not be defended.[126]

The fact-finders' report on reclamation furnished the basis for action by Congress in 1926 tightening the controls on incremental values from public appropriations made for reclamation.[127] In

---

County Land Company, is not susceptible to the kind of land reform the Bureau seems interested in introducing via the back door. Its 160-acre limitation clause is a wholly inadequate club with which to coerce the big landowners into dividing their baronies among the serfs. It scares nobody; it irritates nearly everybody. It bids fair merely to trip up the doughty giantkillers so widely wielding it. One wonders, indeed, why they are so intent on laying about them with this particular shillelagh."
DOWNEY, THEY WOULD RULE THE VALLEY 180 (1947). Under protest, Di Giorgio later agreed to dispose of excess holdings in Delano-Earlimart District. California Farmer, May 15, 1952, p. 533.

122. Cal. Legislature, *Report of the Swamp Land Investigating Committee*, 20th Sess. (1874). See Taylor, *Foundations of California Rural Society*, 24 CAL. HIST. Q. 193 (1945), and documents cited therein. Issues of slavery and Chinese immigration involved the question of size of land holdings. CALIFORNIA COMMISSION ON IMMIGRATION AND HOUSING, LARGE LAND HOLDINGS IN SOUTHERN CALIFORNIA (1919); see also notes 110, 113, 116 *supra* and note 126 *infra*.

123. *E.g.*, U.S. Industrial Commission, Final Report, "Opportunities for Acquiring Land," H.R. Doc. No. 380, 57th Cong., 1st Sess., vol. XIX, at 105–15 (1902); House Committee on Irrigation of Arid Lands, *Report on Reclamation of Arid Lands*, H.R. Doc. No. 1468, 57th Cong., 1st Sess. (1902); U.S. Industrial Relations Commission, Final Report and Testimony, *Land Question in the Southwest*, S. Doc. 415, 64th Cong., 1st Sess., vol. 9, at 8949 (1915); vol. 10, *id.* at 9290 (1915); *Hearings, supra* note 121, at 573–788; *Hearings, supra* note 121; *Hearings, supra* note 120, at 13–23, 37–48.

124. See note 110 *supra*.

125. San Francisco Chronicle, Sept. 17, 1877, p. 3.

126. COMMISSIONER OF THE GENERAL LAND OFFICE ANN. REP. 51 (1905). The passage quoted referred to entries made under both the Desert Lands Act and the Homestead Act.

127. Secretary of the Interior Committee of Special Advisers on Reclamation, *Federal Reclamation by Irrigation*, S. Doc. No. 92, 68th Cong., 1st Sess. (1924). See 44 STAT. 649, 650 (1926), 43 U.S.C. § 423e (1952) which sets forth the contract requirements.

1946 the Senate Small Business Committee published a comparative study in Central Valley showing the deep influence on the character of communities of the scale of agricultural enterprises surrounding them.[128] The Chairman, Senator James A. Murray, introduced the report by saying, "The bearing on the American way of life, which is all-important to all of us who seek to see the virility of this Nation go on unimpaired, is at once apparent."[129]

The issue inherently must be, and will remain, one of policy. It is far more than mere distribution of public dollars and resulting incremental land values, important policy matters as these are. The evidence on this point is overwhelming, world-wide, age-old, and timeless, pervading every branch of government, legislative, administrative, and judicial, and the civic channels through which citizens make their desires known and felt.

It is improbable that American citizens, either as electors or as represented in legislatures, will permit themselves long to be denied opportunity to debate whether control of water and incremental values resulting from public appropriations shall be concentrated in few hands or distributed widely. They took the formulation of water doctrine out of the hands of the California Supreme Court in 1928, when left no other alternative. It is unlikely, and going in the face of history, to expect that they would accept without question the edict of the *Ivanhoe* majority that water and incremental values from water developed by the federal government belong to whoever may be the owners of arid land. It is improbable that they ever intended, or will permit, each and every state to decide this question for itself, or let the national government appropriate in aid of water development contrary to established national policy or not knowing when some state may decide to change accepted rules, perhaps years after the nation has spent and is committed to spend more.

The California Supreme Court majority imposes a doctrine that favors accumulation of water rights and incremental values. The court forbids Congress, the constitutional maker of policy, to distribute water rights widely when serving private lands. The court confronts those who believe in the national policy as embedded in law and tradition with the arduous process of constitu-

---

128. Special Senate Committee, *Small Business and the Community: A Study in Central Valley of California on Effects of Scale of Farm Operations*, 79th Cong., 2d Sess. (1946).
129. *Id.* at viii.

tional amendment as the only means left to preserve it. No precedent supports the court's doctrine, other judicial authority is opposed, and the immediate effects are confusion and impasse.

V. SUPREME LAW OF THE LAND

> Congress has a substantive power to tax and appropriate for the general welfare, limited only by the requirement that it shall be exercised for the common benefit as distinguished from some mere local purpose . . . . Thus the power of Congress to promote the general welfare through large-scale projects for reclamation, irrigation, or other internal improvement, is now as clear and ample as its power to accomplish the same results indirectly through resort to strained interpretation of the power over navigation.
>
> UNITED STATES V. GERLACH LIVE STOCK CO., 1950[130]

Appeal of the *Ivanhoe* case by the Attorney General of California raises a question whether the United States Supreme Court has power in this case to review and reverse the California Supreme Court. Can it do more than say that under reclamation law the federal government is obliged to include the excess land provision in contracts, and that under local law as determined by the highest authority on that subject, viz., the California Supreme Court, irrigation districts in that State are powerless to enter into such contracts? A negative answer would pose the problem of an irresistible force meeting an immovable object, to be solved only by cessation of federal aid to California water development, by congressional abandonment of its effort to distribute the benefits from public expenditures equitably through the excess land provision, or by a change in the California Constitution. In essence, this is precisely where the California decision has left state-federal relations and where opponents of the appeal would have the United States Supreme Court leave them.

An amicus curiae memorandum for the California Farm Bureau Federation declares that "the decision shows very clearly that federal law had nothing to do with the holding. It was pure California law."[131] Other attorneys opposing the appeal state:

> We emphasize at the outset that . . . the Government is simply attempting to proceed by contract with public agencies which are creatures of the State of California. No regulatory or coercive power of the Fed-

---

130. 339 U.S. 725, 738, 20 A.L.R.2d 633, 643–44 (1950) (Justice Jackson).
131. Brief for the Cal. Farm Bureau Federation as Amicus Curiae, p. 14, Ivanhoe Irr. Dist. v. All Parties, *appeal docketed*, 25 U.S.L. WEEK 3343 (U.S. May 13, 1957) (No. 993).

eral Government is brought into play. A valid contract necessarily requires two contracting parties with capacity to make it. The highest court of the state has held that one of the parties, namely the state agency, lacks such power and, under the California Constitution, could not be granted such power by the Legislature. This is the fundamental point to which all argument eventually returns. No action of this Court, we submit, can provide California irrigation districts with powers which they lack.[132]

The first question for examination is whether federal law is involved, which the attorney for the California Farm Bureau Federation denies. Analysis of the *Ivanhoe* opinion does not support him; the reverse is much closer to the truth. Not state law, but the validity of federal law, is in question.

The only state law dealing specifically with federal-state relations over water development does not deny California irrigation districts power to enter into contracts with the United States under reclamation law; on the contrary it authorizes them to do so, incorporating the excess land provision by reference.[133] The only *certain* effect of the *Ivanhoe* decision is to block the operation of the federal excess land provision in California.

In construing the federal excess land provision as "inapplicable," the California Supreme Court invokes the Federal Constitution. The state court decision strongly implies reliance on the

---

132. Brief for Appellees on motion to dismiss appeal, p. 22, Ivanhoe Irr. Dist. v. All Parties, *appeal docketed*, 25 U.S.L. WEEK 3343 (U.S. May 13, 1957) (No. 993).

133. See text at notes 44–51 *supra*. A recent Note, setting forth the variety of views, says a view "sanctioned by some recent Supreme Court expressions . . ." is that "where the state interprets federal law incorporated by reference a federal question is always presented." Note, *Supreme Court Review of State Interpretations of Federal Law Incorporated by Reference*, 66 HARV. L. REV. 1498, 1508 (1953). The United States Supreme Court has held, in reference to a compact between states for control of pollution of waters of the Ohio River, that "the Supreme Court of Appeals of the State of West Virginia, is for exclusively State purposes, the ultimate tribunal in construing the meaning of her Constitution. Two prior decisions of this Court make clear, however, that we are free to examine determinations of law by State courts in the limited field where a compact brings in issue the rights of other States and the United States." West Virginia *ex rel* Dyer v. Sims, 341 U.S. 22, 28 (1950). In view of the twenty-year history of federal reclamation appropriations for California under a forty-year-old California statute authorizing contractual cooperation on federal terms, with Congress committed to further reclamation projects now in process of construction in California, the words of Associate Justice Jackson in a concurring opinion appear relevant:

"Whatever she now says her Constitution means, she may not apply retroactively that interpretation to place an unforeseeable construction upon what the other States to this Compact were entitled to believe was a fully authorized act.

"Estoppel is not often to be invoked against a government. But West Virginia assumed a contractual obligation with equals by permission of another government that is sovereign in the field. After Congress and sister States had been induced to alter their positions and bind themselves to terms of a covenant, West Virginia should be estopped from repudiating her act."

Id. at 35–36.

Federal Constitution in the *Madera* case which accompanies and relies on the *Ivanhoe* decision.[134] It objects to the 160-acre water limitation because under it "large landowners" would be "denied thereby due process and equal protection of the laws . . . ."[135] In the *Santa Barbara* decision also it says "the excess land provisions . . . are inapplicable and if not declared to be so would deprive the landowners of the member units of their property rights without due process of law and constitute a denial of the equal protection of the laws . . . ."[136]

The California Constitution contains no "equal protection of the laws" clause: that is in the Federal Constitution, amendment XIV, sec. 1.[137] Use of "equal protection of the law" to prevent application of the excess land law, therefore, must have been an interpretation of the Federal Constitution.[138] The California Constitution includes a "due process" clause.[139] The California court cited both state and federal due process provisions in the same sentence and called them "similar."[140] There is no indication, however, that the California Supreme Court was relying upon any possible differences in meaning between these state and federal provisions, and that it was not, in fact, interpreting the Federal Constitution to nullify a federal statute in California.[141] If there are any differences and the court was relying on them, it was nullifying a federal statute by testing it against a state constitution, which the supremacy clause of the Federal Constitution forbids.[142]

Further evidence that the California Supreme Court was interpreting federal law is furnished by its reliance on section 8 of the Federal Reclamation Act to destroy the excess land provision.[143]

Apparently the only state precedent without an equivalent in the Federal Constitution which the California Supreme Court em-

---

134. See Madera Irr. Dist. v. All Persons, 47 Cal.2d 681, 688, 306 P.2d 886, 890 (1957).
135. *Id.* at 688, 306 P.2d at 890.
136. Santa Barbara County Water Agency v. All Persons, 47 Cal.2d 699, 713, 306 P.2d 875, 884 (1957).
137. CAL. CONST., art. I, § 11 says: "All laws of a general nature shall have a uniform operation." The California court has said elsewhere that this clause is "similar" to the federal equal protection clause, County of Los Angeles v. Southern California Tel. Co., 32 Cal.2d 378, 388, 196 P.2d 773, 780 (1948), but did not refer to it in the *Ivanhoe* case.
138. Ivanhoe Irr. Dist. v. All Parties, 47 Cal.2d 597, 626, 306 P.2d 824, 841 (1957).
139. CAL. CONST., art. I, § 13.
140. Ivanhoe Irr. Dist. v. All Parties, 47 Cal.2d 597, 625, 306 P.2d 824, 840 (1957).
141. *Id.* at 624–25, 636, 306 P.2d at 840, 847.
142. U.S. CONST., art. VI, cl. 2.
143. See text at note 35 *supra*.

ployed was the provision in the Water Code that water must be distributed ratably,[144] a general requirement enacted much earlier than the specific authorization of irrigation district contracts conforming to reclamation law.[145] This state ground, even if it is accepted for the sake of argument, is inadequate to support the California Supreme Court decision as the court's resort to federal law and Constitution demonstrates.

The second aspect of the argument for dismissal of the appeal is its insistence that the essence of the situation is a contract between two parties,[146] one of which, by decision of its own final authority, is powerless to enter into a contract with the other agreeing to the excess land provision. "No action" by the United States Supreme Court, it is argued with finality, "can provide California irrigation districts with powers which they lack."[147] But the power to contract is not at issue; California irrigation districts have that power by state law, and *Ivanhoe* makes no move to strip them of it.

The new element the California majority injects is barring the excess land provision. The broad language of the majority carries no hint of anything less than preventing recognition of the federal provision in California in any form, contract or otherwise:

> We therefore feel free to declare that in all transactions between the United States and the State of California or its agencies such as the plaintiff district, the parties are dealing with trust property held by the state or by those who have acquired rights to it from the state or otherwise for the benefit of the real owners thereof. . . . Whatever interest or title the United States has acquired to water by appropriation, assignment or by other means of acquisition in furtherance of the execution of its trust relationship with the water users of the state is necessarily subject to the limitations of title herein determined.[148]

---

144. CAL. WATER CODE § 22250 (1956).

145. See text at note 51 *supra*.

146. Brief for California Farm Bureau Federation as Amicus Curiae, p. 22, Ivanhoe Irr. Dist. v. All Parties, *appeal docketed*, 25 U.S.L. WEEK 3343 (U.S. May 13, 1957) (No. 993).

147. Brief for Appellees on motion to dismiss appeal, p. 22, Ivanhoe Irr. Dist. v. All Parties, *appeal docketed*, 25 U.S.L. WEEK 3343 (U.S. May 13, 1957) (No. 993).

148. Ivanhoe Irr. Dist. v. All Parties, 47 Cal.2d 597, 628, 306 P.2d 824, 842 (1957). But the Supreme Court of the United States has said that to hold title in trust for a public purpose, such as use for a park or bandstand, does not bar the United States from taking full title to real property for another governmental purpose: "It makes little difference that the site here sought to be condemned is held by the City in trust instead of in fee." United States v. Carmack, 329 U.S. 230, 239 (1946). Also it has been said that "when the United States acquires, by eminent domain or otherwise, a tract of land in a State, it becomes the owner, and thereafter disposition is within the unfettered discretion of the Congress. No overriding sovereign governmental authority of the State impinges upon that discretion or gives rise to power on the part of courts to interfere with that disposition." Clackamas County v. McKay, 226 F.2d 343, 345 (D.C. Cir.), *cert. denied*, 350 U.S. 904 (1955).

This impairment of federal power by the *Ivanhoe* decision reaches to every alternative available to the federal government to acquire water rights necessary to accomplish reclamation.[149] Besides specifically denying the United States unfettered water rights by assignment from the state itself, the *Ivanhoe* majority reduces federal power to acquire them from the owners otherwise, either by purchase or eminent domain, to an impossibility and absurdity. The "real owners," according to the decision, are "the present and prospective water users of the state who may become entitled thereto under the laws of the state."[150] To identify these owners in order to make them offers of purchase or bring them into court under condemnation proceedings is a plain impossibility.[151] If they could be identified and their water rights condemned, just compensation for rights to unused water that are valueless without great public subsidy would be purely nominal, an outcome that would turn the proceeding into an absurdity.[152]

The substance of the situation is not to be confused with the shadow. It lies not in the formal "debtor-creditor" relationship, but rather in the power of the United States to use whatever legal means may be necessary to carry out a federal reclamation project, through contract or otherwise. The United States Supreme Court placed this on the broadest possible grounds of the general welfare in a recent Central Valley Project, California, decision.[153] The authorizing legislation empowered the Secretary of the Interior to "acquire by proceedings in eminent domain, or otherwise, all . . .

---

149. The use of contracts between irrigation districts and the United States to collect reimbursable costs and effectuate equitable distribution of water under the excess land provision is an expedient and convenience; it was not made standard procedure until nearly a quarter century after the beginning of federal reclamation, by passage of § 46 of the Omnibus Adjustment Act of 1926, 44 STAT. 649, 43 U.S.C. § 423e (1952).

150. Ivanhoe Irr. Dist. v. All Parties, 47 Cal.2d 597, 628, 306 P.2d 824, 842 (1957).

151. See text at note 86 *supra*.

152. "The capital investment to put water on land under the Central Valley Project averages $350 per acre. If an irrigator owns 1,000 acres, the capital investment to serve his land is approximately $350,000. This money is interest-free and the interest cost to the federal government over the pay-out period roughly equals the capital investment. In other words, the interest on $350,000 over a 50-year period is roughly $350,000. This is a direct subsidy to the irrigator. Using the percentages on repayment referred to in Chief Justice Gibson's dissenting opinion, the irrigator will pay back approximately $123,000. The balance of the capital investment will be paid by public power revenues. This amounts to $227,000. Thus, the total subsidy to this 1,000-acre irrigator adds up to approximately $577,000." Letter from Congressmen Clair Engle, George P. Weller, John E. Moss, Harlan Hagen, B. F. Sisk, J. J. McFall to Attorney General Edmund G. Brown, Feb. 4, 1957.

153. United States v. Gerlach Live Stock Co., 339 U.S. 725, 738, 20 A.L.R.2d 633, 643-44 (1950).

water rights . . . necessary . . ." to carry out the project.[154] The *Ivanhoe* case bars the way.

To permit the *Ivanhoe* decision of the California Supreme Court to stand without reversal by the United States Supreme Court not only would diminish the power of the federal government to exercise eminent domain—essential to a sovereign government[155]—for accomplishing its purposes under the general welfare clause, but also would encourage the confusion of authority and destruction of uniformity of application of federal law throughout the nation that the supremacy clause of the Constitution was intended to prevent.

---

154. Act of Aug. 26, 1937, c. 832, § 2, 50 STAT. 850.
155. See United States v. Carmack, 329 U.S. 230, 236–37 (1946).

EXCESS LAND LAW ON THE KERN?

California Law Review

Excess Land Law on the Kern?

A STUDY OF LAW AND ADMINISTRATION OF PUBLIC PRINCIPLE vs. PRIVATE INTEREST

*Paul S. Taylor**

Property is vigilant, active, sleepless; if ever it seems to slumber, be sure that one eye is open.—William Ewart Gladstone, 1891.[1]

No principle commands more ready acceptance than that special interest should yield to the general good. Yet, to declare the principle of public good in a statute is one thing; to administer it effectively is quite another. Causes of failure to realize principle may be many. Among them are unskillful bill drafting, unsound administrative structure, and unbalanced pressures upon administrators. The pressure for relaxation from those placed under limitation by a statute is not matched in strength and persistence by the efforts of adherents to principle and those potentially benefiting from its enforcement. The public is short of memory and, except on rare occasions of great stress, its common interests appear to be weak and diffused. Ownership of property encourages memory and providence, and its concentration invites use of power to serve its interests.

These factors are present on the Kern River in California. Some of them produced concentration of landownership there long ago.[2] The question whether they will also produce failure of the excess land law, or 160-acre water limitation,[3] is still in the balance.

The excess land law is a provision of national reclamation law written as a declaration and instrument of public policy by Congress in 1902, at the instigation of President Theodore Roosevelt.[4] No individual private

---

* Professor of Economics, University of California; consultant to the Office of the Secretary of the Interior and Bureau of Reclamation successively between 1943 and 1952. Klaus G. Loewald and Beverly Starika assisted ably in preparation of this paper. In March, 1958, the California Law Review forwarded a copy of this article as originally drafted to the Department of Justice.

[1] 3 MORLEY, LIFE OF WILLIAM EWART GLADSTONE 469 (1903).
[2] This implies no reflection on present owners of large land holdings, nor is any intended.
[3] 32 STAT. 390 (1902), 43 U.S.C. § 372 (1952), 44 STAT. 649–50 (1926), 43 U.S.C. § 423(e) (1952).
[4] See remarks of Congressman Francis G. Newlands of Nevada, 35 CONG. REC. 6674 (1902).

landowner may receive more water from a federal reclamation project than an amount sufficient to irrigate 160 acres. This is not a restraint on ownership of land, for no one is required to subject himself to its provisions unless willing to do so to obtain publicly-developed water. The restraint lies upon the individual, who is limited to an equitable share of water in the interest of spreading opportunity to others. "The bill is drawn exclusively," said Congressman Eben W. Martin of South Dakota, "for the protection of the settler and actual home builder, and every possible safeguard is made against speculative ownership and the concentration of the lands or water privileges into large holdings . . . ."[5] "This provision," said Congressman Frank W. Mondell of Wyoming, in answer to eastern charges that federal reclamation of the west would hand over its waters to a few, "was drawn with a view of breaking up any large land holdings which might exist in the vicinity of the Government works and to insure occupancy by the owner of the land reclaimed."[6]

Congress applied reclamation law, including the excess land provision, to flood control projects including Kern River, in 1944.[7] However, the executive branch of the federal government has failed to insist on enforcement. It has permitted the Army Engineers—sympathetic to the views of excess landowners there and unsympathetic to those of other local persons who favor reclamation law—to delay, deny, and obstruct. This paper is a commentary on administration of land and water law on the Kern,[8] important as a case study of national significance—especially in the Missouri Valley and eastward to Florida.

I

LAND

[The] land department has been very largely conducted to the advantage of speculation and monopoly, private and corporate, rather than in the public interest . . . . It seems that the prevailing idea running through this office and those subordinate to it was that the government had no distinctive rights to be considered and no special interest to protect . . . . I am satisfied that thousands of claims without foundation in law or equity, involving millions of acres of public land, have been annually passed to patent

---

[5] *Id.* at 6758.
[6] *Id.* at 6678.
[7] 58 STAT. 891 (1944), as amended, 43 U.S.C. § 390 (1952).
[8] Kern River flows into Tulare Lake Basin, its flood waters merging there with those of the Tule, Kaweah, and Kings Rivers; these rivers and basin are in the southern part of the Sacramento-San Joaquin Basin, known also as the Great Central Valley of California. Water, geography, economics, law, and administration are so closely interrelated throughout the area that while the focus of this paper is on the Kern, the treatment must frequently draw upon data and situations that reach beyond the lands that strictly bear that river's name.

upon the single proposition that nobody but the government had any adverse interest.—Commissioner William A. J. Sparks, 1885.[9]

The administration of the law, both in Washington and in the field, was frequently in the hands of persons unsympathetic to its principle, and Western interests, though lauding the [Homestead] act, were ever ready to pervert it.—Paul Wallace Gates, 1936.[10]

Public faith in a causal connection between widespread ownership of land and water and the maintenance of popular government has animated the main stream of legislation for disposal of the American public domain. This faith has been expressed countless times,[11] and combined with the land hunger of a numerous landless population, it has been politically effective in enacting notable legislation to diffuse landownership and protect against land and water monopoly. Its driving power produced the Pre-emption Act of 1841.[12] In 1860 it helped carry to power the Republican Party, which wrote the Homestead Law in 1862[13] and, after forty more years, the National Reclamation Law of 1902.[14]

Congress made exceptions to this policy at times—for example, in granting great tracts of public land to encourage railroad building by private

---

[9] ANNUAL REP. COMM'R GEN. LAND OFFICE 3-4 (1885) (emphasis in original).

[10] Gates, *The Homestead Law in an Incongruous Land System*, 41 AM. HIST. REV. 652, 655-56 (1936).

[11] Never more succinctly than by Daniel Webster in 1820 when he said, at the bicentennial of the landing of the pilgrims: "Our New England ancestors . . . were themselves, either from their original condition, or from the necessity of their common interest, nearly on a general level, in respect to property. Their situation demanded a parcelling out and division of the lands; and it may be said fairly, that this necessary act *fixed the future frame and form of their Government*. The character of their political institutions was determined by the fundamental laws respecting property . . . . The right of primogeniture . . . was . . . abolished . . . . The entailment of estates, long trusts, . . . were . . . seldom made use of. On the contrary, alienation of the land was every way facilitated . . . . The consequence of all these causes has been a great subdivision of the soil, and a great equality of condition; the true basis most certainly of popular government." Webster, *Discourse, Delivered at Plymouth, December 22, 1820. In Commemoration of the First Settlement in New England* 53-54 (3d ed. 1825). (Emphasis in original.) In 1776 Thomas Jefferson had persuaded the Virginia Legislature to abolish entailed estates. He said: "In the earlier times of the colony, when lands were to be had for little or nothing, some provident individuals procured large grants . . . desirous of founding great families for themselves . . . . To annul this privilege, and instead of an aristocracy of wealth, more harm and danger, than benefit, to society, to make an opening for the aristocracy of virtue and talent, which nature has wisely provided for the direction of the interests of Society, and scattered with equal hand through all its conditions, was deemed essential to a well-ordered republic." Foley, The Jefferson Cyclopedia, 307 (1900) citing *Autobiography*, in I WRITINGS OF THOMAS JEFFERSON 36 (1821).

[12] Act of Sept. 4, 1841, c. 16, 5 STAT. 453 (codified in scattered sections of 43 U.S.C.).

[13] Act of May 20, 1862, c. 75, 12 STAT. 392 (codified in scattered sections of 43 U.S.C.).

[14] Act of June 17, 1902, c. 1093, 32 STAT. 388 (codified and amended in scattered sections of 43 U.S.C.); see also the Puerto Rican 500-acre limitation enacted by Congress in 1900, 31 STAT. 715 (1900), 48 U.S.C. § 752 (1952).

enterprise; but, in 1902, it reconsidered that method of disposing of land in large blocks and repudiated it as a deviation from principle not to be repeated, even to obtain construction of great irrigation works which could not otherwise be profitably constructed by private enterprise. The House Committee on Arid Lands recognized that disposition of large blocks of public lands to a single private interest would secure the construction of such irrigation works, but found this sacrifice of public policy too costly.[15]

Recent investigation has furnished fresh support for the view that the historic policy of wide distribution continues to foster sound community values. During the forties, when national policy was under attack in Congress, an intensive study was made comparing two communities based on large scale and family-size farm operations respectively. The results were impressive.[16] The former was highly stratified, the latter more balanced.[17] In the latter community local business, newspapers, and church, veteran, recreational and civic organizations were all more flourishing.[18] "The bearing on the American way of life, which is all-important to all of us who seek to see the virility of this Nation go on unimpaired, is at once apparent," wrote Senator James E. Murray in the foreword of the study.[19]

The excess land provision of reclamation law embodies this national policy by favoring more equally balanced rural communities. Its fate in a

---

[15] House Committee on Irrigation of Arid Lands, *Report on Reclamation of Arid Lands*, H.R. REP. No. 1468, 57th Cong., 1st Sess. 3, ser. 4404 (1902): "If we were willing to abandon our time-honored policy of inviting and encouraging small individual landholdings, and were prepared to turn over all of the public lands under a large irrigation system to the control of a single individual or a corporation, we could undoubtedly secure the construction of extensive works which cannot be profitably constructed by private enterprise under present conditions, but no one contemplates paying so stupendous a price as this for irrigation development."

[16] Senate Special Committee to Study Problems of American Small Business, *Small Business and the Community, a Study in Central Valley of California on Effects of Scale of Farm Operations*, S. COMMITTEE PRINT No. 13, 79th Cong., 2d Sess. (1946); made pursuant to S. RES. 28, 79th Cong., 2d Sess. (1946).

[17] The family-size farm community had twice the proportion of business and professional and white collar workers, three times the proportion of farm operators, and less than half the proportion of agricultural laborers which, in the large-scale farm community, rose to two-thirds of the gainfully employed. Senate Special Committee to Study Problems of American Small Business, *Small Business and the Community, a Study in Central Valley of California on Effects of Scale of Farm Operations*, S. COMMITTEE PRINT No. 13, 79th Cong., 2d Sess. 43–45 (1946).

[18] "The small-farm community is a population of middle-class persons with a high degree of stability in income and tenure, and a strong economic and social interest in their community. Differences in wealth among them are not great, and the people generally associate together in those organizations which serve the community. Where farms are large, on the other hand, the population consists of relatively few persons with economic stability, and of large numbers whose only tie to the community is their uncertain and relatively low-income job. Differences in wealth are great among members of this community, and social contacts between them are rare." *Id.* at 6.

[19] Chairman of Senate Special Committee to study problems of small business. *Id.* at viii.

number of places, among them the Kern River, is currently in jeopardy from administrative quarters.[20]

The history of the administration of both land and water statutes disposing of public domain under pressure of large private interests furnishes disturbing omens of the outcome on the Kern River. In 1905 the Public Lands Commission advised Congress that:[21]

> [T]he land laws, decisions, and practices have become so complicated that the settler is at a marked disadvantage in comparison with the shrewd business man who aims to acquire large properties. Not infrequently their effect is to put a premium on perjury and dishonest methods in the acquisition of land.

Consequently, Commission inquiries revealed, "collusion or evasion" of the law was common practice in the acquisition of large estates, and speculators and corporations were acquiring a larger proportion of the public lands than actual settlers.[22]

This breakdown of public principle reported so regretfully and regularly to Congress probably was nowhere more conspicuous than in the Sacramento-San Joaquin Basin, including Kern River. Historian Paul Wallace Gates of Cornell University writes:[23]

> With great areas of land in the San Joaquin and Sacramento valleys open to cash purchase the opportunity for speculative profits was unparalleled elsewhere; nor was the opportunity neglected . . . . Greatest of all the speculators operating in California was William S. Chapman, whose political influence stretched from Sacramento to St. Paul, Minnesota, and Washington, D.C. Of him it was said, with apparent justice, that land officers, judges, local legislators, officials in the Department of the Interior, and even higher dignitaries, were ready and anxious to do him favors, frequently of no mean significance . . . .

---

[20] Projects for Kings and Kern rivers were authorized under the Flood Control Act of 1944, and constructed by the Army Engineers. See Taylor, *The Excess Land Law: Execution of a Public Policy*, 64 YALE L.J. 477 (1955) (present author's study of maladministration of reclamation law on Kings River).

[21] Public Lands Comm'n Second Partial Rep., *Message from the President*, S. Doc. No. 154, 58th Cong., 3d Sess. 13 (1905).

[22] "It is apparent, in consequence, that in very many localities, and perhaps in general, a larger proportion of the public land is passing into the hands of speculators and corporations than into those of actual settlers who are making homes . . . . Your Commission has had inquiries made as to how a number of estates, selected haphazard, have been acquired. Almost without exception collusion or evasion of the letter and spirit of the land law was involved. It is not necessarily to be inferred that the present owners of these estates were dishonest, but the fact remains that their holdings were acquired or consolidated by practices which can not be defended." *Id.* at 13–14.

[23] Gates, *The Homestead Law in an Incongruous Land System*, 41 AM. HIST. REV. 652, 668–69 (1936).

... The total amount purchased from the Federal government by Chapman, Miller and Lux, Friedlander, E. H. Hiller, and Mitchell was one and a quarter million acres. Forty-three other large purchasers acquired 905,000 acres of land in the sixties in California. Buying in advance of settlement, these men were virtually thwarting the Homestead Law in California where, because of the enormous monopolization above outlined, homesteaders later were able to find little good land.

The early concentration of ownership on the Kern River was the subject of official inquiry by Secretary of the Interior Carl Schurz in 1877; he suspended all land entries at Visalia Land Office pending investigation. The first investigator he sent out was caustically critical of the methods used to obtain land. According to probably the only account of his findings extant:[24]

> Mr. Newcomb discovered that the Desert Land Act of Congress was simply a Ring job, and was made the medium for an organized colossal steal by the Ring, to the prejudice of thousands of honest, *bona fide* settlers, against whom it was so used as to prevent them enjoying the benefits of the letter and spirit of the Act. By arrangement and collusion, the thing was so managed as to furnish from Washington to the Ring here the instant information of the Executive approval of the Act, and in less time, by weeks, than it requires to officially communicate the necessary order to give proper operation to an Act of Congress on this coast, the Ring land-grabbers had been allowed by the officers of the Visalia Land Office to list and locate an immense area of the desert tracts . . . .

The entire matter was reviewed for Secretary Schurz on October 26, 1878, by J. A. Williamson, Commissioner of the General Land Office, who recommended removal of the suspension of land entries. The Commissioner found no violation of the statutory requirement that no one can take more

---

[24] San Francisco Chronicle, Sept. 18, 1877, p. 2; see also *id.*, Sept. 17, 1877, p. 3; *id.*, Dec. 9, 1877, pp. 4, 8; *id.*, Dec. 11, 1877, p. 3; *id.*, Dec. 12, 1877, p. 1; *id.*, Dec. 13, 1877, pp. 2, 4; *id.*, Dec. 16, 1877, p. 8; *id.*, Dec. 17, 1877, pp. 1, 3; *id.*, Dec. 19, 1877, p. 6; *id.*, Dec. 22, 1877, p. 2; *id.*, Dec. 25, 1877, p. 3; *id.*, Dec. 26, 1877, p. 2; *id.*, Dec. 29, 1877, p. 1; *id.*, Dec. 31, 1877, p. 2; *id.*, Jan. 5, 1878, p. 4; *id.*, Jan. 6, 1878, p. 4; *id.*, Jan. 7, 1878, pp. 2, 4; *id.*, Jan. 8, 1878, p. 3; *id.*, Jan. 9, 1878, p. 4; *id.*, Jan. 10, 1878, pp. 2, 4; *id.*, Jan. 11, 1878, pp. 1, 2; *id.*, Jan. 12, 1878, p. 2; *id.*, Jan. 13, 1878, p. 3; *id.*, Jan. 15, 1878, p. 2; *id.*, Jan. 17, 1878, p. 2; *id.*, Jan. 21, 1878, pp. 2, 3; *id.*, Jan. 22, 1878, p. 2; *id.*, Jan. 23, 1878, p. 2; *id.*, Jan. 26, 1878, p. 1; *id.*, Jan. 29, 1878, pp. 2, 4; *id.*, Jan. 30, 1878, p. 2; *id.*, Jan. 31, 1878, pp. 2, 4; *id.*, Feb. 2, 1878, p. 2; *id.*, Feb. 3, 1878, pp. 2, 3, 5, 8; *id.*, Feb. 4, 1878, p. 4.

Archives of the Interior Department contain evidence that Newcomb was paid to go to California to investigate land scandals, and the Chronicle mentions a 300-page report by him, which it summarizes from a Washington dispatch; no copy of the report itself is to be found in National Archives. See also COOPER, LAND, WATER, AND SETTLEMENT IN KERN COUNTY, CALIFORNIA: 1850–1890, at 128–256 (unpublished master's thesis in Univ. of Calif. Library, Berkeley, 1953); UNITED STATES V. JAMES B. HAGGIN, TESTIMONY TAKEN BEFORE THE REGISTER AND RECEIVER OF THE UNITED STATES LAND OFFICE, AT VISALIA, CALIFORNIA (1878); Remarks of delegate Ganz of Illinois, PROCEEDINGS, NINTH ANNUAL SESSION OF NATIONAL IRRIGATION CONGRESS 54–57 (1900).

than one section, that the loan arrangements whereby the lender—a single individual—obtained liens on the lands of the other parties were possibly unenforceable but not illegal, and that the use of "combined enterprises" was a "reasonable and even necessary" means of developing irrigation on desert land.[25]

The Williamson report evidently closed the case. It did not, however, end the issue of wide vs. concentrated landownership. For the nature of the "combined enterprises" referred to by Williamson soon turned out to be a closely held partnership and before long a corporation, rather than an association of landowning neighbors enabled "to enjoy the benefit of the act" by engaging "in common with others" in bringing water to their lands.

Whatever the language of the statute and the facts surrounding acquisition of title to land, this was understood as a defeat of principle. The same year that Williamson made his report, Major J. W. Powell, recognizing

---

[25] "The testimony shows that no one man has nominally claimed to enter more than he is entitled to under the act but that many have entered claims of adjoining tracts, and are jointly irrigating the entire body of land entered.

"There is no evidence which proves that this is not in good faith, and for the real benefit of all.

"It seems that long canals are necessary, and many persons desiring to enter land are unable to build the ditch, and could not afford to do so except in common with others.... It seems reasonable and even necessary, if one man is to have only one section or less; and I think there is nothing in the statute, or the intention of its makers, to prohibit combined enterprises from making valuable a large district of desert land. The only restriction is, that no one can take more than one section.

"It seems that in this case, money has been loaned by one of the parties, Haggin, to others, and a contract made, which is set forth in the evidence, purporting to give him a lien therefor on the land.

"In case the certificates are not assignable, or the claims inalienable before a patent issues, then the contract for a lien on the land is simply void. I think that question is not properly before us in the case.

"The fact that one man encourages others by loans to make claims under the statute, so as to have aid in procuring water and right of way, does not make a case, in my judgment, of entering several tracts for his own use, and does not savor of fraud against the government, but simply enables others and himself to enjoy the benefit of the act, and accomplish what Congress seems to think desirable—the improvement of lands now nearly useless, which would not, and could not, be done by a single person." Letter from Comm'r. J. A. Williamson to Secretary of the Interior Carl Schurz 22-25, October 26, 1878. The San Francisco Chronicle called this "an outrageous decision" by one whose "whole official course" shows "he is always for the wealthy grabber and against the poor settler." (November 5, 1878.) The Visalia Delta was critical (November 1, 1878), and The Tulare Times was favorable, saying "all that is desired is that these barren plains should be made to blossom as the rose." (Quoted in the Visalia Delta, November 8, 1878.) To this the Visalia Delta replied sarcastically with political overtones: "And all that is necessary to make them bloom is to give them away in chunks, the size of whole states, to Carr & Haggin and let them sell them to actual settlers who have use for them. Rah for Tilden and Reform." *Ibid.* Newspaper quotations from COOPER, LAND, WATER, AND SETTLEMENT IN KERN COUNTY, CALIFORNIA: 1850-1890, at 250-52 (unpublished master's thesis in Univ. of Calif. Library, Berkeley, 1953).

widespread fears aroused by such occurrences, pointed out that land monopoly need not inevitably lead on to water monopoly, provided legislators would take measures to prevent it. "The question for legislators to solve," he wrote in his famous official report on the arid west, "is to devise some practical means by which water rights may be distributed among individual farmers and water monopolies prevented."[26] One year later the California Constitutional Convention, after protracted debate on land monopoly, prohibited grants of more than 320 acres of cultivable land to an individual.[27]

The prohibition was a genuine reflection of the public view on sound policy, but it came too late to be effective practically; a pattern of extraordinary concentration of landownership had already become established in California, especially in the southern and western San Joaquin Valley.[28] It survives to this day. In 1947 about twenty-five corporations owned nearly fifty-five per cent of the 192,000 acres in Tulare Lake Basin Water Storage District, and 102 individuals held about thirty-five per cent, all in holdings exceeding 160 acres.[29] In the same year the Bureau of Reclamation listed thirty-four individual and corporate owners of "5,000 or more acres in probable present and future San Joaquin Valley service areas of Central Valley Project," totalling 748,490 acres, and in an overlapping tabulation listed 717,257 acres in "large holdings" on the "upper west side of probable future development and Tulare Lake Basin" held by "land and development companies, banks, oil companies, partnerships and estates, individual and community property holdings of 1,000 acres or more, processors of farm products, railroads, corporation farms and other companies."[30] The chief engineer of Kern County Land Company informed Congress in 1940 that he was chief engineer of fourteen of the fifteen enterprises using water from Kern River, covering 300,000 acres, and that the other enterprise covered about 50,000 acres.[31]

Under these circumstances the opposition between the private interest of excess landowners and the principle of reclamation law dividing water

---

[26] POWELL, REPORT ON THE LANDS OF THE ARID REGION OF THE UNITED STATES 41 (2d ed. 1879). The excess land law is Congress' answer to Powell's question of 1879.

[27] CAL. CONST., art. XVII, § 3 (1879).

[28] See testimony of Paul H. Johnstone, economist of the Bureau of Reclamation, *Hearings on S. 912 before Senate Public Lands Subcommittee*, 80th Cong., 1st Sess. 860 (1947); compare the critical views of Sheridan Downey, *id.* 1236; DOWNEY, THEY WOULD RULE THE VALLEY 163 (1947).

[29] Letter from Commissioner of Reclamation Michael W. Straus to Senator Paul H. Douglas, February 2, 1949, p. 2 (mimeo.).

[30] Testimony of Paul H. Johnstone, *Hearings, supra* note 28, at 864. It is impossible to predict precisely which or how much of these acreages actually need or will be supplied with project water, but the proportion may be high.

[31] Testimony of George L. Henderson, *Hearings on H.R. 9640 before House Flood Control Committee*, 76th Cong., 3d Sess. 578 (1940).

equitably among individuals attains magnitude, feelings become intense, and pressures to distribute water according to property instead of according to people become sustained and pervasive.

II

WATER

The Bureau of Reclamation ... has consistently endeavored to bring about changes and to substitute social experiments which are distasteful to the citizens of this community, who have brought about a state of satisfaction through about 80 years of development .... We have no disposition to deal with the Bureau of Reclamation in any particular. I may even say that we have refused and will continue to refuse to participate in this project if it is assigned to them for construction and operation .... [W]e cannot consent to the invasion of our rights as citizens and of the control of our private properties and do not intend to do so.—George L. Henderson, Chief Engineer of Kern County Land Company, June 5, 1944.[32]

[Y]ou will need no supersleuth to discover that there are strong local interests from that area which seek to avoid application of the Federal reclamation laws to themselves ... by having the works built by an agency other than the Bureau of Reclamation. Naturally large landed interests have been conspicuous in this slightly disguised effort to escape the provisions of the federal reclamation laws which seek to distribute widely the benefits of conserved water. Other local interests at the same time, among whom family-size farmers are conspicuous, have been equally insistent that the antimonopoly and antispeculation features of the Federal reclamation laws shall be maintained without alteration in principle. If my opinion is worth anything, the national interest clearly lies on the side of the family-size farm families.—Secretary of the Interior Harold L. Ickes, June 7, 1944.[33]

Although land in the arid regions is of little value for agricultural purposes without water, no close measurement of the incremental value of add-

---

[32] *Hearings on H.R. 4485 before Senate Commerce Subcommittee*, 78th Cong., 2d Sess. 318–19 (1944). Mr. Henderson qualified himself before congressional committees as "chief engineer of the Kern County Land Co., one of the largest landowners in that area," as "chief engineer of 14 of the 15 canal units, the irrigation units of the Kern River," and as representing "all the irrigation interests of the Kern River in San Joaquin Valley." *Id.* at 305, 317, 319; *Hearings on H.R. 4911 before House Flood Control Committee*, 77th Cong., 1st Sess. 114 (1941); *Hearings on H.R. 4485 before House Flood Control Committee*, 78th Cong., 2d Sess. 751 (1944); see also *id.* at 756.

[33] *Hearings on H.R. 4485 before Senate Commerce Subcommittee*, 78th Cong., 2d Sess. 460 (1944). In 1941 and 1944 spokesmen for Grange, organized labor, and other local interests in Kern County opposed efforts to escape the excess land provision, whether by authorizing the Army Engineers to construct Isabella Dam or otherwise. *Hearings on H.R. 4911 before House Flood Control Committee*, 77th Cong., 1st Sess. 140–51 (1941); *Hearings on S. Res. 295 before Subcommittee of Senate Irrigation and Reclamation Committee*, 78th Cong., 2d Sess. 459–75 (1944).

ing water to the lands held by large owners on the Kern River is presently available. Data that distinguish between the values added by bringing natural stream flow to the land and those added by providing a controlled flow through the regulation of stored waters, or that specify the increment to each owner from water deliveries made possible by operation of Isabella Dam are likewise deficient and disputed.[34] But these values per acre are substantial by any measure for any era from the beginnings of development to the present, and are large in the aggregate for a few owners in the Kern River Valley.

In 1947, a Bureau of Reclamation economist estimated this net increment, allowing around $60 expenditure for levelling land, at around $200 per acre.[35] Using his basis for arriving at net increment and the differential land prices actually prevailing in Tulare County in 1945, the net differential from irrigation appears close to $400 per acre.[36] In 1957, the financial editor of the San Francisco Examiner reported figures pointing to a net differential of $300 per acre, figured conservatively.[37] He also cited income figures suggesting a much higher estimate: "The average acreage leased by the company to its tenants is 267 acres and in a decent crop year the tenant can make a net profit of about $16,000 from it." The landlord's share, he said, "would be about $12,000, minus taxes and other expenses."[38]

In the aggregate, incremental values can be of great importance to owners of large landholdings. At $200 an acre the owner of 10,160 acres would stand to gain approximately $2 million from reclamation if freed of the excess land law which allows him to gain only $32,000. If the $300 or $400 per acre estimates were used, the calculations of aggregate increment would need to be increased by 50 and 100 per cent, respectively. If a landowner already has a partial water supply, the estimates should be reduced to arrive at the increment attributable to improvement from construction of a dam.

These rough estimates and calculations are to indicate that the interest of present large landowners in a firm water supply, provided to them free

---

[34] *Hearings, supra* note 28, at 831–58, 860–911, 939–65, 965–74; DOWNEY, THEY WOULD RULE THE VALLEY 163–70 (1947).

[35] Paul H. Johnstone, *Hearings, supra* note 28, at 904.

[36] *Id.* at 861.

[37] White, "Barony in Valley is 'Precision' Farmer," San Francisco Examiner, June 14, 1957, sec. II, p. 4. Another financial editor writes: ". . . at a cost of $250–350 an acre the company since 1941 has levelled about 110,000 acres of raw grazing land for irrigation. Its lands upgraded from $200 an acre value to $800 or so, and it's now growing high-yield row crops in precision farming." Allen, "Kern County Land Heeds Lady Luck," San Francisco Chronicle, June 13, 1957, p. 19. This estimate appears to include the cost of sinking wells. The water supply coming from wells in the Southern San Joaquin Valley lacks assured permanence; this makes big reservoir projects indispensable.

[38] White, "Barony in Valley is 'Precision' Farmer," San Francisco Examiner, June 14, 1957, sec. II, p. 4.

of excess land limitations, is one of magnitude; the estimates are not intended to imply that a wider distribution of the same incremental values is not of great consequence to farmers, businessmen, and the community at large. On the contrary, the excess land provision was drawn largely with the interests of the latter in mind. Present landowners, however, are on the ground and watchful of their private interests; others are usually dispersed and ill-informed of their less well-defined interests.

Those active in acquiring large blocks of land in Kern River Valley in the eighties were aware of the prospect of incremental gain. To establish ownership of a large block of arid land, therefore, was to create at once a strong and conscious economic interest in the union of water and land. The great landholders on Kern River moved quickly to obtain its waters. Hardly was title to land cleared when the two greatest among them carried their dispute to the California Supreme Court. It was a battle of giants for a division of the natural flow of the stream.[39] Apprehensively, the court in 1886 expressed fears of the imminence of "a monopoly of all the waters of the state by comparatively few individuals . . . controlling aggregated capital, who could either apply the water to purposes useful to themselves, or sell it to those *from whom they had taken it away,* as well as to others."[40]

The decision pointed out the danger but did not solve the issue of monopoly. On the contrary, by declaring the doctrine of riparian rights to be the law of California it gave victory to one of the greatest landowners in Kern Valley. A public controversy broke out, charging that the riparian rights doctrine created a monopoly of water.[41] A leading attorney in water law told of the settlement in retrospect:[42]

> Did Henry Miller rest satisfied with the decision which gave him and his associates all of the water of Kern River? Not at all. He immediately said, "There is more water than we can use, and it does not come at the right time of the year. It comes in a great flood early in the spring, and in the hot

---

[39] The contest for the *controlled* flow would come many decades later when help was sought from the federal government to build Isabella Dam to make storage and regulation of water possible, and is the subject of later portions of this paper.

[40] Lux v. Haggin, 69 Cal. 255, 309–10, 10 Pac. 674, 703 (1886). As protections against water monopoly the doctrines or riparianism and appropriation proved horns of a dilemma, neither of them a solution. This was clear to the United States Supreme Court sixty-four years later when it said: "The State Supreme Court said the law of appropriation would result in monopoly. Lux v. Haggin . . . . If the uneconomic consequences of unlimited riparianism were revealed by court decision [as in Herminghaus v. Southern California Edison Co., 200 Cal. 81, 252 Pac. 607 (1926); Ivanhoe v. McCracken, 47 Cal. 2d 597, 621–2, 306 P.2d 824, 837–8 (1957)], so the effects of unrestrained appropriation became apparent when the flow of rivers became completely appropriated, leaving no water for newcomers or new industry." United States v. Gerlach Live Stock Co., 339 U.S. 725, 750 (1950).

[41] See Proceedings, State Irrigation Convention (San Francisco, May 20–22, 1886).

[42] Treadwell, The Cattle King 93 (1931).

months of summer the river is dry." So he said to his late antagonists, "You builds me a reservoir, and I gives you two-thirds of the water," and the difficulty was solved.

In recognition of the importance of the political issue of monopoly in California in that era, he added the comment: "In this settlement Henry Miller showed that he was not only a great general, but also a great statesman at the peace table."[43] With one of its chief supporting interests eliminated from immediate controversy, the agitation subsided. Concentration of landownership on the Kern had been followed by concentration of control of natural stream flow. The question of rights to controlled flow remained for the future—our present.

Costs of developing water supplies in the arid regions quickly came to exceed what agriculture could afford. Therefore, toward the end of the nineteenth century western landowners and other citizens interested in promoting western development sought aid from the federal government. Their agitation, lasting more than a decade, produced the National Reclamation Act of 1902 as an instrument for providing generous financial aid for water development and incorporating the excess land provision and other safeguards against private monopoly of water.[44] Opponents of the bill charged that large landowners would reap huge incremental gains in land values, but its sponsors—citing the excess land provision in answer—denied emphatically and repeatedly that this would be its effect.[45] It is abundantly clear that the bill would never have passed Congress[46] without this pro-

---

[43] *Id.* at 94. Although the immediate controversy on the Kern ended, dissatisfaction with the riparian doctrine as a guide to public policy survived. However, it was not until 1928, after an unsuccessful attempt by the Legislature in 1913, Cal. Stat. 1913, p. 1012, was blocked by the California Supreme Court in 1926, Herminghaus v. California Edison Co., 200 Cal. 81, 252 Pac. 607 (1926), that the people of the state were able to curb its most extreme aspects by amending the constitution. CAL. CONST., art. XIV, § 3 (1928). See résumé of the effort to overcome this obstacle to water development in Ivanhoe v. McCracken, 47 Cal. 2d 597, 621-2, 306 P.2d 824, 837-8 (1957); United States v. Gerlach Live Stock Co., 339 U.S. 725, 751 (1950).

[44] See Taylor, *The Excess Land Law: Execution of a Public Policy*, 64 YALE L.J. 477, 484-86 (1955).

[45] Congressman George W. Ray of New York, opposing the bill, said, "[T]he very moment that we, at the public expense, establish or construct these irrigation works and reservoir, you will find multiplied by 10, and in some instances by 20, the value of now worthless land owned by those railroad companies . . . ." 35 CONG. REC. 6685 (1902).

[46] Congress was thoroughly familiar with the concentration of landownership in the arid region, and determined to prevent a similar concentration in control of water, as the debates show. The House report on the bill, pointing out that private lands ought to be provided water from public projects, gave this reassurance: "The bill is carefully guarded against the accumulation of large holdings of irrigated lands in single ownership and would compel the breaking up of any large tracts now held for which water rights from Government works are to be obtained by limiting the area of lands the property of any one landowner for which a water right may be acquired to 160 acres." H.R. REP. No. 794, 57th Cong., 1st Sess., ser. 4402, pt. 1, at 7 (1902). See also the unequivocal statement by John E. Raker, California judge and congressman, in PROCEEDINGS, THIRTEENTH NATIONAL IRRIGATION CONGRESS 61 (1905) (Portland, Oregon).

vision to limit private benefit from public water development and to distribute opportunity to make homes on irrigated farms. Without it the law might not have passed the scrutiny of courts concerned with justifying public expenditures for private benefit.[47] In 1926, following the recommendation of the Fact-finders Report, Congress tightened the controls over private receipt of incremental values accruing from public construction of irrigation works.[48]

The great advantage of federal reclamation law to private landowners is that under it they can obtain water they could not otherwise afford. Along Friant-Kern canal, which reaches from the San Joaquin River to the Kern, landowners are currently asked to pay for water less than one-fourth of what its estimated cost would otherwise be.[49] The Chairman of the House Committee on Interior and Insular Affairs and his five Central Valley colleagues pointed out in 1957 that on the Central Valley project landowners repay only about $123 an acre, and are subsidized by the interest-free provision of the law and by contributions to repayment from hydroelectric power users to the extent of about $577 an acre.[50]

Passage of the National Reclamation Act was hailed by many representatives of important economic interests in California as the instrument for developing the waters of the State. A California Promotion Committee, whose prominent sponsors were occupationally classified from "advertising," "banks," "capitalists" to "woollens" and included a private utility, published a pamphlet proclaiming the advantages of reclamation law under the title *"For California"* in 1905. Pointing to the opportunity afforded by the willingness of the federal government to construct irrigation works "even where the land is in private ownership," one of the papers in the pamphlet said:[51]

> In California much of the best land . . . is in huge private holdings. It is believed that every great landowner in California will be willing to sign a contract to subdivide in order that the Government may proceed as rapidly as possible to construct irrigation works . . . . Already owners of more than seventy huge tracts of land have signified to the California Promotion

---

[47] Burley v. United States, 179 Fed. 1 (1910).

[48] *Federal Reclamation by Irrigation*, S. Doc. No. 92, 68th Cong., 1st Sess. 116 (1924); 44 STAT. 649–50 (1926), 43 U.S.C. § 423e (1952).

[49] *Hearings, supra* note 28, at 869.

[50] Letter from Clair Engle, George P. Miller, John E. Moss, Harlan Hagen, B. F. Sisk, and J. J. McFall to California Attorney General Edmund G. (Pat) Brown, February 4, 1957, in Ivanhoe v. All Parties, petition for rehearing of the appellant the State of California, in the Supreme Court of the State of California, L.A. No. 23,043, February 4, 1957, appendix, p. ii.

[51] Ferris, *Reclamation of Swamp Lands*, FOR CALIFORNIA, Sept. 1905, p. 14; see also Senator Francis G. Newlands' address at Red Bluff, June, 1905, SACRAMENTO VALLEY DEVELOPMENT ASS'N, BULL. No. 23, p. 14–18 (1905).

Committee their willingness to subdivide their lands for the benefit of intending settlers. This shows which way the wind blows and may be taken as an indication that when the Government is ready to go ahead our patriotic landed proprietors will be willing and ready to cooperate.

The hopes of the California Promotion Committee proved over-optimistic. On the very eve of its public invitation to cooperation between California large landowners and the federal government, excess landowners launched an attack on the provisions in the National Irrigation Congress in session at Portland, Oregon. The issue was debated thoroughly there and the attack rejected by voice vote "amid great applause."[52] However, the decision did not persuade the large landowners of California.

The only federal reclamation undertaken in California prior to the Central Valley project in the mid-thirties was a small project of 12,000 acres at Orland where private landowners accepted a 40-acre limitation to obtain federal aid. The great landowners on the Kern took no steps to include a dam on their river in the federal Central Valley project to bring water from the Sacramento to the San Joaquin. Instead, after it became clear that the Central Valley project would be constructed under reclamation law including the excess land provision, and after Congress made "flood control" costs non-reimbursable—that is, to be borne by the federal treasury rather than by the beneficiaries—in the Flood Control Act of 1936[53]—large landholding interests in the southern San Joaquin Valley turned their attention toward bringing the Army Engineers into reservoir construction on all rivers from the Kings south to the Kern, as a means of water control. As early as 1940, Congressman Bertrand W. Gearhart, from the Kings River area, introduced a bill at the instance of large landowners to authorize the Army Engineers to construct Pine Flat dam, although the Bureau of Reclamation already held full legal authorization and was "ready for its first or initial appropriation."[54] Flood control law, governing the Army Engineers, did not include reclamation law and its excess land provision *at that time*. Landowners probably expected financial advantages from their choice also,[55] although one spokesman denied it.[56]

---

[52] PROCEEDINGS, THIRTEENTH NATIONAL IRRIGATION CONGRESS 28–30, 60–2 (1905) (Portland, Oregon). See also testimony of Secretary of the Interior, J. A. Krug, *Hearings, supra* note 28, at 991–92.

[53] 49 STAT. 1570 (1936), 33 U.S.C. § 701a (1952).

[54] *Hearings on H.R. 9640 before House Flood Control Committee*, 76th Cong., 3d Sess. 544 (1940); see also *id.* 554.

[55] ". . . these water conservation facilities will be obtained through this program . . . at far less cost than would be the case by any other means." Address of President Ray B. Wiser, California Farm Bureau Federation, PROCEEDINGS, CALIFORNIA WATER CONFERENCE 323 (1945).

[56] Testimony of Charles L. Kaupke, *Hearings on H.R. 3024 before Subcommittee of Senate Appropriations Committee*, 79th Cong., 1st Sess. 999 (1945).

It is not difficult to understand why large landowners usually desire water permanently for all their lands and feel entitled to press for it, including the public help necessary to get it. Their spokesmen are inclined to ignore the considerations that have led public policy to prefer numerous smaller holdings to fewer large ones, to overlook the heavy subsidization of water development by taxpayers and power users, and to equate payment of *reimbursable* costs with full discharge of their public responsibilities. As one said:[57]

> ... these irrigators and their lands are not a part of, and being self-contained and self-sustaining, do not contemplate any connection whatsoever with the Central Valley project, unless it be the extension of favors to less fortunate neighbors who do contemplate use of Central Valley facilities and may be accommodated in the exchange of water. This is a service flowing from and not to these *privately owned projects* and should not by any stretch of the imagination be construed as reason to impose an outside control upon their private affairs .... [T]he water rights, distribution systems, and lands in these projects are privately owned and have been privately developed to a high degree of efficiency at a very great cost, and without any Federal aid. Their owners propose *to buy and to pay for any* reservoir capacity used, or nominal services rendered in connection with these flood-control developments. That being the case, they are *under no obligation* to anyone of a nature to call for their *giving up the control of their lands* or rights or subjecting themselves to the *protective custody* or the social and economic theories *imposed on debtors of some Federal* projects.

The effort to deny the Bureau of Reclamation the right to construct dams on four rivers from the Kings to the Kern, and to award it to the Army Engineers, succeeded, the authorization for these dams being contained in the Flood Control Act of 1944. However, Congress was engaged at the same time in a full scale debate on the excess land provision in the Rivers and Harbors bill, owing to the simultaneous effort of large landowning interests to obtain passage of the Elliott rider exempting the Central Valley project from it.[58] The decision of Congress to reject the rider[59]

---

[57] H. L. Haehl, *Hearing on H.R. 4485 before House Flood Control Committee*, 78th Cong., 2d Sess. 767 (1944) (emphasis added). On another occasion Mr. Haehl identified himself as consulting engineer for 25 or 26 years of the canal company that "distributes about 80 percent of the water of the Kern River for the Kern County Land Co." *Hearings on S. Res. 295 before Subcommittee of Senate Irrigation and Reclamation Committee*, 78th Cong., 2d Sess. 437 (1944).

[58] *Hearings on H.R. 3961 before Subcommittee of Senate Commerce Committee*, 78th Cong., 2d Sess., pt. 4 (1944).

[59] By allowing the entire Rivers and Harbors Bill, carrying the rider, to go down to defeat; this collapse of a bill known colloquially as the "gravy train" is a gauge of the intensity of opposition to lifting the excess land law. The author of the amendment, Congressman Alfred J. Elliott, represented Kern, Kings, and Tulare counties, and was the most active member of the House in the effort to prevent the Bureau of Reclamation from constructing Pine Flat and Isabella dams. Stripped of the Elliott rider, the Rivers and Harbors Bill passed promptly at the opening of the next session of Congress.

was matched by a parallel decision to make reclamation law a part of flood control law, thus applying the excess land provision to irrigation uses of water on projects of the Army Engineers; this is the thesis of the present paper.

The two bills authorizing water development were moving through Congress at the same time, the fate of both of them in some doubt because of intense controversy. They were linked by common subject matter and divided by their governing policies and by the administrative agencies they made responsible for construction.[60] When it appeared that Congress, in spite of Administration support for the Bureau of Reclamation, might authorize construction of multipurpose dams in Central Valley and elsewhere by the Army Engineers, Secretary of the Interior Ickes asked it to apply reclamation law to the projects.[61] It would be superfluous to recite legislative history in detail but for the present denial by the Chief of Engineers that this law applies. The original House report on the Flood Control Bill had professed to take care of reclamation interests:[62]

> Sound public policy requires not only that flood-control storage be under the supervision of the Secretary of War and the Chief of Engineers but also that *storage for the reclamation of arid lands be under the supervision of the Secretary of the Interior* . . . .

> Accordingly, the bill provides that *whenever* in the opinion of the Secretary of War and the Chief of Engineers *any dam and reservoir project* operated under the direction of the Secretary of War *can be consistently used for reclamation* of arid lands, *it shall be the duty of the Secretary of the Interior to prescribe regulations* for the use of the storage available for such purposes, and the operation of any such project shall be in accordance with such regulation. Such amounts as the Secretary of the Interior may deem reasonable shall be charged for the use of such stored water . . . .

The language of the House bill and these professions of the report were unsatisfactory to the Secretary of the Interior. Carefully he insisted on substitution of language of his own to protect reclamation principles.[63] The Senate Commerce Committee responded by inserting in the bill which au-

---

[60] A contest over public power preference for publicly-generated electricity paralleled that over the excess land provision. The public power issue is not a concern of this paper.

[61] *Hearings on H.R. 4485 before Senate Commerce Subcommittee,* 78th Cong., 2d Sess. 313, 457–58 (1944); see also epigraph at note 33 *supra.*

[62] H. REP. No. 1309, 78th Cong., 2d Sess., ser. 10845, p. 8 (1944) (emphasis added).

[63] "I believe that this section should be rephrased in a way that would eliminate possible future uncertainties with respect to its precise meaning and operation. Language that might appropriately be used for this purpose . . . is suggested in my written report." Testimony of Secretary Ickes, *Hearings on H.R. 4485 before Subcommittee of Senate Commerce Committee,* 78th Cong., 2d Sess. 458 (1944); see Letter from Secretary Ickes to Senator Josiah W. Bailey, June 2, 1944, *id.* 310–14.

thorized construction of these projects a new section 8, to replace section 6, using language "generally in accord with existing law and the expressed views of the Secretary of the Interior."[64] The managers for the House, reporting from the conference committee, said:[65]

> This amendment of the Senate replaces section 6 of the House approved bill with certain modified language *substantially as requested by the Secretary of the Interior* and constitutes section 8 of the Senate approved bill. The Senate language *will provide for more effective administration in relation to the various technical features of the Federal reclamation law. It establishes a procedure for the utilization of multiple-purpose projects for irrigation purposes* when the Secretary of War determines upon recommendations of the Secretary of the Interior that a project operated under the direction of the Secretary of War may be utilized for irrigation purposes.

The conference report was approved by Senate[66] and House[67] on the same day.

If further evidence of legislative intent to apply reclamation law to flood control projects were necessary, it is supplied by a colloquy between Acting Majority Leader Senator Lister Hill and Senator John H. Overton. Although the contest in the 78th Congress over application of reclamation law was focused on two separate bills, it involved the closest attention of the same congressional personnel. Congressman Alfred J. Elliott represented the large landowners' opposition both as author of the amendment to the Rivers and Harbors bill to exempt Central Valley and as a principal spokesman before committees of both Houses urging authorization of Kings and Kern River projects to the Army Engineers. Senator John H. Overton not only presided over the Senate Commerce subcommittee that killed the Elliott rider to the Rivers and Harbors bill after extensive hearings, but held personal responsibility for leading the Flood Control bill through the Senate as well. Neither man, nor Senator Hill as party leader, could have misunderstood the nature of the issue as it appeared in either of the bills.

Senator Overton said in response to specific questioning just prior to passage of the Flood Control bill by the Senate:[68]

> The President wrote me and the chairman of the subcommittee in this regard. *However, in view of the fact that the Senate amendment made not only the California projects but all such projects subject to irrigation laws,* and in view of the fact that the House concurred in this action by agreeing to section 8 of the Senate bill, I am sure that the President will feel that

---
[64] S. Rep. No. 1030, 78th Cong., 2d Sess., ser. 10842, p. 4 (1944) (emphasis added).
[65] H. Rep. No. 2051, 78th Cong., 2d Sess., ser. 10848, p. 7 (1944) (emphasis added).
[66] 90 Cong. Rec. 9269 (1944).
[67] *Id.* 9287.
[68] *Id.* 9264 (emphasis added).

we have met the problem that he raised. Section 8 of the bill clearly places reclamation uses of water from these projects *under the Secretary of the Interior and under the application reclamation laws. No project in this bill which may include irrigation features is exempted from the reclamation laws* .... As I stated a while ago, *section 8 of the bill clearly places reclamation uses of waters from all projects authorized in this bill under the Secretary of the Interior and under the applicable reclamation laws.*

Secretary Ickes observed later: "I am satisfied that the foregoing colloquy interprets the law in no uncertain terms. I am satisfied that section 8 ... represented a sweeping victory for the traditional reclamation policy of the Congress."[69]

III

LAND AND WATER ON THE KERN

The Kern County Land Company was born to wealth and by its own efforts it has continued into its maturity, even before the present golden flow of oil royalties came into being .... *"To those who have it shall be given them" is written in the Bible, and this certainly seems the proper formula to apply to the Tevis and Haggin heirs.*—P. J. Fitzgerald, 1939.[70]

The Bureau of Reclamation has not yet been able to make repayment arrangements with local interests under the Kings River procedure [*for "making of repayment arrangements ... with the Bureau ... in accordance with reclamation law"*]. ... *Local irrigators also oppose extension of the*

---

[69] Letter from Secretary of the Interior Ickes to Lt. Gen. Raymond A. Wheeler, Chief of Engineers, War Department, January 22, 1946, H.R. Doc. No. 367, 81st Cong., 1st Sess., ser. 11325, p. 67 (1949).

Section 8 reads as follows: "Hereafter, whenever the Secretary of War determines, upon recommendation by the Secretary of the Interior that any dam and reservoir project operated under the direction of the Secretary of War may be utilized for irrigation purposes, the Secretary of the Interior is authorized to construct, operate, and maintain, under the provisions of the Federal reclamation laws (Act of June 17, 1902, 32 Stat. 388, and Acts amendatory thereof or supplementary thereto), such additional works in connection therewith as he may deem necessary for irrigation purposes. Such irrigation works may be undertaken only after a report and findings thereon have been made by the Secretary of the Interior as provided in said Federal reclamation laws and after subsequent specific authorization of the Congress by an authorization Act; and, within the limits of the water users' repayment ability such report may be predicated on the allocation to irrigation of an appropriate portion of the cost of structures and facilities used for irrigation and other purposes. *Dams and reservoirs operated under the direction of the Secretary of War may be utilized hereafter for irrigation puposes only in conformity with the provisions of this section,* but the foregoing requirement shall not prejudice lawful uses now existing: *Provided,* That this section shall not apply to any dam or reservoir heretofore constructed in whole or in part by the Army engineers, which provides conservation storage of water for irrigation purposes." 58 STAT. 891 (1944), as amended, 43 U.S.C. § 390 (1952) (emphasis added).

[70] FITZGERALD, KERN COUNTY LAND COMPANY, A STORY OF SCIENCE AND FINANCE 29 (2d ed. 1939).

Kings River procedure to other projects, because they are unwilling to make repayment contracts under reclamation law, although they have offered to repay a substantial part of the cost of the project. They feel that provisions of reclamation law regarding acreage limitation and transfer of water rights to the Federal Government are not applicable in an area where irrigation has been practiced locally for many years, where local water rights are established under State law, and where most of the irrigation water to be provided by a Federal project is of a supplemental nature. Consequently, local interests appear to desire that repayment arrangements be made by the Secretary of the Army under the provisions of the *Flood Control Act of 1944, which* do not embrace the requirements of reclamation law.—Lieutenant General R. A. Wheeler, Chief of Engineers, July 27, 1948.[71].

The pattern of extreme concentration of landownership prevalent on Kern River since the settlement of that area continues to provide a natural basis for strong pressures to acquire similarly concentrated rights to controlled deliveries of water. These pressures, visible clearly in the contest over natural stream flow in the eighties, came to the surface again with the prospect of federal reservoir construction on the Kern in the forties. A few holders of rights to most of the natural stream flow of the river asked for construction of a reservoir by the Army Engineers, hoping to obtain federal help in securing the benefits of water control without invoking the policy of equitable distribution. Farmer and labor organizations of Kern County, on the contrary, opposed construction of Isabella Dam by the Army Engineers and favored reclamation law.[72] The latter failed to obtain their first point, but, as will appear below, they succeeded in their second. Nevertheless the pressures founded upon concentrated landownership remain the most influential factor in the administration of law on that river today, and are reflected in a tendency to forget there are any "local interests" on Kern River except those of large landowners.[73]

As early as December 3, 1945, the Chief of Engineers made it plain that,

---

[71] *Sacramento-San Joaquin Basin Streams, California,* H.R. Doc. No. 367, 81st Cong., 1st Sess., ser. 11325, p. 6 (1949) (emphasis added).

[72] *E.g.,* Ralph Abel, *Hearings on H.R. 4911 before House Flood Control Committee,* 77th Cong., 1st Sess. 140–51 (1941); various witnesses, *Hearings on S. Res. 295 before Subcommittee of Senate Irrigation and Reclamation Committee,* 78th Cong., 2d Sess. 459–75 (1944).

[73] *E.g.,* "Custom indicated that had the local interests opposed the authorization of these two [Kern and Kings River], Congress would have thrown them out of the Flood Control Bills, and they would not have been built. The *local interests* consented and asked for their construction, with the understanding that the 160-acre rule would not apply, and that the operation of the facility, subject to flood control, would be in the hands of the local interests." Letter from Eugene E. Marsh to Secretary of the Interior Douglas McKay, U.S. DEPT. INTERIOR, EXCESS LAND PROVISIONS OF THE FEDERAL RECLAMATION LAWS AND THE PAYMENT OF CHARGES, pt. 1, p. 101:2 (May 1956) (prepared at request of Subcommittee on Public Works and Resources, House Committee on Government Operations).

so far as projects authorized in the Flood Control Act of 1944 were concerned, he intended to act as though section 8 of the Flood Control Act[74] did not exist. He said: "The actual agreements for such repayment [for conservation storage] will be between local interests and the War Department. It is not mandatory under the law that these agreements comply with the provisions of the Reclamation Acts."[75] If this analysis of the meaning of flood control law by the Chief of Engineers is given effect by administrators, the concentration of ownership of land long since achieved on the Kern River will be paralleled there—and everywhere in the United States that flood control projects are constructed and concentrated landownership exists—by a like concentration of ownership of rights to controlled flows of water, the very outcome that the excess land provision was designed to prevent.

The arguments the Army Engineers use to support their position have been stated and restated over the years.[76] They boil down to three: (1) Congress authorized Kern River as a *flood control, not a reclamation* project. (2) Congress adopted, by reference to the Chief of Engineers' report, his recommendation that *he* make arrangements for payment. (3) Section 8 of the Flood Control Act, which deals with reclamation law on flood control projects, applies only to *additional works* that might be authorized in the future, *not to works authorized in the act.* These arguments will be examined seriatim.

(1) In order to distinguish a *flood control* project from a *reclamation* project, the Chief of Engineers has argued:[77]

---

[74] Flood Control Act of 1944, § 8, quoted in note 69 *supra*.

[75] Letter from Lieut. Gen. R. A. Wheeler to Governor Earl Warren, in PROCEEDINGS OF CALIFORNIA WATER CONFERENCE 72, 74 (1945).

[76] Letter from Major General E. C. Itschner, Chief of Engineers, to Senator Paul H. Douglas, March 19, 1957; Major General Thomas M. Robins, "The 160-acre limitation . . . does not apply . . . . You do not think the Army Engineers are dumb enough to go against the law." Quoted in reference to Kings River project in Fresno Bee, August 17, 1945, p. 9; Letter from Lieut. Gen. R. A. Wheeler to the Secretary of War, December 2, 1946, H.R. Doc. No. 136, 80th Cong., 1st Sess. 44–47 (1947); H.R. Doc. No. 367, 81st Cong., 1st Sess. xi, xii, 5–7 (1949); Letter from Major General Lewis A. Pick, Chief of Engineers, to Senator Paul H. Douglas, August 31, 1950; Letter from Secretary of the Army Frank Pace, Jr., to Senator Douglas, March 21, 1952, 98 CONG. REC. 9179 (1952); Letter from Brig. Gen. C. H. Chorpening, Asst. Chief of Engineers, to Senator Douglas, May 15, 1952, *Id.* at 9180; Letter from Brig. Gen. J. L. Person, Asst. Chief of Engineers, to Senator Douglas, January 22, 1957. The points covered in these officials' statements correspond closely to a carefully prepared legal analysis arriving at the same conclusion furnished by attorneys (McCutchen, Thomas, Matthew, Griffiths & Greene, by Burnham Enersen) to the Kern County Land Company, May 29, 1954 (processed).

[77] H.R. Doc. No. 136, 80th Cong., 1st Sess. 46–47 (1947). This statement referred to Kings River, but both Kings and Kern projects were authorized by the same act, their waters mingle in Tulare Lake Basin, and there is only slight difference in argument as to the law governing the two projects.

In the first place flood-control benefits of the project are more than sufficient to justify its entire cost. Other conditions include the facts that local water users have incurred expenditures of over $70,000,000 without Federal assistance in developing their irrigation systems; that they are now using by far the greater part of the flow of Kings River under established water rights; and that this project does not involve the development of new lands but is for improving water supply for existing holdings of lands already developed. Thus, in my opinion, land ownerships and farming operations in the area make inappropriate the acreage limitations involved in reclamation law.

These arguments have convinced the Chief of Engineers that the excess land provision is "inappropriate" on Kings or Kern Rivers, but they offer no support to a conclusion that Congress shared this opinion. The opposite is the fact. To answer the main question—whether Kings and Kern projects are covered by reclamation law—it is irrelevant to ask whether or not flood control benefits are more or less than sufficient to justify the project, whether or not the improvement in water supply is for the benefit of lands and irrigation systems already developed at great local cost, whether or not the lands are newly developed, or whether or not water rights have been established previously. Section 8 of the Flood Control Act is concerned explicitly with the irrigation benefits from a project, not with their relation to flood control benefits. Reclamation law never has been concerned with the question whether, when, or at what cost benefiting landowners developed their irrigation systems and lands, except to offer to help them to build reservoirs and irrigation systems. Reclamation law requires that established water rights be recognized,[78] but if landowners choose to ask irrigation water benefits under reclamation law, the law requires equal compliance from all beneficiaries.[79]

The first argument of the Chief of Engineers fails generally, then, because to argue that a flood control project cannot be covered by reclamation law is a non-sequitur; it fails specifically because the facts it states do not

---

[78] 32 STAT. 390 (1902), 43 U.S.C. § 383 (1952).

[79] Argument about water rights tends to obscure the essential question which is the conditions under which Congress has said that individuals can obtain federal help in getting water for their lands. The Warren Act of 1911 covers precisely such a situation as the Kern, authorizing Secretary of the Interior to contract for the *impounding, storage,* and carriage of *non-project water* with "individuals, corporations, associations and irrigation districts," *provided* "that water shall not be furnished from any such reservoir . . . to any one landowner in excess of an amount sufficient to irrigate one hundred and sixty acres." 36 STAT. 925–26 (1911), 43 U.S.C. §§ 523–24 (1952). To do otherwise would be to give owners of *uncontrolled* water the power to require the federal government to give them the *benefits of control* while waiving national policy in their favor. The so-called established water right is not a right to *controlled* flow of water, but only to natural stream flow, a right with which reclamation law does not interfere. Under reclamation law improvement of irrigation by controlling flow is not imposed on anyone; it is provided only through congressional appropriations and request by water users.

distinguish the irrigation benefits on Kern River and similar "flood control" projects from those customarily recognized and covered by reclamation law.[80]

(2) The second argument of the Chief of Engineers is that *he* is responsible for repayment contracts since, in section 10 of the Flood Control Act,[81] Congress approved by reference the recommendation in his project report that "authority to construct should be understood to include authority . . . *to make arrangements for payment* by the State or other responsible agency to the United States *for the conservation storage when used.*"[82] The language of section 10 of the act authorized the Kern River project "substantially in accordance with the recommendations of the Chief of Engineers," and the House report on the bill said the recommendations "attain the force of law through adoption of the report in the bill."[83]

However, the same report also said "sound public policy requires" that "storage for the reclamation of arid lands be under the supervision of the Secretary of the Interior," and the "bill provides" that "it shall be the duty of the Secretary of the Interior to prescribe regulations for the use of the storage" and project "operation" and set the "amounts" to "be charged for the use of such stored water."[84] This appears to establish, in the opinion of the House Committee, the primary role of the Department of the Interior in controlling arrangements for irrigation storage. The case is stronger since this report preceded a strengthening of language of the bill at request of the Secretary of the Interior to assure coverage of flood control projects under reclamation law. Since reclamation law requires the Secretary of the Interior to make repayment contracts,[85] the overriding question is whether Congress applied reclamation law to the Isabella Dam project by including

---

[80] It may be inferred from statements by the Chief of Engineers that he is aware of the irrelevance, while adhering to his position; he avoids saying his conclusion *rests on the arguments* of large landowners that Kern River is a special kind of project. In the epigraph to section III, in text at note 68 *supra*, he recites facts supporting the "feelings" of landowners opposed to the law, but avoids giving these as supports for *his conclusion* that reclamation law does not apply. In the passage quoted in the text at note 77 *supra*, he recites the same facts as support for a mere "opinion" that reclamation law is "inappropriate" on flood control projects.

[81] 60 STAT. 643 (1946), 10 U.S.C. § 1026b-1, 33 U.S.C. §§ 701f, 701j, notes (1952).

[82] *Kern River*, H.R. Doc. No. 513, 78th Cong., 2d Sess. 6–7 (1944) (emphasis added). See also Letter from Secretary of War Robert P. Patterson to Secretary of the Interior, February 15, 1946, S. Doc. No. 113, 81st Cong., 1st Sess. 275, 276 (1949); Letter from Secretary of the Army Frank Pace, Jr., to Senator Paul H. Douglas, March 21, 1952, 98 CONG. REC. 9179 (1952).

[83] H.R. Doc. No. 1309 on H.R. 4485, 78th Cong., 2d Sess., ser. 10845, p. 41 (1944).

[84] *Id.* at 8. For assertion of this legal authority and responsibility of the Secretary of the Interior, see H.R. Doc. No. 367, 81st Cong., 1st Sess., ser. 11325, p. 66 (1949); U.S. DEP'T OF INTERIOR SOLICITOR'S OPINION M-36457, PROPOSED CONTRACT BETWEEN THE UNITED STATES AND THE KINGS RIVER CONSERVATION DISTRICT 2 (July 10, 1957).

[85] *E.g.*, 44 STAT. 649 (1926), 43 U.S.C. 423(e) (1952).

section 8 in the Flood Control Act. This is explored fully below,[86] in light of the Army Engineers' denial that Congress did so.

Actually, the Chief of Engineers has not maintained his position on principle. Under the direction of his superiors, the President of the United States and Secretary of War, he has already surrendered the sole responsibility to make arrangements for repayment on flood control projects in one notable instance. On June 24, 1946, he joined with the Commissioner of Reclamation in a public statement that on Kings River, "under existing congressional authority, the Corps of Engineers will start construction . . . after required payments are insured *by contract, under the reclamation law, between the water users* who are beneficiaries of the development *and the Secretary of the Interior.*"[87]

The present basis for assumption of responsibility by the Army Engineers to conduct negotiations for repayment on Kern River is not *law*, but mutual agreement between the Departments of the Army and the Interior. The Department of the Army has been so flexible as to be prepared to accept the Department of the *Interior* as negotiating agency even on *Kern* River. On October 28, 1954, Secretary of the Army Robert T. Stevens wrote to the Secretary of the Interior that, in April 1954, the Department of the Army had executed an interim contract with local interests on Kern River *"after reaching an informal understanding with representatives of the Department of the Interior that your Department would be responsible for negotiating and executing the long term contract."*[88] Secretary Stevens then asked that responsibility be yielded back to the Army for reasons of which he specified only two: (1) the Army had been conducting negotiations with local interests for *interim* water service, and (2) *local interests preferred* to negotiate with *the Army* rather than with the Interior Department.[89]

---

[86] Text following note 93 *infra*.

[87] H.R. Doc. No. 136, 80th Cong., 1st Sess. 49 (1947) (emphasis added).

[88] U.S. Dep't Interior, Excess Land Provisions of the Federal Reclamation Laws and the Payment of Charges, pt. 1, app. 70 (May 1956) (emphasis added). This "informal understanding" surrendering jurisdiction to the Department of the Interior followed earlier claims of legal authority for the Army by Secretaries Patterson and Pace. See note 82 *supra*. Secretary of the Interior McKay similarly was willing to recede from the claim of legal jurisdiction made by Secretary Ickes, H.R. Doc. No. 367, 81st Cong., 1st Sess., ser. 11325, p. 66 (1949), and supported by argument of regional counsel under Secretary Oscar Chapman. Letter from Leland O. Graham to Karl W. Shattuck, chairman of the negotiating committee, Kings River Water Association, July 24, 1950, U.S. Dep't Interior, Excess Land Provisions of the Federal Reclamation Laws and the Payment of Charges, pt. 2, app. 12:2 (May 1956). See text at note 95 *infra*.

[89] "Local interests . . . advocate most strongly that arrangement for handling the long term contract [for Isabella Dam] be accomplished by the Secretary of the Army and contend that existing law contemplated that such arrangements should be by *this* Department . . . . In view of the circumstances, including the *negotiations which have been conducted* to date by the

Neither consideration is a matter of *law,* nor did Secretary Stevens imply his own belief that it was, as he could easily have done by saying that he agreed with the large landowners' contention that he had responsibility under "existing law." His acceptance of the second consideration reflects again the willingness of the Army Engineers to side with certain local interests against others in effectuating a disputed interpretation—if not an outright violation—of law.

In 1950, after the Regional Counsel of the Bureau of Reclamation responded to a challenge by large water users' representatives on Kings River by making a detailed argument that the law required the Department of the Interior to make the repayment contract,[90] Kings River representatives entered into negotiations with the Bureau of Reclamation. But when a change in administration had taken place, a new Undersecretary of the Interior receded implicitly from the earlier position taken under Secretaries Ickes, Krug, and Chapman, by yielding to Secretary Stevens' request that the Army be allowed to conduct negotiations on the Kern.[91] By 1955, in making arrangements between them for contract negotiations, neither Secretary of the Army Stevens nor Undersecretary of the Interior Davis showed any concern for what the law might prescribe, or any opinion that it prescribed at all. On October 20, 1955, Secretary of the Interior Douglas McKay likewise made no pretense of standing on *law* as his predecessor

---

Department of the Army and the *desires of local interests,* it is considered *desirable* that this Department complete the contract in that case. I would appreciate your confirming that this is agreeable to you." U.S. DEP'T INTERIOR, EXCESS LAND PROVISIONS OF THE FEDERAL RECLAMATION LAWS AND THE PAYMENT OF CHARGES, pt. 1, app. 70:1–2 (May 1956) (emphasis added). Secretary Stevens did not claim *legal* authority for the Army.

Simultaneously the Chief of Engineers was affirming his own opinion that the law conferred authority on him to negotiate the contract in one sentence, and announcing his surrender of it in another: "Existing flood control law under which these two projects [Kings and Kern] were authorized by Congress provided that the Secretary of the Army would make arrangements for repayment to the United States for conservation storage when used. The President, however, has issued instructions in the case of the Kings River or Pine Flat project that repayment arrangements for that project would be made by the Secretary of the Interior. Consequently, the Corps of Engineers is governed regarding the Pine Flat project by the President's decision and by the agreement for carrying it out which was reached between the Secretaries of Army and Interior on 1 February 1947." Letter from Major General Lewis A. Pick to Senator Paul H. Douglas, August 31, 1950.

[90] Letter from Leland O. Graham to Karl W. Shattuck, July 24, 1950; see notes 88 *supra,* 95 *infra.*

[91] "As a result of our recent conferences with Assistant Secretary of the Army George H. Roderick and his staff, we now understand it to be acceptable to your Department, . . . that the Department of the Army negotiate and *execute a repayment contract* with local interests for conservation storage in the Isabella Reservoir, California." Letter from Clarence A. Davis to the Secretary of the Army, February 17, 1955, U.S. DEP'T INTERIOR, EXCESS LAND PROVISIONS OF THE FEDERAL RECLAMATION LAWS AND THE PAYMENT OF CHARGES, pt. 2, app. 71:1 (May 1956) (emphasis added).

Secretary Ickes had done; administrative decision by the President followed by agreement between departments had tossed responsibility for negotiations on Kings River to the Department of the Interior; now agreement between departments without Presidential directive tossed responsibility on Kern River to the Army.[92] The contention of Secretary Ickes and of Regional Counsel Graham that responsibility for negotiation is a matter of law rather than agreement was rejected without public answer.

(3) The third and crucial argument of the Army Engineers is that section 8 of the Flood Control Act, which deals with reclamation law on flood control projects, applies only to *additional works* that might be authorized in the future, not to works authorized in the Act itself.[93]

Did Congress, as the Chief of Engineers contends, apply reclamation law only to future projects *not* authorized in the act and exempt all the projects that *were* authorized? This would be like saying that Congress, in passing section 8 of the Flood Control Act of 1944, was down in the cellar at midnight looking for a black cat that wasn't there. Such a construction is both unflattering to Congress and unable to bear inspection of the language of the statute.

Section 8 consists of three sentences.[94] The first two authorize construction of "additional works" under the reclamation laws and appropriate circumstances and procedures. The third sentence contains no reference at all to "additional works"; it reads: "Dams and reservoirs operated under the direction of the Secretary of War may be utilized hereafter for irrigation purposes only in conformity with the provisions of this section . . . ." Reclamation law, including a passage stating that "the Secretary of the

---

[92] Letter from Secretary of the Interior Douglas McKay to Eugene E. Marsh, October 20, 1955, *Id.*, pt. 1, app. 102. See also Letter from Eugene E. Marsh to Secretary McKay, July 28, 1955, *Id.*, pt. 1, app. 101:3, recommending, in light of the fact that the "larger landowners are strenuously opposed" to negotiating a contract with the Bureau of Reclamation that might apply the excess land provision, that the "simple way out is to have the Bureau withdraw, and permit the U.S. Army Engineers to negotiate the contract." To this, Secretary McKay replied: ". . . the fact that the Army early determined that they would offer *no different terms* than the Bureau of Reclamation would offer minimized many of the reasons which were urged upon the Department as a reason for the change." Letter from Secretary McKay to Eugene E. Marsh, Oct. 20, 1955, *id.*, pt. 1, app. 102:2 (emphasis added).

[93] The Chief of Engineers states: "Section 8 has been analyzed very carefully from the strictly legal viewpoint and it has been concluded that the authority provided therein pertains *only to dam and reservoir projects requiring additional Federal works* to make them useful for irrigation purposes. Such irrigation works may not be undertaken until after a report and findings thereon have been made by the Secretary of the Interior and after specific authorization of the Congress by an authorization Act. *No Federal supplemental irrigation works are involved in the operation of the seasonal irrigation storage provided in Isabella Reservoir, and hence it is considered that this general legislation is not applicable to this project.*" Letter from General E. C. Itschner to Senator Paul H. Douglas, March 19, 1957 (emphasis added).

[94] Section 8 is quoted in note 69 *supra*.

Interior is authorized to construct, operate and maintain, under the provisions of the Federal reclamation laws . . . ," is the only subject of the section. The reference in the third sentence to "Dams and reservoirs" is patently to *all* dams and reservoirs, of which Isabella Dam is the only one on Kern River named in the act. None of the congressional reports or debates on the Flood Control bill mentioned "additional works" or suggested departing from existing reclamation law in order to create a distinction between projects consisting only of "dams and reservoirs" and those consisting of "additional works" such as auxiliary dams, canals, or distribution systems. Unless intended to cover situations *other than* the "additional works" already covered in the first two sentences, the third sentence of section 8 would be unnecessary and without meaning.[95]

On the chance that his first line of defense might fall, the Chief of Engineers offers a second:[96]

> While we do not consider that Section 8 is applicable to the Isabella project we feel that we should point out that if this general authority were considered in direct conflict with Section 10 of the same Act, which authorizes the Isabella project, we would feel that the *specific* authority contained in Section 10 would govern . . . . It is considered that *specific* language would be necessary for each new project in order to make reclamation law applicable thereto unless *general* legislation covering the matter is enacted.

The statement is open to at least two objections. First, the *general* authority, section 8, prescribes the governing law of all flood control projects; the *specific* authority merely attaches authority to "make arrangements" for payment to the authority to construct. Since they do not refer to the same thing, the "general" and the "specific" in this instance are not comparable. Second, the "general" prescription of governing law is in the statute itself, while the "specific" authority to make arrangements for repayment depends upon the weaker ground of adoption by reference. The Army Engineers, in effect, claim power to oblige Congress to discover and

---

[95] Regional Counsel for the Bureau of Reclamation summed up the point as follows: ". . . section 8 of the Flood Control Act of 1944 . . . intended that the section apply to all projects constructed by the Corps of Engineers to the extent that they should be utilized for irrigation purposes. Section 8 provides (1) for the construction of *additional works* pursuant to the Federal reclamation laws, to the extent that additional works are necessary, and it does this by the first two sentences of the section, and (2) for the utilization for irrigation purposes under the Federal reclamation laws of projects constructed by the Secretary of War where no additional works are necessary, and it does this by the third sentence. Only by a strained construction of the statute and an ignoring of the legislative history could it be argued that the Congress intended that where the *same type of benefit* is conferred a *distinction should be made* only on the basis of whether additional features are necessary." Letter from Leland O. Graham to Karl W. Shattuck, July 24, 1950, note 88 *supra*, pt. 2, app. 12:6 (emphasis added).

[96] Letter from General E. C. Itschner to Senator Paul H. Douglas, March 19, 1957.

specifically reject each and every recommendation affecting policy contained in an engineering construction report to which it might not wish to give approval, even to one—in the present instance—beginning in the middle of a paragraph on the last line on page 6 and including the first few lines at top of page 7 of a 42-page House report.[97] Confirmation of such power would offer administrators a field day for law-making, subject only to line-item veto by Congress.

If any doubt that the Flood Control Act of 1944 applies reclamation law to flood control projects survives the preceding analysis of its language, reference to the legislative history of the bill should suffice to resolve it.

The propriety of going to legislative history for clarification is denied by attorneys for large local interests; the Chief of Engineers ignores legislative history, although Secretary Ickes quoted it to him to support a charge that refusal to apply reclamation law to flood control projects "would be in direct violation of the intent of the Flood Control Act of 1944."[98] However, argument that examination of legislative history is unnecessary and inappropriate because the meaning of the statute is clear and unambiguous on its face is untenable. At least two Secretaries of the Interior have publicly asserted an opposite interpretation of the law to that of the Chief of Engineers.[99] One Chief of Engineers acquiesced over his own signature to a contract "under reclamation law" on Kings River, a project without "additional works" authorized under the same statute as Kern River project.[100] None of his successors have publicly repudiated this action, but on the contrary have accepted it by references as recently as 1957.[101]

The Chief of Engineers is left by his own actions and those of his superiors in no position to assert either that clarity of language in the flood control statute renders legislative history immaterial, for it clearly shows

---

[97] H.R. Doc. No. 513, 78th Cong., 2d Sess. 6, 7 (1944). From a congressional viewpoint, Senator Douglas commented: "It is very difficult for me . . . to find any justification for your conclusion, in the absence of any expressed exemption, that the excess land provisions of the Reclamation Law do not apply to the Isabella project, *since the authorizing legislation for that particular project did not repeat the requirements of the Reclamation Law.* Do the Army Engineers seriously maintain that it is essential to repeat the provisions of existing general law in order to make it apply in connection with each new, specific project?" Letter from Senator Douglas to Lieut. Gen. S. D. Sturgis, Jr., Chief of Engineers, Feb. 15, 1957 (emphasis added). General Itschner's reply was in the affirmative. Letter from General E. C. Itschner to Senator Paul H. Douglas, March 19, 1957.

[98] H.R. Doc. No. 367, 81st Cong., 1st Sess. 66-67 (1949).

[99] Secretary Ickes, *ibid.*; Secretary J. A. Krug, S. Doc. No. 113, 81st Cong., 1st Sess. 16 (1949); the argument of Regional Counsel Graham was made under Secretary Oscar Chapman.

[100] H.R. Doc. No. 136, 80th Cong., 1st Sess. 49 (1947).

[101] Letter from Brig. Gen. J. L. Person, Assistant Chief of Engineers, to Senator Paul H. Douglas, January 22, 1957.

the intent of Congress to make reclamation law applicable,[102] or that a flood control project without "additional works" is not covered under reclamation law.

IV

ADMINISTRATIVE STRANGULATION

> ... *two large Federal agencies—the Army Corps of Engineers and the Department of Interior's Bureau of Reclamation—have conflicting jurisdiction in river development work. Operating under separate statutes and appropriations one is primarily concerned with local flood control, the other with irrigation. . . . There have been repeated instances where each competes with the other to begin construction on the same project. The result has been hasty planning, lack of sufficient basic data, duplicating cost of surveying and estimating, failure to consider the entire needs of the area, and the creation of strong and opposing local pressures each seeking special benefits. The end result has been needless delay, confusion, and gross waste of the taxpayers' money. The history of the operation of these agencies in the Columbia and Missouri Valleys and the Central Valley of California provides eloquent testimony to the disastrous consequences of the competition between these Federal agencies. . . . To remove the major areas of overlapping and duplication, we have recommended that the functions of flood control and river and harbor improvement work of the Army Corps of Engineers be consolidated with the Reclamation Service within the Department of the Interior.*[103]
> —Hoover Commission, 1949

The thesis of this paper is that reclamation law, applied to flood control projects by Congress in 1944, is being strangled by confused, irresponsible, and unsympathetic administration in the executive branch of government. The ultimate end of such a course, if permitted to continue, is outright violation of the law.

On October 2, 1957, four years after negotiations for repayment began on Kern River and ten years after negotiations for repayment began on Kings River, the Department of the Army advised the Comptroller General of the United States that it was proceeding, together with the Department of the Interior, to request the Attorney General of the United States to review and furnish his opinion on the question as to *which federal agency* is legally responsible for entering into the repayment contracts covering

---

[102] The legislative history is explored in text from notes 58 to 69 *supra*.
[103] [HOOVER] U.S. COMMISSION ON ORGANIZATION OF THE EXECUTIVE BRANCH OF THE GOVERNMENT, CONCLUDING REPORT 27-29, 43 (May, 1949). See also MAASS, MUDDY WATERS: THE ARMY ENGINEERS AND THE NATION'S RIVERS (1951); Maass, *Kings River Project in the Basin of the Great Central Valley—a Case Study*, COMMISSION ON ORGANIZATION OF THE EXECUTIVE BRANCH OF THE GOVERNMENT, CONCLUDING REPORT, APP. L, TASK FORCE REPORT ON NATURAL RESOURCES, January 1949, app. 7, pp. 149-82 (May, 1957); Maass, *Administering the CVP*, 38 CALIF. L. REV. 666-95 (1950).

irrigation benefits from Army projects and *under which laws*.[104] Two months later, the Comptroller repeated a previous recommendation of a "vigorous effort" to consummate contracts, and told Congress that "should these efforts fail, the matters [should] be referred to the appropriate congressional committee for instruction as to further actions."[105]

Proper administrative procedure in accordance with law is not difficult to discover. By inserting section 8 in the Flood Control Act, Congress covered *authorized* as well as "additional" works, and placed responsibility for concluding repayments on the Secretary of the Interior. President Truman, Secretary of War Patterson, three Secretaries of the Interior, at least one Chief of Engineers, and spokesmen for the interests of large landowners— the latter reluctantly[106]—have supported this view on Kings River. There is no sufficient difference between Kings and Kern projects in geography, economics, history, or statute to distinguish them as to governing law or the location of administrative responsibility for its enforcement. The Chief of Engineers—referring future decision to Congress—has even gone so far as to express his opinion that "the disposal of irrigation water is not properly a permanent function of the Department of the Army but should eventually be administered by the Bureau of Reclamation in accordance with the applicable provisions of reclamation law."[107] Yet the Army Engineers deny that reclamation law applies to Kern River project now, and are permitted by the Secretary of the Army, the Secretary of Interior, and the Chief Executive to reiterate the denial and to hold themselves out as possessing an administrative authority that Congress placed elsewhere.

---

[104] Comptroller General of the United States, Audit Report to the Congress of the United States, Central Valley Basin, California, Water Resources Development Program, Bureau of Reclamation, Department of the Interior and Corps of Engineers (Civil Functions), Department of the Army for the Fiscal Year Ended June 30, 1956, December 11, 1957, p. 10, note 1.

[105] *Id.*, p. 10. For reasons given in this article the author disagrees with the unsupported statement of the Comptroller General that the Army Engineers bear responsibility for negotiating a repayment contract on Kern River, *Id.*, pp. 9, 34.

[106] It is not clear to what extent this reluctance was overcome by legal argument of the Regional Counsel of the Bureau of Reclamation under Secretary Chapman that the law made the Bureau of Reclamation responsible, as compared with the offer of Secretary McKay to permit excess landowners "to comply with the provisions of the Reclamation Law *without disposing of their excess land holdings.*" Letter from Secretary McKay to Eugene E. Marsh, Oct. 20, 1955, U.S. Dep't Interior, Excess Land Provisions of the Federal Reclamation Laws and the Payment of Charges, pt. 1, app. 102:1, 2 (May, 1956) (emphasis added). In Taylor, *The Excess Land Law: Execution of a Public Policy,* 64 Yale L.J. 477 (1955), I argued that the McKay contract was a violation of reclamation law. McKay's successor, Secretary Fred A. Seaton, has rejected the contract, saying: "I cannot justify an aggravation of a prior practice in an effort to remedy an absence of legal authority. What I am concerned about is the process by which inferences are based on inferences and there is a whittling away at a principle until all that is left is a pile of shavings." New York Times, July 13, 1957, p. 10.

[107] Lieutenant General R. A. Wheeler, H. R. Doc. No. 367, 81st Cong., 1st Sess. 6 (1949).

Behind a facade of arguments in which law, the preferences of administrators, and the feelings of some—but not other—local interests are mingled almost indiscriminately, there is the spectacle of two agencies of the same government competing for authorizations to construct dams. Interests based on large landholdings, by giving or withholding their support, use this defective administrative structure and poorly drafted legislation to play one agency against the other for private advantage. Public principle and public interest are the victims of the pressures given elbow room by these defects. In an effort to correct this unsound organization of government the Hoover Commission recommended that the function of flood control and river and harbor improvement work of the Army Corps of Engineers be consolidated with the Reclamation Service within the Department of the Interior.[108]

Both the Army Engineers and the Bureau of Reclamation have recognized the difficulty of obtaining repayment contracts under reclamation law. The former have opposed delay in construction of flood control projects until contracts conforming to reclamation law were signed,[109] and their counsel was followed on Kings and Kern rivers. The consequences are no repayment for dams completed years ago and uncertainty whether reclamation law will be complied with at all. The Army Engineers would be satisfied with obtaining money for the treasury. The Department of the Interior has stood for both policy and money; Secretary Ickes characterized congressional reclamation policy as concerned primarily with policy —the creation of farm homes.[110]

Very recently the Solicitor of the Department of the Interior has given legal confirmation of the position taken by Regional Counsel of the Bureau of Reclamation in 1950,[111] and supported in this paper, viz., that reclamation law applies to flood control projects and requires the Secretary of the Interior to enforce it. On July 10, 1957, the Solicitor said:[112]

> The statutory authority that you as Secretary exercise in connection with flood control projects providing irrigation benefits is derived from the Flood Control Act of 1944, particularly section 8. 43 U.S.C. 390. Dams and res-

---

[108] See epigraph at note 103 *supra*.
[109] *E.g.*, H.R. Doc. No. 367, 81st Cong., 1st Sess. xii, xiii (1949).
[110] "The reclamation policy of the Congress is not concerned solely, nor indeed, primarily with repayment. It is concerned with the wide distribution of economic opportunities arising as a result of the construction of reclamation structures. It is concerned with the creation of farm homes. It strives against the monopolization of benefits by a privileged few." *Id.* 68; *cf.* Memorandum—Statement of Differences, prepared by the Army, *id.* xii, xiii.
[111] See note 95 *supra*.
[112] Elmer F. Bennett, U.S. Dep't of Interior Solicitor's Opinion M-36457, Proposed Contract Between the United States and the King's River Conservation District 2 (July 10, 1957).

ervoirs operated for flood control purposes under the direction of the Secretary of the Army after December 22, 1944 may be utilized by you for purposes of irrigation under that Act only in conformity with the provisions of the Federal reclamation laws. Act of June 17, 1902, 32 Stat. 388 and Acts amendatory thereof or supplementary thereto. The specific provision with which you must comply under this mandate is found in section 46 of the Omnibus Adjustment Act of 1926 as amended. 43 U.S.C. 423e.

In drawing attention to large landowners who are opposed to reclamation law and administrators who are unsympathetic, it would be easy to overlook the contrasting attitude of most water users and of sympathetic administrators. The difference is crucial. When water contracts that included the excess land provision were presented to irrigation districts along Friant-Kern Canal in the southern San Joaquin Valley there were no rejections. On the contrary, the popular vote at the polls in 13 districts on 20 contracts was 5,753 to 551, a ratio of more than ten to one favoring acceptance of the contracts.[113]

Contrary to some predictions, acceptance of water under reclamation law has proceeded even farther. In the intensity of the effort to remove the excess land law from Central Valley in 1947, Senator Sheridan Downey said:[114]

> The conclusion is inescapable; the Di Giorgio Fruit Corporation, like the Kern County Land Company, is not susceptible to the kind of land reform the Bureau seems interested in introducing via the back-door. Its 160-acre limitation clause is a wholly inadequate club with which to coerce the big landowners into dividing their baronies among the serfs. It scares nobody; it irritates nearly everybody. It bids fair merely to trip up the doughty giantkillers so widely wielding it. One wonders, indeed, why they are so intent on laying about them with this particular shillelagh. There is plenty of water in the Central Valley for the DiGiorgio holdings as well as for all other project farms, excess and non-excess alike.

However, in 1952, the DiGiorgio Fruit Corporation signed a contract for water with Delano-Earlimart district agreeing to sale of its excess holdings

---

[113] Senator Thomas H. Kuchel says that Corning district in the Sacramento Valley is prepared to accept the excess land provision voluntarily, despite the California Supreme Court decision against its validity. Sacramento Bee, June 22,.1957, p. D-6.

[114] DOWNEY, THEY WOULD RULE THE VALLEY 180 (1947). Senator Downey ignored the fact that Congress intended to spread the benefits of reclamation beyond local landowners to include persons anywhere in the nation seeking opportunity to farm on reclamation projects. However, citizens in other states who might like to farm on the project if they were informed of the opportunity are politically ineffective as compared with large landowners on the spot; they furnish no support to administrators trying to enforce the law. While Senator Downey directed political attack upon administrators sympathetic to the law, his logical target was Congress, which refused his proposal to change the law.

in compliance with reclamation law. The Corporation did so "under protest in order to get supplemental water for its crops, mostly grapes."[115]

Electors on the Kings and Kern rivers should be offered the opportunity that electors were given on Central Valley Project to vote on repayment contracts consistent with reclamation law, not denied it. The executive branch of the federal government, particularly the Secretary of the Interior, bears the responsibility his Solicitor confirmed on July 10, 1957, to see that this opportunity is provided.

---

[115] *The Bureau Coerces DiGiorgio*, CALIFORNIA FARMER, May 17, 1952, p. 533.

THE EXCESS LAND LAW

Legislative Erosion
of Public Policy

THE EXCESS LAND LAW: LEGISLATIVE EROSION OF PUBLIC POLICY

PAUL S. TAYLOR*

I

1902

... by the perversion of the existing land laws the sources of water supply are gradually being monopolized by the owners of cattle herds and the controllers of the great cattle ranges. Their purpose is to obtain the title to the water and by this means to control the land, prevent settlement, and perpetuate the monopoly which they now hold. If the Government does not act promptly it will be difficult for it to move at all.... Irrigation means the multiplication of the small homes and of the small herds....
—Congressman Francis G. Newlands of Nevada[1]

... and so we find behind this scheme, egging it on, encouraging it, the great railroad interests of the West, who own millions of acres of these arid lands, now useless, and the very moment that we, at the public expense, establish or construct these irrigation works and reservoirs, you will find multiplied by 10, and in some instances by 20, the value of now worthless land owned by those railroad companies, the title to which they obtained through grants from the Government for building great transcontinental railroad lines.
—Congressman George W. Ray of New York[2]

The roots of current controversy over the excess land provision lie deep in American history; their presence was better known long ago than now. A quarter of a century before Congress passed the law, Major John Wesley Powell, in his famous report on the arid region in 1879, warned: "The question for legislators to solve is to devise some practical means by which water rights may be distributed among individual farmers and water monopolies prevented."[3]

In the original Congressional debates of 1902 over whether the federal government should aid the reclamation of western waters,

---

*Professor of Economics, University of California; consultant to the Office of the Secretary of the Interior and Bureau of Reclamation successively between 1943 and 1952. Klaus Loewald and Beverly Stirina assisted ably in preparation of this paper.
    1. Co-sponsor of the National Reclamation Bill, 35 CONG. REC. APP. 256 (1902).
    2. Leading spokesman against the National Reclamation Bill, 35 CONG. REC. 6685 (1902).
    3. POWELL, REPORT ON THE LANDS OF THE ARID REGION OF THE UNITED STATES 41 (2d ed. 1879).

friends and opponents of the bill to grant public aid agreed with Major Powell; neither was willing to allow those who had amassed large holdings of arid and semi-arid lands to gain a similar monopoly of water. Friends of public reclamation believed that by dint of clear purpose and careful bill-drafting they were simultaneously undermining current monopoly of land and erecting a permanent barrier to future monopoly of water.[4] Opponents prophesied that, nothwithstanding the excess land provision and other precautions, the practical outcome of federal reclamation would be vast concentration of water rights and of private gain.[5] Beneath the concern over prevention of water monopoly lay appeals to the long national tradition of using land—and now water—resources to create opportunity and independence for more families[6] as a means of assuring a free and stable society[7] and of nourishing patriotism.[8]

The framers of reclamation law devised the excess land provision as first among their instruments for preventing monopoly. The provision states: "No right to the use of water for land in private ownership shall be sold for a tract exceeding one hundred and sixty acres to any one landowner. . . ."[9] They employed as additional

---

4. Congressman Frank W. Mondell of Wyoming, chairman of the committee in charge of the bill. 35 CONG. REC. 6677, 6678, 6680 (1902); see also address of Senator Francis G. Newlands before Red Bluff Banquet, SACRAMENTO VALLEY DEVELOPMENT ASS'N, Bull. No. 23, pp. 14-15 (1905).
5. See text at note 2 *supra*.
6. *E.g.*, Senator Henry C. Hansbrough of North Dakota, co-sponsor of the bill, said: "It is argued by some that as wealth grows larger in a few hands the opportunities of the laboring classes to secure employment are multiplied. Doubtless this contention is based upon sound reasoning, but looking a little beyond immediate benefits, it appears that the tendency under such conditions is to dwarf self-reliance in the masses and to make the mere service of opulent employers by the great army of breadwinners the fulfillment of all human ambition. I think it is the duty of the legislator to pursue a policy under which the greatest possible number of our people may be provided with the means of independent employment, by which the aspirations of the individual may be encouraged and developed." 35 CONG. REC. 1386 (1902).
7. *E.g.*, Congressman John Dalzell of Pennsylvania said reclamation "would relieve us of the greatest danger to our social stability which confronts us today—the danger arising from the possible throwing out of employment of a multitude of men in some period of business depression, such as we passed through a few years ago. In such times as that strikes and riots are inevitable, and we have had experience enough in the past to show their danger." 35 CONG. REC. 6739 (1902). Congressman Newlands said that if lands were conveyed to private corporations to obtain private construction of irrigation works "we would have fastened upon this country all the evils of land monopoly which produced the great French revolution, which caused the revolt against church monopoly in South America, and which in recent times has caused the outbreak of the Filipinos against Spanish authority." 35 CONG. REC. 6734 (1902).
8. *E.g.*, Congressman Wesley L. Jones of Washington said: "Manhood, patriotism, love for family, and love for country flow from such a measure, and are infinitely more to be desired than the few dollars we propose to spend." 35 CONG. REC. 6755 (1902).
9. 32 STAT. 389 (1902), 43 U.S.C. § 431 (1952). This provision was inserted in the bill at the personal instance of President Theodore Roosevelt; it had not been a part of earlier drafts. Congressman Newlands, said the President, "was somewhat in doubt as to whether the bill was sufficiently guarded in the interest of homeseekers. . . . We all wanted to prevent monopoly and concentration of ownership, and the result was that certain changes were made absolutely satisfactory

instruments to achieve the same purpose: (1) use of public enterprise to supplement private enterprise; (2) prohibition of commutation, an alternative that had seriously damaged the operation of homestead land policy by permitting substitution of cash payment for observance of anti-monopoly policy; (3) tightening the habitancy requirements of reclamation projects above those prescribed by homestead law; and (4) making water rights appurtenant to the land irrigated and beneficial use the basis, measure, and limit of the right.[10]

With one hand reclamation law confers generous financial benefits on irrigators.[11] With the other it asks those who request water from a federal project to comply with the anti-monopoly and anti-speculation policy embodied in the excess land provision.[12] No landowner is required to sell any of his land,[13] but in case of voluntary private sale, the Secretary of the Interior is made responsible for controlling private receipt of incremental values arising from construction of the project.[14] In the years since passage of the original Act of 1902 Congress has often reiterated its approval of federal reclamation policy[15] and even tightened the original controls on private monopoly and speculation.[16] It heeded the advice of the Fact-finders report,[17]

both to the Executive and to the Irrigation Committee, and intended only to carry out the intentions of both." 35 CONG. REC. 6674 (1902).
   10. These are elaborated elsewhere. See Taylor, *The Excess Land Law: Execution of a Public Policy*, 64 YALE L.J. 477, 484-86 (1955).
   11. *E.g.*, Congressman Engle, chairman of the House Interior and Insular Affairs Committee, and five other Central Valley Congressmen, have estimated that in the Central Valley project, California, a landowner repays only $123 an acre to the federal government, receiving a "direct subsidy" of $350 which is the "interest cost to the federal government" of providing "interest-free" money to him, and an additional subsidy of $227 paid by "public power revenues." Letter from Congressman Engle *et al.* to Attorney General Brown of California, February 4, 1957.
   12. Section 46 of the Omnibus Adjustment Act of May 25, 1926 requires that repayment contracts between the United States and irrigation districts shall "provide that all irrigable land held in private ownership by any one owner in excess of one hundred and sixty irrigable acres shall be appraised in a manner to be prescribed by the Secretary of the Interior and the sale prices thereof fixed by the Secretary on the basis of its actual bona fide value at the date of appraisal without reference to the proposed construction of the irrigation works; and that no such excess lands so held shall receive water from any project or division if the owners thereof shall refuse to execute valid recordable contracts for the sale of such lands under terms and conditions satisfactory to the Secretary of the Interior and at prices not to exceed those fixed by the Secretary of the Interior; and that until one-half the construction charges against said lands shall have been fully paid no sale of any such lands shall carry the right to receive water unless and until the purchase price involved in such sale is approved by the Secretary of the Interior. . . ." 44 STAT. 649 (1926), 43 U.S.C. § 423 (e) (1952).
   13. Under flexible administrative interpretations, excess landowners have sometimes been supplied water for 160 acres even if unwilling to sign recordable contracts in compliance with legal requirement for obtaining water for lands in excess of that amount. U.S. BUREAU OF RECLAMATION, DEP'T OF INTERIOR, LANDOWNERSHIP SURVEY ON FEDERAL RECLAMATION PROJECTS 47 (1946).
   14. See note 12 *supra*.
   15. *E.g.*, in 1906, 1910, 1911, 1912, 1914, 1916, 1924, 1926, 1927, 1937, 1939, 1940, 1943, 1944, and 1945. U.S. BUREAU OF RECLAMATION, DEP'T OF INTERIOR, *op. cit. supra* note 13, at 62.
   16. Notably in 36 STAT. 926 (1911), 43 U.S.C. § 524 (1952); 37 STAT. 266 (1912), 43 U.S.C. §§ 542-44 (1952); 44 STAT. 649 (1926), 43 U.S.C. § 431 (1952). U.S. BUREAU OF RECLAMATION, DEP'T OF INTERIOR, *op. cit. supra* note 13, pt. II, at 29.

whose secretary, John A. Widtsoe, wrote in 1928: "In the future it will be even more necessary to insist that large holdings shall not receive water from government supplies, unless divided into farm units of proper size, and offered to intending purchasers at reasonable terms."[18]

This continuing support of the aims of reclamation policy, on the one hand, has been countered by pervasive and consistent efforts on the part of large landowners to escape the anti-monopoly and anti-speculation provisions of the law, on the other. As forecast by opponents of federal aid in 1902, large landowners have resisted public policy with increasing success. In their effort they have pressed against all branches of government—executive, judicial and legislative alike. Aware that the policy of wide distribution of ownership of land and water rights has become imbedded in national mores as well as statutes, their efforts to destroy the excess land provision have as common characteristics the giving of lip-service to the idea of equitable distribution of resources and the avoidance of the appearance of challenging it.[19]

I have examined elsewhere pressures on administrators for relaxation of enforcement[20] to the point of outright violation of the statute.[21] The drive against the excess land provision through the judiciary culminated in a 1957 decision by the California Supreme Court declaring it unconstitutional for a California irrigation district to agee to comply with the federal excess land provision.[22] I have questioned the validity of this decision elsewhere.[23] The present article analyzes efforts to break down the excess land law in the third branch of government through legislation.

---

17. *Federal Reclamation by Irrigation*, S. Doc. No. 92, 68th Cong., 1st Sess. 116 (1924).

18. WIDTSOE, SUCCESS ON IRRIGATION PROJECTS 113 (1928).

19. *E.g.*, Senator Sheridan Downey, in the midst of his drive to exempt the Central Valley from the provision, wrote: "I favored it myself until personal investigation revealed its impracticability and its dangers." DOWNEY, THEY WOULD RULE THE VALLEY 1 (1947). See text *infra* at note 32.

20. Taylor, *supra* note 10, at 501-06. See also my paper which has been accepted by the California Law Review for publication in May, 1958.

21. Secretary of the Interior Fred A. Seaton advised Philip A. Gordon, Kings River Conservation District, by letter dated July 12, 1957: "The Department continues to recognize and support the basic concept of Reclamation Law that full and final payment of the obligations of a district to the federal government ends the applicability of the acreage limitations." The unsoundness of this interpretation of the law has been shown in Taylor, *supra* note 10, at 489-501, 512-13.

22. Ivanhoe Irrigation Dist. v. All Parties and Persons, 47 Cal. 2d 597, 306 P.2d 824 (1957).

23. Taylor, *Destruction of Federal Reclamation Policy? The Ivanhoe Case*, 10 STAN. L. REV. 76 (1957).

II
1905 - 1947

> In California much of the best land for Government irrigation is in huge private holdings. It is believed that every great landowner in California will be willing to sign a contract to subdivide in order that the Government may proceed as rapidly as possible to construct irrigation works under the National Reclamation Act. Already owners of more than seventy huge tracts of land have signified their willingness to subdivide their lands for the benefit of intending settlers. This shows which way the wind blows and may be taken as an indication that when the Government is ready to go ahead our patriotic landed proprietors will be willing and ready to cooperate.
>
> —John W. Ferris, C.E., 1905[24]

> The conclusion is inescapable; the DiGiorgio Fruit Corporation, like the Kern County Land Company, is not susceptible to the kind of land reform the Bureau [of Reclamation] seems interested in introducing via the back door. Its 160-acre limitation clause is a wholly inadequate club with which to coerce the big landowners into dividing their baronies among the serfs. It scares nobody; it irritates nearly everybody. It bids fair merely to trip up the doughty giant killers so widely wielding it.
>
> —Senator Sheridan Downey, 1947[25]

The unity in opposing water monopoly between opponents and friends of federal aid in 1902 was not shared by some large landholders. Their unwillingness to comply with the excess land provision in order to obtain water, although unexpressed while the fate of federal aid to reclamation was in the balance, was not long in showing itself after aid was assured. Barely three years later they asked the National Irrigation Congress, the original citizen-backers of reclamation, to recommend elimination of the provision. They personified their appeal in the figure of an eastern Oregon farmer "whose gray and wrinkled beard and horny hands are evidences of the toil to which he has been subjected for forty years."[26] However, a spokesman favoring the law was more persuasive to the delegates; he recited the hard political fact that the western states' delegations in Congress seeking passage of the reclamation bill had "secured its adoption and presentation to Congress solely and entirely upon the question that the great land monopolists in the United States would be prohibited from getting the benefit of it . . . and thereby prevent the homeseekers from getting homes."[27] After extended debate the National Irrigation

---

24. *The Reclamation of Swamp Lands*, FOR CALIFORNIA, Vol. II, No. 10, p. 14 (Sept. 1905).
25. DOWNEY, *op. cit. supra* note 19, at 180.
26. Delegate Zera Snow, in PROCEEDINGS OF 13TH NATIONAL IRRIGATION CONGRESS 60 (1905).
27. Delegate John E. Raker, *id.* at 61.

Congress refused "amid great applause" to tamper with the excess land law.[28]

For 36 years no efforts were made in Congress to eliminate the excess land provision. During most of that time the Reclamation Service constructed projects where excess lands were not generally involved or where their owners consented to comply with the law. As F. H. Newell, first chief of the Service, said to the Irrigation Congress in 1905:

> I have been told again and again that . . . the large landowners will not agree to divide; but in every case where the matter was laid straight before them . . . they have yielded; and I am convinced that they will do it. At any rate there is ample room in the United States where the people will do it, so that there is no trouble of disposing of the Reclamation Fund in the United States within the next ten years. . . . [T]he department will never consent to expend any money until the people who own the land are willing to sub-divide it, and to express their willingness by a definite guarantee. . . . If the people . . . the commercial bodies . . . and your prominent men will take some move which will bring to bear public opinion and influence, we will have this thing settled almost immediately.[29]

Where opposition to the excess land provision was substantial, federal reclamation lagged; where it was not, it advanced to the limits of available funds.

The first Congressional attack on reclamation law, made in 1938, set a tactical pattern for local inroads upon it. In that year Congress exempted the Colorado-Big Thompson project from the excess land provision, or rather those lands within it that would receive water supplementing existing supplies.[30] The sponsors of the exception expressed approval of reclamation law in principle; there were no public hearings, or at least none were published; an Acting Secretary of the Interior Department, E. K. Burlew, signed the departmental report instead of Secretary Harold L. Ickes; there was no debate in House or Senate, nor record vote.[31]

---

28. *Id.* at 62. Saying that "The story hasn't changed a bit," Secretary of the Interior Krug summarized the 1905 debate in persuading the Senate to kill an attack on the excess land law in 1947. *Hearings Before the Senate Public Lands Subcommittee on S. 912*, 80th Cong., 1st Sess. 991-92 (1947).
29. PROCEEDINGS OF THE 13TH NATIONAL IRRIGATION CONGRESS 29-30 (1905). In 1937 Congress authorized the Central Valley Project where excess land holdings are extensive, without waiting to secure either repayment contracts or the cooperation of excess landowners, acting under the twin pressures of unemployment and acute water shortage.
30. 52 STAT. 764, 43 U.S.C. § 386 (1952). The meaning of supplemental water was not defined. See text *infra* at note 38.
31. S. REP. No. 1921, H.R. REP. No. 2620, 75th Cong., 3d Sess. 1 (1938); 83 CONG. REC. 8323, 8832 (1938). In 1944 Secretary Ickes defended the excess land provision staunchly and personally, as did Secretary Krug in 1947. *Hearings Before the Senate Commerce Subcommittee on H.R. 3961*, 78th Cong., 2d Sess. 529, 536-37 (1944) (Ickes); *Hearings Before the Senate Public Lands Subcommittee on S. 912*, 80th Cong., 1st Sess. 991, 1026 (1947) (Krug).

The Senate report deferred to the principle of limiting water supplies to *public* lands by saying, "This provision was entirely appropriate to conditions to which it was intended to be applied,"[32] and by portraying the supplying of water to privately owned and irrigated lands with deficient supplies as "quite different from that of the earlier reclamation projects."[33] These genuflections were diversionary. They were directed toward irrelevant sections of reclamation law applying to public lands[34] not involved in the bill immediately before the Senate; they ignored the relevant sections applying to private lands[35] that were the subject of the bill. Their effect, if not intention, was to present the bill as a reasonable exception to general principle and to obscure the fact that it cut into the very heart of the law.

The suggestions, expressed publicly for the first time in 1938 on the Colorado-Big Thompson project,

(1) that reclamation law was intended originally to apply only to water furnished to public land and not to private land;
(2) that it applied originally to a sole supply of new water rather than to a supplemental supply; and
(3) that later projects each differ in some essential way from the earlier projects generally embraced by the law,

have been made so persistently ever since 1938 to support other exemptions[36] that they merit evaluation.[37]

The very language of the statute denying sale of water rights "for land in *private* ownership" in excess of 160 acres refutes the first suggestion. (Emphasis added.) The second has been refuted logically by Ralph B. Wertheimer, who reached the following conclusion:

[T]here is no difference in principle between a supplemental and a primary supply insofar as the wisdom of applying acreage limitations and anti-speculation provisions is concerned. Pressure to relax the restrictions in such cases may be viewed as a flank attack upon the whole policy, for in the future many million acres which the Bureau of Reclamation expects to irrigate will receive supplemental supplies.[38]

---

32. S. REP. No. 1921, *supra* note 31 at 1. See text *supra* at note 19.
33. S. REP. No. 1921, *supra* note 31 at 1.
34. 32 STAT. 388 (1902), 43 U.S.C. §§ 391, 411 (1952).
35. 32 STAT. 389 (1902), 43 U.S.C. §§ 419, 431, 439, 461 (1952).
36. See *e.g.*, DOWNEY, *op. cit. supra* note 19, at 4.
37. Points (1) and (2) are evaluated immediately in the text; evaluation of point (3) is necessarily diffused through the text, *infra*, as each project is taken up. Perhaps the only conclusion about point (3) that can be drawn certainly is that sponsors of special project exemptions find it useful to assert the existence of some essential difference.
38. WERTHEIMER, *Legislative and Administrative History of Acreage Limitations and Control of Speculation on Federal Reclamation Projects*, in ACREAGE LIMITATION IN THE CENTRAL VALLEY, A REPORT ON PROBLEM 19, at 37 (Central Valley Project Studies, Berkeley, September 25, 1944, mimeo.). Congressman Engle sees no difference in "moral basis" between "supplemental" and "original" water. See text *infra* at note 145.

The fact is that all water furnished by federal reclamation law supplements existing supplies whether from underground, other surface sources or the sky.³⁹

Historical evidence is as clear as statutory language and logic that reclamation law was intended to cover supplemental water. Francis G. Newlands, co-sponsor of the original bill in the House, speaking in 1905 as Senator from Nevada, was explicit:

> We realized in the framing of that Act that it would not be fair to apply it only to the public domain, for within reach of every Governmental project lie lands in private ownership, thirsting for water to be supplied by National aid, and we felt it was as much the duty of the National Government to supply *agricultural communities that were thus imperiled* as to create new agricultural communities.
>
> And so we provided that water rights could be secured for lands in private ownership within reach of Government projects, to be guarded against monopoly by preventing any proprietor from securing water rights for more than 160 acres, the amount of land fixed in the bill.⁴⁰ (Emphasis added.)

If there are any reasons why the principle of wide distribution of water rights in reclamation law should be altered to permit substantial distinctions between owners of public and of private land,⁴¹ or between more and less supplementation of other water supplies, they were not offered in support of the Colorado-Big Thompson exemption. "Supplemental water" was used as a formula to weaken the law, not as a reason for doing it.

Analysis of the committee reports on the Colorado-Big Thompson exemption bill reveals serious defects in the information on which Congress relied. In an earlier act authorizing the Colorado-Big Thompson project Congress had required execution of contracts with prospective water users prior to construction. The Senate report on the exemption bill objected that this imposed a requirement impossible to fulfill "in a project which was intended to open land to settlers *who could not come upon the land until the project was*

---

39. The House report on the reclamation bill recognized the large amount of semi-arid, *i.e.*, partially watered, irrigable land in private ownership, notably in Nebraska and Kansas, and proposed to include them. H.R. REP. No. 1468, 57th Cong., 1st Sess. 1 (1901).
40. SACRAMENTO VALLEY DEVELOPMENT ASS'N, *op. cit. supra* note 4, at 14, 15. The Warren Act of 1911 expressly applies the excess land provision even to water used for irrigation prior to construction of a federal project, provided it is impounded in a project reservoir or delivered through a project canal or ditch. 36 STAT. 925, 926 (1911), 43 U.S. C. §§ 523-24 (1952).
41. The distinction in present law lies in greater generosity to owners of private lands than to those who receive public lands. On private lands the limit of water furnished is set at 160 acres; on public lands the Secretary of the Interior may reduce the size of entries to as low as 10 acres, as may be appropriate to "represent the acreage . . . reasonably required for the support of a family. . . ." 32 STAT. 389 (1902), 43 U.S.C. § 434 (1952); 34 STAT. 519 (1906), 43 U.S.C. § 434 (1952).

completed."⁴² (Emphasis added.) Since the requirement of contracts prior to construction is a common means of assuring compliance with law, the logical remedy for the difficulty of *identifying individual water users in advance* of their arrival on the project would have been to amend the authorization statute to require execution of contracts containing the excess land provision *with irrigation districts;* this has been standard procedure since 1926.⁴³ The Senate Report, instead of choosing the easy and logical remedy offered by statutory precedent, chose the drastic and illogical alternative of eliminating the excess land provision.

The House report contributed no more to clarity than the Senate report. It incorporated a letter from the Acting Secretary of the Interior stating (1) that the excess land provisions had been "intended, primarily at least," for application to "new lands"; (2) that the average holding on the project was only 96 acres, and farms in excess of 160 acres were "relatively few in number"; (3) that since the land had been "settled for more than 50 years" and was likely to respond without legislative requirement to a "tendency toward subdivision" there was "no practical need" for the excess land provision;⁴⁴ and (4) that enactment of the bill "would not be inconsistent with the policy and purposes of the excess-land provisions of the Federal reclamation laws."⁴⁵

The Acting Secretary's first statement was untrue in any legally significant sense.⁴⁶ His second statement gives no support to his conclusion: a low average size of farm with relatively few large holdings is consistent with the concentrated landownership at which the excess land provision was aimed. His third statement contains at least two serious defects: (1) existence of a tendency to natural subdivision of farms in the absence of legal requirement is highly debatable, and (2) mere duration of settlement has no relation to the existence or non-existence of either large landholdings or speculative increments in value from public expenditures.⁴⁷ The Acting Secretary's fourth statement, that the exemption bill was not inconsistent with reclamation policy, is untrue. Nevertheless, the House Commit-

---

42. S. REP. No. 1921, *supra* note 31, at 2.
43. 44 STAT. 649 (1926), 43 U.S.C. 423 (e) (1952).
44. The Senate Report chose to emphasize the tendency, not to subdivision, but to *agglomeration:* "By reason of the normal farming development in such a large area, there are many individuals owning and cultivating in excess of 160 acres of land."
45. H.R. REP. No. 2620, 75th Cong., 3d Sess. 1 (1938).
46. See text *supra* at notes 36-40.
47. The argument that incremental values, if any, are small because large landholdings are few and have been settled a long time seems covered by Wertheimer's comment that it is like arguing "a violation of a principle really isn't a violation if the sums are sufficiently small." WERTHEIMER, *Legislative and Administrative History of Acreage Limitations and Control of Speculation on Federal Reclamation Projects,* in ACREAGE LIMITATION IN THE CENTRAL VALLEY, A REPORT ON PROBLEM 19, at 48 (Central Valley Project Studies, Berkeley, September 25, 1944, mimeo.).

tee "adopted" the Acting Secretary's letter as a "statement of facts" and "as affording a sufficient history."[48]

With the issues thus confused and beclouded, and the breach in historic water policy obscured if not concealed, Congress passed the exemption without debate.[49] The real clue to passage of the bill appears to be the concentrated pressure behind it rather than sound premises and logic. The Senate report observed, "In order that the contracts for repayment of the cost shall be provided as required by law, it is necessary that these farmers with tracts in excess of 160 acres shall become parties to the contract and purchasers of the water."[50] In that "existing situation" the Senate Committee was ready to sacrifice national policy to the objections of large landholders.[51]

Two years later Congress granted a second exemption, on the Truckee and Humboldt projects in Nevada. As before, it was made to appear in the reports to Congress and the public that no breach of essential purpose of the law was being proposed. As before, no public hearings were held or at least none were printed. As before, an Acting Secretary of the Interior, A. J. Wirtz, rather than Secretary Ickes made the departmental report on the bill.[52] He was more cautious on this occasion than Acting Secretary Burlew had been before him. He avoided taking position on the exemption, declining to say whether the Nevada projects were "wholly similar to the Colorado-Big Thompson Project so as to justify similar treatment," while recognizing "sufficient similarity so that I cannot interpose an objection. . . ."[53] He walked the fence similarly in leaving unanswered the question whether supplying "supplemental water" justified exemption to avoid "disruption of an established community." [54]

On the floor of the Senate, Senator Carl Hatch interpreted the Acting Secretary's neutrality to mean, "The Department of the Interior has reported favorably on the bill."[55] The only reason the Senator gave for granting exemption was, "A person must have more land than 160 acres in order to farm successfully and carry on live-

---

48. H.R. REP. No. 2620, *supra* note 45.
49. 83 CONG. REC. 8323, 8832 (1938); 52 STAT. 764 (1938), 43 U.S.C. § 386 (1952).
50. S. REP. No. 1921, *supra* note 31, at 2.
51. See text *infra* at note 179.
52. H.R. REP. No. 3036, 76th Cong., 3d Sess. 2 (1941).
53. *Id.* at 1.
54. *Id.* at 2. Construction engineers on the Nevada projects advanced a number of arguments, most of them made familiar on the Colorado-Big Thompson project, viz., communities were already established, incremental values would be small, project water would be supplemental, 160 acres was too small for the hay and livestock agriculture of Nevada. WERTHEIMER, *op. cit. supra* note 47, at 41-42.
55. 86 CONG. REC. 13681 (1940).

stock feeding operations."[56] No facts to support this contention appear anywhere in the legislative record. Although the logic of his argument supported no more than raising the limit above 160 acres, he suggested no higher figure; instead, he supported a complete exemption. On this presentation of a basis for action, Congress granted a complete exemption without debate or record vote.[57]

The third drive for legislative exemption was aimed in 1944 at the great Central Valley Project in California. It relied tactically on surprise, which was successful in the House. Although extensive hearings had been held on the Rivers and Harbors Bill of 1944, none of the testimony concerned the excess land provision, for the bill before the committee proposed no exemption.[58] After hearings had been concluded, however, and just as the bill went to the floor of the House, a Committee amendment was added exempting the Central Valley project.[59] Its author, Congressman Alfred J. Elliott, told the House (1) that the majority of "our farmers own more than 160 acres"; (2) that more than 160 acres was necessary "to make a decent living"; (3) that the provision should be removed so "that the small farmer can afford to pay for the water" and (4) so "the large farmer will not have part of his land destroyed"; (5) that he had the "full support of my people who are going to pay for this project in the San Joaquin Valley"; and (6) that the limitation itself was "socialistic."[60]

The first[61] and second[62] points were contrary to fact. The third point was unnecessary because reclamation law provides implicitly, if not explicitly, that charges shall not be above the capacity of benefited landowners to pay.[63] The fourth point failed to disclose how

---

56. *Ibid.* Congressman Scrugham of Nevada, sponsor of the bill, gave a similar reason. 86 CONG. REC. 13646 (1940).
57. 86 CONG. REC. 13647, 13681 (1940); 54 STAT. 1219 (1940).
58. H.R. REP. No. 3961, 78th Cong., 2d Sess. 1 (1944).
59. Section 4 of H.R. REP. No. 3961, 78th Cong., 2d Sess. (1944) became known as the "Elliott Rider" from its sponsor, Congressman A. J. Elliott of the southern San Joaquin Valley, California.
60. 90 CONG. REC. 2923 (1944).
61. In 1940, 89 percent of the ownership units of irrigable land in Madera, Tulare and Kern Counties (the latter two in the Congressman's district) were below 160 acres. Many very large holdings were in or adjacent to the Congressman's district; 34 of these totaled close to three-quarters of a million acres. Testimony of Paul H. Johnstone in, *Hearings, supra* note 28, table 4 at 862, table 7 at 864.
62. A folder distributed in the mid-forties by the Fresno Chamber of Commerce recommended as "economic units appropriate to derive the total income necessary to support a home and family from a single crop" the following: figs, 60-80 acres; apricots or peaches, 30-40 acres; oranges, 20-30 acres; cotton, 120-160 acres; alfalfa, 80-120 acres; grapes and raisins, 30-60 acres; grain and flax (generally dry farmed or sometimes irrigated), 320 acres. Testimony of M. C. Hermann in, *Hearings, supra* note 28, at 149-52.
63. Congress has been at great pains to assure that repayment charges shall not exceed the capacity of irrigators, *e.g.*, by: (1) making financial feasibility depend in part on what can "probably be repaid by the water users," 53 STAT. 1194 (1939), 43 U.S.C. § 485 (h) (1952); (2) by approving "variable payments" geared to fluctuations in agricultural income, 53 STAT. 1187 (1939), 43 U.S.C.

the excess land provision would destroy any land, nor is the probability of such destruction apparent. The fifth point is at least questionable. The Congressman was attacked vigorously by some of his constituents at congressional hearings three months later,[64] carried his own primary by barely 700 votes at the next election,[65] and gave up office at the end of the term. The sixth point was a departure from the tactics employed in earlier successful attempts to obtain exemptions: instead of upholding the principle of wide distribution of water rights it levelled a charge of "socialistic."[66]

Urged by Congressman Elliott, the House overrode a compromise that would have permitted exemption of lands owned and irrigated annually ever since 1937 when the Central Valley project was authorized, *i.e.*, confining the limitation to "new" lands as in the Colorado-Big Thompson Act. It then passed the complete exemption.[67]

Without the advantage of surprise, the fate of the Elliott rider became a different story. The Senate Commerce Committee held extended hearings and killed the rider.[68] Senator Downey then held hearings of his own in California but failed to find the solid support he had hoped for.[69]

By holding open hearings in Washington and in California as well, the Senate provided channels of public information the House had not opened. After the public learned that the principle of wide distribution of ownership of water rights was in jeopardy due to the proposed exemption, public opinion became effective. Senator Robert M. LaFollette, Jr. blocked the exemption, telling the Senate:

> ... I am not willing to concede that the fundamental policy of the United States Government for the development of reclamation projects out of the Treasury of the United States should be altered, and the conditions under which those projects were started should be changed by a rider on a rivers and harbors bill, which excludes consideration by a committee of the United States Senate which knows most about reclamation, and is primarily responsible for the land policy of the United States. . . .[70]

---

§ 485 (1952); and (3) by scaling downward payments that have proved to exceed the capacity of irrigators, 44 STAT. 636 (1926), 16 U.S.C. § 404 (c) (1926).

64. *Hearings Before Senate Irrigation and Reclamation Subcommittee*, 78th Cong., 2d Sess. 459-90 (1947), pursuant to S. Res. 295.

65. CALIF. SECRETARY OF STATE, STATEMENT OF VOTE, PRIMARY ELECTION, June 4, 1946, at 17.

66. Theodore Roosevelt defended the excess land provision on precisely opposite grounds, "because [he was] against the doctrines of the extremists, of the socialists . . . because [he wished] to see the country continued as a genuine democracy. . . ." 7 TRANSACTIONS OF THE COMMONWEALTH CLUB OF CALIFORNIA 108 (1912).

67. 90 CONG. REC. 2924 (1944).

68. *Hearings Before Senate Commerce Subcommittee on H.R. 3961*, 78th Cong., 2d Sess. 536-37, 573-788 (1944); S. REP. No. 903, 78th Cong., 2d Sess., ser. 10842 (1944).

69. *Hearings Before Senate Irrigation and Reclamation Subcommittee on S. Res. 295*, 78th Cong., 2d Sess. (1944).

70. 90 CONG. REC. 9499 (1944). Senator Hatch, supporting Senator LaFollette,

Burdened fatally with the rider, the entire Rivers and Harbors Bill failed of passage.[71]

In the 80th Congress, Senator Downey renewed his effort to exempt Central Valley from the excess land provision. Broad support was laid by obtaining sponsorship of all six Senators from California, Colorado, and Texas for a bill exempting one project in each of these states. Testimony extending to 1300 pages was taken. Strong resistance, however, kept the bill from leaving committee.[72]

III
1949 - 1956

> I fear that if this piecemeal abandonment of our traditional reclamation policy continues, America may find that our Government is providing the funds . . . while large holders of land dictate the policies. . . . This would certainly be against the public interest. . . . I sincerely hope that before the Senate or House Interior Committees grant any further exemptions that hearings be held . . . that the views of those concerned with the public interest as well as those who have a stake in individual projects be heard. . . .
> —Senator Paul H. Douglas of Illinois[73]

Adherence of Congress to reclamation law when under heaviest fire in 1944[74] and 1947 spread the attacks upon its principles beyond the legislature to both administration and judiciary.[75] The diversion was only temporary; in 1949 a separate bill was introduced to obtain for San Luis Valley, Colorado,[76] the exemption that failed earlier when the proposal was tied to the Central Valley exemption bill in the 80th Congress.[77]

Secretary of the Interior J. A. Krug opposed separate consideration of the San Luis exemption and asked instead for a general Congressional reconsideration of a more flexible basis for applying the law to special cases. He recognized the existence of "somewhat unique"

---

said: "The Senator from Wisconsin is *stressing the fact of changing the fundamental law, and I want to emphasize that point again,* because the Senator from California [Downey] has said here on the floor that officials of the Reclamation Service are trying to strait jacket the people of California. The people of California came to the Congress of the United States and obtained the appropriations *under the reclamation laws.* No one here is trying to do anything to California." (Emphasis added.) *Ibid.*

71. 90 CONG. REC. 9493-9500, 9555-56. Minus the rider it passed easily in the following session. 59 STAT. 10 (1945).

72. *Hearings, supra* note 28. See also Taylor, *Destruction of Federal Reclamation Policy? The Ivanhoe Case,* 10 STAN. L. REV. 103 (1957).

73. 103 CONG. REC. 13095 (daily ed. Aug. 12, 1957).

74. Congress defeated the Elliott Rider and simultaneously applied reclamation law to irrigation uses of flood control projects. 58 STAT. 891 (1944), 33 U.S.C. § 701 (f), (j) (1952).

75. Taylor, *The Excess Land Law: Execution of a Public Policy,* 64 YALE L.J. 501-06 (1955); Taylor, *Destruction of Federal Reclamation Policy? The Ivanhoe Case,* 10 STAN. L. REV. 76 (1957).

76. S. 1385, 81st Cong., 1st Sess. (1949).

77. S. 912, 80th Cong., 1st Sess. (1947).

conditions on a portion of San Luis Project and mentioned "irrigation practices not readily adaptable to farm units of 160 irrigable acres, or 320 irrigable acres for man and wife . . . ," but he "opposed . . . the appropriation of interest-free funds from the Federal Treasury to encourage or perpetuate industrial, factory-sized, corporate or large scale irrigated farming operations."[78] No hearings were held on the bill, or at least none were published.

The Senate Report recited, and the House Report repeated:
1. The United States does not own any of the water supplying the project; this water is in private or local ownership.
2. The United States does not supply any new unappropriated water to the project.
3. The United States does not own any of the lands under the project.
4. There are no industrial, factory-size, corporate operated farms.
5. The farms under the project are family-operated.
6. The situation is not complicated with land speculation.
7. The landowner cannot make a decent living under the existing acreage limitation.[79]

The reference to absence of "new" water obscured the service of the public project in regulating use of "old" water; reference to absence of *public* lands was irrelevant since the law applies to *private* lands. The reference to absence of private speculation denied the inevitable accrual of incremental values from project construction. The House report recited that the San Luis Valley was not marked by extreme concentration of ownership, perhaps to suggest that a small enough violation of principle is not really a violation. At any rate, no inference was drawn that lack of extreme concentration might make securing compliance easier. The report cited figures, without giving the source, claiming that 160 or even 320 acres were insufficient to provide a decent living for a family.[80] It offered no comment on or refutation of a statement to the Senate in 1947 by the regional supervisor of the Bureau of Reclamation that "some 26 to 35 ownerships . . . would benefit by lifting of the excess land limitations so that there are a large number that need . . . more lands for setting up an adequate basis for economic farming units. . . . [T]here are a good many of those farmers who have been able to develop an economy whereby they could do pretty well with somewhere around 160

---

78. S. REP. No. 825, 81st Cong., 1st Sess. 2 (1949). No reference was made, either in the report or in the statement by the Secretary of the Interior, to the testimony by the Bureau of Reclamation regional supervisor in 1947. See text *infra* at notes 81 and 86.

79. *Id.* at 3. H.R. REP. No. 1361, 81st Cong., 1st Sess. 2 (1949): ". . . the average net annual farm earnings from a 120-acre tract is $656, from a 160-acre tract is $930, and from a 320-acre tract is $1,630."

80. H.R. REP. No. 1361, 81st Cong., 1st Sess. 4 (1949). See text *infra* at note 86.

acres."[81] The report noted the presence in San Luis Valley of numerous "owners of these small tracts [who] cannot live on the earnings from their land. They lease to other farm operators and work for other farmers or in the neighboring towns."[82] The conclusion of the report was uninfluenced by their admitted need for more land and water which a reclamation project might have helped to provide. Explanation of the bill by its sponsors on the House floor followed the lines of the reports, a now familiar pattern, implying that the bill really was not invading principle, when it was.

Senator Edwin C. Johnson of Colorado argued on the Senate floor that the bill was in the interest of the small owner "because the project is not feasible without the larger rancher, and no money can be obtained from him unless we pass the bill and permit him to come in, because he will sit out on the side lines and get his water, since he already has the water rights and owns them."[83] The Senator ignored the fact that rights to unregulated water are far less valuable than, and confer no legal rights to, a regulated flow provided under reclamation law."[84] He argued, in effect, that Congress ought to take the initiative in yielding national policy when large landowners object, rather than oblige large landowners to conform to national policy in return for federal aid. Under insistent objections from Senator Paul H. Douglas of Illinois, the bill as passed by the House was amended to restrict the scope of the intended exemption and passed.[85]

President Truman pocket-vetoed the bill, saying, "Most of these existing farm units will be fully capable of supporting a farm family at an acceptable standard of living, once a regulated water supply is made available." Recognizing that a larger acreage might be necessary to support a family adequately on some project lands, he pointed out, "In striving to meet the problems of a small part of the area, [the bill] would relax the existing acreage limitations for a much larger block of lands where adequate family-size farms can be maintained within these limitations."[86] He rejected "new land" as a basis for making exceptions to a law "assuring that the benefits of the irrigation systems will inure to family-size farming enterprises. This is true whether the purpose of the particular project is to open up new land for settlement by providing an original water supply, or to stablize an existing irrigation economy as in the case of the San Luis Valley project." In the absence of the excess land provision, he said, "the heavy

---

81. *Hearings, supra* note 72, at 914-15.
82. H.R. REP. No. 1361, 81st Cong., 1st Sess. 2 (1949).
83. 95 CONG. REC. 11082 (1949). The same argument, viz., that large landowners should be granted an exemption to coax them into the project for the benefit of smaller landowners, was rejected on the Central Valley Project. 90 CONG. REC. 2923 (1944). See text *infra* at note 179.
84. 36 STAT. 926 (1911), 43 U.S.C. § 524 (1952).
85. 95 CONG. REC. 11081-83, 13309 (1949).
86. *Id.* at 15046.

investments of interest-free funds being made for the reclamation program would lose much of their justification." Like Secretary Krug, he hoped Congress would consider general rather than special legislation, "so as to authorize appropriate adjustments in maximum acreages, where necessary, under carefully worked-out standards, which could be applied not only to the San Luis Valley project, but also to other projects in which some adjustment may be warranted" to meet "special and unique situations . . . without doing violence to the basic and often reaffirmed principle of maintaining the family-size farm. . . ."[87]

Blocked by presidential veto in 1949, the effort to exempt the San Luis Valley was resumed in 1951. The attorney for the water conservancy district presented the issue as one between "the people" of his district and the government: the people, he said, "will not approve a repayment contract . . . unless their project is exempted from the land-limitation provisions of the reclamation laws."[88] The Senate report drew the issue as one between the excess landowners on one hand and the Congress and small owners on the other, and gave the whip hand to the excess landowners. It regarded owners of rights to use natural flows who pooled them for storage for regulated releases at more appropriate times as "penalized" by the excess land provisions rather than as helped by the project dam. It minimized the importance of the excess land provisions as an "at best, temporary law"; assuming, erroneously, the impermanence of the excess land provision,[89] it argued that its application "for a few years only" would "benefit no one" in the San Luis Valley.[90] It incorporated, but had no comment to make on, a letter from the Secretary of the Interior recommending "strongly" against a project exemption, and, instead, inviting consideration of amendment of the basic laws so "as to preserve and, perhaps even more positively, promote their underlying policy."[91]

The Senate report made a gesture of supporting reclamation law by censuring the Bureau of Reclamation for completing the dam despite President Truman's veto of the exemption in the 81st Congress and without a prior repayment contract. The report—and Congress—thus threw the blame on the Bureau without trying to retrieve the situation by standing on the law and letting excess landowners wait for regulated water until they complied with it.

---

87. *Id.* at 15045-46.
88. S. REP. No. 1594, 82d Cong., 2d Sess. 3 (1952). "The people" referred, evidently, to excess landowners.
89. *Id.* at 4. For a contrary view see Taylor, *The Excess Land Law: Execution of a Public Policy*, 64 YALE L.J. 489-501 (1955).
90. S. REP. No. 1594, 82d Cong., 2d Sess. 4 (1952).
91. *Id.* at 5. The House report blamed the Bureau of Reclamation for proceeding with the project when objections to the excess land provision were foreseen as early as 1940 when the project was authorized, and in other respects virtually repeated the Senate report. H.R. REP. No. 2145, 82d Cong., 2d Sess. 4 (1952).

The bill, modifying without wholly lifting the excess lands provision, passed both Houses without debate.[92] As a result of Senator Douglas' objections in the previous session, it substituted, in lieu of the standard excess land provision, a limitation to a quantity of "supplemental or regulated water" reasonably necessary to irrigate 480 acres. Besides, it declared the legislation to be "special," *i.e.,* not a precedent, and "not to be considered as altering the general policy of the United States" as expressed in the excess land provision.[93]

The 83d Congress in 1954 produced a rash of bills proposing modification of the excess land provision, a number of them proposing to exempt "an existing agricultural economy" or "supplemental water."[94] Two of these bills passed; they exempted the Owl Creek, Wyoming, and Santa Maria, California, projects, respectively.[95]

No hearings were held on the bill proposing to exempt Owl Creek project from the excess lands provision, or at least none were published. The Department of the Interior told House and Senate Committees it had "no information that would enable it to assure . . . that all opposition . . . would be overcome" by exempting the project from the excess lands provision.[96] The Bureau of the Budget told the Senate Committee "it does not appear that the 160-acre limitation is an immediate problem" and that an exemption "is not necessary at this time."[97] On the face of the record no one except the congressional sponsor of the bill was urging its passage, not even the excess landowners. Nevertheless, Committees of both Houses recommended passage. The House passed the bill with no debate.[98]

In the Senate, Senator Frank Barrett, of Wyoming, argued that because of the shortness of the growing season, viz., 88 days, landowners "have objected to the construction of the project, because . . . the limitation of 160 acres of land" would make it "uneconomical."[99] No evidence was presented to support the conclusion. Senator Wayne Morse, of Oregon, asked and was given assurances that the bill "could in no way be considered a precedent for the modification of the 160-acre limitation with respect to public lands."[100] The Senate passed the bill and it became law.[101]

---

92. 98 CONG. REC. 6321, 7287 (1952).
93. 66 STAT. 282 (1952), 5 U.S.C. 171 (f) (1952).
94. S. 2855, H.R. 2235, 4721, 7129, 7521, 7619, 7620, 7622, 9862, 10172, 83d Cong., 2d Sess. (1954).
95. 68 STAT. 890, 1190.
96. S. REP. No. 1790, 83d Cong., 2d Sess. 3 (1954); H.R. REP. No. 1248, 83d Cong., 2d Sess. 3 (1954). See also Owl Creek Irr. Dist. v. Bryson, 71 Wyo. 30, 253 P.2d 867 (1953). The court, in dictum, viewed the constitutionality of the excess lands provisions unfavorably.
97. S. REP. No. 1790, 83d Cong., 2d Sess. 4 (1954).
98. 100 CONG. REC. 3241 (1954).
99. *Id.* at 14091.
100. *Ibid.* Since Senator Morse subsequently defended the excess land provision as applied to *private* lands on more than one occasion, his reference to *public* lands in this instance probably was without significance.
101. *Ibid.*

Efforts to exempt the Santa Maria project, California, had begun in 1953 with hearings to authorize construction of the project, at which legal counsel for the Santa Maria Valley Water Conservation District pleaded for removal of the excess land provision. To support his plea, the district counsel argued that the 13 owners of approximately 26 per cent of the land, while deriving "substantial benefits" from the project, regarded these as insufficient "to persuade them to sell their land in order to make the project possible."[102] Congressman Clair Engle, of California, in a colloquy with the district counsel, brought out the point that since project water would be distributed "wholly underground," "there would be no way of preventing the landowners . . . from participating in the benefits, *if the dam was built.*"[103] (Emphasis added.) In other words, if Congress decided to build the dam without requiring compliance from excess land owners first, *then* there would be no way to keep them from getting water if they refused to comply. Only witnesses favoring exemption were heard.

Congressman John F. Shelley, of California, insisted successfully on amending the bill so as to lift the excess land provision only "so long as the water utilized on project lands is acquired by pumping from the underground reservoir,"[104] in order "to make it completely clear that we were in no way compromising the Congress' traditional position in opposition to attempts to eliminate the 160-acre limitation as a cornerstone of national reclamation policy."[105] Since the sole purpose of the project was to improve water supplies for pumping, the amendment was an ineffective gesture in face of ultimate decision to build the dam without requiring prior compliance.

Congressman Engle recognized that inability to control underground water required the government "to have the contract in their hand . . . prior to the time they started construction. . . ."[106] Although willing to insist on prior agreement to assure financial repayment, evidently he was not prepared to insist on it to assure compliance with national policy.[107]

Indeed, no one in the House raised, as alternative to immediate authorization of the project, the obvious possibility of delaying con-

---

102. District counsel offered agreement by excess landowners not to "create a new excess ownership." *Hearings Before House Interior and Insular Affairs Subcommittee on H.R. 2235 and 2259*, 83d Cong., 1st Sess. 57-58, 67 (1953).
103. *Id.* at 66.
104. 100 CONG. REC. 1149, 1150 (1954); 68 STAT. 1190 (1954).
105. 100 CONG. REC. A950 (1954).
106. *Hearings, supra* note 102, at 63.
107. ". . . we cannot find any practical way to apply the 160-acre limitation. . . ." 100 CONG. REC. 1145, A865 (1954). Authors of the Senate report wore similar blinders: "The committee is aware of the fact that it is infeasible, both physically and legally, to attempt to enforce the land-limitation provisions . . . where project supplies are commingled with waters to which project landholders have a prior right." S. REP. No. 1789, 83d Cong., 2d Sess. 3 (1954).

struction to give the combined public opinion of their neighbors and their own growing need for water a chance to persuade the excess landowners to comply with the law.[108]

Counsel for the Santa Maria District said that Assistant Secretary of the Interior Fred G. Aandahl, as well as Regional Director Richard L. Boke, had advised him the Department would not oppose "appropriate exceptions" to the excess land provision, but neither indicated "just what they would approve."[109] Congressman Engle, however, assumed full responsibility saying, "The Secretary of the Interior did not recommend taking off the land limitation. We took it off. They voiced no objection."[110]

Senator Morse opposed the exemption, posing the real alternative, viz., whether the excess landowners or Congress should yield. Citing the Veterans of Foreign Wars and others in California whose opposition to the bill had come to his attention, he said:

> The opponents of the bill say . . . there is no reason to assume all will not agree to execute the contracts . . . that if the people in the area want the project for the common good, it should be up to the local people to secure agreement on the part of the 13 who hold 25 percent of the land in the area as excess land. It should not be a case of Congress being blackjacked into making an exception, by a threat on the part of one or a handful of persons who might say that they will not agree, unless they can have an exception which will allow them to draw water out of the project financed by Federal dollars to be used on land far in excess of the 160-acre limitation.[111]

His attempt to kill the exemption failed by vote of 17 to 45, 34 not voting;[112] the project was exempted from the excess land provision so far as waters are pumped from underground, "in view of the special circumstances" of the Santa Maria project.[113]

The next Congress, the 84th, authorized and exempted the Washoe, Nevada, project from the excess land provision, substituting an interest payment on water supplied to excess lands not to exceed the increased capacity of the lands to repay, and applying only to "supplemental" water.[114]

---

108. Congressman Engle, by clear implication rejected the alternative. The "three owners on the west side of the Santa Maria Valley who have the big part of the land," he said, had a water supply "good for another 20 years, at least," and could "stay outside the district and put the pumps down anyway." 100 CONG. REC. A865 (daily ed. Feb. 3, 1954). No consideration, apparently, was given to the alternative of requiring compliance while delaying application of the law for, say, ten or twenty years. *Cf.* Analysis of Santa Maria Project, California, prepared by Dr. Paul S. Taylor for the National Council on Agricultural Life and Labor at 2-3, Jan. 15, 1954.
109. *Hearings, supra* note 102, at 58.
110. 100 CONG. REC. 1144, A864 (1954).
111. *Id.* at 15020.
112. *Id.* at 15024.
113. 68 STAT. 1190 (1954).
114. 70 STAT. 775 (1956). For the background of the interest charge to excess

The Senate report on the bill recited "ample precedent" for exemption of lands receiving supplemental water, naming the Colorado-Big Thompson, Truckee and Humboldt, Nevada, exemptions, as well as the San Luis Valley, Colorado, modification.[115] The first two had been justified as exceptions to principle,[116] and the latter, while declaring the reasons for departure from the usual language of the excess lands provision were "special" and not an alteration of principle,[117] had merely raised the acreage figure. The Senate report recited:

> Supplemental water lands under the Washoe project are in the same category as those covered by the congressional precedents cited and the committee concludes the exemption in this instance is fully justified *as preserving the principle of acreage limitations of the reclamation law.*[118] (Emphasis added.)

Thus Congress, without hearings or debate on the excess land provision, turned exceptions distinguished originally from general principle into precedents to support a further invasion of the general principle.[119]

IV
1956 - 1957

> I grant you, you start kicking the 160-acre limitation and it is like inspecting the rear end of a mule: You want to do it from a safe distance because you might get kicked through the side of the barn. But it can be done with circumspection, and I hope we can exercise circumspection.
> —Congressman Clair Engle, of California, 1955[120]

As early as 1954, Congressman Engle set out on the difficult, if not impossible, task of finding an acceptable middle ground between special interest and general principle. He sought it by levying an interest charge on excess landholders in lieu of requiring disposal of their excess holdings in return for water. He wanted, according to the press, to stand between the "extremists on either side," to be "realistic" about those who see the 160-acre limitation as a vehicle to revamp the California agricultural economy and those determined to maintain the status quo.[121] He would permit excess landowners to

---

lands, see text part IV; also *Hearings Before the Subcommittee on Irrigation and Reclamation of House Interior and Insular Affairs Committee on H.R. 6028,* 84th Cong., 1st Sess. 74-76 (1955).
115. S. Rep. No. 1829, 84th Cong., 2d Sess. 7 (1956).
116. See text *supra* at notes 33 and 53.
117. See text *supra* at note 93.
118. S. Rep. No. 1829, 84th Cong., 2d Sess. 7 (1956).
119. See text *infra* at notes 167 and 185.
120. *Hearings Before the Subcommittee on Irrigation and Reclamation of the House Committee on Interior and Insular Affairs on H.R. 104, 384 and 3817,* 84th Cong., 1st Sess. 70 (1955).
121. Sacramento Bee, July 12, 1954, p. 10, col. 1. The words in quotes were attributed to Congressman Engle; the others are a paraphrase of the reporter's words.

obtain water without limitation by paying an interest charge on water costs, leave them in possession of the power revenue subsidy, and remove the controls upon them limiting speculation in incremental land values. He offered no concession to those "extremists" who believe that use of water itself should be distributed widely and speculation controlled, these being the aspects of existing law excluded from his formula. His hope, evidently, was to draw the fires from under eastern opposition to western reclamation by weakening a "favorite" argument—"that the east is paying interest on the government's money invested in reclamation . . . and that the benefits sometimes go to wealthy operators."[122]

A year later the Congressman described the response to his initial effort as one that drew him no friends from either side:

> Last year I put a bill in to provide that as an alternate to this business of having a man necessarily sign a recordable contract, he could agree to pay interest on that portion of the land which was in excess of the usual limitation. Well, it did not get any loud cheers from anywhere. In fact, it was met with a resounding silence. The landowners did not like it because they did not want to pay the interest, and those who have been the great crusaders for the 160-acre limitation, regarded it as some kind of political sacred cow, accused me of being a defaulter on a principle that has become a part of Democratic doctrine in the last 25 years. So I got shot at from both sides. I still think it is sound.[123]

The second response was more favorable, from one side. Witnesses hostile to the excess lands provision who were present at the 1955 hearing gave the proposal immediate, if somewhat grudging, support. Speaking for a "majority, if not all," of a group present from the National Reclamation Association, one of them said that "perhaps *if we had to have* a land-limitation provision" the interest-payment formula "would be the simplest way to solve it and . . . do the least violence to the established setup."[124] (Emphasis added.)

The new proposal soon found support, at least by clear implication, from a new Presidential Advisory Committee on Water Recources Policy. Fixing attention on a single financial aspect of reclamation in relation to the family-size farm, it recommended "no interest-free funds" "to farmland in excess of a family-size farm."[125] Consistent

---
122. *Ibid.*
123. *Hearings, supra* note 120, at 63.
124. *Id.* at 63-64.
125. Presidential Advisory Committee on Water Resources Policy, Dec. 22, 1955, p. 34. This Committee, appointed by President Eisenhower and composed of Secretaries Benson, Wilson and McKay, took a much narrower view of encouraging the family-size farm than the citizens on the Water Resources Policy Commission appointed five years earlier by President Truman. The latter recommended broadly in 1950 that "The benefits of Federal financial assistance" through reclamation "should go only to family-sized farms," urged that this principle, "together with other antispeculation and antimonopoly provisions" should be "maintained," "enforced," and "extended" to reclamation by "drainage, or other

with this view, the formula substitutes a limited financial incentive for compliance with the policy of wide distribution as an absolute condition of receiving permanent water.[126]

The Engle formula became law in the Democratic 84th Congress as part of the Small Reclamation Projects Act.[127] A similar bill for federal financing of "small" projects had nearly passed the preceding Republican Congress[128] without Administration objection to omission of any excess lands provision.[129] When the bill reappeared in the 84th Congress it included the formula.[130] Congressman Engle, a Democrat, described it as "a partnership arrangement" between federal and local interests, and named as "co-author" Republican Congressman A. L. Miller, of Nebraska, author of the bill in the 83d Congress.[131] Republican Congressman John Phillips, of California, said it was "primarily in line with the philosophy of this side of the aisle."[132] An eastern Republican Congressman, objecting mainly to any excess lands provision at all, opposed application of the bill to any but the 17 western reclamation states.[133] However, the House passed the bill, applying it to all 48 states.

The Senate Report neither mentioned the proposed departure from the traditional excess lands provision nor commented on the recommendation in a letter it printed from the Bureau of the Budget that cautioned, "it would seem appropriate that any legislation providing an exception to the excess land provisions . . . be considered on an overall policy basis rather than in connection with piecemeal legislation dealing only with loan financing of small reclamation projects."[134]

Senator Richard L. Neuberger, of Oregon, however, made the formula an issue in the Senate by attaching a separate statement to

---

methods," and recommended that 160 acres "should be considered as a maximum." A Water Policy for the American People, Vol. I, p. 14.

126. See text *infra* at notes 149 and 150, for discussion whether the formula, on balance, provides a net incentive for distribution or agglomeration of landholdings.

127. 70 STAT. 1044 (1956), 43 U.S.C. § 422 (Supp. IV 1956). Also in the Washoe, Nevada, Project Authorization and Exemption Act, 70 STAT. 775, 43 U.S.C. § 614 (Supp. IV 1956). The Barrett interest-formula, proposed as a substitute for the standard excess land provision on all reclamation projects in S. 2541, sec. 3 (85th Cong.), is essentially the same as the formula in the Small Reclamation Projects Act.

128. H.R. 5301, 83d Cong., 2d Sess. (1955), authored by Congressman Miller of Nebraska, passed the House and was reported favorably to the Senate where it died. 100 CONG. REC. 13163 (1954).

129. Secretary of the Interior McKay made no objection; the Bureau of the Budget merely noted the omission as a fact. S. REP. No. 2472, 83d Cong., 2d Sess. 4 (1955); H.R. REP. No. 2443, 83d Cong., 2d Sess. 10 (1955).

130. H.R. 5881, 84th Cong.

131. 101 CONG. REC. 7134 (1955).

132. *Id.* at 7136.

133. Congressman Saylor of Pennsylvania. *Id.* at 7145-57.

134. S. REP. No. 1073, 84th Cong. 1st Sess. 8 (1955). The letter referred to earlier bills omitting an excess land provision, rather than to the draft containing the formula.

the Committee report saying that any projects authorized under the bill ought to be subject to the usual excess lands provision.[135]

On the Senate floor, Senators Morse and Douglas succeeded in incorporating the traditional excess land provision in place of the Engle formula.[136] However, the Senate conferees[137] joined with the House conferees[138] to drop the Morse-Douglas amendment,[139] placing its supporters in an unfavorable tactical position to carry on the fight against the formula. Later, Senator Morse described the influence of this on the outcome:

> ... the bill was reported to the Senate on May 4, 1955, but the bill was not scheduled for consideration until July 28, 1955, in the closing days of the session of the Senate. I think there is real doubt that Senate passage would have been possible had an extended debate developed on the proposed amendment.
>
> The bill remained in conference almost 1 year. Once again it came to the floor of the Senate very late in the session, on July 20, 1956. In the confusion of the closing days of the session the 160-acre provision was lost in the shuffle. Public supporters of the anti-monopoly provision had little opportunity to mobilize....[140]

Final passage of the bill in the Senate came under circumstances so unusual that Senator Douglas described them to the Senate immediately after the vote:

> At the time the conference report was agreed to, I was not on the floor, although I had given notice that I wished to be notified when the conference report was brought up. Through an unavoidable error, that was not done. The Senator from

---

135. *Id.* at 10.

136. Except on old irrigation projects. 101 CONG. REC. 11820-29 (1955) Senator Douglas argued for a wide distribution of landed property, warned that removal of the traditional limitation would be "striking a blow at the economic foundations of democracy," and expressed disbelief that "because the small farmers [are] having difficulties, we should help put them out of business." *Supra* at 11828.

137. Senators Anderson of New Mexico, Bible of Nevada, Watkins of Utah and Barrett of Wyoming. Senator Anderson later explained: "I think I might remind the Senator from Illinois that there was no yea-and-nay vote on his amendment. . . . If a yea-and-nay vote had been had on the floor, the Senator's 160-acre amendment would have met the same fate, I am quite certain. . . . [He] was very anxious to have his amendment included. We agreed to take it to conference and see if the House conferees would agree to it." "The House was adamant in refusing to accept" the Morse-Douglas amendment "because it is not a practical limitation to apply when supplemental water is being supplied." 103 CONG. REC. 6737 (daily ed. May 23, 1957). *Cf.* Congressman Engle's statement in text *infra* at note 145.

138. Congressmen Engle of California, Aspinall of Colorado, O'Brien of New York and Miller of Nebraska. Public expressions by at least three Senate conferees suggest that the Morse-Douglas amendment found little support among either House or Senate conferees.

139. 102 CONG. REC. 10096-97 (1956). Although covered by general language in the report, no specific mention was made of the preference given the Engle formula passed by the House over the Morse-Douglas amendment passed by the Senate.

140. 103 CONG. REC. 6740 (daily ed. May 23, 1957).

New Mexico is perfectly innocent in the matter. He should in no sense be blamed for it. But the truth is that the conference report was agreed to with a very small attendance of Senators on the floor, and I did not have an opportunity to inquire about the bill as I had hoped to do.[141]

Questioned by Senator Douglas about elimination of the Morse-Douglas amendment, Senator Clinton Anderson, of New Mexico, replied that while the "exact language" of the Senate amendment had been "eliminated," he was "certain . . . that on all new land . . . the 160-acre limitation will apply."[142] The statute discloses no language that fits the Senator's description. Senator Anderson termed the Engle formula "as close to a 160-acre limitation as it can come and still recognize supplemental water rights."[143] Less enthusiastically, Senator Douglas characterized it as "at least an improvement over some procedures," *i.e.*, evidently preferable to complete exemptions of one project after another, by "piecemeal" procedures.[144]

Congressman Engle, having received initial and continuing support from those unfriendly to the excess land provision, has sought to gain support also from those who place higher value on policy than on money. As the objections of Senators Douglas, Morse and Neuberger to enactment of his formula show, he has not met with great success in this quarter. He began as early as 1955 by aligning himself against exemption of "supplemental" water.

> I cannot agree that there is any difference in the application of an acreage limitation from the standpoint of a moral basis for supplemental water than for an original water supply, because the moral basis for the 160-acre limitation, or any limitation, is the fact that there is a Federal subsidy given to those lands.[145]

Thus, like the supporters of the traditional provision, he founds his formula on a "moral" basis. "The moral basis of the 160-acre limitation," he says, "is to prevent unjust enrichment resulting from the subsidies to irrigation provided by interest-free Federal money and

---

141. 102 CONG. REC. 13659 (1956). Nearly a year later Senator Douglas referred again to this situation saying, "I have always felt very unhappy about the speed with which that report was acted on by the Senate, before I could reach the floor, make a protest, and ask the Senate to stand by its original decision." Senator Anderson replied, "There was no attempt to slide past the Senator from Illinois." 103 CONG. REC. 6737 (daily ed. May 23, 1957).

142. 102 CONG. REC. 13659 (1956).

143. 102 CONG. REC. 13660 (1956). *Cf.* Congressman Engle's criticism of exemption of "supplemental" water, in text *infra* at note 145.

144. 102 CONG. REC. 13659 (1956). Since the 84th Congress, when Congressman Engle became chairman of the Interior and Insular Affairs Committee, no outright exemptions of projects have gone through the House; the Engle formula has been included in every bill omitting the traditional excess lands provision.

145. *Hearings, supra* note 120, at 62. However, he supported the Santa Maria, California, exemption of a project supplementing underground waters; see text *supra* at note 107.

public power revenues."[146] The "moral" basis of defenders of traditional policy, by contrast, is the more inclusive ground of wide distribution of *resources,* as well as of *moneys.*

It is conceivable that, given strength of purpose and sufficient skill on the part of its authors, a money incentive formula could be devised that would influence excess landowners to reduce their holdings to family-size farms as a method of escape from the weight of the payments levied upon excess holdings. It would not be easy to do this, nor is there any evidence that the Engle formula is likely to accomplish it.

The danger of destroying policy by a money alternative is familiar. Substitution of money for compliance with habitancy requirements destroyed the anti-monopoly policy of the Homestead Law.[147] Known as "commutation," this exchange of policy for money was forbidden by Congress in the National Reclamation Act in order to prevent a repetition of destruction.[148]

When the Engle formula was broached to the House Committee in 1955 Congressman William A. Dawson, of Utah, offered as his judgment that it would destroy anti-monopoly and anti-speculation policy. The formula, he said, probably would "break down the 160-acre limitation" because large landowners would prefer paying the interest charge to disposing of their excess holdings, and it might even encourage land agglomeration:

> . . . to say that these large landowners are going to pay interest on their excess and, therefore, it is going to result in breaking up the large ownerships just is not true. For this reason: that there are plenty of other benefits in this bill which they have not been receiving up to this point that they would get even though paying the interest.
>
> For instance, they get the advantage of the nonreimbursable items, which may be considerable but which are not repaid back at all.
>
> Furthermore, up until this point they are not getting in on any cheap Government money. By "cheap," I mean if they pay interest, they are still only going to pay 2½ percent or something in that neighborhood, which is very reasonable money. That could even be *encouragement for people to get into big ownerships and to take on more acreage, because the other benefits are so great that it could encourage them.*[149] (Emphasis added.)

---

146. Letter from Congressman Engle *et al.* to Attorney General Brown of California, February 4, 1957. The Engle formula does not include repayment by excess landowners of the frequently substantial subsidy from power users and other sources made possible by reclamation law.
147. Gates, *Homestead Law in an Incongruous Land System,* 41 AM. HIST. REV. 655-56 (1936).
148. 32 STAT. 388 (1902), 43 U.S.C. § 432 (1952).
149. *Hearings, supra* note 120, at 69-70. Congressman Dawson might have mentioned also that omission from the formula of the speculation controls of the excess land provision exposes purchasers of land in family-size farm acreages to

The analysis of the Engle formula by Congressman Dawson appears to be corroborated by at least one large landowner, who has welcomed a prospect of being able to pay an interest charge in lieu of disposing of excess holdings. Citing a letter from the Southern Pacific Railroad to the Bureau of Reclamation, the Sacramento Bee said the Railroad "would favor the so-called 'Engle Formula'" because it is holding approximately 150,000 irrigable acres "for long range purposes and is not prepared to commit it for sale under the usual bureau recordable contract which would require disposal of lands in excess of 160 acres for which bureau water was received."[150] In other words, the interest payment prescribed by the formula provides insufficient incentive, in the opinion of the corporation, to induce it to dispose of excess holdings and so distribute water resources widely in line with traditional policy. This judgment appears to be reliable; the formula does not specify a money incentive strong enough to preserve national policy.

For the present the breach in traditional policy seems to be limited to "small projects."[151] But, as Senator Douglas remarked, "small projects do not mean small farmers."[152] Besides, efforts inspired by outside pressures on administrators of the law to widen the breach created by the Small Projects Act are possible, if not in clear prospect. An official of an organization opposed to the excess lands provision said the limitation on loans under the Act to $5 million per unit of a project "may leave the way open to construction of larger projects where such projects can be divided into two or more features or units."[153]

Senators supporting the Engle formula against replacement by the standard excess land provision have not tried to persuade supporters of the provision that the formula will really preserve the

---

capitalization in the price charged them by excess landowners, of the benefits of interest-free money that reclamation law intended should go to the family-size farmer.

150. October 17, 1956, p. A2, Cols. 1, 2. The Valley Labor Citizen, of Fresno, remarked editorially: "And in the process, the SP would take a long step toward regaining its long-lost political dictatorship of California. This is what the Engle formula would do." Nov. 29, 1957, p. 6, Col. 1. Refusal of this single landowner to accept water unless standard reclamation law is replaced by an interest-payment formula may jeopardize feasibility of the entire San Luis, California project. (Assistant Secretary of Interior Fred G. Aandahl, Hearings before House irrigation and reclamation subcommittee, on H.R. 6035 and H.R. 7295, 85th Cong., 2d Sess. 41, 42).

151. And others to which it has been specifically applied, e.g., Colorado-Big Thompson, San Luis (Colo.), Santa Maria (Calif.), Humboldt-Truckee (Nev.), Texas-Mercedes, projects.

152. 103 CONG. REC. 6737 (daily ed. May 23, 1957).

153. Paraphrase of views of Robert T. Durbrow, Secretary of the Irrigation Districts Association of California, on H.R. 5301, 83d Congress, the precursor of H.R. 5881, 84th Congress, by the organ of the Association, Western Water News, July, 1954, p. 2. The Senate Committee said, on the other hand, that it "heard evidence to the effect that there was neither opportunity nor intention on the part of local interests to expand such enterprises into major reclamation developments on a step-by-step basis." S. REP. No. 1073, 84th Cong., 1st Sess. 2 (1955).

policy. On the contrary, they have taken the offensive against the excess land provision itself, concentrating argument on its application to "supplemental" water or to lands "already under cultivation."[154] In doing this they are following a lead given by the author of the Engle formula when he first broached it in 1954. He was seeking a "common sense" approach, he said, to "avoid all the government red tape and legal difficulties involved in applying the limitation to an *established agricultural area where the water supplied is supplemental* to existing but insufficient supplies."[155] (Emphasis added.)

It is apparent that in supporting the formula, in continuing to speak of "supplemental water," and in resisting the excess lands provision, a thought survives of retrieving the Congressional defeats of Central Valley exemptions in 1944 and 1947. Senator William Knowland, of California, who co-sponsored the 1947 Central Valley exemption bill with Senator Sheridan Downey, observed that in California "what is involved is purely a supplemental supply of water."[156] He made the long-familiar genuflection to an historic excess lands provision he would have approved but that never existed: he believed the "160-acre limitation . . . is an excellent public policy" where "new public lands are being brought into development for the first time, to prevent land speculation, and so forth,"[157] *i.e.,* where the limitation—directed solely at supplying water to *private* land—never applied. Senator Anderson said the excess land limitation is "not a practical limitation to apply when supplemental water is being supplied," and referred to Central Valley and Colorado-Big Thompson projects as cases in point. The potentially far reach of the device of the doctrine of "supplemental" water did not escape Senator Douglas, who said:

> The argument that the 160-acre limitation did not apply in the case of supplemental water confused the Senator from Illinois for some years, until he went to California and the Southwest and discovered what the real situation was. Virtually all of the land has some water on it, either from natural causes, by rainfall, or by pumping underground water through wells.
>
> If it is said that the 160-acre limitation applies only where there is no water, either from the heavens or from subsurface deposits, then one is really saying that the 160-acre limitation should not apply at all. . . .[158]

---

154. 101 CONG. REC. 11823 (daily ed. July 28, 1955).

155. Sacramento Bee, July 12, 1954, p. 10, col. 1. *Cf.* text *supra* at note 145. The argument on "supplemental" water has been used in virtually every attempt to remove the excess lands provisions, successful and unsuccessful alike, since the Colorado-Big Thompson exemption of 1938.

156. 101 CONG. REC. 11823 (daily ed. May 23, 1955).

157. *Ibid.*

158. 103 CONG. REC. 6737, 6738 (daily ed. May 23, 1957).

As the debate has proceeded, it has become clearer that supporters of the formula find virtually no place suited to application of the historic principle of wide distribution of water resources. Senator Arthur V. Watkins, of Utah, explained:

> The fact is that now in the West practically all new land or public land that could be brought under cultivation has already been brought under cultivation. I would say roughly that probably 70 percent or 80 percent of the projects now are furnishing water as a supplemental supply for areas which are of the kind the Senator from Arkansas has described in Arkansas or in the Mississippi delta. That is also true of the whole Central Valley in California. It is true in my State. It is true in Arizona where new lands are being brought in. It is true of practically every 1 of the 17 Western States.[159]

Senator Anderson, like Senator Watkins, believed the provision should not be applied to lands "already under cultivation," but might properly be applied to "new" lands. With an empty gesture of approval toward the historic reclamation law, Senator Anderson indicated why he regarded it as no longer applicable:

> Of course, what the able Senator from Illinois said about the *historic* American policy in our reclamation program is true. *I agree with him.* But we were dealing with a *completely different* situation in the early days of reclamation. There was a time when an individual could file a desert entry. Try to find a piece of ground in the United States on which to file a desert entry today. At one time I filed a desert entry, and I allowed other members of my family to file them. In all, we filed on a total of some 10,000 acres available in the Rio Grande Valley. That was in 1922 or 1924. But there has not been an acre of that type of land available for 15 years.[160] (Emphasis added.)

Convinced that the Engle formula is insufficient as an incentive to persuade owners to dispose of their excess lands and to preserve national policy from erosion, and that it is no more to be welcomed than the camel's nose inside the tent, Senator Douglas saw no reason at all to abandon principle:

> ... this is the issue which I am trying to have established: that the *resources* which the United States Government furnishes for irrigation should be used, insofar as possible, to foster and protect the family-sized farms, rather than to foster and protect the huge estates and the enormous land holdings which characterize certain portions of California and the Southwest. ... We wish to try to hold on to the smaller, self-sufficing farms, which produce independence of thought, because men have their living under their feet. ... .[161] (Emphasis added.)

---

159. 101 CONG. REC. 11823 (daily ed. July 25, 1955).
160. 103 CONG. REC. 6735, 6736 (daily ed. May 25, 1957).
161. *Id.* at 6734-35.

Opponents of the excess land provision argued that technological forces are making the farms of federal reclamation beneficiaries larger. Senator Douglas replied that this is irrelevant: "the legal question was not how large a man's holdings should be, but under what conditions would the Government furnish him water?"[161a]

V
1957 - 1958

If the big landowners in the valley lose out in this particular fight [to exempt Central Valley project from the excess lands provision], they have several other proposals to accomplish their end. One of them is . . . [to] authorize the Army to add irrigation . . . to its present navigation and flood-control powers. . . . This would circumvent the 160-acre rule, since the Army is not bound by that restriction.[162]

Another proposal, said to have originated among the big landowners of Fresno County, is for the State of California to take over the Central Valley project, paying the entire bill. This, too, would sidestep the 160-acre limitation.
—Business Week, May 13, 1944[163]

The tactics employed by large landowners to destroy the excess land provision are remarkable for their consistency; they follow lines described publicly nearly 14 years ago. The first of these, the effort to obtain project by project exemptions, was begun in 1938 and 1940, interrupted by defeats, and resumed. Continuing the work of the eroding principle of the two preceding Congresses, the current 85th Congress already has exempted valley lands on the East Bench, Montana, project.[164] The method of obtaining the exception resembles predecessors. A hearing attended by spokesmen for local districts and representatives of the Interior Department was held but apparently not printed. Evidently everyone present approved an

---

161a. 103 Cong .Rec. 6738. "High efficiency may be obtained in many instances on small farms where custom work by specialized machines is used or where cooperative ownership of certain equipment leads to reasonable costs. Comparability of income for the family on a small farm often is achieved by combining farming with other occupations." U.S. Dept. Agr. statement on "Size of farms on federal reclamation projects," Memorandum of the chairman of the subcommittee on irrigation and reclamation to members of the Senate committee on interior and insular affairs, April 25, 1958, p. 46.

162. Congress subsequently bound the Army Engineers to observe the excess land provision. 58 STAT. 891 (1944), as amended, 43 U.S.C. § 390 (1952).

163. Valley Divided, Business Week, No. 767, May 13, 1944, p. 24. Business Week described a fourth tactic for escape from the excess lands provision: "Still other landowners are sinking wells around their holdings in order to be prepared to pump irrigation water from the raised water table, thus getting a free ride on the Central Valley project." Ibid. However, pumping underground waters has never destroyed the effectiveness of state irrigation district boundaries, at least in California; and apparently has never persuaded those on whose behalf it was made that it could be sufficiently effective to render other means of removing the excess lands provision unnecessary to achieve its defeat. See Taylor, *160-acre Water Limitation and the Water Resources Commission*, 3 WESTERN POL. Q., 435-49 (1950).

164. P.L. 112, 85th Congress.

exemption.[165] Sponsors of the bill assured Congress that it created no "precedent."[166] Perhaps the assurance was given in response to skepticism expressed earlier in the same session by Senator Morse, that "Exceptions are bad precedents."[167] There was no debate in either House.[168] With an undocumented request before it for adjustment of the excess land provision upward to permit "suitable family livelihood," and permit irrigators to "meet the cost of water service," Congress gave a *complete* exemption.

The Fryingpan-Arkansas bill passed the Senate with an exemption of regulated waters for lands "which now have an irrigation water supply from sources other than a Federal reclamation project." A public hearing was held and printed. The average size of irrigated farm was reported to be 70 acres, with one-eighth of the 322,000 acres of the project in excess holdings. The relation of these facts, if any, to the desirability or undesirability of the bill was not indicated. The Interior Department expressed no opinion of its own although it observed that the bill raises an issue of policy because it proposes a departure from the Warren Act of 1911.[169] It suggested that the Senate might wish to consider using the Engle formula.[170] The Senate Committee recommended exemption from the excess land provision "In view of the costs" of "continuous examinations of titles necessary for enforcing land limitation regulations as against the extent and origin of these holdings, chiefly of families, as well as other factors. . . ."[171] With this record before it, the Senate passed the bill without debate on the exemption.[172] There it rests.

The Columbia Basin Act of 1957 differs substantially from most other bills modifying the excess lands provision described herein, since it granted a readjustment of the acreage limitation figure upwards, rather than complete exemption. It raises the permissible acreage held by an individual or corporation that may be furnished water to 160 acres, and by a family to 320 acres.[173] Hearings were held and printed; thoughtful reasons were given why the limitation should be raised. The action of Congress in raising the limit was related logically to the case made for altering the excess land pro-

---

165. S. REP. No. 574, 85th Cong., 1st Sess. 3 (1957).
166. 103 CONG. REC. 9810 (daily ed. July 2, 1957).
167. 103 CONG. REC. 6741 (daily ed. May 23, 1957).
168. 103 CONG. REC. 10574 (daily ed. July 15, 1957). Evidently no one proposed to restrain public liberality by even so little as inclusion of the Engle formula.
169. 36 STAT. 926 (1911), 43 U.S.C. § 524 (1952).
170. *Hearings Before Irrigation and Reclamation Subcommittee of Senate Interior and Insular Affairs Committee on S. 60*, 85th Cong., 1st Sess. 6 (1956).
171. S. REP. No. 325, 85th Cong., 1st Sess. 7 (1957). *Cf.* text *supra* at note 47.
172. 103 CONG. REC. 9414-32 (daily ed. June 27, 1957).
173. H.R. REP. No. 810, 85th Cong., 1st Sess. 3 (1957). Congressman Engle opposed the bill on the ground that it would provide "unjust enrichment," through water subsidized by the federal government at $1,000 an acre, but did not propose adoption of his formula.

vision.[174] It preserved the principle of wide distribution of water. In this respect the Columbia Basin Act is unique.

In March, 1958, Congress exempted the Mercedes division, Texas project, from the historic excess lands provision.[175] The Senate held no hearings on the bill, or at least none were published; the House held hearings but these were not published. A bill to exempt an adjacent Valley Gravity project, Texas, had failed after published hearings in 1947.[176] The Bureau of the Budget recommended that "it would be preferable to deal with the question of land limitations on an overall rather than a project-by-project basis."[177] Congress received information that 28 landowners on the project have holdings in excess of 320 acres. Evidently ability to support a family on less than 160 acres is not in question, for the principal crops are "citrus (grapefruit and oranges), vegetables (cabbage, carrots, tomatoes), and cotton."[178] That is to say, exemption was clearly at the expense of the family-size farm, not for its protection. The law substitutes the Engle formula for the excess lands provision, although the public record discloses no reason why this historic protection should not apply.[179]

Congressman John Saylor of Pennsylvania told the House that the project met "every requirement that the reclamation acts have laid down. It is not one that has had to have exceptions made for it."[180] Congressman Aspinall of Colorado responded to an inquiry whether costs of the project would be interest-free "except as to land in excess of 160 acres."[181] Replying in the affirmative, Congressman Aspinall added, "That is the reclamation law and has been since 1902."[182] Almost immediately, as committee chairman, he introduced committee amendments substituting, in lieu of the historic excess land provisions as they have stood since 1902, the new Engle formula charging interest against landholdings in excess of 160 acres.[183]

The Texas, Mercedes, exemption is clearly in the tradition of the

---

174. 71 STAT. 590 (1957). Whether the particular change in acreage figure that Congress approved was justified is a question of fact and judgment.
175. 104 CONG. REC. 4112 (daily ed. March 18, 1958); 104 CONG. REC. 3714 (daily ed. March 13, 1958).
176. *Hearings, supra* note 28.
177. S. REP. No. 603, 85th Cong., 1st Sess. 5 (1957); H.R. REP. No. 1002, 85th Cong., 1st Sess. 5 (1957).
178. S. REP. No. 603, 85th Cong., 1st Sess. 4, 5 (1957).
179. In another connection the author of the formula has offered an explanation that may or may not be intended to apply here: "With reference to the so-called Engle formula: This applies . . . where one large landowner, by refusing to sign a recordable contract, could prevent forty or one hundred little ones from getting necessary water." Valley Labor Citizen of Fresno, Jan. 3, 1958, p. 4, col. 1. As Klaus Loewald has replied, this "in effect enables one large landowner to dictate public policy on public expenditures." *Supra* Jan. 10, 1958, p. 4, col. 1. *Cf.* text *infra* at note 201; also footnote 150.
180. 104 CONG. REC. 3714 (daily ed. March 13, 1958).
181. *Ibid.*
182. *Ibid.* The Congressman was in error.
183. *Ibid.*

first tactic of large landowners to escape national policy.[184] Congress was warned against the cumulative effect of this tactic on policy in 1954 by Senator Morse: "It is all very well to say that every rule has its exception. But when a rule becomes honeycombed with exceptions, it ceases to be a rule."[185]

At least two other bills aimed at weakening or destroying the excess land provision have been introduced in the 85th Congress. Senator Joseph C. O'Mahoney, of Wyoming, introduced S. 1996 to authorize as well as to exempt Kendrick project, Wyoming. A hearing was held, but apparently not printed. The Interior Department approved an exemption because of the "marginal quality of the project lands" used in a "short growing season" for "hay and pasture," making it "difficult, if not impossible" to "have an economic size of farm capable of furnishing a reasonably adequate level of living."[186]

Senator Frank Barrett, of Wyoming, introduced a bill to give the Secretary of the Interior, upon request of the governor of the State in which a reclamation project is located, authority to determine that more than 160 acres is necessary for support of an "average sized family at a suitably profitable level," and to raise the figure above 160 as appropriate, taking into consideration elevation, climate, topography, soils, crops, and earning capacity.[187] This would jeopardize the judiciality of any decision by a Secretary of the Interior, by making it easy to confront him with a recommendation from a Governor, made perhaps under local pressure, for a decision for which Governors carry no legal responsibility. A better way to amplify irresponsibility for federal public policy would be difficult to find. The bill damages reclamation law in other ways by substituting the interest formula for the excess land provision when a project delivers "supplemental" water, or water to lands that have been "cultivated." It is unlikely that any remnants of the policy of wide distribution of water resources, and hardly any of wide distribution of federal moneys, could survive passage of the Barrett bill.[188]

As counter-offensive to these inroads on national policy that employ the first tactic, viz., exemption or virtual repeal, Senators Douglas, Morse and Neuberger have introduced S. 1425 to repeal the Engle formula in the Small Projects Reclamation Act, and have asked for broad hearings on the excess lands provision.

The second tactic of large landowners, as described in Business Week in 1944, is to empower an agency not governed by the excess

---
184. See text *supra* at note 161.
185. 100 CONG. REC. 15019 (1954).
186. S. REP. No. 838, 85th Cong., 1st Sess. 5 (1957). Earlier, Senator O'Mahoney had supported the excess land provision, as Senator Douglas pointed out. 103 CONG. REC. 6738 (daily ed. May 23, 1957).
187. S. 2541, 85th Cong., 1st Sess. (1957).
188. See text *supra* at notes 149, 150.

land provision to exercise the same functions and confer the same financial benefits as the Bureau of Reclamation. A conspicuous example has been the use of the Army Engineers, who, although covered by Congress under reclamation law in 1944,[189] have refused to this day to apply the excess land provision.[190]

The 84th Congress created a comparable situation by authorizing the Secretary of Agriculture to make loans covering the local share of costs of small "works of improvement" under the Watershed Protection and Flood Prevention Act.[191] The House Agriculture Committee declared its belief that under the bill "Federal assistance should be substantially comparable to that provided for under reclamation acts and similar legislation."[192] In face of this recommendation, and without debate upon it, Congress omitted the standard instrument of reclamation policy, viz., the excess lands provision. Thus Congress offers federal assistance to water development in western states from two sources under differing laws. This sets the stage for the same destructive competition through dual agencies that the Hoover Commission of 1949 condemned when it recommended consolidation of the Army Engineers with the Bureau of Reclamation, the combined reclamation agency to be a part of the Department of the Interior.[193]

This breach of water policy was not made without thought of how the gates of federal financial assistance for water development in the East might be thrown open without incurring for excess landowners there the anti-monopoly and anti-speculation protections that have been offered generally in justification of federal aid to irrigation since 1902.[194]

The third tactic to permit large landowners to escape the excess lands provision, named in Business Week in 1944, viz., making use of a state, is now under serious legislative and executive consideration in California.[195] A first proposal—that the State purchase Central Valley project from the Federal government—appears to be dor-

---

189. 58 STAT. 891 (1944), 43 U.S.C. § 390 (1952).

190. Kings River Project in the Basin of the Great Central Valley—A Case Study, Hoover Commission on Organization of the Executive Branch of the Government, Appendix L, Task Force Report on Natural Resources, January, 1949, Appendix 7.

191. 70 STAT. 1088 (1956), 16 U.S.C. §§ 1003, 1004 (Supp. V 1958).

192. H.R. REP. No. 1810, 84th Cong., 2d Sess. 3 (1956).

193. See note 190 *supra,* concluding report, May, 1949, pp. 27-29, 43.

194. Debates on the Watershed Protection Bill, H.R. 8750, do not disclose consideration of the excess lands provision. 102 CONG. REC. 6879, 13642 (1956). However, some senators and congressmen outside the western reclamation states opposed carrying the excess land provision eastward in debates on the Small Reclamation Projects bill. 101 CONG. REC. 7145-46, 11823-24 (1955).

195. The California judiciary, in effect, has already approved this by divided vote of its supreme court. See Taylor, *Destruction of Federal Reclamation Policy? The Ivanhoe Case,* 10 STAN. L. REV. 76 (1957).

mant.[196] However, a second proposal—that the State construct new works rather than the Federal Government—is receiving active consideration in the Legislature. The proposed State Feather River project in the Central Valley watershed is an example. The Legislature has defeated attempts to incorporate an excess lands provision in Feather River legislation,[197] made appropriations for relocating railroad tracts and readying the site for a dam, but has not yet decided to appropriate for State construction. The financial obligation of such a project would be very heavy[198] for the State of California to carry, and it is uncertain how much federal financial assistance would be given by Congress, or on what terms. Proposals for obtaining federal contributions have been made;[199] whether, if granted by Congress, these would carry the excess lands and public power preference policies of federal reclamation law is uncertain. Senator Morse has said he would oppose them unless they did:

> ... it is not fair or right to expect that the federal government should bear the burden of non-reimbursable costs for flood control, for example, and surrender, give away, the power facilities or the anti-monopoly irrigation policy of federal law. . . . One senator at least, stands here who will oppose such a give-away of funds and policy.[200]

While the motivation of proposals to use the State of California as an instrument for avoiding reclamation policy of wide distribution of resources and benefits is clear, the prospect for their acceptance by both the State of California and the Congress of the United States is uncertain. Finance and policy remain central issues, as they were in 1902 when western states sought and obtained federal aid for water development under the terms of the National Reclamation Act.

VI
1958

What was the reason for cancellation of the 160-acre limitation on these . . . federal projects? Simply because the landowners and water users flatly refused to accept it. Is the

---

196. Hugh G. Hansen, Central Valley Project: Federal or State? Report Prepared for California Assembly Interim Committee on Conservation, Planning and Public Works, Vol. 13, No. 6, Chs. 5, 10, May, 1955.

197. CALIFORNIA LEGISLATURE ASSEMBLY JOURNAL 809 (daily ed. Jan. 22, 1957).

198. Hugh Hansen, using the lowest cost estimates, says: ". . . the annual obligations for principal and interest on a 50-year 3 percent bond issue of $1,133,000,000 as proposed for the complete Feather River Project and Southern California diversion system would amount to $44,000,000 per year. A complete failure of net project revenues would thereby involve a risk equal to 3.1 percent of the 1954-55 state budget, and a partial failure correspondingly less." See note 196 supra, at 280 ,281.

199. "It is expected Congressman Clair Engle . . . who was responsible for the request [for $40 million for flood control on Feather River] in last year's measure, will move for an amendment to have it made a part of the present bill." Sacramento Bee, Jan. 10, 1957, p. 1, col. 6.

200. Senator Morse, Water and America's Future, address before the Commonwealth Club, San Francisco, pp. 4, 5, Feb. 15, 1957.

Santa Maria project to be abandoned because of this situation? Hardly. . . .

Thus falls another invulnerable shibboleth of straw without even a gesture of hail and farewell!
—State Senator J. Howard Williams, of California, 1953.[201]

. . . the question before the Senate is a very simple one. We simply say to this area of California, "Get busy with local public opinion, which, after all, is your great policeman when you really want to bring a community betterment; and make perfectly clear to the 13 excess-landholders that they have the duty—and a patriotic duty it is, too—to yield to the rule that what promotes the welfare of the greatest number is the policy which those who have any real interest in the development of a community should follow."
—Senator Wayne Morse, of Oregon, 1954.[202]

The twentieth century opened with a victory for friends of federal aid to western water development, who assured eastern skeptics that their fears of land and water monopoly were groundless. In midcentury the outcome forecast by the skeptics is in the balance. Large western landed interests appear confident of their ability to sustain the flow of federal money whether the principle of anti-monopoly and antispeculation survives or not. They have evidence to support them; Congress decides whether they are right.

It is a mistake to suppose that landowners and water users on reclamation projects generally are unwilling to comply with the excess lands provision in order to obtain water. In the southern portion of Central Valley, for example, where resistance to compliance has been most vocal, the electors of 13 water districts voted more than ten to one at the end of the forties and in the early fifties to accept water contracts including the excess land provision, and another district indicated its willingness to accept it, notwithstanding a state supreme court decision that it could not legally do so.[203] One of the great corporate landowners, reported by former Senator Sheridan Downey as adamant against the law,[204] has signed a recordable contract to dispose of excess holdings as required by law to get water.[205] So long as men are encouraged in the executive, judicial, or legislative branches of government to believe that escape from the law is a possibility, compliance will be resisted, but the contention that the excess lands provision is unenforceable is groundless.

---

201. The Vanishing American, p. 22, Annual Convention, Irrigation Districts Association of California, Palm Springs, Nov. 12, 1953 (processed).

202. 100 CONG. REC. 15022 (daily ed. Aug. 18, 1954).

203. Ivanhoe Irrigation Dist. v. All Parties and Persons, 47 Cal. 2d 597, 306 P.2d 824 (1957); Sacramento Bee, June 22 ,1957, p. D6, col. 4.

204. DOWNEY, THEY WOULD RULE THE VALLEY 180 (1947).

205. "The Bureau Coerces Di Giorgio," California Farmer, May 17, 1952, p. 533.

Congress, of course, cannot at the same time preserve and undermine its own policy, simultaneously declare a faith in wide distribution of water resources, and act as if it had an obligation to vote money for projects on which excess landowners announce they will not comply with the law. Nor can it raise or abolish the acreage limitation figure without exposing itself to demands for more appropriations to put more water on less and less productive lands under more and more marginal conditions.

Nor can Congress make its decisions on the basis of the adequacy of 160 irrigated acres to support a family, virtually ignoring current interpretations that allow water for 160 acres for perhaps each member of a family, and profess to defend the family-sized farm.[206]

Without making it clear whether they believe that fact and logic support a higher acreage limitation figure or none at all, opponents of the excess land provision have argued that technological forces are making the farms of federal reclamation beneficiaries larger. Senator Douglas replied that this fact is true but irrelevant to the principle of a limitation: "[T]his is not a limitation upon the amount of land a man can own. . . . It places a limitation upon the number of acres to which the Government will furnish water."[207]

In the Central Valley, and in many areas where the excess lands provision is most seriously contested, 160 irrigated acres is a large farm by any standard of measurement, including the use of modern technology, and 320 acres is extremely large.[208] Beyond that are ownerships that fairly merit Senator Douglas' query whether we wish to extend public aid to encourage "giantism" in agriculture.[209]

To continue the present erosion of policy is to depart farther and farther from the original reclamation purpose of providing opportunity on the land for the landless.[210] It is to substitute provision of

---

206. 101 CONG. REC. 11827 (1955). Columbia Basin Act recognizes the absurdity of the current interpretations of 160 acres to as many individuals as there may be in a family, by defining a family as "a group consisting of either or both husband and wife, together with their children under eighteen years of age. . . ." 57 STAT. 16 (1943), 16 U.S.C. § 835 (b) (1952).

207. 103 CONG. REC. 6733-34 (daily ed. May 23, 1957).

208. In 1945 when Central Valley project was under construction, the average selling price of 160 acres of non-irrigated land in Tulare County was $12,472, and of irrigated land $85,757. *Hearings, supra* note 28, table 1, p. 861. Average size of irrigated farms in California, according to the 1954 census, was 83.4 acres.

209. Bureau of Reclamation data given Congress in 1947 indicates 34 "Known ownerships of 5,000 or more acres in probable present and future San Joaquin Valley service areas of the Central Valley project," totalling 748,490 acres. *Hearings, supra* note 28, table 7, p. 864.

210. ". . . these lands are being opened to settlement for all the people, whether they now reside in the East, South, or West. The farm boys in the East want farms of their own. It gives them a place where they can go and build homes without being driven into the already overcrowded cities to seek employment. It will provide a place for the mechanic and wage-earner to go when the battle for their daily wages becomes too strenuous. . . ." 35 CONG. REC. 6672 (1902). *Cf.* text *supra* at notes 1-8.

water for the landed, the more land the more water, opening the purses of taxpayers and power consumers to furnish it.[211]

The steps taken by Congress in eroding the principle of widespread distribution of rights to the use of water expose a shabby side of the legislative process. Forms are observed at the minimum, and content is shoddy. Reliance on *ex parte* testimony, unconcern for solid documentation of crucial questions, carelessness of fact, irrelevance of fact and argument to decision, evasion of primary issues and principle, sensitiveness to resistance by powerful private interests garbed as solicitude for the less powerful, reluctance to use the power of the public purse to sustain declared public purpose, avoidance rather than encouragement of an informed public, leaving to a handful of members of the Congress the responsibility for rejection or adherence to policy—these are not adornments of a great parliament but they characterize two decades of erosion.

A great policy—one that bears the names of Jefferson, Lincoln, and Theodore Roosevelt[212]—should not go out this way. Daniel Webster called wide distribution of landownership "the true basis, most certainly, of popular government."[213] Contemparary decision is lighted not only by our national past but by a critical world today. On underdeveloped continents the lack of widespread landownership is among the chief sources of the free world's insecurity.[214]

Only informed and conscious deliberation can replace erosion by decision. If, as some members of Congress suggest, historic water policy is "outdated" and "impractical," that fact—if it is a fact—should be faced. Senator Douglas, doubting, has said:

> We have gone very far . . . in reversing—without openly saying we are doing so—this historic American policy of fostering the family-sized farm. I regard this as one of many tendencies in America which are extremely dangerous and against the public interest. . . .
> If we wish to vote for giantism, we should go ahead and vote that way, but let us know, and let the country know, precisely what it is we are voting for.[215]

---

211. *Cf. supra* note 11; see also Taylor, *Destruction of Federal Reclamation Policy? The Ivanhoe Case*, 10 STAN. L. REV. 77, 93 (1957).

212. U.S. BUREAU OF RECLAMATION, DEP'T OF INTERIOR, LANDOWNERSHIP SURVEY ON FEDERAL RECLAMATION PROJECTS, PART III, HISTORICAL BACKGROUND OF RECLAMATION LAW AND POLICY WITH RESPECT TO EXCESS LAND LIMITATION (1946).

213. Quoted in Small Business and the Community, A Study in Central Valley of California on Effects of Scale of Farm Operations, Report to the Senate Special Committee to Study Problems of American Small Business, 79th Cong., 2d Sess. (1946).

214. *Cf.* General MacArthur's memorandum of Dec. 9, 1945, ordering the Imperial Japanese Government to submit "a program of rural land reform" to "remove economic obstacles to the revival and strengthening of democratic tendencies, establish respect for the dignity of man," and "insure that those who till the soil of Japan shall have more equal opportunity to enjoy the fruits of their labor." LANDOWNERSHIP SURVEY, *op. cit. supra* note 212, at 95.

215. 103 CONG. REC. 6734-35 (daily ed. May 23, 1957).

THE EXCESS LAND LAW

Pressure vs. Principle

The Excess Land Law: Pressure vs. Principle

Paul S. Taylor*

"LATENT CAUSES OF FACTION"[1]

Now I have struck the crux of my appeal [for the excess land law]. I wish to save the very wealthy men of this country and their advocates and upholders from the ruin that they would bring upon themselves if they were permitted to have their way. It is because I am against revolution; it is because I am against the doctrines of the Extremists, of the Socialists; it is because I wish to see this country of ours continued as a genuine democracy; it is because I distrust violence and disbelieve in it; it is because I wish to secure this country against ever seeing a time when the 'have-nots' shall rise against the 'haves'; it is because I wish to secure for our children and our grandchildren and for their children's children the same freedom of opportunity, the same peace and order and justice that we have had in the past.—Theodore Roosevelt, 1911[2]

We talk about political democracy, but we cannot have it without economic democracy. We cannot have political freedom of choice for the individual without economic freedom of choice for the individual. Therefore, I say again today on the floor of the Senate, if I were to be asked to name one thing—if I were limited to the naming of one thing only—which I think is the greatest guarantee of the perpetuity of our democratic form of government, what I would name would be private home ownership in the city and family-farm ownership in the country. On that type of ownership, I think, is dependent, more than we sometimes fully realize, our whole system of political and economic freedom of choice for the individual.—Senator Wayne Morse, 1959[3]

The long contest between those who strive to preserve the excess land provisions of federal reclamation law, now in their fifty-eighth year, and those who seek to avoid or destroy them has been rising to a pitch of intensity in California not reached since the middle forties. This issue is the gist of litigation that made its way from the California Supreme Court in 1957 to the United States Supreme Court in 1958,[3a] and now lies again before the California Supreme Court in 1959. The issue occupied four days of debate

---

* Professor of E... .mics, University of California, Berkeley; consultant to the Office of the Secretary of the In. rior and Bureau of Reclamation successively between 1943 and 1952. Elizabeth Dickerson Huttman, Klaus G. Loewald and Beverly Starika assisted in preparation of this paper.

[1] THE FEDERALIST NO. 10 (Madison).

[2] Theodore Roosevelt, speaking of the excess land law that he inspired personally as President in 1902. 7 TRANSACTIONS OF THE COMMONWEALTH CLUB 108 (1912–13).

[3] 105 CONG. REC. 6894 (daily ed. May 7, 1959).

[3a] Ivanhoe Irr. Dist. v. McCracken, 357 U.S. 275 (1958), *reversing sub nom.* Ivanhoe Irr. Dist. v. All Parties, 47 Cal. 2d 957, 306 P.2d 824 (1957).

on the floor of the United States Senate, from May fifth to twelfth, 1959. Later the same month it entered the legislative debate on the Governor's water program in Sacramento. It permeates negotiations for repayment contracts on Kings River under a disputed administrative order granting immunity from the excess land law to water districts upon discharge of their debt to the Government.

This contest reverberates, in one form or another, in every branch of government—judicial, legislative, and executive—and at every level of government—federal, state and local. It is pervasive because our entire society, like the law, rests on a principle of wide distribution of property. It cuts deeply because the aggregations of landownership that challenge the principle are large, powerful and often geographically concentrated.

The excess land law prescribes that "water shall not be furnished from any [federal] reservoir or delivered through any such canal or ditch to any one landowner in excess of an amount sufficient to irrigate one hundred and sixty acres."[4] This provision does not affect furnishing water to lands of 160 acres or less in single ownership. Man and wife are entitled to water for 160 acres each. Any landowner within reach of a federal project may obtain water for up to 160 acres, no matter how much land he owns. An owner of more than 160 (or 320) acres of land wishing water to irrigate the excess, may obtain it by agreeing to sell the excess within 10 years at a price appraised to exclude enhanced values resulting from the project; the choice is his. The Supreme Court of the United States has said that

> ... the claim of discrimination in the 160-acre limitation, we believe ... overlooks the purpose for which the project was designed. The project was designed to benefit people, not land. It is a reasonable classification to limit the amount of project water available to each individual in order that benefits may be distributed in accordance with the greatest good to the greatest number of individuals. The limitation insures that this enormous expenditure will not go in disproportionate share to a few individuals with large land holdings. Moreover, it prevents the use of the federal reclamation service for speculative purposes.[5]

The concentration of ownership of irrigable western lands has concerned Congress from the beginning of federal reclamation and provided the reason for statutory protections against water monopoly, notably the excess land law. As Congressman Oscar W. Underwood, throwing Southern support to Western reclamation, said in 1902:

> If this policy is not undertaken now, this great Western desert will ultimately be acquired by individuals and great corporations for the purpose of using it for grazing vast herds of cattle. They will acquire the waterways

---

[4] Warren Act, 36 Stat. 926 (1911), 43 U.S.C. § 523 (1952).
[5] Ivanhoe Irr. Dist. v. McCracken, 357 U.S. 275, 297 (1958).

and water rights for the purpose of watering stock and become land barons. Then it will be impossible to ever convert it into homestead lands for our own people or to build up the population of this Western country. I believe the passage of this bill is in the interest of the man who earns his daily bread by his daily toil. It gives him a place where he can go and be free and independent; it gives him an opportunity to be an owner of the soil and to build a home. Those are the class of men we must rely on for the safety of the nation. In times of peace they pay the taxes and maintain the Government; in times of peril and strife they are the bulwark of the nation, and it is justice to them that this legislation be enacted into law.[6]

Congressman Underwood was speaking of the family type farm, a tradition that stretches unbroken through American history and spreads across the pages of congressional debate from colonial times to this day.

Throughout its history the concentration of landholdings in California has impeded development of the national family farm pattern in that State. This concentration remains generally characteristic to the present day of the irrigable lands of Central Valley which are the focus of this Article.[7]

In the latest congressional debates, Senator Paul Douglas of Illinois, battling to save the excess land provision in the San Luis, California project bill, cited tables showing that units of 1,000 acres or more comprise 69.8 percent of 1,135,000 acres in Kern County that include "possible areas of service by irrigation from the San Luis Reservoir south of the Federal service area." A single company owns 16.3 percent of the area.[8] These ownerships are covered broadly under the current phrase "Kern County interests."

The economic stakes at issue in preservation or destruction of the excess land law are large. Among them are public subsidies that six California Congressmen[9] have estimated at $577 per acre on Central Valley project. Thus the 160-acre excess land law permits an individual to receive public subsidy from Central Valley project in the amount of $92,320 (or $184,640 for man and wife), but prohibits more.

This Article continues a series analyzing the excess land law and the successive attacks upon the law through the executive, judicial and legis-

---

[6] 35 CONG. REC. 6672 (1902), remarks of Congressman Underwood.

[7] Taylor, *Foundations of California Rural Society*, 24 CALIF. HIST. SOC'Y Q. 193 (1945).

[8] 105 CONG. REC. 6886 (daily ed. May 7, 1959). Earlier statistics of like import appear in DOWNEY, THEY WOULD RULE THE VALLEY 164 (1947). Close to three-quarters of a million acres were owned by 34 individuals and corporations in 1947 "in the probable present and future San Joaquin Valley service areas in Central Valley Project (CVP);" none of these holdings were under 5,000 acres.

[9] Letter from Representatives Clair Engle, John Moss, Harlen Hagen, B. F. Sisk and J. J. McFall to Attorney General Edmund G. (Pat) Brown, Feb. 4, 1957, reproduced in 44 CALIF. L. REV. 772 (1957). On San Luis unit, the cost (and, presumably, subsidy) estimates by Senator Douglas are very much higher. 105 CONG. REC. 6884 (daily ed. May 7, 1959).

lative branches of government.[10] It brings the simultaneous pressures in all branches, and at all levels, at the close of the 1950's, into a single focus.

I

CONGRESS

The owners of the big estates cannot get what they want by State action alone. They also need Federal help, and they think they can come to Washington, with no one greatly concerned over the issue and push their proposal through Congress on favorable terms to themselves.—Senator Paul Douglas, 1959[11]

As one pauses in this debate to refresh his memory in regard to some of the great scandals in the field of natural resources in our history, and when one thinks of the oil scandals and the oil "steals," the Teapot Dome, the great land frauds, the various types of "steals" of which the powerful economic vested interests of the country have been guilty throughout our history . . . let the RECORD show that I think that if our amendment [to retain the excess land provision at San Luis] is not adopted, the bill will be a water "steal" by the various large landowners the Senator from Illinois has just now listed in the RECORD.—Senator Wayne Morse, 1959[12]

I support the 160-acre limitation too.—Senator Clair Engle, 1959[13]

Battles over federal water development in California in the 1940's and early 1950's revealed strong opposition by great landowning interests to federal reclamation, because the federal excess land law controls incremental land values and requires ultimate disposal of excess lands.[14] Plans prepared by the Bureau of Reclamation for a San Luis unit to be added to the Central Valley project were sent to Congress by President Harry S. Truman as early as 1949.[15] For several years they lay dormant, until a new administration came to power in 1953, ending the New Deal-Fair Deal era and proposing a policy of "partnership" between the federal government and State and local agencies. Simultaneously, Secretary Douglas McKay was offering a relaxed interpretation of the excess land law that held prom-

---

[10] The prior articles by the author are: *Excess Land Law on the Kern?*, 46 CALIF. L. REV. 153 (1958); *The Excess Land Law: Legislative Erosion of Public Policy*, 30 ROCKY MT. L. REV. 1 (1958); *Destruction of Federal Reclamation Policy? The Ivanhoe Case*, 10 STAN. L. REV. 76 (1957); *The Excess Land Law: Execution of a Public Policy*, 64 YALE L.J. 477 (1955).

[11] 105 CONG. REC. 6738 (daily ed. May 5, 1959).

[12] 105 CONG. REC. 6886 (daily ed. May 7, 1959). See also *id.* at 6895; 105 CONG. REC. 7056 (daily ed. May 11, 1959).

[13] *Id.* at 7054.

[14] See note 10 *supra*. See also DOWNEY, *op. cit. supra* note 8. A running fight over public versus private generation and distribution of hydroelectric power generally has paralleled that over the excess land law.

[15] U.S. Bureau of Reclamation, Dep't of the Interior, *Central Valley Basin Report*, S. Doc. No. 113, 81st Cong., 1st Sess. 129–30 (1949).

ise of easy avoidance.[16] In this atmosphere, both friends and opponents of the excess land law came before Congress in 1955 and 1956 to discuss further federal water development in Central Valley.[17] Even these hearings held by the Senate on the San Luis unit developed little agreement on what should be the nature of partnership on the project, or indeed, whether there should be any partnership at all. The testimony of two important witnesses before the Senate committee illustrates the disagreement:

Master of the California Grange, George Sehlmeyer, favored *federal* construction partly as a means of preserving the excess land law, and opposed *State* construction, partly at least, because he feared that State construction would be used to circumvent the law. Asked whether "one of the reasons why the *State* is moving in [to supplement or replace federal development] is to get rid of the land limitation?" he replied, "I think *that was an important factor* . . . ."[18]

A California assemblyman from Kern County, Patrick Kelly, favored State development as strongly as the Grange master favored *federal* construction. He said, "As an inherent part of the development of its natural resources under the *sovereignty of the State* of California, it is suggested that the management and control of all of the elements of the California State water plan, including the San Luis unit thereof, should be vested primarily with the State of California."[19] The hearings failed to produce a committee report.

Similar differences over policy appeared at Senate hearings 2 years later, in 1958. On one hand, the California State Federation of Labor insisted on construction of San Luis project "under reclamation law without deviation or evasion" and protested against any attempt to persuade Congress to relieve the State of California from the obligation required of all to observe the excess land law when using federal facilities.[20]

On the other hand, a member of the Kern County Water Commission and chairman of the Water Problems Department of the Kern County Farm Bureau presented a resolution of the California Farm Bureau Feder-

---

[16] See *infra*, text at note 92.

[17] *Hearings on S. 178 Before the Irrigation and Reclamation Subcommittee of the Senate Committee on Interior and Insular Affairs*, 84th Cong., 2d Sess. 1 (1956).

[18] *Id.* at 175–78. (Emphasis added.) The other factor, he said, was to avoid federal "power" policy.

[19] *Id.* at 252. (Emphasis added.)

[20] Testimony of C. J. Haggerty, secretary-treasurer, California State Federation of Labor, *Hearings on S. 1887 Before the Irrigation and Reclamation Subcommittee of the Senate Committee on Interior and Insular Affairs*, 85th Cong., 2d Sess. 185–86 (1958) [hereinafter cited as *1958 Hearings on S. 1887*]. See also *Hearings on S. 1425, S. 2541 and S. 3448 Before the Irrigation and Reclamation Subcommittee of the Senate Committee on Interior and Insular Affairs*, 85th Cong., 2d Sess. 155–59 (1958) [hereinafter cited as *1958 Hearings on S. 1425, S. 2541 & S. 3448*].

ation declaring that "cooperation should be only on the basis of *control of the projects and properties by the State of California*." He recommended construction by the *State*, and agreed that if the Senate committee did "not take the Kern County amendments . . . the California Farm Bureau Federation . . . *could not approve and support the bill*." Summarizing, he said:

> Fundamentally, it is our position that any . . . authorizing legislation, and any agreement thereunder, shall recognize the *right of the State* to construct, operate, and control the mainline facilities of the State project; and that *the State shall exercise control with respect to determination and administration of the right to the use of water.*[21]

California has had no general legislation providing subsidies to irrigation nor any excess land provision.[22] Federal financing, on the contrary, is very generous under reclamation, and carries an excess land provision. When federal subsidies are spurned by local interests, it is for special reasons. Unmistakably the real bone of contention over San Luis project was the excess land law, and the desire to enforce or avoid it influenced the choice between federal and State projects, and when the choice was made, raised the question which law should govern them into an issue.

The bill, S. 1887, which reached the Senate floor in the 85th Congress was a compromise. It provided for federal construction and offered the benefits of federal financing to all interests in California. It offered to its friends the application of the excess land law to one area to be served by the federal project; it offered to its opponents the exemption of waters flowing to another area, outside the federal project.[23]

The principal instrument of exemption, inserted apparently in response to the views from Kern County interests, was an amendment added by the Senate committee just as the bill reached the floor on August 15, 1958. By this procedure, the legislation proposed on the most controversial issue escaped some of the attention it would have drawn if made public earlier. The amendment read, in part:

> Sec. 7. The provisions of the Federal reclamation laws shall not be applicable to water deliveries or to the use of drainage facilities serving lands under contract with the State to receive a water supply, outside of the San Luis service area . . . .[24]

Senators Douglas and Morse tried on the Senate floor to strike out section 7 together with a clause applying the excess land law except when "inconsistent with this act." California Senators demanded retention of

---

[21] Testimony of Allen Bottorff, *1958 Hearings on S. 1887*, at 101–09. (Emphasis added.)
[22] Financing the water program enacted in June 1959 depends on popular approval of a bond issue in 1960. San Francisco Chronicle, June 23, 1959, p. 34, col. 1.
[23] 104 CONG. REC. 17723–35 (1958).
[24] *Id.* at 17724.

section 7 as necessary protection to their State from what they called federal imposition. They minimized discussion of excess lands. When Senator Morse inquired of Senator Kuchel as to the "present pattern of landownership" and "size of the land holdings" in the area to be exempted from the excess land law—an area known generally and from public records to consist of vast landholdings—the latter replied: "It is not known to me . . ." and changed the subject to a prospective State water program.[25]

Senators Douglas and Morse failed to preserve the excess land law. The Senators from California, with active help from Senator Clinton P. Anderson, chairman of the Senate committee, overrode Senators Douglas and Morse to secure Senate passage of the bill with the exemptions from reclamation law desired by spokesmen for Kern County interests. The House, however, failed to act, so the bill died with the expiration of the 85th Congress.

A revised San Luis bill, S. 44, was prepared in the 86th Congress and presented originally in identical form to both Houses. Essentially it represented the same compromise embodied previously in S. 1887 of the preceding session. The section carrying the exemption passed in preceding session had been omitted from the original draft submitted to the 86th Congress by "inadvertence," as Senator Kuchel explained.[26] It was restored, and proved again to be the main issue in the Senate.

This time the outcome of debate on the floor of the Senate was precisely the reverse of the outcome in August, 1958. After 4 days of debate conducted mainly by Senators Kuchel and Engle of California on one side, and Senators Douglas of Illinois and Morse of Oregon on the other, the Senate eliminated the identical exemption from the excess land law it had approved 9 months earlier.[27]

---

[25] *Id.* at 17733. Extensive data on size and pattern of landholding appear, for example, in *Hearings on S. 912 Before a Subcommittee of the Senate Committee on Public Lands*, 80th Cong., 1st Sess. 861 (1947); *1958 Hearings on S. 1425, S. 2541 & S. 3448*, at 181.

[26] 105 CONG. REC. 6726 (daily ed. May 5, 1959).

[27] It is not entirely clear whether Senators Kuchel and Engle were equally devoted to the particular means of removing the excess land limitation represented by § 6(a), S. 44 (§ 7, S. 1887, 85th Cong., 2d Sess. (1958)). During the debate in the 86th Congress Senator Morse said: "The junior Senator from California, in my judgment, has never gone as far as the senior Senator from California has gone in respect to section 6(a). He has left me with the impression that he would be perfectly willing to have section 6(a) come out of the bill, because he does not believe it makes any difference whether it stays in or comes out. Of course, the junior Senator from California is in a position that many of us find ourselves in from time to time. He would like to go along with his colleague, because his colleague, the senior Senator from California, happens to be the leader in the fight for section 6(a), and therefore the junior Senator is not advocating deleting section 6(a). But certainly he has made it clear in the debate that he has no objection if it comes out. In other words, he is not insisting that it stay in." Senator Engle replied, "The distinguished Senator from Oregon has represented my position correctly." 105 CONG. REC. 7168 (daily ed. May 12, 1959). At another point, Senator Engle said, "I want to make a record which is very plain indeed that in my opinion the section is

Congressional hearings and debate reveal the complexities of the excess land problem that tend to obscure a simple principle, and that have led even specialists almost to despair.[28] To follow the course of the San Luis bills of 1959 through Congress is an exercise in clarification.

The San Luis bills were drawn and presented on an assumption that there were to be two projects, represented by water deliveries to a "Federal service area," and to a "State service area," respectively. Some of the facilities, however, including a reservoir, canal, and pumping plant were designated as "joint-use facilities." The State of California was expected to make financial contributions toward the cost of construction and to share the use of federal facilities to transfer water from northern sources to southern areas of delivery.[29]

The argument for an exemption from the excess land law, led on the floor of the Senate by Senators Kuchel and Engle, comprised four main points: (1) The State project is separate, except for joint use of certain facilities, from the federal projects; (2) federal law should not be imposed on the State project; (3) any policy governing distribution of water and benefits from the State projects should be left to the State to decide; and (4) everyone (or nearly everyone) interested in the project is agreed upon the bill.

(1) Senator Kuchel stated the first point in these words:

> [T]wo systems—one a Federal project in being; the other, a State project about to get underway—would both be served at San Luis, the point where they cross, by a single storage reservoir whose cost of construction and operation would be shared by both governments.[30]

---

surplusage. It is merely a statement of what the law is." To Senator Douglas' demand, "If it is surplusage, then eliminate it," Senator Engle replied, "The people affected want this additional assurance." 105 CONG. REC. 6738 (daily ed. May 5, 1959). The identity of the interests affected is discussed *infra*, text at note 178. Senator Richard Neuberger of Oregon, a member of the Senate committee that had approved S. 44, joined Senators Douglas and Morse. See *id.* at 6734; 105 CONG. REC. 7172 (daily ed. May 12, 1959).

[28] In speaking of the San Luis bill in the 85th Congress, Senator Clinton P. Anderson, chairman of the subcommittee, said: "You understand that a person who is not a lawyer, and I am not a lawyer, has a great deal of difficulty following all these things. I try my best to find what is in it that strikes down the limitation. I cannot find it." *1958 Hearings on S. 1425, S. 2541 & S. 3448*, at 159.

[29] See S. 44, H.R. 301, H.R. 5687 and H.R. 7155, 86th Cong., 1st Sess. (1959).

[30] 105 CONG. REC. 6725 (daily ed. May 5, 1959). See also 105 CONG. REC. 6888 (daily ed. May 7, 1959); 104 CONG. REC. 17731 (1958).

Whether one, several, or many federal facilities are desired for eventual use as part of the State project is not wholly clear. The 1956 State Water Plan regards Folsom Reservoir on the American River, constructed by the federal government and an integral part of Central Valley, as part of the State project for delivering water from northern sources to areas south of San Luis: "These large foothill reservoirs, including Folsom, are considered to be features of the California Aqueduct system but will also serve some local purposes." See 2 CAL. WATER RESOURCES BD., BULL. NO. 3, REPORT ON THE CALIFORNIA WATER PLAN 9–239 (preliminary ed. 1956).

If the State system were physically separate from the federal system, of course federal law would not apply to the State system, but it was *not* separate. The fact that it was not separate became crucial. As Senator Kuchel acknowledged with evident regret, "If there were two reservoir sites, and if the State developed one reservoir site and the federal government developed the second reservoir site, so there would be two parallel systems, each with a storage reservoir, there would be no problem."[31] But since the projects were joined, Senators Kuchel and Engle were obliged to ask for an exemption from federal law, and in order to support their request, to try to create an image of separation in which the physical fact of joint-use would be minimized or overlooked. Senator Engle tried to do this by describing the supposed financial separation of State and federal systems. He argued:

> [T]here will not be a plugged nickel of Federal money in the State project, and everything the State does in order to put a bucketful of water on a square foot of land will be paid for with State money. That is the reason why we have a provision in the bill that the Reclamation law shall not apply to a wholly divisible, completely separate program that is paid for, lock, stock, and barrel—powerhouse and all—by the State taxpayers. . . . All the Federal Government has done has been to build the first story of the structure. The second story goes on at no cost to the Federal Government. . . . The State government will pay every nickel of its share. Not a penny of it will be charged to the Federal taxpayers. . . . The projects are completely severable. They do not overlap or intermix.[32]

A few days later Senator Engle, in pressing his argument again, spoke of "projects built by the State government, projects for which the State has paid every cent.[33]" To this, Senator Douglas replied:

> Previously, they have been saying this would be a 100 percent State project. But it turns out to be nothing of the sort. A large part of the basic cost of the Oroville project is to be charged to the Federal government, in the case of the flood control, and possibly navigation costs; and only the residue, or the irrigation costs, are to be borne by the State government. And as I shall shortly suggest, perhaps even some of these irrigation costs of the so-called State project will also be thrust on the Federal government . . . . This shows what an illusion it is to call this a separate State project . . . .[34]

Senator Engle volunteered that he had sponsored the law authorizing a federal nonreimbursable flood control contribution to the State project,

---

[31] 105 CONG. REC. 7071 (daily ed. May 11, 1959). See also Senator Morse's remark: "If there is a case of solely State waters, of course it does not apply; that is up to the State legislature to determine." *Id.* at 7074; 105 CONG. REC. 7168 (daily ed. May 12, 1959).

[32] 105 CONG. REC. 6731, 6732 (daily ed. May 5, 1959). Senator Douglas remarked during this colloquy that it would be "impossible to have a second story without the federal expenditures on the foundation and the first story."

[33] 105 CONG. REC. 7056 (daily ed. May 11, 1959).

[34] *Id.* at 7057, 7058.

and was "proud" of it.[35] Senator Douglas inserted in the Record a page and a half of material that Senator Engle had inserted in the Record as Congressman in 1957, proposing that the federal government should make interest-free contributions to the State project as well.[36] The Engle proposal of 1957, if adopted, would have preserved the generosity of federal reclamation law to the State and dispensed with policy.

(2) Senator Kuchel, directing his remarks toward Senator Frank J. Lausche of Ohio, who had joined debate on the side of Senators Douglas and Morse, stated the second point in his and Senator Engle's argument for an exemption from the excess land law:

> We believe that when one reservoir is jointly used by the State and by the Federal Government it is unconstitutional for the Federal Government to tell the State of the Senator from Ohio or my State how it shall use its water in a State system, when the water comes from that system.[37]

This argument resembles one used by former Senator Sheridan Downey to support the Elliot-rider exemption of Central Valley project from the excess land law in 1944, which Senator Carl Hatch of New Mexico disposed of in these words:

> [T]he Senator from California has said here on the floor that officials of the Reclamation Service are trying to straitjacket the people of California. The people of California came to the Congress of the United States and obtained the appropriations under the reclamation laws. No one here is trying to do anything to California.[38]

No proposal was before the Senate in 1959 to impose federal law upon a California State project. The language of section 6(a) showed on its face that this was not the issue:

> The provisions of the Federal reclamation laws *shall not be applicable to water deliveries* or to the use of drainage facilities serving lands under contract with the State to receive a water supply, outside of the Federal San Luis unit service area described in the report of the Department of the Interior, entitled "San Luis Unit, Central Valley Project," dated December 17, 1956.[39]

Senators Douglas and Morse made it clear that the only issue before the Senate was whether an area in California should be made an exception to existing reclamation law.

The Warren Act of 1911, whose terms section 6(a) would breach

---

[35] *Id.* at 7057.
[36] *Id.* at 7058, 7059.
[37] 105 Cong. Rec. 6888 (daily ed. May 7, 1959).
[38] 90 Cong. Rec. 9499 (1944).
[39] S. 44, 86th Cong., 1st Sess. § 6(a) (1959). (Emphasis added.) See 105 Cong. Rec. 6729 (daily ed. May 5, 1959).

specifically, was designed to provide the basis for cooperation in reclamation between the federal government and other agencies, public and private, corporate and individual. Federal cooperation was offered on the basis of compliance with federal policy, *i.e.*, that "water shall not be furnished from any such reservoir or delivered through any such canal or ditch to any one landowner in excess of an amount sufficient to irrigate one hundred and sixty acres. . . ."[40]

(3) The third point in the argument of Senators Kuchel and Engle was that authority to determine policy on the State project belonged, and should be left, to the State. Senator Kuchel said the bill "should unequivocably declare that Federal laws will not in any way or manner affect lands which may be supplied from features which are a part of the California water plan." He demanded that "the water for storage in this reservoir which is to be used by the State of California in the State system, paid for by the people of California, and almost completely to be used for domestic purposes, shall be governed by the law of the State of California, and by the law of the State of California alone."[41]

Senator Douglas, rejecting Senator Kuchel's view, including his opinion that the State water would be "almost completely for 'domestic' use," said:

> The State of California has no acreage limitation law. . . . We can be certain that if and when water is put on the second block of land, it will be put on land owned by the large landholders.[42]

> [I]f the State wants to adopt its own acreage limitation, that will be fine. Let the State do so first, however, and then let it come back to us. Let us not destroy the federal land policy now, before the State acts, on the basis of hope.[43]

He was not optimistic that the California Legislature would pass a limitation:

> Since it was not possible to pass any legislation there upholding the 160-acre limitation in the past, I cannot believe that the California Legislature, much as it has improved, will pass such a law in the future.[44]

Senator Engle suggested a more favorable prospect in the State legislature, by introducing a telegram from Governor Edmund G. Brown of California, giving support to Senator Kuchel and himself in the view that policy in the State service areas "should come as a result of State legislation." Governor Brown said: "I intend, at an appropriate time and before contracts are executed, to take this matter up with the California Legis-

---

[40] Warren Act, 36 Stat. 925, 926 (1911), 43 U.S.C. § 523 (1952).

[41] 105 Cong. Rec. 6726 (daily ed. May 5, 1959).

[42] 105 Cong. Rec. 7165 (daily ed. May 12, 1959).

[43] 105 Cong. Rec. 7061 (daily ed. May 11, 1959). See also *id.* at 7076.

[44] 105 Cong. Rec. 6890 (daily ed. May 7, 1959).

lature in order to preclude the undesirable results which I have described . . ." and expressed his belief "that the California Legislature . . . is . . . opposed to any unjust enrichment or monopolization of benefits by owners of large landholdings as a result of either Federal or State operation."[45]

Senator Douglas observed that "it is one thing for the Governor to propose such a program, and it is quite another thing for California to enact such a law. Until California comes forward with a law at least as good as the Federal law, I do not believe we should give up the protection the Federal law affords."[46]

(4) Senator Kuchel presented the bill as a measure bearing united approval, federal and State, legislative and executive, Republican and Democrat, and endorsed by past and present officials. Besides himself, a Republican, and Senator Engle, his Democratic colleague, he included among those who had approved the bill the Republican Secretary of the Interior, the Democratic Governor of California, and former Governor, Goodwin J. Knight, a Republican.[47] At another point he included the name of former Democratic Senator Sheridan Downey as further evidence of bi-partisan support for his position.[48]

Senators Neuberger, Morse, and Douglas inserted evidence in the Record that groups and individuals in California supported them in their opposition to alteration of the excess land law, as proposed by Senators Kuchel and Engle. Among these were statements from the California Labor Federation,[49] Grange,[50] Water and Power Users Association,[51] Young Democrats,[52] Democratic Council,[53] party officials,[54] clubs and individuals.[55]

---

[45] *Ibid.*

[46] 105 CONG. REC. 7069 (daily ed. May 11, 1959). See *infra*, text at notes 77–79, reciting the rejections of acreage-limitiation proposals by the California Legislature both prior and subsequent to these debates in the United States Senate.

[47] 105 CONG. REC. 6725 (daily ed. May 5, 1959).

[48] 105 CONG. REC. 7162 (daily ed. May 12, 1959). It is generally believed in California that one of the main reasons Senator Downey did not run for re-election to the Senate in 1950 was the opposition he aroused by persistent efforts to remove the excess land limitation governing the Central Valley project. See remarks of Senator Douglas, 105 CONG. REC. 7069 (daily ed. May 11, 1959).

[49] 105 CONG. REC. 6735 (daily ed. May 5, 1959); 105 CONG. REC. 7054–55 (daily ed. May 11, 1959).

[50] *Id.* at 7053, 7079.

[51] *Id.* at 7079.

[52] 105 CONG. REC. 6735 (daily ed. May 5, 1959); 105 CONG. REC. 7052 (daily ed. May 11, 1959).

[53] *Ibid.*

[54] *Id.* at 7052, 7078.

[55] 105 CONG. REC. 6735 (daily ed. May 5, 1959); 105 CONG. REC. 7165, 7169 (daily ed. May 12, 1959). See also 105 CONG. REC. 6889 (daily ed. May 7, 1959); 105 CONG. REC. 7053, 7062, 7063, 7073 (daily ed. May 11, 1959).

Sponsors of removal of the excess land provision from the area to be served with waters of the State system using federal facilities avoided discussion of the great concentration of landownership there. On this, the very substance of the issue, Senators Kuchel and Engle tended to be evasive or silent.[56]

Senators Douglas and Morse, on the contrary, spread the facts regarding extreme concentration of ownership extensively on the Record, and appealed strongly to the Senate to preserve national policy as a support to democratic institutions and popular government.[57] Senator Douglas said:

> The power of those holding the land will be enormously increased.[58] . . . The American system is that the person who farms the land should, insofar as possible, be the farm owner. That is the basis on which democracy was established in the Mississippi Valley; but that basis of agrarian democracy does not exist in large areas of California.[59]

Senator Douglas appealed to the California Senators "not to come into this Chamber shackled with the chains of the Southern Pacific Land Co., the Boston Ranch Co., the Kern County Land Co., the Standard Oil Co., the other oil companies, and other large landowners . . .,"[60] and offered to debate the issue with them in California.[61] He summarized the case for preservation of the excess land law in these words:

> What is it in the Federal reclamation law that the two Senators from California want to avoid? They say they do not want the Federal reclamation law to apply in this 500,000-acre block of land—of course they never tell us precisely where or how much it is—which will be brought in after the initial 440,000 acres are.

---

[56] 105 CONG. REC. 6889 (daily ed. May 7, 1959); 105 CONG. REC. 6733 (daily ed. May 5, 1959). At one point in the debate Senator Kuchel stated that the people who wanted the exemption and who would be "affected" by it were not "the big landowners of the Central Valley," but "the city government of the city of Los Angeles." *Id.* at 6738. The excess land law applies to irrigation for agriculture, not to the domestic or industrial uses of water which are given as the chief interests of Southern California. Nevertheless, statements were made in the name of the Metropolitan Water District of Southern California insisting on the language of § 6(a) "to increase the confidence of our people" in view of the "confusion" over applicability of federal and State laws, and also in the name of the Los Angeles Chamber of Commerce "for protection against Federal domination in State water matters." *Hearings on H.R. 301, H.R. 302, H.R. 5681, H.R. 5682, H.R. 5684, and H.R. 5687 Before the Irrigation and Reclamation Subcommittee of the House Committee on Interior and Insular Affairs*, 86th Cong., 1st Sess. 98–99 (1959); *Hearing on S. 44 Before the Irrigation and Reclamation Subcommittee of the Senate Committee on Interior and Insular Affairs*, 86th Cong., 1st Sess. 94–95 (1959).

[57] 105 CONG. REC. 6732, 6733, 6738 (daily ed. May 5, 1959).

[58] *Id.* at 6737, 6739. See also 105 CONG. REC. 7164 (daily ed. May 12, 1959).

[59] 105 CONG. REC. 7058 (daily ed. May 11, 1959).

[60] *Id.* at 7062. See also 105 CONG. REC. 6885 (daily ed. May 7, 1959); 105 CONG. REV. 7166 (daily ed. May 12, 1959).

[61] 105 CONG. REC. 7071 (daily ed. May 11, 1959); 105 CONG. REC. 6889 (daily ed. May 7, 1959). Senator Douglas said: "I hope the Democratic Party of California does not come out in defense of the large landowners." *Ibid.*

Why? There is only one answer—because they do not want the 160-acre limitation to apply. The Senators will not come out openly and say that, but that is the reason.

There is no question of States' rights involved. As a matter of fact, we know California does not have any law on this subject at present.

Knocking out section 6(a) would not replace the Federal reclamation law with a State law. A vacuum would be left. . . . We do not want a vacuum in the law, because into that vacuum will rush the big landowners with their possession of tens of thousands of acres, in some cases over a hundred thousand acres so that they will get an increase in the value of their land, to the extent of $600 an acre, on an average, which will mean enormous benefits. From whom? These benefits will come from the taxpayers of the country as a whole.

In this process the entire irrigation and reclamation program of the country will be so besmeared and discredited that an indignant public will repudiate the whole thing.[62]

The debate ran on during 4 days, until the Douglas-Morse-Neuberger amendment to preserve reclamation law won by a division.[62a] Senator Douglas warned that "if section 6(a) comes back into the bill, I believe it will be found that the Senator from Illinois, the Senators from Oregon, and other Senators will be quite vigorous in their opposition."[63] Nevertheless, the House committee, with six members dissenting, retained the section the Senate had eliminated.[64]

---

[62] 105 CONG. REC. 7076 (daily ed. May 11, 1959).

[62a] 105 CONG. REC. 7170 (daily ed. May 12, 1959).

[63] *Id.* at 7175.

[64] H.R. REP. No. 399, 86th Cong., 1st Sess. 25 (1959). The disputed provision of the House bill was § 7 of H.R. 7155. Congressman B. F. Sisk, author of the San Luis bill in the House, announced in July that he would not seek action before the 1960 session. This decision was reached in consultation with the two Senators and the Governor of California, the House leadership and chairmen of the Interior and Irrigation and Reclamation Committee and Subcommittee, respectively. Congressman Sisk expressed "regret" over the "five months delay," but called delay the "best strategy to insure the earliest actual construction of the project which is so important to the San Joaquin Valley and to the success of the California Water Plan." In explanation he said: "It is not easy to secure approval of any federal reclamation proposal. Because of its size, San Luis naturally will be the subject of extensive debate and the time of its presentation is important." Fresno Bee, July 31, 1959, p. 4-A. He said it "would be difficult to advance" the bill "with other major legislation still pending as Congress moves toward adjournment." San Francisco Chronicle, Aug. 1, 1959, p. 4, cols. 3, 4. In May, Senator Lausche had pointed out specifically that "there are Senators who would vote for the bill" provided it preserved national policy. 105 CONG. REC. 6890 (daily ed. May 7, 1959). After Senate decision to preserve policy, the project carried easily by voice vote. Dissent from the House report was grounded, not on opposition to the project, but on unwillingness to accept the insistence of the majority, including the author of the bill, on rejection of the Senate decision to preserve national policy.

II

STATE LEGISLATURE

[N]o one would believe that shrewd, calculating business men would invest their money on the strength of land rising in value while unimproved, for even the farmer himself has to abandon it who endeavors to add to its value without water. At the same time, purchasers are not lacking who would add it to their already extensive dry domain and the people, in the next legislature, will find themselves confronted by an array of force and talent to secure to capital the ownership of the water as well as of the land, and the people will at last have it to pay for....—Visalia Delta, May 5, 1877[65]

At one stage in the bitter debate, Assemblyman Jesse M. Unruh (Dem—Los Angeles) declared, "At times we have to rise above principle." He had been twitted by Assemblyman Lloyd W. Lowrey (Dem—Rumsey) for opposing the latter's water acreage amendment which is part of both the State and national Democratic platforms.—Earl C. Behrens, 1959[66]

Congress and State legislature play correlative and changing roles in California water development. "Partnership" began, in the limited sense of a creditor-debtor relationship, when federal reclamation started to pour funds into the State, and the legislature, in order to facilitate receiving them, authorized State water districts to enter into repayment contracts in compliance with federal reclamation law.[67] The Central Valley Project Act of 1933, approved by legislature and voters alike, gave the State Water Project Authority the "full power to do any and all things necessary in order to avail itself of such [federal] aid, assistance and cooperation under *Federal legislation now or hereafter enacted by Congress.*"[68] On May 26, 1936, the State senate and assembly memorialized Congress in identical resolutions to make continuing appropriations to assure completion of the Central Valley project which President Franklin D. Roosevelt had made "reimbursable in accordance with the Reclamation Law."[69]

No one in California, apparently, ever has dissented from the general and officially expressed desire to encourage the flow of federal funds into the State for water development. Attitudes toward federal policy for distributing water and preventing speculative gain, however, have differed sharply. As early as 1937, Kern County interests sought ways of obtaining

---

[65] Page 2, col. 3.
[66] San Francisco Chronicle, June 18, 1959, p. 15, col. 1.
[67] CAL. WATER CODE §§ 23175-302. These sections were first enacted in 1917. Cal. Stat. 1917, c. 562. The first federal reclamation project in California was begun before World War I at Orland, in the Sacramento Valley; a 40-acre water limitation was applied.
[68] CAL. WATER CODE § 11500. (Emphasis added.)
[69] CAL. SENATE JOUR., Extraord. Sess. 13-14, 35-36 (1936).

federal aid and at the same time avoiding the excess land law, whether through administrators[70] or through Congress.[71]

Use of the State of California for this purpose was attempted about 1944 in the form of a proposal that it should purchase Central Valley project from the federal government.[72] State purchase of Central Valley project suffered from the disadvantage in winning popular support that it proposed substitution of State for federal funds for *past* construction.[73] More recently a State Feather River project, proposing use of State funds for *future* construction has proved more attractive. Yet efforts have proceeded in the face of great resistance and, very slowly, to obtain, successively, legislative authorization of a State Feather River project in 1951,[74] an appropriation of $25,190,000 for acquisition of land and relocation of highway in 1957,[75] and an appropriation to begin construction in 1959.[76]

In 1957 an amendment to incorporate an excess land provision in the Feather River Project bill was tabled in the assembly without debate by vote of 46 to 25. Assemblyman Francis C. Lindsay, author of the bill, opposed the amendment on the ground that it was not the time to raise questions of policy. He "urged the legislators to defer policy arguments about power and other matters until their spring session and concentrate during this short January meeting on a simple form of appropriation, merely providing the money asked by Governor Goodwin J. Knight...."[77]

The legislature acted similarly in 1959. As if to validate Senator

---

[70] Testimony of Roland Curran, secretary-manager, Central Valley Project Association, *Hearings on S. 912 Before a Subcommittee of the Senate Committee on Public Lands*, 80th Cong., 1st Sess. 1310 (1947). For an account of even earlier objections to the excess land law, see testimony of Secretary of the Interior J. A. Krug, *id.* at 991.

[71] The possibility that Congress might rebuff them appeared early. See *Hearings on H.R. 3961 Before a Subcommittee of the Senate Committee on Commerce*, 78th Cong., 2d Sess. 529–788 (1944).

[72] This "proposal, said to have originated among the big landowners of Fresno County, is for the State of California to take over the Central Valley project, paying the entire bill. This, too, would sidestep the 160-acre limitation." Business Week, May 13, 1944, p. 24. See also BUREAU OF PUBLIC ADMINISTRATION, UNIVERSITY OF CAL., CENTRAL VALLEY PROJECT: FEDERAL OR STATE? (May, 1955) (report prepared by Hugh G. Hansen, for the bureau, for California Assembly Interim Committee on Conservation, Planning and Public Works, pursuant to House Resolution No. 177, 1953). About the same time the California Legislature memorialized Congress by joint resolution to pass the Elliot rider exempting Central Valley project from the excess land law. Cal. Stat. 1945, c. 24, p. 285.

[73] Senator Morse: "Various State takeover proposals were made. These fell because they were far too big a chunk for California's taxpayers to swallow." 105 CONG. REC. 7166 (daily ed. May 12, 1959).

[74] Cal. Stat. 1951, c. 1441, § 2.

[75] Cal. Stat. 1957, c. 15, § 1.

[76] Oakland Tribune, June 21, 1959, p. 1, col. 2.

[77] Sacramento Bee, January 23, 1957, p. A-6, col. 2. Public policy amendments, sponsored by Assemblyman Lloyd Lowrey, who sponsored the excess land amendment, failed of passage twice in eight hours. 1 CAL. ASSEMBLY JOUR., Reg. Sess. 808, 809 (1957).

Douglas' prophecy early in May in Washington, that the California Legislature would not approve excess land legislation, the State senate defeated an excess land amendment to Governor Brown's water program bill on May 29th. Its sponsor, State Senator Virgil O'Sullivan, argued that without a State acreage limitation " 'we are going to make a few millionaires and add to the millions some already have.' " Leading the fight for the Governor's bill, Senator Hugh M. Burns told the State senate this was " 'neither the time nor the legislation' " in which to deal with acreage limitation, and the amendment was defeated, 25 to 10.[78]

The assembly also declined to approve excess land (and public power preference) proposals. Assemblyman John A. O'Connell "contended the legislature should decide the issues *before* the state votes on the proposed $1,750,000,000 bond issue . . . ." The Assembly Water Committee, however, referred both bills for "interim study."[79] Thus the 1959 session of the legislature ended with passage of a proposal, silent on policy, asking the people to finance State water projects by a bond issue.

Congressional procedure usually is to pass an authorization bill first, declaring policy. Appropriations to finance construction of the authorized project are considered afterwards. Congress followed this customary procedure in passing the National Reclamation Act of 1902, which was an authorization bill. It could not have passed Congress except for the inclusion of an excess land policy. The debates show this, and it has been attested to by a competent witness, John E. Raker, judge and later Congressman. He said in 1905: "The committee of seventeen [western members of Congress] that originally planned and arranged the adoption of the National Irrigation Law secured its adoption and presentation to Congress solely and entirely upon the question that the great land monopolies in the United States would be prohibited from getting the benefit of it."[80]

When the State of California planned its first great State water project in 1933, the legislature joined policy to finance in the bond issue for $170,000,000 that it submitted to the voters for a State Central Valley project.[81] The successful campaign for passage of the referendum relied heavily on its policy provisions to win support for the bond issue.[82]

---

[78] Sacramento Bee, May 30, 1959, p. A-6, col. 1. A public power preference amendment also sponsored by State Senator O'Sullivan was defeated by 21 to 16.

[79] Sacramento Bee, June 3, 1959, p. A-10, col. 5. (Emphasis added.)

[80] PROCEEDINGS, THIRTEENTH NATIONAL IRRIGATION CONGRESS (Portland, Oregon) 61, (1905).

[81] CAL. WATER CODE §§ 11464, 11500. This policy, in this instance, was public power preference; excess land policy had not been raised as an issue at that time, *but see supra*, note 68.

[82] CAL. LEGISLATIVE COUNSEL, REFERENDUM MEASURE TO BE SUBMITTED TO THE ELECTORS OF THE STATE OF CALIFORNIA AT SPECIAL ELECTION TO BE HELD TUESDAY, DEC. 19, 1933 (voters' guide, distributed by Cal. Secretary of State), on file in Bureau of Public Administration Library, University of California, Berkeley.

Governor Brown, however, rejected this procedure in 1959, by opposing inclusion of policy in his bond issue measure. When the legislature followed the Governor's recommendation by defeating policy in the State senate, Governor Brown approved: "Some of the principles (in the amendments) are sound," he said, "but they don't belong in bond legislation designed to provide financing, not to settle every water argument in the state."[83]

Just after the legislature passed the water bill, a leading California newspaper that had supported the Governor's program said that action on policy should come earlier than had been planned. It said editorially that, among other matters, acreage limitation "ought to be resolved *before* the voters are asked to pass on the bond issue."[84] The California Labor Federation, too, pressed for early action. It supported its request by a political warning: "If the Governor fails to propose, or is unsuccessful in securing anti-enrichment protections, he may go down as the Democratic Governor who put California in the water and power business for the enrichment of landed monopolists rather than the people of the State of California."[85]

The absence of policy from the bond issue might be sufficient to defeat it, since people like to know the purpose for which they spend money. So far as concerns excess land policy, a few weeks earlier Senator Morse had raised a question whether "This evanescent project, . . . this alleged State project we are dealing with . . . is merely a vision created in the hope that it can somehow transform everybody's water to water reserved only for a few people."[86]

The passage of the Governor's water program by the legislature advanced the prospects for State water projects, but these remained exposed to objections on many and diverse grounds, and uncertain.[87] The

---

[83] Sacramento Bee, May 30, 1959, p. A-6, col. 1.

[84] Sacramento Bee, June 20, 1959, p. B-20, col. 1. (Emphasis added.)

[85] San Francisco Chronicle, June 21, 1959, p. 18, col. 5.

[86] 105 CONG. REC. 7166 (daily ed. May 12, 1959). Ernest A. Engelbert, of the University of California at Los Angeles, writes: "States operate under a handicap in the resources field because a general suspicion exists that the States are not strong enough to protect the public interest. Historically speaking, this is well-justified. . . . Furthermore, interest groups dealing in natural resources appear to dominate state legislatures and administrative agencies in a number of states, particularly in the West. . . . [T]he Federal Government can counter-balance undesirable state and regional pressures with political pressures from other regions and nationally." BUREAU OF PUBLIC ADMINISTRATION, UNIVERSITY OF CAL., CENTRAL VALLEY PROJECT: FEDERAL OR STATE? 286-87 (May, 1955).

[87] The fate of the water bond issue depended on many considerations besides the excess land law, important as this was. The San Francisco Chronicle, for example, which had been neither unfriendly to passage of the water bill by the legislature, nor friendly to an excess land provision, said editorially within a week: "Beyond dispute, the water bill as written and adopted under pressure leaves scores of the most pertinent questions unanswered. Unless they are answered to our satisfaction, this newspaper cannot conscientiously support this bond issue." San Francisco Chronicle, June 23, 1959, p. 34. The same editorial page carried excerpts from a talk by Samuel B. Morris, formerly general manager and chief engineer of the Los Angeles Department of Water and Power, under the heading "Water Bill Says Nothing About Payoff."

next step is a giant bond issue of $1,750,000,000, or about twice the size of federal investment in Central Valley in the last twenty years. The bonds are general obligation, not revenue bonds. Sectional and other differences of interest and opinion remain. These are among the serious considerations that cast doubt upon the outcome of popular vote on the Governor's bond issue in 1960.

III

EXECUTIVE

*[T]he present acreage limitation . . . should be complied with, until the District has fully discharged its obligations to the Federal Government.—*Secretary of the Interior Fred A. Seaton, 1957[88]

*My concern is with the use of an administrative order to overturn an act of Congress. . . . Neither the 81st nor the 82nd Congress accepted Congressman Werdel's twice-offered invitation to approve the interpretation that Secretary McKay advanced, and that you are offering to water users now. . . . Within the past thirty days . . . the Senate has struck down after four long days of searching debate an exemption from the excess land law on lands adjacent to Kings River . . . . You will realize my shock, therefore, Mr. Secretary, to learn from a news dispatch . . . that your subordinates are again offering to honor the protested interpretation of law on Kings River that will turn the statutory limitation into a mockery.—*Senator Paul Douglas, 1957, 1959[89]

Secretary of the Interior Fred A. Seaton has authorized negotiation of repayment contracts on Kings River and Tulare Lake project[89a] that will not require large landholders to dispose of their excess holdings to obtain water as prescribed by the excess land law.[90] The limitation will not apply when a district has "fully discharged its [financial] obligations to the Federal government," apparently whether payments are completed after the customary 40 years of interest-free installment payments or by a single lump sum prepayment.[91]

---

[88] Letter from Secretary of the Interior Seaton to Philip A. Gordon, president, board of directors, Kings River Conservation District, July 12, 1957, copy on file in Bancroft Library, University of California, Berkeley. (Emphasis added.)

[89] Letter from Senator Douglas to Secretary of the Interior Seaton, Dec. 16, 1957, reproduced in *Hearings on S. 1425, S. 2541, and S. 3448 Before the Subcommittee on Irrigation and Reclamation of the Senate Committee on Interior and Insular Affairs*, 85th Cong., 2d Sess. 23 (1958) [hereinafter cited as *1958 Hearings on S. 1425, S. 2541 & S. 3448*]; Letter from Senator Douglas to Secretary of the Interior Seaton, June 9, 1959, copy on file in Bancroft Library, University of California, Berkeley.

[89a] This project was authorized by the Flood Control Act of 1944, ch. 665, § 10, 58 Stat. 891, 901.

[90] Letter from Secretary Seaton to Philip A. Gordon, *supra* note 88.

[91] Newspapers report contract negotiations in progress that offer Kings River districts the option of avoiding disposal of excess lands by prepayment, and an expectation among Sacramento regional officials of the Bureau of Reclamation that the contracts will be approved by the Secretary. See *infra*, text at note 169.

Douglas McKay, Secretary Seaton's immediate predecessor, tendered the same offer with but a single difference. Secretary McKay was ready to permit either *individual* excess landholders or entire *districts,* by making a lump sum prepayment, to avoid the necessity of disposing of their excess holdings.[92] Secretary Seaton has made this option available only to *districts.* Both grounded their authorization on the argument that when financial obligations are met, the law does not require continued compliance with the 160-acre limitation.

In an exchange of correspondence with Senator Paul Douglas,[93] Secretary Seaton set forth the grounds on which he relies in defending his authorization of such negotiations:

> You will appreciate, I am sure, my reluctance to overturn by administrative order, an interpretation of 43 years' standing which could have been modified legislatively by Congress on numerous occasions while considering bills or enacting laws pertaining to that subject. This does not infer that I disagree with the basic interpretation that has been so long applied. But even if I were in disagreement, I do not believe it would be proper for me to overturn at this late date a construction tacitly approved by Congress and thereby unsettle many property rights in the West.[94]

The arguments advanced may be conveniently summarized: (1) the interpretation of the law relied on is one of 43 years' standing; (2) the interpretation has "tacit" congressional support in the form of (a) approval of contracts containing the disputed provision, and (b) failure to act to change the law to counteract the administrative ruling; (3) property rights, built on the interpretation, would be unsettled by its abandonment. These arguments will be considered seriatim.

---

[92] Letter from Secretary of the Interior McKay to C. J. Haggerty, secretary-treasurer, California State Federation of Labor, March 2, 1954, copy on file in Bancroft Library, University of California, Berkeley.

[93] Letter from Senator Douglas to Secretary of the Interior Seaton, Dec. 16, 1957, reproduced in *1958 Hearings on S.1425, S.2541 & S.3448,* at 23. Senator Douglas placed the correspondence in the Record on April 30, 1958; at that time he had received no reply to his last letter to the Secretary, written 16 months earlier, which the Secretary said he had referred to Department of the Interior Solicitor Elmer F. Bennett "for consideration and reply."

[94] Letter from Secretary of the Interior Seaton to Senator Douglas, October 21, 1957, reproduced in *id.* at 21. This statement is in part a repetition of a thesis stated 3 years earlier by Secretary McKay, who said that "in view of the period of time that has elapsed since the ruling mentioned above and the actions that have been taken directly or indirectly in reliance upon it, it is my view that the Department is constrained to follow the precedents already set, *unless they should clearly be demonstrated to be wrong* or unless the law is changed." Letter from Secretary of the Interior McKay to George Sehlmeyer, master, California State Grange, March 2, 1954, reproduced in U.S. DEP'T OF THE INTERIOR, EXCESS LAND PROVISIONS OF THE FEDERAL RECLAMATION LAWS AND THE PAYMENT OF CHARGES, pt. 1, app. 61:2 (May, 1956) [hereinafter cited as EXCESS LAND PROVISIONS]. (Emphasis added.) No evidence can be found that the opinion has ever come before the courts. Secretary Seaton was willing (at least for the sake of argument) to go one step beyond Secretary McKay by waiving the condition, "unless ... clearly ... demonstrated to be wrong."

(1) The Secretary's first argument is that the interpretation of the law on which his action rests is one of "43 years' standing." The reference date is unconvincing. The first departmental expression of opinion on the subject is found in an administrative hearing held in 1913. It was there stated that the completion of payment had no effect on the applicability of the excess land limitation, and that "the language on this point is *susceptible of but one construction*...."[95] In 1914, an opinion of Reclamation Service Counsel, Will R. King[96]—the basis of Secretary Seaton's argument—was submitted, but it lay dormant for many years without action in reliance on it. In 1947, thirty-three years after the opinion was written and only 12 years before the time at which Secretary Seaton is speaking, the Commissioner of the Bureau of Reclamation, Michael W. Straus, was uncertain as to the proper interpretation of the law; he was unwilling to rely on the 1914 King Opinion without further legal advice.[97] The Commissioner has since placed the beginning of concern over the question in 1947, with the most intense activity being delayed until the end of 1951 and the beginning of 1952.[98]

At least through 1952, Straus' original doubts as to the reliability of the interpretation were widely shared by California interests. Congressman Thomas H. Werdel introduced bills in 1950[99] and in 1951[100] to assure that in relation to Kings River the completion of payments would remove the limitation of the excess land law. Neither bill passed.

The failure of these bills in Congress did not deter either Secretary McKay or Secretary Seaton from authorizing negotiation on the basis that completion of payment would remove the excess land limitation. They had some further legal support, however. A 1947 memorandum of Interior Department Associate Solicitor Felix Cohen—given in reply to Commis-

---

[95] Keebaugh & Cook, 42 L. Dec. 543, 545 (1913). (Emphasis added.) For a review of early opinions, see also U.S. BUREAU OF RECLAMATION, DEP'T OF THE INTERIOR, LANDOWNERSHIP SURVEY ON FEDERAL RECLAMATION PROJECTS 32–42 (1946).

[96] Edwin E. Kaine, 43 L. Dec. 339 (1914). This has been accepted subsequently as the only authoritative expression on the matter. The earlier ruling has been ignored, and it is as if King's opinion had been substituted for it. It was King's opinion which formed the only basis for the Cohen Memorandum. See *infra*, text at note 102.

[97] See *infra*, note 102.

[98] "Reclamation has now been engaged in seeking resolution of this matter for six years and most intensively *for 13 months without success*." Letter from Commissioner of the Bureau of Reclamation Michael W. Straus to Secretary of the Interior McKay, Feb. 4, 1953, reproduced in EXCESS LAND PROVISIONS, *op. cit. supra* note 94, pt. 1, app. 56:1. (Emphasis added.)

[99] H.R. 7915, 81st Cong., 2d Sess. (1950). See *infra*, note 100.

[100] H.R. 413, 82d Cong., 1st Sess. (1951). These were identical bills, introduced March 29, 1950, and January 3, 1951, respectively. Proposed to make mandatory acceptance of lump sum payment and "in consideration of" this payment specified that the water users of Kings River would receive right to the "perpetual use for irrigation purposes, in such manner as such water users deem desirable, of the entire flow (including flood waters) of the **Kings River, subject only to**" United States flood control regulation of Pine Flat Dam.

sioner Straus' inquiry[101]—relied on the King Opinion of 1914 without examination or question.[102] In addition, Secretary Seaton had received from Solicitor Elmer F. Bennett the advice that "further review" of the interpretation of the law embodied in the King-Cohen Opinion was not "warranted at this time."[103]

Nevertheless, Secretary McKay remained sufficiently unsure of the legality of the interpretation to leave office in the Spring of 1956 without signing the Kings River contract which his subordinates had negotiated on terms he had previously authorized.[104] On July 12, 1957, Secretary Seaton refused to sign the contracts which Secretary McKay had left unsigned. He noted that "a very large part, approximately one-fourth" of the lands on the Kings River project, is in excess holdings.[105] The contract

---

[101] See *supra*, text at note 97.

[102] Felix S. Cohen, Associate Solicitor, U.S. Dep't of the Interior, Memorandum M-35004 to Commissioner, Bureau of Reclamation, Oct. 22, 1947, reproduced in EXCESS LAND PROVISIONS, *op. cit. supra* note 94, pt. 1, app. 27. The memorandum was given in reply to Commissioner Straus's question: "Does the payment in full of construction charges against 'excess lands' free such lands of the acreage limitations of the reclamation laws . . . ?" The answer given was in the affirmative. Associate Solicitor Cohen relied on King's 1914 Opinion without examination or question. In turn, the Cohen Opinion has been relied on since 1947. Hereinafter, the interpretation of the reclamation law embodied in these opinions will be referred to as the "King-Cohen Opinion."

It should be noted that the phrasing of the Commissioner's question is inharmonious with the language of a later decision of the Supreme Court of the United States. He speaks of freeing lands;" the Supreme Court said that the reclamation law was "designed to benefit people, not land." Ivanhoe Irr. Dist. v. McCracken, 357 U.S. 275, 297 (1958).

[103] Memorandum accompanying Letter from Secretary of the Interior Seaton to Senator Douglas, Oct. 21, 1957, reproduced in *1958 Hearings on S. 1425, S. 2541 & S. 3448*, at 21. The King-Cohen Opinion rests on grounds the author has analyzed in detail, concluding that "it is difficult to find reasonable ground either in the law or its legislative history to explain why administrators have accepted . . . [it], apparently without question." Taylor, *Excess Land Law: Execution of a Public Policy*, 64 YALE L.J. 477, 501 (1955). This analysis need not be repeated here. However, it may be noted that data discovered in subsequent research strengthen an answer previously given. King had supported his interpretation by analogy to what he alleged to be fact, viz., that Congress *never* had placed a limit in prior land laws on "the amount of land which a man may own *after having complied in full with the provisions of the law in order to acquire the title*. . . ." Edwin E. Kaine, 43 L. Dec. 339, 340 (1914). (Emphasis added.) King overlooked at least four contrary examples: one from the homestead laws of 1889, 25 Stat. 854, 43 U.S.C. § 214 (1952); another in reclamation laws barely 3 years prior to his giving the opinion, 36 Stat. 925 (1911), 43 U.S.C. § 524 (1952); the third, a 5000-acre limitation on corporate landownership in territories, the Act of May 3, 1887, ch. 340, § 3, 24 Stat. 476; and the fourth, a 500-acre limitation on corporate landownership in Puerto Rico, 31 Stat. 715 (1900), 48 U.S.C. § 752 (1952).

[104] The Flood Control Act of 1944, 58 Stat. 901, 33 U.S.C. §§ 701f, j notes (1952) had authorized lump sum payment on Kings River without specifying any consequences as to policy.

[105] Letter from Secretary of the Interior Seaton to Philip A. Gordon, president, board of directors, Kings River Conservation District, July 12, 1957, copy on file in Bancroft Library, University of California, Berkeley. It should be remembered that on this point there is little difference between Secretaries Seaton and McKay.

in question "extended to each water user, would reduce the statutory limitations to a mere shadow. This would make the test, not one of public policy, but solely one of the financial capability of each landowner to purchase immunity from the statutory restrictions."[106] This record suggests that the administrative interpretation of the law is neither certain nor of "long standing." At least, Secretary Seaton's predecessors have not indicated by their behavior that it was—not even Secretary McKay.

(2) The second ground on which Secretary Seaton relies is that Congress has given "tacit" approval to the interpretation embodied in the King-Cohen Opinion. Beginning in 1949, apparently, clauses have been written into some repayment contracts providing that, on completion of the payments, the excess lands provisions become inoperative. The precise number of contracts actually drawn up in this fashion is not available, but Commissioner Straus has stated that the clause was to be found in "dozens of repayment contracts."[107] On the other hand, an official listing shows that, in the 4-year period between 1949 and 1952, only eleven such contracts were submitted to Congress and approved by it.[108] After the change in the national administration at the beginning of 1953, thirteen more were given approval in less than 2½ years.[109]

The nature of the congressional approval of these contracts suggests that little, if any, consideration was given to the clause in question, because —if for no other reason—the occasion for the submission of these contracts to Congress was not the inclusion of provisions embodying the disputed interpretation.[110] Secretary Seaton, in elaborating his argument, states that congressional approval has been given "tacitly," because if Congress had objected to the administrative interpretation of the law, it could have modified it "on numerous occasions while considering bills or enacting laws pertaining to that subject."[111] Senator Douglas, in reply, remarked that the memorandum accompanying the Secretary's letter cited "no instances

---

[106] *Ibid.*

[107] Commissioner of the Bureau of Reclamation Michael W. Straus, Memorandum for the Record, Feb. 6, 1953, reproduced in EXCESS LAND PROVISIONS, *op. cit. supra* note 94, pt. 1, app. 54:1. Significantly, Commissioner Straus also spoke of these contracts as "recently approved." Letter from Commissioner Straus to Secretary of the Interior McKay, Feb. 4, 1953, reproduced in EXCESS LAND PROVISIONS, *op. cit. supra* note 94, pt. 1, app. 56.

[108] *Id.*, pt. 1, at 49–54.

[109] *Ibid.*

[110] "These contracts have been executed during the period from 1949 to 1955 and as such, of course, are representative of contracts under a relatively small portion of the total of reclamation projects. Part of these contracts were submitted to and approved by the Congress pursuant to Section 7 of the Reclamation Project Act of 1939. *Their authorization* in this manner *was occasioned by the inclusion of substantive provisions unrelated* to the express recognition which they contain concerning the payment of charges and the application of *the excess land limitations.*" *Id.* at 49–50. (Emphasis added.)

[111] See *supra*, text at note 94.

of Congress' express knowledge, discussion or recognition of the King interpretation. To construe a failure to act as a tacit approval under these circumstances is surely more of an exercise in mind reading—the subconscious mind, I mean—than in logical argument."[112] It may be added that the Secretary, for all his zeal in finding evidence of tacit congressional *approval,* appears to have overlooked the rather convincing evidence of congressional disapproval to be found in the repeated rejection of bills explicitly embodying the interpretation.[113]

(3) The final phase of Secretary Seaton's argument is that Western property rights built upon the administrative interpretation of the law would be unsettled if it were now abandoned. It would be more accurate to speak of unsettling the hopes and expectations of property owners holding, or hoping to hold, excess land.[114] The interpretation of the laws on which these hopes are based was not acted on until it found a place in contracts drawn up 47 years after the original passage of the reclamation law.[115] Rumors of its application on Kings River brought sharp protest.[116] Under criticism, Secretaries Chapman and McKay refrained from actually applying the interpretation to the conspicuous excess land holdings of the Kings River project.[117] It is unlikely that either would have failed to protect property rights by standing firm on the King-Cohen interpretation had they believed there were any legally recognizable property rights to protect. Instead, Secretary Seaton refused in 1957 to sign the Kings River project contract, negotiated under Secretary McKay, with the contested interpreta-

---

[112] Letter from Senator Douglas to Secretary of the Interior Seaton, Dec. 16, 1957, reproduced in *1958 Hearings on S. 1425, S. 2541 & S. 3448, op. cit. supra* note 89, at 23. See also *id.* at 23-24, where Senator Douglas says: "I would prefer, as I think you would, to be able to rely on administrative responsibility for a continuous check of the correctness of its own interpretations of statute, rather than require a continuous and meticulous congressional investigation of the administration of law that Mr. Bennett's argument seems to invite if not necessitate."

[113] See *supra,* text at notes 99, 100.

[114] Non-enforcement of the excess land laws is familiar and confers benefits on those for whom the law did not intend them, but these benefits are not property rights. The limitation on corporation landownership in Puerto Rico went unenforced for close to four decades, but no recognizable rights were acquired thereby. People v. Hermanos, Inc., 309 U.S. 543 (1940). A spokesman for Tulare Lake Basin Water Storage District has recognized "lax" and "entirely missing" enforcement among possible "solutions" at hearings in which his preferred solution was to remove the law by congressional action. "[It] . . . would not be a safe solution here. Landowners could not rely on continued future non-enforcement." Testimony of S. T. Harding, *Hearings on S. Res. 295 Before the Subcommittee on Irrigation and Reclamation of the Senate Committee on Interior and Insular Affairs,* 78th Cong., 2d Sess. 363 (1944).

[115] 32 Stat. 390 (1902), 43 U.S.C. § 372 (1952), re-enacted, 44 Stat. 649 (1926), as amended, 43 U.S.C. § 423(e) (1952). See *supra,* note 107.

[116] See statement of M. C. Hermann, quartermaster-adjutant, Department of California, Veterans of Foreign Wars, read into the Record by Congressman John F. Shelley, 97 CONG. REC. 6351-52 (1951). See also EXCESS LAND PROVISIONS, *op. cit. supra* note 94, pt. 1, app. 29:32–:53, :63, :100.

[117] See *supra,* text at note 104.

tion because it offered exemption from the law to individual excess landowners. He was apparently undisturbed at that time by any thought that he might be unsettling property rights established under these contracts.

An inquiry into the various pressures exerted on the relevant officials is more revealing than further examination of the legal arguments advanced. The source of the pressure is excess landowning interests seeking to escape from the legal limitation on their share of benefits from federal reclamation projects. Pressures are exerted, not only by direct resistance to signing contracts, but also in various other ways. The Bureau of Reclamation has suffered severely in some instances, notably on Kings and Kern Rivers, by losing to Army engineers congressional authorization to construct these projects.[117a] The influence of excess landholders seeking to avoid disposal of excess holdings was decisive against the Bureau in both instances. In the heat of the conflict over enforcement of the excess land law in Central Valley in 1948, a Senator persuaded Congress to deprive Commissioner Straus and Sacramento Regional Director for the Bureau of Reclamation, Richard Boke, of their salaries for 5 months by attaching a rider to an appropriation bill excluding them from the payroll and leaving them uncertain whether they would ever be returned to it.[118]

The following is an example of how the influence exerted by these interests have shaped the course of repayment contract negotiations relating to Kings River project in the past 7 years. On January 18, 1952, Commissioner Straus wrote:

> No ... agreement has been reached, and it is the hope of the water users to get this conservation water for free without any repayment and outside of all the reclamation law, including the 160-acre clause .... The Kings River group is negotiating with the philosophy that, if, in truth, they are ever required to make any payment or recognize any part of the Reclamation law, they would go the "lump sum settlement" route, and thereby divest themselves of the acreage restriction obligation. This has troubled the Bureau of Reclamation which is under numerous mandates to negotiate to a successful conclusion with the Kings River group. The particular relationship to the acreage restriction clause has so troubled Regional Director Boke that he has written the attached memorandum of policy inquiry ....
> In the absence of any recognition of any kind of Reclamation law or any agreement as to any repayment by water users for Pine Flat water, I am of the tactical opinion that we should effect and conclude a "lump-sum repayment" contract under the philosophy of the Associate Solicitor's Opinion M-35004. By that procedure, I believe we would come nearer serving public interest than we would if, on imminent completion of the Kings

---

[117a] See Taylor, *Excess Land Law on the Kern?*, 46 CALIF. L. REV. 153, 167 (1958).

[118] The author has described these events elsewhere. See Taylor, *supra* note 103, at 501–06. The re-election of President Truman in 1948 was the decisive event that brought about their reimbursement and restoration.

River Dam, the water users enjoyed the benefit of that conservation water with no repayment and no recognition of any Reclamation law.[119]

In other words, the decision on the part of the Commissioner to act in accord with the disputed interpretation allowing relief from the operation of the 160-acre limitation was not founded on a belief that the law required him to do so, or even that the action was good policy,[120] but that it was a proper *tactic* necessary in response to the determination of the landowners to "escape certain of the harshest applications of the 160-acre rule," *i.e.*, the necessity of disposing with all excess holdings in order to obtain water. Pressure was having its effect, particularly on the Bureau.[121]

Secretary Chapman had found it "gratifying" in relation to earlier negotiations,[122] based on the escape-hatch interpretation of the reclamation law, to report that this had made it possible for landowners to bring "themselves into compliance with the acreage limitation provisions."[123] On the other hand, apparently sensitive to local political concern spotlighted by protests by eight California Congressmen, he reassured them that "in the entire State of California no situation exists on a Federal Reclamation project where Administrative Letter 303 has been applied or is being considered."[124] On October 21, 1952, the Bureau of Reclamation never-

---

[119] Letter from Commissioner Straus to Secretary Chapman, Jan. 18, 1952, reproduced in EXCESS LAND PROVISIONS, *op. cit. supra* note 94, pt. 2, exhibit 20:2, :3. Three years earlier a Hoover Commission task force report had pointed to difficulties arising from the attitude of excess landholders on Kings River: "It may well be that the Federal Government will never turn a thin dime for a large part of the irrigation benefits provided by this project, and the benefits will accrue to the present owners of land rather than to the small independent farmer around whom the whole philosophy of Federal reclamation has been built." Maass, *Kings River Project in the Basin of the Great Central Valley—a Case Study*, [HOOVER] U.S. COMM'N ON ORGANIZATION OF THE EXECUTIVE BRANCH OF THE GOVERNMENT, CONCLUDING REPORT, APP. L, TASK FORCE REPORT ON NATURAL RESOURCES, January 1949, app. 7, at 178 (May, 1957).

[120] "I do not know whether this theory [lump sum payment] settles the water users' obligations . . . which also embrace compliance with the 160-acre law." Letter from Commissioner of the Bureau of Reclamation Straus to Secretary of the Interior Chapman, Jan. 18, 1952, reproduced in EXCESS LAND PROVISIONS, *op. cit. supra* note 94, pt. 2, exhibit 20:1, :2.

[121] "Although it is true that Mike [Commisissioner Straus] has been crucified on this cross before, I fear I detect a weakening in the Bureau's position, possibly because it is feared that continuing to stand pat on this and other matters may jeopardize a large future construction program." Letter from Arthur A. Maass, assistant professor of government, Harvard University, to Joel Wolfsohn, assistant to the Secretary of the Interior, Oct. 28, 1951, reproduced in EXCESS LAND PROVISIONS, *op. cit. supra* note 94, pt. 1, app. 32:3.

[122] Commissioner of the Bureau of Reclamation Straus, Administrative Letter No. 303, Dec. 16, 1947, reproduced in EXCESS LAND PROVISIONS, *op. cit. supra* note 94, pt. 1, app. 26. See also *id.*, pt. 1, apps. 27, 28; Letter from Richard L. Boke, Regional Director, Bureau of Reclamation, to Commissioner of the Bureau of Reclamation Straus, Oct. 31, 1951, *id.*, pt. 1, app. 31.

[123] Letter from Secretary of the Interior Chapman to Congressman John F. Shelley, March 29, 1951, reproduced in *id*, pt. 1, app. 29:2.

[124] *Ibid.* On November 21, 1951, he advised James G. Patton, president of the National Farmers Union, that the Department, the Bureau, and he, personally, were strongly committed to the family-size farm principle, and that he was "confident that no responsible official of the

theless communicated to the Kings River Conservation District its willingness to accept lump sum payment with the understanding that such payment "would remove the excess land restriction of Reclamation Law."[125] In correspondence with Secretary Chapman at about the same time, Commissioner Straus argued that the "mitigation," allowed under the King-Cohen Opinion, would represent compliance with the reclamation law. He said that this ruling was "the vehicle of the Department in enunciating its policy," and that the King-Cohen Opinion has been "approved by the Secretary of the Interior, and that thereby it was entrenched as policy until modified."[126] In a later letter, he taxed the Secretary with having "consistently withheld commitment" on the Kings River negotiations and, represented that the basis of these negotiations was "established Department policy and practice consistent with" the King-Cohen Opinion "construing the Federal statutes. . . ."[127]

A personal protest to President Truman by President James G. Patton of the National Farmers Union brought the cleavage between the Bureau and the Department into focus.[128] Secretary Chapman soon made it clear that a sharp division on the policy of accepting prepayment as a means of avoiding the excess land law existed between Department and Bureau.[129] He denied that the Department had "formalized is policy" in this respect.

Bureau of Reclamation has proposed that the provisions of Reclamation law be subverted or evaded." Letter from Secretary of the Interior Chapman to James G. Patton, Nov. 21, 1951, reproduced in *id.*, pt. 1, app. 38. At the same time, he advised the Bureau of Reclamation that he was "not in favor of discarding the 160-acre limitation" and assumed that "no commitments are being made on behalf of the Bureau or the Department which will in any way deviate from the provisions of the law and the policy which we have supported here consistently." Letter from Secretary of the Interior Chapman to Commissioner Straus, Nov. 21, 1951, reproduced in *id.*, pt. 1, app. 35.

[125] Letter from Jack W. Rodner, District Manager, Bureau of Reclamation, to Kings River Conservation District, Oct. 21, 1952, reproduced in *id.*, pt. 2, exhibit 27:2.

[126] Letter from Commissioner Straus to Secretary of the Interior Chapman, Jan. 18, 1952, reproduced in *id.*, pt. 1, app. 36:1, :2. See also *id.*, app. 40.

"I cannot see the Department sanctioning a ruse (lump sum payment) to get around the law. . . . Like Ickes, Secretary Chapman has always taken a good stand on these matters. . . . I do not think the Secretary should allow the Bureau to weaken. I hope you can help shore them up." Letter from Arthur A. Maass to Joel Wolfsohn, Oct. 28, 1951, reproduced in *id.*, pt. 1, app. 32:2, :3. See also *id.*, apps. 33, 34.

[127] Letter from Commissioner Straus to Secretary of the Interior Chapman, Dec. 4, 1952, reproduced in *id.*, pt. 1, app. 46.

[128] At that time, Patton presented a letter of protest to President Truman relating to Kings River contract negotiations. It stated that "unless you act fast and decisively, your Administration is about to go down in history, ironically, as the one that pulled the plug on American family farm policy and sent it down the drain, instead of the one that defended it heroically to the last against all attacks." Letter from James G. Patton, to Harry S. Truman, Nov. 24, 1952, reproduced in *id.*, pt. 1, app. 46:4.

[129] Commissioner Straus claimed later that Secretary Chapman told him orally on January 6, 1953, to "disregard the order" of December 23, 1952 that acceptance of prepayment anywhere, including Kings River specifically, was contrary to Department policy. Commis-

For the purpose of correcting the record, I wish to point out that the [King-Cohen] opinion does not in itself set forth any policy, and since it does not contain any policy pronouncement, there was no occasion for the submission of the opinion to the Secretary of the Interior for approval, and it was not so submitted.[130]

The sharpness of this division may be pointed up by a comparison of the following:

(1) *Commissioner Straus:*
[T]he Commissioner reviewed some of the highlights of past battles over acreage limitation; said he viewed the "lump-sum payment clause" in reclamation contracts as a politically necessary escape hatch, but nevertheless a "phony" because it would almost never be used; said that without such "safety valves" as this, the acreage limitation principle would be wiped completely off the books by Congress . . . .[131]

(2) *Secretary Chapman:*
The present policy of the Department of the Interior . . . should now be entirely clear. Except in those situations noted in the preceding paragraph,[132] lump-sum or accelerated payment of construction charges is not to be used as a means of avoiding the acreage limitation provisions of reclamation law.[133]

Secretary McKay, however, chose to erect Secretary Chapman's "exceptions" into the general policy of the Department. In doing so, he said

---

sioner Straus, Memorandum for the Record, February 6, 1953, reproduced in *id.*, pt. 1, app. 54:2. See also *id.*, app. 55. A member of the Program Staff doubted that Secretary Chapman had withdrawn the order on policy, noting that the original remained in the Secretary's files and had been referred to "affirmatively and with emphasis" as stating "clear Department policy," in a letter to Senator Douglas, dated January 19, 1953. Letter from Fred A. Clarenbach, Program Staff of the Department of the Interior, to the files, Feb. 3, 1953, reproduced in *id.*, pt. 1, app. 55:1, :2.

[130] Letter from Secretary of the Interior Chapman to Commissioner Straus, Dec. 23, 1952, reproduced in *id.*, pt. 1, app. 47. In Patton's opinion, Secretary Chapman's statement was insufficient because, while affirming satisfactory policy on Kings River, effective during the reing days of the outgoing administration, it left the King-Cohen Opinion (note 102 *supra*) and Administrative Letter No. 303 (note 122 *supra*) undisturbed. See Letter from James G. Patton to Secretary of the Interior Chapman, Jan. 12, 1953, reproduced in *id.*, pt. 1, app. 52. See also *id.*, pt. 1, apps. 49–53.

[131] Letter from Fred A. Clarenbach, Program Staff of the Department of Interior, to the files, Feb. 3, 1953, reproduced in *id.*, pt. 1, app. 55:1.

[132] See Letter from Secretary Chapman to Harry S. Truman, Dec. 24, 1952, reproduced in *id.*, pt. 1, app. 48, where the situations are discussed. Secretary Chapman mentioned the conclusion of the Cohen Opinion as to the law, and acknowledged that the Department, under Administrative Letter No. 303, had accepted "an accelerated payout from some excess landowners in . . . some of the older projects." Pressures upon him from persons and organizations supporting the principle of the law evidently were too little and too late to be wholly effective. *Ibid.*

[133] The Secretary acknowledged acceptance of accelerated payment "in certain situations," and described them as "exceptions" to policy. Letter from Secretary Chapman to Senator Douglas, Jan. 17, 1953, reproduced in *id.*, pt. 1, app. 50.

that he was "constrained to follow the precedents already set."[134] The use of the lump sum payment device to avoid the excess land limitation was felt to be "not novel, nor did it originate . . . 'with the present administration of the Department.'"[134a] Although, as noted above,[135] Secretary Seaton repudiated a Kings River contract negotiated under this philosophy, that offered *individual* landowners exemption from the law, he simultaneously proposed the terms for new negotiations. The difference between the basis of the old negotiations, and that of the new, was slight. Where Secretary McKay had authorized exemption from the limitation to both *individuals* and *districts,* the new offer was extended to *districts* only.[136]

Despite Secretary Seaton's ringing words in refusing to sign the already negotiated contract,[137] he did not point out that two-thirds of all excess lands on the Kings River project are concentrated in a single district; that of all lands of that district they constitute about 90 percent; and that they represent about 90 percent of the voting power, which is based on assessed valuation. He did not explain how the evident prospect that this entire district—Tulare Lake Basin Water Storage District—would choose pre-

---

[134] Letter from Secretary of the Interior McKay to George Sehlmeyer, master, California State Grange, March 2, 1954, reproduced in *id.,* pt. 1, app. 61:2.

[134a] Letter from Assistant Secretary of Interior Aandahl to C. J. Haggerty, secretary-treasurer, California State Federation of Labor, Aug. 6, 1954, reproduced in *id.,* pt. 1, app. 64:2. "We assure you that the present administration of the Department has no intention, by this decision or any other, '. . . to break the back of family farming in California and the west.'" *Ibid.* In 1957, there were 266,302 acres in excess holdings on the Kings River project. These could provide 160-acre farms for 1,664 families or for 3,328 farms of 80 acres each, which approximates closely the average size of irrigated farms in California. Letter from Secretary of the Interior Seaton to Philip A. Gordon, July 12, 1957, copy on file in Bancroft Library, University of California, Berkeley.

[135] See *supra,* text at note 104.

[136] See *supra,* text at note 91. Secretary Seaton has employed the same tactic twice at critical points, viz., played down or ignored the more important question and played up the less important one: (1) Rejecting the McKay contract in 1957, he passed over the central question whether excess landowners could avoid disposing of excess lands by payment; instead, he called "the overriding issue" whether they could do this as individuals or only through district action. (2) Seeking legal advice from the Attorney General of the United States in 1958, he ignored the central question again; instead, he asked whether reclamation law applied to Kings River, the answer to which no Secretary of the Interior before him has doubted—not even Secretary McKay.

[137] See *supra,* text at note 106. Secretary Seaton had also said that "I am fully aware that over the years there have been legal opinions presented and approved which have permitted individual landowners to avoid the excess land limitations of the law by a prepayment of their administratively allocated share of construction costs. However, I cannot justify an aggravation of a prior practice in an effort to remedy an absence of lawful authority . . . . I conceive it to be . . . my duty as Secretary, to exert every effort to see that applicable laws are complied with. Where discretion may be vested in the Department or the Secretary, that discretion should be exercised to obtain compliance with the principles on which the legislation is enacted. What I am concerned about is a process by which inferences are based on inferences and there is a whittling away at a principle until all that is left is a pile of shavings." Letter from Secretary of the Interior Seaton to Philip A. Gordon, *supra,* note 134a.

payment to avoid disposing of excess lands could be reconciled with the principles he recited as reasons for rejecting the contracts offering exemptions to individuals.

The small margin of difference between the authorization for negotiations from the two Secretaries is reflected in the similarity of their arguments in justification of their actions. Commissioner Straus had argued that allowing the law to be avoided was an "escape hatch" advisable in face of determined resistance from excess landholders. Secretary McKay, by contrast, said that he was, in this matter, "constrained to follow . . . precedents;" Secretary Seaton said that it would not be "proper" for him to "overturn at this late date" the administrative interpretation of the law. This "long-standing interpretation," however, had been rejected by Secretary Chapman only a few years before and in the face of pressure sufficient to make the Bureau of Reclamation turn to it as a necessary tactic.

It is clear that Secretary Seaton's defense of his actions cannot be justified on the terms he has chosen for that purpose. Law and precedent fail to provide a solid foundation for claims that officials are constrained to allow the avoidance of the excess land limitation of the law by the device of lump sum payment of the costs of construction or by completing those payments over a 40-year period.

IV

WATER DISTRICT

The property owners in the Tulare Lake Basin Water Storage District . . . see no way to clearly meet the financial requirements of any contract with the Bureau, in order to avoid the application of the 160-acre limitation rule. Many of the property owners in other irrigation districts near Fresno . . . do not own in excess of 160 acres, and apparently they have the majority of representation on the Kings River Water Association, and may have been giving . . . the impression that there is no objection to negotiating a permanent contract with the Bureau. However, the larger landowners, and especially those in the Tulare Lake Basin Water Storage District, are strenuously opposed to this procedure.—Eugene E. Marsh, 1955[138]

We doubt if we will ever get all the ins and outs of this water and irrigation business through our heads . . . after the question and discussion period which followed the talks it seemed we knew even less.—Cutler-Orosi Courier, 1951[139]

The federal government completed construction of Pine Flat Dam in

---

[138] Letter from Eugene E. Marsh, attorney at law, McMinnville, Oregon, to Secretary of the Interior McKay, July 28, 1955, reproduced in U.S. DEP'T OF THE INTERIOR, EXCESS LAND PROVISIONS OF THE FEDERAL RECLAMATION LAWS AND THE PAYMENT OF CHARGES, pt. 2, exhibit 40:3 [hereinafter cited as EXCESS LAND PROVISIONS].

[139] (Orosi, Cal.), Aug. 23, 1951, p. 1, cols. 1, 5, under the lead, "Kings River Water Users Hear New Organization Explained at Reedley Meeting." The "new organization" was the Kings River Conservation District.

1954 for the benefit of water users on Kings River and Tulare Lake project at a cost of around $40 million. More than a score of districts or agencies distribute water to the lands of the project. They receive water under annual interim contracts, arranged through an overall district created in 1951, known as the Kings River Conservation District (KRCD). Neither the KRCD nor the individual districts have made arrangements for repayment of construction charges and permanent water supplies, although correspondence on the subject dates from as early as 1946.[140] The reason for this extraordinary delay is the determined and persistent opposition of excess landowners to inclusion of the standard excess land provisions in the contracts, as required by reclamation law.

The concentration of this economic interest is impressive. Approximately two-thirds of the 266,302 excess acres on the project are located in Tulare Lake Basin. Fifty-two owners hold 196,466 excess acres, or almost three-quarters of the excess lands on the project. This concentration creates a strong economic interest in defeat of the excess land law on Kings River. About one-fourth of all the million acres on the Kings River and Tulare Lake project are in excess holdings.[141]

Most of the lands of the Kings River project area, however, are in parcels of less than 160 acres. Their owners constitute almost 92 percent of all landholders and are unaffected by the federal requirement of an agreement to dispose of excess lands as a condition of obtaining water. Their desires and interests might easily have led them, uninfluenced by others, to execute permanent contracts, as districts along the Friant-Kern Canal did close to a decade ago to secure permanent water rights from the Central Valley project. Some smaller landowners on Kings River have worked actively to obtain compliance with reclamation law, but in general their leadership has been fitful and unskillful.

Until 1951 the Kings River Water Association (KRWA) was the only organization coextensive with the project area and therefore the only one with even an appearance of speaking for all interests on the river. KRWA administered the distribution schedules of unstored water, without limitation of water deliveries based upon size of ownership. Although the purpose of the project was to improve water rights by a more efficient use of the river, the law requires equitable redistribution as a condition of their improvement. The spokesmen of KRWA opposed redistribution as an interference with established water rights,[142] thereby ignoring the increment attributable to the project.

---

[140] EXCESS LAND PROVISIONS, *op. cit. supra* note 138, pt. 2, at 5.

[141] Letter from Secretary of the Interior Seaton to Philip A. Gordon, president, board of directors, Kings River Conservation District, July 12, 1957.

[142] KINGS RIVER WATER ASS'N, KINGS RIVER—FACTS AND FALSEHOODS 6–9 (1950); testimony of Charles L. Kaupke, engineer and watermaster, KRWA, *Hearings on H.R. 4485 Before a Subcommittee of the Senate Committee on Commerce,* 78th Cong., 2d Sess. 305 (1944); KINGS RIVER PINE FLAT ASS'N, REPORT ON KINGS RIVER PROJECT (1943).

The original tactic of KRWA resistance was to persuade Congress to authorize the Army Engineers rather than the Bureau of Reclamation to construct the Pine Flat project.[143] The attempt to disassociate the law governing Pine Flat from the law governing Central Valley project required physical separation of the projects, as well as use of separate construction agencies. Physical separation was not achieved easily. Pine Flat was included in the plans of both State[144] and federal[145] governments for unified water development of Central Valley. The Friant-Kern Canal of the Central Valley project intersects the Kings River and could easily bring water to lands on Kings River and Tulare Lake that need it urgently.[146] Nevertheless, because of resistance to reclamation law, the intersecting streams have been held separate artificially by siphoning Friant-Kern waters underneath the waters of the Kings River. However, these two devices—separate construction agencies and physical separation of projects—did not prevent Congress from applying the excess land law to Kings River,[147] although they contributed to extraordinary postponement of its execution.

Since these tactics were undependable as means of avoiding the excess land law, large landholding interests found it desirable to keep negotiations with the Government in local hands that could be relied upon to resist completion of contracts accepting the excess land law. This required preventing individual districts from making contracts with the United States that they had power and genuine interest to conclude. Districts with the least excess lands, having least interest in resistance, would probably sign first. Few districts would be willing indefinitely to risk their own

---

[143] On April 24, 1941, after the Bureau of Reclamation held a legal authorization to construct Pine Flat Dam, Charles L. Kaupke, then secretary and engineer, Kings River Pine Flat Association, told Congress that "rather than accept the provisions of the Bureau project, we would forego a project on Kings River." *Hearings on H.R. 4911 Before the House Committee on Flood Control,* 77th Cong., 1st Sess. 181 (1941). A telegram from Tulare Lake Basin Water District, dated May 7, 1945, said: "Over the several past years we have been required to incur much expense in order to assist in preventing this project from being undertaken by the Bureau of Reclamation." *Hearings on H.R. 3024 Before a Subcommittee of the Senate Committee on Appropriations,* 79th Cong., 1st Sess. 991 (1946).

[144] CAL. DIV. OF WATER RESOURCES, REPORTS ON STATE WATER PLAN, BULL. NO. 29, SAN JOAQUIN RIVER BASIN 261–65 (1931) (prepared pursuant to Cal. Stat. 1929, c. 832, § 1).

[145] S. Doc. No. 113, 81st Cong., 1st Sess. 216 (1949).

[146] Testimony of Louis T. Robinson (Kings County farmer), *Hearings on S. 178 Before the Subcommittee on Irrigation and Reclamation of the Senate Committee on Interior and Insular Affairs,* 84th Cong., 2d Sess. 140–41 (1956).

[147] 58 Stat. 891 (1944), 43 U.S.C. § 418 (1952). See 41 OPS. ATT'Y GEN. 56 (1958); Maass, *Kings River Project in the Basin of the Great Central Valley—a Case Study,* [HOOVER] U.S. COMM'N ON ORGANIZATION OF THE EXECUTIVE BRANCH OF THE GOVERNMENT, CONCLUDING REPORT, APP. L, TASK FORCE REPORT ON NATURAL RESOURCES, January 1949, app. 7, at 149–82 (May, 1957). See also Taylor, *Excess Land Law: Execution of a Public Policy,* 64 YALE L.J. 477 (1955); Taylor, *Excess Land Law on the Kern?,* 46 CALIF. L. REV. 153 (1958).

future water supplies while adjacent districts were signing contracts to make theirs secure. Each contract signed by an individual district on Kings River for a permanent water supply would weaken the power of the remaining districts to hold out. Districts resisting longest would progressively lose support for their resistance, and risk losing their own future water supplies to districts signing earlier, which by compliance with the law would be entitled to priority in permanent distribution of water.[148]

Along the Friant-Kern Canal, where the situation was comparable, resistance to the acceptance of permanent contracts containing the excess land law was beginning to crumble at the first determined efforts of the Bureau of Reclamation to conclude them. In 1948 two districts along the Friant-Kern Canal signed four contracts containing the excess land provision and ratified by popular vote of 188 to 1 the only one requiring ratification.[149] Three districts approved contracts in 1949 by a combined vote of 1,072 to 183.[150] Five districts signed contracts in 1950, with a total popular vote for approval of 1575 to 121.[151] Similar action by at least some of the neighboring Kings River districts could reasonably have been anticipated in the absence of measures to delay or prevent it.

The direct power of excess landholders, based on their holdings and their votes, is distributed very unequally within the several water districts on Kings River. In Fresno, the most populous irrigation district, only about 13 per cent of all lands are held in tracts of above 160 acres in size, and only about 6 per cent above 320 acres. The district consists of about 240,000 acres, and, in 1944, there were 12,400 landowners.[152] Since

---

[148] "My recent trip in the Kings River area convinced me that there is a growing number of land owners who, having observed *just this summer* the benefits derived or to be derived by those who have contracted for Friant-Kern water, are now ready to enter into similar contracts for Pine Flat water. Several irrigators with whom I spoke stated that they are getting fed up with KRWA, feel that organization is asking them—the smaller and majority of farmers in the area—to pull chestnuts out of the fire for the big boys, and actually seek advice on how they can break away and contract with the Bureau." Letter from Arthur A. Maass to Joel Wolfsohn, October 28, 1951, reproduced in Excess Land Provisions, *op. cit. supra* note 138, pt. 1, app. 32:1.

[149] Lindsay-Strathmore Water District. The other district was South San Joaquin Municipal Utility District. Contracts covered water service, distribution system, or were supplementary or amendatory. Bureau of Reclamation Regional Office (Sacramento), California Elections on Reclamation Water Contracts (April, 1952), on file in Sacramento regional office.

[150] Ivanhoe, Lindmore, Orange Cove. *Ibid.*

[151] Exeter, Lindsay-Strathmore, Stone Corral, Terra Bella, and Tulare. Three districts (Delano-Earlimart, Lower Tule, Saucelito) signed in 1951 approving by a combined vote of 750 to 49. Porterville approved by 58 to 42, but failed to give the necessary two-thirds majority until the following year. In 1952, five districts (Delano-Earlimart, Ivanhoe, Lindmore, Lindsay-Strathmore, and Porterville) approved contracts by a vote of 744 to 125. Saucelito rejected a supplementary, or amendatory, contract by a vote of 33 to 45. *Ibid.*

[152] Computations made from data in letter from C. Sam Johnson, assessor-collector, Fresno Irrigation District, to Charles L. Kaupke, May 20, 1944, reproduced in *Hearings on H.R. 3024 Before a Subcommittee of the Senate Committee on Appropriations*, 79th Cong., 1st Sess. 1001–03 (1946), and testimony of Charles L. Kaupke, *Hearings on S. 912 Before a Subcommittee of the Senate Committee on Public Lands*, 80th Cong., 1st Sess. 176 (1947). Since

all electors vote in irrigation districts, the power of excess landowners, except as they influence others, is meager.

At the other extreme from Fresno is the least populous district on Kings River, the virtually uninhabited Tulare Lake Basin Water Storage District. The district consists of 192,000 acres. Around 90 percent of all its lands, or approximately 270 square miles, is in holdings in excess of 160 acres.[153] Votes are cast, not by polling the electors, of whom there are few if any, but by counting votes reckoned in units of $100 of assessed valuation. Manifestly the power of excess landowners to guide the actions of Fresno or other irrigation districts is far less direct and sure than their power to guide the actions of Tulare Lake Basin Water Storage District in which they hold the power directly.

Since 1946 the KRWA had engaged in correspondence and negotiations directed toward conclusion of a contract on terms satisfactory to its leadership, *i.e.*, excluding the excess land provision.[154] This procedure was initially successful, but the usefulness of the KRWA in preventing acceptance of contracts by individual districts having power to make them was limited by the fact that it could not offer to serve the districts as an alternative contracting agency. It lacked legal powers required to support the financial obligations assumed in contracts. In this situation the KRWA sought a more effective instrument to prevent individual districts from concluding contracts complying with the excess land law, and thus breaking the solid front of resistance. The means the association chose was a new district on Kings River with legal power to contract with the United States. A bill was prepared for submission to the State legislature to create the Kings River Conservation District, including within it the lands of previously existing districts, yet without extinguishing the districts themselves or diminishing their legal powers. Individual districts already had the power to contract, but the new district offered a unified and legally qualified alternative.[155]

---

[153] Letter from Commissioner of the Bureau of Reclamation Michael W. Straus to Senator Douglas, Feb. 2, 1949, copy on file in Bancroft Library, University of California, Berkeley.

[154] EXCESS LAND PROVISIONS, *op. cit. supra* note 138, pt. 2, exhibits 1–4.

[155] "The KRWA is in a sense an extra-legal organization which repesents all of the irrigation districts in the Kings River water service area. All of the districts have given the Association power of attorney to negotiate for them on Pine Flat. It is this power of attorney that many of the irrigators and some of the irrigation district directors want to recapture so they can negotiate directly with the Bureau for a regular contract. At the last session of the California legislature a bill was passed to establish a single irrigation district for the entire Kings River area. (In effect, giving legal status to the KRWA.) I was unable to obtain definite evidence, but believe that this bill was pushed through by KRWA supporters to prevent the imminent possibility of one or more of the existing districts breaking away from the Association and signing a regular contract with the Bureau. If one were to break away, the Association's solid front would thus be pierced, and its effectiveness, badly damaged." Letter from Arthur Maass to Joel Wolfsohn, Oct. 28, 1951, reproduced in EXCESS LAND PROVISIONS, *op. cit. supra* note 138, pt. 1, app. 32:2.

Press and other available reports do not yield indications that this explanation for creating KRCD was ever offered generally to the water users of Kings River area. The customary procedure of forming irrigation or other water districts by vote of electors or landowners was avoided in forming the Kings River Conservation District, and the proposal to establish the KRCD was taken directly to the State legislature.

Local Kings River press furnishes a front-page account of how the KRWA described and presented its KRCD Bill to a small community within the project area. Three speakers addressed the meeting. According to the local account the first speaker, who was sponsor of the bill in the legislature, told the people that above all, KRCD would keep control of the Kings River water in the hands of the people.[156] The second speaker, described as "a Fresno attorney who helped draw up the bill," but unnamed, stated that "until recent dates no one contested the rights of the water users but with the advent of the federal government into the picure in California we find it necessary to set up a legal entity."[157] The local account gives no indication that he gave a reason for the necessity. Existing districts were legal entities with powers to contract to obtain water, and were not to be abolished.

The Kings River water master told the meeting, " 'I hope we can run our affairs so that we never lose control of our water rights.' . . . 'This country is becoming socialized faster than you think,' [and] that if the federal government can get control of the water, together with the power rights on our rivers, they (the bureaucrats) can control just about any kind of an economy they want."[158]

The local reporter, remarking that "we [newspaper writers] don't know much about this water business," said he grasped one idea from the meeting that appeared to furnish solid foundation: "To our mind one of the biggest features of the [KRCD] plan is the retaining of control by the people."[159] Apparently no mention of the excess land law was made to the meeting, and no question raised whether, in the phrases "control of our

---

[156] Assemblyman William Hansen, sponsor of Cal. Assembly Bill 340, Reg. Sess. (1951), as reported in Cutler-Orosi Courier (Orosi, Cal.), Aug. 23, 1951, p. 1, col. 2.

[157] Id. at p. 1, cols. 3, 4.

[158] Charles L. Kaupke, quoted *ibid.* Two months later the quartermaster-adjutant of the California Department, Veterans of Foreign Wars, replying to this argument of the KRWA, said: "Do not be misled by the endless repetition of spoksemen on Kings River that the Bureau of Reclamation is going to deprive any water users of their water rights. There is purpose behind the repetition, but the statement, on the face of it is false. Reclamation law specifically requires the Bureau to respect those water rights, and the courts of the United States are open to anybody who thinks his rights are not being protected as required by law." Statement of M. C. Hermann before a subcommittee of the House Public Lands Committee, at Sacramento, Cal., Dec. 19, 1950, in 97 CONG. REC. 13, 14 (1951).

[159] Cutler-Orosi Courier, (Orosi, Cal.), Aug. 23, 1951, p. 1, col. 7.

water rights" and "control by the people," a distinction between individuals owning more, and those owning less than 160 acres of land, might be important.

The presentation by the KRWA to the State legislature of the necessity for creating a new district apparently was consistent with that made to the meeting at Reedley, and not much more illuminating. The bill recited that the legislature "finds and determines" that formation of an overall district will benefit "the lands thereof," and that "it is necessary to have a political entity embracing the areas having rights to said waters created in order to protect such rights...."[160] Neither the necessity, nor the "benefit" to "the lands" were clarified further in the bill, nor apparently otherwise. The water master for the KRWA told the Assembly Committee on Conservation, Planning and Public Works at a lengthy hearing that "the issue has nothing to do with the 160-acre limitation." His reasoning was that "the same contract would be signed, whether by one district or its many components."[161]

The day after the hearing, an editorial in the San Francisco News said:

> Ordinarily irrigation and water districts are formed by vote of the landowners of the proposed district, a democratic process that has prevailed from the very inception of the district plan of utility development.... Why has this unusual procedure been resorted to? Some residents of the area believe it is intended to drive a wedge into the heart of the Central Valley Project thereby preventing the CVP from being, as originally intended, an integrated, comprehensive water plan for the whole interior basin of the state.... [W]e see no reason for departing from the time-honored custom of letting landowners vote on formation of water districts. The Legislature should be sure it knows what the real purpose and effect of this proposal is before voting finally upon it.[162]

The legislature created the Kings River Conservation District that, before long, superseded the KRWA in negotiating with the Bureau of

---

[160] Cal. Assembly Bill 340, Reg. Sess. (1951).

[161] Sacramento dispatch: "Kings River Water District Action Delayed," San Francisco News, March 29, 1951, p. 9, col. 1. "Charles Kaupke, water master of the Kings River Water Association, told the committee the members of his association—including irrigation districts, storage districts, mutual water companies and individual farmers—want the district because they want a single legal entity to contract with the Federal Government for water contracts when Pine Flat Dam is completed in 1953.... Committee members queried why local residents couldn't vote on forming the district, before the Legislature okehed [sic] it. Wallace D. Henderson (D., Fresno) urged that this step be tried. Harlan Hagan [sic] (D., Hanford) protested that land owners who are not water users are getting blanketed into the district without say-so. O. M. Davis, a Kerman rancher, declared that the bill in effect represents a plot by the Kings River Water Association and the Pacific Gas and Electric Co. to prevent this area from becoming a part of Central Valley. Assemblyman Hansen hit back at Mr. Davis as a disgruntled campaign opponent of two years back."

[162] San Francisco News, March 30, 1951, p. 20, col. 2.

Reclamation. Changes in personnel in the positions of leadership were few as between KRWA and KRCD, policies remained the same, and resistance to the excess land law was more solid than before.[163]

The KRCD picked up where the KRWA had left off. On September 10, 1952, the KRCD rejected draft number four of the proposed repayment contract on the ground that it was "based upon principles which are not acceptable to the owners of water rights in the Kings River Service Area." The principle "acceptable" to the board of directors of KRCD was an "understanding" that "lump sum payment . . . would entitle the Kings River water users to all the storage space in the Pine Flat Reservoir, subject only to flood control operations by the army engineers; and that the Bureau of Reclamation, in consideration of such payment, would no longer claim that the project was in any manner subject to reclamation laws."[164]

During the next 6 weeks, negotiations took a fresh turn. The District Manager of the Bureau of Reclamation threatened, in face of rebuff by the KRCD, to undertake negotiations with individual districts. At the same time he offered to accept lump sum payment and to agree that this would "remove" the excess land law.[165] He added: "[W]e have gained the impression that this assurance opened the way to completing the contract."[165a] The general election of 1952, which followed closely, produced a change of administration, and negotiations were ended for more than a year.

Secretary of the Interior Douglas McKay resumed negotiations with KRCD on November 9, 1953, offering that advance lump sum payment would render the excess land laws "inoperative." His successor, Secretary Seaton, rejected the contract on July 12, 1957, offering a slightly different interpretation of the law.[166] Secretary McKay would have permitted *individual landowners* to avoid the law by completing their payments; Secretary Seaton was willing to permit only *districts* to do this.[167]

---

[163] Elections to directorships of water districts are held separately at odd times, and attendance of more than 10% of persons eligible to vote is extraordinary. The turnout of voters for the KRCD election was somewhat larger than usual, but very small measured by the turnout at general elections.

[164] Letter from Philip A. Gordon, president, board of directors, Kings River Conservation District, to Jack W. Rodner, District Manager, Bureau of Reclamation, Sept. 10, 1952, reproduced in EXCESS LAND PROVISIONS, *op. cit. supra* note 138, pt. 2, exhibit 26:1. The second Werdel bill (H.R. 413, 82d Cong., 1st Sess. (1951)), validating this "understanding," had failed of passage in the then current Congress.

[165] Letter from Jack W. Rodner to Kings River Conservation District, Oct. 21, 1952, reproduced in EXCESS LAND PROVISIONS, *op. cit. supra* note 138, pt. 2, exhibit 27:2, :3. Before leaving office, Secretary of the Interior Chapman rejected lump sum payment on Kings River. See Taylor, *Excess Land Law: Execution of a Public Policy*, 64 YALE L.J. 477, 506-09 (1955).

[165a] *Ibid.*

[166] Letter from Secretary of the Interior Seaton to Philip A. Gordon, July 12, 1957, copy on file in Bancroft Library, University of California, Berkeley.

[167] See *supra* note 88.

Secretary McKay's willingness to render the excess land law "inoperative" by completion of money payments eliminated the resistance of excess landholding interests on Kings River and Tulare Lake project to conclusion of a contract by the KRCD with the Bureau of Reclamation. Secretary Seaton's interpretation rendered the Kings River Conservation District not only useless to them, but an obstacle.

The problem of getting non-excess landholders to join with excess landholders in prepayment, for the purpose of helping the latter at a substantial and unnecessary cost to the former—since reclamation law charges no interest on deferred payments—had been a concern of excess landholders since at least 1951. Secretary McKay had dissolved the problem entirely by offering to accept payments by *individual* excess landholders under a single contract with KRCD which would not require any non-excess landowners to pay cash to help excess landowners avoid the law. Secretary Seaton restored the problem, in part, by agreeing to accept *district* payments only. This would require *some* non-excess landowners to advance cash, if the excess landholders of the district were to escape the law.

The response of KRWA to Secretary Seaton's offer was to resume its role as spokesman for Kings River and Tulare Lake interests, to lay aside its creature, the Kings River Conservation District, and to prepare for the previously avoided *individual* district contracts.

On May 19, 1959, the attorney and secretary for the KRWA announced that the new contract " 'would allow water agencies to sign individually.' " He said that " 'some of the water agencies will want a 40-year interest-free payment contract, and others will want a lump sum payment contract.' " Upon completion of payments the districts " 'would not be bound by the water delivery limitation.' " While contracts would be signed by individual districts, the KRWA secretary said, " 'if it goes through I expect all the agencies will sign at the same time.' "[168] Two weeks later news reports said that regional officials of the Bureau of Reclamation in Sacramento were "optimistic over chances of top level approval" of the contracts in Washington.[169]

The probable reason why KRWA preferred individual district contracts to an overall KRCD contract is not far to seek. Under the terms approved by Secretary Seaton, about 127 owners of excess lands in Tulare Lake Basin Water Storage District could easily obtain a prepayment contract. If necessary, they could outvote about 635 owners of non-excess lands, on the voting basis of $100-units of assessed valuation.[170] By so

---

[168] Fresno Bee, May 20, 1959, p. 12-A, col. 1.
[169] Fresno Bee, June 8, 1959, p. 7-A, col. 1.
[170] Statement of M. C. Hermann, quartermaster-adjutant, Department of California, Veterans of Foreign Wars, read into the record by California Congressman John F. Shelley, 97 CONG. REC. 6351-52 (1951).

doing they could render the excess land law inoperative at a stroke on about two-thirds of all the excess lands of the project area.

V

PROCESS

When one faces up to the policy and collects any and all statements and pronouncements on the principle of the 160-acre law, one is impressed by the unanimity of support for it from Members of Congress and representatives of the executive establishment. Witness the statements by all members of this committee during this session today. In the light of this support for the principle of the small farm and the 160-acre law, efforts to escape the provision should have rough going in our Federal Government.—Arthur A. Maass, 1958 [171]

Senator Kuchel, I think in this very room you have people who in the main must be satisfied and in agreement before any real progress can be made on the San Luis project. There is one segment of opinion represented by the State Grange, Mr. Sehlmeyer, who is a very admirable man, who does not endorse any type of State project because the State does not have an acreage limitation law. . . . However, I think agreement could be achieved without the agreement of Mr. Sehlmeyer, and I think it has to be achieved . . . regardless of whether this Congress passes an authorization bill or not, because . . . the State has so many locks on various aspects of progress that the State acceptance has to be present for any progress to be made.—Congressman Harlan Hagen, 1958 [172]

Procedure for arriving at public decisions may determine the decision itself. The balance of interest against principle may be controlled by procedure. The excess land law, representing the principle of wide distribution of resources and control of unjust enrichment, suffers damage continuously from faulty procedure.

The principal means by which the pressure of interests works against principle and policy, as represented by the excess land law, is simple and effective. The common method, as Dr. Arthur Maass of Harvard University testified to the Senate Irrigation and Reclamation Subcommittee, is "*specifically by not facing up to the issue directly* in the light of full public discussion and debate."[173] Among the examples cited by Dr. Maass were (1) "proposals to avoid the limitation entirely by lump-sum payout" which "should be widely discussed for what they are and not considered as a

---

[171] Testimony of Arthur A. Maass, *Hearings on S. 1425, S. 2541, and S. 3448 Before the Subcommittee on Irrigation and Reclamation of the Senate Committee on Interior and Insular Affairs*, 85th Cong., 2d Sess. 91 (1958) [hereinafter cited as *1958 Hearing on S. 1425, S. 2541 & S. 3448*.]

[172] Testimony of Congressman Harlan Hagen, *Hearings on S. 1887 Before the Subcommittee on Irrigation and Reclamation of the Senate Committee on Interior and Insular Affairs*, 85th Cong., 2d Sess. 42 (1958) [hereinafter cited as *1958 Hearings on S. 1887*].

[173] Testimony of Arthur A. Maass, *1958 Hearings on S. 1425, S. 2541 & S. 3448*, at 90.

technical matter of contract . . . ;" (2) "partnership bills" in which "public and congressional discussion" have not "focused public attention on the . . . quite intentional result . . . to repeal, exempt, or modify the 160-acre law;" (3) the proposed two-price system for water, because it offers too much "opportunity for deception;" and (4) the proposal to allow administrators "greater flexibility," because an administrator needs "desperately a firm and unequivocal statute close up behind him" as protection from the "tremendous pressures on administrative agencies."[174]

The legislature carries two related but separable functions: (1) to declare the principle or standard by which private pressures can be limited or curbed in the public interest, and (2) to strike a balance among the pressures of interests. In preparation and consideration of the San Luis bill[175] the two functions became confused; procedure appropriate to the balancing of pressures was employed where principle was at stake. The chairman of the Senate committee on the bill, faced by diverse interests and opposed views on principle, admonished those who came before him: "First of all, you ought to be able to agree between yourselves voluntarily. If you cannot do that I do not think you ought to go further with it then."[176]

The chairman's admonition was heeded, and an agreement produced. Agreement was achieved, however, by excluding those groups, such as the California Grange and Labor Federation, that stood solid for principle. Congressman Harlan Hagen described how, and among whom, agreement was reached:

> This compromise was the binding agreement of a representative of California's Governor, the two California Senators, Congressman Sisk, and myself, and representatives of San Luis, Kern County, and Los Angeles water interests, arrived at in a March 13 meeting attended by representatives of the Bureau of Reclamation.[177]

The price of agreement, predetermined by the procedure that included some and excluded others, was sacrifice of principle. Not complete sacrifice,

---

[174] *Id.* at 89–92. The author has analyzed the process elsewhere in a detailed description that need not be repeated. See Taylor, *Excess Land Law: Legislative Erosion of Public Policy*, 30 ROCKY MT. L. REV. 1 (1958).

[175] See *supra*, text at note 23.

[176] Remarks of Senator Clinton P. Anderson, *1958 Hearings on S. 1887*, at 172.

[177] Testimony of Congressman Harlan Hagen, *Hearings on S. 44 Before the Subcommittee on Irrigation and Reclamation of the Senate Committee on Interior and Insular Affairs*, 86th Cong., 1st Sess. 29 (1959). Governor Brown claimed a share in the agreement: "For the first time in these long discussions . . . Californians come before you united, offering a single plan with unanimous support. In conferences during the past 2 weeks, representatives of the Westlands Water District, the Metropolitan Water District of Southern California, and Los Angeles Department of Water and Power, the State Farm Bureau Federation, and Kern County interests have worked with my administration and the authors of this legislation to remove potential sources of conflict. The bill before you reflects the minor amendments to which all concerned have agreed." H.R. REP. No. 399, 86th Cong., 1st Sess. (to accompany H.R. 7155) 7 (1959).

however, for the agreement included an estimate by the interests sharing responsibility for its making, of the concessions to principle that were necessary to secure passage of the bill if opposed in Congress by friends of the excess land law. The estimate proved erroneous, at least in the Senate, which refused to exempt San Luis project from reclamation law in early May.

The Interior and Insular Affairs Committee of the House of Representatives faced the same issue on May 29, 1959. The majority insisted on retaining the specific exemption from reclamation law in the House bill (H.R. 7155, section 7) that Senators Douglas and Morse had removed from the Senate bill (S. 44, section 6(a)).[178] It argued that its retention would "contribute to clarity and advance construction of the projects." In doing so, it relied on the procedure that produced agreement among interests by excluding those who would disagree on grounds of principle.[179]

The House report tried to widen another door of escape. This was the administrative order of Secretary Seaton that could free the State from compliance with the excess land law by prepayment.[180] The report appropriately might have asked Congress to validate this administrative interpretation, as Congressman Werdel had done in the 81st and 82d Congresses, unsuccessfully.[181] Instead, it said no legislation was "pending" before

---

[178] See *supra*, text at note 64.

[179] The report said that preparation of the bill "involved bringing together . . . many diverse interests and points of view," and for this reason the author "should be given considerable latitude in the way he expresses the position that is arrived at. . . ." This resembles the explanation given for retaining the exemption in the Senate, viz., that "the people affected want this additional assurance." H.R. REP. No. 399, 86th Cong., 1st Sess. (to accompany H.R. 7155) 15–16 (1959); 105 CONG. REC. 6738 (daily ed. May 5, 1959).

[180] Like the Secretary, the majority of the committee rests its view finally on an administrative ground, rather than on statute; it says the administrative order "is now so well fortified by history that it can probably be successfully attacked by no one except Congress. H.R. REP. No. 399, *supra* note 179, at 14. Secretary Seaton's Solicitor argued that no court had declared the doctrine invalid; the committee majority conceded that the doctrine had "not been construed in any reported judicial decision." *Ibid*. The House report omits mention of documented analyses that arrive at a conclusion contrary to that of Secretary Seaton and itself. See, *e.g.*, correspondence between Senator Douglas and Secretary of the Interior Seaton, reproduced in *1958 Hearings on S. 1425, S. 2541, & S. 3448*, at 20–25; H.R. REP. No. 399, 86th Cong., 1st Sess. 11–16 (1959); Taylor, *The Excess Land Law: Execution of a Public Policy*, 64 YALE L.J. 477 (1955).

[181] H.R. 7915, 81st Cong., 2d Sess. (1950); H.R. 413, 82d Cong., 1st Sess. (1951). The House report and the California Labor Federation, opposed in their views toward the excess land provision, unite in recognition of the concert of tactics in Congress, State legislature and Interior Department, and in the dominating influence of the agreement among "many diverse interests and points of view." H.R. REP. No. 399, 86th Cong., 1st Sess. 15, 16 (1959). The Federation, in a reference to a "three-pronged attack" manifested in the San Luis bills, Seaton interpretation, and California State water program legislation, stated: "These three drives are not necessarily coordinated, but, significantly, each of them would serve the same end: monopolization of irrigation water furnished by public monies . . . . We appreciate the fact that some of those supporting H.R. 7155 have accepted the questionable language as the price they must

Congress or "ever" had been introduced to "overrule the departmental interpretation."

The House report added no substantial support either to the defense of the exemption by Senators Kuchel and Engle, or to the defense of Secretary Seaton's proposed action on Kings River. The majority of the House committee could not change existing law by expressing an opinion; and it refrained from asking Congress for statutory authority. Instead it encouraged Secretary Seaton to proceed in his offer permitting excess landholders on Kings River, and elsewhere, to avoid the excess land law.[182]

The arenas in which public decisions are made in America are informal and formal, and they are numerous. Legislatures, courts, and the offices of administrators are not sequestered, but exposed in varying degrees to winds as diverse as those bearing the results of agreements among interests, and those carrying the score in straw polls on questions of principle.[183] They are not open equally to winds from all quarters except as public discussion and debate is assisted, rather than avoided.

The principle of equitable and wide distribution of benefits and resources is simple, but legal language and the details of projects invest it with an appearance of complexity. In this obscurity, principle can fail to receive necessary consideration in congressional channels where it passes in review. Senator Morse asserted this was true of the San Luis exemption: "The sad fact is that I believe the Senate Committee on Interior and Insular Affairs never gave consideration to the points . . . which the Senator from Illinois . . . has brought out so eloquently on the floor of the Senate."[184]

---

pay to gain support from certain interests in California. We do not doubt the sincerity of these men, but we cannot accept their assurances, and we do not believe that the whole framework of future California water development should be lashed to their political commitments." California Labor Federation, Statement on Water Issues 1, 4 (ca. July 15, 1959), copy on file Bancroft Library, University of California, Berkeley (mimeo).

[182] Senator Engle earlier took the position of advising "'river officials to sign a contract with the government and pay off the cost of the project within ten years. Then the 160 acre limitation will not apply.'" Fresno Bee, Feb. 12, 1959, p. 1, col. 3.

[183] As aftermath of the legislative proceedings in the shadow of the agreement among interests, the San Francisco News reported the opinion of a party leader: "The Governor, at the budget session next winter, must make good on his promise that there'll be no 'unjust enrichment' to large landholders from the water program. If he gets that, he can go all the way. If he doesn't, he'll be just another politician." San Francisco News, June 18, 1959, p. 6, col. 3. See also San Francisco Chronicle, June 21, 1959, p. 1, col. 2, and p. 18, col. 5; *id.*, July 5, 1959, § 2, p. 6, col. 5. The Chronicle, conducting a straw poll on water development, reported that 58.9% of those polled on the question "Should the 160-acre limitation apply to irrigation water?" answered yes, and 21.5% answered no. *Id.*, June 29, 1959, p. 32.

[184] 105 CONG. REC. 7074 (daily ed. May 11, 1959). Senator Douglas said: "The owners of big estates cannot get what they want by Senate action alone . . . and they think they can come to Washington, with no one greatly concerned over the issue and push their proposal through Congress on favorable terms to themselves." 105 CONG. REC. 6738 (daily ed. May 5, 1959). See also Taylor, *The Excess Land Law: Legislative Erosion of a Public Policy*, 30 ROCKY MT. L. REV. 1, 13 (1958).

Pressure against principle produces curiously incongruous political behavior. A Congressman authors a bill proposing partnership between the federal government and a State, and containing an exemption from the excess land law. A governor approves the partnership bill, including the exemption. The Congressman, *while sponsoring* the *federal* exemption, wires State legislators urging them to adopt *State* "safeguards" using the "federal limitation" as a "pattern," and explaining that "had the State enacted such limitations" his task as Congressman "would have been immeasurably assisted."[185] The governor blocks efforts in his legislature to enact the safeguards the Congressman urges,[186] and proposes action *later* to prevent "any unjust enrichment or monopolization of benefits by large landholdings as a result of either Federal or State operation."[187] Congressman and governor, in office on a party platform approving the federal excess land law, support an executive interpretation that would reduce it to a mere shadow.

The issue is not one of the sincerity of public men in their professions of devotion to principle. Devotion to principle becomes impossible or ineffective when pressures rule and responsible organs of government allow confusion of issues, rather than assist their clarification in the arenas of public discussion and debate.

Public principles and policy are forged in these arenas and in them alone can public principles be maintained against pressures that flourish on silence and confusion. Defeat of the exemption by the Senate was a demonstration.

> *There were only a few people who listened to the debates. . . . Yet the extraordinary thing is that as the facts were developed one could see the opinion of the Senate change. . . . The analysis of the bill spread by a process of osmosis through the Senate as a whole, so that those who did not hear the debates nevertheless read the RECORD, or colleagues upon whom they relied relayed information to them. . . . There has been too much of an idea, Mr. President, that important public matters should be settled off the floor, should be settled by secret arrangements, and that debate itself should be minimized and curtailed, being at best useless and at worst actually harmful. I hope our experience in this debate will encourage other Senators from time to time, when they feel strongly about a measure and feel informed about that measure, to take the floor of the Senate and to express their convictions honestly and accurately.*[188]—Senator Paul Douglas, 1959

---

[185] Congressman B. F. Sisk, quoted in Valley Labor Citizen (Fresno), July 3, 1959, p. 6, col. 2.

[186] California Labor Federation, Weekly Newsletter, June 26, 1959, p. 7, col. 3.

[187] Letter from Edmund G. (Pat) Brown to Senator Engle, May 7, 1959, reproduced in H.R. REP. No. 399, 86th Cong., 1st Sess. 15 (1959).

[188] 105 CONG. REC. 7175 (daily ed. May 12, 1959).

THE EXCESS LAND LAW

A Note
On Pressure vs. Principle
In the Courts

THE EXCESS LAND LAW: A NOTE ON PRESSURE VS. PRINCIPLE IN THE COURTS *

PAUL S. TAYLOR
University of California

... although the Supreme Court of the United States has now determined that the Federal Government, on its part, has authority to enter into the contracts in question, the authority of the state agencies so to contract is controlled EXCLUSIVELY *by state statutory and constitutional provisions. In our view, this Court has previously held that state irrigation districts lack the authority under California law to enter into these contracts. . . .*

Opening brief (against the excess land law) on further proceedings in the Ivanhoe case in the Supreme Court of California, on remand from the Supreme Court of the United States, 1959[1]

The legal fencing which is now going on in the Central Valley litigation is obscuring the real problems. . . . California needs greater water development, more water . . . to be distributed to as many people as possible as soon as possible. . . . To urge on the one hand that the Federal Government complete the project at a cost now estimated to be $676,018,000, and to argue on the other, that State agencies cannot as a matter of Sate law and policy co-operate in a plan which the State has for years known was contemplated, is to commit an act of duplicity of which I am incapable. . . . I tell you as bluntly as I can, that the adoption of the arguments contrary to mine can saddle legal millstones around the neck of this State capable of depriving it of the chance of solving its own water problems.

Edmund G. Brown, Attorney General of California, 1951[2]

---

* Related papers by the present author on the excess land law are: "Central Valley Project: Water and Land," *Western Political Quarterly*, II (1949), 228; "The 160-Acre Water Limitation and the Water Resources Commission," *Western Political Quarterly*, III (1950), 435; "Excess Land Law: Execution of a Public Policy," 64 *Yale Law Journal* 477 (1955); "Destruction of Federal Reclamation Policy, The *Ivanhoe* Case," 10 *Stanford Law Review* 76 (1957); "Excess Land Law on the Kern," 46 *California Law Review* 153 (1958); "Excess Land Law: Legislative Erosion of Public Policy," 30 *Rocky Mountain Law Review* 1 (1958). The present note is companion to an article to be published in the *California Law Review*, August, 1959, under the title, "Excess Land Law: Presssure v. Principle." Elizabeth Dickerson Huttman and Beverly Starika assisted in preparation of this paper.

[1] Opening brief [against the excess land law] on further proceedings of defendant-respondents on L.A. No. 23043 etc., *Ivanhoe Irrigation District* v. *All parties and persons, etc.*, by Horton & Knox, W. R. Bailey, Green, Green & Bartow, Sherman Anderson, Wm. P. Butcher, and Brobeck, Phleger & Harrison, March 16, 1959, p. 2. (Italics supplied.)

[2] Statement on the Central Valley validation cases, to the Joint Interim Committee on Water Problems of the Legislature, in *Report* of a Special Subcommittee on Irrigation and Reclamation . . . on Central Valley Project, California, as a result of hearings held October 29, 30, and 31, 1951 (Sacramento, California), pp. 107, 112, 119. The Attorney General identified one of the firms of attorneys participating in 1959 in the opening brief, *supra*, epigraph at note 1, as having represented Di Giorgio Fruit Farms, Inc. in 1951. (*Ibid.*, p. 114.) This corporation has been conspicuous in the controversy over the excess land law for many years. Although former Senator Downey described it as proof against application of the excess land law in 1947, it signed a recordable contract in compliance with the law in 1952 to obtain immediate water supplies for its excess holdings in Delano-Earlimart district. See Paul S. Taylor, "Excess Land Law on the Kern," 46 *California Law Review* 153, 183, 184 (1958).

COURTS ARE final arbiters of some controversies, but on great issues of public policy they sometimes are found in the middle. This is true in the dispute over the excess land law.³ Many California districts already were receiving water under contracts validated by California courts, and hundreds of millions of federal dollars had been poured into California for reclamation, before a California court decided in 1952 that the contracts under which the water was obtained were invalid in one important respect.

McCracken, a bachelor owning 309 acres in the Ivanhoe Irrigation District, went to court when the District, complying with its contract with the United States, refused to furnish him with Central Valley Project water for more than 160 acres unless he would agree to dispose of the excess acreage according to law. The trial court upheld McCracken.⁴

If politics, pressures and personalities are excluded from the courtroom, they are not absent from the corridors leading to it. Fred N. Howser, Attorney General of California, stood wtih McCracken rather than the Ivanhoe Irrigation District in the Superior Court. His successor, Edmund G. Brown, of opposite party affiliation, reversed Howser's position, and switched the support of the State from McCracken to the District. For doing so he was attacked sharply. The *Los Angeles Times* warned, without deterring him, that the "underlying issue is whether the Federal Bureau of Reclamation in its vigorously pursued policy of 'seize water and electric power to gain political domination' is to be permitted to gain a strangle hold on California's internal resources." ⁵

The change in position of the Attorney General evidently did not change the outcome. In 1957 a bare majority of the Supreme Court of California upheld the trial court in declaring the contracts invalid.⁶ Then the United States Supreme Court reversed the state Supreme Court in a unanimous decision, 8–0, in 1958.⁷ Back in the state Supreme Court, attor-

---

³ "No right to the use of water for land in private ownership shall be sold for a tract exceeding 160 acres to any one landowner...." 32 *Stat.* 389. The National Reclamation Act was passed in 1902 to provide opportunity for families to make homes on the land. Incidental to achieving this purpose, as the House report on the bill specified, "The bill... would compel the breaking up of any large tracts now held for which water rights from Government works are to be obtained by limiting the area of lands the property of any one landowner for which a water right may be acquired to 160 acres." (H.R. Rep. No. 794, 57th Cong., 1st Sess., ser. 4402, pt. 1, p. 7.)

⁴ *Ivanhoe Irrigation District v. All parties and persons,* in the Superior Court of the State of California, in and for the County of Tulare, No. 39627, July 31, 1952.

⁵ Editorial, March 7, 1951. The California Water and Power Users Association asserted in 1959 that the Tejon Ranch, owned "approximately 40 per cent" by the "Times-Mirror Corporation and Chandler and Sherman interests," could obtain $14 million of "unjust enrichment" from public water development in the absence of an excess land limitation. *Fresno Bee,* May 31, 1959, p. 11A.

⁶ *Ivanhoe Irrigation District v. All parties and persons,* 47 Cal. 2d 597 (1958); see also Paul S. Taylor, "Destruction of Federal Reclamation Policy? The *Ivanhoe* Case," 10 *Stanford Law Review* 76 (1957).

⁷ *Ivanhoe Irrigation District v. McCracken,* 357 U.S. 275.

neys for opponents of the excess land law are demanding in 1959 that the state court reaffirm the invalidity of contracts that contain it. This demand threatens to pit the Supreme Court of a state against the Supreme Court of the United States in the classic stand-off between an irresistible force and an immovable object.[8] Of course the United States Supreme Court might not approve this outcome, even if the state Supreme Court should assent.

The latest phase of these proceedings in the Ivanhoe case before the California Supreme Court is unusual in a number of respects. Attorneys representing opponents of the excess land law asked a lower court to reaffirm a result previously reversed by a higher court.[9] They advanced their proposal on grounds previously submitted to the higher court without altering the result.[10] They appealed to the lower court to save the higher court from outside criticism by "reversing" it.[11] Their proposal, if accepted, would create a legal stalemate between the state and federal governments.[12]

It is a curious feature of the entire Ivanhoe proceedings that apparently it has remained for this latest phase, and for those who argue that contracts accepting the 160 (or 320) acre limitation are contrary to state law and beyond reach of the Legislature, to mention for the first time the 320 acre land limitation in the California Constitution. This provision prescribes that *lands* granted to settlers shall be "in quantities not exceeding three hundred and twenty acres" each.[13] If the Constitution approves ownership of 320 acres of land as an appropriate dividing line controlling

---

[8] See epigraph at note 1, *supra*.

[9] ". . . we ask that, following such consideration of the decision of the Supreme Court of the United States in relation to this Court's prior decision as may be appropriate, this Court's judgments of invalidity be reaffirmed." (Opening brief, p. 2, cited note 1, *supra*.)

[10] "A valid contract necessarily requires two contracting parties with capacity to make it. The highest court of the state has held that one of the parties, namely the state agency, lacks such power and, under the California Constitution, could not be granted such power by the Legislature. This is the fundamental point to which all argument eventually returns. No action of this Court, we submit, can provide California irrigation districts with powers which they lack." (Brief for appellees on motion to dismiss appeal, p. 22, *Ivanhoe Irrigation District v. All Parties*, appeal docketed, 25 *U.S. Law Week* 3343 (May 13, 1957) (No. 993).

[11] "Problems of federal-state relationships . . . cannot be considered in isolation from the events of our times. It would be futile to attempt to blind ourselves to the widespread concern that has been voiced in responsible quarters with respect to the increasing authority being drawn into the central government and the consequent diminishing powers of the states of our federal union. . . .

"On this background, we submit the appellants do a disservice to the Supreme Court of the United States in attempting to extend its decision in these cases beyond the strictly limited points which it purported to determine." Reply brief on further proceedings . . . of defendant-respondents in L.A. No. 23043 . . . on remand from Supreme Court of the United States, April 1, 1959, p. 23.

[12] "The contracts are invalid, not because the United States lacks capacity, but because the state agency lacks the capacity; and in this field it takes two to make a bargain." Opening brief, p. 11, *supra*, note 1. See also epigraph at note 1.

[13] California Constitution, Art. XVII, Sec. 3.

distribution of *land*, it appears difficult to argue that the same or a similar dividing line controlling distribution of *water* is contrary to the Constitution. However, the opponents of the excess land law in the current state proceedings are willing to undertake the task.¹⁴

If the question were one of action by the Legislature, the "absence of any such [water] limitation" might merit this stricture in the brief: "Where the people of California have desired to distribute state property with reference to the holdings of the distributee, they have shown themselves capable of saying so." But the people in fact have said, through their Legislature, and more than once, that they were willing to have water distributed as prescribed by Congress, which is with reference to the holdings of the distributee.¹⁵

The question posed by implication by the attorneys' briefs is incorrectly drawn. The issue is not whether the Constitution *prescribes* distribution of water in the manner it prescribes distribution of land, but whether the Constitution *forbids* the Legislature to distribute water "with reference to the holdings of the distributee." When the State Constitution permits a 320 acre ownership criterion to govern public distribution of land, it can hardly forbid the constitutionally-approved body for lawmaking, the Legislature, to make use of the same criterion of land ownership to govern public distribution of water.

The opinion of the United States Supreme Court gives unmistakable clues to the guides it might apply to the Ivanhoe case, should it return to them a second time. It said it is "clear" that the judgments of the California Supreme Court "do not rest on an adequate state ground," and "the suggestion that state law prevented the water districts and agencies of the State from entering into the contracts" would not "change this conclusion.¹⁶ The United States Supreme Court said also that among the questions it need *not* determine, was this: "whether *a State* could [prevent water districts and agencies of the State from entering into the contracts

---

¹⁴ "Where the people of California have desired to distribute state property with reference to the holdings of the distributee, they have shown themselves capable of saying so. Thus Article XVII, Section 3 of the State Constitution provides that lands belonging to the State, which are suitable for cultivation, shall be granted to actual settlers, 'and in quantities not exceeding three hundred and twenty acres to each settler, under such conditions as shall be prescribed by law.' The absence of any such limitation in the case of the constitutional provisions dealing with water manifestly cannot be disregarded." (Opening brief, p. 17, footnote 11, *supra*, note 1.)

¹⁵ Cal. Water Code, Secs. 11500, 23175–23302 (1956).

¹⁶ 357 U.S. 290. The briefs of attorneys for those opposed to the law, notwithstanding the language in the decision of the Supreme Court of the United States, insist that the state Supreme Court already has decided the incapacity of water districts to contract in compliance with the excess land law on *state grounds*: "The validity of the contracts is ultimately controlled by state statutory and constitutional provisions. So tested, as this Court has held, the contracts are invalid." (Opening brief, pp. 22, 18; reply brief, 2. Cf. note 14.)

by 'state law' and] in that manner frustrate the consummation of a federal project constructed at its own behest." [17]

The insistence of attorneys for excess landholders that the jurisdictions of the state and federal governments over the respective parties to contracts between them are mutually exclusive, if accepted by the state Supreme Court, would raise again the question of federal supremacy. Since the present writer has discussed this, as well as other aspects of the original decision by the state Supreme Court, elsewhere, his comments need not be repeated here.[18]

The clash of views between state and United States courts is fundamental, not technical, as is generally true on great issues. The Supreme Court of the United States said that federal reclamation is "designed to benefit *people*, not *land*." [19] The opposite view, as argued in the briefs asking the California Supreme Court to declare the contracts invalid again, holds that state water law "looks to the *land* for the use it can make of the waters and contains no exception based upon the *identity of the landowner*."[20]

The progress and duration of proceedings in the courts, as well as their final legal outcome, are important. Support of litigation requires time and resources. Resources are very unequal between large landholding citizens and small or landless ones.[21] A concentrated interest has great advantages over a diffused one in protracted contests. The ordinary citizen, interested in the principles to govern the use of public funds to which he contributes as taxpayer, is unlikely to be accorded any standing in court at all, even if he has resources to meet court costs.

---
[17] 357 U.S. 290 (Italics supplied). Associate Justice Jackson, in a concurring opinion, has denied the right of a state court to determine, without federal review, state law affecting an interstate compact to control water pollution of the Ohio River: "Whatever she now says her Constitution means, she may not apply retroactively that interpretation to place an unforeseeable construction upon what the other States to this Compact were entitled to believe was a fully authorized act. Estoppel is not often to be invoked against a government. But West Virginia assumed a contractual obligation with equals by permission of another government that is sovereign in the field. After Congress and sister States had been induced to alter their positions and bind themselves to terms of a covenant, West Virginia should be estopped from repudiating her act." *West Virginia ex rel. Dyer* v. *Sims,* 341 U.S. 22, 28 (1950).

[18] Paul S. Taylor, "Destruction of Federal Reclamation Policy? The *Ivanhoe* Case," 10 *Stanford Law Review* 76, 106–111 (1957). Recently the United States Supreme Court has repeated the earlier language of Chief Justice Marshall: "It is of the very essence of supremacy to remove all obstacles to its action within its own sphere, and so to modify every power vested in subordinate governments, as to exempt its own operations from their own influence." *Public Utilities Commission* v. *United States,* 355 U.S. 534, 544 (1958).

[19] *Ivanhoe Irrigation District* v. *McCracken,* 357 U.S. 275, 297 (1958) (Italics supplied).

[20] Opening brief, p. 17 (Italics supplied).

[21] "We must make it so that the poor man will have as nearly as possible an equal opportunity in litigating as the rich man; and under present conditions, ashamed as we may be of it, this is not the fact." William Howard Taft, quoted in Final Report and Testimony of the U.S. Commission on Industrial Relations, Senate Document No. 415, 64th Cong., 1st Sess., I, 47 (1916).

If the California Supreme Court should reaffirm its original decision, as attorneys for excess landholding interests urge it to do, and should the decision stand, the course of legislative action would be gravely affected. In the past, the Supreme Court of California has been jealous of its own power over water law, and unfriendly to determination of water law by the Legislature. The Legislature tried in 1913 to trim from the state court's riparian doctrine of 1886 what the United States Supreme Court has called its "canine element," i.e., the power of riparian owners to assert a right to the full flow of a stream "no matter how unreasonable." [22] The state Supreme Court struck down the legislation of 1913 in 1926.[23] A constitutional amendment was adopted in 1928 to accomplish what the Legislature had tried vainly to do in 1913.[24]

The 1959 Legislature, considering the Governor's water program, rejected an excess land law.[25] Strong appeals were made, therefore, to adopt excess land legislation at a later session, and the Governor declared his intention to submit proposals. When the Assembly postponed action on an excess land bill, it arranged for an interim study of the problem that forecast possible later consideration.

If the courts accept the position of attorneys for excess landholders in current proceedings in the Ivanhoe case, the Legislature is powerless, and all efforts to persuade it to pass an excess land law will be useless and a delusion. The people, if they want a water limitation to parallel the constitutional land limitation, will have no recourse except to try to write it into the Constitution alongside the land limitation, through the arduous, slow and costly process of amendment.

---

[22] *United States v. Gerlach Live Stock Co.*, 339 U.S. 725, 751, 20 A.L.R. 2d 633, 650 (1950) (Justice Jackson); *Ivanhoe Irrigation District v. All Parties*, 47 Cal. 2d 597, 622, 306 P. 2d 824, 838 (1957).

[23] *Herminghaus v. Southern California Edison Co.*, 200 Cal. 81, 252 Pac. 607 (1926), cert. dismissed, 275 U.S. 486 (1927).

[24] California Constitution, Art. XIV, sec. 3.

[25] The California Labor Federation states that "Some 63% of the lands in the potential service area of the aqueduct are in ownerships of greater than 1,000 acres each. . . . Yet, at the insistence of the Brown Administration, the state legislature rejected efforts in both houses to enact anti-enrichment protections for the taxpayers." (Weekly newsletter, Vol. 1, No. 22, June 26, 1959, p. 7).

EXCESS LAND LAW

Secretary's Decision?

EXCESS LAND LAW: SECRETARY'S DECISION? A STUDY IN ADMINISTRATION OF FEDERAL-STATE RELATIONS

Paul S. Taylor*

I. Focus of Decision

For many years the two governments have peacefully and wholeheartedly cooperated in the planning and construction of this huge [Central Valley] project. In the very truest sense of the terms it is and has been a cooperative project. Certainly there is no conflict between the legislative branches of the two governments. . . . The federal Congress . . . has determined . . . that the 160-acre limitation is a basic part of federal policy. The state Legislature has adopted this concept as state policy by specifically authorizing irrigation districts to enter into contracts for project water that contain the 160-acre limitation. . . .
—California Supreme Court, 1960[1]

As we understand, neither the Bureau of Reclamation nor the State Administration desires to apply the Federal excess land provisions to the State service area [of San Luis Project, a part of Central Valley Project]. We are informed that an agreement is now being negotiated which, as we understand, on one ground or another, will permit State law to apply.
—Opinion of Counsel, Report of Chas. T. Main, Inc., to California Department of Water Resources, 1960[2]

Survival of a national policy—the distribution of water "in accordance with the greatest good to the greatest number of individuals"[3]—is at stake again, this time in administrative decisions affect-

---

*Professor of Economics, University of California, Berkeley; consultant to office of the Secretary of the Interior and Bureau of Reclamation, successively, between 1943 and 1952. Don Vial kindly read the manuscript, and Henry A. Dalton assisted in its preparation; the author alone is responsible. On October 25, 1961, the editors of the U.C.L.A. Law Review sent a copy of this article as originally drafted to Secretary of the Interior Stewart Udall.

[1] Ivanhoe Irrigation District v. All Parties, 53 Cal.2d 692, 714-15, 3 Cal. Rptr. 317, 330 (1960).

[2] Chas. T. Main, Inc., Final Report, General Evaluation of the Proposed Program for Financing and Constructing the State Water Resources Development System of the State of California Department of Water Resources, 2229-1-2A, app. 29, October 1960 [hereinafter cited as Main Report].
State legislation has approved at least six times the acceptance of federal contracts containing acreage limitation by *water districts*. Legislation has not specifically given this approval to a *state* contract, as proposed at San Luis. See Personal testimony of Paul S. Taylor prepared for presentation before State Assembly Water Committee, Sacramento, California, April 11, 1961, at 8, 9. However, the federal government might contract with water districts for use of San Luis facilities already empowered to accept acreage limitation. See text accompanying notes 30, 46 *infra*.

[3] Ivanhoe Irrigation Dist. v. McCracken, 357 U.S. 275, 297 (1958).

ing reclaimed areas within the Central Valley of California on the Kings and Kern rivers, and at San Luis. The policy is embodied in the excess land, or 160-acre, provisions of federal reclamation law that limit distribution of water to each individual to an amount sufficient to irrigate 160 acres.

Agreement and harmony on this policy has prevailed at times among legislative, executive and judicial branches, and between state and federal governments. At other times, sharp conflict has pervaded the processes of legislation on California water development and thrown these branches and levels of government into curious and changing alignments with, or against each other. In 1959, the California Supreme Court was able to report (and itself to exemplify) complete agreement between legislative and judicial branches of state and federal governments in *favor* of applying national policy in Central Valley. Two years earlier, prior to reversal by the United States Supreme Court, the state court's position had been otherwise.[4] In 1960 legal counsel advised the State of California of the existence of complete agreement between executive agencies of state and federal governments but in *opposition* to application of national policy.

Meanwhile, the federal administration has changed; a California reclamation project has run the gauntlet of Congress; and an interlocking state water program has run the gauntlet of the California legislature. While Congress decided in favor of acreage limitation, the legislature decided against it and the Governor decided against it in his contract with the Metropolitan Water District in southern California. Today conflict over policy is sharp between Congress and the California legislature and executive. The decisions to be made next are in the hands of the executive branch of the federal government. They may determine the survival of an effective national policy in California and in the nation.

The heat of controversy had so obscured the true character of acreage limitation as the instrument of historic national land and water policy that it required the United States Supreme Court to restate the policy with simple clarity. The purpose of acreage limitation is to distribute the benefits of federal expenditures for reclamation widely among individuals.[5] The principle of widespread distribution of benefits is timeless. Congress offered to extend these benefits — not only to settlers on public domain—but upon request, to those private landowners who would accept as their proper and generous share an

---

[4] Ivanhoe Irrigation Dist. v. All Parties, 47 Cal.2d 597, 306 P.2d 824 (1957).
[5] The words of the Supreme Court were: "[T]hat benefits may be distributed in accordance with the greatest good to the greatest number of individuals. The limitation insures that this enormous expenditure will not go in disproportionate share to a few individuals with large land holdings. Moreover, it prevents the use of the federal reclamation service for speculative purposes." Ivanhoe Irrigation Dist. v. McCracken, 357 U.S. at 297.

amount of water no greater than sufficient to irrigate 160 acres.[6] Congressman Frank W. Mondell, in charge of the Reclamation Bill in 1902, reassured the House that reclamation would not be used to support water monopoly:

> It is a step in advance of any legislation we have ever had in guarding against the possibility of speculative landholdings and in providing for small farms and homes on the public land, while it will also compel the division into small holdings of any large areas . . . in private ownership which may be irrigated under its provisions.[7]

The acreage limitation provisions of the reclamation law do not compel or force any private landholder to do anything. They neither confiscate nor expropriate land. Any excess landowner, knowing the terms on which Congress offers to provide water, is free to accept or to decline; he is not free to enlarge his own share at the expense of others beyond a sufficiency for 160 acres, or to reach for uncontrolled windfalls from public expenditures.

Congress has provided that individual landowners — including those who decline to ask for water for their *excess* lands — receive enough subsidized water to irrigate up to 160 acres. Employing the subsidy estimate of $577 per acre, a man and wife owning 160 acres each can obtain water bearing a total subsidy of $184,640.[8] However, substantial inducement is offered landowners to ask for additional water for their excess lands. By accepting acreage limitation — whether they own 10,000 acres, 50,000 acres, or any other acreage of irrigable land — they can obtain the use of subsidized water for their entire holdings for 10 years before selling the excess above 160 acres at a fair price, appraised to exclude increments in value created by the project. A leading opponent of acreage limitation acknowledged the generosity of this privilege to Congress. Referring to a large landholder in Central Valley, the Chief Counsel of Imperial Irrigation District said: "I will give you my own opinion of Jack O'Neill's willingness to sign the 160 acre limitation. He thinks if he gets water for

---

[6] Senator Francis G. Newlands, co-author of the Reclamation Act, said at Red Bluff, California, in 1905: "We realized . . . it would not be fair to apply it [reclamation] only to the public domain, for within reach of every Governmental project lie lands in private ownership . . . guarded against monopoly by preventing any proprietor from securing water rights for more than 160 acres . . . to destroy land monopoly; not only prevent the monopoly of public land, but to break up the existing land monopolies throughout the arid region." SACRAMENTO VALLEY DEVELOPMENT ASSOCIATION, BULL. No. 23, 14-18.

[7] 35 CONG. REC. 6677 (1902).

[8] This estimate excludes flood control subsidy. Letter from Congressmen Clair Engle, George P. Miller, John E. Moss, Harlan Hagen, B. F. Sisk, J. J. McFall to California Attorney General Edmund G. Brown, Feb. 4, 1957, in 44 CALIF. L. REV. 772 (1959).

10 years on there without having to sell it, he can make enough money out of it so he can afford to sell it at any old price."[9]

Some excess landholders, nevertheless, regard limitation of their opportunities under federal reclamation as too severely restricted. They have sought in various ways to escape acreage limitation while retaining the liberal financial benefits of federal reclamation law. Their methods have included demands for outright exemption, and use of the Army Engineers and the State of California in lieu of the Bureau of Reclamation.[10] As an alternative they have sougth congressional and administrative approval of money payments. In the Small Projects Reclamation Act they succeeded in obtaining the privilege, known as the Engle formula, of making interest payments in lieu of other compliance with acreage limitation. They have sought congressional and administrative acceptance of full payment of construction charges in lieu of other compliance with acreage limitation on Kings and Kern rivers and at San Luis, but so far have not obtained it.

Proposals of this kind for undermining acreage limitation are phrased in language that needs clarification. "Full payment of construction charges" by water users is not the same as "payment of full costs of construction" of the reclamation works that provide them with irrigation water. The discrepancy between them is often great. Water users' organizations on Kings River are being asked to repay less than one-third the actual cost of Pine Flat dam. Although 63 per cent of *reimbursable* costs of construction on Central Valley Project are allocated to irrigation, the irrigators — i.e., private landowners — have been asked to repay only 17 per cent.[11] Others must repay what the benefited landowners do not. On Central Valley Project, power users and municipal and industrial water users pay the difference between 17 per cent and 63 per cent of reimbursable costs. Federal taxpayers pay non-reimbursable costs, principally for flood control and for provision of interest-free money for irrigation.

For administrative convenience, reclamation policy is applied and financial repayment is arranged through the same contract executed between water users' organizations and the United States. This arrangement of convenience has fostered a contention that policy depends upon repayment and ceases with the final installment. The foundation of public policy, however, is not money but principle.

---

[9] Statement by Harry W. Horton, *Hearings on S. 1425, 2541, 3448, Before Subcommittee on Irrigation and Reclamation of Senate Committee on Interior and Insular Affairs*, 85th Cong., 2d Sess. 87, 88 (1958). [Hereinafter referred to as *1958 Hearings on S. 1425*.]

[10] See text accompanying notes 29-33 *infra*. See also Taylor, *Excess Land Law: Legislative Erosion of Public Policy*, 30 ROCKY MT. L. REV. 480, n.163 (1958).

[11] See 38 CALIF. L. REV. 728, 730-732 (1950) (citing H. R. Doc. No. 146, 80th Cong., 1st Sess. 23 (1947)).

Acreage limitation is the instrument of policy, not a form of collateral to assure repayment.[12] The demand of excess landholders that "full payment" be accepted as "full satisfaction" of acreage limitation, is a spurious claim that final payment of a fraction of the construction cost should extinguish a public policy that does not depend on cash. The current demand by excess landholders upon the Secretary of the Interior for approval of this claim is the occasion for this article.

On January 20, 1961, the day he entered the office of the Secretary of the Interior, Secretary Stewart L. Udall found himself facing at least two critical decisions affecting application of the excess land provisions. Only the day before, on his last day in office, Secretary Fred A. Seaton had said that he had made one of these decisions. He had approved repayment contracts on Kings and Kern rivers recognizing that completion of full payment of construction charges by water users' organizations renders the excess land laws inoperative. But Secretary Seaton was careful not to make his approval final, for he withheld "execution [of the contracts] . . . until the Attorney General's views are received. . . ."[13] In other words, he had not made a final decision, but had left that to the incoming administration. A few days later the Attorney General for the new administration sent the contracts back to the desk of the new Secretary without opinion.

The crucial point at stake in this first decision — whether payment of money can satisfy policy—is that the law requires agreement by landowners to dispose of their holdings above 160 acres per individual at a fair appraised price as prerequisite to obtaining federal project water for their *entire* holdings. If it should be finally decided that full payment of the financial obligations of water users renders these provisions inoperative, then it would be possible for water users' organizations to avoid national policy entirely by promptly paying up in full. Naturally many excess landholders desire this option.[14] Furthermore, if water agencies on Kings and Kern rivers are permitted to escape acreage limitation by pre-payment in full, they can do so in other areas of federal reclamation — including the federal San Luis service area. In addition, the State of California can relieve excess landholders, in the state service area of the San Luis Project, from the limitation by paying the state's share of the

---

[12] Taylor, *Excess Land Law: Execution of a Public Policy*, 64 YALE L.J. 477, 512-514 (1955).

[13] U.S. Dep't of Interior, Information Service, January 19, 1961.

[14] For example, the manager of the Land Department of the Southern Pacific Company, L. Frandsen, owning close to 150,000 acres in the San Luis Valley, testified that his company desired "the alternative of paying interest on the federal irrigation investment and thus be allowed to retain their land holdings and obtain water for them." *Hearings on S.44 Before Senate Subcommittee on Irrigation and Reclamation*, 86th Cong., 1st Sess. 101 (1959). See also Fresno Bee, Sept. 27, 1961.

cost concurrently with construction.[15] This is the import of the decision Secretary Udall must now make.

If the Secretary of the Interior accepts the doctrine that full payment renders the excess land laws inoperative, further decisions on acreage limitation on the San Luis Project will have been stripped largely of substance. But if he rejects it he still faces a second decision, of importance substantively as well as in principle.

The San Luis Project Act of 1960 authorizes him to enter into a contract with the State of California covering designing and constructing joint-use facilities — dam, reservoir, pumping plant, and canal — and to permit their use for delivery of water to a so-called state service area.[16] In passing the bill, Congress refused to exempt those water deliveries and drainage facilities serving lands under contract with the state lying outside the federal San Luis unit service area from the application of federal reclamation law.[17] The Secretary is responsible, therefore, for including provisions in the contract that will determine the manner and extent of application of federal reclamation law to the state service area.

These two decisions involve vast economic interests. Probably the greatest concentrations of ownership of remaining irrigable land in the United States lie within the adjacent areas of the Kings, Kern, and San Luis projects. Senator Douglas placed figures in the *Congressional Record* showing that in Kern County alone — including possible areas of service south of the federal San Luis service area — 64.2 per cent of 2,135,000 acres was owned in lots of over 1,000 each, and 31.7 percent was held by four landowners.[18] Their financial stake in avoiding disposal of their excess lands is great. Public subsidies alone amounted to $577 per acre on the Central Valley Project, and have been estimated at $591 an acre on the San Luis unit.[19] Increments in land values from availability of water are likely to range from $500 to $1500 an acre, depending on fertility of soil, suitability for high value crops, and other factors affecting the quality of the land.[20] Besides, additional incremental values may be in

---

[15] See text accompanying note 120 *infra*.

[16] 74 Stat. 156 (1960). All waters from the state project reaching the southern San Joaquin Valley and southern California must flow through these facilities.

[17] S. 44, § 6(a); H.R. 7155, § 7, 86th Cong. (1959).

[18] 105 CONG. REC. 7670 (1959).

[19] See also the statement of Harvey O. Banks, California State Engineer, to Senator James E. Murray, June 18, 1956, *Hearings on S. 178 Before Subcommittee on Irrigation and Reclamation of Senate Committee on Interior and Insular Affairs*, 84th Cong., 2d Sess. 37 (1956) [hereinafter cited as *1956 Hearings on S. 178*].

[20] For estimates of the magnitude of economic interests at stake, see Taylor, *Destruction of Federal Reclamation Policy? The Ivanhoe Case*, 10 STAN. L. REV. 76, 92, (110); Personal testimony of Paul S. Taylor, *supra* note 2, at 2-4.

prospect for those who can retain ownership during years of strong population and economic growth.

These concentrated economic interests are the chief source of conflict over the excess land law at every level and in every branch of government whenever and wherever a decision affecting it is to be made.[21] Naturally intensity of feeling surrounds the issue. It was exemplified recently on one side by a resolution of the Feather River Project Association that unless Congress would exempt the state service area from acreage limitation, the Association should oppose federal construction of the San Luis Reservoir.[22] It was exemplified on the other side by descriptions that Senators Douglas and Morse applied to exemption, calling the attempt, if successful, a "public catastrophe" and "great water steal."[23]

II. State Project

> I support the position that the Federal Government should respect the water laws of California. If elected governor I will do everything in my power to have the department of water resources and the water rights board sustain the State's position as upheld by the recent decision of the Supreme Court of California [rejecting the 160-acre limitation] in the Ivanhoe and related cases. . . . My opponent, the present attorney general [Edmund G. Brown] of California, has himself abandoned, and sought to get the irrigation districts to abandon, this position.
> —Senator William F. Knowland, Candidate for Governor of California, 1958[24]

> Gov. Brown is determined that the state water program, his great achievement, shall not fall on a technical point of federal law. . . . Every voter in California shall have his say on this in November when a proposition to authorize $1.75 billion in bonds will be on the ballot. The water agencies hold the fate of the bond issue . . . they could influence voters in their districts for or against the bond issue; or by refusing to negotiate contracts for water, they could shake the financial structure of the program so that bonds could not be sold, even if they were authorized . . . they have hung back with their

---

[21] See Taylor, *Excess Land Law: Pressure vs. Principle*, 47 Calif. L. Rev. 499 (1959).

[22] "[I]f federal legislation is adopted without such a provision as Section 7, then the state should proceed to construct the San Luis Reservoir and other joint-use facilities as part of the state project, with the right of the federal government as may be agreed upon, to provide the necessary storage capacity therein to serve its federal San Luis service area." *Feather River Project Association Resolution*, February 12, 1960, in 4 Feather River Project Ass'n Newsletter No. 2 (1960). Members of the Board of Directors included spokesmen in opposition to acreage limitation for some of the largest landowning corporations in Central Valley.

[23] 105 Cong. Rec. 7670 (1959).

[24] Address by Senator Knowland, Oakland, Calif., March 21, 1958, in 104 Cong. Rec. A2705 (1958). In 1947 Senator Knowland co-sponsored S.912 with Senator Sheridan Downey to exempt Central Valley Project from acreage limitation. Attorney General Brown obtained unanimous reversal by the United States Supreme Court of the California Supreme Court's rejection of acreage limitation in the *Ivanhoe* case. He won the Governorship over Senator Knowland on a platform that declared: "We re-affirm our support of federal Reclamation Laws providing for 160-acre limitation to insure equitable distribution of water and avoid the evils of land speculation and monopoly, and to prevent undue profit at public expense." *California Democratic Party Platform*, 1958, p. 14.

contracts, and that is why Gov. Brown will wage his all-out fight for Section 7 [to exempt the state service area from the 160-acre limitation]. He must retain the active support of the water agencies to win the water ballot next November. These mighty water agencies and associated organizations have made the terms. They have picked the ground on which the governor must do battle. It is rough ground, and it is a measure of the governor's courage and sagacity in this matter that he is willing to fight on it.
—*Gov. Brown's "All-out" Fight*, editorial, Los Angeles Times, 1960[25]

The State of California carried on extensive water investigations beginning in the 1920's and in 1930 proposed a state water plan, of which Central Valley development was a major part.[26] In 1933 the legislature, and the voters by referendum as well, approved a state revenue bond issue of $170 million to construct the first unit of Central Valley Project.[27] Unable to market the bonds, the state—through its spokesmen including the State Engineer—appealed to the federal government to undertake construction of this initial unit, *viz.*, Shasta Reservoir, Delta cross-channel, Tracy pumps, Delta-Mendota canal, Friant Reservoir, Madera and Friant-Kern canals. This the federal government proceeded to do in 1935, assigning Central Valley Project to the Bureau of Reclamation.[28]

In the Spring of 1944, when the first full-scale effort to persuade Congress to remove acreage limitation from Central Valley was in progress, led by Congressman Alfred J. Elliott and Senator Sheridan Downey of California, a national business journal described plans attributed to California's "big landowners" for a four-pronged attack upon the law. The methods for destroying or avoiding acreage limitation were: (1) specific congressional exemption; (2) use of the Army Engineers as the construction agency, since its basic legislation did not include the acreage limitation provisions of reclamation law; (3) use of the State of California as owner, or operator, of Central Valley Project to "side-step the 160-acre limitation;" and (4) use of

---

[25] Feb. 28, 1960. "If Brown could ram through the water program that Knight failed to accomplish . . . (and) ring up a smashing victory on his new tax program, then the door of the White House might swing wide." Editorial, Calif. Farmer, April 25, 1959, p. 432, col. 2.

For recent indications of the enduring and deep-seated political character of the acreage limitation issue see Earl C. Behrens, "The Federal 'Price' for Aiding San Luis Project?" San Francisco Chronicle, November 26, 1961, p. 9; Edward H. Dickson, "160 Acre Limitation Has Long Political History," Fresno Bee, November 12, 1961; Ruth Finney, "Trouble Looms for San Luis," San Francisco News-Call-Bulletin, November 10, 1961, p. 21; Fresno Bee, October 13, 1961.

[26] Division of Water Resources, Calif. Dep't of Public Works, Bull. No. 25, Report to Legislature of 1931 on State Water Plan, in JOURNAL OF CALIF. SENATE & ASSEMBLY, 49th Sess. app. 3 (1931).

[27] Cal. Stat. 1933, chs. 918, 1042.

[28] MONTGOMERY & CLAWSON, HISTORY OF LEGISLATION AND POLICY FORMATION OF THE CENTRAL VALLEY PROJECT; Bureau of Agricultural Economics, U.S. Dep't of Agriculture, March 1946, 82-92.

pumps to draw upon underground water supplies rather than the surface waters delivered by a federal project.[29]

Attacks upon the excess land law exhibiting each point in this varied pattern have been unfolding successively, or simultaneously, ever since. The results of each tactic so far can be summarized briefly as follows:

Tactic (1): Congress rejected attempts at specific exemption of Central Valley in 1944, 1947, 1959 and 1960.[30]

Tactic (2): In 1944 Congress extended the acreage limitation provisions of reclamation law to govern also the irrigation features of projects constructed by the Army Engineers.[31] The Army Engineers denied for years that Congress had done this, but the Attorney General confirmed it on December 15, 1958.[32] In the meantime, the position taken by the Army Engineers obstructed application of the law to reservoirs on the Kings and Kern rivers completed in 1954. Now the decision lies with Secretary Udall whether to accept or reject the Kings and Kern contracts as approved conditionally — but not finally — by Secretary Seaton.

Tactic (3): Use of the state of a means of avoiding acreage limitation is now being put fully to the test. At the moment its prospect for success depends on the nature of the contract with the State of California which the Secretary of the Interior is willing to approve for joint-use of the San Luis Project.

Tactic (4): Reliance on pumps has provided water from underground for large areas for many years, without acreage limitation. However, in 1956, and again in 1958, the President of Westlands District was appealing for federal help due to the insufficiency and poor quality of the pumped water, and professed willingness to accept federal acreage limitation law to get it.[33]

The remainder of this paper is devoted to consideration of the attempt to employ tactic number (3), use of the state as a means of escape from acreage limitation.

The original state Central Valley Project Act, approved by the

---

[29] *Valley Divided*, Bus. Week, May 13, 1944, pp. 21, 24. The proposal that the state "take over the Central Valley project, paying the entire bill," was "said to have originated among the big landowners of Fresno County...."

[30] H.R. 3961, 78th Cong., 2d Sess. (1944); S. 912, 80th Cong., 1st Sess. (1947); S. 44, H.R. 7155, 86th Cong., 2d Sess. (1960).

[31] Act of Dec. 22, 1944, ch. 665, § 8, 58 Stat. 891.

[32] 105 CONG. REC. 7862-66. See also Taylor, *Excess Land Law on the Kern?*, 46 CALIF. L. REV. 153 (1958).

[33] "The near tragic situation I outlined before you 22 months ago has steadily worsened. Our water table has receded further and the use of deep well water of high mineral content is continuing to cause deterioration of our agricultural lands." Statement of J. E. O'Neill, *Hearings on S. 1887 Before the Subcommittee on Irrigation and Reclamation of the Senate Committee on Interior and Insular Affairs*, 85th Cong., 2d Sess. 89 (1958) [hereinafter cited as *1958 Hearings on S. 1887*].

legislature and people in 1933, carried with it approval of not only state construction, but also of federal construction under reclamation law, of which acreage limitation is an essential part. In fact, the California legislature had approved acreage limitation at least five times, and the voters once, between 1917 and 1943, by authorizing acceptance of federal aid for water development under reclamation law.[34] In 1944, however, the California State Engineer "speaking personally and not for the water project authority" began to voice opposition to acreage limitation. In that year he supported an effort to exempt Central Valley, saying that the limitation was "inapplicable and unworkable for much of the Central Valley Project," and needed to be "radically amended or eliminated." He told Congress, "The necessity of change or elimination of this feature of the law, applying to Central Valley, has been repeatedly brought to the attention of the United States Bureau of Reclamation for many years."[35] The State Engineer did not mention the state legislative record on acreage limitation, nor the fact that under these laws the federal government long before had taken responsibility for construction of the Orland Project in Central Valley, applying to it a forty-acre limitation, nor the more recent fact that the legislature had memorialized Congress to appropriate funds for the Central Valley Project "reimbursable in accordance with the reclamation law" during the years when the State Engineer and other spokesmen for the state were actively seeking federal aid for Central Valley.[36] The State Engineer's opposition to acreage limitation was shared by large land-owning interests and, from the thirties, apparently by some officials of the Bureau of Reclamation as well.[37]

---

[34] Cal. Stat. 1917, ch. 160, §§ 1, 4; Cal. Stat. 1933, ch. 918, § 2; Cal. Stat. 1933, ch. 1042, § 15; Cal. Stat. 1935, ch. 615, §§ 2, 3; Cal. Stat. 1937, ch. 922, § 2; Cal. Stat. 1943, ch. 372. Section 15 of the 1933 Central Valley Act, approved separately at the polls by the people, empowered the state Water Project Authority to accept federal cooperation in "construction, maintenance and operation and in financing" of the Central Valley Project "under federal legislation now or hereafter enacted by Congress." Cal. Stat. 1933, ch. 1042 § 15.

[35] Statement by Edward Hyatt, State Engineer and Executive Officer, Water Project Authority of the State of California, *Hearings on H.R. 3961 Before a Subcommittee of the Senate Committee on Commerce*, 78th Cong., 2d Sess. 635 (1944).

[36] CALIF. SENATE JOURN., Extraord. Sess. 1936, at 13, 14, 35, 36.

[37] Statement of Roland Curran, Secretary-Manager, Central Valley Project Association, *Hearings on S. 912 Before a Subcommittee of the Senate Public Lands Committee*, 80th Cong., 1st Sess. 1310 (1947). The State Engineer supported construction by the Army Engineers on Kings River in preference to the Bureau of Reclamation at a time when the Army Engineers were resisting, and the Bureau of Reclamation supporting acreage limitation. "In 1944, the Bureau of Reclamation asked an appropriation to start work on the Pine Flat project. No state official showed concern or backed the request. . . . By 1946, state officials, who had been silent throughout efforts on the part of the Bureau of Reclamation to get funds for Pine Flats, began an active drive to get money appropriated to the Army Engineers for this

The first major effort to use the state itself as an instrument for avoiding acreage limitation assumed the form of a proposal that the state take over the Central Valley Project which was being constructed by the federal government.[38] The State Chamber of Commerce, the Farm Bureau Federation, and later the California Water Council composed of representatives from irrigation districts, chambers of commerce, municipal governments and other organizations interested in water problems, were conspicuous among its supporters.[39] In 1945 Secretary of the Interior Harold L. Ickes identified the reasons, in his opinion, for the proposal that the state operate the Central Valley Project:

> It is the age-old battle over who is to cash in on the unearned increment in land values created by a public investment. . . . [T]heir principal objective is to avoid application to the Central Valley of California of the long-established reclamation policy of the Congress which provides for the distribution of the benefits of great irrigation projects among the many and which prevents speculation in lands by the few.[40]

This initial effort slowed to a walk after the terms on which the Department of the Interior would be willing to withdraw in favor of the state were fully realized. Secretary Ickes advised Governor Earl Warren:

> If the state has arrived at a financial position where it is ready to reimburse the United States Treasury for expenditures already made in behalf of the people of California, and is further prepared to guarantee the additional financing necessary to complete the project within a reasonable number of years, the Department of the Interior is prepared to withdraw from the project. Before we hand back these responsibilities to the state, however, we feel that sufficient evidence should be presented to prove the willingness and ability of Californians to shoulder the burdens of this great enterprise.[41]

The Bureau of Reclamation made it clear that congressional approval, required to turn over the federal project to the state, would involve discussions over continuance, under state operation, of acreage limitation and other federal policies, as well.[42]

---

project. In January, 1946, Northcutt Ely, the state's Washington lobbyist . . . read a telegram from [State Engineer] Hyatt saying 'the need is urgent, in order to prevent further flood damage.'" Statement of Finney, San Francisco News, October 16, 1948.

[38] MONTGOMERY & CLAWSON, *op. cit. supra* note 28, at 117-128.

[39] San Francisco News, December 18, 1946. The Water Council asked for, "State control . . . and exemption of CVP . . . from the 160 acre limitation law."

[40] Letter from Harold L. Ickes to Frank Clarvoe, editor, San Francisco News, October 31, 1945.

[41] Letter from Harold L. Ickes to Governor Earl Warren, March 7, 1945.

[42] U.S. Bureau of Reclamation, U.S. Dep't of Interior, Answers to Questions Submitted to that bureau by the Central Valley Project Committee 3, 4, in MONTGOMERY & CLAWSON, *op. cit. supra* note 28, at 116-17. The move for state purchase came to a dead stop in 1953 when Secretary of the Interior Douglas McKay said he was "not optimistic," and remarked that Shasta Dam "is worth a lot more than the book value." Noting the opposition of "some people" to federal management and acreage limitation, the *Oroville*

A second (the present) phase of the attempt to use the state to avoid acreage limitation began in 1951 when the state legislature approved Feather River as a state project.[43] A few years earlier, in 1945, the Federal Bureau of Reclamation had included development of Feather River in its plan for the Central Valley Basin, and in 1949 President Harry S. Truman had transmitted the plan to Congress.[44] The prospect of federal construction on Feather River, therefore, was coming closer. Besides, the Bureau of Reclamation was receiving the approval of more and more California water users and voters for contracts incorporating acreage limitations. On December 17, 1947, the voters of the Coachella Valley County Water District approved a contract by 1133 to 19. Two water users' districts in the San Joaquin Valley had accepted Central Valley Project repayment contracts containing the limitation in 1948, one of them through its board of directors and the other by popular vote of 188 to 1. Three more districts signed similar contracts in 1949, and five more in 1950; voters approved overwhelmingly.[45] These events revealed a severely concentrated, rather than broadly popular, basis for resistance to acreage limitation.

Acreage limitation and other questions of policy were not a significant part of the public discussions surrounding state authorization of the Feather River Project. However, state authorization was one possible way to place the Feather River Project beyond reach of this apparent trend toward water users' acceptance of federal policy. Unless the legislature should close a possible legal gap in state policy[46] by specifically extending acreage limitation to the Feather River Project, voters in water districts receiving Feather River Project water might not even be asked to express themselves on acceptance of water under acreage limitation.

Engineering considerations and possible conflicts with the federal government over physical aspects of Feather River development were discussed, but these were not among the reasons for state authorization. On the contrary, Governor Earl Warren explained carefully to

---

Mercury Register said, "From our viewpoint, purchase of the Central Valleys Project would mean an extension of the state's credit to a point where it would be unable to finance the big Oroville dam—the Feather River Project." Sacramento Bee, October 29, 1953, p. 36 col. 5.

[43] Cal. Stat. 1951, ch. 1441, § 2.

[44] Bureau of Reclamation, U.S. Department of Interior, Central Valley Basin—a Comprehensive Report on the Development of the Water and Related Resources of the Central Valley Basin for Irrigation, Power Production, and Other Beneficial Uses in California, and Comments by the State of California and Federal Agencies; see S. Doc. No. 113, 81st Cong., 1st Sess. 59 (1949).

[45] Taylor, *The Excess Land Law: Pressure vs. Principle*, 47 CALIF. L. REV. 499, 531 (1959).

[46] Epigraph accompanying note 1 *supra*. See also text accompanying note 2 *supra* and note 130 *infra*.

Congress that there was no "conflict with any federal program." "That Feather River project is a tremendous project. It involves multiple-purpose dams exactly the same as our Central Valley project does, the development of power and water and many other features."[47]

There is a considerable difference in the means of financing federal and state projects. For example the availability of interest-free money under federal law amounts to an advantage in favor of federal over state construction of around a half-billion dollars on the Feather River Project.[48] Public discussions in California, at the time of state authorization of the Feather River Project and ever since, have been remarkably free of this particular financial aspect — a deterrent rather than motive for a state project.

Of course financial aspects of the Feather River Project were mentioned. Governor Warren spoke to Congress in 1951 of California's readiness to carry a larger share of the costs of its own water development. "I just want you to know that we want to be as self-reliant as we can. We don't want to come to Congress when it isn't necessary." Describing the state Feather River Project as "in consonance with the reclamation program and the flood control program," and apparently aware that as a state project without acreage limitation, Feather River was ineligible for federal interest-free irrigation funds, he said, "We will do it without asking the federal government to appropriate any money except insofar as federal interest might direct it in regard to navigation, flood control or salinity control."[49]

Instead of discussing in California the additional costs Californians would be obliged to bear if it were constructed as a state project, more public emphasis has been laid there upon the alleged reluctance of Congress to finance more irrigation development in that state, and upon the possibility of persuading Congress to make contributions to a state project for flood control, far less in amount than

---

[47] Testimony given October 29, 1951, *Report of a Special House Subcommittee on Irrigation and Reclamation on Central Valley Project, California, as a result of hearings held October 29, 30, and 31, 1951*, at 29, 30. [Hereinafter cited as *1951 House Special Report*.] Eight years later, Senator Clair Engle was even more emphatic about the harmony between state and federal programs than the Governor had been. "The federal San Luis unit," he told the Senate, "is part and parcel of the overall state water plan. . . ." 105 CONG. REC. 7486 (1959).

[48] The basis for this estimate is the prospect that by 1990 water deliveries under the state project will be devoted about 40 percent to irrigation and 60 percent to urban uses. Federal investment for irrigation is interest-free under reclamation law. See Main Report, *supra* note 2, at 7, 8; Personal Testimony of Paul S. Taylor, *supra* note 2, at 14, 15.

[49] *1951 House Special Report. supra* note 47, at 27-30. Later, Congressman Engle advocated unlimited federal assistance to the state project, including interest-free money for irrigation costs as available presently only under reclamation law. 103 CONG. REC. A7668, A7669 (1957); 105 CONG. REC. 7855-57 (1959).

the interest-free money for irrigation for which a state project is ineligible. Both subsidies are available to a federal project.

Congressman Clair Engle, emphasizing reluctance of Congress to authorize a federal Feather River Project, attributed this to three causes: (1) unwillingness "to step in when the state has expressed an interest"; (2) unwillingness to increase already large appropriations for California water development; and (3) opposition from congressional supporters of the "Upper Colorado Project hanging on the edge of defeat due to the opposition from Southern California."[50] The first and third were responses to California's own actions.

Progress on the state Feather River Project has been hesitant and slow. A sense of urgency appears to be lacking. About five years after authorization, the state arranged for relocation of highway and railroad, works which are still uncompleted. In 1961 the state let contracts for two diversion tunnels. These works are also "preliminary to the actual construction of Oroville dam."[51]

Among the more important effects of the 1951 state authorization of the Feather River Project, apparently, has been that it deterred the Bureau of Reclamation from constructing that project. As Senator Kuchel said in 1956, "I venture the guess that if the state had not indicated its interest in Oroville, we would have had long before last year's flood a federal dam at Oroville."[52]

---

[50] "Engle Declares Federal FRP Is Empty Hope," Sacramento Bee, Feb. 3, 1956, p. 3, col. 1. *Time Magazine* indicated another possible reason for lack of enthusiasm among western Congressmen for aiding California water development. By its account, a federal report on Western Water Exchange, authorized by Congress to plan large-scale, united western water development, was pigeon-holed in 1951 "probably because California is afraid of the effect the report may have on its struggle with Arizona for the last dribbles of water in the lower Colorado River. . . ." Time Magazine, July 30, 1951, p. 50.

[51] N. Y. Times, August 20, 1961, p. 75.

[52] *1956 Hearings on S.178, supra* note 19, at 179. About two months earlier, Governor Knight had asked the state legislature for funds for relocation of railroad and highway, and surveys and construction plans. "He quoted Congressman Clair Engle . . . as telling him . . . California's chance of government help will be enhanced immensely if he can report affirmative appropriation action by the state legislature and not simply that state authorities still are studying the vast FRP undertaking. Governor Knight . . . emphasized an equally important factor . . . the crying need for Northern California flood protection and the fact that legislature originally approved the FRP five years ago and has taken no substantial action since. . . . 'I'm going to see that the people of this great valley get flood protection if I don't do anything else as governor,' Knight said. 'Floods don't wait for the settlement of hair splitting technicalities.'" He "expressed hope" for grants of $300 million or more "in federal money ultimately" for flood control and San Luis Dam construction. Sacramento Bee, March 13, 1956, p. 1. Four years later, an editorial of the *San Francisco Chronicle*, entitled "Governor Brown Deplores Floods," stated: "The Governor of California, who was an early and vigorous critic of the water plan when it was broached under a previous administration—but who has now adopted it and plainly regards it as his own— . . . has said that the present winter rains imply floods that could become catastrophic . . . and he has ominously added: . . . 'I ask some of the newspapers who have editorialized against it [the bond issue]

III. Federal Project

> For the first time in these long discussions with which many of you are most familiar, Californians come before you united, offering a single plan with unanimous support.
> —Governor Edmund G. Brown, 1959[53]

> Mr. [Senator Thomas] Kuchel: Who, in God's name, speaks for the people of California? Does a Democratic Governor? Do the two Senators from California?
> Mr. [Senator Paul] Douglas: No.
> —Congressional Record, 1959[54]

> Senator Kuchel: How do we judge the acceptance of the people of California, Congressman Hagen? How do we do that?
> Representative Hagen: Senator Kuchel, I think in this very room you have people who in the main must be satisfied and in agreement before any real progress can be made on the San Luis project. There is one segment of opinion represented by the State Grange, Mr. Sehlmeyer, who is a very admirable man, who does not endorse any type of State project because the State does not have an acreage limitation law. . . . However, I think agreement could be achieved without the agreement of Mr. Sehlmeyer, and I think it has to be achieved before any progress could be made regardless of whether this Congress passes an authorization bill or not, because in my judgment the State has so many locks on various aspects of progress that the State acceptance has to be present for any progress to be made.
> —Senate Hearings before the Subcommittee on Irrigation and Reclamation, 1958[55]

The moves made during the late fifties and early sixties toward a new state water plan have not rested on the assumption that the state should undertake construction of all parts of the plan. On the contrary, the Feather River Project is the only large construction within the plan for Central Valley that the state legislature has said the state itself will undertake. This particular responsibility was assumed, as noted above, in spite of the heavy financial burden it imposes on the state, and the substantial financial advantage it would be to its citizens to make Feather River a federal project. A special House subcommittee—taking note of this burden upon the state a few months after the legislature acted—said its members were "surprised to learn that the legislature of the State of California author-

---

to take note. The responsibility will be theirs.'" The editorial expressed "a disbelief that Providence has sent the winter rains to drum up votes for his bond issue—which contemplates spending precious little of its $1.75 billion for purposes of flood control." February 11, 1960, editorial page, cols. 1, 2. Construction of a dam on Feather River had not started in 1961.

[53] *Hearings on S. 44 Before the Subcommittee on Irrigation and Reclamation of the Senate Committee on Interior and Insular Affairs,* 86th Cong., 1st Sess. 11 (1959) [hereinafter cited as *1959 Hearings on S. 44*].

[54] 105 CONG. REC. 7851 (1959).

[55] *Hearings on S. 1887 Before the Subcommittee on Irrigation and Reclamation of the Senate Committee on Interior and Insular Affairs,* 85th Cong. 2nd Sess. 42 (1958) [hereinafter cited as *1958 Hearings on S. 1887*]. Congressman Hagen did not mention the California Labor Federation, long an active supporter of acreage limitation. Governor Brown said, "I have made no attempt to answer every conceivable question or satisfy all extremists."

ized a project for the total estimated capital cost of $1,270,000,000 on which the State Engineer testified he did not know whether the project was economically or financially feasible."[56]

State authorization of the Feather River Project has not ended federal efforts elsewhere in Central Valley toward completion of its water development. These have continued, principally on Trinity River, and have been supported by spokesmen for the state. A bill in the 87th Congress, S. 103 by Senator Kuchel, proposed additional federal construction within the state plan at both Auburn Reservoir on the American River, and the Folsom South Canal.[57]

The state Feather River Project does not stand by itself, separate from San Luis, in any significant respect. It would be at least as accurate to say that at San Luis a single project is divided into two, as to say that at San Luis two projects meet.[58] The Feather River Project is dependent physically upon construction of San Luis Reservoir as a means of getting water southward into the southern San Joaquin Valley and beyond. As State Engineer Harvey O. Banks said, "San Luis Reservoir is as essential to the Feather River Project as Shasta Reservoir is to the Central Valley Project."[59] State authorization of the Feather River Project, in recognition thereof, included authorization of San Luis in 1951 as a part of a whole.[60]

In 1956, Governor Goodwin J. Knight asked Congress to construct the San Luis unit "in such a manner that it can be integrated

---

[56] *1951 House Special Report, supra* note 47, at 9. A few months earlier the State Engineer's report had concluded that: "The Feather River Project and associated Santa Clara-Alameda and San Joaquin Valley-Southern California Diversion Projects are not financially feasible on the basis of revenue derived from water charges and the sale of electric power at the rates assumed in the report unless the Federal and State Governments contribute to the cost of the projects funds in substantial amounts in the interest of flood control and water development on the basis of state-wide concern." Report on Feasibility of Feather River Project and Sacramento-San Joaquin Delta Diversion Projects proposed as features of the California Water Plan 126, May 1951.

[57] 13 WESTERN WATER NEWS No. 5, 1, 4 (1961).

[58] Senator Kuchel told the Senate on May 5, 1959, "Thus two systems—one a federal [Central Valley] project in being; the other, a state project about to get under way—would both be served at San Luis, the point where they cross—by a single storage reservoir whose cost of construction and operation would be shared by both governments." 105 CONG. REC. 7483 (1959). A resolution presented to the Senate by the San Bernardino County Board of Supervisors, stated: "Whereas the San Luis dam is an essential part of said Feather River Project . . . the state [should] construct, operate, manage, and control the San Luis Dam and Reservoir as part of the Feather River Project." *1956 Hearings on S. 178, supra* note 19, at 14.

[59] Statement of Harvey O. Banks to Senator James E. Murray, June 18, 1956, *1956 Hearings on S. 178, supra* note 19, at 36.

[60] "It is an authorization under which the State could, if appropriations are made available, construct all of the works at San Luis to serve the entire service area in the westerly-southerly end of the San Joaquin Valley, including the San Luis service area and areas in Kern County and southern California." Statement of Harvey O. Banks, *1958 Hearings on S. 1887, supra* note 55, at 58.

with the state's Feather River Project. . . ."⁶¹ From the state standpoint, federal construction of the San Luis Project was one means of lightening the heavy financial burden that a totally state-constructed Feather River Project would impose.⁶² But water policy as well as money was involved. Despite the financial advantages of federal construction to the state and its water users, in Washington several witnesses from his own state failed to support Governor Knight and were so effective that Congress was influenced to postpone action on the Governor's request.⁶³

These California witnesses were fearful of federal aid sought by Governor Knight in the form of federal construction. A spokesman for the Kern County Farm Bureau, for example, told Congress the Bureau preferred state construction of San Luis because federal authorization of San Luis "will cause undue delay in the construction and earliest usefulness of the Feather River Project. . . ."⁶⁴ The source of the "undue delay" was unexplained, but it became clear that a primary objective of these witnesses was to obtain use of San Luis facilities "under state law," *i.e.*, without acreage limitation. Assemblyman Patrick Kelly, of Kern County, apparently with the same end in view, asked Congress for a loan to enable the state to undertake "immediate construction, operation, management and control . . . of its natural water resources" including the San Luis dam, reservoir, and aqueducts.⁶⁵ Assemblyman Kelly called his proposal "in accord" with the partnership recommendation of President Eisenhower's Advisory Committee on Water Resources Policy on "partnership" dated January 17, 1956.

In these ways "control" of the San Luis reservoir emerged as the

---

⁶¹ *1956 Hearings on S. 178, supra* note 19, at 7.

⁶² *I.e.*, the same financial pressures that weighed heavily against state purchase of the federal Central Valley Project favored appeal to the federal government to build San Luis! "It was, of course, unrealistic to think at any time that the state would be able to buy the project—and at the same time do other big things to which the state is committed. . . . Government management is onerous, of course, and to some people the 160 acre limitation is practically confiscatory. These are the ones who are pushing the idea of a purchase." Editorial, Oroville Mercury Register, in Sacramento Bee, Oct. 29, 1953.

⁶³ *1956 Hearings on S. 178, supra* note 19, at 178, 263, 270, 274, 275, 294.

⁶⁴ Statement of Allen Bottorff, *1956 Hearings on S. 178, supra* note 19, at 216, 219. The position taken by the Kern County Farm Bureau and State Assemblyman from Kern County was consistent with testimony of President Dwight M. Cochran of the Kern County Land Company against acreage limitation before the California Assembly Interim Committee on Water, November 5, 1959: "[W]ith acreage limitation, the Feather River Project will never succeed. . . . Acreage limitation would prevent farmers from purchasing water for large acreages of their land. Under such circumstances, it is doubtful that the program could be self-liquidating. Not enough water could be sold."

⁶⁵ *1956 Hearings on S. 178, supra* note 19, at 252. "I did not say, or it is not stated here, 'interest-free loan.' It says 'loan agreement', which is entirely different . . . because some of that loan could possibly be on an interest basis." *Ibid.*

dividing issue. Federal and state financing and construction were considered in the light of resulting federal or state control and, application or avoidance of acreage limitation. The interests in Kern County, where concentrated ownership of land is conspicuous, demanded state control. Their proposals became known as the "Kern County concept," by which "the state would build and operate the joint-use features and the United States would pay to the state its appropriate share of construction costs and be entitled to use a proportionate part of the jointly used project capacities."[66] Mayor Norris Poulson of Los Angeles supported state construction financed by a federal loan under the "partnership" plan, because, "the federal government must not upset our program and attempt to dictate how California will make use of its own water within its own boundaries." When Senator O'Mahoney remarked: "All the federal government should do is pay the money," Mayor Poulson replied, "Well, no comment."[67]

The Master of the California Grange, on the contrary, wanted federal construction of both the San Luis and Feather River projects in order to assure federal control and acreage limitation. Asked by Senator Arthur Watkins of Utah if he meant that "one of the reasons why the state is moving in is to get rid of the land limitation," Grange Master George Schlmeyer replied this "was an important factor and . . . the other factor is power."[68]

Any possible doubt that acreage limitation was a principal issue was removed two years later when State Engineer Banks presented a San Luis bill to Congress that included for the first time, a section specifically exempting from federal acreage limitation those lands

---

[66] *1956 Hearings on S. 178, supra* note 19, at 14-32. See also *1958 Hearings on S. 1887, supra* note 55, at 56, 57, 103.

[67] *1956 Hearings on S. 178, supra* note 19, at 20. *Cf.* the comment by Secretary of the Interior Harold L. Ickes on the early proposal that the state take over federal Central Valley Project: "I do not wish to dwell at length on all the false assumptions and unwarranted conclusions contained in the State Chamber's statement, but there are three or four additional claims that I can not ignore . . . it certainly is naive for the State Chamber to expect the Federal Government to hand over the State the two revenue-producing facilities—irrigation and power—while retaining responsibility for flood control, navigation, salinity control, and fish and wildlife development which the State Chamber says 'are not reimbursable costs and are, under any circumstances, gifts from the Federal Government.'" Letter from Harold L. Ickes to Frank Clarvoe, Oct. 31, 1945.

[68] *1956 Hearings on S. 178, supra* note 19, at 178. *Cf.* Secretary Ickes description in 1945 of the proposal that the State should take over the Central Valley Project from the Federal government, in which he linked the opponents of acreage limitation and public power preference as chief supporters of the effort. Letter from Harold L. Ickes to Frank Clarvoe, Oct. 31, 1945. See also Senator Wayne Morse's statement in 1959: "There has been . . . as much objection to the anti-monopoly preference clause in regard to federally generated power as to the antimonopoly land law. The same groups oppose both of these laws. The same groups have devised many devious interpretations; have written legislation which they have attempted to get the Congress to enact." 105 CONG. REC., 7686 (1959).

"under contract with the state to receive a water supply."⁶⁹ This proposal for coupling federal construction with the explicit exemption of a state service area from acreage limitation was an alternative to the Kern County concept of avoiding acreage limitation through state construction.⁷⁰ It was a compromise on finance and on policy. Federal construction included liberal financial aid to the state and acreage limitation for one San Luis area on the one hand, while on the other hand guaranteeing exemption to huge landholdings including those in Kern County.

The Senate debated and authorized the federal San Luis Project on these terms on August 15, 1958. Senator Watkins of Utah, overlooking the financial pressures that had led the state to ask for federal construction of San Luis as a means of helping the state Feather River Project, praised the state Feather River Project and state water plan and offered congratulations to California's Senators on the fact that their state "will build this project, and a still larger project which will cost in the neighborhood of $11 billion, and do it on its own . . . without calling upon the federal government."⁷¹

The exemption was challenged. Senators Kuchel, Knowland and Clinton P. Anderson each justified it, using generally similar language, *viz.*, "land which may be served by state operations only, under the state's water plan, upon which, of course, state law should apply";⁷² "an attempt to impose federal legislation upon a state in the case of purely intrastate waters";⁷³ "in the areas where the state puts up the money, without cooperation by the federal government, the state naturally has its own rights under its own laws."⁷⁴ Senators Douglas and Morse demanded removal of the exemption, without success.

Nine months later the Senate, after four days of debate, would reverse itself by refusing the same exemption it had accepted the year before.⁷⁵

IV. 86TH CONGRESS

[T]he amendment which we propose would apply the 160-acre limitation not merely to the initial 440,000 acres to be brought into cultivation, but

---

⁶⁹ *1958 Hearings on S. 1887, supra* note 55, at 54.
⁷⁰ *1956 Hearings on S. 178, supra* note 19, at 195; *1958 Hearings on S. 1887, supra* note 55, at 56, 57.
⁷¹ 104 CONG. REC. 17730 (1958).
⁷² 104 CONG. REC. 17727 (1958).
⁷³ 104 CONG. REC. 17735 (1958).
⁷⁴ 104 CONG. REC. 17731 (1958). In a California court the federal government has asserted its ownership of the right to use all unappropriated water within California. City of Fresno v. State Water Rights Bd., Fresno County Superior Court No. 105.245. See Harold W. Kennedy, *Federal Claims against California's Unappropriated Water*, as reported by the County Counsel of Los Angeles County, May 5, 1960 (mimeo).
⁷⁵ S. 1887 died with the 85th Congress for lack of action by the House. It reappeared in the 86th Congress as S. 44 and H.R. 7175.

> with respect to any additional land brought into cultivation which will use Federal facilities as a part of the system of distributing water, even though there may be State improvement superimposed upon the Federal system.
> —Senator Paul Douglas, May 7, 1959[76]
>
> [T]here is merit in the position . . . that some persons could argue in a judicial proceeding that if at this late date section 6(a) [exempting the state service area from federal law] were stricken from the bill it would constitute an intention on the part of the Senate to make Federal law apply.
> —Senator Thomas Kuchel, May 11, 1959[77]
>
> Has any explanation been given by the proponents of the bill why they feel that the 160-acre limitation should not apply, and why they feel that the holders of great acreages of land ought to have the benefit of irrigation under a policy different from that stipulated in the Federal law?
> —Senator Frank Lausche, May 7, 1959[78]

Senator Paul Douglas, of Illinois, co-sponsor of an amendment to eliminate exemption of the state service area from the 1959 San Luis bill, together with Senators Wayne Morse and Richard Neuberger of Oregon, stated repeatedly that the effect of their amendment would be to apply the federal 160-acre limitation to the state service area.[79] Senator Kuchel was apprehensive that this might be so and placed in the *Congressional Record* a telegram from a California attorney opposed to application of federal law, stating that, "Logically, the only valid argument for deletion of section 6(a) is that federal law should control water service by the state."[80] Senator Engle denied the claim of Senator Douglas (and fear of Senator Kuchel), saying that "it makes no difference whether section 6(a) is in the bill or out of the bill, because the federal law will not apply to the state-serviced areas anyway."[81] He said, "[T]he section is surplusage. It is merely

---

[76] 105 CONG. REC. 7668 (1959).

[77] *Id.* at 7989. Senator Kuchel conceded on the floor of the Senate: "I telephoned persons who represent public agencies in California, trying to ascertain if there were a way in which we could do what it sometimes seemed to me, from statements in the *Record*, the Senator from Oregon wanted to do, and yet, at the same time, to avoid what the Senator from Illinois frankly says he desires to do.

"Here is an instance in which persons who are skilled lawyers in my State, and who represent public agencies, believe that the Senator from Illinois, in the position he takes, would have some vigorous supporters if the legislation got into the court, in contending that judicial adoption of the Douglas-Morse amendment would mean that the Federal reclamation law would cover all the waters coming out of the dam which is provided for by the bill." *Id.* at 7870.

[78] *Id.* at 7672. Although California's Senators were patently opening the door to escape from acreage limitation, neither was willing to accept characterization as an opponent of that law. Senator Engle said, "I support the 160-acre limitation." *Id.* at 7854. Senator Kuchel responded to a colloquy between Senators Lausche and Douglas: "The case should not be stated that way. . . . The question is as simple as this . . . we believe that the State of California, through its Governor and its legislature, ought to determine what the restrictions for use of water through a state system should be. It is exactly that simple. It is that easy to state." *Id.* at 7671.

[79] *Id.* at 7496, 7666, 7668, 7673.

[80] *Id.* at 7987, 7988 (Stanley W. Kronick to Senator Thomas Kuchel, May 9, 1959).

[81] *Id.* at 7673.

a statement of what the law is." Senator Douglas responded, "If it is surplusage, then eliminate it."[82]

Senator Kuchel implied that approval or rejection of specific exemption would be a "policy decision" by Congress.[83] Senator Engle cited a telegram from Governor Brown in support of his own position that no policy decision was involved and debate over section 6(a) was therefore useless:

> Upon the basis of my own legal analysis and that of all my legal advisors I am convinced that . . . with or without the language contained in section 6(a) under S. 44, the federal reclamation laws do not . . . apply to the state facilities and state service areas of the project.[84]

Apparently the interests opposed to elimination of section 6(a) did not share the Governor's and Senator Engle's view that federal law would not apply to the state service area without specific congressional exemption. An editorial in the *Los Angeles Times* on February 28, 1960, stated:

> Gov. Brown's water lawyers assure him that an acreage limitation would not apply to the state parts of Feather River Project, but the water agencies have vigorously expressed their doubts. . . . The results of Mr. Brown's all-out fight for Section 7 [House equivalent of section 6(a) in the Senate version] will be felt for the rest of this century.[85]

The compelling reason why neither Senator Engle nor Senator Kuchel would voluntarily eliminate section 6(a) apparently was the insistence of excess landholding interests on its retention. As noted before, inclusion of a specific exemption was essential to induce supporters of the Kern County concept to accept federal rather than state construction of the San Luis Project.[86]

Senators Engle and Kuchel were evasive, however, when questioned as to the identity of those seeking the "assurance" that congressional exemption would provide. When Senator Douglas asked the former, "Who are they? What people?," the latter interjected, "I will tell the Senator what people they are. They are the people of

---

[82] *Id.* at 7496. See also 7857, 7858, 7994.

[83] *Id.* at 7993, 7989.

[84] *Id.* at 7994.

[85] § 2, p. 4, col. 1. After the Senate had eliminated section 6(a) it reappeared in the House San Luis bill as section 7 of H.R. 7155. The Feather River Project Association would accept nothing less than specific exemption; even when the Senate had eliminated exemption before approving the San Luis Project, the Association resolved that, failing to obtain congressional exemption, the state should construct the San Luis Project itself, allowing federal government to use the joint facilities. 4 Feather River Project Association Newsletter, No. 2, Feb. 29, 1960.

[86] See text accompanying note 70 *supra*. Faced with diverse California views in 1956 and 1958, Senator Clinton Anderson, Chairman of the Irrigation and Reclamation Subcommittee, had been unwilling to proceed toward authorization of a federal project, even when requested by a Governor. *1958 Hearings on S. 1887, supra* note 55, at 172.

southern California." Asked if he meant "the big landowners of Central Valley . . . the Kern County Land Company? The big land interests?," Senator Kuchel replied, "I do not mean them. I mean the city government of the city of Los Angeles." Senator Douglas responded, "How would the people of Los Angeles be hurt by omitting section 6(a), which would in effect provide a 160-acre limitation in the Central Valley?" Senator Kuchel then changed the subject by asking if state, rather than federal law ought not to apply.[87] When Senator Douglas asked Senator Engle again, additional assurance "to what people?," the latter's reply was, "To the people of southern California." Senator Douglas responded, "Was it to the people of southern California, or to the large landowners in the Central Valley and the railways and the oil companies, who have dominated politics in California for 70 years?" Senator Engle's answer was to reiterate that, "They wanted us to restate the law," but he himself "never believe[d] in restating the law."[88]

The reluctance of the California senators does not obscure the ample evidence in the public record and elsewhere that excess landholding interests wanted the additional assurance of congressional exemption. Indeed, no interests other than excess landholding interests are directly affected by the law and have a stake in its removal.[89] Senator Morse ascribed the purpose of section 6(a) to "the intention of the large landowners of California . . . to scuttle the 160-acre

[87] 105 CONG. REC. 7496, 7497 (1959). At the hearings, Warren Butler, Vice Chairman of the Board of Directors of the Metropolitan Water District of Southern California had testified: "Let me say parenthetically, gentlemen, that our concern south of the Tehatchapic does not involve this 160-acre limitation as it does north of the Tehatchapic." *1959 Hearings on S. 44, supra* note 53, at 71, in 105 CONG. REC. 7987 (1959) (inserted by Senator Kuchel). The possibility that state project water might be delivered in Orange County to the 93,000 acre Irvine Ranch is not to be excluded. An engineering report of May 1961 was concerned with a "specific program" to transport Metropolitan Water District water to the Irvine Water District. It spoke of water from the Colorado River, but the Director of the State Division of Water Resources had said in 1959 that the insufficiency of Colorado River water for "satisfaction of Orange County's ever increasing water requirements" would necessitate "the early importation of water from northern California." The referee of the United States Supreme Court has recommended reduction of California's entitlement to Colorado River water, reducing the prospect of water for the Irvine Ranch area from that source; the Metropolitan Water District has contracted for northern California water for delivery in southern California, raising the already strong prospect that state project water will reach Orange County. STATE OF CALIFORNIA DEPARTMENT OF WATER RESOURCES, BULL. No. 70, ORANGE COUNTY LAND AND WATER USE SURVEY, 1957; Santa Ana Div., Calif. Div. Water Resources, Boyle Engineering Report Upon Water Transportation Facilities Required for Supplemental Colorado River Water Supply to Irvine Ranch Water District, May 1961; *cf.* "Hot Words Over Irvine Ranch Plans," San Francisco Chronicle, Oct. 14, 1961, p. 2, col. 1.

[88] 105 CONG. REC. 7673 (1959).

[89] Private power interests have a large stake in defeat of reclamation law and in curbing the Bureau of Reclamation, because reclamation law and projects carry antimonopoly power, as well as acreage limitation, provisions. See text accompanying note 68 *supra*.

limitation."⁹⁰ The compromise agreement referred to by Congressman Hagen — made immediately preceding introduction of the San Luis bill in the 86th Congress with section 7 an essential part — represented a "binding agreement of a representative of California's Governor, the two California Senators, Congressman Sisk, and myself, and representatives of San Luis, Kern County, and Los Angeles water interests, arrived at in a March 13 meeting attended by representatives of the Bureau of Reclamation."⁹¹

The Feather River Project Association, insistent throughout that section 6(a) was not surplusage and that congressional exemption was essential, has three directors at large with two of them spokesmen before congressional or state legislative committees for large landowning corporations.⁹² Senator Douglas filled pages of the *Record* with names and statistics, including a table showing that these two corporations together owned close to 400,000 acres in Kern County "including possible areas of service by irrigation from San Luis Reservoir south of [the] Federal service area."⁹³

The Senate eliminated section 6(a).⁹⁴ Nevertheless, the identical proposal to exempt the state service area from acreage limitation reappeared in the House San Luis bill as section 7 of H.R. 7155. The House Committee, by a divided report from which six members dissented, recommended adoption of section 7. Its report included a lengthy statement supporting a conclusion that section 7 was "surplusage," that it "in nowise changes established principles of reclamation law," and that its inclusion "is not to be interpreted as indicative of a belief on the Committee's part that without it the excess land provisions of the federal reclamation laws would be applicable to the state-served lands."⁹⁵

The chief reliance of the Committee in expressing this view was upon the opinion given by Associate Solicitor of the Department of Interior Felix S. Cohen, on October 22, 1947, offering the prospect that, "[U]pon full payment of construction obligation under a joint-liability repayment contract, the lands receiving water . . . are . . . relieved of the statutory excess-land restrictions."⁹⁶ The San Luis bill

---

⁹⁰ 105 CONG. REC. 7871 (1959).

⁹¹ Supplementary statement of Congressman Harlan Hagen, in *1959 Hearings on S. 44, supra* note 53, at 28, 29.

⁹² George L. Henderson testified for Kern County Land Company. *Hearings on H.R. 4885 Before a Subcommittee of the Senate Committee on Commerce,* 78th Cong., 2d Sess., 317 (1944). J. P. Van Loben Sels testified before the California Assembly Committee on Water on Nov. 5, 1959, for the Southern Pacific which, with its subsidiary land company, owned about 150,000 acres, "mainly located in the southern San Joaquin Valley."

⁹³ 105 CONG. REC. 7670 (1959).

⁹⁴ See Taylor, *Excess Land Law: Pressure vs. Principle,* 47 CALIF. L. REV. 499, 502-512 (1959).

⁹⁵ H.R. REP. No. 399, 86th Cong., 1st Sess. 11, 15, 16 (1959).

⁹⁶ *Id.* at 13, 14. The Committee drew support also from a telegram from Gov-

afforded a ready means of taking advantage of Cohen's and the Committee's view — if accepted — by providing that, "The State will ... have paid its entire share of the cost of constructing the joint facilities prior to its utilization of them for storage and delivery of water."[97]

The House Committee protected against both routes of escape from acreage limitation, the surplusage theory and specific exemption. As the authors of S. 44 had done, it deferred to the difficulties of "bringing together as many diverse interests and points of view ... as the San Luis project involves ... ," saying:

> The Committee recognizes that the inclusions of surplusage is usually undesirable in a bill, but it also recognizes that the author of a bill ... should be given considerable latitude in the way he expresses the position that is arrived at, more latitude than the Committee might give itself if it were to start drafting a bill ab inito.[98]

The difference was not incidental but crucial.

The House rejected the Committee's recommendation on a roll call vote after two days of debate and thus joined the Senate in eliminating the specific exemption.[99] During debate a good deal was said by Congressmen Aspinall, Hosmer, Hagen, Lipscomb, Moss and Sisk to indicate that in their opinion, section 7 was "surplusage" and it made no difference in reclamation law whether it was left in or stricken out.[100] However, the vigorous and intensive debate in both houses; the rejection of exemption despite its acceptance by the committees of both houses; and the record of the roll call vote in the House, leave little ground — if any — for relying on the legislative history of the 86th Congress for support of the view that in denying

---

ernor Brown stating similar views that Senator Engle had placed in the *Record* during Senate debate. 105 CONG. REC. 7857 (1959); 106 CONG. 10461 (1960).

[97] H.R. REP. No. 399, *supra* note 95, at 11. The report cited "concurrence in this view of the law" by Secretary of the Interior Fred A. Seaton. However, Secretary Seaton left to Secretary Udall the final decision whether or not to act on this view of the law on Kings and Kern rivers, and at San Luis.

[98] *Id.* at 15, 16.

[99] 106 CONG. REC. 10560, 10563, 10564 (1960). Three votes were taken on the Ullman amendment to eliminate section 7. The first showed 81 ayes, 84 noes. The second showed 139 ayes, 122 noes. The third roll call vote showed 215 ayes, 179 noes, 38 not voting. The Committee Chairman, Congressman Wayne Aspinall, voted "present."

[100] E.g., by Congressman Aspinall, *id.* at 10450, Hosmer, *id.* at 10458, Hagen, *id.* at 10463, 10560, Lipscomb, *id.* at 10470, Moss, *id.* at 10471, Sisk, *id.* at 10560. Of these, Hosmer, Hagen and Lipscomb voted to retain section 7; Moss and Sisk voted to eliminate it; Aspinall voted "present." Congressman Saylor of Pennsylvania, had introduced a motion in committee to apply acreage limitation to the state service that failed, but he voted against elimination of the exemption. *Id.* at 10464.

exemption, Congress intended to permit exemption of the state service area.[101]

V. LEGISLATURE, 1957-1961

> I am, and I believe that the California Legislature also is, opposed to any unjust enrichment or monopolization of benefits by owners of large land holdings as a result of either Federal or State operation. . . . I intend, at an appriate time and before contracts are executed, to take this matter up with the California Legislature in order to preclude the undesirable results which I have described. . . .
> —Governor Edmund G. Brown, May 7, 1959[102]

> While there has been a big improvement in California in the selection of more Democratic, liberal, and progressive State legislators, in view of the past record we are not justified in depending on the frail reed of State action. What is likely to happen is that there will be no defense, and the big landowners will now take over.
> —Senator Paul Douglas, May 11, 1959[103]

When the California legislature grappled with proposals in 1933 to construct the first big unit of Central Valley development, it decided issues of policy and finance simultaneously. As part of the same law it approved not only the issuance of revenue bonds to finance the project, but also a state public power preference, a federal power preference and acreage limitation as well.[104] It referred its decision on both policy and finance to the people of the state who voted their approval. During recent consideration of proposals for state water development, however, the legislature has followed a different procedure and with a different result. Instead of coupling decisions on policy with those on finance as in 1933, the legislature has kept them separate. In 1960 the legislature referred only its decision on finance to the voters. Between 1957 and 1961, it defeated all proposals to adopt acreage limitation and gave the people no opportunity to say whether they approved or disapproved.

This striking contrast between the current defeat of policy and its previous approval in 1933 cannot be explained by rising popular ob-

---

[101] "We understand that recommendations are being made that the contract for joint utilization of the San Luis Dam and Reservoir be modified to require acreage limitations in areas to be served by the State of California. As you know, Congress rejected this provision at the time the joint partnership venture was authorized as part of the Central Valley Project." Letter from R. L. Minckler, Chairman, Statewide Water Resources Committee, California State Chamber of Commerce, to Secretary Stewart L. Udall, Sept. 12, 1961.

[102] 105 CONG. REC. 7673 (1959).

[103] 105 CONG. REC. 7861 (1959).

[104] CAL. STAT. 1933, ch. 1042. In 1933 the conspicuous antimonopoly policy issue was public power generation with preference for public distribution; acreage limitation was inconspicuously included by adoption of federal law by reference in the state statute. Referendum measures to be submitted to the electors of the State of California at special election to be held Tuesday, December 19, 1933, as compiled by Fred B. Wood, Legislative Counsel, and distributed by Frank C. Jordon, Secretary of State, Sacramento, 1933. In recent debate over the Feather River and San Luis projects the balance in public concern has been the reverse—over acreage limitation more than public power preference.

jections to acreage limitation. On the contrary, popular acceptance is clear and it is not diminishing. Previous to 1957, the legislature had approved acreage limitation seven times, memorialized against it only once, and allowed two bills to die in 1947 that proposed to prohibit irrigation districts from accepting contracts containing acreage limitation. The California Democratic Party platform supported acreage limitation in 1958, as it had since 1944, and Democratic candidates were generally victorious that year. The Governor won by approximately 3 to 2 over his Republican opponent who specifically opposed acreage limitation. In addition, fifteen popular votes in irrigation districts, recorded to 1951, total majorities of better than seven to one in favor of accepting Central Valley contracts with acreage limitation.[105] In 1952 five more districts approved contracts by a total vote of 744 to 125, and one rejected a supplementary contract by 33 to 45.[106] As recently as June, 1957, Senator Kuchel said that, when it found its legal capacity to contract with the United States impaired by a state supreme court decision against acreage limitation, Corning District in Sacramento Valley was willing to accept acreage limitation voluntarily to obtain federal project water.[107]

It was, and remains, decidedly to the financial advantage of California's water users to accept water under federal reclamation contracts.[108] Nothing in the record suggests that a change since 1933 in popular opinion toward acreage limitation accounts for the current defeat of policy. Instead this defeat is owing to the skillful tactical manipulation by its opponents in relying *exclusively* on the legislature, where they had strength, and in avoiding popular decision.

Attempts were made in the legislatures of 1957 and 1959 to approve application of acreage limitation to the state water project. But these failed. The arguments against adoption were procedural rather than substantive; they avoided open opposition to the principle of acreage limitation, as Senators Kuchel and Engle avoided it in debates on the San Luis bill by asking that the state be allowed to decide. It was urged in the legislature, for example, that policy arguments for acreage limitation should be deferred so as to permit the

---

[105] Statement of Edmund G. Brown, Attorney General of the State of California, in *1951 Report of the House Special Subcommittee on Irrigation and Reclamation* 110 (Sacramento).

[106] *California Elections on Reclamation Contracts* (April 1952), on file in Sacramento Regional Office, Bureau of Reclamation.

[107] Sacramento Bee, June 22, 1957, p. D-6, col. 1.

[108] In 1951 Attorney General Edmund G. Brown estimated the advantage along Friant-Kern canal to be the difference between $3.50 and $8.75, or $5.25 per acre-foot. *Report of the House Special Subcommittee on Irrigation and Reclamation* 113 (Sacramento). "[U]nits are anxious to get permanent contracts because it has been estimated they will pay only a little more than half as much for [water under] their permanent agreements [as under interim agreements under reclamation law]." Fresno Bee, Sept. 27, 1961, p. 1, cols. 1, 2.

legislature to concentrate on "appropriation"; that water bond legislation was "neither the time nor the legislation" for consideration of policy; and that "at times we have to rise above principle."[109] Although urged to place water on the agenda of the 1960 session of the legislature, Governor Brown declined, thus foreclosing debate on acreage limitation for that session.[110] As a result, the $1.75 billion state water bond issue that received popular approval by a small margin in November of 1960 was minus policy.

Governor Brown made his decision against acreage limitation public at the opening of the 1960 session.[111] On January 20th he announced his "plan of attack" in a television broadcast to the people of the state. The attack commenced with abandonment of acreage limitation and substitution of a two-price differential with higher charges against landownerships in excess of 160 acres. He likened his proposal to "the principle of differential water rates for large and small farmers . . . already in effect in federal law in the small projects act sponsored by California's Senator Clair Engle."[112]

---

[109] Governor Brown said: "Some of the principles are sound, but they don't belong in bond legislation designed to provide financing, not to settle every water argument in the state." See Taylor, *Excess Land Law: Pressure vs. Principle*, 47 CALIF. L. REV. 499, 516 (1960). In a similar vein State Senator Richard Richards, participating in debate on acreage limitation and public power preference at the February 1960 Fresno convention of the California Democratic Council, referred to these as "glib policy issues." In December, immediately after the water bond election, he wrote: "We cannot afford any more wrangling on policy. . . ." Western Water News, Dec. 1960, p. 3, col. 4.

[110] "Highly dubious advice has gone to Governor Brown from the Director of Water Resources, Harvey O. Banks, in his recommendation that the 1960 Legislature should not be opened to discussion of and action upon water problems. . . . Banks' recommendation to the Governor happens to be in line with Brown's own preference. . . . Labor leaders have been insisting that before organized labor votes for water bonds the Federal 160-acre limitation must be imposed to prevent 'unjust enrichment' of big landholders in the San Joaquin Valley. The California State Chamber of Commerce just last week went on record opposing the 160-acre limitation. . . . The Governor should swallow his dislike of a brawl in a presidential year and call upon the legislature to go once again into the thick of the California water controversy." Editorial, San Francisco Chronicle, Dec. 8, 1959, p. 20, col. 1.

[111] Addressing the Feather River Project Association, he said: "I want to do everything I can to prevent such unjust enrichment, but I quite frankly am not at all sure that I know what the best method is. Simple acreage limitation doesn't really meet this problem head-on. As one of the acreage limitation's longtime defenders in litigation I know it has its faults as well as its virtues. In order to discover whether there isn't some much better approach, I want to announce to you here today that I am setting up a task force among the experts in State government to study this problem and come up with a recommendation as soon as possible. Ralph Brody, my special water counsel, is already working on a plan of attack." (Undated, apparently during second half of 1959.) The Governor spoke also of power preference policy: "My position in favor of power purchase preference for public agencies is well known. How and where it should apply in this project, however, is a matter requiring further detailed study."

[112] "I firmly believe that we have the responsibility to see that no one receives a disproportionate or lion's share of the benefits from a publicly-financed project. In addition, I think that the development of small farms should be encouraged. I believe we can attain those just and fair ends without trying to

When the Engle formula had first been proposed, its ineffectiveness for controlling enrichment and spreading ownership was immediately pointed out. Congressman William A. Dawson of Utah, a member of Congressman Engle's committee, described it, not as a means of controlling concentration of benefits, but as an "encouragement to take on more acreage because the other benefits are so great...."[113] Nevertheless, the Governor incorporated his water price differential in a contract with the Metropolitan Water District of Southern California — concluded four days before the November election at which the voters approved the state water bond issue.[114] Apparently the water charge differential incorporated in the contract is not only ineffective for accomplishing its professed purpose, but may also lack legal force. The opinion of counsel in the *Main Report* —submitted to the Governor just before the water bond election— states: "The law of California fails to authorize a contractual provision requiring or permitting the Department, an irrigation district or other water agency to impose a price differential based on the size of landholdings."[115]

In the 1961 session of the legislature that opened a few weeks after passage of the $1.75 billion water bond issue, bills to provide acreage limitation were introduced and several hearings were held in the Assembly. The bills either were killed or died in committee.[116]

The Feather River Project of the State of California has no acreage limitation, and the contract between the state and the Metropolitan Water District contains clauses that, if honored, will prevent effective compliance with federal acreage limitation law. If a contract

---

obligate or coerce anyone to sell or divide his land in order to get water. We are therefore establishing a fair price differential to take care of this situation. On land in excess of 160 acres, the price to be charged shall be the cost of delivering the water, including the market value of the power used to pump it to this land. For all others — which shall include the overwhelming majority of customers in both the cities and farm areas — the price shall be cost of delivering the water, including only the actual cost of the power to pump it rather than the market value of that power, less the amount of the benefit from any sale of power outside the project." Address by Governor Edmund G. Brown, California Water Program Bond Issue, NBC TV and Radio Network Broadcast, Jan. 20, 1960.

[113] *Hearings on H.R. 104, 384, and 3817 Before Subcommittee on Irrigation and Reclamation of House Committee on Interior and Insular Affairs,* 84th Cong., 1st Sess. 70 (1955). See also Taylor, *Excess Land Law: Legislative Erosion of Public Policy,* 30 ROCKY MT. L. REV. 1, 21 (1958).

[114] Apparently to reduce to very small dimensions any prospect that an administrator might ever find excess lands receiving project water to which to apply the surcharge, the contract creates a presumption that most or all non-project waters, not subject to acreage limitation, go presently to excess lands. Contract between the State of California Department of Water Resources and the Metropolitan Water District of Southern California for a water supply, executed Nov. 4, 1960, p. 30.

[115] Main Report, *supra* note 2, app. 34. AB 1829, introduced to authorize the differential price system based on size of landholding, died in the 1961 session.

[116] AB 1326, AB 2019, AB 2224. AB 1326 approximated federal acreage limitation law. Power preference bills also died in committee.

between the United States and the State of California should accept these conditions, acreage limitation would not apply to the state service area. As the President of the Feather River Project Association said, in effect, when Congress rejected exemption of that area,

> [T]he federal Bureau of Reclamation may be able, under the new legislative history established during the recent House and Senate debate, to enter into a contract which will include the basic principle fought for by those in the State project area—namely the *single application of state law to water deliveries in that area by the state*.[117]

VI. Administrative Decision

> [I]n view of the action which deleted Section 7 before its passage, whatever rights the state will have in future joint federal-state facilities and with respect to water deliveries in the state Feather River Project service area, *must then depend entirely upon the language of the contract* which may be executed between the state and federal government.
> —Allen Bottorff, President, Feather River Project Association, 1960[118]

> Mr. Senator [Paul] Douglas: I have seen enough of the operations in the Department of the Interior in Pine Flats, and so forth, to know it is one thing to get it in the law, and it is another thing to get it carried out as you face a mighty combination of landowners.
> ....
> Mr. Senator [Clair] Engle: There will be a Democratic administration soon, and the law will be enforced.
> Mr. Douglas: It will be enforced a little better, but nor necessarily well, because sometimes Democratic Secretaries of the Interior go sour, too. . . .
> ....
> Mr. Douglas: . . . [I] wish to pay tribute to those . . . people who have been boycotted and blacklisted in the valley and throughout California because of opinions which they have held. . . . Without them the victory which was won this afternoon would not have been possible.
> —Congressional Record, 1959[119]

If the present Secretary of the Interior should wish not to apply acreage limitation to the state service area, legal opinions are on record approving such a decision and counselling him how to accomplish that end. They come from sources both within and outside the Department of the Interior. They hold that full payment of the construction charge obligation renders the excess land provisions of reclamation law inoperative. Applied to the Kings and Kern river contracts now on the Secretary's desk, these opinions would support contracts permitting water users' organizations — at their option — to relieve excess landholders of the obligation to agree, as a condition of receiving project water, to dispose of their excess lands at a fair

---

[117] 4 Feather River Project Association Newsletter, May 31, 1960, p. 3. (Emphasis in original.)
[118] *Ibid.* (Emphasis in original.)
[119] 105 Cong. Rec. 7495, 8000, 8001 (1959). Referring to her defeat in the race for U. S. Senator against Richard M. Nixon, Senator Douglas said: "There are heroic public figures such as Helen Gahagan Douglas, who went down to political defeat in 1950 in part because she stood for this [160-acre] principle." *Id.* at 8000. Referring to Governor Edmund G. Brown, of California, he said: "Pat Brown, as attorney general, made a great fight to uphold the 160-acre limitation. I could not believe that as Governor he would do something contrary to his policy as attorney general. I hope the Democratic Party of California does not come out in defense of the large landowners." *Id.* at 7675.

appraised price. Making full payment would provide this relief. Applied to the San Luis contract to be negotiated between the State of California and the United States, these opinions would relieve excess landholders in the state service area under a provision of the San Luis Project Act that "conditions the integration of the [federal] facilities with the state's Feather River and related projects upon the state providing funds to pay an equitable share of the cost of the San Luis Project joint facilities at the time they are built or enlarged."[120] The prospect of rendering acreage limitation law inoperative through payments made concurrently with construction underlay claims by the House Committee report on the San Luis bill, and by some senators and congressmen during debate, that exempting the state service area was "surplusage."

Secretary Seaton, in approving the form of repayment contracts with thirty-two water user entities on Kings and Kern rivers providing that full payment renders acreage limitation inoperative, said on January 19, 1961, that he was relying on the consistent views of all the chief legal advisors of the Department for nearly a half century.[121] The support these opinions afforded, however, is far less than appears, as Secretary Seaton himself recognized. In the same statement announcing his approval of the contract forms he said he was withholding "execution on behalf of the government until the Attorney General's views are received," because he was "aware . . . of conflicting views strongly held by some. . . ."

Senators Douglas and Morse have attacked the opinions of King, Cohen and Bennett cited by Secretary Seaton. Senator Douglas supported his own views in a notable exchange of correspondence with the Secretary that apparently closed with the latter's unfulfilled promise on December 24, 1957, that Solicitor Elmer F. Bennett would continue it.[122] Senator Morse described the King opinion as "merely an administrative opinion shared by a few administrative employees . . . never . . . seriously defended in the Congress,"[123] and noted that Cohen had accepted King's instructions "without inquiry." Quoting

---

[120] U.S.D.I. Information Service release, Jan. 19, 1960, 1, 2; see 74 Stat. 156 (1960).

[121] The most notable of the opinions supporting him were by: Chief Counsel Will R. King in 1914, Instructions, 43 Land Decisions 339 (1914); Associate Solicitor Felix S. Cohen in 1947, Memorandum to Commissioner, Bureau of Reclamation, No. M-35004, Oct. 22, 1947; and Solicitor Elmer F. Bennett in 1957, Memorandum to Commissioner, Bureau of Reclamation, No. M-36457, July 10, 1957; Memorandum from the Solicitor to the Secretary, undated, attached to letter, Secretary Seaton to Senator Paul H. Douglas, Oct. 21, 1957; see *Hearings on S. 1425, S. 2541, and S. 3448, Before Subcommittee on Irrigation and Reclamation of Senate Committee on Interior and Insular Affairs*, 85th Cong., 2d Sess., 21, 22 (1958). [Hereinafter cited as *1958 Hearings on S. 1425*.]

[122] *1958 Hearings on S. 1425, supra* note 121, at 20-25.

[123] 105 Cong. Rec. 7686 (1959).

from a statement by Secretary Seaton approving the "lump sum theory" — that prepayment in full renders the acreage limitation law inoperative — Senator Morse told the Senate: "I am sure that the Secretary of the Interior under this administration, given the wide range of authority to negotiate agreement as set forth in this legislation, will find some way to subvert reclamation laws in regard to the San Luis area."[124] After Secretary Douglas McKay enunciated it, the present writer, examining elsewhere the doctrine that full payment renders acreage limitation inoperative, concluded it utterly lacks legal foundation and is tantamount to "complete subversion of the law."[125]

Although some Secretaries of the Interior have said they accept the doctrine, none has yet been willing to put his name to documents making it a finally and legally binding Department policy. Secretary Oscar Chapman refused to accept "lump-sum or accelerated payment . . . as a means of avoiding . . . acreage limitation" on Kings River.[126] Secretaries McKay and Seaton, although endorsing the doctrine and saying they would accept it in Kings and Kern river contracts, nevertheless withheld signatures that would have given final approval.

Excess landholding interests to whom approval of the King-Cohen-Bennett doctrine would be of advantage apparently have long shared with the Secretaries this lack of confidence in its legal soundness. The congressional representative of Kern and adjacent counties, where landownership is concentrated, introduced bills in 1950 and 1951 seeking from Congress the legal authority the King-Cohen doctrine said they already had, *viz.*, to accept full payment in satisfaction of acreage limitation on Kings and Kern rivers.[127] Similar unwillingness of some California interests in 1959 and 1960 to accept a San Luis bill without "additional assurance" of specific congressional

---

[124] *Id.* at 7688. He said he was opposed to letting "big landowners buy their way out from under the 160-acre laws" to get "priceless water for any amount of land by an elaborate legalistic rationalization." *Id.* at 7689. Congressmen, spokesmen for organized labor and other groups, and individuals, also have protested the King-Cohen-Bennett doctrine of accepting money in satisfaction of policy.

[125] Taylor, *Excess Land Law: Execution of a Public Policy*, 64 YALE L.J. 477, 481 (1955), Ivanhoe Irrigation Dist. v. McCracken, 357 U.S. 275, 292 (1958); see Taylor, *Excess Land Law: Pressure vs. Principle*, 47 CALIF. L. REV. 499, 517-528, 535-540 (1959). The analysis is not repeated here.

[126] Taylor, *Excess Land Law: Pressure vs. Principle*, 47 CAL. L. REV. 499, 526 (1959). He permitted individual excess landowners on some old projects to bring "themselves into compliance with the acreage limitation provisions" by making full payment and Secretary McKay extended a similar offer broadly. Secretary Seaton condemned this, however, saying, "I cannot justify an aggravation of a prior practice in an effort to remedy an absence of legal authority. What I am concerned with is a whittling away at a principle until all that is left is a pile of shavings." Letter from Secretary Seaton to Philip A. Gordon, July 12, 1957. But he approved acceptance if payment was made by districts. See also Taylor, *Excess Land Law: Execution of a Public Policy*, 64 YALE L.J. 477, 480 (1955).

[127] H.R. 7195, 81st Cong.; H.R. 413, 82nd Cong. Neither bill passed.

exemption suggests continued lack of confidence in the doctrine among directly-affected interests.[128]

The doctrine has been given support recently by legal opinion outside the Interior Department. Counsel in the *Main Report* states that the excess land provisions "do not apply to waters to be delivered from the San Luis Project to state service areas." Counsel conceded, however, that "deletion of sections 7 and 6a of the [San Luis] bills somewhat clouds the foregoing conclusion."[129]

The *Main Report* examines two principal lines of argument supporting its opinion. One of these, not involving the King-Cohen-Bennett doctrine, holds that cooperation between California and the federal government is outside the Warren Act, which prescribes for cooperation under reclamation law between the federal government, irrigation districts and other entities. "[It] could well be argued," says the opinion of the *Main Report*, "that section 542 limits its cooperative provisions to irrigation districts, water users' associations, corporations, entrymen or water users' and that the State of California is not properly included within any of those classifications." The opinion, however, balanced against this the contrary argument that "the state comes within the general classification of 'water user' and the act applies to a project such as San Luis because of use of such a broad term as 'water user.'" The opinion then reinforces this contrary argument by observing that the United States also "may have agreements for the use of San Luis Reservoir with 'irrigation districts' or 'water users' associations,' apart from any agreement with the state." Since these agreements would be explicitly within the Warren Act, a theory of avoidance subject to simple administrative choice to employ another arrangement to escape it and founded on the shadowy distinction between a state and other water-using entities, has virtually no support at all.[130]

Examining the other line of argument, the *Main* opinion attaches weight to the King-Cohen-Bennett doctrine and quotes a passage from the House Committee report on the San Luis bill referring to an "administrative practice . . . now so well fortified by history that it can probably be successfully attacked by no one except Congress," and to the absence of legislation introduced to "overrule the departmental interpretation."[131] But departmental construction of a statute does not acquire legal force if it is "obviously or clearly wrong."[132] When Sec-

---

[128] See text accompanying notes 85-89, *supra.*
[129] Main Report, *supra* note 2, at 29.
[130] Senator Morse told the Senate: "I do not believe that this [state project] entity is any different from an irrigation district — which is a state agency, with governmental powers." 105 CONG. REC. 7992 (1959).
[131] H.R. Rep. 399, 86th Cong., 2d Sess., 14 (1960); Main Report, *supra* note 2, at 29. See also text accompanying note 95, *supra.*
[132] United States v. Finnett, 185 U.S. 236, 244 (1902); *1958 Hearings on S. 1425, supra* note 121, at 24.

retary Seaton made substantially the same argument in 1957, Senator Douglas responded saying: "You speak of your 'reluctance to overturn' an administrative interpretation 'by administrative order.' My concern is with the use of an administrative order to overturn an act of Congress."[133] Hence, it would seem that the opinion of counsel in the *Main Report* adds nothing of consequence to the insufficient foundations of the King-Cohen-Bennett doctrine.

The *Main Report* observes that, "[N]either the Bureau of Reclamation nor the state administration [its client] desires to apply the federal excess land provisions to the state service area . . ." and that, "[A]n agreement is now being negotiated which, as we understand, on one ground or another will permit state law to apply." Immediately following its quotation of passages reiterating the King-Cohen-Bennett doctrine in the House report, and undeterred by concession that the legality of its conclusion is "somewhat clouded," it recommends bold procedure:

> At any rate, it would seem apparent that the state should strive to obtain as part of its agreement with the federal government a provision that none of the waters supplied from the San Luis Reservoir, or from any of the aqueducts constituting a part of that project, to state service areas should be subject to the excess land provisions. It is true that if in fact the Bureau of Reclamation did not have the authority to enter into such a contract, the agreement might be open to challenge. However, as a practical matter, such a challenge in the courts need not be anticipated in the normal course of events.[134]

The opinion of counsel in the *Main Report*, it appears, merits more serious attention as advice to a client on how to attain a desired end than as impartial analysis to determine the law.

It is germane to the question — whether claims are well founded that the state service area, or any part of it, is legally entitled to exemption from federal acreage limitation — to inquire if there really is any state project separate and apart from the federal Central Valley Project of which San Luis is an integral part. Senators Kuchel and Engle were at pains to claim a clear separation of state from federal projects, notwithstanding their admitted physical union at San Luis. They supported their claim on three grounds citing separation of *lands*, *finances*, and *physical facilities*, respectively.

As to *lands*, Senator Engle argued:

> I am speaking of the lands on which the water is delivered. They are completely severable. That is why we have said to the state, 'Put up your money if you so desire, and build a second story on the dam, increase its size, and spread the water out on lands in the state projects.[135]

---

[133] *1958 Hearings on S. 1425, supra* note 121, at 23, 24. The present writer has concluded elsewhere that "administrative practice" accepting the King-Cohen-Bennett doctrine is clearly wrong. Taylor, *Excess Land Law: Execution of a Public Policy*, 64 YALE L.J. 477, 512-514 (1955); Taylor, *Excess Land Law: Pressure vs. Principle*, 47 CALIF. L. REV. 499, 517-528 (1959).

[134] Main Report, *supra* note 2, at 29. This appears in accord with the views of

However, the separateness of land areas receiving water is irrelevant to reclamation law. The vital concern of reclamation law and its acreage limitation provisions is with water and the individuals who receive it; land area is simply a convenient measure of the maximum amount of water an individual is permitted to receive.[135]

As to *finance*, Senator Engle argued that separation of state and federal projects was complete. He assured the Senate that:

> [T]here will not be a plugged nickel of federal money in the state project, and everything the state does in order to put a bucketful of water on a square foot of land will be paid for with state money. That is the reason why we have a provision in the bill that the reclamation law shall not apply to a wholly divisible, completely separate program that is paid for, lock, stock, and barrel — powerhouse and all — by the state taxpayers. . . . The state government will pay every nickel of its share. Not a penny of it will be charged to the federal taxpayers. . . . All the federal government has done has been to build the first story of the structure. The second story goes on at no cost to the federal government.[137]

Senator Douglas obtained immediate acknowledgement from Senator Engle that it was not "possible to have a second story without the federal expenditures on the foundation and the first story."[138] Later he pressed his argument home:

> Previously, they have been saying this would be a 100 percent state project. But it turns out to be nothing of the sort. A large part of the basic [flood control] cost of the Oroville project is to be charged to the federal government. . . . [T]here is a possible further federal subsidy in the case of the Oroville Dam — namely, through interest-free payments to the so-called state irrigation project. That is a subsidy from the federal government. This shows what an illusion it is to call this

---

the President of the Feather River Project Association, who testified as a member of the Kern County Farm Bureau and Water Commission before Congress in 1958 in favor of the Kern County concept. See text accompanying note 117 *supra*; *1958 Hearings on S. 1887, supra* note 33, at 100. Apparently the *Main Report* did not misunderstand the attitude of the state administration; Governor Brown urged President Eisenhower to sign the San Luis bill in a telegram stating: "Immediately upon your signing of the bill, State representatives and the local office of the Department of Interior will commence negotiation of a contract which should lay to rest any fears arising as a result of amendments to the bill made immediately prior to its passage." Press release, Governor Edmund G. Brown, May 27, 1960.

[135] 105 Cong. Rec. 7490 (1959). For Senator Kuchel's similar argument founded on difference in lands to be served, see *1959 Hearings on S. 44, supra* note 53, at 23, 25; 105 Cong. Rec. 7484 (1959).

[136] "The project was designed to benefit people, not land." Ivanhoe Irrigation Dist. v. McCracken, 357 U.S. 275, 297 (1958).

[137] 105 Cong. Rec. 7490 (1959).

[138] *Ibid.* Senator Engle responded by pointing out that San Luis proposed "a fine partnership" in which "The state government will pay every nickel of its share." *Ibid.* Senator Kuchel said, "The State of California is indebted for what the Congress of the United States has done with federal reclamation in the state. . . . Now, under the leadership of the incumbent Governor of California — and, I may say, in the same fashion as under his two Republican predecessors — the people of my state are about to embark on a $11 billion state water system. They are willing to bond themselves, and pay that money themselves, for a state system." 105 Cong. Rec. 7672.

a separate state project, from which federal land policy should be excluded, as section 6(a) seeks to do.[139]

Then Senator Douglas placed in the *Record* material inserted previously by Senator Engle as a Congressman, proposing federal "interest-free loans for irrigation" for the state project as well as "outright grants for flood control, which is a traditional responsibility of the federal government."[140] The claim of financial separation falls to the ground when examined in light of these realities.

As to *physical separation* of state and federal projects, it was impossible to deny their union at "the one [San Luis] site the Creator has made available."[141] The physical bonds between state and federal projects are even more numerous and extensive. The state report, for example, says that "large foothill reservoirs" in the American River Basin, "including Folsom are considered to be features of the California Aqueduct System. . . ."[142] Folsom Reservoir is an existing part of the federal Central Valley Project. The state report says that "from the siphon . . . water would be conveyed by canal and tunnel into the head of the existing Sly Park Reservoir. . . ."[143] Sly Park Reservoir, too, is part of the Central Valley Project. In addition, the state report says that "water for export would be conserved largely in Auburn Reservoir immediately above the head of the North Fork arm of Folsom Reservoir."[144] Senator Kuchel requested the 87th Congress to authorize Auburn Reservoir as a federal project.[145] As noted above, San Luis itself — authorized as a federal project in 1960 — was authorized originally as a state project in 1951.[146]

It is difficult at the present time to ascertain the specific items included within the state water plan that might touch or use a federal

---

[139] *Id.* at 7855.

[140] Secretary of the Interior Harold L. Ickes commented on an earlier proposal that flood control and navigation were federal "responsibilities" on Central Valley Project, and that irrigation and power were state "functions": "The State Chamber's statement recommends restoration to the State of California of those Central Valley project facilities that are 'properly state functions,' which a footnote alleges to be irrigation and power. . . . It certainly is naive for the State Chamber to expect the federal government to hand over the state the two revenue-producing facilities — irrigation and power — while retaining responsibility for flood control, navigation, salinity control, and fish and wildlife development which the State Chamber says 'are not reimbursable costs and are, under any circumstances, gifts from the federal government.'" Letter from Harold L. Ickes to Frank Clarvoe, October 31, 1945. pp. 1-3.

[141] 105 CONG. REC. 7485 (1959). Apparently more as a diversion of attention from this crucial fact than as a point of law, Senator Kuchel argued that joint construction would be "in the interests of the people of the United States and the people of California." *Ibid.*

[142] STATE OF CALIFORNIA, PUBLICATIONS OF STATE WATER RESOURCES BOARD, BULL. No. 3, REPORT ON THE CALIFORNIA WATER PLAN, VOLUME II, 9-239 (Prelim. Ed. 1956).

[143] *Id.* at 9-258.

[144] *Id.* at 9-240.

[145] Text accompanying note 57.

[146] Text accompanying note 60.

unit directly, or might even become a federal unit as San Luis has become. The state plan is not clear as to the specific units within it; as Senator Engle intimated, its own present judgments are not final.[147] It is not in the nature of plans to be "final," and especially when the plan is motivated so largely by a desire both to take full advantage of the financial generosity of federal reclamation law, and to avoid its acreage limitation provisions. This lack of finality is illustrated by exchanges between Senators Douglas and Engle. The former asserted that state project water would flow through the federal Delta Mendota Canal.[148] Senator Engle denied this, saying this was "not the present plan." He said that the state would "build their own canal."[149] Senator Douglas cited a federal report assigning priority to enlargement of the federal Delta Mendota Canal over construction of a separate canal. Senator Engle then shifted his argument to one of *financial* separation, saying, "Of course it makes no difference whether a separate ditch is built or the present canal is enlarged. In either event the state will pay the cost."[150]

Senator Douglas named other points of probable physical union between federal and state projects, saying:

> [T]he Delta Cross Channel is to be used . . . (and water elevated) with power developed from the dams and falls of water up north. . . . [The] additional state outlay, if it should be made would not get to first base if there were not a prior huge federal investment. To claim that this action is entirely distinct from the federal outlay is, to my mind, "moonshine." In addition to that, the previous outlays on Shasta, Keswick, Nimbus, Folsom, and Trinity, which is still under construction, will make water and power available to what is alleged to be a purely State system but which will not be in fact purely a state system but will be a joint system.[151]

Neither Senator Kuchel nor Senator Engle gave an immediate, direct response, but the latter denied at one point in debate that water would be elevated with the Tracy pumps using Central Valley power.[152] State Engineer Harvey O. Banks had told Congress in 1956 that the state desired to "contract for the use by the state of Central Valley project power facilities."[153]

Statements of Senators Engle and Kuchel in presenting the San Luis bill to Congress indicate how inextricable from one another the

---

[147] Text accompanying note 149.
[148] 105 CONG. REC. 7496 (1959).
[149] *Ibid.* Senator Douglas argued that "one cannot cut the dam in two any more than Solomon's child could be cut in two. . . . One cannot build a second story unless one has a first story." *Id.* at 7490.
[150] 105 CONG. REC. 7672 (1959).
[151] *Id.* at 7671. Senator Douglas' characterization of the Feather River-San Luis development as a "joint system" left little ground under Senator Kuchel's suggestion that federal law might not apply north of San Luis Reservoir, even if section 6(a) were deleted. He did not press this point again. *Id.* at 7672, 7851.
[152] *Id.* at 7854.
[153] *1956 Hearings on S. 178, supra* note 19, at 44, 46.

state and federal projects are and how intrinsically desirable it is, if not inevitable, that each should take full advantage of the other. "[Federal] Central Valley project is part and parcel of the overall state water plan...," said Senator Engle.[154] The San Luis bill, said Senator Kuchel, seeks "to pave the way for the integration of the San Luis unit with the Central Valley project of the California state water plan."[155]

Physical and financial separation, clearly, are not facts but rather fictions asserted to support argument for removing federal acreage limitation law from a so-called state service area. Senator Douglas summarized the situation by saying: "[T]his is not the injection of a federal provision in a purely state project, but the assertion of federal protections in a largely federal project."[156] Senator Morse told the Senate:

> [T]he state development cannot take place without the federal development, so we have inseparabilities.... The fact is that this project was born of the federal government....[157] I would only add that this almost becomes one of the 'now you see it, now you don't' affairs when a discussion is had of a federal interest in a state project.[158]

"This alleged state project we are dealing with, therefore," he said on another occasion, "is merely a vision created in the hope that it can somehow transform everybody's water to water reserved only for a few people ... [they] think they have discovered a way around the law."[159]

The present Secretary faces the latest phase in a long-drawn out series of efforts to enable excess landholders to obtain water from public projects without agreeing to dispose of their excess lands as required by federal law. A spokesman for excess landholders once remarked to a friend of the present author, "You have to win every time; we have to win only once." This view of strategy affords an explanation of the variety and persistence of attacks in Congress, upon and through administrators, through the courts, through the state and through its agencies. But the responsibility of an administrator is to accomplish the objectives of law and policy laid down by Congress.

The Secretary of the Interior can advance the application of law on Kings and Kern rivers by presenting the thirty-two districts there with contracts like those approved so overwhelmingly by district di-

---

[154] 105 CONG. REC. 7486 (1959).
[155] *Id.* at 7484.
[156] *Id.* at 7497.
[157] *Id.* at 7492.
[158] *Id.* at 7495.
[159] *Id.* at 7992.

rectors and voters along the Friant-Kern and Madera canals a decade ago.[160] That will provide them opportunity to decide whether they wish firm water rights under reclamation law. If they accept the contracts, excess landholders within them are free individually to choose whether they wish to comply with reclamation law in order to obtain project water beyond an amount sufficient for 160 acres; usually it is financially very advantageous for them to do so. However, if either districts or individuals decline water on these terms, the Bureau of Reclamation will be free to dispose of it to others who accept it under the law.

This procedure should end a nearly half-century old contention that full payment renders acreage limitation inoperative, a contention no Secretary has been willing firmly to approve, but nevertheless one which has supported long delays in application of the law.

Courts are open to challenge of the Secretary's decision by either side, but the abilities of excess landholding and small landholding interests actually to carry a challenge through the courts are markedly different. Apparently the *Main Report* had in mind the difficulties of small landholders when forecasting that if a decision adverse to acreage limitation should be written into the San Luis contract, appeal to the courts would be unlikely. Reclamation law, however, is intended to be administered for the *benefit* of small landowners, not to place them at a disadvantage.

The San Luis contract, like the Kings and Kern contracts, should apply acreage limitation without qualification to the entire state service area. The State of California would have opportunity under reclamation law of choosing whether to participate in the San Luis Project or not. If the State of California should decline to participate in the San Luis Project, the San Luis Act permits the Secretary of the Interior to report to Congress that he intends to proceed with the federal project after ninety days.[161] As an alternative, the Secretary could recommend delay until a modified, perhaps enlarged, program of federal construction could be placed before Congress. In any case, firm insistence on compliance with law is more likely to advance than to retard water development in the West, which is the purpose of reclamation law.

The prospect of avoiding acreage limitation has encouraged obstruction and delay rather than development. However, growing awareness of water needs and the high costs of meeting them, in

---

[100] Taylor, *Excess Land Law on the Kern?*, 46 CALIF. L. REV. 153, 183, 184 (1958); Taylor, *Excess Land Law: Pressure vs. Principle*, 47 CALIF. L. REV. 499, 528-37 (1959). The Secretary could virtually assure that, except by his own choice, no excess landowner on Kings River would be deprived of opportunity to obtain project water, by offering a single contract to the all-embracing Kings River Conservation District.

[101] 74 Stat. 156, 157 (1960).

California as elsewhere in the West, may impel communities there to seek broader planning, financial and engineering bases than single states can well afford. It is possible as well—given time and a clear statement of choices — that pressures within California favoring construction under reclamation law, as revealed in public hearings and debates, may assert themselves in the same direction, and that together these forces may prove sufficient to change the state's position.

Straws are visible in the wind. A broad strategy of federal development, recently rejected, may become acceptable. California is contesting the adverse decision of a Supreme Court referee in its dispute over division of Colorado River water with Arizona, but cannot be sure of the outcome. The Mountain Counties Water Resources Association is attacking the state Feather River Project, and proposing that California lead other western states in requesting federal aid to develop the waters of the Columbia River for the needs of California.[162] This proposal from "counties of origin" of northern California waters amounts to a request for resumption of the Western Water Exchange report plans of the Bureau of Reclamation, shelved in 1951, apparently in response to California influence.[163] That year California was girding for the contest with Arizona. That same year saw district after district within the state accept water under acreage limitation, and decision by the legislature to authorize a state project unprotected by acreage limitation.

The record of the past decade reveals the state project as a hugger muggery, portrayed publicly as a great and generous state gesture to meet an imperative need, but the decade has seen no actual construction on the dam itself. In the meantime, though appeals for more and more federal aid, the size of the state's announced undertaking has been whittled down step by step. Its concealed purposes have remained a source of delay both actual and threatened and have led the state into an impasse, provided the Secretary of the Interior enforces reclamation law. The character of the project has obliged those who spoke for it to proclaim to Congress a fictitious separation of

---

[162] Letter from Vernon Campbell to Joseph Jensen, President, Metropolitan Water District, July 26, 1961, p. 3. "To try to rob the people of Northern California of the water they must have for their own area development eventually will result in endless litigation more bitter and futile than that between California and Arizona. . . . California State Project water will be very expensive, not only because the project works will be costly but also because interest charges will at least double the cost of construction, making the water too expensive for agricultural use and very high in cost for domestic and industrial use. California must have more water than the state produces. The Columbia River has the water. California should lead the way in the promotion of the Columbia River Project and should without delay contact the other Colorado River States and secure their cooperation in presenting the proposal to the Congress." *Ibid*. See also BALLIS, CALIFORNIA WATER PLAN: AN EVALUATION 6 (1960), on file in Public Affairs Institute, Washington, D. C.

[163] Text accompanying note 50.

state from federal projects in order to have recourse to an appeal to states' rights as means of parrying direct attacks upon the concealed purposes of the San Luis bill. It has obliged officials to abandon party platform and state policy, leaving statute book and contract between the state and its water agency, alike, stripped of all protections against concentration of private enrichment and of ownership of resources developed at public expense. The law places no responsibility upon a Secretary of the Interior for salvaging a state project of that particular kind in his endeavors to promote reclamation.

ADDENDUM: THE SECRETARY DECIDED

> Such an agreement must be submitted to Congress before appropriations for the San Luis Project are made. The reaction of Congress and its relevant committees is more a political than a legal problem.
> —Opinion of Counsel, Report of Chas. T. Main, Inc. to California Department of Water Resources, 1960.[1]

The state argued to the Solicitor in late November that acreage limitation does not apply to the state service area.[2] Its brief dismisses as an "apparently easy inference" a contrary conclusion that acreage limitation does apply—derived from language of the statute saying "the Secretary shall be governed by the federal reclamation laws," and from action of Congress in striking the qualifying phrase: "except so far as the provisions thereof are inconsistent with this Act." The brief relies on the report of the House Committee which said, in accepting the deletion of exceptions by the Senate, that "such deletion will do no harm" to the Committee's position against acreage limitation.[3]

The state supports its own position from the statute with these words: "the state cannot be restricted in the use of its allocated capacities 'for water service outside the federal San Luis unit service area.' 74 Stat. 158 (1960)."[4] But this is not what section 3(f) of the statute says; the statute is much more restrictive than the state claims. It says:

> The *rights to the use of* capacities of the joint-use facilities of the San Luis unit *shall be allocated* to the United States and the State, respectively, in such manner as may be mutually agreed upon . . . The State shall not

---

[1] See note 2 of the original text *supra*. This addendum was prepared on January 3, 1962, before texts of the Solicitor's opinion, and statements by the Attorney General and Secretary of the Interior were available.

[2] Letter from B. Abbott Goldberg, Deputy Director-Contracts, Department of Water Resources, to Frank J. Barry, Solicitor, U.S. Department of the Interior, November 29, 1961.

[3] *Ibid*. The brief argues also that no reclamation statute prior to the San Luis Act of 1960 applies to the state service area.

[4] *Ibid*.

be *restricted in the exercise of its allocated right* to the use of the capacities of the joint use facilities for water service outside the Federal San Luis unit service area.[5]

This language empowers the Secretary of the Interior to agree with the state upon an "allocated right," not an unrestricted "use." The Secretary—governed by reclamation law, with no exceptions and with exemption of the state service area specifically rejected— cannot confer upon the state by contract more than reclamation law permits.

The Secretary executed a contract on December 30, 1961, without provision for acreage limitation.[6] The *Main Report* of 1960 mentions the Department of Justice as among "potential litigants" who might protest action. Attorney General Robert F. Kennedy, however, has removed himself from this class by concurring in the Secretary's action.[7] The *San Francisco Chronicle* by remarking that the "New Year's Eve agreement . . . saved the Governor's bacon, as Secretary Udall was well aware," bears out the observation of the *Main Report* that the reaction of Congress may be "more a political than a legal problem." The *Chronicle* acknowledges that the Secretary's and the Attorney General's decision "may be shaky legally but . . . it is sound and practical."[8]

What are the criteria by which the committees of Congress to which the contract has been referred for review will decide whether or not to disapprove it? Will decision be according to their own preferences? As the Committee was composed in 1959, its members were against applying acreage limitation to the state service area. One member of the earlier Committee (Senator Richard Neuberger) opposed the Committee report when the bill reached the floor, and helped the Senate strike out both the Committee provision for exceptions to reclamation law and a specific exemption. What weight will the Senate Committee attach to the 1959 defeat of its own recommendations? The House Committee, with six dissenting members, said in 1960 that the actions by the Senate after four days of debate were without legal significance and, included the same proposal for

---

[5] 74 Stat. 158 (1960). (Emphasis supplied.)

[6] Whether the Secretary also relied on the state's reasoning for doing so is presently unknown.

[7] The Main Report, *supra* original text note 2, observes that the validity of interpreting the law so as to free the state service area "has been severely challenged." *Id.* at 28 n.14. Attorney General Kennedy states that "strong arguments can be made to the effect that they [Congress] did not intend to abandon the [160-acre] policy even within the area to be serviced by the state," and urged the Secretary to seek a "clear determination" from Congress. San Francisco Chronicle, December 31, 1961, p. 10, col. 3.

[8] Editorial, *Two Kinds of San Luis Water*, San Francisco Chronicle, January 3, 1962.

specific exemption in its bill that the Senate had rejected. What weight will the House Committee attach to the 1960 rejection of its own proposal by the House? What are the responsibilities of committees to actions of Congress with which they may disagree? What weight shall they attach to opinions of a Solicitor and of an Attorney General who apparently are not wholly of one mind on the state of the law?

Those members of Congress who worked to preserve acreage limitation in 1959 and 1960 may now find themselves on more difficult terrain. The Secretary and Attorney General have held their past victories to be lacking in legal effect, and the committees of Congress—whose recommendations were overthrown in 1959 and 1960—need only remain silent for ninety days to support the contract without acreage limitation. This situation has few precedents, if any. It touches the very heart of our constitutional procedure for arriving at and executing public decisions through separate, coordinate branches of government.

In making their decision, the Secretary and Attorney General might have chosen to endeavor to apply acreage limitation in the contract and thus leave it to the state or excess landowners to take it to the courts if so desired, or if necessary allow Congress to take up the San Luis Project afresh on leveler ground. Whether or not such a choice of alternatives would have preserved the law, at least it would have been in the spirit of reclamation law. The Secretary and the Attorney General did not do so. The *Main Report* anticipated this outcome in 1960, saying:

> It is true that if in fact the Bureau of Reclamation did not have the authority to enter into such a contract, the agreement might be open to challenge. However, as a practical matter, such a challenge in the courts need not be anticipated in the normal course of events.[9]

In another decision on December 30th Secretary Udall held that, after forty years, completing repayment of construction costs charged against private landowners may render excess land laws inoperative. However, he rejected prepayment as a means of escape from acreage limitation on Kings and Kern rivers. Prepayment, he said, would "completely frustrate" the intent of acreage limitation.[10]

Although disapproving frustration in this complete form, the Secretary's approval of the acceptance of money in satisfaction of the requirements of policy *at any time* inverts the true relation between government and private beneficiaries of public reclamation, as perceived by the courts. When *public* expenditures for reclamation of

---

[9] Main Report, *supra* original text note 2, at 29.
[10] San Francisco Chronicle, December 31, 1961, p. 10, col. 2.

private lands were challenged as unconstitutional, they were justified in court on two principal grounds, *viz.*, the expenditures promoted development, and acreage limitation assured wide distribution of their benefits.[11] How can calling on the public to subsidize private beneficiaries be justified if repayment of a portion of the cost by beneficiaries can extinguish the policy that justifies the public subsidies the beneficiaries do not repay?

This issue is not being threshed out in a vacuum. The federal official signing the state contract on December 30th hailed application of acreage limitation to the *federal* San Luis service area as conducive to "family farms" and to "diversified farming like the eastern part of the valley," in contrast to "large farms with migrant workers living in labor camps."[12] Apparently neither he nor anyone else remarked on possibly contrasting results from allowing the *state* service area to develop free of acreage limitation. The *Wall Street Journal* said, "Had the Udall decision gone the other way, California was expected to pull out of the San Luis project, which might have seriously jeopardized its efforts to sell state water bonds."[13] The *Chronicle* remarked:

> One major difference mentioned at yesterday's ceremony is that ranches receiving *federal* water from the project will pay $7 or $7.50 per acre-foot at canalside. *State* water will cost about $18 to $20 an acre-foot at canalside in Kern County to small users.[14]

---

[11] Burley v. United States, 179 Fed. 1, 7, 8, 11, 12 (1910).
[12] San Francisco Chronicle, December 31, 1961, p. 10, col. 1.
[13] January 2, 1962, p. 6, col. 3.
[14] San Francisco Chronicle, December 31, 1961, p. 10, col. 3.

EXCESS LAND LAW

Calculated Circumvention

Excess Land Law: Calculated Circumvention

Paul S. Taylor*

FEDERAL RECLAMATION began as a program to help "farm boys" who "want farms of their own" obtain them "without being driven into the already overcrowded cities to seek employment."[1] Begun as a turn-of-the-century "war on poverty," reclamation is administered currently on important projects in apparent forgetfulness of this purpose.[2] On these projects it has become a program largely to subsidize reclamation of great landholdings primarily for the benefit of their owners. This Article is a study of current circumvention of the antimonopoly provisions of reclamation law in two areas within the Central Valley Project.[3]

The study concerns contracts between the United States and the Westlands Water District, a portion of the Federal Service Area of the San Luis Unit which, in turn, is a portion of the Great Central Valley Project. The Westlands District is located on the west side of California's San Joaquin Valley. The pattern of circumvention with which this Article deals is also evidenced by the contract between the United States and the Glenn-Colusa Irrigation District regarding diversion of water from the Sacramento River.

At Westlands, a half-million privately owned acres threatened with return to "sagebrush" and "desert" are currently under federal reclamation at an authorized cost to the public of nearly a half-billion dollars. There, the antimonopoly excess land laws are being violated wholesale. An excuse for the violation has already been arranged.

At Glenn-Colusa, the same antimonopoly excess lands laws are being frustrated. The means of frustration may be different, but the circum-

---

* Professor of Economics, Emeritus, University of California, Berkeley; consultant to the Office of the Secretary of the Interior and Bureau of Reclamation 1943-52. Letters and various other cited documents not otherwise available to the public are being filed under the title of this Article at the Bancroft Library, University of California, Berkeley, and are indicated herein by an asterisk (*).

[1] Congressman Oscar W. Underwood, of Alabama. S. Doc. No. 446, 57th Cong., 1st Sess. 21 (1902).

[2] Secretary of the Interior Stewart L. Udall listed his Department's contributions toward the "war on poverty" in testimony on the Economic Opportunity Bill in April 1964. He spoke of assistance to Indians and employment opportunities for youth on public lands, but failed to mention the vast Bureau of Reclamation program. *Hearings on H.R. 10440 Before House Subcommittee on War On Poverty of Committee on Education and Labor*, 88th Cong., 2d Sess. 341-61 (1964).

[3] Present administrators of the Department of the Interior failed also to require observance of the excess land law in the contract between the United States and the State of California after Congress had denied exemption. See note 30 *infra*.

vention is no less conspicuous.⁴ Circumvention in the Federal Service Area and along the Sacramento, however, have this in common: No challenge to national antimonopoly policy has been raised or deliberated in Congress; no word of any statute has been altered.

I

ANTIMONOPOLY POLICY: THE EXCESS LAND LAW

The purpose of the federal reclamation program, launched by Congress in 1902,⁵ is to provide national assistance to develop the water resources of the West. Its principal financial instrument is a subsidy from the national treasury in the form of long-term interest-free loans. The value of this subsidy to beneficiaries is substantial, roughly equal to the amount of the investment itself. In addition, there are other large subsidies from power users, municipalities, and taxpayers that reduce the cost of water to irrigators.⁶ As originally presented to Congress and the courts, the main justifications for undertaking federal reclamation are two-fold: (1) it promotes national development in the West; and (2) its benefits are distributed widely among the many, and are not monopolized by the few.⁷ In the words of Theodore Roosevelt, who inspired the excess land provisions and first signed reclamation into law, "every dollar is spent to build up the small man of the West and prevent the big man, East or West, coming in and monopolizing the water and land."⁸

The legal instrument for effectuating the antimonopoly policy of the reclamation law is the excess land provisions. By the original Reclamation Act, "no right to the use of water for land in private ownership shall be sold for a tract exceeding one hundred and sixty acres to any one landowner . . . ."⁹ It should be noted that this provision limits the size of ownership of land entitled to receive water, not the scale of operations.¹⁰

---

⁴ Letter From Martin H. Blote to Secretary of the Interior Udall, January 30, 1964 (*) [hereinafter cited as *Blote to Udall*].

⁵ 44 Stat. 649, 650 (1926), 43 U.S.C. § 391 (1958).

⁶ See, e.g., Note, 38 CALIF. L. REV. 728, 730-32 (1950).

⁷ See House Committee on Arid Lands, *Report on Reclamation and Arid Lands*, H.R. REP. No. 1468, 57th Cong., 1st Sess. 3 (1902); Burley v. United States, 179 Fed. 1, 7-8 (1910).

⁸ THEODORE ROOSEVELT, 7 TRANSACTIONS OF THE COMMONWEALTH CLUB 102 (1912-13).

⁹ 44 Stat. 649 (1926), 43 U.S.C. § 431 (1958).

¹⁰ A spokesman for large landholding interests of California asserted that "[T]he excess land provisions apply only to the record ownership of land. There is no statutory limitation on the amount of land that may be leased and farmed under the projects." S. T. Harding, *Hearings on S. Res. 295 Before Senate Subcommittee on Irrigation and Reclamation*, 78th Cong., 2d Sess. 358 (1944) [hereinafter cited as *1944 Hearings on S. Res. 295*]. Opponents of the excess land law also have taken an opposite view in arguing against the excess land law; e.g., "We sincerely feel that such a limitation, if imposed, . . . would . . . fail to recog-

In 1924 a special advisory committee issued what has come to be known as the Fact Finders Report, recommending revisions of reclamation law.[11] The main purpose of reclamation was reiterated: "to provide opportunities for homestead making for rural-minded people. Making a homestead, a place able to support a family and desirable for family life, must remain the central thought of . . . Federal reclamation."[12]

The Fact Finders' proposals for revision were intended: (1) to simplify Federal administration of projects by giving water users a larger sense of participation and responsibility through their own organizations;[13] (2) to strengthen controls over private speculation, which had "added greatly to the farmer's burdens" in seeking to win his "homestead from the desert;"[14] and (3) to assure more effective enforcement of the excess land provision by requiring that "no reclamation project should hereafter be authorized until all privately owned land in excess of a single homestead unit for each owner shall have been acquired by the United States or by contract placed under control of the Bureau of Reclamation . . . ."[15]

These suggested revisions were influential in the rewriting of reclamation law two years later when Congress passed the Omnibus Adjustment Act.[16] It prescribed execution of contracts between the Secretary of the Interior and irrigation districts prior to water deliveries to new projects, and thus provided the needed "sense of participation."[17] It established new controls over private speculation. Water rights were denied to otherwise eligible lands if they were created by subdivision of ineligible excess lands, unless the subdivided lands were sold at a price appraised "without reference to the proposed construction" of the project.[18] Most important, the act tightened the language of the excess land

---

nize the startling agricultural trends of the past several decades which have shifted farming away from family type operations on small plots to the mass production science necessary to feed and clothe the rising population." D. B. McHenry, Hearing Before California Assembly Committee on Water (1959). See also Los Angeles Times, June 7, 1964, p. 6-G, col. 1.

[11] Report by the Committee of Special Advisers on Reclamation, S. Doc. No. 92, 68th Cong., 1st Sess. (1924).

[12] *Id.* at 111.

[13] *Id.* at 103-08.

[14] *Id.* at 114-16.

[15] *Id.* at 116. This recommendation applies to the Secretary of the Interior to whom it was made, and to Congress. Congress chose to adopt this recommendation for at least one project, leaving it otherwise within administrative discretion. Leaving this discretion to the Secretary has exposed him to severe pressures from large landholders to exercise his discretion in their favor, rather than to create more opportunity for small farmers' families. See text accompanying notes 107-13 *infra.*

[16] 44 Stat. 636 (1926), 43 U.S.C. § 423 (1958).

[17] 44 Stat. 649 (1926), 43 U.S.C. § 423(e) (1958).

[18] *Ibid.*

provision, and added a device to facilitate effective enforcement. Reclamation law now prohibits not only the sale of a water right, but also forbids excess lands from receiving project water unless the owner authorizes the Government to sell these lands.[19]

The Act of 1926 also reduced the financial obligations of settlers on many reclamation projects, an evidence of more congressional concern for effectuating the policies of the Reclamation Program than for recovery of costs. Under the Act, repayment of the federal investment by beneficiaries, without interest, is accomplished through contracts executed between the United States and organized water users' districts having power to raise revenue. Although these contracts customarily recite the duty of the district to observe the excess land law, this recitation does not of itself enforce the law. More is required, and it is provided for in the 1926 Omnibus Act.[20]

The enforcement device created by this Act provides that the only way landowners can render their excess lands eligible to receive reclamation project water is by individually executing recordable contracts with the United States. These contracts, executed in return for the right to receive subsidized water, authorize the Secretary of the Interior to sell lands in excess of 160 acres, at appraised prices excluding incremental values added by the proposed construction of the irrigation works.

The statute imposes a clear and unqualified requirement that "no such excess lands so held shall receive water from any project or division if the owners thereof shall refuse to execute valid recordable contracts for the sale of such lands under terms and conditions satisfactory to the Secretary of the Interior . . . ."[21]

II

RECLAMATION ISSUE AT SAN LUIS: ADMINISTRATION

San Luis is but the most recent in a long succession of units authorized by Congress under reclamation law as part of federal development of the Central Valley's water resources.[22] Although dispute over application of the excess land law has come sharply into focus at San Luis, division over the question did not originate there. Because of the existence of large western landholdings, antimonopoly policy has been a prominent issue in federal reclamation from its legislative beginnings.[23] Nowhere has the

---

[19] *Ibid.*
[20] *Ibid.*
[21] *Ibid.*
[22] See *Central Valley Basin: A Comprehensive Departmental Report on the Development of the Water and Related Resources of the Central Valley Basin, and Comments from the State of California and Federal Agencies*, S. Doc. No. 113, 81st Cong., 1st Sess. (1949).
[23] See Taylor, *Central Valley Project: Water and Land*, 2 W. POL. Q. 229, 238-45 (1949).

issue been the object of more heated or more protracted debate than in the Great Central Valley of California. The greatest concentration of ownership of irrigable lands in the United States is there, especially in the San Joaquin Valley of which the Federal San Luis Service Area[24] is a part.

Seventy percent of the lands of the Federal San Luis Service Area are ineligible under the excess land law to receive project water because they are held in ownerships exceeding 160 acres and their owners have not executed recordable contracts to make them eligible. A single owner, the Southern Pacific, holds nearly 120,000 acres. Other holdings are also very large; in all about 250,000 acres of the Federal Area are owned in excess amounts.[25]

In pleading initially for congressional authorization of the 483 million dollar San Luis Project, spokesmen in the House and Senate portrayed the dire need for water of all the people in the Federal Service Area, and of all the lands. Congressman B. F. Sisk, of California, described the bleak future facing the 10,500 rural people and 12,500 townspeople who "will have to leave and seek livings and homes elsewhere, . . . starved out of existence by lack of water." "Most of the cultivated land which is the basis of their economy," he said, "will revert to desert."[26] Senator Clair Engle, of California, spoke of ground waters being " 'mined' to the point of exhaustion" by pumping; of "consuming a capital resource"; and of the necessity of appealing for a federal " 'rescue' project" to "save good cropland from returning to sagebrush and sand."[27]

As discussion of the San Luis authorization bill proceeded in Congress, it developed that winning support for financing the project depended more on allaying doubts that the excess land law actually would be applied, than upon the distressed appeals to rescue the land from return to "sagebrush and sand."[28] These doubts concerned two land areas of the project, and two branches of the federal government. The first con-

---

[24] Lands served directly by the federally-administered project are designated as Federal Service Area; those served directly by the State-administered project are called State Service Area. Both federal and state projects use "joint facilities" including reservoir, canals, and pumps.

[25] Assistant Secretary of the Interior Kenneth Holum, *Hearing Before Senate Committee on Interior and Insular Affairs . . . on Proposed Contract Between the Secretary of the Interior and Westlands Water District for Construction of a Water Distribution and Drainage Collector System in the San Luis Unit, Central Valley Project, California*, 88th Cong., 2d Sess. (July 8, 1964) [hereinafter cited as *1964 Westlands Hearing*]. See also testimony of Taylor, *1964 Westlands Hearing* at 140.

[26] *Hearings on H.R. 301 Before House Subcommittee on Irrigation and Reclamation*, 86th Cong., 1st Sess. 13 (1959).

[27] 105 CONG. REC. 7485 (1959).

[28] See 105 CONG. REC. 8001 (1959).

cern was application of the excess land law to the so-called State Service Area.[29] The bill authorized joint use of the San Luis facilities not only for the Federal Service Area, but also by the State of California, and proposed legislative exemption of the State Service Area. The Senate debated the proposed exemption for four days, and the House for two. Both bodies refused legislative exemption.[30] There was no attempt to gain exemption of the excess land law for the Federal Service Area.

The second concern of Congress was whether the executive branch of Government could be relied on to enforce the excess land provision in either the State or Federal Service Area. The record of nonenforcement was long,[31] and pressures from excess landholding interests to prevent executive enforcement had been unremitting.

As early as 1944 State Engineer Edward Hyatt, speaking for the California Water Project Authority, told Congress that exemption of the Central Valley Project was "expected," if not by legislative decision, then by executive action.[32] Three years later he testified that the State Authority was in sympathy with "the vast majority of the people who are affected," *i.e.*, the excess landowners, and pronounced the law "unjust and harsh and unworkable."[33]

Legislators friendly to the excess land provision expressed deep distrust of the executive during debate on the San Luis authorization bill. Democratic Senator Wayne Morse, of Oregon, said he was "sure that the Secretary of the Interior" of the current Republican Administration, "given the wide range of authority to negotiate agreements . . . will

---

[29] See note 24 *supra*.

[30] See 105 CONG. REC. 7483-98, 7665-91, 7849-77, 7986-8000 (1959); 106 CONG. REC. 10448-71, 10559-66 (1960). Nevertheless, Secretary Udall failed to require observance of the excess land law in the contract he executed with the State of California on December 30, 1961. 108 CONG. REC. 5717-21 (1962). See Taylor, *Excess Land Law: Secretary's Decision? A Study in Administration of Federal-State Relations*, 9 U.C.L.A.L. REV. 1 (1962).

[31] See 1964 *Westlands Hearing* at 146-47. See also Taylor, *The Excess Land Law: Execution of a Public Policy*, 64 YALE L.J. 477, 501-06 (1955).

[32] "During these early years the water project authority studied the subject and discussed it informally with officials of the Bureau. The necessity of change or elimination of this feature of the law as applied to the Central Valley project was repeatedly brought to the attention of the Bureau. It was expected by the water project authority and others active in the furtherance of the project in California that, if it was finally determined that the excess-land provisions would be legally construed to apply under the terms of authorization of the project, that the excess-land provisions either would be removed by congressional action as in the case of similar projects such as the Colorado, Big Thompson project in Colorado and the Boca Dam project in Nevada, or by executive decision or action as in the case of the All-American Canal unit of the Boulder Dam project in California." *1944 Hearings on S. Res. 295*, at 27.

[33] *Hearings on S. 912 Before Senate Public Lands Subcommittee*, 80th Cong., 1st Sess. 27 (1947) [hereinafter cited as *1947 Hearings on S. 912*].

find some way to subvert reclamation laws in . . . the San Luis area."[34] Democratic Senator Clair Engle, of California, offered an opinion that under a future Democratic Secretary "the law will be enforced,"[35] but Democratic Senator Paul Douglas, of Illinois, was skeptical that the problem was one of political party. "Sometimes Democratic Secretaries . . . go sour, too," he said, adding: "If I may say so, I notice that the interests that are trying to operate against the welfare of the country have representatives inside both parties and they operate inside both."[36]

Senator Douglas was specific as to his fears: The Southern Pacific, notably, might receive project water for its excess lands without agreeing to subdivide them as required by law.[37] Whether he knew it or not, the Senator was echoing doubts expressed fifty-seven years earlier by Congressman George W. Ray, of New York. Unconvinced by assurances of western spokesmen pleading in 1902 for a national reclamation program, that the excess land laws would result in "breaking up any large land holdings" in the vicinity of reclamation projects,[38] Ray led the opposition to all federal reclamation. "We find behind the scheme," he had said, "the great railroad interests of the West, who own millions of acres of . . . arid lands . . . ." The value of these lands, he asserted, "will be multiplied by 10" and even "by 20" at the "very moment that we, at the public expense . . . construct these irrigation works . . . ."[39]

Spokesmen for the San Luis project regularly gave assurances that the law would be applied, as their predecessors had answered the skeptics of 1902. At the first presentation of the San Luis project to the Senate in 1958, Senator Wayne Morse, of Oregon, inquired whether the project would be economically feasible with Southern Pacific excess land holdings ineligible to participate.[40] Senator Thomas H. Kuchel, of California, responded that "in my judgment, they will be compelled to participate through the force of public opinion." Senator Clinton P. Anderson, of New Mexico, added immediately that "in my judgment, the Southern Pacific will reverse its decision . . . and will subdivide its lands."[41]

---

[34] 105 CONG. REC. 7688 (1959).

[35] *Id.* at 7495.

[36] *Ibid.*

[37] *Ibid.*

[38] 35 CONG. REC. 6678 (1902).

[39] 35 CONG. REC. APP. 256 (1920). In 1960 Congress authorized public investment of about $483 million to reclaim the San Luis Federal Service Area which had an assessed valuation of about $20 million. On October 20, 1964, landowners approved Westlands construction contract by vote of 12,399,817 to 388,328, each vote representing $1 of assessed valuation. Westlands District includes approximately four-fifths of the entire Federal Service Area. See Fresno Bee, September 16, 1964, p. 10-c, col. 1.

[40] See 104 CONG. REC. 17733 (1958). See also note 44 *infra.*

[41] 104 CONG. REC. 17733 (1958).

At the following Congress when the San Luis authorization bill was brought again before the Senate, Senator Kuchel renewed his assurances:

> It should be made crystal clear that the federal acreage limitations will be enforced in the case of those benefiting from the Federal project in this joint venture . . . . [T]here is every intention on the part of the authors of the bill to have the Federal Reclamation law apply completely to every drop of water which goes into the San Luis Dam and which thereafter is to be used on properties lying within the expanded Federal reclamation area.[42]

As will appear, it is one thing for the legislative branch of government to decide to apply reclamation law to a project; but it turns out to be quite another for the executive branch actually to apply it.

III

ENFORCEMENT: TWO MEANINGS

Before long it became clear that there was disagreement as to the meaning of "enforcement" of reclamation law. On the one side, Senator Douglas and his colleagues apparently meant execution of recordable contracts by excess landholders agreeing to dispose of their excess lands.[43] Senator Kuchel apparently meant something else. He denied that Senator Douglas was "correct," and said that excess landowners were permitted by law to elect either to ask for water by executing recordable contracts, or to decline to ask. "When a Federal reclamation project is created . . . if I am . . . a large landowner, I do not have to take supplemental water if I do not wish to do so."[44]

---

[42] 105 CONG. REC. 7484 (1959).

[43] "I believe in making the Southern Pacific Railway Co. obey the law. It has stated pretty directly that it does not intend to obey the law. The big estates do not want to accept it." *Ibid.* "The Boston Ranch does not want to accept it. They want to have tens of thousands of acres held under one ownership and still secure the irrigation waters." *Id.* at 7667.

[44] 105 CONG. REC. 7491-92 (1959). The complexities of detail in reclamation law and its application, confused rather than clarified the debate, and in so doing helped pave the way toward circumvention of the law. Another important example is the confusion between "financial feasibility" and "economic feasibility," which was shared by both sides in the Senate debate. "Financial feasibility" has never been seriously in question at San Luis; excess landowners, including the Southern Pacific, are willing to meet financial obligations to the United States. "Economic feasibility," on the other hand, concerns a relationship between project costs and benefits to eligible lands adjudged to be either favorable or unfavorable to authorization of construction of the project. Expending full authorized San Luis costs of $483 million to benefit only 30% of the San Luis lands, because 70% are legally ineligible to receive project benefits, raises per acre costs, and reduces "economic feasibility." Project costs are about $1,000 an acre, provided all lands qualify as eligible to "receive water" ($483 million authorized to develop about 496,000 acres). If, however, eligible lands remain at only 30% because 70% are ineligible, costs per acre rise to $3,333.

Geology of the San Luis Service Area furnishes the clue to an explanation of how both sides in Senate debate could proclaim their devotion to reclamation law with apparently equal fervor, yet at the same time disagree so completely on the question whether law would be enforced or violated. A ground reservoir fed by underground sources and seepage from water applied to the surface underlies the Federal San Luis Service Area. Once in the ground reservoir, water is physically available through pumping to both eligible and ineligible lands. Against this geological background, two contrary interpretations of "enforcement" have been advanced.

"The situation in question," said Senator Kuchel, "does not involve a violation of acreage limitation law. That ought to be made abundantly clear."[45] Senator Morse insisted there was violation. Under the Westlands Water District contract with the United States, he said, application of the acreage limitation would be limited to "surface water" and would unlawfully ignore the "undue enrichment that the large landowners would receive from a raising of the underground water level." Owners of ineligible lands "would take the water out with . . . pumps" without regard for the excess land law. "That is the gimmick."[46]

On another occasion Senator Kuchel clarified beyond any doubt his own meaning of obedience to the excess land law, and established agreement with Senators Morse and Douglas on the exact point of difference between himself and them. "Underground seepage of water delivered to their neighbors is not . . . a 'delivery' within the meaning of the acreage limitation . . . ," he wrote. "The material fact is whether or not they receive project water by surface delivery and . . . until they ask for that privilege there is no way to force them to sign a recordable contract to dispose of excess land."[47]

This Article will establish that there is no legal justification for the view that deliveries of ground water at San Luis are exempt from the excess land law and that the law is currently being violated through official nonenforcement.

This alters the measure of "economic feasibility" vastly. Usually "economic feasibility" affects legislative or administrative decisions whether or not to proceed with a project. During Senate debate the matter was thoroughly confused, and "economic feasibility" or infeasibility apparently carries little present weight with the Secretary of the Interior. In 1959 Senator Kuchel sought to reassure his opponents by quoting Senate Interior Committee Counsel Stewart French, in an ambiguous passage reading: "Refusal of Southern Pacific to [execute a recordable] . . . agreement would in no way jeopardize the project." Senator Kuchel was clearly misled in adding to this statement the qualifying phrase, "from the standpoint of economic feasibility." See 105 CONG. REC. 7492 (1959).

45 110 CONG. REC. 17915 (daily ed. Aug. 7, 1964).
46 *Id.* at 17919.
47 Letter From Senator Thomas H. Kuchel to J. B. Neilands, May 13, 1964 (*).

IV

LEGAL FOUNDATIONS OF CIRCUMVENTION

The language of reclamation law, already quoted,[48] requires the Secretary of the Interior to prevent ineligible lands from receiving project water. The language of the statute makes no distinction between water received at the surface and water received underground. The legislative history of the reclamation law offers no evidence of congressional intent to distinguish between surface and underground deliveries of water at San Luis or elsewhere on Central Valley Project.[49] On the contrary, Congress has reserved to itself the power to make any such distinction, project by project. Citing congressional exemption of the Santa Maria, California, Project where "water utilized on project lands is acquired by pumping from the underground reservoir," the United States Supreme Court observed, "significantly, where a particular project has been exempted because of its peculiar circumstances, the Congress has always made such exemption by express enactment."[50]

Administrators of the San Luis unit, nevertheless, have taken it upon themselves, in applying the excess land law, to distinguish between deliveries of water at the surface, and deliveries by seepage from the surface into the ground reservoir.

Commissioner of Reclamation Floyd E. Dominy has advised the Senate that although recordable contracts will be required to qualify excess lands to receive surface deliveries of water, these will not be required of those who, instead, "choose to continue pumping" from underground waters that will have been improved by "deep percolation losses from surface water applications," including surface applications of project water.[51] The Department of the Interior, represented before the Senate Interior Committee by Assistant Secretary Kenneth Holum and Solicitor Frank J. Barry, supported this position, which was embodied in the contracts to carry out the project between the Department of the Interior and Westlands Water District.[52]

---

[48] See text accompanying note 21 *supra*.

[49] No bill to make this distinction on Central Valley Project has been introduced. The most extensive argument on practical difficulties of enforcement under ground reservoir conditions was advanced by Senator Sheridan Downey, of California, during efforts from 1944 to 1947 to persuade Congress to exempt Central Valley Project from the excess land law. These attempts failed. See *1947 Hearings on S. 912*; *1944 Hearings on S. Res. 295*; DOWNEY, THEY WOULD RULE THE VALLEY (1947).

[50] Ivanhoe Irr. Dist. v. McCracken, 357 U.S. 275, 292 (1958) (referring to exemption of ground water by 68 Stat. 1190 (1954)).

[51] Letter From Commissioner of Reclamation Floyd E. Dominy to Senator Henry M. Jackson, Chairman, Senate Interior and Insular Affairs Committee, May 26, 1964, cited at 110 CONG. REC. 17497 (daily ed. Aug. 5, 1964).

[52] *1964 Westlands Hearing* at 15-44.

The views of the Manager-Chief Counsel of Westlands Water District, Ralph M. Brody, were in accord with those of Commissioner Dominy and the Interior Department spokesmen before the Committee. He, too, recited the legal prohibition of water delivery to ineligible lands;[53] he conceded that water "applied at the surface as a result of project activities" will seep into the underground;[54] he denied that execution of recordable contracts is required by law as precondition of construction or for receiving project seepage water; he insisted that neither temporary nor even permanent refusal of excess landowners to qualify their lands by executing recordable contracts, although receiving underground project waters, contravenes the excess land law.[55]

Senator Thomas H. Kuchel, of California, as noted earlier, was explicit in declaring the existence of a legal distinction between surface and underground water deliveries.[56] He grounded his position, he said, "upon the advice of the Solicitor's Office of the Department of the Interior and after consultation with counsel on the staff of the Senate Interior Committee."[57]

The Westlands water service contract of June 5, 1963, provides specifically that project water pumped from underground is outside the scope of the excess land law "if such water reached the underground strata . . . of excess land as an unavoidable result" of furnishing project water to eligible lands. Assistant Secretary Kenneth Holum justified this as "the standard Central Valley contractual clause."[58]

This exclusion of "unavoidable" delivery of water into the ground reservoir from application of the excess land law, apparently first received official legal attention in the middle nineteen-forties. At that time Senator Sheridan Downey, of California, was leading a vigorous and persistent, but unsuccessful campaign to persuade Congress that the difficulties of applying the excess land law to water received by ineligible lands through the ground reservoir justified congressional exemption of Central Valley Project from the law.[59] In 1947 the Chief Counsel of the Bureau of Reclamation, Clifford E. Fix, submitted a statement to the Senate Committee then holding hearings, reviewing the "legal basis for assessment of excess landowners by irrigation districts."[60] Chief Counsel Fix con-

---

[53] *Id.* at 101, 114, 115.
[54] *Id.* at 113. Assistant Secretary Holum estimated on July 9, 1964, that about 7.5% of surface water would seep into the ground reservoir. *Id.* at 25. On October 7, 1964, he estimated percolation at "between 10 and 15 percent." *Id.* at 179.
[55] See *id.* at 101, 114.
[56] See text accompanying note 47 *supra*.
[57] Letter From Senator Thomas H. Kuchel to J. B. Neilands, May 13, 1964 (*).
[58] *1964 Westlands Hearing* at 20-21.
[59] See note 49 *supra*.
[60] *1947 Hearings on S. 912*, at 1270-96.

cluded, on the main point at issue, that the power of a district to assess landowners for benefits does not depend on delivery of water to their own lands. He quoted with apparent approval an earlier hypothetical statement by Commissioner of Reclamation Harry A. Bashore, namely, "if . . . the physical introduction of project water on and under project lands has for its principal purpose, and its principal result is, the furnishing of irrigation water to eligible lands, with the incidental, and evitable [inevitable?] result that the underground water supply of ineligible excess lands is benefitted," that result is not to be construed as furnishing water contrary to the excess land law.[61] At the opening of his statement, Chief Counsel Fix had cautioned that "so far as underground waters are concerned," he was dealing with "potential" rather than actual "legal questions."[62] On this slender incidental consideration, the words of the "unavoidable" excuse clause, now in the Westlands contract, began to appear in Central Valley Project water district contracts.

Although the words are the same as those used in earlier Central Valley contracts, project conditions at San Luis are fundamentally different. The two conditions that Commissioner Bashore attached to his interpretation are unfulfilled at San Luis: (1) benefit to underground waters is not "incidental" but planned as a major purpose of the San Luis Project;[63] and (2) the "principal purpose" and "principal result" are not furnishing water to eligible lands at San Luis but rather to the seventy percent of lands that are ineligible. The administrative precedent, therefore, is not applicable.[64]

The effort to discover a legal foundation for distinguishing between surface and underground water deliveries on the San Luis unit resembles the midnight search in the cellar for the black cat that is not there. In mid-summer of 1964, Secretary of the Interior Stewart L. Udall and

---

[61] *Id.* at 1274.

[62] *Id.* at 1270.

[63] See note 101 *infra* and accompanying text.

[64] "This appears to be the genesis of the 'unavoidable clause.' No reference is made in the quoted ruling to any applicable law permitting this evasion of the 'excess land law.' Congressional will cannot be relied upon in this matter because that will through the years has been unalterably opposed to the perpetuation of land and water monopolies. In simple terms executive fiat has been indulged in to create an exception to the excess land laws where none actually exists. Insidious though that evasion may be in the light of the law, the precedent stemming from the evasion is far worse. As is so frequently the case, a contempt for the law breeds further violation." Statement by Senator Gaylord Nelson on the Westlands Water District construction contract of 1963, 110 CONG. REC. 17495 (daily ed. Aug. 5, 1964). The United States Supreme Court incidentally referred to the "unavoidable" clause in 1958, citing it as one item in evidence among others (*e.g.*, "subsidy" for reclamation) for concluding that the excess land law does not result in "damage constituting taking of property without compensation." Ivanhoe Irr. Dist. v. McCracken, 357 U.S. 275, 266, 295, 296. *Cf.* Testimony of Solicitor Frank J. Barry, *1964 Westlands Hearing* at 37.

Solicitor Frank J. Barry finally joined others in the search, virtually conceding its administrative futility by asking Congress to join also.

Responding to request by the Senate Interior Committee on August 1, 1962, for a study and report on the excess land law, the Secretary advised the Committee on June 30, 1964, that "both Congress and the Executive Branch have on occasion exhibited a degree of concern for the excess-land owner which may be difficult to reconcile with the policies embraced by the excess land laws."[65] The Secretary cited first among the "facets of excess land law or policy which merit further inquiry," that excess landowners have "not been required to comply with Federal excess land laws or to sign a recordable contract" when project waters "stabilize the underground, or reduce the rate at which it is being mined."[66]

Thus the Secretary of the Interior apparently now makes no claim that the distinction between receiving water at the surface and receiving it underground is founded on law.[67] Solicitor Barry explained the Secretary's views to the Senate Interior Committee: "I want to point out to you that this letter was sent to the full committee for the purpose of alerting the Committee to the fact that . . . [indirect receipt of water by stabilization of the ground water table] is a problem and that consideration should be given to it." It seems that Solicitor Barry, the chief legal officer of the Department of the Interior, was unprepared four years after the passage of the San Luis Authorization Act, to state whether or not he supports a legal distinction between surface and ground waters. He told the Senate that he did "not want to give a legal opinion here"; that he "would prefer to study this matter with considerable care"; that he had "discussed this matter at considerable length with the people" on his staff, had "studied the matter myself," and could not "say at this point whether it is illegal . . . to supply water under these conditions, or whether we can legally require . . . a recordable contract."[68]

V

PARALYZED ADMINISTRATION

Secretary Udall has advised Congress that the "executive branch," upon occasion, has "exhibited a degree of concern for the excess-land

---

[65] Letter From Secretary Stewart L. Udall to Senator Henry M. Jackson, June 30, 1964, Acreage Limitation Policy, Study Prepared by the Department of the Interior Pursuant to a Resolution of the Senate Committee on Interior and Insular Affairs, Committee Print, xiii [hereinafter cited as *Acreage Limitation Policy*].

[66] *Id.* at xi.

[67] *Ibid.*

[68] *1964 Westlands Hearing* at 34. Solicitor Barry's uncertainty on July 8, 1964, contrasts sharply with Senator Kuchel's certainty on May 15, 1964, relying upon "advice of the Solicitor's Office," that the law distinguishes between surface and underground water deliveries. See text accompanying note 57 *supra*.

owner . . . difficult to reconcile" with the excess land law, and suggested that a part may have been played by "careful planning to take advantage of . . . exceptions to the acreage limitations."[69]

Inability to devise adequate administrative procedures to enforce the law is not a sufficient explanation for its breakdown. As there is no legal basis for exempting ground water deliveries at San Luis, the simplest way for the Secretary to insure enforcement is to require excess landowners to execute recordable contracts before he spends public funds to construct the project. Indeed, under the ground reservoir conditions that characterize the Federal Service Area, the Secretary appears to have no practicable, effective alternative. Congress, by requiring one-hundred percent compliance by holders of excess lands as a condition precedent to construction of an earlier project has even provided the Secretary with legislative precedent for this procedure.[70]

The Secretary of the Interior, however, has been following an opposite course at San Luis. If continued, this can lead only to violation of the excess land law. The Secretary has allowed four years to pass since Congress authorized the San Luis Project[71] without requesting execution of any recordable contracts.[72] He has, however, asked Congress for authorization to spend 157 million dollars beyond the 290 million dollars authorized in 1960 for construction now under way to build water distribution and drainage systems within the Federal Service Area[73] for privately-owned lands, seventy percent of which are ineligible to receive the project benefits—surface and ground water—he is preparing to confer. In addition, he has joined with others to ask Congress, and has obtained, an appropriation of 1.5 million dollars to begin construction.[74]

The Commissioner of Reclamation has explained to Congress that it is not his intention to ask excess landholders for recordable contracts prior to construction. In support of this he cited procedures adopted at other times and under other circumstances. He noted that earlier Central Valley Project contracts "establish no specific time prior to which large landowners must have placed their excess lands under recordable contract . . . . In the normal course the majority . . . are executed shortly before irrigation facilities have reached a stage of completion where water deliveries can be made."[75] The Commissioner failed, however, to advise

---

[69] *Acreage Limitation Policy* xiii.

[70] 52 Stat. 211 (1938), 43 U.S.C. 600(a) (1958).

[71] 74 Stat. 156 (1960).

[72] One excess landowner has requested and executed a recordable contract making 480 acres eligible to receive water. Letter From Assistant Secretary of the Interior Kenneth Holum to Rev. James L. Vizzard, S.J., National Catholic Rural Life Conference, July 9, 1964 (*).

[73] 110 Cong. Rec. 17495-96 (daily ed. Aug. 5, 1964).

[74] *Id.* at 17912-22.

[75] *Id.* at 17497. See also text accompanying notes 84-86 *infra*. The Commissioner's refer-

Congress of the probability, if not certainty, that the procedure he proposed would frustrate the objectives of the excess land law.

First, even apart from the ground water problem, the Central Valley and other experience point to the legal inadequacy of the "normal course" of procedure, namely, to construct a project first and ask for recordable contracts later. In April 1964, twenty years after completion of Shasta Dam, the Bureau began to execute district contracts with Sacramento River diverters. Some unfavorable aspects of these long-delayed contracts are described below.[76] No recordable contracts have been signed, and apparently few are expected, although large land holdings are prevalent along the Sacramento.[77]

In the spring of 1964, ten years after completion of Pine Flat and Isabella Dams, district contracts were executed. Whether recordable contracts will be obtained remains to be seen. Recordable contracts were obtained along the Friant-Kern and Madera canals with great difficulty in the late nineteen-forties and early nineteen-fifties, mainly through determination of administrators of the Department of the Interior at that time to enforce the law. On other reclamation projects—notably in Imperial Valley, California, constructed a quarter-century ago, and in the Salt River Valley, Arizona, constructed a half-century ago—no recordable contracts have been requested or offered.[78] Enforcement of the excess land law is entirely absent.

Second, on the San Luis Federal Service Area, geological conditions prevent administrative control of water distribution as between eligible

---

ence to Central Valley Project precedent was misleading. Central Valley procedure itself was not "normal" for reclamation projects, but exceptional. As the Chief Counsel of the Bureau of Reclamation had explained in 1947, the "conventional policy requirement" of even district contract execution—let alone contracts with individual landowners—"prior to the commencement of construction" was "waived" on Central Valley Project, specifically because the "public works program" to reduce unemployment, which supplied funds to begin the project, "required that money be expended with greater speed" than insistence on prior contracts "would have permitted." *1947 Hearings on S. 912*, at 1271.

[76] See text accompanying notes 137-50 *infra*.

[77] See 110 CONG. REC. 17501 (daily ed. Aug. 5, 1964).

[78] Testimony of Northcutt Ely, *Hearings on H.R. 3961 Before Senate Commerce Subcommittee*, 78th Cong., 2d Sess. 632 (1944). See also testimony of Taylor, *1964 Westlands Hearing* at 144. On February 24, 1933, under a ruling by Secretary of the Interior Ray Lyman Wilbur, application of the excess land law to Imperial Irrigation District was waived. Solicitor Fowler Harper criticised this in 1945. (M.33902, May 31, 1945, 16, 17). The Department of Justice, apparently, also disagreed in 1957 pleadings before the United States Supreme Court. (*Arizona v. California*) On May 7, 1964, 31 years after the waiver by Wilbur, an Acting Commissioner of Reclamation, referring to the original ruling and its criticism by the Justice Department, wrote that "the continuing press of other matters had caused us to defer a current study of the Imperial situation. We hope, however, to review this matter in the future as the circumstances of time permit." Letter From G. G. Stamm to Rowland Watts (*).

and ineligible lands. Water applied at the surface on eligible lands in the Federal Service Area seeps into the ground reservoir from which it becomes available for use on ineligible lands by pumping from wells already installed. "Normal" procedure of executing contracts "shortly before irrigation facilities have reached a stage of completion where water deliveries can be made," therefore, is entirely unsuited to obtaining compliance with law.[79] Delay in obtaining compliance with the excess land law reduces bargaining power of the Bureau of Reclamation almost to the vanishing point.

In the absence of firm legal justification for distinguishing between project waters received at the surface and those received underground, the present administrative paralysis at San Luis becomes intelligible only in terms other than law. When pressures from excess landholding interests find response among administrators of the excess land law, no recordable contracts are asked and the result is frustration of the law.[80]

Ground water conditions on the Federal Service Area have been recognized by some Bureau of Reclamation officials for a quarter of a century as conducive to circumvention of the excess land law. Similar recognition by excess landholders invites serious efforts toward such circumvention. At least, spokesmen for excess landholding interests have long testified to their hope and expectations, and to a willingness of some administrators to share them.

As early as 1937, according to a Kern County spokesman,

> We were assured by officials of the Bureau of Reclamation that, as there were no public lands in the area and that at least half of the project water would be used, of necessity, for recharging the groundwater table and as there was no legal or physical way in which any land owner could be prevented from pumping what waters underlay his surface lands, that we could count with certainty that before the project was completed, the acreage limitations would be removed. Until 1944 this was the general understanding.[81]

In 1944 a large landowner, now Chairman of the Board of Directors of the Westlands Water District, advised Congress that a high engineering official of the Bureau of Reclamation had indicated, in accepting 25,000 dollars from private large landholding interests to share costs of water surveys in the area, "that the 160-acre limitation was not to be taken seriously. It was their [reclamation officials'] suggestion."[82]

---

[79] Testimony of Taylor, *1964 Westlands Hearing* at 132, 142-44, 146-47.
[80] *Cf.* Taylor, *supra* note 31, at 501-06. See also *1964 Westlands Hearing* at 146-47.
[81] Testimony of Roland Curran, *1944 Hearings on S. 912*, at 1310.
[82] Testimony of Russell Griffin, *Hearing Before Senate Military Affairs Subcommittee on Central Valley Water Project* 93 (Mimeo. by Bureau of Reclamation, Sacramento, April 7, 1944).

A month later a national magazine noted, in a discussion of tactics planned by "the big landowners in the valley . . . . to accomplish their end," that "landowners are sinking wells around their holdings in order to be prepared to pump irrigation water from the raised water table."[83]

Again, in July of the same year, a spokesman for Tulare Lake Basin Water Storage District, adjacent to Westlands District, testified that "no means either legal or physical have been suggested for preventing the continuation of such pumping. . . . The Bureau of Reclamation and others . . . have admitted that the excess land provisions will not be effective in such ground water areas."[84] The distinction between "legally applicable" and "practically effective" was carefully avoided.

Success of this tactic for circumvention of the excess land law is dependent, of course, upon a particular sequence of administrative actions. Specifically, success depends upon obtaining administrative delivery of surface water that will seep into the ground reservoir prior to administrative insistence upon execution of recordable contracts. By not insisting on execution as a precondition to construction, it will be far more difficult to obtain enforcement if it is later decided to apply the law to underground "deliveries." Perhaps it is hoped that the practical difficulties then encountered will marshal a legal interpretation of the statute favorable to the excess landholders, much as Senator Sheridan Downey in the nineteen-forties had hoped that such difficulties could be marshaled to produce legislative exemption.

In sum, the so-called "normal" procedure, accepted as appropriate by the Bureau of Reclamation, and followed since the San Luis Act passed in 1960, leads to circumvention of the excess land law on the Federal Service Area, as foreseen and planned. The Commissioner of Reclamation, apparently undetered by either prospective illegality or financial irresponsibility in his course of inaction, is content to delay asking for recordable contracts until "irrigation facilites have reached a stage of completion where water deliveries can be made."[85] Apparently he is ready to risk heavy public investment for construction of canals that may never be placed in service legally, but once constructed are likely to be used illegally.[86]

---

[83] *Valley Divided*, 767 BUSINESS WEEK 24 (May 13, 1944).
[84] Testimony of S. T. Harding, *1944 Hearings on S. Res.* 295, at 358.
[85] See text accompanying notes 71-75 *supra*.
[86] The risk is increased by granting the District a veto over federal construction of water distribution and drainage systems to serve the district, in which 70% of the lands are ineligible to receive water and voting is by assessed valuation. The potential effectiveness of the veto in producing either wasteful construction or law violation, or both, is enhanced by the prevalence of "checker-board" landownership by the Southern Pacific, arising from original land grants to railroads.

There appears to be no adequate legal justification for distinguishing between surface deliveries and purposeful ground deliveries. It appears equally certain, given the geological conditions at San Luis, that there can be only one effective means of enforcing the excess land law. Without substantiating their position on the law applicable to these geological conditions, proponents of the Westlands contracts have offered complex rationalizations in support of the current course of administration. The remainder of the present Article examines the defenses, rationalizations, and methods by which the law is being circumvented on the Federal San Luis Service Area.

VI

GEOLOGY: AID TO CIRCUMVENTION

The geological conditions of the San Luis Service Area have been offered by both the Commissioner of Reclamation and the Westlands Water District as support for the argument that economic pressures will compel excess landowners to execute recordable contracts in order to receive surface water. The administrators apparently believe that it is unnecessary to substantiate their position on the distinction between ground and surface deliveries since the economic pressures to receive surface deliveries will result in compliance with the law. Through this reasoning they seek to justify their unwillingness to insist upon execution of recordable contracts prior to construction.[87] In light of this argument, a brief review of the geological factors in the San Luis Federal Service Area is appropriate.

The ground reservoir underlies the entire San Luis Service Area.[88] Recognizing that this condition distinguishes San Luis from previous units of the Central Valley Project in the San Joaquin Valley, the San Luis project emphasizes replenishment of ground water as a major aim. The District water service contract recites that "ground water underlying the District is seriously depleted and in need of replenishment," and that "an additional water supply to meet these present and potential needs can be made available by and through the works constructed and to be constructed by the United States." It allots an additional amount of water up to 117,000 acre-feet annually in order to replenish ground waters, should estimates of seepage from water delivered at the surface and reduction of overdraft from surface deliveries prove low.[89] The Bureau of

---

[87] See text accompanying notes 94-97 *infra*.

[88] Bureau of Reclamation, Sacramento, *Geology and Ground-Water Resources, San Luis Service Area, Central Valley Project* 17 (Feb. 1963).

[89] Contract Between the United States and Westlands Water District Providing for Water Service 2, 8 (June 5, 1963) (*).

Reclamation plans to provide facilities "for integrating ground water with surface water," to integrate about "400 existing deep wells . . . into the distribution system," and to mix "well water" with "surface project water in the main laterals."[90]

The Commissioner of Reclamation explains that the water supply of the area will be derived from three sources: (1) pumped water from the deep zone (the water table will be raised from a present level of about 450 feet to about 300 feet, by a combination of reduced pumping drafts on "nondistrict natural recharge," and seepage from surface deliveries); (2) "project surface water"; and (3) "groundwater supply resulting from deep percolation losses from surface water applications."[91]

Studies by the Geological Survey corroborate the presence of ground water reservoir conditions favorable to the success of San Luis project as planned. Water seeps downward and laterally. Its direction of flow underground can be influenced by pumping. A layer of less permeable Corcoran clay divides the San Luis reservoir into an upper and lower zone. This has been cited to support argument that little, if any, surface water will reach the pumps that draw upon waters in the lower zone.[92] However, the Geological Survey indicates that the deep zone is rechargeable from surface applications of water, whether by lateral movements or by percolation assisted by punctures through the clay made by 1,000 active, and by 2,000 abandoned wells.[93]

The Commissioner of Reclamation, who has used his knowledge of these geological conditions to plan a project to integrate fully the supply of surface waters with the replenishing of ground waters, claims: (1) that surface water applications will seep underground; (2) that applications of surface water combined with seepage will raise the water table, bringing waters that have been moving steadily out of economical reach of pumps; and (3) that he does not intend to deny project water to ineligible lands provided it reaches them via the ground reservoir.[94] The Commissioner does not intend to insist, prior to construction of the project, upon

---

[90] Memorandum From Commissioner of Reclamation Floyd E. Dominy to the Secretary of the Interior, April 23, 1964, cited at 110 CONG. REC. 17496 (daily ed. Aug. 5, 1964).

[91] See Letter From Commissioner of Reclamation Floyd E. Dominy to Senator Henry M. Jackson, May 26, 1964, cited at 110 CONG. REC. 17497 (daily ed. Aug. 5, 1964).

[92] Letter From Ralph M. Brody, Manager-Chief Counsel, Westlands Water District, to Senator Frank E. Moss, Chairman, Senate Subcommittee on Irrigation and Reclamation, June 11, 1964 (*). See Testimony of Ralph M. Brody, *Westlands Hearing* at 113.

[93] United States Dept. Interior, California Department of Water Resources, *Geological Survey Water Supply Paper* 1618, "Use of Ground-water Reservoirs for Storage of surface water in the San Joaquin Valley, California" 24, 41-45, 81-88, 117-19 (1964).

[94] See Letter From Commissioner of Reclamation Floyd E. Dominy to Senator Henry M. Jackson, Chairman, Senate Interior and Insular Affairs Committee, May 26, 1964, cited at 110 CONG. REC. 17497 (daily ed. Aug. 5, 1964).

execution of recordable contracts necessary to qualify the seventy percent of presently ineligible lands to receive the ground water benefits the project will confer upon them. He offers, as a substitute, an expectation that economic pressures to obtain surface deliveries will result in execution of recordable contracts. These pressures, it is argued, will arise from the cost differential favoring surface over pumped water, and from *ad valorem* taxes levied on all lands within the district whether they receive surface water or not.[95] The Commissioner of Reclamation states in support of his view, and the Manager-Chief Counsel of Westlands Water District agrees, that the District will apparently raise funds for repayment to the United States by using a combination of toll charges for water delivered by surface to eligible lands, and *ad valorem* assessments on all district lands to cover the insufficiency of funds collected from tolls.[96] This manner of raising funds obliges owners of eligible lands to pay twice, and owners of ineligible lands but once. An opportunity to obtain cheaper water is undoubtedly an incentive to execute recordable contracts, but the proposed measures to raise district funds appear more likely to operate in an opposite direction. It is improbable that a district controlled by excess landholders owning seventy percent of the lands and voting by assessed valuation, would manipulate the means and measure of shared repayment to their own disadvantage.

An element of uncertainty in the effectiveness of the pressures is conceded by acknowledgment that "it is impossible" to "predict at this time the extent and sequence that may characterize the rate at which" the Southern Pacific (and presumably other excess landholders) "will embrace the recordable contracting program."[97]

In substance, the Commissioner confesses that project water will reach ineligible lands via the ground reservoir, as Senator Sheridan Downey pointed out long ago.[98] This is precisely what reclamation law would seem

---

[95] See also testimony of Ralph M. Brody, *1964 Westlands Hearing* at 113-15.

[96] 110 CONG. REC. 17497 (daily ed. Aug. 5, 1964); Testimony of Ralph M. Brody, *1964 Westlands Hearing* at 102; Testimony of Assistant Commissioner of Reclamation G. G. Stamm, *id.* at 30-32.

[97] See note 91 *supra*. See also note 111 *infra*.

[98] Senator Sheridan Downey of California argued in 1947 that "there is no way of preventing the excess-land owner from getting ground-water benefits once . . . placed in a common ground table." DOWNEY, THEY WOULD RULE THE VALLEY 102 (1947). Although owners of excess lands on the Orland Project, operating successfully in the Central Valley since about 1909, had voluntarily accepted a forty-acre limitation, Senator Downey dismissed as "naive" a "hope" expressed by Assistant Commissioner of Reclamation William E. Warne that on the Central Valley Project "excess landowners voluntarily would give a recordable option to the Secretary simply to promote the general community interest." *1947 Hearings on S. 912*, at 1216-17. The Senator also rejected as "illogical and inconsistent" the assertion by Bureau officials, conformable to law, "that if the limitation cannot be applied . . . water should be denied . . . ." *Id.* at 1200. Apparently fearful that the excess land law

expressly to forbid.[99] It remains to assess the total argument that no violation of law is occurring at San Luis.

VII

LEGISLATIVE POLICY ABANDONED: A BRIEF SUMMARY

Those who contend there is no violation of the excess land law at San Luis have made the two principal arguments already examined. The first is that the excess land law in no case applies to water received through the ground reservoir. This has already been shown to be legally tenuous. Even conceding, *arguendo,* that "unavoidable" ground deliveries might be judicially exempted from the statute, this seems totally inappropriate in the San Luis project[100] where ground water will be replenished by design,[101] thereby bringing project water to already installed pumps. The second is that whether or not the law applies to underground deliveries, economic pressures eventually will compel execution of recordable contracts by excess landowners desirous of receiving surface water. Assuming, again *arguendo,* that such pressures are a proper substitute for strict legal enforcement, we have seen[102] that there is small probability that these pressures will operate to compel execution of recordable contracts by excess landowners receiving substantial groundwater benefits.

Two further arguments have been made: (1) timing of requests for execution of recordable contracts is wholly within official discretion; and (2) execution of recordable contracts is entirely a matter of choice by excess landowners, a choice to be exercised after construction is underway.

As to the first, there is noteworthy agreement between officials of the Interior Department and officials of the Westlands Water District in respect to their unwillingness to require execution of contracts as a condition precedent to construction. There can be little doubt that a prompt demand for contracts would remove the possibility that the Secretary will allow violations of the excess land law. The question of timing of the request for these contracts has, however, produced a remarkable array of explanations for the Secretary's reluctance to make such demand.

---

might be enforced administratively by denial of water to ineligible lands, the Senator worked indefatigably for congressional exemption.

[99] See text accompanying notes 48-68 *supra.*
[100] See Statement by Senator Gaylord Nelson quoted at note 64 *supra.*
[101] "Ground water underlying the district is seriously depleted and in need of replenishment, and . . . an additional water supply to meet these present and potential needs can be made available by and through the works constructed and to be constructed by the United States." Westland Water Service Contract, June 5, 1963 (*).
[102] See text accompanying notes 87-99 *supra.*

Solicitor of the Interior Frank J. Barry advised the Senate:

> Suppose that . . . someone on the Westlands District . . . feels that he wants to see whether his ground water will be sufficiently improved by the project so that he can derive water from the underground rather than sign a recordable contract. Now, he has unlimited time.[103]

Senator Gaylord Nelson, of Wisconsin, asked the Interior Department spokesman: "Why . . . not insist that the contracts all be signed before we launch into a $150 million project?" In reply, Assistant Commissioner of Reclamation G. G. Stamm said, "The law does not require it," but acknowledged that the law "does not prohibit it."[104]

Solicitor Barry conceded that the Secretary could simply say "I am not going to build a project until I am satisfied." He also volunteered that "if Congress wants to prescribe" that the Secretary is not to "build a project until [he has] everybody signed up," he, the Solicitor, "probably would cheer, personally." However, he would "advise the Secretary . . . that this is not a legally valid ground to object to this contract, notwithstanding . . . that there are people who hold another view."[105]

The Solicitor discussed the Secretary's powers of administrative discretion in respect to execution of recordable contracts, but failed to advise the Senate that Congress itself, upon at least one occasion in 1938, had required "that construction work is not to be initiated . . . until . . . contracts shall have been made *with each owner* of more than one hundred and sixty irrigable acres . . . by which he . . . shall be obligated to sell all of his land in excess . . . ."[106] In the same Senate hearing, while Senator Kuchel was presiding, this Congressional mandate was quoted. The witness pointed out that this congressional mandate buttresses the exercise of discretionary power of the Secretary to insist on prior execution of contracts when necessary, as at San Luis, to prevent violation of law.[107] Notwithstanding this quotation of the statute and a colloquy on the sub-

---

[103] Referring to Central Valley experience, Solicitor Barry added that an excess landowner "may wait ten, fifteen or more years before he calls for project water. The delay is deliberately availed of by landowners to determine by actual experience whether they will have sufficient benefits from the stabilization of the ground water to stave off the need for ever calling for direct delivery of water and thereby subjecting their lands to reclamation law." *1964 Westlands Hearing* at 34.

[104] *Id.* at 32.

[105] *Id.* at 36.

[106] 52 Stat. 211 (1938), 43 U.S.C. § 600(a) (1958). [Emphasis added.] The original transcript of 1964 Westlands hearing records this response by Solicitor Frank J. Barry to a question from Senator Kuchel: "So far as I know, this has never been [the last three words are stricken by pen]—no one has ever required that recordable contracts be secured before the project is constructed." (p. 56). The entire quotation from the transcript is omitted from the printed hearing. (p. 35). See also statute cited note 70 *supra*.

[107] Testimony of Taylor, *1964 Westlands Hearing* at 137-38.

ject between witness and presiding Senator on July 8, 1964, Senator Kuchel, while pleading with the Senate to approve an appropriation to begin construction at Westlands on August 7, 1964, said Congress had never passed such a law.[108]

As to the second argument, the Manager-Chief Counsel of Westlands District, in harmony with the view of Solicitor Barry and Senator Kuchel, emphasized that execution of contracts prior to construction is "not a statutory requirement," that an excess landowner is not required to execute a contract "if he does not desire . . . water," and that "the law contemplates a choice upon his part."[109]

At the July 8, 1964 hearing before the Senate Interior and Insular Affairs Committee, when the Westlands contract was under attack, Manager-Chief Counsel Brody stated that "Mr. Russell Giffen, the Chairman of our Board of Directors . . . said . . . he intended to sign a recordable contract, that he was morally obligated to do so . . . ." He added that Producers Cotton Oil Company "was of the mind to sign . . . and intended to, and I know there has been no change in attitude . . . ." He said also that "Mr. Diener, another Board member, as far as I am aware, intends to sign a recordable contract," and that "I have had discussions with a considerable number of landowners who see that they have no alternative."[110] Mr. Brody qualified his information with a vague statement, that "I cannot conceive of any landowner, no matter what his intentions . . . actually signing [a recordable contract] until the [ground?] water became available, or until he wanted water for his land." Then he held up the spectre of a lone hold-out, or even "any portion of the landowners," whose refusal to sign might "defeat the very purpose for which the project is being built, and that is to serve those people who are eligible."[111]

---

[108] "Congress has never required . . . that the landholders in every block of property within that district sign such a contract . . . . If we wish to ask Congress to make every single landowner, as a condition precedent, sign a contract, let a bill be introduced . . . . But, do not single out one irrigation project in my State, and do not say that we are not going to approve the item for this project . . . ." 110 CONG. REC. 17918 (daily ed. Aug. 7, 1964).

[109] Testimony of Ralph M. Brody, *1964 Westlands Hearing* at 114. He added that "Congress wisely concluded that through the taxing power of the districts . . . [excess landowners] would be forced through economic circumstances to execute a recordable contract." No evidence for this view was cited, and there appears to be none.

[110] *Id.* at 109-10.

[111] *Id.* at 110. A greater fear was possible administrative creation of "situation and circumstances" (by demanding execution of recordable contracts, or in lieu thereof, the designation of the particular 160 acres chosen from among total landholdings to receive project water) that would lead to quick decision. This administrative action would tap the same economic necessity of landholders for water that they relied upon originally to persuade Congress to authorize spending $483 million for their benefit, conditioned by the excess land law. Objecting to this administrative procedure, Mr. Brody testified: "They

The apparent contradictions between intending to sign *later*, and unwillingness to sign *now* in order to assure the start of construction, and between earlier distressed pleadings for authorization by Congress to prevent return of lands to sagebrush, and later insistence upon a "right to choose between compliance or non-compliance at one's pleasure," were not explained. Neither was it clear how much weight the Senate Committee should attach to a sense of moral obligation felt by an official of Westlands District owning excess lands, nor how widely the feeling was shared by other excess landholders in the district. Mr. Brody did not say in 1964 whether, in his opinion, Southern Pacific would be among those landowners whose unwillingness to sign might stand in the way of serving "those people who are eligible." Five years earlier, however, while authorization of San Luis project was pending, Senator Clinton P. Anderson, of New Mexico, had expressed an opinion that the company would "subdivide" its lands under the excess land law, for "no corporation in its right mind would take that land out of cultivation . . . ."[112]

Reviewing the opinions expressed it appears that Senator Sheridan Downey's early description of escape from the excess land law by getting ground waters first and then deciding afterwards whether to sign recordable contracts fits San Luis today. As Solicitor Barry stated on July 8, 1964, "delay is sometimes deliberately availed of to stave off the need . . ." to comply with the law in order to obtain surface water. This means of circumvention assumes, as previously noted, that Congress is willing to authorize the project and appropriate funds, and that the Secretary of the Interior is willing to proceed with construction without knowing which lands are eligible to benefit under the law, or at San Luis, knowing that seventy percent of the lands are ineligible. Both assumptions appear to be realized; Secretary, Congress and large landholders join in shunning the inquiry that would determine officially and quickly the willingness of excess landowners to render their lands eligible. Federal reclamation law and its avowed purposes are not being debated, repealed and disavowed. They are merely being abandoned.

VIII

STATUTORY PROCEDURES IGNORED

The contracts between the United States and the Westlands District deviate from certain procedural requirements of the San Luis Act. The

---

want this thing to happen overnight. These holdings were not built up overnight. It took a long time and it will take a long time . . . to be broken up. . . . You cannot physically force a man to put his name to a contract. All you can do is to create a situation and circumstances under which he is going to find it impossible for him to continue economically . . . to operate as he has in the past." *Id.* at 102.

[112] 104 CONG. REC. 17733 (1958).

effect of these deviations may facilitate the circumvention of the excess land law on the Federal Service Area.

Because of ground water conditions, the natural and imminent prospect of water deliveries to the Westlands District will improve the ground reservoir and raise the water table throughout the entire Federal Service Area, of which it is a part. Westlands does not include about 105,000 acres of the Federal Service Area which lie largely if not entirely within the West Plains District.

The San Luis Act specifies that the Secretary of the Interior shall transmit to Congress "a contract" for construction of water distribution and drainage systems within the covered area. No provision is made for *two* contracts within the same Federal Service Area.[113] Nevertheless, Assistant Commissioner of Reclamation G. G. Stamm told the Senate Interior Committee that the Bureau expects to "have contracts with both the Westplains . . . and the Westlands Water District." These two areas together, he said, include "all of the [San Luis] Federal Service Area . . . essentially in one irrigation district."[114]

The effect of this deviation is not trivial. The 105,000 acres of the Federal Service Area lie mostly or all within the Westplains District with which a contract for construction of distribution and drainage systems has yet to be executed. Irrespective of the expressed intentions of the Bureau, Westplains is currently without legal provision for construction of project facilities. Meanwhile, Westlands District has preempted 157 million dollars of the 192 million dollars authorized by Congress in 1960 to serve the entire Federal Service Area. The balance of 35 million dollars may not be sufficient to complete the San Luis project. The San Luis Act assigns no priority to Westlands District, but the effect of administrative action is to give it priority.

Notwithstanding this priority of construction, benefits to the Westplains area will accrue from improved ground water. The failure of the Bureau of Reclamation to follow prescribed procedure leaves this area without legal arrangements for construction and without methods for obtaining compliance with the excess land laws. This facilitation of circumvention is all the more startling when one considers that a single landowner, the Southern Pacific, owns about 55,000 acres, or over half of the total acres in the excluded area.

Deviation from the procedures prescribed by Congress goes even farther. The San Luis Act requires that Congress approve fully executed

---

[113] 74 Stat. 156 (1960). But see testimony of Brody, *1964 Westlands Hearing* at 109. "There has never been a requirement that there be one district or one contract to cover an entire project service area."

[114] *1964 Westlands Hearing* at 22.

contracts with the water districts before the project is begun.[115] In transmitting legal arrangements with Westlands District to Congress, the Department of Interior submitted not one fully executed contract, but two "contracts": (1) a water service contract, fully executed, but submitted to Congress only by reference; and (2) a "form" or "proposed" contract—but not an executed contract—for construction of distribution and drainage systems. Nevertheless, Secretary of Interior Stewart L. Udall described the construction contract document as "a contract" in transmitting it to Congress.[116] Secretary Kenneth Holum called it a "contract" and a "form";[117] Commissioner of Reclamation Floyd E. Dominy called it a "form" or "proposed" contract, but also referred to it as "a contract."[118] Congress did not discuss this departure from legally prescribed procedure publicly during the ninety-day period during which the Westlands documents lay before it in the summer of 1964, and may not even have observed it.

The seriousness of this failure to follow statutory procedure may appear shortly. On October 9, 1964, Assistant Secretary Holum advised Senator Henry M. Jackson, Chairman of the Senate Interior Committee that Secretary Udall had "determined that certain modifications should be made in the water service contract" executed with Westlands District on June 5, 1963, that lay before Congress for the prescribed ninety days in 1964. He expressed no intention to resubmit it to Congress after administrative revision.[119] On October 20, 1964, Westlands Water District voted on, and approved, the original "proposed" or "form" construction contract that lay before Congress for ninety days.[120]

The hand of Congress will be removed from enforcement of the excess land law on the Federal San Luis Service Area unless the contractual arrangements actually covering that area are placed properly before it. Until now they have not been, due to a failure to adhere to legally prescribed procedure.

---

[115] 74 Stat. 156 (1960).

[116] Letter From Secretary Udall to President pro-tem. of the Senate Carl Hayden, April 24, 1964, *1964 Westlands Hearing* at 3.

[117] *1964 Westlands Hearing* at 15, 17.

[118] *Id.* at 3, 5.

[119] On the contrary, he hoped that by amending the water service contract only, and not the "form" or "proposed" construction "contract," he might avoid resubmittal, notwithstanding alterations from the text originally before Congress for the required ninety-day review. Letter From Assistant Secretary Kenneth Holum to Senator Henry M. Jackson, Chairman, Senate Interior Committee, October 9, 1964, at 177; Memorandum, Holum to Udall, October 7, 1964, at 177-80.

[120] "Westlands Farmers Okeh Water Pact," Fresno Bee, October 21, 1964, p. 1, col. 3. Landowners voted 475 to 25 in favor of the contract (by assessed valuation, $1 per vote, the result was 12,399,817 to 388,328). Authorized federal investment in San Luis unit is $483 million.

IX

LEGISLATIVE OVERSIGHT: CIRCUMVENTION COMPLETED

The requirement that a contract for construction of water distribution and drainage systems shall lie before Congress for ninety days before it can be made effective is known as "legislative oversight." At San Luis, legislative oversight has proved to be double-edged. The excess land law and the prospect it holds there for creation of few thousand family-size farms operated by their owners—the original promise of federal reclamation—are the victims. The damage is worse than executive violation of law. Through legislative oversight the violation subtly gains the formal appearance of congressional concurrence.

Two Westlands contracts, transmitted by Secretary Udall on April 23, 1964, lay before the Senate and House for ninety days as prescribed by law.[121] The House Interior Committee approved them almost immediately, without hearing. However, no item to begin construction of Westlands water distribution and drainage systems appeared in the public works appropriation bill passed soon thereafter by the House. The Senate Interior Committee, after two months had elapsed, held a one-day hearing on Westlands contracts on July 8, but the Committee itself remained silent. A few days before expiration of the required ninety days of legislative oversight the Senate Appropriations Committee, without hearing, proposed a 1.5 million dollar token item to begin construction at Westlands, and the Senate passed it. A vigorous attempt by opponents of Westlands contracts to strike the item from the bill was defeated, fifty-seven to twenty-three.[122]

Presumably, the purpose of ninety-day "legislative oversight" is to give Congress opportunity to verify, in advance of execution, that proposed administrative measures shall conform to law and will achieve the purposes of law. On the San Luis unit of the Central Valley Project, Congressional inaction during the running of the ninety-day period has apparently resulted in precisely the opposite—circumvention and violation—not in fulfillment of law.[123] Such circumvention and violation de-

---

[121] The San Luis Authorization Act of June 3, 1960, 74 Stat. 160 (1960), specifies submission of "a contract" to Congress for legislative oversight. Without explanation the Secretary of the Interior submitted two Westlands "contracts." A construction and repayment "contract" was submitted on May 1, 1964. A second contract, executed on June 5, 1963 to cover water distribution service, was submitted by reference only. The latter contains many of the provisions most destructive to effective enforcement of the excess land law. See 110 CONG. REC. 17495-97 (daily ed. Aug. 5, 1964). See also text accompanying notes 115-18 supra.

[122] 110 CONG. REC. 17922 (daily ed. Aug. 7, 1964). The House agreed to the item in conference, and it was included in the bill as passed by Congress.

[123] Cf. Taylor, supra note 30; 108 CONG. REC. 5708-09 (1962).

pends upon a willingness within the executive branch of government to allow circumvention and upon a similar willingness—or simply lack of knowledge—of those members of the Congress astride the channels through which legislative action is exercised. The process of circumvention within the Federal San Luis Service Area can be clearly charted.

First, the Congress originally decides what the law shall be through customary legislative procedures. It decided in 1960, after assurances that excess land law would be applied, that it would authorize and finance construction of the San Luis project.

Second, executive administrators of reclamation, in conjunction with the Westlands District, prepare two contracts that simultaneously recite the law as written and confess non-enforcement, offering as an excuse for making ground water available to ineligible lands, the "unavoidable clause." These are submitted to Congress.

Third, the contracts, referred to committees, lie before Congress under a time limitation of ninety days. Failure to act allows the Secretary of the Interior to proceed under the contracts. In this posture the excess land law is not faced directly but tangentially and incidentally to other matters: interior committees are concerned with promoting construction of projects and appropriations committees with financing them. Law and policy are not prime considerations under this kind of legislative oversight.

Originally, the full Congress held the whip hand over the San Luis project. Ability to insist upon the excess land law lay in the power to withhold authorization and finance from the project. This power was used on the San Luis bill. Under legislative oversight the whip is gone; the balance of political power is shifted. With authorization and finance in hand, incentive to act politically without regard to law is unchecked. Public principle and policy stand exposed to special interest and stark political pressure.[124]

A facade of official and party unanimity was thrown by Senator Kuchel over his appeal, on August 7, 1964, for an appropriation to begin construction at Westlands. He spoke, he said, "on behalf of" his Democratic colleague, Senator Pierre Salinger, "of the government of the State of California, of the Department of the Interior, of the Budget Bureau, of the administration of the late President Kennedy, and of the incumbent Johnson administration."[125] The appeal succeeded; the appropriation to

---

[124] In a similar situation, also under the San Luis Act of 1960, legal counsellors advised the State of California that "The reaction of Congress and its relevant committees is more a political than a legal problem." Chas. T. Main, Inc., *Final Report, General Evaluation of the Proposed Program for Financing and Constructing the State Water Resources Development System of the State of California Department of Water Resources* 222-1-2A, app. 29 (1960).

[125] The facade is contrived; it does not represent united popular support. In 1964 the

begin construction was passed, and the Westlands contracts survived. The original statute remains but goes unenforced, its ends unachieved. Only a change of executive intent, or perhaps a difficult citizens' appeal to the courts appear as possible ways to alter this outcome.

"The life of the law is in its enforcement."[126] In these proceedings of the San Luis project, of which recent legislative appropriation to begin construction mark the culmination, "the law" has not been changed. Rather, as Roscoe Pound said long ago, "the limits of effective legal action" have been exceeded.[127] Law has failed at San Luis, not in legislative deliberations on policy, not before the bench,[128] but at the bar of politics. This is because of a peculiarly effective combination of factors within the federal government operating in harmony with the purposes of a state-created water district—a district dominated by excess landholders whose financial interest in circumventing the excess land law is obvious.[129]

Interior Department and Westlands District, standing together before Congress, were opposed by farm, labor, and other popular organizations. This has been so for a long time, but pressures upon public officials are often severe, as the history of the excess land law demonstrates. In 1951 California Attorney General Edmund G. Brown supported his decision to press an appeal to the United States Supreme Court from state court decisions against the excess land law, by reciting the "better than 7 to 1" popular vote in Central Valley Irrigation districts favoring acceptance of water contracts carrying the excess land provision. (For compilation of these statistics, see *1951 Report of Special House Subcommittee on Irrigation and Reclamation . . . on Central Valley Project, California*, as a result of hearings held Oct. 29-31, 1951, Sacramento, Cal. at 110-11 (*)). In 1958 he was elected Governor on a platform that reaffirmed support of the "160-acre limitation to insure equitable distribution of water and avoid the evils of land speculation and monopoly." But after election he said, in 1960 that "we can attain those just and fair ends without trying to obligate or coerce anyone to sell or divide his land in order to get water." (Address by Governor Edmund G. Brown, California Water Program Bond Issue, NBC-TV and Radio Network Broadcast, Jan. 20, 1960. Wording of quotation taken from mimeo text of speech supplied by Office of the Governor to author, p. 4 (*).)

An explanation has been offered for lack of firm adherence to platform and the record of popular opinion by J. Blaine Quinn, Master of the California State Grange: "We fear that it was the pressure of immense money groups and the threat of withdrawal of financial support needed by political parties that prompted this about face." Christian Science Monitor, March 28, 1962, p. 18, col. 5.

[126] Pound, *The Limits of Effective Legal Action*, 22 PA. BAR ASS'N REP. 221, 239 (1916).
[127] *Id.* at 237.
[128] *Cf.* Ivanhoe Irr. Dist. v. McCracken, 357 U.S. 275 (1958).
[129] The value of the interest-free money subsidy provided to irrigators by reclamation law is about $1,000 per acre on the San Luis Federal Service Area. The benefits of circumvention of the law include not only participation in this subsidy without legal limitation, but also uncontrolled access to incremental land values accruing to permanently watered lands in the fastest growing state in the nation. The author's view has been criticised publicly by Ralph M. Brody, of Westlands Water District. Answering the author's letter to the editor of the Washington Post on July 23, 1964, entitled "Circumventing the Law," Mr. Brody dismissed the author's thesis as "part of a pattern of misrepresentations to the public and the Congress . . . . There is to be no 'planned' or other delivery of project water to those

Enforcement fails at San Luis, not because of popular opposition, as during Prohibition, but because of concentrated and powerful opposition operating upon the law-making and law-enforcing mechanisms. The facade of official unity professed by Senator Kuchel contrasts with a remarkable alignment of popular organizations against his position, among them the AFL-CIO, National Grange, National Farmers Union, and the National Catholic Rural Life Conference.[130] Lacking both effective review during legislative oversight, and official executive support, these organizations and others favoring antimonopoly water law are seriously disadvantaged in their efforts to preserve excess land law from violation.[131] They face not only obstacles of cost and effort in going to court, but problems of standing to be heard in court at all.[132] More, however, than the discomfiture of private citizens unable to show the special interest necessary to obtain standing in federal court may be at stake. Judicial control of public officers becomes itself uncertain. "The question we are putting," as Professor Jaffe writes, "is essentially one as to the 'necessary and proper' role of the judiciary."[133] Failing practicable judi-

---

ineligible to receive it . . . Mr. Taylor simply does not know the physical facts . . . Mr. Taylor's $1000 an acre subsidy simply does not exist." "Westlands Water Contract," Washington Post, August 29, 1964, p. A-8, col. 6.

[130] See also "Windfall Stirs Reaction," Sacramento Union, Aug. 5, 1964, p. B-2, col. 6; "Conflict Over California Land," *id.*, Aug. 9, 1964, p. C-2, col. 6. Broad popular support for the excess land law has been manifested ever since attacks upon the application of the law in Central Valley began in the 1940's. See authorities cited in Taylor, *Destruction of Federal Reclamation Policy? The Ivanhoe Case*, 10 STAN. L. REV. 76, 130, n.120 (1957).

[131] Senator Paul Douglas pointed to a fundamental difficulty, absence of the usual participation of opposed interests in proceedings where their interests are at stake: "I think we all know the practical difficulties in such a situation as this. The land is owned at present by a relatively small number of persons and corporations, each one of which owns an enormous amount of land . . . They are organized . . . powerful . . . do not wish to have their holdings broken up . . . and . . . can marshal tremendous resources in support of their position and against anyone who tries to stand against them. . . . Those who might benefit from the acreage limitation . . . the small farmers who would come into being if the huge estates were broken up are persons in the future . . . Since they exist only in the future and not in the present, they lack voices and are in a sense unrepresented." 108 CONG. REC. 5711 (1962). See also Taylor, *supra* note 31, at 501-06.

[132] It should be noted that federal law requires (44 Stat. 649 (1926), 43 U.S.C. § 423(e) (1958)) and California law permits (CAL. WATER CODE §§ 22670, 23225) the bringing of a suit to confirm the district contract and assessments made thereunder. Availability of these suits, however, does not resolve the standing problem because typically the district sues the existing landowners ("All Persons"), and the potential landowners are still not represented. Furthermore, any independent suit by a taxpayer to vindicate the general public interest would probably fail for lack of plaintiff's standing to raise the issue. See generally Jaffe, *Standing to Secure Judicial Review: Public Actions*, 74 HARV. L. REV. 1265 (1961).

[133] "The law of standing raises acute questions concerning . . . judicial control of public officers. It is accepted . . . that the primary role of judicial review is the protection of interests specially affected by allegedly illegal official action . . . . But when the plaintiff is not able to satisfy the requirement of special interest, when he brings his action as a repre-

cial review, the fate of public policy lies uncertainly in the relatively unchecked hands of often severely pressured administrative officials.

X

SACRAMENTO DIVERTERS: PATTERN OF CIRCUMVENTION

Among recently executed agreements that show a pattern of circumvention and otherwise reflect the present intent of reclamation administration, Westlands contracts do not stand alone. Nor is legislative oversight a necessary channel to the achievement of circumvention. With ingenuity and administrative willingness to avoid the law, varied techniques are found that accomplish the same destructive ends. Contracts executed by the Secretary of the Interior in the spring of 1964 with diverters from the Sacramento River, who have been receiving water since 1944 when Shasta Reservoir began operation, promise to prove as fatal to the excess land law as the Westlands contracts.

Glenn-Colusa Irrigation District is the largest of the water districts serving the extensive landownerships along the Sacramento River. The Glenn-Colusa contract, executed by the Secretary of the Interior in 1964, may be regarded as a prototype contract with Sacramento River diverters. Nearby is the Orland project, undertaken about 1909 under agreement with excess landholders to accept a forty-acre limitation. Contrast between Orland and Glenn-Colusa, in respect to enforcement of the excess land law and its acceptance by large landholders, could hardly be more striking.

There are about 170 Sacramento River diverters representing thousands of individual users and involving about one-half million acres using about 2.3 million acre-feet of water annually.[134] With construction of the Central Valley Project assured in 1935, use of Sacramento River water increased rapidly. By 1951 it was three times the 300,000 acre-feet increase expected by the State of California and Reclamation officials, and "would have caused the river to be dry for about forty miles in July, 1951 if stored water had not been available from Shasta Reservoir. . . ."[135] Negotiations for agreement between the diverters and the Bureau of Reclamation began in 1944, but were broken off by withdrawal of the

---

sentative of the general public, . . ." he has difficulty in obtaining standing in court to present his case as a party to a suit. Jaffe, *supra* note 132, at 1265.

[134] Summarization of the situation is available in a Letter From Secretary of the Interior Stewart L. Udall to Comptroller General Joseph Campbell, November 29, 1963 (*) [hereinafter cited as *Udall to Campbell*].

[135] *1951 Report of Special Subcommittee on Irrigation and Reclamation . . . on Central Valley Project, California*, as a result of hearings held Oct. 29-31, 1951, Sacramento, Calif. at 4.

Bureau's offer of settlement in 1946. After a number of intervening steps, negotiations were resumed in 1961 and led to execution of contracts in 1964.[136]

The principal means employed in the Glenn-Colusa contract to minimize, if not totally destroy the effectiveness of the excess land law, is to give diverters an excessive allotment of Sacramento River water. Water granted by the contract is divided into "base supply" and "project supply." Neither the excess land law nor an obligation to pay the United States apply to the "base supply." Both, however, attach to the "project supply." The Secretary granted Glenn-Colusa water users "about six acre-feet per irrigable acre," or 720,000 acre-feet annually as "base supply."[137] Only 75,000 acre-feet are considered to be "project supply."

Measured by several criteria, the "base supply" allotted to Glenn-Colusa appears excessive. The approximately six acre-feet per acre granted to Glenn-Colusa District is double the California average water use per acre reported by the census, and 2.3 times the Central Valley average of 2.6 acre-feet per acre. The 75,000 acre-feet considered "project supply" in Glenn-Colusa is only 9.4 percent of total supply. Only five months earlier Secretary Udall advised the Comptroller General that "under the proposed agreements about thirty percent would be considered as supplied from the Central Valley Project," or more than three times this proportion.[138] The 720,000 acre-feet "base supply" is about seventy percent greater than the largest pre-project diversion of 423,954 acre-feet recorded in 1943. It is about forty-two percent above the Bureau's original offer of 507,734 acre-feet made in 1944-46, based on the total of maximum monthly diversions during the five years preceding operation of Shasta Reservoir. Leading landowners in the Glenn-Colusa district were recorded at the time as "very happy" with the original offer.[139] In critical months the river would be dry, except for Central Valley Project.[140] This dependability in water supply provided by Central Valley

---

[136] These steps are summarized in *Udall to Campbell.*

[137] Letter from Secretary of the Interior Stewart L. Udall to Paul S. Taylor, March 27, 1964 (*) [hereinafter cited as *Udall to Taylor*]. The Secretary called this allotment "not unreasonable considering the losses involved in the extensive canal system, and that rice, which uses large quantities of water, is the principal crop grown in the District." The contract grants the district the right to recapture waste, seepage and return flow waters, as does Westlands contract. Recapture of heavy return flows is customary in Glenn-Colusa.

[138] *Udall to Campbell.* The Glenn-Colusa contract accounts for more than one-third of the total water used by Sacramento River diverters.

[139] *Blote to Udall.* Mr. Blote was in charge of measuring diversions between 1924 and 1944, and then served the Bureau of Reclamation until 1961, first as Watermaster, then as Regional Supervisor of Irrigation and Power.

[140] "An inspection of the flow records of the Sacramento River indicates that in many of the last years the Sacramento River would have been dry 50 to 60 miles above Sacramento were it not for the water released from storage at Shasta Dam." *Blote to Udall.*

Project is reflected in the character of agriculture that can be practiced in the district.

A second method of weakening effectiveness of the excess land law is by substituting for the statutory prohibition that no ineligible lands shall "receive water," a "quantity-of-water" measure. This measure is to be applied, not to water received at the lands themselves, but to water delivered to the district. This administrative invention permits "averaging" by the district to the advantage of excess landholders, in lieu of specific enforcement against ineligible lands.[141]

A third means of undermining the excess land law is by defining the 75,000 acre-feet "project supply" as limited to water delivered to the district only in the months of July and August. This opens opportunity to store "base supply" deliveries in June in the shallow surface basins, or reservoirs used in rice-growing, for release to ineligible lands in July or August. Surrender of United States title to waste, seepage and return flow waters within the district, which are availed of customarily on the Sacramento, is a fourth means of facilitating circumvention.[142]

Other, and serious objections to Glenn-Colusa contract have been made. One of these is the charge that excessive water allotments afford opportunity to sell unneeded water to others.[143] Responses by the Interior Department to this charge are unconvincing. Secretary Udall said the contracts do not "provide for resale of water to municipal users."[144] Assistant Secretary of the Interior Kenneth Holum rejected the criticism, saying the "contracts do not confer a water right under State law which could be used to sell surplus water."[145] He added, as reassurance, that the "contract provides that no sale or disposal can be made for use out-

---

[141] A similar device is provided in Westlands Water Service Contract, June 5, 1963, § 27(b)(ii). Martin H. Blote has said that manipulation of estimates is also encouraged. "I can see no valid basis for permitting Glenn-Colusa Irrigation District and other Sacramento River diverters to treat acreage limitations of federal reclamation law simply as arithmetical calculations, as you now do in article 19(c). Kern River interests actually acquired long ago and put to beneficial use the entire flow of the Kern River. The Corps of Engineers by their own hydrologic claims, yielded only an insignificant amount (about 50,000 acre-feet) of so-called 'new water' for agricultural purposes." *Blote to Udall.*

[142] See text accompanying note 147 *infra.*

[143] "In California a water right is a property right, and can be disposed of as such, and I cite sales of the Miller and Lux water rights . . . ." *Blote to Udall.*

[144] *Udall to Taylor.* It is relevant to note that the charge is not that the contracts "provide for resale," but that they permit it.

[145] Letter From Assistant Secretary of the Interior Kenneth Holum to Congressman Jeffrey Cohelan, March 31, 1964 (*). The contracts may not confer the water rights, but Secretary Udall spoke of "water rights" repeatedly in his description to the Comptroller General of the problem of executing contracts with Sacramento River diverters. *Udall to Campbell.* Attorney Martin McDonough, of the Sacramento River and Delta Water Association, praised settlement of "so vast and complicated a water rights problem without lawsuits." Sacramento Union, June 26, 1964, p. B-16, col. 1-2.

side that [designated] area without obtaining the written consent of the United States." He failed to say that Acting Secretary of the Interior James K. Carr had approved a memorandum containing this statement: "Such consent has been promised to the District by means of a separate letter to be given to the [Glenn-Colusa] District at the time of execution of the proposed contract."[146]

Glenn-Colusa contract had not been signed two months before its circumvention of the excess land law was publicly noted. Reporting a meeting of the California Central Valley Flood Control Association, the *Sacramento Union* described it as "an historic compromise" between the Bureau of Reclamation and Sacramento Valley farmers, *i.e.*, excess landholders. The "compromise . . . apparently will see the farmers get the use of federal water without having to break up their farms. . . ." The *Union* described some of the devices of circumvention: "The Yolo County farmers plan to use the federal water only on a 160 acre plot—but they believe the same water can be reused on other land because it does not pick up contamination from the earth in other fields." The *Union* added that the landholders "also expect to use ground water and other water supplies for their additional acreage and do not believe they will have to breakup their holdings."[147]

Reclamation officials apparently agree with the landowners that the excess land law has been rendered ineffective by the Sacramento diverters contracts. The *Union* said: "Robert Pafford, director for Region Two of the Bureau of Reclamation, said that he does not believe many of the landholdings will be broken up except for some through economic factors." Referring to Westlands, the *Union* said "Similar contracts are also being prepared for users of San Luis Project water." The *Union* summed up the meaning of the Sacramento River diverters' contracts, allowing them to avoid the excess land law, in these words: "Thus a battle which has been waged since 1944 when Shasta Dam was built ended."[148]

Secretary of the Interior Udall, however, had conveyed another impression than the *Sacramento Union* reported, when describing the same contracts only a few months earlier in anticipation of their execution. On the eve of execution of the first Sacramento River diverters contracts he said that "when the contracts are signed" this "deplorable situation" of "taking Central Valley Project water without paying for it and without complying" with reclamation law "will be rectified."[149] Rectification, it

---

[146] Memorandum from Commissioner of Reclamation Floyd E. Dominy to the Secretary of the Interior, December 19, 1963, approved by Acting Secretary of the Interior James K. Carr, December 27, 1963.
[147] Sacramento Union, June 26, 1964, p. B-16, col. 1-2.
[148] *Ibid.*
[149] *Udall to Taylor.*

appears, was accomplished with the help of two major concessions to water users: (1) by abandoning attempts "to collect now for all diversions of project water made during the past nineteen years," and (2) by agreeing to "an historic compromise" that "apparently will see" the owners of excess lands "get the use of federal water without having to breakup their farms. . . ."

The Department of the Interior still insists that "no 'claims' are being 'cancelled' " on the Sacramento River, and "none of the Sacramento River diverters are 'being relieved of their indebtedness to the Federal Government."[150] However, along the Sacramento another understanding prevails. The *Sacramento Union* states that "[T]he Bureau of Reclamation is offering to waive all charges for project water drawn previously by farmers if they sign a 1964 contract. The Bureau has told thirty potential signers that to get the waiver they must sign the 1964 contract."[151]

XI

LAW AND INSTITUTIONS: SHAMBLES

In the long and tortuous course of circumvention of excess land law, words have been emptied of their meaning, statutes of their content, procedures of their certainty, parties of their principles, and constitutional functions of their integrity. Ethics and law have been trampled.[152] It need occasion no surprise that the question of conflict-of-interest has been raised, in both an ethical and legal sense.[153] Confidence in reclamation,[154] and in government as well,[155] has been diminished.[156]

---

[150] Assistant Secretary of the Interior Kenneth Holum to Rev. James L. Vizzard, S.J., National Catholic Rural Life Conference, July 9, 1964 (*).

[151] Sacramento Union, June 26, 1964, p. B-16, col. 1-2.

[152] Russell Griffen, now chairman of Westlands Water District Board, questioned the ethics of certain Bureau officials in his testimony before the Senate Military Affairs Committee in 1944. Referring to financial contributions by westside landowners to water surveys, at invitation of officials, he said: "It seems to me that the Bureau was completely in bad faith in taking that $25,000, knowing that they were going to support as vigorously as they have the 160-acre limitation, knowing that our district could not accept that." Testimony Before Subcommittee on Central Valley Water Project of Senate Military Affairs Committee, San Francisco, April 7, 1944, 93. (Mimeo by Bureau of Reclamation, Sacramento).

[153] "Former Solicitor Bennett of Interior was counsel for the irrigators although just out of office." Letter From James G. Patton, president, National Farmers Union, to President Lyndon B. Johnson, July 29, 1964, cited at 110 CONG. REC. 17920 (daily ed. Aug. 7, 1964). Among relevant sources are: Letter From Secretary Udall to Senator William Proxmire, September 13, 1954 (*); Letter From Solicitor Frank J. Barry to Elmer F. Bennett, April 13, 1962 (*); Elmer F. Bennett to Solicitor Frank Barry, Jan. 26, 1962 (*); *Udall to Campbell*; Letter From Campbell to Udall, Jan. 21, 1964 (*).

[154] At its fortieth annual convention in St. Louis, Missouri, on Aug. 27, 1964, the National Catholic Rural Life Conference adopted a resolution stating that "if, in the very near future, there are no concrete and adequate indications of a return to effective protection

The Federal Service Area of the San Luis unit of the Central Valley Project and the Sacramento River diverters are not the only instances of failure of the executive branch of our government to enforce the law against delivering water to ineligible lands.[157] At San Luis and along the Sacramento, however, the violation is unusually dramatic in its revelation of long-calculated, substantial circumvention coming to fruition before our very eyes. To thwart legislation by exercising administrative discretion beyond tolerable limits is familiar and simple. To achieve the same ends by manipulations involving the federal executive, a state-created water district, and the Congress itself, is unusual and more complex. The former is repeated on the Sacramento. The latter is enacted at San Luis.

A final outcome fatal to law is not inevitable in either area. The Administration has been asked to investigate violation of conflict-of-interest statutes on the Sacramento.[158] Power of decision on the Federal Service Area still lies with the Executive as this Article is written. The Administration has gone so far as to ask and receive from Congress a financial appropriation to complete the circumvention, but the power of choice remains—either to continue on course and violate the law while preserving its forms, or to reverse and sustain its substance.

Subsequent to the July 8, 1964, hearings on Westlands contracts, administrators have indicated they will respond to some of the more serious attacks made upon them. Secretary Udall, for example, approved a memorandum by Assistant Secretary Holum on October 7, 1964, pro-

---

of the family farm and of the anti-monopoly provisions of basic reclamation law, the Conference will be forced to reconsider and to oppose any further appropriation of federal funds for reclamation projects in the Western States" (*).

[155] "It seems that big money has some governmental heads of both California and the United States in the palm of their hands. Would that we had enough men in the official family of California as well as the United States who would be true to their oath of office and preserve the interests of all the people." Editorial by J. Blaine Quinn, Master, California State Grange, California Grange News, May 10, 1964, cited at 110 CONG. REC. 17503 (daily ed. Aug. 5, 1964).

[156] Some relevant questions that deserve inquiry have not been touched upon in this Article. For example: (1) Has the Secretary of the Interior, in the Sacramento River contracts, exceeded his authority under Constitutional provisions placing navigable streams under the jurisdiction of Congress, and under § 10 of the Rivers and Harbors Act of 1890, 30 Stat. 1151 (1899), 33 U.S.C. § 403 (1958), forbidding "creation of any obstruction, not affirmatively authorized by Congress, to the navigable capacity of any ... waters"? (2) Has the Secretary exceeded law or the limits of good judgment in the Sacramento River settlements, by making piecemeal allotment of water rights to a particular interest group of irrigators, prior to broader consideration of all interests in the Sacramento River from its headwaters to San Francisco Bay, including interests in irrigation, industrial use of water, navigation, recreation, and protection from water pollution?

[157] Testimony of Taylor, *1964 Westlands Hearing* at 146-47.

[158] See note 153 *supra*.

posing important revisions in the Westlands water service contract.[159] Among these are elimination of the "unavoidable" excuse clause, weighting of *ad valorem* taxes so as to raise the economic incentive of excess landholders to execute recordable contracts, scaling down of the share of irrigation requirements of eligible lands to be met by project water deliveries and elevation of the share to be met by district pumping—so as to diminish the rate of ground water replenishment—and consolidation of Westlands and West Plains districts. No mention was made of an intention to make prompt request for execution of recordable contracts, or—in the alternative—immediate designation by excess landowners of which 160 acres is to receive permitted project water.

How effectively these proposals can be carried out in negotiations between the Department of the Interior and districts representing the landowners of the Federal Service Area remains to be seen. Strict compliance by the Interior Department with the procedural requirements of the San Luis Act would mitigate the effect of pressures upon administrators to weaken enforcement of the excess land law. Will Congress insist upon exercising its power to review changes in the Westlands contracts and thereby keep the channels open to countervailing pressures from both supporters and detractors of the excess land laws? Or will the Secretary be allowed to forge changes without resubmission for the ninety day oversight period and thereby continue the pattern of acquiescence by two branches of our federal government in what must be termed a legal and institutional shambles?

---

[159] Amendment of water service contract, Westlands Water District, Central Valley Project, California, Memorandum from Assistant Secretary, Water and Power Development, to Secretary of the Interior, Oct. 7, 1964, in *1964 Westlands Hearing* at 177-80.

WATER, LAND, AND ENVIRONMENT
IMPERIAL VALLEY

natural resources journal

Published four times a year by The University of New Mexico School of Law

WATER, LAND, AND ENVIRONMENT IMPERIAL VALLEY: LAW CAUGHT IN THE WINDS OF POLITICS**

PAUL S. TAYLOR°

PUBLIC RECLAMATION

These lands are being opened to settlement for all the people, whether they now reside in the East, South, or West. The farm boys in the East want farms of their own . . . where they can . . . build homes without being driven into the already overcrowded cities. . . . If this policy is not undertaken now, this great Western desert will ultimately be acquired by individuals and great corporations. . . . [The National Reclamation Act] is in the interest of the man who earns his bread by his daily toil. It gives him a place where he can . . . be free and independent . . . an owner of the soil. . . . Those are the class of men we must rely on for the safety of the nation. (Congressman Oscar Underwood, of Alabama. 1902)[1]

Water and land are separated west of the hundredth meridian. It is costly to bring them together at the place and time needed to render them productive, and the costs—with scarcely an exception—are beyond the resources of local interests. A decade of popular agitation was needed to persuade Congress to open the door to the national treasury to finance reclamation. Before consenting, Congress insisted upon the explicit condition that the benefits should be distributed to the many, not monopolized by the few.

The Homestead Act of 1862[2] offered a precedent: its aim was to assure widespread distribution of benefits from the disposal of public lands. To achieve this Congress offered a quarter section of land (160

°Professor of Economics, *Emeritus,* University of California, Berkeley; Consultant to the Office of the Secretary of the Interior and Bureau of Reclamation between 1943 and 1952.
°°Martha Chase assisted in preparation of this paper and the Institute of Business and Economic Research, University of California, Berkeley, gave support.
1. S. Doc. No. 446 Ser. 4249, 57th Cong., 1st Sess. 376 (1902). Southern support of western reclamation was essential. The authorization bill passed by only 146 to 55—150 recorded as present or not voting. Of the yea votes 57, or 39 percent, came from South Atlantic and South Central states. Congressman Underwood was a member of rising influence in the House.
2. Act of May 20, 1862, ch. 75, 12 Stat. 392.

acres) to any family which would live upon and develop it. The citizens who gathered almost annually at Irrigation Congresses during the 1890's pointed repeatedly to the already marked concentration of western land ownership in private hands, a concentration planned largely in anticipation of the coming of water and the "many fold" increases in land values to the owners it would bring with it. In light of this concentration of land ownership the Irrigation Congresses insisted time and again that reclamation plans should not promote a similar concentration of benefits from the arrival of water.[3]

Congress and the White House made clear that they shared the conception of public policy held within the citizens' movement. The House Committee on Reclamation of Arid Lands rejected private construction of irrigation works, not as financially infeasible, but as a step toward private monopoly. It declared:

> If we were willing to abandon our time-honored policy of inviting and encouraging small individual land holdings, and were prepared to turn over all of the public lands under a large irrigation system to the control of a single individual or a corporation, we could undoubtedly secure the construction of extensive works which can not be profitably constructed by private enterprise under present conditions, but no one contemplates paying so stupendous a price as this for irrigation development.[4]

As the reclamation bill was moving through Congress President Theodore Roosevelt made plain to its sponsors that he, too, wanted to assure adequate safeguards against private monopolization of benefits.[5] On the floor of Congress western spokesmen gave emphatic assurance that the acreage limitation and residency provisions in the bill would guard "against the possibility of speculative landholdings and . . . compel the division into small holdings of any large areas . . . in private ownership which may be irrigated under its provisions."[6]

Eastern opponents of the reclamation bill remained skeptical of the adequacy of these provisions. Their spokesman charged that:

> We find behind this scheme, egging it on, encouraging it, the great railroad interests of the West, who own millions of acres of these arid lands, now useless, and the very moment that we, at the

---

3. Taylor, *Water, Land, and People in the Great Valley*, 5 American West 24 (1968); Taylor, *Reclamation: the Rise and Fall of an American Idea*, 7 American West 27 (1970); Taylor, *Reclamation: Aspirations vs. Achievements*, 115 Cong. Rec. 34489 (1969).
4. H.R. Rept. No. 794 Ser. 4402, 57th Cong., 1st Sess., 3 (1902). *See also* Taylor, *Central Valley Project: Water and Land*, 2 Western Pol. Q. 241 (1949).
5. 35 Cong. Rec. 6674 (1902).
6. 35 Cong. Rec. 6677 (1902).

public expense, establish or construct these irrigation works and reservoirs, you will find multiplied by 10, and in some instances by 20, the value of now worthless land owned by those railroad companies. . . . [7]

Congress overrode these doubts and launched reclamation as a nationally financed program in 1902. The condition upon which it was willing to do so is set out in the following public policy statement, found in the National Reclamation Act:

No right to the use of water for land in private ownership shall be sold for a tract exceeding 160 acres to any one landowner, and no such sale shall be made to any landowner unless he be an actual bona fide resident on such land, or occupant hererof residing in the neighborhood . . . .[8]

PRIVATE RECLAMATION

Congressman Gilbert M. Hitchcock, of Nebraska: "Then, you think there should not be any limit to the profits that the private corporation should be permitted to earn while taking the public waters of the river and irrigating and controlling largely the public lands?" Anthony Heber, California Development Company, Imperial Valley: "I am opposed to the Government interfering, in every instance, with the private property and the private profits of any private corporation.—Congressional hearing, 1904."[9]

In the history of western reclamation the Imperial Valley is a great exception. The Desert Land Act[10] made public land available to settlers on condition they would irrigate it. Motivated by prospects of speculative gain, private capital undertook to supply the water to the coming settlers. At the beginning, the necessity for construction of a reservoir to store floodwaters was not evident. The initial cost of diverting public water from the nearby Colorado River for sale to the settlers was low, and within the grasp of private capital. Water began to flow into the Valley in 1901, one year before Congress laid down public policy in the National Reclamation Act. Consequently, controls were absent.

The feasibility of private development at the beginning was a product of exceptional geographic factors, and men experienced in

---

7. 35 Cong. Rec. 6685 (1902).

8. *Reclamation and Irrigation of Lands by Federal Government*, 43 U.S.C. 431 (1971). Not until 1926 did Congress control speculative profits from sale of "excess" lands by setting pre-project value as the sale price. Reclamation and Irrigation of Lands by Federal Government, 43 U.S.C. 423(e) (1971). *See also* Taylor, *The Excess Land Law: Execution of a Public Policy*, 64 Yale L. J. 477 (1955).

9. *Hearings Before House Committee On Irrigation Of Arid Lands*, H.R. Doc. No. 13627, 58th Cong., 2nd Sess. 63 (1904).

10. 43 U.S.C. 321 *et seq.* (1964).

administration of large landholdings took advantage of them.[11] Imperial Valley lay well beneath the bed of the Colorado River, and mostly below sea level. The necessary original investment, therefore, was modest—a few hundred thousand dollars. With teams and scrapers the developers made a cut in the soft silt of the river embankment and dug a short canal. This sufficed to release a stream of water which ran down hill through the canal, into a cleared-out old overflow channel and onto the desert below. Upon arrival of the first waters the developers encouraged settlers to buy government land at $1.25 an acre. To reward their own investment they sold the settlers rights to receive delivered water without which their land was toally unproductive.

Privately-provided irrigation produced the effects Congress had anticipated and sought to avoid. By the late twenties Imperial Valley was not a traditional homogeneous community of farmers working their own land, but a polarized, divided society. Operation and ownership of land were concentrated in few hands; the laboring landless were numerous. About a third of the population was of Mexican origin, largely of Mexican birth, and composed almost entirely of field laborers. Control of production of two principal crops—melons and lettuce—already was concentrated in the hands of as few as 56 and 67 growers, respectively, with average acreages of 667 and 336. Investigation at the height of the Valley's private development revealed that:

> Mexicans come principally as . . . gangs of hand laborers . . . a class apart . . . the coincidence of class, racial, and cultural differences . . . combine to maintain a social ostracism, which . . . accentuate[s] the domiciliary . . . isolation, . . . delay[s] the rapprochement of the two cultures . . . and retard[s] the blurring of the class line.[12]

Concentration of land ownership and operation has continued to grow. By 1969, the size of the average irrigated farm in Imperial County was 494 acres, more than three times the 142-acre average in the State of California. Of the 438,000 irrigated acres in the Valley, about 800 owners held 233,000, or more than half, in parcels exceeding 160 acres.

From the beginning the developers of the Valley found the uncertainty of their right to divert Colorado River water to be an

---

11. "The men who brought the first farmers into the Colorado Desert in 1901 . . . Charles Robinson Rockwood and C. N. Perry were construction engineers for the Southern Pacific Railroad, familiar with handling men, money, and materials. Anthony Heber and Sam Fergusson were land agents of the Kern County Land Company." Hosmer, *Triumph and Failure in the Colorado Desert*, 3 American West 34, 38-39 (1966).

12. Taylor, Mexican Labor in the United States: Imperial Valley 33, 94 (1928).

impediment in their efforts to raise capital.[13] To remove this obstacle they appealed to Congress in 1904 to declare the Colorado River "non-navigable," and consequently beyond federal jurisdiction. After a hearing marked by opposition from the newly formed Reclamation Service and its supporters, Congress rejected the appeal.[14] Thereupon the developers turned to Mexico and cut an intake beyond the jurisdiction of the United States, just below the international boundary.[15]

The new cut in riverbank silt was made without a protective headgate, and disaster soon struck. In 1905 the river's floodwaters widened the intake into a breach that poured the entire flow of the Colorado into the Valley to form a fast enlarging Salton Sea. Complete inundation of Imperial Valley impended. The original developers, aided by (and ultimately controlled by) the Southern Pacific Company, whose railroad tracks traversed the Valley, worked to close the breach. This finally was accomplished in 1907.

On the eve of the final effort toward closure, President Theodore Roosevelt advised Congress that the making of the cut in Mexico:

> in a bank composed of light soil above a depression . . . without controlling devices, was criminal negligence. . . . The ownership of the property in Imperial Valley, both farmers and towns-people, together with the Southern Pacific company, and the California Development have combined to call upon the government to assist the California Development Company to the extent of erecting permanent works to insure protection in the future.

The President recommended that:

> The reclamation service should be authorized to take steps at once for the construction of an irrigation project under the terms of the Reclamation Act for the lands in the Imperial Valley, and in the lower Colorado River Valley.[16]

---

13. "The bankers tell me, 'You get Congress to simply declare that stream is not navigable, and then you can have all the money you want.'" *Supra* note 9, at 60.

14. "If this legislation should be enacted, you will have granted away forever the entire magnificent Colorado River." Hearings on H.R. 13627, *supra* note 9 at 88. "If the policy of the Government is to be sustained and carried out, the Reclamation Bureau will have to take up this enterprise, because the small enterprises will get just enough land in frequent spots and just enough water to make it impossible for the Government to carry out on proper lines what would be absolutely impossible for the individual or corporation here to carry out." Hearing on H.R. 13627, *supra* note 9, at 59.

15. "It is my earnest desire to worship at our own altar and to receive the blessing from the shrine of our own Government, but if such permission is not granted, of necessity I will be compelled to worship elsewhere." Hearing on H.R. 13627, *supra* note 9, at 87.

16. Message on the Imperial Valley situation sent to Congress on January 12, 1907 by President Roosevelt, on the unfriendly attitude of the United States Government towards the

Congress did not follow the President's recommendation of a federal reclamation project, but in 1910 authorized him to spend up to one million dollars—most of which he expended—for the purpose of protecting lands in the Imperial Valley and elsewhere along the lower Colorado River.[17]

LEGISLATION

> Allow the water sources . . . to pass under unrestricted control of monopolists, and the land to be reclaimed . . . might as well be granted to them at once, for the ownership of the water virtually gives them the land, and that is what they expect to achieve.[18]

The danger to the Imperial Valley from inundation by flood waters had been merely postponed, and after an interval of years, California spokesmen in Congress raised the hazard and proposed a remedy. Congressman Phil D. Swing, representing the Valley, and Senator Hiram Johnson, of California, became sponsors of bills to authorize the Secretary of the Interior to construct a dam and reservoir to restrain flood waters at Boulder Canyon, and a canal to conduct water from the Colorado River to the Valley without passing through Mexico. A canal entirely on American soil would forestall enlargement of Mexican water rights beyond those created by the original developers when they cut the intake south of the border.[19] The reservoir not only would protect the Valley from repetition of the 1905-07 disaster, or worse, but also would provide water needed for irrigation in the slack season.

> Secretary of Interior Hubert Work reported on January 4, 1928: Imperial and Coachella Valleys, during May, June, and July of each year, are threatened by destruction by flood. In September and October Imperial Valley is threatened by, and has actually suffered, millions of dollars loss from drought. . . . The great reservoir will catch and hold the flood water [and] will guarantee

---

Imperial Valley. (April 1907,42-45). Imperial Valley spokesmen rejected the President's charge of "criminal negligence." They said that since by refusing to declare the Colorado River "non-navigable" the Government had "ruined the credit of . . . [the California Development] company and made it powerless to build suitable headworks, it is not extravagant to state that the Government is responsible for the runaway Colorado River and the Salton Sea." Letter from L. M. Holt to President Roosevelt, *Id.* at 17.

17. Law of June 25, 1910, ch. 441, 36 Stat. 883.

18. H.R. Rep. No 3767, 51st Cong., 2nd Sess., (5); *Report of House Select Committee on Irrigation of Arid Lands in the U.S.*, H.R. 12210 (1891).

19. Senator Sam G. Bratton, of New Mexico, described the purpose of the All-American Canal: "to discontinue the enlargement of these [water] rights in Mexico." 70 Cong. Rec. 326 (1928).

lower basin communities, especially Imperial Valley, a dependable water supply. . . .[20]

The Supreme Court noted additional benefits received by Imperial Valley lands from construction of Hoover Dam, which checked "erosion of land and the deposit of silt which fouled waters, choked irrigation works, and damaged good farm land and crops."[21]

Reservoir storage was important to irrigate land already under cultivation, as well as to reclaim new land. Senator William H. King, of Utah, supporting the project, told Congress:

> The low water is wholly inadequate to irrigate the land in the Imperial Valley. . . . The result is that there is a diminution of the quantity of crops produced upon all of the land. Therefore it is important not only for the bringing new lands under cultivation that there should be storage facilities, but it is vitally important to those who have primary rights that they should have storage facilities and storage of water.[22]

In 1928, after several years' deliberation, Congress passed the Boulder Canyon Project Act [23] authorizing the Secretary of the Interior to build a reservoir, a power plant, and an All-American Canal. The Act provided: that the project was to be "reimbursable, as provided in the reclamation law:" for "payment of all expenses of contruction, operation and maintenance of said canal and appurtenant structures in the manner provided in the reclamation law;" that reclamation law is defined as the 1902 law and acts "amendatory and supplementary thereto;" and that "this act shall be deemed a supplement to the reclamation law, which said reclamation law shall govern the construction, operation, and management of the works herein authorized, except as otherwise herein provided."[24] "Reclamation law" thus includes the acreage limitation and residency requirements adopted in 1902.

PUBLIC ADMINISTRATION

> I conceive it to be . . . my duty as Secretary, to exert every effort to see that applicable laws are complied with. Where discretion may be vested in the Department or the Secretary, that discretion should be exercised to obtain compliance with the principles on which the legislation is enacted. What I am concerned about is a process by which inferences are based on inferences and there is a whittling away at a principle until all

---

20. 70 Cong. Rec. 8541-2 (1928).
21. Arizona v. California, 373 U.S. 546, 553 (1962).
22. 70 Cong. Rec. 74 (1928).
23. Boulder Canyon Project Act, 45 U.S.C. 617a, 617c(b), 617k, 617m (1964).
24. *Id.*

that is left is a pile of shavings. (Secretary of the Interior Fred A. Seaton, 1957)[25]

The initial response at the Department of the Interior to the references to reclamation law in the Boulder Canyon Project Act[26] was one of the acceptance and apparent approval. Attorney Northcutt Ely, Interior Secretary Ray Lyman Wilbur's Executive Assistant and representative in negotiation of water contracts under the act, recorded these views on November 4, 1930:

> The Reclamation Law's limitation of 160 acres to a particular owner presents a serious problem, in view of the fact that this, being an existing project, includes many farms with larger area. I see nothing to do but enforce it unless the Imperial Irrigation District can get new legislation. In any event, enforcement of this requirement would undoubtedly have a salutary effect on suspected speculative activities in that locality.[27]

In due course, however, an Imperial Irrigation District attorney solicited an opposite response, i.e., that the 160-acre limitation did not apply.[28] Following an exchange of views within the Interior Department, but without a formal solicitor's legal opinion, Ely ordered for the Secretary's signature a letter approving nonapplication of acreage limitation to Imperial Valley. Secretary Wilbur signed it on February 24, 1933.[29]

In 1944, fourteen years after he had written that Congress had indeed applied acreage limitation to Imperial Valley, and that its application would be a "salutary" control over speculation, Ely testified to Congress that in administering reclamation law to Imperial Valley, acreage limitation simply "has been ignored."[30]

Coachella Valley is served by an extension of the All-American Canal northward beyond the Imperial Valley. Secretary Wilbur's 1933 letter had covered an early impending contract between the United States and the Imperial Irrigation District only. In 1945, his successor, Secretary Harold L. Ickes, faced a similar decision of whether or not to apply acreage limitation to Coachella Valley as the All-American Canal was extended to that area. The opinion of

---

25. *Hearings Before Senate Subcommittee on Irrigation and Reclamation*, on S. 1425, 2541, and 3448, 85th Cong., 2nd Sess., Appendix C, 26, 27 (1958).
26. 45 U.S.C. 617 *et seq.* (1964).
27. 71 Interior Dec. 528 (1964).
28. "He doesn't want any formal ruling, of course, if the Solicitor were to hold that the limitation applies so far as Imperial Irrigation District is concerned." Richard Coffey, District Counsel, to Porter W. Dent, Assistant Commissioner, Bureau of Reclamation, Feb. 4, 1933. 71 Interior Dec. 527 (1964).
29. 71 Interior Dec. 529-30 (1964).
30. *Hearings on H.R. 3961 Before Senate Commerce Subcommitee*, 78th Cong., 2nd Sess., 632 (1944).

Solicitor Fowler Harper, upon which Secretary Ickes relied as to Coachella Valley, repudiated the Wilbur ruling on Imperial Valley:

> . . . the letter of Secretary Wilbur . . . was written solely for the purpose of giving partisan help to the Imperial Water District, as the delay of the final confirmation of the contract held up construction of the All-American Canal. Besides, the time of the Hoover Administration was near its close . . . in view of section 14 of the Boulder Canyon Project Act, which makes that act supplementary to the Federal reclamation law, the excess-land provisions contained therein are carried into operation with respect to the Coachella Valley . . . .[31]

The mid-forties was a period of extended public debate over application of acreage limitation law. Its focus at that time was the Central Valley Project in California, but the implications and repercussions of the contest were far broader. Attempts to obtain Congressional exemption of Central Valley Project were pressed hard, especially in 1944 and 1947, but they failed. President Harry S. Truman's prospects for election to another term were in great doubt, and in 1948 his support of acreage limitation was to become an issue.[32]

In the midst of this situation a spokesman for the Veterans of Foreign Wars—an organization supporting acreage limitation, with veterans given preference in access to land—asked now Secretary of Interior J. A. Krug to follow the logic of the Harper decision of 1945, reverse Secretary Wilbur's ruling of 1933, and apply acreage limitation to Imperial as well as to Coachella Valley. In response, Secretary Krug stood by the Ickes decision to apply acreage limitation to Coachella Valley, but declined to reverse Secretary Wilbur's Imperial Valley decision, saying "we must allow that inconsistency, if such there be, to continue." He explained that

> . . . inasmuch as the Secretary of the Interior then charged with the administration of law construed the acreage limitation as not being applicable to lands of the Imperial Irrigation District under the facts as he then understood them, and it being clear that the then owners and subsequent purchasers of irrigable lands in the Imperial Irrigation District were entitled to rely upon advice from the Secretary and thus establish an economy in the district consistently with that advice, they should not now be abruptly advised that the economy of the project is to be changed under a

---

31. 71 Interior Dec. 533, 548 (1964).
32. Taylor, *Excess land law: Legislative Erosion of Public Policy*, 30 Rocky Mt. L. Rev. 1, 11-13 (1958); Taylor, *Excess Land Law: Execution of a Public Policy*, 64 Yale L. J. 477, 501-503, text at n. 144 (1955).

contrary ruling of the present officer charged with the adminstration of the law.[33]

In declining to follow the clear import of Harper's 1945 opinion that acreage limitation law applied to Imperial Valley as well as to Coachella, Secretry Krug thus gave weight to two practical aspects of the situation stemming from the Wilbur decision. The first was concern for the injury that reversal would do to "owners and subsequent purchasers" of Imperial Valley land. The second was the fifteen-year duration of an administrative interpretation upon which he believed they now "were entitled to rely." Although declining to disturb the Wilbur administrative ruling, Secretary Krug did not close the legal issue, adding, "that action might now be subject to valid question."[34]

Thus the Secretary left the final outcome in a shroud of uncertainly that prevails to this day. In balancing interests affected by his decision, he chose to give greater weight to the interest of land "owners and subsequent purchasers" in nonenforcement than to the opposed interest of the "man who earns his bread by his daily toil" seeking through access to the land "a place where he can . . . be free and independent." The latter were not vocal and he did not mention them.[35]

In 1957, nine years after Secretary Krug declined to apply acreage limitation to Imperial Valley, Solicitor General J. Lee Rankin examined the Wilbur decision critically, and arrived at the same conclusion as Solicitor Harper, that the law applied to Imperial Valley:

---

33. Secretary J. A. Krug to M. C. Hermann, Department Quartermaster Adjutant, Veterans of Foreign Wars, California, April 27, 1948, 71 Interior Dec. 548-9 (1964).

34. *Id.* at 549. Surviving uncertainty over application of acreage limitation to Imperial Valley soon was reflected in political campaigning, as reported in a Valley newspaper: "Rep. Richard Nixon visited Saturday in the Valley with members of the Imperial County Republican Central Committee . . . regarding his possible candidacy for senator in the 1950 election. . . . Two statements made by Nixon should prove popular with people of Imperial Valley. Nixon declared he is against the 160-acre limitation of ownership of lands demanded by the bureau of reclamation, and that he is against the Department of Interior's grab for power." Brawley News, Oct. 31, 1949.

35. *See supra* note 32 and epigraph at *supra* note 1. In 1958, a decade later, Chief Counsel Harry W. Horton, of Imperial Irrigation District, was to tell Congress that whatever the economic hardship suffered by owners of excess land from compliance with acreage limitation, it is balanced by the economic gains received from reclamation of their lands. Explaining the avowed readiness of a prominent San Joaquin Valley owner of excess lands to comply with the law by selling them within the customary ten years after receiving water, Horton said: "Let us lay the cards on the table. . . . I will give you my own opinion of Jack O'Neill's willingness to sign the 160-acre limitation. He thinks if he gets water for 10 years on there without having to sell it, he can make enough money out of it so he can afford to sell the land at any old price." *Hearings on S.1425, S.2541, and S.3448 Before the Senate Subcommittee on Irrigation and Reclamation*, 85th Cong, 2nd Sess. 87-8 (1958).

> [F]or the reasons stated in Solicitor Harper's opinion, as well as for others, no conclusion seems permissible other than that the limitations of the reclamation law upon the quantity of privately owned lands which might receive irrigation water under the All-American Canal are applicable in the Imperial Valley . . . .[36]

The Interior Department administrators of reclamation law, however, were unmoved. Early in 1958, within months of the issuance of Solicitor General Rankin's opinion, Solicitor of Interior Elmer F. Bennett repeated the reasons given by Secretary Krug in 1948 for not enforcing the law, notwithstanding the Wilbur "decision might now be subject to valid question." Bennett said he had:

> not had occasion to undertake a legal analysis of the respective views heretofore expressed by Secretary Wilbur and former Solicitor Harper. Whatever the conclusion might be, to my mind the time has long since passed when it is realistic and practicable to do so . . . The negotiations leading to the [original] contract were lengthy and extensively in the public view. . . . Water has been delivered to the lands of Imperial District pursuant to the contract since the early 1940's. I am not aware that any administrative action has been proposed or taken either by the preceding administration or by this one to recognize or enforce application of the 160 acre limitation to the lands of the Imperial Irrigation District. . . . There must surely arise a point of time, again I believe long since past, when the contract . . .became binding upon the United States and the District. To treat otherwise at this date could have far-reaching effects.[37]

Continuance of administrative inaction in applying acreage limitation to Imperial Valley, however, did not suffice to assure owners of excess lands there that they could rely confidently on survival of the Wilbur opinion and regard the issue as permanently at rest. A year after Solicitor General Rankin said the limitation legally applies to the Valley, Senator Clinton P. Anderson, as chairman of the Senate Subcommittee on Irrigation and Reclamation, issued a memorandum reprinting the opposed Wilbur and Harper opinions.[38]

Five days later, on April 30, 1958, the Subcommittee opened hearings on three acreage limitation bills. Imperial Irrigation District Chief Counsel Harry W. Horton appeared as witness on the opening

---

36. Memorandum in behalf of the United States with respect to relevance of noncompliance with acreage limitations of reclamation law, No. 10 Original, Arizona v. California 357 U.S. 902 (1957); 71 Interior Dec. 466, 555 (1964).
37. 71 Interior Dec. 550-53 (1964).
38. Acreage limitation-reclamation law. Memorandum of the Chairman of the Subcommittee on Irrigation and Reclamation to Members of the Senate Committee on Interior and Insular Affairs, Apr. 25. 1958, 11-24.

day to say, "I hope that in any report made by this committee there will be no presumptions indulged in in favor of Mr. Harper's opinion."³⁹

After the lapse of another three years Senator Anderson again raised the question of applicability of the law. In a letter to Secretary of the Interior Stewart L. Udall, he stated:

> I have had some complaints from Southern California that the acreage limitation provisions of the Reclamation law have not been enforced in . . . the Coachella and Imperial Valleys. Would you kindly advise me if these areas are subject to acreage limitation provisions, and if so, the status of land ownership within them?⁴⁰

Secretary Udall responded nine months later, on May 15, 1962, regretting that the Senator's letter "unfortunately" had been "misplaced," and mentioning the Wilbur, Harper and Rankin opinions and the Krug letter to the Veterans of Foreign Wars. The Secretary concluded:

> The continuing press of other matters has caused us to defer a current study of the Imperial situation. We hope, however, to go into it in the future, as circumstances of available staff and time permit.⁴¹

Two and a half years later Solicitor of Interior Frank J. Barry issued an opinion thoroughly covering administrative action and inaction between 1930 and 1964. After reviewing the Wilbur ruling, Harper opinion, Krug letter, Rankin opinion, Bennett letter, and Anderson-Udall exchange, he came to this unqualified conclusion:

> The Boulder Canyon Project Act by its plain terms incorporates those provisions of law which impose acreage limitations on lands served from federal reclamation projects. The Boulder Canyon Act works, including the All-American Canal, Imperial Dam and appurtenant structures, are federal reclamation facilities. Nothing in the history of the Project Act and nothing in the legislative history of reclamation law modifies what has been expressed by Congress as its plain intent.
>
> The interpretation in the Wilbur letter of the meaning of the Project Act was clearly wrong and could not effect a change in the statutes enacted by Congress. The fact that the Department has

---

39. *Hearings on S.1425 et al., supra* note 25, at 83.
40. 71 Interior Dec. 496, 556 (1904). "This question arose again at the Senate hearings on S.1658 last April (1964) when Senator Kuchel of California asked if the excess land laws apply under the Boulder Canyon Project Act. The Senator stated that the question was, in his view, an important one." 71 Interior Dec. 499 (1964).
41. 71 Interior Dec. 556-58 (1964).

failed for over 30 years to enforce the excess land laws acreage limitations in Imperial Valley cannot legitimize a violation of public policy contrary to the spirit and the letter of the law.[42]

Secretary Udall accepted the Barry opinion. The statute, now validated for at least the time being, gave the Secretary of Interior the responsibility and power to deny water to those owners of excess lands failing to execute recordable contracts complying with the law.[43] Had he chosen to cease delivery of water to lands not in compliance, the courts were open to owners of excess lands in order to contest the denial immediately. However, the administrative arm of government followed another and slower procedure. The Interior Department attempted for several years to negotiate a contract with Imperial Irrigation District incorporating acreage limitation.

Failing these efforts, it brought suit to enforce compliance, meanwhile continuing delivery of water to excess lands. Years elapsed after the Barry opinion before the suit finally came up for trial in 1970; it was decided in its fourth year of litigation on January 5, 1971.[44]

JUDICIAL REVIEW: I

If no action were taken at all . . . to [exempt] Central Valley [from acreage limitation law], I imagine that the course would be exactly as it has been on the Salt River project and in Imperial Valley: that the law would remain on the books, the prohibition of delivery of water to holdings in excess of 160 acres, and that somehow the lands under cultivation would continue to be cultivated . . . the law would simply have to be ignored, as it has been ignored on these other supplemental water projects. (Northcutt Ely, 1944)[45]

In its 1970 argument before federal district Judge Howard B. Turrentine in United States v. Imperial Irrigation District[46] the Justice Department characterized the 1933 Wilbur ruling that the acreage limitation did not apply to Imperial Valley as politically motivated:

---

42. M-36675, Dec. 31, 1964. 71 Interior Dec. 496, 518 (1964).
43. Barely two years prior to enactment of the Boulder Canyon Project Act, Congress had restated acreage limitation law in these words: ". . . no such excess lands so held shall receive water from any project or division if the owners thereof shall refuse to execute valid recordable contracts for the sale of such lands under terms and conditions satisfactory to the Secretary of the Interior and at prices not to exceed those fixed by the Secretary of the Interior . . . ." Reclamation and Irrigation of Lands by the Federal Government, 43 U.S.C. 423(e)(1971).
44. United States v. Imperial Irrigation District 322 F. Supp 11 (S.D. Cal. 1971), came before Judge Howard B. Turentine, nominated to the federal bench in San Diego by President Richard Nixon on Feb. 19, 1970. *Cf. supra* note 34.
45. Testimony given as attorney for the State of California Water Project Authority at the *Hearings on H.R. 3961, 632 Before Senate Commerce Subcommittee, 78 Cong., 2d Sess., (1944).* 322 F. Supp. 11 (S.D. Cal. 1971).
46. 322 F.Supp. 11 (S.D. Cal. 1971).

Thus, the Wilbur letter must be considered for what it was: A partisan effort by a lame duck administration to effect, by administrative interpretation, an exemption that proponents of the [Boulder Canyon] Project Act never dared risk seeking directly.[47]

Judge Turrentine chose to define the issue otherwise. His goal, he said, was to determine "whether Congress intended in the Project Act to apply acreage limitation to privately owned lands in the Imperial Valley."[48] In deciding in favor of the Wilbur ruling that the acreage limitation was inapplicable, he at first rejected the argument that the decision should rest upon the reasonableness of an administrative practice of long-standing, a ruling deferred to by Secretary Krug in 1948,[49] and by Solicitor Bennet in 1958.[50] Nevertheless, returning later to the same question, Judge Turrentine noted that the Wilbur "interpretation was followed during the incumbencies of six successor Secretaries and four Presidential administrations" despite "doubts [that] never crystallized into an official repudiation."[51]

Enactment of a law does not assure its enforcement. Congress, having opted for acreage limitation in order "to prevent monopoly and to diffuse ownership,"[52] was vetoed by administrators of both

---

47. U.S. Plaintiff's reply brief to landowners' brief no. 1, and landowners' brief no. 2, 124, United States v. Imperial Irrigation District, 322 F Supp. 11 (S.D. Cal. 1971). "As former counsel for Imperial Irrigation District, Congressman Swing had devoted a major protion of his professional life toward obtaining federal assistance for Imperial Valley interests. . . . As congressional sponsor of the Boulder Canyon Project Act bills, he desires to protect large landowners in his district from a settled policy of federal reclamation law (in enacting section 46 of the 1926 Omnibus Adjustment Act only two months later, the same Congress reaffirmed its policy of restricting the distribution of federal benefits from reclamation projects), yet he is astute enough to realize that a specific congressional exemption from acreage limitations would not be enacted; hence, he inserted measures that incorporate generally the reclamation law but leaves certain specific policies of that law unstated, the calculated risk being that an exemption stands a better chance of being effected through administrative or a judicial construction than it does through congressional enactment. . . . This is the classic case of an attempt to obtain 'by ingenious interpretation and insinuation, that which cannot be obtained by plain and expressed terms.' Dubuque & Pac. R.R. v. Litchfield, 64 U.S. 66, 88-90 (1860)." United States Plaintiff's Reply Brief, 4, 5, United States v. Imperial Irrigation District, 322 F. Supp. Reply Brief, 4 , 5, United States v. Imperial Irrigation District, 322 F. Supp 11 (S.D. Cal. 1971).
48. United States v. Imperial Irrigation District 322 F. Supp. 11 (S.D. Cal. 1971).
49. See text at notes 28, 34, 42.
50. See text at note 37.
51. United States v. Imperial Irrigation District, 322 F. Supp. 11 (S.D. Cal. 1971). The decision finds support in United States v. Midwest Oil Co., 236 U.S. 459, 472-473 (1914) from which it quotes as follows, that "government is a practical affair, intended for practical men . . . officers, lawmakers, and citizens naturally adjust themselves to any long-continued action of the Executive Department, on the presumption that unauthorized acts would not have been allowed to be so often repeated as to crystallize into a regular practice. That presumption is not reasoning in a circle, but the basis of a wise and quieting rule that, in determining the meaning of a statute or the existence of a power, weight shall be given to the usage itself even when the validity of the practice is the subject of investigation."
52. USDI-BR Landownership survey on federal reclamation projects, 66 ff. (1946).

parties. When the issue came before Judge Turrentine, he sided with the administrators, citing as his support the administrative decisions, rather than the legislative enactment.

Describing his task as one of statutory interpretation, Judge Turrentine took note of language in the Boulder Canyon Project Act[53] that made it "a supplement to the reclamation law,'""reclamation law" being described as the original 1902 Act and acts "amendatory thereof and supplemental thereto." "Reclamation law," it said, "shall govern the construction, operation, and management of the works herein authorized, except as otherwise herein provided."[54] Judge Turrentine emphasized the final excepting clause.

The Project Act spelled out numerous details of constructing, contracting, and repayment applicable to Boulder Canyon Project. It made no express mention of acreage limitation which, by contrast, is applicable generally to all reclamation projects. Judge Turrentine, however, recognized no distinction between a manifest necessity to recite in each project act those provisions applicable uniquely to it, on the one hand, and an absence of necessity to repeat in each project act those provisions applicable to all projects generally, on the other. On the contrary, he argued that because a provision of general application such as acreage limitation was so "important," it was as necessary to recite it in each project statute as to recite those provisions that were of unique application. He said:

> . . . the only item in sec. 46 [of the Omnibus Adjustment Act of 1926] not expressly provided for in the Project Act is the acreage limitation, an issue of social policy and not mere technical details of contracting. It is unlikely that Congress would relegate an issue as important as acreage limitation for private lands to indirect inclusion.[55]

Thus the decision rests on the faulty argument that since no acreage limitation was written into the statute, an acreage limitation would not apply. A more reasoned approach would be to note the distinction between provisions of reclamation law uniquely applicable and those generally applicable, then the logical search would have been for a *specific exemption*, which is absent from the statute.[56]

---

53. Reclamation and Irrigation of Lands by Federal Government, 43 U.S.C. 431 (1971).
54. United States v. Imperial Irrigation District, 322 F. Supp. 11 (S.D. Cal. 1971).
55. *Id.* at 17-18.
56. The Turrentine decision recited other arguments in justification of its conclusion, *e.g.*: the Justice Department's contention that because the Project Act "created a federal subsidy . . . the Act must be strictly construed against" those receiving subsidized water as invalid, because "the Act set in motion a great project conferring many and important benefits on all parties involved, including the United States;" Congress "for more than 30 years was fully aware" of the Wilbur ruling, which was called to its attention at appropriation and other

JUDICIAL REVIEW: II

> In short, this timely movement, looking to the reclamation of Arid America, thus giving "land to the landless," ranks in real importance with the foremost public measures of the times . . . . (Harrison Gray Otis, Ninth National Irrigation Congress, Chicago, 1900.)[57]

A second decision by Judge Turrentine soon followed. Dr. Ben Yellen and several score landless persons in Imperial Valley, participating in *Imperial Irrigation District* Case originally as *amicus curiae*, sought change of status. Their purpose was to be able to appeal the decision, should the government decide against doing so. On March 29, 1971, with the government's decision yet unannounced, Judge Turrentine denied Yellen *et al.* the right to intervene.

The court held that the "interest" of the Valley residents was "extremely speculative and remote," and "no greater than that possessed by the general public." Furthermore, the probable course of litigation, and of administration of sale of excess lands, should his previous decision be reversed, would be lengthy. Also, the "applicants have shown no present ability to purchase and no prior offers within the past twenty years to purchase farm land in the Imperial Valley at market value." Besides, exercise of the "usual right of a seller to choose his purchaser" might exclude the particular applicants for intervention. The court added "there would quite likely be a veterans' preference for entry which would put a large class ahead of the present applicants." Finally, the court noted that it "has observed the vigorous representation by counsel for United States in urging that acreage limitation applies . . . and finds that the interest of applicants, if any, has heretofore and is now being adequately represented. . . ."[58]

A few days later the Justice Department, supported by Solicitor of the Interior Mitchell Melich, abandoned its representation of the

---

hearings, yet it took no action; a Congressional practice of express exemption, project by project, is not controlling because it did not "come into vogue until 1938," a decade after passage of the Boulder Canyon Project Act; Senator Johnson in 1928 (although assuring the Senate that two bills before it held "like purposes and like designs") substituted ("to preserve orderly legislative procedure") the one "without an express acreage limitation provision" for the other containing one, yet no one pointed to or objected to "this significant difference"; the Bureau of Reclamation "never flagged in its support of the Wilbur ruling"; Imperial Valley lands held "perfected rights" to receive water under the Colorado River Compact which acreage limitation would invade. (In adopting 43 U.S.C. 528 (1911) Congress found "perfected rights" no impediment to limitation of the acreage on which an individual landowner might have the right to receive water.) United States v. Imperial Irrigation District, 322 F. Supp. 11 (S.D. Cal. 1971).

57. Proceedings of the Ninth National Irrigation Congress at Chicago, at 240 (1900).
58. United States v. Imperial Irrigation District, Civil No. 67-7-T (S.D. Cal., filed Mar. 29, 1971).

interests of persons seeking access to land by announcing it would not appeal the loss of the government's case.

CONGRESS

Senator John H. Overton, of Louisiana: You say the act . . . [authorizing Central Valley Project in 1937] made no reference to the reclamation law?

Northcutt Ely: Not the excess-land provision. It provided that the project should be contructed in accordance with the reclamation law . . .

Senator Overton: Well, the reclamation law contained the excess land, does it not?

Mr. Ely: Yes. . . .

Senator Overton: So that if it was subject to the reclamation, it would be subject to the excess land.

Mr. Ely: Well, I think the correct legal opinion is exactly what you have expressed. (Congressional hearing, 1944.)[59]

While the inapplicability of the acreage law to Imperial Valley was repeatedly cited to Congress, the validity of that position went unchallenged. *(United States v. Imperial Irrigation District,* 1971.)[60]

In 1971, while the Justice and Interior Departments were pondering the loss of the government's case, one interested member of Congress addressed letters to each department urging that they appeal the Turrentine decision. Senator Clinton P. Anderson, chairman of the Senate subcommittee on water and power resources, was pressing further a question he had raised in 1958 and in 1961. His earlier inquiries had contributed to the government's decision to attempt to enforce the law in the suit which met defeat in the decision of 1971.[61]

Each branch of government was being drawn more tightly into the vortex of the excess land issue. The legislative branch had written the laws establishing policy beginning in 1902. The administrative branch had said in 1933 that Congress failed to apply this policy to Imperial Valley, in 1945 that it had applied it to Coachella Valley served by the same project works, and in 1964 that Congress had intended to apply it to Imperial Valley as well. The judicial branch, which had not spoken until 1971, sided with the original administrative interpretation of 1933, and against those of 1945 and 1964.

---

59. *Senate Commerce Subcommittee Hearings on H.R. 3961, supra* note 45, at 624-25.
60. 322 F. Supp. at 27.
61. *See* text at notes 38 & 40.

It was becoming evident that reclamation policy was at stake, not only in Imperial Valley but elsewhere as well. First to point this out was Chief Counsel Reginald L. Knox, of Imperial Irrigation District. Hardly had Solicitor Barry issued his 1964 opinion that the law applies to the Valley, than the Imperial Irrigation District News reported:

> If the opinion of Solicitor Frank Barry is correct, it also applies to all areas receiving water from the Colorado River, including land in the Metropolitan Water District which supplies water to some extremely large holdings on the coast. According to Knox, there has never been any reference to that area, but if the opinion is correct, it would necessarily apply there also.[62]

Senator Anderson went beyond Knox's inclusion of large southern California landholdings in assessing the potential impact of the Turrentine decision. The Senator pointed out that the decision undermined policy on reclamation projects generally throughout the West. He wrote the Attorney General:

> . . . nearly all Federal reclamation projects for many years have been authorized by statutes employing language similar to that used in the Boulder Canyon Project Act which the District Court held did not incorporate the excess-land limitations by reference. . . . It has never been questioned that the language in these authorizing acts which is substantially identical to section 14 of the Boulder Canyon Project Act makes the excess-land limitations of the Federal reclamation laws applicable. The District Court's opinion now, for the first time, raises a substantial question regarding whether the Department of the Interior, the Congress and the water user groups seeking project authorizations have been in error in assuming that authorizing a project subject to the Federal reclamation laws made excess-land limitations applicable.[63]

Among the projects to which the Turrentine decision on excess land law would apply, Senator Anderson named the Central Arizona Project and upper basin projects authorized in the Colorado River Basin Act, and the Central Valley Project in California. Furthermore, he said to Solicitor of Interior Melich:

> A second area of uncertainty introduced by the opinion deals with the relationship between excess-land limitations and pre-project use of water. These uncertainties are westwide in their implications. . . . Certainly, any suggestion that supplemental

---

62. 26 Imperial Irrigation District News 1 (Feb., 1965).
63. Letter from Senator Clinton P. Anderson to Attorney General John N. Mitchell, Mar. 26, 1971.

water projects should be exempt from the excess land laws by Congress would engender great controversy. When such an attempt was made back in the middle '40's, involving principally the Central Valley Project, it was rejected by the Congress but the turmoil that ensued plagued the reclamation program for many years. A lower court holding that can be read as possibly having such an effect similarly can be expected to give rise to extensive controversy in connection with future authorizations which could have a substantial adverse impact upon the reclamation program. . . . As for the merits of the legal question, there is substantial doubt concerning the legal validity of the Court's holding as demonstrated by the fact that the Solicitor General of the United States in the Eisenhower Administration felt it necessary to state to the Supreme Court's Special Master hearing Arizona v. California that, in his opinion, excess-land limitations are fully applicable.[64]

The Justice Department, through the Assistant Attorney General, Land and Natural Resources Division, responded. Rejecting Senator Anderson's appeals to protect public policy from frustration by either the judicial or administrative branches of government, he placed responsibility for such a result upon the legislative branch itself. Specifically he charged Congress with failure to face the issue of policy squarely and to draft legislation clearly. He said:

If the enforced subdivision and sale of privately owned lands in excess of a limited acreage which will receive the benefits of a federal reclamation project continues to be a viable and fundamental policy of the reclamation program, there is crying need for congressional action today so declaring and to preclude frustration of the policy by administrative or judicial interpretation of statutes the age of which leave them open to attack as allegedly archaic and not reflective of modern realities . . . the Statutes at Large are replete with case after case in which the Congress itself has omitted to address the problem. Indeed, in some instances where the problem has actually come up for debate, it has been left without resolution by the pending legislation, with both the proponents and the opponents of acreage limitation being content to avoid a showdown in the apparent hope that their remarks in the legislative history would lead to an administrative or judicial resolution in accord with their respective views.[65]

---

64. Anderson to Mitchell Melich, Mar. 26, 1971.
65. He added that "there is . . . need for modern legislation clarifying whether it continues to be congressional policy that the break up of pre-existing excess holdings of privately owned lands is a condition to their receipt of project benefits. There is also need for further legislation so that no funds will be appropriated for, and constjuction will not be begun on, any project to which Congress intends acreage limitation to apply without there first being executed the

Thus spokesmen for the judicial, the administrative and the legislative branches of government each sought to lay responsibility for the death of public policy upon the others. The judicial branch charged the legislative with defective bill drafting and an obligation, unfulfilled, to monitor enforcement by the administrative branch. The administrative branch laid blame on the legislative branch for having opened the door to frustration of policy by administrative and judicial interpretation. And a member of the Congress appealed vainly to the administration not to abandon its support of public policy as written, but to press on through the judicial hierarchy for a favorable decision.

The Justice Department, as noted above and after failure of landless applicants for intervention to gain a right to appeal in their own behalf, decided against appeal by the government. Solicitor General Erwin N. Griswold explained: "The decision does not in any way affect the Government's position with respect to reclamation projects in other areas where different facts are involved."[66] He made no reference to Imperial Irrigation District Chief Counsel Knox's early warning that the decision would involve some extremely large holdings on the coast of southern California,[67] or to Senator Anderson's charge that the Turrentine decision already endangered public policy on Colorado Basin and Central Valley projects and jeopardized authorization of future reclamation projects.[68]

PUBLIC RELATIONS

My feeling on this case is to get it tried and on its way to the Supreme Court.
--Judge Howard B. Turrentine, San Diego Union, September 26, 1970.

The decision favoring IID is expected to be appealed, perhaps as far as the U.S. Supreme Court. Both sides made statements in December they would appeal if they lost.
--Brawley (California) News, January 6, 1971.

. . . lifting of the 160-acre limitation is going to send land costs

---

contracts essential to the execution of this policy." Assistant Attorney General Shiro Kashiwa to Senator Clinton P. Anderson, Apr. 16, 1971. Reclamation and Irrigation of Lands by Federal Government 43 U.S.C. 418 (1971) states "That before any contract is let or work begun for the construction of any reclamation project hereafter adopted the Secretary of the Interior shall require the owners of private lands thereunder to agree to dispose of all lands in excess of the area which he shall deem sufficient for the support of a family upon the land in question . . . ."

66. United States Dep't. of Justice Release, Apr. 9, 1971. The Justice Department was faced by an opposite decision, whether or not to appeal, at the end of 1972. *See* note 106, *infra*.

67. 26 Imperial Irrigation District News 1 (Feb. 1965). Congressman Victor V. Veysey, Congressman representing Imperial Valley, and Senator John Tunney, formerly Congressman representing Imperial Valley, supported denial of appeal. Sacramento Bee, Feb. 25, 1971.

68. *See* note 58, *supra*.

soaring—after years of comparatively low values while the ranchers sweated out their case.
--Los Angeles Times, February 22, 1971.

The Nixon administration has an agricultural time bomb in its pocket. Very soon, it will have to decide who to drop it on. . . .
--Sacramento Bee, February 22, 1971.

The decision to abandon the government's case for applying acreage limitation to Imperial Valley met sharply opposed views. Carl Bevins, board chairman of Imperial Irrigation District, said promptly that the ruling "is very gratifying. . . . It was almost my feeling IID and Valley farmers had a just case inasmuch that, before the Department of Justice's action in 1964, our position was upheld by five Interior Secretaries."[69]

Once the decision against appeal was announced, criticism appeared from the other side. The New Republic carried an article on May 8 entitled "Water, Water for the Wealthy."[70] On May 28, Mrs. Stephen L. Stover, a protesting Kansas woman, brought the article to the attention of Solicitor General Griswold. He responded with an elaborate exposition in justification of his decision against appeal.

First, he characterized the New Republic article as a "one sided presentation" from which one "would not know ... that ... irrigation of the Imperial Valley was started about 1900 and was virtually completed by 1920, without any participation by the federal government." The development of "large land holdings" on the "expensive project" was "natural." Furthermore, while public construction of the All-American Canal "was undoubtedly an advantage for the Valley," it "did not result in the reclamation of a single acre of desert land."[71]

Application of acreage limitation law, however, is not dependent upon reclamation of land, but upon receiving water. The language of the statute is : "no such excess lands so held shall receive water . . . if the owners thereof shall refuse to execute valid"

---

69. Brawley News, Jan. 6, 1971. Similarly, the California Feature Service published by Whittaker & Baxter on Apr. 26, 1971, issued a draft editorial stating:
"In 1964 . . . someone in government for some incredible reason decided the Wilbur ruling was wrong and instigated a suit to impose the limitation, a move that would have wrecked the prosperity of the valley. It was that suit the judge rejected. Wisely, if belatedly, the government decided not to appeal. It would have been a tragic caricature of democratic government had the belated and unsupportable federal suit succeeded."
70. Water, Water for the Wealthy, The New Republic (1971).
71. Solicitor General Erwin N. Griswold to Mrs. Stephen L. Stover, June 1, 1971. 117 Cong. Rec. S21299, (daily ed. Dec. 10, 1971). Apparently the Congressional allocation of $1 million in 1910 to protect lower Colorado basin areas from flooding, and Imperial Valley from the hazard of complete inundation was either overlooked or regarded as irrelevant. See text at note 17.

contracts agreeing to disposal of the excess "on the basis of its actual bona fide value . . . without reference to the proposed construction of the irrigation works. . . ."[72]

The Solicitor General further advised Mrs. Stover that no question was seriously raised about it until about 30 years after Secretary Wilbur's decision.

Against this statement must be set, *inter alia,* Solicitor of Interior Harper's decision in 1945, Solicitor General Rankin's opinion in 1957, and Senator Anderson's memorandum of 1958 and inquiry of 1961 addressed to the Secretary of the Interior.[73]

Summarizing his justification, Solicitor General Griswold stated:

> I considered the matter carefully and thoroughly, and over a considerable period of time. As a result of my consideration, I became convinced that (a) we would not win the case in the court of appeals, and (b) we should not win it.

This statement contrasts sharply with much evidence that was available at the time. Perhaps most notable of all, it contrasts with statements by Executive Assistant Northcutt Ely, who facilitated effectuation of the Wilbur ruling of 1933. As noted before, Attorney Ely in 1930 recorded as his view (a) that he could "see nothing to do but enforce [acreage limitation in Imperial Valley]. . . unless the Imperial Irrigation District can get new legislation," and (b) that enforcement "would undoubtedly have a salutary effect on suspected speculative activities in that locality."[74]

JUDICIAL REVIEW: III

Let's ask ourselves "what is the environment?" In short, it is everything—everything that was here before man—plus all the changes man has wrought, both directly and indirectly. In addition, and not to be overlooked, it must include man himself. (Secretary of the Interior Rogers C. B. Morton, 1971)[75]

---

72. Reclamation and Irrigation of Lands by Federal Government 43 U.S.C. §423(e) (1971). "Occasionally one recalls the warnings he received in law school, among them the danger in paraphrasing statutory language. . . . I recall no general provision in the law that limits the excess land law to lands 'reclaimed through a federal project. . . .' Of course a great many reclamation projects involve the supply of supplementary water to land already in cultivation. To the best of my knowledge it has never been thought that this fact exempted the project from the provision of the excess land law." Joseph L. Sax, Professor of Law, University of Michigan, to Solictor General Griswold, September 1, 1971. 117 Cong. Rec. S21299 (daily ed. Dec. 10, 1971).
73. *See* text at notes 31, 36, 38, 40.
74. 71 Interior Dec. 496, 528 (1964).
75. Remarks before Great Issues Forum, University of Southern California, United States Dep't of Interior Release, Apr. 22, 1971.

The 1902 Reclamation Act establishes in the same sentence two requirements that a landowner must meet to be entitled to receive water from a reclamation project. The first is acreage limitation. The second is residency, *i.e.*, he must "be an actual bona fide resident on such land, or occupant thereof residing in the neighborhood of said land."[76]

On April 9, 1971 Solictor General Griswold announced his decision not to appeal the Turrentine ruling. Griswold, after studying the problem "carefully and thoroughly, and over a considerable period of time," based the decision not to appeal on his professed belief that the appeal could not be won.[77]

On November 23, 1971, barely six months later, another judge, sitting in the same Federal District Court as Judge Turrentine, and likewise interpreting reclamation law, held that the residency requirement applied to Imperial Valley and to other lands receiving water under the Boulder Canyon Project Act.[78]

This second suit, *Yellen v. Hickel*, was before Visiting Judge William D. Murray, of Montana. Plaintiffs were the same landless Imperial Valley residents to whom Judge Turrentine previously had denied right to intervene. The government, as defendent charged with failure to enforce the law, argued unsuccessfully that they should be denied standing in court again.[79] The court granted plaintiffs summary judgment.

Many conclusions reached in the two decisions were directly opposed. On the central issue—the applicability of national reclamation policy to Imperial Valley—the first held that the Boulder Canyon Project Act did not apply acreage limitation; the second held that the same act applied residency.

Reclamation law provides both national policy and the details of financial repayment; the latter often vary from project to project. Both are important, but they are not identical in nature. Policy is distinguished largely by its general and enduring application. Financial arrangements are of more particular and immediate application. Judge Murray observed that the Omnibus Adjustment Act of 1926,[80] for example, had as a main purpose "to provide relief to settlers then residing on the land. There is no indication the Act was intended to change the policy of the reclamation law."[81] Similarly, the Boulder Canyon Project Act freed Imperial and Coachella Valley

---

76. 43 U.S.C. 431 (1971).
77. Griswold to Stover, *supra*, note 70.
78. Yellen v. Hickel, 335 F. Supp. 200 S.D. Cal. (1971).
79. *Id.* at 203.
80. Act of May 25, 1926, ch. 383, 44 Stat. 636.
81. Yellen v. Hickel, 335 F. Supp. (S.D. Cal. 1971).

lands of obligation to pay for water delivered through the All-American Canal.[82]

Quoting water law authority Joseph L. Sax, Judge Murray pointed to the fundamental distinction between policy and finance: "It is important to note . . . that reclamation laws are 'designed to promote federal policies of permanent importance and not merely to secure an investment interest.' "[83]

The Murray opinion counters one line of argument after another employed in the Turrentine decision. The Department of the Interior, Murray held,

> . . . cannot repeal an Act of Congress. . . . The fact that residency has not been required by the Department of Interior for over 55 years cannot influence the outcome of this decision. Failing to apply the residency requirement is contrary to any reasonable interpretation of the reclamation law as a whole, and is destructive of the clear purpose and intent of national reclamation policy. It is well settled that administrative practice cannot thwart the plain purpose of a valid law.[84]

Judge Turrentine attached weight to "Congressional knowledge and approval of the Wilbur interpretation" that removed acreage limitation from Imperial Valley, observing that:

> At no time from 1933 to the present has Congress taken any action in derogation of the propriety of the Wilbur interpretation or of the long standing administrative practice which followed it . . . Congress would hardly have ignored the Department's failure to enforce an important provision of reclamation law.[85]

Judge Murray, on the contrary, refused to lay responsibility to monitor enforcement on Congress. He said:

> It has been held that an administrative interpretation of a statute was binding on the court where it has been impliedly upheld by re-enactment of the statute. . . . However, Congressional re-enactment of a statute, without expressed consideration or reference cannot give controlling weight to an originally erroneous administrative interpretation of the statute.[86]

Further, he found the initial 1902 policy enactment by Congress to be in full force and effect, not superseded by any subsequent enactment:

> Statutory construction of Section 5 [1902] and Section 46 [1926] reveals no repugnancy whatever. Section 5 requires that there is

---

82. Boulder Canyon Project Act, 43 U.S.C. §617 (1971).
83. Yellen v. Hickel, 335 F. Supp. 200, 205 (S.D. Cal. 1971).
84. Id. at 207, 208.
85. United States v. Imperial Irrigation District, 322 F. Supp. 11, 26-27 (S.D. Cal. 1971).
86. Yellen v. Hickel, 335 F. Supp. 200, 207 (S.D. Cal. 1971).

no right to use water on tracts of any one owner of over 160 acres and no water shall be sold to anyone not occupying the land or residing in the neighborhood. Section 46 establishes a system whereby the Secretary no longer sells to individuals, but to irrigation districts instead, and provides for a situation not contemplated in the original Act where water would be supplied through the irrigation district to private landowners of more than 160 acres in addition to settlers on public lands opened up for entry under the original reclamation law. There is no inconsistency in applying the requirements of Section 5 at the same time with those of Section 46. . . . A literal reading of both statutes then reveals no implied intent on the part of Congress that the earlier statute would be repealed by Section 46. . . . The plain language of the Omnibus Adjustment Act of 1926 does not repeal Section 5 of the 1902 Act, nor is any legislative intent to do so exhibited in the Act's background.[87]

Conspicuous aspects of the history of reclamation in Imperial Valley are the absence between 1902 and 1971 of a challenge in the courts by the landless themselves, and of relaxed administration of a law designed to provide settlers with ready access to land. As if to answer Judge Turrentine's denial of intervener status to landless Imperial Valley residents, Judge Murray pointed out that the greater the difficulty of citizens in obtaining standing, the greater would be the latitude given bureaucratic officials to defeat legislative policy:

> National policy, as expressed in the reclamation laws, is to provide homes for people. Homes are possible only where speculation and monopolization are not possible. The 160 acre limitation and the national policy which it reflects have been upheld by the Supreme Court. . . . The residency requirement in Section 5 . . . is a second expression of that national policy. Its repeal by implication would be contrary to the purpose for which Section 5 was enacted. . . . Failure to enforce residency subverts the excess land limitation. . . . Through the use of corporations, trusts and cotenancies flagrant violations of the purpose of this limitation are possible. Each of these farms may be used to by-pass the acreage limitation. The policy behind reclamation law to aid and encourage owner operated farms requires enforcement of the residency requirement to prevent these violations. See Sax, The Federal Reclamation Law in 11 Waters to Water Rights . . . 217-224. . . . Rather than indicate the validity of the administrative ruling [against residency], the lapse of time serves to dramatize the unavailability of relief in the past and points toward the need for increased access to the court in the future.[88]

---

87. *Id.* at 203, 204. *Cf.* Kashiwa to Anderson, *supra*, text at note 64.
88. Yellen v. Hickel, 335 F. Supp. 200, 208 (S.D. Cal. 1971).

Both Turrentine and Murray emphasized the importance of national reclamation policy. From this common ground their conclusions diverge. Judge Turrentine argued that, considering the importance of national policy of acreage limitation, its express inclusion in the Boulder Canyon Project Act was to be expected and its absence in express language was evidence that Congress had intended not to apply it to the project. Judge Murray argued the opposite; absence of its express repeal was evidence of Congressional intent to include it by reference. It sufficed that "The Boulder Canyon Project Act . . . provides that the Act shall be deemed a supplement to reclamation law which shall govern the construction, operation and management of the works authorized."[89]

JUDICIAL REVIEW: IV

. . . [i]t is conceded by all thinking men that the comfort and contentment of our laboring classes depend upon keeping open opportunities for all who want them to get homes on the land. As Carlyle said:

> Ye may boast o' yer dimocracy, or any ither 'cracy, or any kind o' poleetical rubbish; but the reason why your laboring folks are so happy is that ye have a vast deal 'o land for a verra few people.
> —Congressman William A. Reeder, of Kansas, speaking on the Reclamation bill, 1902[90]

The landowners of Imperial Valley, believing that their interests were not sufficiently protected by the government, requested and were granted permission to intervene on their own behalf. A full trial on the merits was then held. (Judge William D. Murray, 1972)[91]

The 1902 Congress prescribed the acreage limitation and the residency requirement in the same sentence, but these two related issues were raised separately in the two district court decisions discussed above. As the Imperial Valley litigation proceeded, these issues came closer together, the lines between those affected by the litigation became more distinct, and the interested parties began increasingly to question the role that the executive branch of government was playing. First the landless had sought to intervene in court to protect their own interests in acreage limitation fearing, justifiably, that the government would fail their cause by declining to appeal the Turrentine decision. Now in the Murray court it was nonresident landowners who were unwilling to leave protection of

---
89. Id.
90. 35 Cong. Rec. 6739 (1902).
91. Yellen v. Hickel, 352 F. Supp. 1300 (S.D. Calif. 1972).

their interests solely in government hands even though the government remained a party to the case and technically on their side.

In the full trial on the merits that followed his original partial summary judgement, Judge Murray gave careful attention to five specific contentions of the intervening landowners:

> The issues being reconsidered are: (1) the issues of standing and res judicata, (2) the scope of Section 5 of the 1902 Reclamation Act (the residency requirement), (3) the effect of the Boulder Canyon Project Act . . . on the Imperial Valley, (4) the rule of Udall v. Tallman, 380 U.S. 1 (1965) which requires deference to longstanding administrative constructions, and (5) the equal protection argument.[92]

A. *The Issues of Standing and Res Judicata.*

Nonresident Imperial Valley landowners sought standing to intervene before Judge Murray. They sought also to have standing denied to the landless plaintiffs, on the ground that only landowners were directly affected. The court, however, granted standing to both:

> Obviously the landowners, the beneficiaries of the present state of affairs, are not going to press for enforcement of Section 5. If the plaintiffs are not granted standing to bring this suit, the Department of the Interior will in effect be given a license to disregard the law, as well as an immunity from challenge by the intended beneficiaries of the legislation in question.[93]

As for res judicata, the court held that a 1933 California state court decision against applying Section 5 of the 1902 Reclamation law to Imperial Valley[94] was not binding upon federal courts. It held further that the state court's ruling already had been overthrown by the United States Supreme Court.[95] The latter, Judge Murray said, had decided that language authorizing the Central Valley project—language similar to that used in authorizing the earlier Boulder Canyon project—incorporated the acreage and residency provisions of Section 5 of the 1902 Reclamation law. "The precise question of whether the term 'construction, operation and maintenance' includes the delivery provisions of Section 5 has been decided by the United

---

92. *Id.*
93. *Id.*, at 1-3. "The present value of farm land in Imperial Valley ranges from $600 to $1200 per acre. When the Secretary of the Interior becomes obligated to prohibit the District from delivering irrigation water to lands owned by non-residents, there will be an immediate and substantial decline in the market value of farm land."
94. Hewes v. All persons, No. 15460 Dep't 2, (Super. Ct. Cal. County of Imperial, May 24, 1933).
95. Ivanhoe Irrigation District v. McCracken, 357 U.S. 275 (1958).

States Supreme Court in Ivanhoe Irrigation District v. Mc-Cracken. . . ."[96]

B. *The Scope of the Residency Requirement of Section 5 of the 1902 Reclamation Act.*

Section 5 of the 1902 Reclamation law refers to the *sale* of water to landowners, who are required to be residents. The landowners contended there was no *sale* of water in Imperial Valley, only delivery, and that the residency requirement thus did not apply to them. They argued further that since Congress had reenacted the acreage limitation specifically, while failing to mention the residency requirement, Section 5 had been superseded.

The court rejected both contentions. Judge Murray noted that in Ivanhoe Irrigation District v. McCracken there was no *sale* of water, but only procedural prescriptions governing water deliveries. "The formation of 'districts,'" he said, "is merely for administrative expediency. It is not meant to thwart the policy of Section 5."[97] The court quoted from *Ivanhoe* the statement that "where a particular project has been exempted (from reclamation law) because of its peculiar circumstances, the Congress has always made such exemptions by express enactment."[98]

Judge Murray then noted the close relationship between acreage limitation and residency as twin instruments for effectuating reclamation policy. First he quoted the Supreme Court's description of Congressional policy as "requiring that the benefits . . . be made available to the largest number of people, consistent, of course, with the public good," and to be "accomplished by limiting the quantity of land in a single ownership to which project water might be applied."[99] Immediately he added: "Residency, the companion requirement of the 160 acre limitation, will also further the policy of making the benefits from the act available to the largest number of people."[100]

The nonresident landowners argued that the residency requirement was a mere threshold requirement, disappearing within a few years or upon completion of final payment. Rejecting this contention, the court declared: "To so limit it, would be contrary to the whole tenor of Reclamation Law."[101]

---

96. Opinion, 118 Cong. Rec. E9067, E9068.
97. Id. at E9068.
98. Id.
99. Id.
100. Id.
101. Id.

C. *The Effect of Boulder Canyon Project Act on Imperial Valley.*

The landowners contended specifically that they held perfected water rights, a claim barring enforcement of residency. The court doubted the existence of any such rights in Imperial Valley at the time of the passage of the Boulder Canyon Project Act, and, in any case held the right "irrelevant because it need only be shown that the Imperial Irrigation District is deriving a benefit from the use of a government facility for reclamation law to be applicable."[102]

D. *The Rule of* Udall v. Tallman,[103] *Requiring Deference to Longstanding Administrative Constructions.*

The landowners contended that the Supreme Court, by its decision in the *Tallman* case, required deference to the 1933 administrative interpretation of Secretary of the Interior Ray Lyman Wilbur, who said acreage limitation was inapplicable to Imperial Valley, an interpretation no Secretary challenged until 1964. Judge Murray rejected the relevance of *Tallman* to the case at bar since *"Tallman* dealt with the construction of an administrative regulation," whereas "Section 5, far from being an administrative regulation, is an expression of national policy."[104]

E. *The Equal Protection Argument.*

Landowners argued that "a durational residency requirement would penalize their constitutionally protected right to travel." Judge Murray, however, found that the cases cited in support of their contention "involved laws which discriminate between *old* and *new* residents," and "say nothing about laws which discriminate between *residents* and *non-residents* as Section 5 does," which is "a permissible classification."[105]

Summing up, the court said:

> No conceivable purpose would be served by freeing the landowners from this [residency] requirement after they have acquired the immense benefits of federal subsidy. The law was not intended to provide supplemental income to former residents who have returned to San Diego, Burbank and other locations far removed from the Reclamation project. Accordingly, the residency requirement should not be waived upon final payment of construction costs of the project. Such a practice would reduce

---

102. Opinion, 118 Cong. Rec. E9069. "If this court had jurisdiction to determine this issue, it would hold that private landowners within the Imperial Valley Irrigation District have no vested and present perfected right to a continued supply of Colorado River water for irrigation purposes precluding application of the residency requirement of Section 5 of the Reclamation Act of 1902." Findings of Fact and Conclusions of Law, 16.
103. 380 U.S. 1 (1965).
104. Opinion, 118 Cong. Rec. E 9069.
105. *Id.*

the statutory limitations to a mere sham. Section 5 would then be nothing more than a financial test tailored to suit the more affluent who can afford to accelerate their payments, move off the project and reap the benefits of a federal subsidy. The policy of the Reclamation Law will best be advanced by imposing a durational requirement upon recipients of water from federal projects, even after the construction costs have been paid.[106]

In conclusion, Judge Murray reemphasized his reliance upon the language of reclamation law and its interpretation by the United States Supreme Court:

> Over the years the interpretations of Section 5 have been very much in conflict . . . . As a consequence of these conflicts, this court must look at the law itself and interpret it consistently with the Supreme Court's holding in *Arizona v. California* and *Ivanhoe Irrigation District v. McCracken.* . . .[107]

PERSPECTIVE

> . . . the requirement of residence . . . and that relative to the holding of more than one farm unit . . . are specific requirements of law, which the Service is necessarily compelled to enforce. . . . These laws having been frequently discussed . . . during the last ten years and more, they should have been known to all . . . persons purchasing land within the project. . . . Personally I think the law as to residence should be repealed. (First Assistant Secretary of the Interior E. C. Finney to Senator Samuel D. Nicholson, of Colorado, January 20, 1923.)

> Property is vigilant, active, sleepless; if ever it seems to slumber, be sure that one eye is open. (William Ewart Gladstone.)[108]

In 1902 the political problem of persuading Congress to open the doors of the national treasury to bring public waters to arid private

---

106. *Id.*, E 9068.
107. *Id.*, E 9069.
The Justice Department is faced again, as by the Turrentine decision, with making its own decision whether or not to appeal. Commenting on the import of the pending determination by the Justice Department, Congressman Jerome R. Waldie observed:
> "Now if the Justice Department insists on appellate review of the Murray decision, then what it is really saying is that when the administration's policy of interpreting the Reclamation Act in a manner favorable to corporate interests is upheld at any judicial level, then such decisions will be embraced. But when the intent of the law is held to be inimicable to those powerful interests, then the Justice Department will pursue the case to great lengths, seeking a reversal, and rendering the decision meaningless in the interim. . . . I am embarrassed that private parties have had to assume what should be the proper role of the Government in seeking judicial enforcement of the Reclamation Act. I will do whatever I can to bring pressure upon the Justice Department . . . and to bring to the public's attention what I consider to be law enforcement for the privileged few." 118 Cong. Rec. E9257 (daily ed. Nov. 8, 1972).

108. Morley, 3 Life of William Ewart Gladstone 469 (1903).

lands west of the hundredth meridian was solved.[109] The solution was to condition the release of funds, and thus water, upon compliance by its beneficiaries with traditional American land policy favoring actual settlers over speculators and monopolists. The purpose, in words of the Supreme Court fifty-six years later, was to "benefit people, not land," to prevent "use of the federal reclamation service for speculative purposes," and to assure that "this enormous expenditure will not go in disproportionate share to a few individuals with large land holdings."[110]

Linked to concern for equitable distribution of benefits was a desire to promote political stability. Congressman Francis G. Newlands of Nevada, sponsor of the reclamation bill, stressed the stabilizing influence of the public policy written into it:

> Lord Macauley said we never would experience the test of our institutions until our public domain was exhausted and an increased population engaged in a contest for the ownership of land. . . . Convey this land to private corporations and doubtless this work would be done, but we would have fastened upon this country all the evils of land monopoly which produced the great French revolution, which caused the revolt against church monopoly in South America, and which in recent times has caused the outbreak of the Filipinos against Spanish authority.[111]

The policy condition established by Congress rested on two requirements: a limitation on water deliveries to 160 acres per individual, and residency by the receiving landowner. Although the

---

109. Congressman James M. Robinson, of Indiana: "This bill affects us adversely who live outside the arid section." 35 Cong. Rec. 6734 (1902). In 1905 Judge (later Congressman) John E. Raker, of California, told the Thirteenth National Irrigation Congress: "The committee of seventeen that originally planned and arranged the adoption of the National Irrigation Law secured its adoption and presentation to Congress solely and entirely upon the question that the great land monopolies in the United States would be prohibited from getting the benefit of it." Proceedings of the Thirteenth National Irrigation Congress at Portland, Oregon, at 61 (1905).

110. Ivanhoe v. McCracken, 357 U.S. 275, 292 (1958).

111. 35 Cong. Rec. 6734 (1902). As President in 1902 Theodore Roosevelt signed the National Reclamation Law. In 1911 he gave the Commonwealth Club of California his reasons for approving its antimonopoly provisions:
> "I wish to save the very wealthy men of this country and their advocates and upholders from the ruin that they would bring upon themselves if they were permitted to have their way. It is because I am against revolution; it is because I am against the doctrines of the Extremists, of the Socialists; it is because I wish to see this country of ours continued as a genuine democracy; it is because I distrust violence and disbelieve in it; it is because I wish to secure this country against ever seeing a time when the 'have-nots' shall rise against the 'haves'; it is because I wish to secure for our children and our grandchildren and for their children's children the same freedom of opportunity, the same peace and order and justice that we have had in the past." 7 Transactions of the Commonwealth Club 108 (1912-13).

Supreme Court in 1958 had only the first of these requirements formally before it, the court's opinion referred approvingly to Section 5 of the 1902 Act which prescribed both "as re-enacted in the Omnibus Adjustment Act of 1926."[112]

Imperial Valley is but one among many localities served by federal reclamation where the condition attached by Congress to supplying public funds and water goes unobserved.[113] It is one of only three projects where the issue is currently under litigation.[114] So far, two opposed administrative rulings on the application of the law to Imperial Valley are matched by two opposed federal district court rulings. The outcome is pending on appeal.

This near-paralysis of public policy raises questions that go to the heart of the functioning of processes upon which democratic government depends. Does it suffice, as one court has suggested, to rest on the view that "law enforcement may better be left to the public officials. Any dereliction in duty by those officials is always subject to review by their superiors and to correction by impeachment, removal or by a refusal to re-elect"?[115] Are the "superiors" free of outside pressures or thoroughly resistant to them? "Washington is the political cynosure of the nation, and federal officials are . . . susceptible to the pressures of public exposure."[116] From which side do the strongest pressures come—from those favoring, or from those opposing observance and enforcement of law, and how much do pressures depend upon what law is in question?

John Gaus has suggested that public administration, its competence improved by a "good budget staff and a good personnel office," can "do more to preserve the liberties of the people than a good court, because they will be in operation long before a potential wrong is done." The question remains, however: Are pressures to undermine public policy from above and/or from the outside at times irresistible even by competent administrative staffs? Gaus himself answered the

---

112. Ivanhoe v. McCracken, 357 U.S. 275, 297 (1958).
113. For example: (1) Sacramento River diverters. *See* Taylor, *Testimony before House Subcommittee on Conservation and Natural Resources*, 91st Cong., 1st sess., 229-237 (1969); (2) San Luis unit, CVP. *See* Taylor, *Excess Land Law: Calculated Circumvention*, 52 Calif. L. Rev. 978 (1964); Taylor, Testimony Before Senate Committee on Interior and Insular Affairs, July 29, 1966; (3) Central Arizona Project. Congressman Donald L. Jackson, of California, quoting a Los Angeles Mirror editorial of July 9, 1949: "Some 55 percent of these 260,000 acres are owned by only 420 men. So what their scheme amounts to is simply subsidizing 420 wealthy landowners." 95 Cong. Rec. A4668 (1949).
114. U.S. v. Tulare Lake Canal Co. Civil No. 2483-ND (E.D. Cal. 1972) (Tulare Lake Basin); Bowker *et al.* v. Morton, Civil No. C-70 1274 (O.J.C. 1972) (California State Water Project).
115. State v. Miller, 164 Ohio St. 163, 128 N.E.2d 47, 51-52 (1955).
116. FCC v. Sanders Bros. Radio Station, 309 U.S. 470 (1940). *See* Jaffe, *Standing to Secure Judicial Review: Public Actions*, 74 Harv. L. Rev. 1265, 1313 (1961).

question by hastening to add that staffs and courts are "not alternatives."[117]

Congress created the office of Comptroller General of the United States to oversee acts of administrators executing its laws. This official is charged with reporting to Congress "every expenditure or contract made by any department or establishment in any year in violation of law." But creation of machinery to oversee law enforcement does not assure its use for the purpose intended.[118]

In each of the three branches of government the availability of proper procedures is of greatest importance. But availability does not alone assure equitable protection of diverse interests and preservation of public policy. Speaking of the judicial branch, Louis Jaffe has observed that, "Reliance on judicial control means reliance on rather unusual spurts of energy and expenditures of time and money by individual citizens or taxpayers."[119] Besides a sense of injury,

---

117. Gaus, Reflections on Public Administration, 110, 115 (1947).

118. 31 U.S.C. §53(c) (1971). The Comptroller General reported to Congress that on the San Luis unit of Central Valley Project the Bureau of Reclamation

> "may have difficulty in obtaining recordable contracts from several ineligible landowners who own substantial acreage in the service area and that, therefore, 76 percent of the irrigable land in the Westlands service area may not become eligible for project water . . . three landowners who together owned about 25 percent of the acreage had not signed recordable contracts, although some of this land could be served by the existing distribution system if the land were owned by eligible landowners." He made no comment on the Bureau's failure to observe an unrepealed 1914 law prescribing that "before any contract is let or work begun for the construction of any reclamation project hereafter adopted the Secretary of the Interior shall require the owners of private lands thereunder to agree to dispose of all lands in excess of the area which he shall deem sufficient for the support of a family upon the land in question. . . ."

Reclamation and Irrigation of Lands by Federal Government 43 U.S.C. §418 (1971). Neither did the Comptroller General cite Senator Kuchel, of California, who said in debate on the Senate floor with Senator Paul H. Douglas, of Illinois, over the latter's doubt that acreage limitation actually would be enforced on San Luis unit:

> "The Senator from Illinois understands, does he not, that under Federal reclamation law, when a project such as this one is authorized by Congress, the Secretary of the Interior is required in advance of construction to enter into contracts with the landowners—the farmers—in the area, so that there will be no question about the engineering and economic feasibility of the project? The Senator is aware of that requirement of the law, is he not?" 105 Cong. Rec. 7862 (1959).

Instead, the Comptroller General suggested that Congress give consideration to a proposal by the largest corporate landowner on the project that, for a moderate payment, owners be allowed to retain and to receive water for their entire excess holdings. Questionable aspects concerning construction and operation of the San Luis unit CVP, 16. Feb. 12, 1970.

119. 74 Harv. L. Rev. 1265, 1287 (1961). Between service as President and as Supreme Court Justice, William Howard Taft said: "We must make it so that the poor man will have as nearly as possible an equal opportunity in litigating as the rich man; and under present conditions, ashamed as we may be of it, this is not the fact." Final report of the Commission on Industrial Relations, 52 (1915). In the same spirit the Senate Subcommittee on Migratory Labor entitled recent hearings *Migrant and Seasonal Farmworker Powerlessness* (1970).

knowledge of what to do, organization and financial resources are necessary to meet substantial costs of often prolonged procedures.

Imbalance in political power between the landed and the landless is notable. Awareness of this fact is the key to historic national land policy. In 1820 Daniel Webster, citing the first two centuries since arrival of the Pilgrims, said: "The consequence of all these causes has been a great subdivision of the soil, and a great equality of condition; the true basis most certainly of popular government."[120]

The importance of equitable distribution of landownership has not disappeared in the modern era of reclamation. Commenting on a proposed extension of reclamation in Arizona where acreage limitation and residency requirements have long gone unobserved,[121] Congressman Donald L. Jackson, of California, told the House in 1949:

> . . . it does seem that when a large number of individual landowners have substantial holdings in the proposed project and spend considerable money for the promotion of that project in lobbying the Congress of the United States it is something that should be looked into by the Members of the House of Representatives.[122]
>
> o o o
>
> Think of it, 140,000,000 American citizens paying income taxes for the benefit of 420 rich Arizonians, each one getting a $500,000 chunk of your money, for nothing.[123]

A decade later, in 1959, Senator Paul H. Douglas, of Illinois, spoke with equal emphasis of the relative political powerlessness of the landless to protect their own interest in the fruits of an enforced excess land law:

> I know of the pressure in California in support of large farms and large agricultural holding. . . . The advocates of such holdings are powerful, whereas the small farmers who might use that land are in the future; and they are therefore, for the present, nonexistent. It is always hard for the indefinite future to compete with the powerful present.

And again he said:

> I have seen enough of the operations of the Department of the Interior . . . to know it is one thing to get . . . [acreage

---

120. Webster, Discourse Delivered at Plymouth 53, 54 (3d ed. 1825). In commemoration of the first settlement in New England, given Dec. 22, 1820.
121. Statement of Klaus G. Loewald, *Hearings on S.1425, S.2541, and S.3448 Before Senate Subcommittee on Irrigation and Reclamation* 85th Cong., 2nd Sess., 230-238 (1958).
122. 95 Cong. Rec. 10131 (1949).
123. 95 Cong. Rec. A4668 (1949).

limitation] in the law, and it is another thing to get it carried out as you face a mighty combination of landowners.[124]

The winds of politics have bent the law in Imperial Valley for a long time.

---

124. 104 Cong. Rec. 17732 (1958); 105 Cong. Rec. 7495 (1959).

MEXICAN MIGRATION
AND THE
160-ACRE WATER LIMITATION

Mexican Migration and the 160-Acre Water Limitation

Paul S. Taylor*

The author traces the parallel histories of the Mexican migration and U.S. land reclamation practice, focusing on the contrast between the asserted goals of public land reclamation policies and actual patterns of ownership. He urges Mexican Americans to take an active role in seeking enforcement or reform of the reclamation laws.

For more than 50 years, Mexican immigrants and *braceros* have been a primary labor source for irrigated farms of the western United States. Fleeing the turmoil of a Mexican agrarian revolution, more Mexicans than at any prior or subsequent time came to this country between 1912 and 1930. They came to the land which Congress, through the National Reclamation Act of 1902, had intended to provide for the landless. Regrettably, this Act has gone largely unenforced and the national purpose embodied therein unfulfilled. Ironically, migrants from Mexico and their descendants now occupy a position in the United States much like that which spurred their flight from Mexico, a position which the National Reclamation Act sought to prevent.

Historical accidents as well as weaknesses in legislation and its administration have thwarted the distribution of landownership among the many. At the same time structural and technological changes in agriculture have been diminishing the numbers of working farmers and farm workers, and generating pressures which tend to reinforce the existence of large agglomerations of land.

Yet in opposition to this general trend, a few Mexican-American farm workers have acquired farms which they operate with notable success. Whether such projects signal a new trend is a question for the future; the answer will depend on the winds of politics, law, economics, and the shaping of purpose among farm workers themselves.

---

* Professor of Economics Emeritus, University of California, Berkeley; consultant to the Office of the Secretary of the Interior and Bureau of Reclamation successively between 1943 and 1952. Martha Chase and Stefan Jovanovich assisted in preparation of this paper. The Institute of Business and Economic Research and the Committee on Research of the University of California, Berkeley, gave support.

I

No right to the use of water for land in private ownership shall be sold for a tract exceeding one hundred and sixty acres to any one landowner, and no such sale shall be made to any landowner unless he be an actual bona fide resident on such land, or occupant thereof residing in the neighborhood of said land . . . .

National Reclamation Act (1902)[1]

* * *

The Nation shall have at all times the right to impose on private property such limitations as the public interest may demand . . . . For this purpose necessary measures shall be taken . . . to divide large landed estates . . . to develop small landed holdings . . . to establish new centers of rural population with such lands and waters as may be indispensable to them . . . .

Mexican Constitution (1917)[2]

Despite the serious obstacles that have impeded its practical effect, the declared policy in both the United States and Mexico for over two generations has been that land should be distributed among working farmers. Beginning with the Preemption Act of 1841,[3] the United States Congress passed three significant pieces of legislation attempting to effectuate this policy. The Preemption Act was enacted to halt the practice of acquiring paper title to lands already developed by settlers. These titled speculators had forced the settler either to share land whose value he had improved by his labors or to give it up. The Homestead Act,[4] passed in 1862, opened 160 acres of public land to each actual settler on condition that he reside on the land and develop it. Finally, Congress passed the National Reclamation Act in 1902. It imposed a residency requirement and 160-acre limit on individual landholdings to receive water from federal reclamation projects.[5]

Urging adoption of these limitations, the bill's sponsors had cited recent Latin American and Philippine revolts against land monopolies. Failure to include acreage limitation in the reclamation bill to prevent monopoly "would have fastened upon this country all the evils of land monopoly which produced the great French revolution, which caused the revolt against church monopoly in South America and which in recent

---

1. 43 U.S.C. § 431 (1902).
2. CONSTITUCIÓN FEDERAL art. 27 (Mexico, 1917), *translated in* E. SIMPSON, THE EJIDO: MEXICO'S WAY OUT 66 (1937).
3. Act of Sept. 4, 1841, ch. 16, 5 Stat. 453.
4. Act of May 20, 1862, ch. 75, 12 Stat. 392.
5. 43 U.S.C. § 431 (1902).

times has produced the outbreak of the Filipinos against Spanish authority," said Congressman Francis Newlands of Nevada.[6]

Congressional debate made reference to other dangers to stability. Congressman John Dalzell of Pennsylvania pointed out:

> [A reclamation program] would draw off the surplus of unemployed labor in the East in any period of hard times, and . . . act as a safety valve and preserve stable conditions beneficial to both labor and capital. It would relieve us of the greatest danger to our social stability which confronts us today—the danger arising from the possible throwing out of employment of a multitude of men in some period of business depression, such as we passed through a few years ago. In such times as that strikes and riots are inevitable, and we have had experience enough in the past to show their danger.[7]

The desire was to preserve an open door of opportunity on the land. Thomas F. Walsh, President of the private National Irrigation Association, described anticipated benefits to "farmers' boys growing to manhood, who want the same chance . . . that their fathers had in the earlier days when land was easy to get in the great Mississippi Valley; or . . . tenant farmers, longing to own the land they cultivate."[8] Congressman Wesley Jones of Washington stressed the importance of what had come to be called the "agricultural ladder." He pictured reclamation as a way to preserve the opportunity for people to advance.

> The great result from this bill will be the happy homes that will be built in our own country and more loyal citizens to our flag and the principles it represents. To take the fruits of one's toil and give to another, to work from day to day and eke out a mere miserable existence for oneself and family, to live without hope of bettering one's condition, is not conducive to noble manhood or loyal citizenship.[9]

This view of the reclamation bill and a proper role for farm labor was not unanimous. Gilbert M. Tucker, editor of *The Country Gentleman* magazine, spoke for eastern farmers who depended on hired laborers to work their farms and who feared "absorption by the free lands of the men and women who ought to supply, and in the normal condition of things would supply, an abundance of labor, at moderate wages, for established farmers."[10]

The issue was clear: Was the tiller to have a chance at independence on a farm of his own? Congress answered affirmatively by passing the reclamation bill to irrigate arid western lands. The bill's sponsors gave unstinted assurances that the acreage limitation and residency

---

6. 35 CONG. REC. 6734 (1902). The Mexican revolution had not yet broken out.
7. *Id.* at 6739.
8. S. DOC. NO. 446, 57th Cong., 1st Sess. 29 (1902).
9. 35 CONG. REC. 6755 (1902).
10. *Id.* at 6724.

requirement would effectively provide an opportunity for independent, individual farm ownership. Congressman Eben W. Martin of South Dakota said: "The bill is drawn exclusively for the protection of the settler and actual homebuilder and every possible safeguard is made against speculative ownership and the concentration of the lands or water privileges into large holdings."[11]

Congressman Frank Mondell of Wyoming assured Congress:
> [The acreage limitation and residency provisions were] drawn with a view of breaking up any large land holdings which might exist in the vicinity of the Government works and to insure occupancy by the owner of the land reclaimed. . . .
>
> No law ever presented to any legislative body has been so carefully drawn with a view of preventing the possibility of speculative ownership in lands. . . .[12]

Thus, historic national land policy was formulated to be applied to the irrigation of arid and semiarid western lands, both public and private.

II

> *Comrades: A little more than four months ago the Red Banner of the Proletariat floated on the battle fields of Mexico, sustained by emancipated workers, whose aspirations are epitomized in the sublime cry—"Land and Liberty."*
>
> *Liberal Party Manifesto (1911)*[13]

The course of agrarian affairs in Mexico stands in contrast to that in the United States. In 1910, rebellion followed the ousting of Dictator-President Porfirio Diaz. The following year, an illiterate sharecropper named Emiliano Zapata catalyzed open and widespread agrarian revolt. He issued his Plan de Ayala as a warning to Diaz's replacement Francisco Madero, a warning of the urgent necessity to press for agrarian reform.

The Plan declared:
> Let Señor Madero—and with him all the world—know that we shall not lay down our arms until the *ejidos* of our villages are restored to us, until we are given back the lands which the *hacendados* stole from us during the dictatorship of Porfirio Diaz, when justice was subjected to his caprice. We shall not lay down our arms until we cease to be the unhappy tributaries of the despotic magnates and landholders of Morelos . . . .[14]

---

11. *Id.* at 6758.
12. *Id.* at 6678.
13. *Translated in* SIMPSON, THE EJIDO: MEXICO'S WAY OUT 49 n.14 (1937).
14. *Id.* at 51. Zapata was assassinated in 1919.

For a decade Mexico was in turmoil as one leader replaced another. Whether agrarian reform would emerge as the central issue from military and political struggles for power was uncertain until Venustiano Carranza issued the Decree of 1915. Supporting the agrarian aspirations of the Mexican masses, the Decree took its place along with Zapata's Plan as a forerunner to article 27 of the Mexican Constitution.[15] But despite proclamations and even a constitutional provision, realization of substantial land distribution came slowly, and spasmodically.

Not until the late 1930's, when President Lazaro Cardenas "distributed more land to the peasants than had been distributed in all the years since the beginning of the Revolution,"[16] was major progress made in the land reform program. This distribution occurred after the high tide of emigration to the United States in the 1920's and during a period of repatriation under the impact of depression in the United States.[17] At least temporarily, Mexico's political safety valve of emigration had ceased to function.

III

Goodbye, my beloved country,
Now I am going away;
I go to the United States,
where I intend to work.

Corrido, *An Emigrant's Farewell (late 1920's).*[18]

* * *

What they say about us
is nearly all the truth,
but we left the country
from sheer necessity.

Corrido, *Defense of the Emigrants (late 1920's).*[19]

In 1850, just after the treaty transferring title to the Southwest, there were fewer than 14,000 people of Mexican birth in the United

---

15. *Id.* at 54. The decree recognized that villagers had been unable to protect their property and were left with no "recourse but to hire themselves out at ridiculous wages to the powerful landlords." *Quoted in id.* at 57.
16. L. SIMPSON, MANY MEXICOS 288 (1952).
17. During the years 1930-33, Mexico officially reported 306,628 repatriates. Taylor, *Mexican Labor in the United States: Migration Statistics*, 12 UNIV. CAL. PUBL. ECON. (1934). *See also* A. HOFFMAN, UNWANTED MEXICAN AMERICANS: REPATRIATION PRESSURES DURING THE GREAT DEPRESSION (1973).
18. Taylor, *Songs of the Mexican Migration*, in PURO MEXICANO 222 (J. Dobie ed. 1935).
19. *Id.* at 238.

States.[20] Over 12,000 of these resided in the southwestern states and territories where the Spanish pattern of large land grants prevailed. During the second half of the nineteenth century, migration from Mexico was meager and mainly confined to within 100 miles of the border, with migrants crossing and recrossing the border frequently. Not until 1908 did the United States Immigration Service even report the annual number of Mexican immirgants.

By the early 1900's construction of railways from the interior of Mexico to the international border enabled more people to migrate. The flow was largely seasonal, migrants moving both ways, serving the labor needs of railway track construction and working the adjacent crops in the United States. This transborder movement began prior to the end of the Diaz regime and the outbreak of revolution in Mexico; still, the influence of agrarian dissatisfaction could already be discerned. A distinguished American observer commented in 1908:

> What is sometimes called the "peon country" (the group of States . . . [newly opened to emigration by the Mexican railways]) appears to be precisely where these little villages of feudal tenants are most common, and one of the most interesting secondary effects of the tide of emigration starting northward from this section to the United States is its probable influence in breaking up the patriarchal organization of agriculture and landholding in Mexico.[21]

The real surge of Mexican migration to the United States followed the displacement of Diaz in 1910. From 1905 to 1910, the United States Immigration Service had reported an estimated 21,732 immigrants from Mexico. Between 1915 and 1920 the number rose to 91,075. The Mexican Revolution, United States entry into World War I, and the enactment of quota laws in the 1920's limiting immigration from Europe stimulated immigration from Mexico. Between 1925 and 1930 the number of recorded Mexican immigrants reached 238,527, 10 times the number that had come 20 years earlier.[22] The tightening of border controls,[23] and the Great Depression brought heavy return movement to Mexico. Between 1930 and 1935, emigration from the United States expanded and immigration fell to a low of 19,200. The level of immigration was not to increase again significantly until the 1950's.[24]

---

20. BUREAU OF CENSUS, STATISTICS, xxxvii (1850) (the figure given is 13,317).
21. Clark, *Mexican Labor in the United States*, 78 U.S. BUREAU LABOR BULL. 468 (1908).
22. L. GREBLER, J. MOORE & R. GUZMAN, THE MEXICAN-AMERICAN PEOPLE 64 (1970) [hereinafter cited as GREBLER] (the first figure for 1905-10 is an estimate).
23. Taylor, *More Bars Against Mexicans?*, 64 THE SURVEY 26 (1930).
24. GREBLER, *supra* note 22, at 64.

IV

> *American laborers will not generally submit to the standard of living acceptable to the [immigrant] migratory farm labor of the West.*
>
> United States Immigration Commission (1911).[25]

* * *

> *If the farm labor of which we are now desperately in need could be secured from the congested centers within the United States we would not be here asking for help.*
>
> Harry A. Austin, Secretary, United States Sugar Manufacturers' Association (1926).[26]

* * *

> *Somebody, somewhere, has to do hard physical labor because it is here to be done. . . . Under our present system of education, we must either bring somebody in here to do our hard work or we must go elsewhere for our foodstuffs and clothing.*
>
> Ralph H. Taylor, Executive Secretary, Agricultural Legislative Committee, California (1928).[27]

The high tide of immigration that brought 678,291 reported immigrants from Mexico between 1911 and 1930,[28] coincided with notable agricultural development in the five southwestern states of Arizona, California, Colorado, New Mexico, and Texas. The development was stimulated by federal reclamation of water resources, both underground and stored flood waters, and it spread rapidly to arid and semiarid lands. Production of fruits and vegetables which were to be sold largely in eastern markets, and of sugar beets, which enjoyed protective tariffs, expanded. Cotton growing, historically confined to the Cotton Kingdom of the South, rapidly moved west to Arizona and California.

The labor requirements for each of these crops were high in peak seasons but low in slack. The lack of continuous employment in the same crop and the same area made seasonal migration from region to region common.

This pattern, already familiar to the West, was directly attributable to the high concentration of landownership. James Bryce described this land and labor pattern prevalent in California as early as 1889:

---

25. IMMIGRATION COMM'N, IMMIGRANTS IN INDUSTRIES, S. DOC. NO. 633, 61st Cong., 2d Sess. 151 (1911).
26. *Hearings on Seasonal Agricultural Laborers from Mexico Before the House Comm. on Immigration and Naturalization*, 69th Cong., 1st Sess. 251-52 (1926).
27. *Hearings on Immigration from Countries of the Western Hemisphere Before the House Comm. on Immigration and Naturalization*, 70th Cong., 1st Sess. 307 (1928).
28. 1973 IMMIGRATION AND NATURALIZATION SERVICE ANN. REP. 54.

When California was ceded to the United States, land speculators bought up large tracts under Spanish titles, and others, foreseeing the coming prosperity, subsequently acquired great domains by purchase, either from the railways which had received land grants, or directly from the government. Some of these speculators, by holding their lands for a rise, made it difficult for immigrants to acquire small freeholds, and in some cases checked the growth of farms. Others let their land on short leases to farmers, who thus came into a comparatively precarious and often necessitous condition; others established enormous farms, in which the soil is cultivated by hired labourers, many of whom are discharged after the harvest—a phenomenon rare in the United States, which is elsewhere a country of moderately sized farms, owned by persons who do most of the labour by their own and their children's hands. Thus the land system of California presents features both peculiar and dangerous, a contrast between great properties, often appearing to conflict with the general weal, and the sometimes hard pressed small farmer, together with a mass of unsettled labour, thrown without work into the towns at certain times of the year.[29]

During the 1890's, westerners gathered nearly every year at national irrigation congresses to seek ways to promote irrigation. They asserted that with the coming of water this landownership and labor pattern would be broken. As stated above, the devices Congress chose to enable more people to own land were the requirement that individuals receive water for no more than 160 acres and that they be residents on the land or in the neighborhood.[30]

Writing these requirements into the 1902 statute, however, did not assure the occupation of western irrigated lands by farmers tilling their own soil. Several factors explain this gap between policy goals and their realization during this period of intensifying Mexican immigration. First, early projects in the Southwest, of which Imperial Valley was the largest, were privately constructed prior to passage of the 1902 Act. Therefore, federal reclamation law did not apply to them. Second, the construction of federal reclamation projects proceeded slowly. During the first 27 years of federal reclamation, while Mexican immigration was rising to the peak of the 1920's, only $240 million was spent on irrigation projects. During the next 27 years, *after* immigra-

---

29. 2 J. BRYCE, THE AMERICAN COMMONWEALTH 427 (7th ed. 1923).
30. Taylor, *Water, Land and the People in the Great Valley*, 5 AM. WEST 24 (1968). *See also* epigraph accmmpanying note 1 *supra*. For land and labor background, see M. Cooper, Land, Water and Settlement in Kern County, California: 1850-90, Nov. 6, 1953 (unpublished master's thesis in the Graduate Social Science Library, Univ. of Cal., Berkeley); *Hearings on Violations of Free Speech and Rights of Labor Before a Subcomm. of the Senate Comm. on Education and Labor*, 74th Cong., 3d Sess. 19,777 (1940) [hereinafter cited as *Hearings on Free Speech*].

tion had slackened, $3.2 billion was spent.[31] The great California Central Valley Project, for example, was not begun until the mid-1930's, and still is incomplete. Third, the Arizona Salt River Project was authorized in 1903 under reclamation law, but the law's acreage limitation and residency provision have never been enforced there.[32] Fourth, not until 1928 was Imperial Valley brought under reclamation law in the Boulder Canyon Project. Whether the law is to be enforced there is an issue currently before the courts.[33]

With construction of reclamation projects retarded and the antimonopoly and residency provisions of the law unenforced, immigrant Mexicans entering western agriculture filled the labor niche planned for them by large landed employers. As Bryce had noted in the 1880's, landless laborers were employed seasonally in ever larger numbers and denied access to landownership. According to the 1970 census, only 4.3 percent of those born in Mexico and only 6.7 percent of the second generation, those born in the United States of Mexican parents, had become farmers or managers in the five southwestern states.[34] The result of this agricultural labor pattern is the polarization of rural society in the western United States. While in the country as a whole, the average percentage of "farm personnel" belonging to the "lower class" in 1959 was 31.1 percent, in California the percentage was 55.7, and in Arizona 71.4. In Imperial Valley, California, where reclamation law is unobserved, the "lower class"

---

31. THE LIBRARY OF CONG. LEGIS. REF. SERV., 86TH CONG., 1ST SESS., REPORT TO THE HOUSE COMM. ON INTERIOR AND INSULAR AFFAIRS: RECLAMATION—ACCOMPLISHMENTS AND CONTRIBUTIONS 50 (Comm. Print No. 1, 1959).

32. When Congress was considering expansion of reclamation in that area in 1949, Congressman Donald Jackson of California explained:

Not one acre . . . would be available to veterans or other worthy Americans who wished to find farm homes. The great landowners, individuals, and corporations, own it and it is reasonable to assume in the light of past history, that they would take the profits from it.

It is true that under reclamation law, each individual ownership is entitled to 160 acres of irrigated land. . . .

True, the Bureau of Reclamation says that the 160-acre law will be enforced if the Arizona project is built. But we know that this law has never been enforced there. There is no reason to believe it will be enforced in the future. Rather, there is every reason to believe that it will not be enforced.

95 CONG. REC. 10,128 (1949). See also Hearings on S. 1425 Before the Subcomm. on Irrigation and Reclamation of the Senate Comm. on Interior and Insular Affairs, 85th Cong., 2d Sess. 231 (1958) [hereinafter cited as Hearings on S. 1425].

33. Compare Yellen v. Hickel, 352 F. Supp. 1300 (S.D. Cal. 1972) with United States v. Imperial Irrigation Dist., 322 F. Supp. 11 (S.D. Cal. 1971), appeals docketed and joined, Civil No. 73-1333 (9th Cir., Nov. 29, 1972) and Civil No. 73-1388 (9th Cir., Dec. 14, 1972). See also Taylor, Water, Land and Environment, Imperial Valley: Law Caught in the Winds of Politics, 13 NAT. RES. J. 1 (1973).

34. 1970 BUREAU OF CENSUS, SUBJECT REPORTS, PERSONS OF SPANISH SURNAMES 61, 78.

mostly of Mexican birth or parentage, reached 87.3 percent.[35]

V

This excess [urban] labor force grew larger over the years . . . as the growth of agribusiness forced more small farmers and farm workers off the land.
          Ira Eisenberg (1974).[36]

* * *

[M]*ore than a year ago, 30 Chicano farm worker families formed a strawberry co-op, borrowed $175,000 from Wells Fargo Bank and $100,000 from the federal government.*

Today, the bank loan is paid off, the co-op owns its own machinery and the workers are looking this year for an income between $9,000 and $11,000 a family . . . .
          Joel Tlumak (1972).[37]

Over the years Mexican immigrants to the United States have generally gathered together in *barrios*, neighborhoods where inherited culture and language survive through daily use. Rarely did immigrants apply for United States citizenship. Ultimate return to Mexico was thought of as normal, however improbable in actuality. Thus, in contrast to the previous experience of most migrations to the United States from Europe, Mexican assimilation was retarded for almost two generations.[38] Until they realized that their future lay in the United States, Mexican Americans had little reason to concern themselves with the land acquisition opportunity afforded them under reclamation law.[39]

Mexican Americans have accepted the role of farm wage worker though they have not been content with this role. Their record is one of protest in the form of strikes, boycotts, and a succession of attempts

---

35. Smith, *A Study of Social Stratification in the Agricultural Sections of the U.S.*, 34 RURAL SOCIOL. 496, 506-08 (1969).

36. Eisenberg, *The People and the Police*, San Francisco Sunday Examiner & Chronicle, May 26, 1974 (California Living), at 8.

37. San Francisco Sunday Examiner and Chronicle, Aug. 27, 1972, at 1, col. 6.

In the Salinas-Watsonville area, government funds (your tax dollars) are being used to help the disadvantaged get into farming. This is either good or bad depending upon one's political, social and economic point of view. It might be a good investment if a few hundred thousand of your dollars would get some families off welfare and into a productive, tax-paying position.

CAL. FARMER, June 17, 1972, at 7.

38. It is perhaps characteristic that a Mexican-American . . . whose parents had immigrated . . . remembers continual family discussion of an early return to the homeland, until he himself, at the age of eighteen, recognized that "he was here to stay."

GREBLER, *supra* note 22, at 63-64.

39. To this day no Mexican American has challenged in court the failure of administrators to enforce acreage limitation and residency provision along the Salt River in Arizona. *Cf.* the statement of Congressman Jackson quoted *supra* note 31.

to organize and bargain collectively with their employers.[40] Nonenforcement of reclamation law cannot be accurately explained by the indifference or inaction of the landless—Mexican Americans among them. The central problem arose from the fact that potentially irrigable lands had largely passed into private hands long before public reclamation became a reality. This created special interests resistant to the controls over monopoly and speculation incorporated in the 1902 reclamation law. As early as 1877, this fact was noted in California's Central Valley:

> [N]o one would believe that shrewd, calculating businessmen would invest their money on the strength of this land rising in value while unimproved, for even the farmer himself has to abandon it who endeavors to add to its value without water. At the same time, purchasers are not lacking who would add it to their already extensive dry domain and the people . . . will find themselves confronted by an array of force and talent to secure to capital the ownership of the water as well as of the land, and the people will at last have it to pay for.[41]

An early study by the Bureau of Reclamation disclosed a 759 percent increase in land value attributable to irrigation.[42] To prevent these windfall profits by large landowners, Congress prescribed in 1926 that the sale price of excess lands be limited to their value "without reference to the proposed construction of the irrigation works."[43] Enactment of the 1926 statute did not assure its enforcement, nor end disputes over the allocation of the additional value, however.

The longer the owners of excess lands were allowed by administrative ruling to postpone sale after the coming of water, the greater the chance for gain. As Harry W. Horton, Chief Counsel of Imperial Irrigation District, testified to Congress in reference to a ruling allowing 10 years time to sell the excess:

> Let us lay the cards on the table . . . . I will give you my own opinion of Jack O'Neill's willingness to sign the 160-acre limitation. He thinks if he gets water for 10 years on there without having to sell it, he can make enough money out of it so he can afford to sell it at any old price.[44]

---

40. *See* E. GALARZA, MERCHANTS OF LABOR (1964); E. GALARZA, SPIDERS IN THE HOUSE AND WORKERS IN THE FIELD (1970). *See also Hearings on Free Speech, supra* note 30, at 17,207-20.
41. The Visalia Delta [Cal.], May 5, 1877, at 2, col. 3.
42. *Hearings on Exemption of Certain Projects from Land-Limitation Provisions of Federal Reclamation Laws Before a Subcomm. of the Senate Public Lands Comm.*, 80th Cong., 1st Sess. 204 (1947).
43. 43 U.S.C. § 423(e) (1926).
44. *Hearings on S. 1425, supra* note 32, at 87-88.

Nearly a quarter of a century after enactment of the original reclamation law a citizens' committee of special advisers appointed by the Secretary of the Interior had recommended that "weaknesses in the original law [should] be corrected, since they are largely responsible for the difficulties that have arisen and are still apparent in the execution of the reclamation act."[45] Their report had stated:

> Although the Reclamation Service attempted to compel the subdivision of these privately owned lands into the units fixed by law, yet the legal enforcement was found difficult; and what was still worse, in many cases the owners of the land capitalized the Government expenditures and the liberality of its terms of repayment by selling the lands to the settlers at much higher prices than could otherwise have been obtained. The benefits of the reclamation act, therefore, went in such cases almost entirely to these speculative owners . . . .[46]

In 1926, within two years of the committee report, Congress had sought to rectify this weakness by prescribing that the windfall profits from reclamation projects initiated after 1926 should not go to owners of excess land. It declared:

> [A]ll irrigable land held in private ownership by any one owner in excess of one hundred and sixty irrigable acres shall be appraised . . . and the sale prices thereof fixed by the Secretary on the basis of its actual bona fide value at the date of appraisal without reference to the proposed construction of the irrigation works . . . .[47]

Here again a reclamation statute was to prove wanting. No civil or criminal penalties were prescribed for violation of the law by a recipient of project water. Administrative interpretations of the meaning of "without reference to the proposed construction of the irrigation works" were arrived at in a relaxed atmosphere. Neither observance nor enforcement was forthcoming. In 1965, for example, when the DiGiorgio Corporation was divesting itself of excess lands in Delano-Earlimart and Arvin-Edison water districts in California's Central Valley, the corporation distributed a fact sheet among prospective purchasers. With reference to sale prices it said: "The Bureau has indicated that it will not withhold approval for any transaction within reason."[48]

The issue persists: Should the excess landowner, the purchaser of excess land, or the public treasury receive the profit created by reclamation? In *Ivanhoe v. McCracken*,[49] the United States Supreme Court

---

45. S. Doc. No. 92, 68th Cong., 1st Sess. 38-39 (1924).
46. *Id.*
47. 43 U.S.C. § 423(e) (1926).
48. Letter from Di Giorgio Corp. to all interested parties, Aug. 27, 1965, on file in *California Law Review* offices.
49. Ivanhoe v. McCracken, 357 U.S. 275 (1958).

indicated that the benefit was not to inure solely to the large landowner. According to the Court:

> The project was designed to benefit people, not land. It is a reasonable classification to limit the amount of project water available to each individual in order that benefits may be distributed in accordance with the greatest good to the greatest number of individuals. The limitation insures that this enormous expenditure will not go in disproportionate share to a few individuals with large land holdings. Moreover, it prevents the use of the federal reclamation service for speculative purposes.[50]

In 1970, the Public Land Law Review Commission recommended the acreage limitation and residency requirement be abandoned in an age of expensive technology which requires large land holdings to make agricultural industry economically feasible.[51] Three years later the National Water Commission professed that "it would not do to abolish the limitation if the effect would be to confer large windfall gains on reclamation farmers;"[52] *i.e.*, upon private landowners. On the other hand, it recommended waiver of acreage limitation at the option of irrigation districts or landowners if money payments were made, though the payments admittedly "would not fully recapture the subsidy granted to irrigation water."[53]

Subsidy and windfall profits are not the same. While the Natural Water Commission recommended abolition of subsidy on future projects, it was silent on windfall profits. Apparently it relies on its contractor who, in substance, holds the view that reclamation law is unconcerned with windfall profits. For despite the 1926 language requiring that the sale price of excess land be set "without reference to the proposed construction of the irrigation works," the contractor contends:

> A landowner has a right to be compensated . . . for what the market determines [his excess land] . . . to be worth. . . . The advent of project water is typically discounted in land value long years before the arrival of the water on the project lands. This being the case, the [purchaser of] . . . pre-project lands would pay close to a price for land that reflected its post-project value. . . .[54]

Apparently the National Water Commission accepts this view of the innocuousness of congressional legislation.

---

50. *Id.* at 297.
51. PUBLIC LAND LAW REVIEW COMMISSION, ONE THIRD OF THE NATION'S LAND 182-84 (1970).
52. NATIONAL WATER COMMISSION, WATER POLICIES FOR THE FUTURE 148 (1973).
53. *Id.* at 149.
54. H. HOGAN, THE ACREAGE LIMITATION IN THE FEDERAL RECLAMATION PROGRAM 289 (Nat'l Tech. Inf. Serv. Publ. 1972). The National Water Commission stated that the "background and operation of the acreage limitation . . . [were] taken largely" from the report of Mr. Hogan. NATIONAL WATER COMMISSION, *supra* note 52, at 142.

An alternative to the views of the two Commissions was placed before both Houses of Congress but did not receive a hearing. This proposal, called the Reclamation Lands Authority Act, built upon the 1926 language "without reference to the proposed construction of the irrigation works," and would have made it administratively effective by authorizing the government itself to purchase the excess lands. This would have diverted the windfall profits created by public reclamation into the public treasury,[55] and assured a lower investment cost to the landless person acquiring a farm under reclamation law.

VI

> *This timely movement, looking to the reclamation of Arid America, thus giving "land to the landless," ranks in real importance with the foremost public measuers of the times.*
>
> *Harrison Gray Otis (1902)*[56]

* * *

> *Applicants [for permission to intervene in suit to compel observance of acreage limitation law] have shown no present ability to purchase and no prior offers within the past twenty years to purchase farm land in the Imperial Valley at market value . . . .*
>
> *Judge Howard B. Turrentine (1971).*[57]

Despite comprising one-third of the population of Imperial Valley and most of its agricultural labor force, Mexican Americans did not challenge nonobservance of reclamation law in the Valley. The Government acted first. Based on a 1964 opinion by the Solicitor of the Interior, the Government, after some 30 years of nonenforcement, brought suit in 1967 to enforce acreage limitation in the Valley.[58]

The next move was made by a Valley physician from Brooklyn who undertook active support of the Government's case. "Dr. Yellen rounded up 123 non-landowners—many of them farm-workers who could not get jobs because the big growers use illegal Mexican labor—and hired a lawyer to file an *amicus* brief on their behalf . . . ."[59] A local newspaper reported:

> Most of the petitioners are farm workers who have been or are now employed as agricultural laborers . . . . None presently own farm land anywhere in the United States.

---

55. S. 2863, H.R. 5236, 92d Cong., 1st Sess. (1971); 117 CONG. REC. 11,201-02 (1971) (remarks of Rep. Kastenmeier).
56. Proceedings of the Ninth National Irrigation Congress, Chicago, 240.
57. Ben Yellen, Application to Intervene, United States v. Imperial Irrigation Dist., Civil No. 67-7-T (S.D. Cal., March 29, 1971).
58. United States v. Imperial Irrigation Dist., 322 F. Supp. 11 (S.D. Cal. 1971), *appeal docketed*, Civil No. 73-1388 (9th Cir., Dec. 14, 1972).
59. Kinsley, *Ben Yellen's Fine Madness*, 2 Wash. Monthly, January 1971, at 44.

Most of the privately-owned irrigable land within Imerpial Irrigation District is owned by persons who do not reside on or near such lands. All of the petitioners desire to own land of their own upon which to engage in farming; and to be able to purchase irrigable lands within IID which will be sold if the government obtains a favorable decision in the case.[60]

In 1971 federal district court Judge Howard B. Turrentine ruled against the Government and held that the acreage limitation does not apply to privately-owned land in Imperial Valley.[61] Anticipating that the Government might not appeal, Dr. Yellen sought to intervene and thereby allow the landless to appeal. Judge Turrentine denied the motion,[62] the Government did not appeal.[63]

Meanwhile, Yellen and his landless litigants raised the issue of residency in a separate suit. Residency is the companion requirement to acreage limitation and compels the water receiver to be "an actual bona fide resident on such land, or occupant thereof residing in the neighborhood of said land . . . ."[64]

Despite Judge Turrentine's holding the acreage limitation inapplicable to Imperial Valley, Judge William D. Murray held the residency provision applicable to the Valley and to reclamation projects generally. Judge Murray wrote:

> Failure to enforce residency subverts the excess land limitation. . . . Through the use of corporations, trusts and cotenancies flagrant violations of the purpose of this limitation are possible. Each of these farms may be used to by-pass the acreage limitation. The policy behind reclamation law to aid and encourage owner operated farms requires enforcement of the residency requirement to prevent these violations.
>
> . . . .
>
> The fact that residency has not been required by the Department of Interior for over 55 years cannot influence the outcome of this decision. Failing to apply the residency requirement is contrary to any reasonable interpretation of the reclamation law as a whole, and it is destructive of the clear purpose and intent of national reclamation policy. It is well settled that administrative practice cannot thwart the plain purpose of a valid law. Rather than indicate the validity of the administrative ruling, the lapse of time serves to dramatize the

---

60. Brawley Advertiser [Cal.], August 9, 1967, at 1, col. 6.
61. United States v. Imperial Irrigation Dist., 322 F. Supp. 11 (S.D. Cal. 1971).
62. See note 57 supra.
63. See Hearings on Farmworkers in Rural America Before the Subcomm. on Migratory Labor of the Senate Comm. on Labor and Public Welfare, 92d Cong., 1st & 2d Sess., pt. 3A, at 833 (1971-72) [hereinafter cited as Hearings on Farmworkers].
64. 43 U.S.C. § 431 (1902). See also epigraph accompanying note 1 supra.

unavailability of relief in the past and points toward the need for increased access to the court in the future.[65]

The companion issues of acreage limitation and residency have now advanced to the Ninth Circuit Court of Appeals.[66] That court has joined them for a common hearing, and in addition has granted litigant standing to Yellen and his landless. Whichever way the Circuit Court decides, appeal to the Supreme Court may be expected.

Against these significant steps toward judicial recognition of the stake of landless persons in gaining access to land in the Imperial Valley, stands the absence of challenge by the landless of other valleys who allow widespread nonenforcement of reclamation law to continue.[67]

VII

[We small farmers and farm workers] have so many problems in common and so many common interests that we should unite for our joint survival.

Dolores Huerta, Vice President of United Farm Workers Organizing Committee (1972).[68]

* * *

The working farmer who does his own work, and whose product when placed on the market comes into competition with products of other farmers, prefers high wage scales so that the cost of labor entering into the goods of his competitors will force up the selling price of goods and hence give to him the high returns.

R.L. Adams, Professor of Farm Management (1939).[69]

Among Mexican Americans there has been no movement to acquire land for farming. The attention of those engaged in agriculture has been absorbed in the daily problems of employment, wages, housing and working conditions. Recently, however, a small number of

---

65. Yellen v. Hickel, 335 F. Supp. 200, 208 (S.D. Cal. 1971) (citations omitted). *See also* Yellen v. Hickel, 352 F. Supp. 1300 (S.D. Cal. 1972).

66. *See* note 33 *supra.*

67. Exceptions are rare. On February 7, 1970, Joe Ramon and Bruno Cavazos, farm workers owning five and 17 acres respectively, brought suit in Northern California Federal District Court to compel enforcement of the 160-acre law in the Delano-Earlimart Irrigation District, but the case has not been pressed. Ramon v. Delano-Earlimart Irrigation Dist, Civil No. C-70-299 (N.D. Cal., filed Feb. 7, 1970).

In the same District Court, four family farmers—not Mexican Americans—filed a similar suit to enforce federal reclamation law with respect to the California State Water Project. Bowker v. Morton, Civil No. C-70-1274 (N.D. Cal., Aug. 2, 1973). Following district court decisions adverse to plaintiffs, the Ninth Circuit granted leave to appeal. Bowker v. Morton, Civil No. 75-8126 (9th Cir., May 2, 1975).

68. *Hearings on Farmworkers, supra* note 63, pt. 3C, at 1784.

69. *Hearings on Free Speech, supra* note 30, at 17,218.

labor-intensive cooperative farming projects have been undertaken, and initial results have raised excited hopes for expansion.

> [An 80-acre strawberry cooperative in the Salinas-Watsonville area] produces revenues of $650,000 to $700,000. Approximately half of that is expense . . . . The remaining $350,000 then is rechanneled back as farm income. The farm income then is the income earned as a result of the labor they have invested. So therefore, each family approximately will be making $8,000 to $10,000 next year with about a $2,000 net equity in the cooperative.[70]

A second project has attracted the attention of farm workers in the Fresno area. As described in *Las Noticias*:

> They decided to grow 5 acres of cherry tomatoes. . . . Just as planned, everyone is working long hours, 7 days a week to make this the best crop in the valley. The result has been a complete success. So far the harvest of the 5 acres has been producing well over $1,000 per day in sales, and in the daily marketing reports for tomatoes, the price that Rancho El Bracero receives is always one of the top prices in the valley. The 40 acres is completely level now, and as soon as the harvest is over, the coop will plant a fall crop of grain on the full 40 acres. In 1974 they will be ready for full vegetable production.
>
> All of the coop members are very proud and happy to be working for themselves on their own farm. This is certainly the main reason for their tremendous success in farming.[71]

Enthusiastic accounts of a few projects, however, do not alter the fact that overwhelmingly Mexican Americans in agriculture remain landless workers for wages. Their daily conditions are affected directly by their ability to organize in unions. In a 1972 colloquy between Senator Adlai E. Stevenson III, and Dolores Huerta, of the United Farm Workers Union, the issues and alternatives emerged clearly.

> Senator Stevenson. The United Farm Workers Organizing Committee has been very active in organizing farmworkers for the purpose of collective bargaining and the improvement of working conditions, but do you think that a dream of the farmworker is not to work for a wage but it is to own his own land, and to farm it with his own hands?
>
> Ms. Huerta. It is a nice dream, but where do you get the money to buy the land? . . .
>
> . . . .
>
> Senator Stevenson. If the Federal programs are available, why shouldn't farmworkers take advantage of them, get the credit that they need both for the acquisition of land equity, and become farm owners?

---

70. *Hearings on Farmworkers, supra* note 63, pt. 1, at 158.
71. Las Noticias, Sept. 1973 (Organ of West Side Planning Group, Inc., 1476 N. Van Ness, Fresno, California, 93728, a nonprofit community economic development corporation).

Ms. Huerta. That would be beautiful, Senator, if it could become a reality.

. . . .

Senator Stevenson. You seem to be more interested and preoccupied with simply negotiating and improving the working conditions of wage earners.

Ms. Huerta. Senator, if we are having trouble getting wages of $1.90 and $2 an hour for farmworkers . . . and you are talking now about making it possible for them to get money to buy land, this is a beautiful dream and I think we have to be practical.[72]

Are improvement of working conditions of farm workers, and enhancement of access to one's own land, mutually exclusive alternatives? In forming their practical answer to this question Mexican Americans will have to weigh their own interests, and decide what effort they will make to obtain effective enforcement of a reclamation policy that has been on the books for two full generations.

If a national policy is to be effective under the American system of government, each of the three branches of government must fulfill its relevant functions. If Mexican Americans conclude they have interests in reclamation law that are not now being properly served, they should approach the administration, the legislature, and the courts. They can protest the lax enforcement of the laws in the media, or in communications to congressional committees. Administrators may respond to pressures that may jeopardize their project authorizations or appropriations.[73]

Mexican Americans may conclude that reclamation law itself requires amendment to improve its enforceability, to redistribute excess land to the landless, to broaden its public service, to finance public education in the land grant tradition, or to preserve open space and family-size-farms on prime agricultural land. They then should evaluate pending legislation in the Congress,[74] and give or withhold their active support.

The courts are available to redress and forestall violations by administrators who fail to observe and enforce the acreage limitation and residency requirement of reclamation law. Mexican Americans can bring suit for enforcement of the law in other reclamation areas as they have done in Imperial Valley.[75] In ways such as these, Mexican

---

72. *Hearings on Farmworkers, supra* note 63, pt. 3C, at 1773-74.
73. W. WARNE, THE BUREAU OF RECLAMATION 218-22 (1973).
74. *See, e.g.,* 117 CONG. REC. 11,201 (1971) (remarks of Rep. Kastenmeier).
75. Taylor, *Water, Land, and Environment, Imperial Valley: Law Caught in the Winds of Politics,* 13 NAT. RES. J. 1 (1973). Among documented yet judicially unchallenged examples of apparent nonenforcement of acreage limitation law are the following, each involving substantial amounts of land: (1) Salt River Valley, Arizona. *See,* 95

Americans can make their United States citizenship effective in serving their best interests and in giving meaning to their participation in the social, political, and economic life of this nation.

CONG. REC. 10,126 (1949); *Hearings on S. 1425, supra* note 32, at 231-38. (2) Southern California. *See* Statement of Chief Counsel Reginal L. Knox, Imperial Irrigation Dist., in Imperial Irrigation District News, Feb. 1965, at 1. (3) Sacramento River diverters, California. *See Hearings on H.R. 3300 Before a Subcomm. of the House Comm. on Interior and Insular Affairs*, 90th Cong., 1st Sess., at 686-87 (1967).

PUBLIC POLICY
AND THE
SHAPING OF RURAL SOCIETY

PUBLIC POLICY AND THE SHAPING OF RURAL SOCIETY

By Paul S. Taylor*

> *This article traces the social and economic history of the family farm, concentrating on relevant governmental actions. The author examines the Homestead Act of 1862 and the Reclamation Law of 1902 and their administrative interpretations. He determines that although the intention of the acts was to support the family farm, the administrators have failed to carry out this purpose. The author concludes that political and economic realities demand that Congress declare and administrators enforce a policy favorable to the family farm or this institution will be lost as a way of life.*

Introduction

> [I]n the absence of any national policy or regional plan, the agribusiness corporations have simply availed themselves of technological change to maximize profits and have left society to cope with the human consequences.
>
> New York Times Editorial, December 27, 1971.[1]

Is declaration of public policy toward rural society, and its effective implementation, necessary? Or can the outcome be left safely to the unrestrained forces of technology and the market?

Answers to these questions lie in the historical development of the farming culture in the United States. Study reveals the conflicting characters of an industrialized farm or plantation society and a family farm society. In recognition of this conflict, the United States Congress, since the Homestead Act of 1862, has consistently declared when disposing of public land or authorizing public development of public waters that an essential element of sound rural society is the family farm operated by actual residents upon their own land. Unfortunately, Congress has often failed to support its own policy. Furthermore, the implementation of policy often has been frustrated by bureaucratic misinterpretation if not defiance of congressional mandate.

Backdrop of History

"The magic of property turns sand into gold," the classic saying of Arthur Young, has been widely accepted, yet some of its market

---

* Professor of Economics Emeritus, University of California, Berkeley. Martha Chase assisted in preparation of this paper, and the Institute of Business and Economic Research and Committee on Research of the University of California aided.

1. N.Y. Times, Dec. 27, 1971, at 26, col. 1 (Editorial).

place decisions have been challenged from time immemorial. Not least among these have been decisions resulting in landownership by the few and landlessness among the many. "Woe unto them that join house to house," said the prophet Isaiah, "that lay field to field till there be no place, that they may be placed alone in the midst of the earth."[2] The Roman Pliny voiced an identical concern in 77 A.D. Peasant revolts spotted the Middle Ages and surfaced in the French Revolution. Control over land tends to give control over the labor that makes it productive, and to shape the very foundations of rural society.

Our own twentieth century has witnessed both revolution founded on landlessness, and land reform intended to draw the fires of such extremism. In its second decade revolutions almost simultaneously overturned the governments of Mexico in the New World and Russia in the Old. The slogan of the former was "Land and Liberty," and of the latter, "Peace, Bread, and the Land."

In the fifth decade, under General Douglas MacArthur, commander of an army of occupation, Japan administered a thorough land reform on the principle that "to the tiller belongs the soil." At almost the same time and in rapid succession, Mainland China and North Vietnam went through Communist revolutions grounded on peasant dissatisfactions.[3]

The United States, too, has experienced both the stabilizing and the divisive influences of differing relationships of man to land. From earliest settlements in the seventeenth century, opposed patterns of rural society—the family farm and the plantations—spread over the lands of the North and the South. Eventually these societies clashed in bitter warfare.

In the New England colonies, farmers as a rule owned the land they tilled by their own labor and the labor of their families. Celebrating the bicentennial of the landing of the Pilgrims, Daniel Webster drew these conclusions:

> [Our New England ancestors] were . . . nearly on a general level in respect to property. Their situation demanded a parcelling out and division of the lands, and it may be said fairly, that this necessary act *fixed the future frame and form of their government.* . . . The consequence has been a great subdivision of the soil, and a great equality of condition; the true basis most certainly of popular government.[4]

---

2. *Isaiah* 5:8.
3. HOUSE GOVERNMENT OPERATIONS COMM., FOREIGN OPERATIONS AND GOVERNMENT SUBCOMM., COMMUNIST STRATEGY AND TACTICS OF EMPLOYING PEASANT DISSATISFACTION OVER CONDITIONS OF LAND TENURE FOR REVOLUTIONARY ENDS IN VIETNAM, 91st Cong., 2d Sess. (Comm. Print 1970).
4. D. WEBSTER, *First Settlement of New England,* in THE LIFE, EULOGY, AND ORATIONS OF DANIEL WEBSTER 113-14 (1854).

As settlement spread across the Middle West, the New England pattern expanded with it. A century after Webster, the superintendent of the Wisconsin State Historical Society defined the prevailing rural character in terms now well familiar:

> [S]tudy . . . reveals agriculture as one of the main supports of American democracy because it is an occupation embracing millions of freemen who own property and cultivate land on a somewhat equal basis. . . . A farm represents a "living," . . . but neither an actual nor a potential modern "fortune." . . . [T]he family-sized farm is the American ideal and means in effect that the owner and his son or sons can perform the actual work of tillage, the female members of the household smoothing the way by providing home comforts, assisting about chores, or in field or meadow as pressure of work may dictate. Hired men are rather the exception than the rule in this typical agriculture. So far as they are employed, it is usually with the instinctive purpose of raising the labor force to the normal family plane rather than in the hope of abnormally expanding the business beyond the family-farm norm.[5]

The distribution of landownership pattern that came to characterize the South contrasted sharply with that of the North. Large plantations rather than family farms came to dominate the South. Plantations produced commodities such as tobacco or cotton for export rather than for local markets or to provide food and fiber for the farm family. They were worked by slave laborers belonging to often absentee masters, and under the immediate supervision of local overseers and drivers.

The plantation system was challenged unsuccessfully as early as 1732 by the British founders of Georgia, last of the Thirteen Colonies. Disapproving of the plantation societies as they had developed in Virginia and the Carolinas, the Georgia Trustees in London decided instead to place a 500 acre ceiling on landownership, to settle their new colony with families on generally fifty acre farms and to forbid slave labor.

South Carolina planters and aspiring planters in Georgia, however, brought pressure in Parliament, and ultimately succeeded in terminating the Trustees' family farm plan. When it came to an end in 1752, plantations of up to 2000 acres appeared quickly, and slaves poured in to work them.[6] From these beginnings along the eastern seaboard, plantation society spread westward over the southern black belt of Alabama, the delta lands of Mississippi and Louisiana, and onto the Brazos River bottoms of eastern Texas.

A century after defeat of Georgia's planned family farm society and on the eve of civil war, South Carolina's Senator Hammond gave Congress the Southern view of the plantation system:

---

5. J. SCHAFER, THE SOCIAL HISTORY OF AMERICAN AGRICULTURE 289-90 (1936).

6. P. TAYLOR, GEORGIA PLAN 1732-1752, at chs. 8, 9 (1972).

> In all social systems there must be a class to do the mean duties, to perform the drudgery of life. That is, a class requiring but a low order of intellect and but little skill. Its requisites are vigor, docility, fidelity. Such a class you must have, or you would not have that other class which leads progress, refinement, and civilization. It constitutes the very mud-sills of society and of political government; and you might as well attempt to build a house in the air, as to build either the one or the other, except on the mud-sills.[7]

As the war moved into its later stages, President Abraham Lincoln, too, noted the contrast between Southern and Northern rural societies. In his second inaugural address he said:

> One eighth of the whole population were colored slaves, not distributed generally over the Union, but localized in the southern part of it. These slaves constituted a peculiar and powerful interest. All knew that this interest was somehow the cause of the war.[8]

In the Far West even before the Civil War, a distinctive pattern of man's relation to land was being laid down. At the conclusion of the war with Mexico a variant of the South's plantation appeared quickly in California. Slave labor was rejected, but concentrated landownership and dependence upon landless laborers were accepted. In 1854 the *California Farmer* expressed the prospect in these words:

> California is destined to become a large grower of cotton, rice, tobacco, sugar, tea and coffee and where shall the laborers be found? Americans will not become the working men of our . . . rice and our cotton plantations. . . . At the south, this is the work of the slave, but . . . California is a free state. . . . Then where shall the laborers be found? The Chinese! . . . that population, educated, schooled and drilled in the cultivation of these products are [sic] to be to California what the African has been to the south. This is the decree of the Almighty, and man cannot stop it.[9]

A generation of land grabbing followed this early forecast.[10] The land and labor pattern of rural society that resulted was described by James Bryce in the 1880's:

> When California was ceded to the United States, land speculators bought up large tracts under Spanish titles, and

---

7. CONG. GLOBE, 35th Cong., 1st Sess. 962 (1858).
8. 8 A. LINCOLN, THE WRITINGS OF ABRAHAM LINCOLN 329-30 (A. Lapsey ed. 1888).
9. CALIFORNIA FARMER, May 26, 1854, at 164, *quoted in* Fuller, *The Supply of Agricultural Labor as a Factor in the Evolution of Farm Organization in California*, in Hearings Before a Subcomm. of the Senate Comm. on Education and Labor on Violations of Free Speech and Rights of Labor, 76th Cong., 2d, 3d Sess. pt. 54 (1940).
10. Gates, *The Homestead Law in an Incongruous Land System*, 41 AM. HIST. REV. 652, 668-69 (1936); Cooper, Land, Water, and Settlement in Kern County, California, 1850-1890, 1954 (dissertation, University of California, Berkeley).

others, foreseeing the coming prosperity, subsequently acquired great domains by purchase, either from the railways which had received land grants, or directly from the government. Some of these speculators . . . made it difficult for immigrants to acquire small freeholds, and in some cases checked the growth of farms. . . . [O]thers established enormous farms, in which the soil is cultivated by hired labourers, many of whom are discharged after the harvest—a phenomenon rare in the United States . . . . Thus the land system of California presents features both peculiar and dangerous, a contrast between great properties, often appearing to conflict with the general weal, and the sometimes hard pressed small farmer, together with a mass of unsettled labour, thrown without work into the towns at certain times of the year.[11]

This pattern of rural society has persisted in California and spread to Arizona, Florida and scattered areas where fruits and vegetables are intensively produced.[12] The operators of these agricultural industries were well aware of the contrast between their methods and those of the North and Middle West. In 1939 the *Western Grower and Shipper* declared, "The incidents of husbandry, the family-sized farm with all its glamor, is a lovely idyll—elsewhere than most sections of California."[13] The dependence of this type of industrialized farming upon landless laborers was attested to before Congress by the spokesman for the California Agricultural Legislative Committee. Opposing legislation to restrict free entrance of immigrants from Mexico, he said:

Somebody, somewhere, has to do hard physical labor because it is here to be done. . . . Under our present system of education, we must either bring somebody in here to do our hard work or we must go elsewhere for our foodstuffs and clothing.[14]

As in the Southern plantation belt, Far Western industrialized agriculture has proved productive of crops for distant markets. It is marked by large landownerships, large-scale operating units, and

---

11. II J. BRYCE, THE AMERICAN COMMONWEALTH 427 (1924) (footnote omitted). *See also* R. FELLMETH, POLITICS OF LAND (1973).
12. Taylor, *Migratory Farm Labor in the United States*, 44 MONTHLY LABOR REV. 537-49 (March 1937).
13. WESTERN GROWER & SHIPPER (Oct. 1939). *See also Hearings Before a Subcomm. of the Senate Comm. on Education and Labor on Violations of Free Speech and Rights of Labor*, 76th Cong., 2d, 3d Sess. pts. 47, 54 (1940).
14. *Hearings Before the House Comm. on Immigration & Naturalization on H.R. 6465: Immigration from Countries of the Western Hemisphere*, 70th Cong., 1st Sess. 307 (1928) (testimony of Ralph H. Taylor).

Seasonal dependence upon migratory labor prevailed on the Great Plains wheat belt from the late 1860's until the middle 1920's when mechanical harvesting ended the necessity for hand labor. P. Taylor, Origins of Migratory Labor in the Wheat Belts of the Middle West and California: Second Half of Nineteenth Century in *Hearings Before the Subcomm. on Migratory Labor of the Senate Comm. on Labor and Public Welfare on Migrant and Seasonal Farmworker Powerlessness*, 91st Cong., 1st, 2d Sess. pt. 8C at 6258-98 (1970).

by recurrent and apparently unending friction between growers and farmworkers.[15]

Thus the period from the first settlement to the 1860's saw the emergence of three types of American rural society—the Northeastern family farm, the Southern plantation, and the Far Western pattern falling in between. The three types grew relatively uninfluenced by government regulation but rather in response to economic forces of the time. It was in this context that Congress moved to spread the Northern pattern as it deliberated on the Homestead Act.

Homestead Act of 1862

Slavery cannot exist except with the system of large farms, and your homestead bills establish the system of small farms with which free labor is inseparably connected.
—Carl Schurz' Paraphrase of Slaveholders' Opposition to Homestead Bills 1860[16]

In years preceding the Civil War, national land policy was under recurrent congressional debate. The nation's frontier was moving westward, and an underlying issue was whether national land policy should favor expansion of the New England family farm pattern or the southern plantation-slave-labor system. The family farm pattern won out when Congress passed and President Abraham Lincoln signed the Homestead Act in 1862.[17] The new law was designed to favor the actual settler on the land, and was passed after southern representatives had left Washington with the outbreak of war. Historian Benjamin H. Hibbard has described the Homestead policy:

> Settlers finally could acquire farms of 160 acres free of all charges, except a minor fee to be paid when filing the claim. To insure permanency of settlement the law specified that before title to the land was gained the individual must live on the homestead for five years.[18]

Although the intent to insure permanency was clear, the device to achieve it was inadequate. Pointing to the critical weakness, Hibbard notes that the public policy controls ended once title had passed from the government to a landowner:

> With the feeling that all land should be made private property as rapidly as possible . . . that *laissez faire* is the best

---

15. R. De Toledano, Little Cesar (1971); E. Galarza, Merchants of Labor (1966); E. Galarza, Spiders in the House and Workers in the Field (1970); Senate Comm. on Education and Labor, Violations of Free Speech and Rights of Labor, Employers' Associations and Their Labor Policies in California's Industrialized Agriculture, S. Rep. No. 1150, 77th Cong., 2d Sess. pt. 4 (1942).
16. *Quoted in* B. Hibbard, A History of the Public Land Policies 382 (1924) [hereinafter cited as Hibbard].
17. Ch. 75, 12 Stat. 392.
18. Hibbard, *supra* note 16, at 385.

guide in deciding questions . . . there was little opportunity for the development of a conscious, workable, vigorous land policy. A land policy means social control over one of the greatest instruments of production. . . .
. . . .

That the land issue is not settled once for all by and through private ownership is demonstrated in the history of most countries of which we have knowledge, and conspicuously in the struggles going on around us to-day [1924]. Not only do Russia and Mexico furnish evidence of the persistence of the land problem long after land has once been put into private hands, but countries much more stable exhibit tendencies almost as pronounced and not greatly different in character. For example, within a quarter century there has been a virtual revolution in the land system of Ireland, supervised and financed through government . . . in Denmark . . . in New Zealand . . . Australia. . . .[19]

As the nation's agricultural frontier moved westward across the hundredth meridian, the insufficiency and undependability of rainfall began to impede successful homesteading by family farmers under the terms of the Homestead Law. Congress thereupon passed a succession of measures designed to encourage private or state development of water resources, in part by allowing larger farms in the arid and semiarid belt than the 160 acres practicable in the humid belt.

Yet as it turned out, these statutes failed to achieve either substantial irrigation or establishment of actual settlers on the land. As to the latter, historian Arthur B. Darling concluded that "in spite of every measure yet devised, the nation's resources in land were accumulating in large tracts owned by a few wealthy individuals and corporations."[20] Allowing settlers to acquire full ownership in less than five years by paying the regular price "was to prove a loophole in the law through which many worked their way into possession of large areas of the public land."[21] Acquisition of full title by homesteading for five years briefly retarded but did not prevent this process.

Reviewing the effect of the Homestead Act in 1937, a Presidential committee reported that tenancy in the United States grew from 25.6 percent in 1880 to 42.1 percent in 1935.[22] "While aggravated by the depression," said President Franklin D. Roosevelt,

---

19. *Id.* at 562-63.
20. Darling, *Irrigation,* in I THE PUBLIC PAPERS OF FRANCIS G. NEWLANDS 54-55 (A. Darling ed. 1932).
21. *Id.* at 52.
22. NATIONAL RESOURCES COMM., FARM TENANCY 96 (1937) [hereinafter cited as FARM TENANCY]. The Committee's findings of fact were reprinted as H.R. Doc. No. 149, 75th Cong., 1st Sess. (1937) [hereinafter cited as H.R. Doc. No. 149]. In North Dakota the percentage of tenancy had increased from 2.1 to 39.1 and in South Dakota from 4.4 to 48.6. FARM TENANCY, *supra,* at 96; H.R. Doc. No. 149, *supra,* at 96.

"the tenancy problem is the accumulated result of generations of unthinking exploitation of our agricultural resources, both land and people."[23] The Report noted that "In some of our States, among them a number settled under the homestead system little more than a generation ago, it is estimated that the equity of operating farmers in their lands is little more than one-fifth; nearly four-fifths is in the hands of landlords and mortgage holders."[24] The Report continued, "The land policy adopted by this country, under which title to practically all of the agricultural land of the Nation passed to private owners in fee simple absolute, has proved defective as a means of keeping the land in the ownership of those who work it."[25] The Report recommended placing restrictions upon the too rapid transfer of property in fee.

These recommendations received general, although not unanimous, support. As a member of the committee, E. A. O'Neal, President of the American Farm Bureau Federation, gave only limited approval. Recording specific dissent, he said:

> I cannot approve . . . withholding the transfer of title to any purchaser who is able to pay the principal indebtedness for which he obligated himself. . . . I regard restriction on alienation of lands as contary to sound American jurisprudence. . . . By and large, I am of the conviction that a man who owns a proper equity in a farm . . . is capable of the responsibilities of . . . ownership. Other policies relating to the use of agricultural land should be approached from the standpoint of education and demonstration rather than through limitations on the right of ownership.[26]

Limitations on the right of land ownership, to which O'Neal objected, are neither new nor few. The Virginia Legislature in 1776 abolished primogeniture and entailed estates. Thomas Jefferson, sponsor, said:

> In the earlier times of the colony, when lands were to be obtained for little or nothing, some provident individuals procured large grants . . . desirous of founding great families for themselves . . . . To annul this privilege, and instead of an aristocracy of wealth, of more harm and danger, than benefit, to society, to make an opening for the aristocracy of virtue and talent, which nature has wisely provided for the direction of the interests of Society, and scattered with equal hand through all its conditions, was deemed essential to a well-ordered republic.[27]

---

23. FARM TENANCY, *supra* note 22, at 26; H.R. Doc. No. 149, *supra* note 22, at iii.
24. FARM TENANCY, *supra* note 22, at 3; H.R. Doc. No. 149, *supra* note 22, at 2.
25. FARM TENANCY, *supra* note 22, at 6; H.R. Doc. No. 149, *supra* note 22, at 6.
26. FARM TENANCY, *supra* note 22, at 23; H.R. Doc. No. 149, *supra* note 22, at 27.
27. T. JEFFERSON, AUTOBIOGRAPHY (1821), *reprinted in* I THE WRITINGS OF THOMAS JEFFERSON 36 (A. Bergh ed. 1907). Congress limited corporate landownership in territories in 1887 to 5,000 acres. Act of March 3, 1887,

Long after Jefferson, the Homestead Act explicitly expressed ownership of land by actual settlers as its policy goal. However, by making its protections little more than threshold requirements, it failed to achieve sustained success for its declared policy. Public controls ended when title passed to the first landowner, opening the door to subsequent purchase of large blocks by speculators. In light of this experience Congress deliberated carefully over the conditions it would attach to appropriations of public funds to finance western water development.

NATIONAL RECLAMATION ACT OF 1902

> *Lord Macauley said we never would experience the test of our institutions until our public domain was exhausted and an increased population engaged in a contest for the ownership of land. That will be the test of the future, and the very purpose of this bill is to guard against land monopoly and to hold this land in small tracts for the people of the entire country . . . . Convey this land to private corporations and doubtless this work would be done, but we would have fastened upon this country all the evils of land monopoly which produced the great French revolution which caused the revolt against church monopoly in South America, and which in recent times has caused the outbreak of the Filipinos against Spanish authority.*
>
> —CONGRESSMAN FRANCIS G. NEWLANDS, 1902[28]

The next major land legislation following the Homestead Law of 1862 was the National Reclamation Act of 1902. This time Congress sought to close the loopholes that left public policy with merely threshold rather than enduring support. The statute specifies simply that

> No right to the use of water for land in private ownership shall be sold for a tract exceeding 160 acres to any one landowner, and no such sale shall be made to any landowner unless he be an actual bona fide resident on such land, or occupant thereof residing in the neighborhood of said land . . . .[29]

Furthermore Congress expressly forbad "commutation" of the residence requirement on reclamation projects in return for cash payment.[30]

The language of this reclamation statute contains no hint that its controls over monopoly and absentee ownership were intended to expire at any time. In addition, the legislative history of the reclamation bills confirms that Congress intended to permanently close the loopholes that had become visible when the Homestead Act left the family farm exposed to the forces of the marketplace.

---

ch. 340, 24 Stat. 476. Corporate landownership in Puerto Rico was limited to 500 acres in 1900. Act of May 1, 1900, ch. 23, § 3, 31 Stat. 716. Congress continued this limitation in 1917. Act of March 2, 1917, ch. 145, 93 Stat. 964, 48 U.S.C. § 752 (1970).
  28. 35 CONG. REC. 6734 (1902).
  29. 43 U.S.C. § 431 (1970).
  30. 43 U.S.C. § 432 (1970); *see* Taylor, *Excess Land Law: Execution of a Public Policy,* 64 YALE L.J. 477, 513 (1955).

With a long look into the future, Senator Hansbrough of North Dakota said in 1902:

> It is argued by some that as wealth grows larger in a few hands the opportunities of the laboring classes to secure employment are multiplied . . . . [B]ut looking a little beyond immediate benefits, it appears that the tendency under such a condition is to dwarf self-reliance in the masses and to make the mere service of opulent employers by the great army of breadwinners the fulfillment of all human ambition. I think it is the duty of the legislator to pursue a policy under which the greatest possible number of our people may be provided with the means of independent employment, by which the aspirations of the individual may be encouraged and developed.[31]

In similar vein, Congressman Martin of South Dakota said, "The policy of the Government is to build up communities of many settlers with small holdings, and not to encourage the prosecution of agriculture by large corporations."[32]

Congressman Frank W. Mondell of Wyoming emphasized that the strictness of the reclamation bill as compared to the Homestead Act would assure achievement of public policy goals:

> No law ever presented to any legislative body has been so carefully drawn with a view of preventing the possibility of speculative ownership in lands. . . . [W]e have thrown further safeguards around the public lands than . . . [the author of the Homestead Law] felt necessary in his act . . . .[33]

Congressman Francis G. Newlands of Nevada told how President Theodore Roosevelt, who was personally familiar with North Dakota, had taken a hand during consideration of the reclamation bill to tighten its language:

> It passed in the Senate . . . and then President Roosevelt, who is entirely familiar with that region and knows its wants, invited in consultation some members of the Irrigation Committee of the House, regardless of party. He was somewhat in doubt as to whether the bill was sufficiently guarded in the interest of homeseekers.
>
> It was a question simply of construction. We all wanted to preserve that domain in small tracts for actual settlers and homebuilders. We all wanted to prevent monopoly and concentration of ownership, and the result was that certain changes were made absolutely satisfactory both to the Executive and to the Irrigation Committee, and intended only to carry out the intentions of both.[34]

---

31. 35 CONG. REC. 1386 (1902).
32. *Id.* at 6750.
33. *Id.* at 6678. Likewise, in the Senate, Senator William A. Clark of Wyoming said, "The present proposed bill is far more stringent in its operation than was the homestead law . . . ." *Id.* at 2222.
34. *Id.* at 6674.

A statute, however, has only the effect given it by its administrators. Notwithstanding the unqualified language of the Reclamation Act and its legislative history, administrators have limited the duration of residency requirement. According to a Reclamation Decision of 1917: "After approval of the application further residence is not required of such applicant," and upon transfer of ownership of the land receiving water "it is immaterial whether or not the transferee be 'an actual bona fide resident on such land or occupant thereof residing in the neighborhood.' "[35] Thus since 1917 administrators have treated the residency requirement as no more than a threshold requirement expiring with the acquisition of a water right.

This early administrative determination opened loopholes which allowed for absenteeism and tenancy under reclamation law. Such loopholes were comparable to the Homestead Act's statutory termination of residency requirements upon completion of five years in residence or earlier commutation cash payment.

Judicial review of this administrative interpretation came only after more than a half century. In 1971 federal district Judge William D. Murray held that administrators

> cannot repeal an Act of Congress. . . . The fact that residency has not been required by the Department of Interior for over 55 years cannot influence the outcome of this decision. Failing to apply the residency requirement is contrary to any reasonable interpretation of the reclamation law as a whole, and is destructive of the clear purpose of a valid law.[36]

This decision is currently under review by the Ninth Circuit Court of Appeals.

Limitation of water received by an individual landowner to an amount sufficient to irrigate 160 acres is the companion requirement of residency. As with residency, question has arisen among administrators whether at some time this condition terminates. In 1957 Secretary of the Interior Fred A. Seaton said that "The Department continues to recognize and support the basic concept of reclamation law that full and final payment of the obligation of a district to the Federal Government ends the applicability of the acreage limitations."[37]

The repayment obligation laid upon irrigators is normally discharged over forty years without interest. Such repayment, as

---

35. *In re* J.W. Merritt (Truckee-Carson), I FED. RECLAMATION LAWS ANN. 67 (Reclamation Decision July 25, 1917).
36. Yellen v. Hickel, 335 F. Supp. 200, 207-08 (S.D. Cal. 1971). *See also* Taylor, *Water, Land, and Environment, Imperial Valley: Law Caught in the Winds of Politics*, 13 NATURAL RESOURCES J. 1 (1973).
37. *Hearings Before a Subcomm. on Irrigation and Reclamation of the Senate Interior and Insular Affairs Comm. on S. 1425, S. 2541, and S. 3448* at 26, 27 (1958) (Appendix C) [hereinafter cited as *S. 1425 Hearings*].

discussed below, does not cover or terminate the subsidy to irrigators.[38]

Official challenge of the Secretary's termination of public policy upon repayment came quickly from a member of Congress. Senator Paul H. Douglas of Illinois stated in an open exchange of correspondence with the Secretary:

> It seems plain to me that Congress reserved to itself the authority to make any modifications in application of the excess-land provisions and has not conferred on anyone else the power to declare any date at which the application of the provision terminates, whether upon completion of financial aspects of a transaction or otherwise.[39]

Then he repeated Secretary Seaton's own statement amazingly made in this same context: "What I am concerned about is the process by which inferences are based on inferences, and there is a whittling away at a principle until all that is left is a pile of shavings."[40]

Administrative termination of acreage limitation upon pay-out remains unchallenged in the courts, although failure to apply acreage limitation to particular projects is currently under judicial review.[41] Thus both requirements of the Reclamation Act intended to insure widespread ownership of the land—the absentee ownership provision and the acreage limitation—have been frustrated and circumvented by administrators who have a long and varied record of "whittling away" at national water policy rather than infusing it with life.[42]

HERITAGE

> It has been demonstrated historically and is true in many countries today that those who control the land end up controlling the country.
>
> —SENATOR GAYLORD NELSON OF
> WISCONSIN, 1968[43]

---

38. See text accompanying notes 60-62 *infra*. See also Page, *Acreage Limitation: Policy Considerations*, 38 CALIF. L. REV. 728, 730 n.13 (1950).
39. S. 1425 *Hearings*, supra note 37, at 20-25.
40. *Id.*
41. Bowker v. Morton, No. C-70-1274 (1973) (appeal pending 9th Cir.); United States v. Tulare Lake Canal Co., 340 F. Supp. 1185 (E.D. Cal. 1972) (appeal pending 9th Cir.); Yellen v. Hickel, 335 F. Supp. 200 (S.D. Cal. 1971) (appeal pending 9th Cir.), *joined with*, United States v. Imperial Irrigation Dist., 322 F. Supp. 11 (S.D. Cal. 1971) (appeal pending 9th Cir.).
42. *Hearings Before a Subcomm. of the House Comm. on Government Operations on the Nation's Estuaries: San Francisco Bay and Delta, Calif.*, 91st Cong., 1st Sess. 229-33 (1969) (statement of Paul S. Taylor); Taylor, *Excess Land Law: Calculated Circumvention*, 52 CALIF. L. REV. 978, 1008-14 (1964); Taylor, *The 160-Acre Law*, 114 CONG. REC. 24142-146 (1968); Taylor, *The 160-Acre Limitation*, 119 CONG. REC. 5343-46 (1973).
43. *Hearings Before the Subcomm. on Monopoly of the Senate Select Comm. on Small Business on the Effects of Corporation Farming on Small Business*, 90th Cong., 2d Sess. 199 (1968) [hereinafter cited as *1968 Hearings*].

> *Corporations and big commercial farmers have the capital to introduce modern technology rapidly with consequences which are unplanned and unprovided for. . . . The entrance of diversified corporations into agriculture has not produced better or cheaper or more varied food. America does not become a healthier, more diversified, more self-reliant society by reducing farmers to the status of corporation dependents . . . .*
>
> —Editorial, New York Times, December 27, 28, 1971[44]

The legacy of the Homestead and Reclamation Acts, as explained above, included on the one hand, expression of a national policy favoring wide distribution of landownership among actual settlers, and on the other hand, the absence of statutory and administrative controls essential to make this policy effective and enduring. The net result was to leave the outcome largely to the play of private forces in the marketplace and the arena of politics.

The *New York Times* recently described the current situation, noting that

> [a] million family-sized farms were consolidated out of existence in the 1950's and another million in the 1960's. . . . Small towns which live by serving farmers have also suffered. It has been estimated that one small town businessman goes under for every six farmers who quit farming.[45]

Land and water laws are not the only legislative expressions that shape actual public agricultural policy. Some of the other acts have also brought unfavorable results. For example, tax laws favor entry of nonfarm corporations into agriculture. A recent North Central States Agricultural Extension publication entitled *Who Will Control U.S. Agriculture?* summarizes the adverse effect of tax laws on family farms:

> In principle, all kinds of farmers—small and large, part-time and full-time, operating farmers and so-called Wall Street investors—are equally eligible to use tax rules to their own gain. . . . However, the deductions and concessions have their greatest attraction and deepest impact for high-tax-bracket investors who have a sizeable nonfarm income in addition to their farm operations—irrespective of whether they are basically farmers or non-farmers. This is true because tax rates are graduated, and because losses in farming are deductible from income received from other sources.[46]

---

44. The mechanical cotton picker, the Times notes, in addition to displacing marginal farmers, swept most sharecroppers, laborers paid a share of the crop, into the cities where "their migration contributed significantly to the welfare and housing crisis." N.Y. Times, Dec. 27, 1971, at 26, col. 1-2 (Editorial). From three-quarters of a million in 1930, the number of sharecroppers shrank so rapidly that by 1969 the census no longer separately reported them. United States Dep't of Commerce, Bureau of the Census, 15th Census of the United States, vol. 7, at 156, table 7 (1930).
45. N.Y. Times, Dec. 28, 1971, at 28, col. 1-2 (Editorial).
46. University of Illinois (Champaign-Urbana), College of Agricul-

Agricultural subsidy legislation also has had the effect of displacing family farms. Conceived in the early 1930's as a program to relieve family farmers caught in the depths of depression, an elaborate system of farm subsidies has unfolded with generally unanticipated adverse effects upon them. Its practical impact on the nation's farms has been described in a Brookings Institution staff report:

> Since farm subsidies accrue roughly in proportion to sales, it follows that the bulk of subsidies go to that fifth of farmers with the highest average income . . . [to that small group of farmers with incomes averaging $20,000]. [B]ecause the value of the subsidy tends to get reflected in farmland prices, the subsidies are gradually translated into capital gains for long-term holders of land, while recent purchasers and renters receive a much smaller benefit, losing at least part of the subsidy in higher carrying costs or rents.[47]

In the course of time extensive inequities appeared in the distribution of subsidies. At the top of the scale in 1968 a single corporation in Kings County, California, received payments of 3,010,042 dollars,[48] and in adjoining Fresno County 487 payees each received 5,000 dollars or more for a total of 16,392,595 dollars.[49]

This situation, including these extreme examples, has brought the subsidy program under critical legislative review. In two stages, Congress lowered the subsidies which could be paid to farmers. First, it reduced the ceiling to 55,000 dollars for each wheat, feed grains and cotton subsidy program.[50] It then lowered to 20,000 dollars "[t]he total amount of payments which a farm shall be entitled to receive under one or more of the annual programs . . . ."[51]

TURE, COOPERATIVE EXTENSION SERVICE, HOW FEDERAL INCOME TAX RULES AFFECT OWNERSHIP AND CONTROL OF FARMING 1 (North Central Regional Publication 37, Special Publication 32, July 1974). *See also Hearings Before the Subcomm. on Migratory Labor of the Senate Comm. on Labor and Public Welfare on Land Ownership, Use, and Distribution: Farmworkers in Rural America, 1971-1972,* 92d Cong., 1st, 2d Sess. pt. 3A, at 1065 (1972) [hereinafter cited as *Farmworkers in Rural America*].
  A recent study concludes that in California's Westlands Water District,
> [a]lthough the Reclamation Law was designed to preserve the family farm, there is much evidence that the administration of the Reclamation Law is such that the small farmer is not the major beneficiary of the lower water costs. . . . Altogether the interpretation and administration of the Reclamation Law has substantially favored the large landowner, while the initial objectives of the Reclamation Law—to assist the small-scale farmer and foster the family farm—are not being achieved.

J. Jamieson, S. Sonenblum, W. Hirsch, M. Goodall, & H. Jaffe, Some Political and Economic Aspects of Managing California Water Districts 277-78 (1974).
  47. C. SCHULTZE, THE DISTRIBUTION OF FARM SUBSIDIES 3 (1971).
  48. *Hearings Before the Subcomm. of the Senate Comm. on Appropriations on H.R. 11612, Department of Agriculture and Related Agencies Appropriations for Fiscal Year 1970,* 91st Cong., 1st Sess. pt. 3, at 114 (1969).
  49. *Id.* at 126.
  50. Agricultural Act of 1970, Pub. L. No. 91-524, 84 Stat. 1358.
  51. 87 Stat. 221, 7 U.S.C. § 1307 (1970).

Nevertheless, for a generation the subsidy program has favored larger farms, whether corporate or not. Joined to inadequate statutory land law, administrative laxity in the enforcement of water law, the incidental effects of income tax law, and the increasing availability of technology, the subsidy program has contributed to the weakening of family farming and diminished widespread landownership by resident farmers.

Perennial Issue

I do not believe that we should concern ourselves only with trying to decide what the future of American agriculture is going to be—but what it should be. We should not accept any trend as inevitable. Trends are made by our public policy, not born of the wedding of inscrutable and uncontrollable forces.
—Tony T. Dechant, President, National Farmers Union, 1968[52]

[T]he form of agricultural organization that maximizes profit may not necessarily be the form desired for society.
—Recent American Experience in Agrarian Reform, 1966[53]

In the political arena strong interests oppose each other over the issue: what should be our agricultural structure? The character of our rural society depends upon the answer.

What difference does it make whether rural society is founded upon family-size farms or upon large-scale corporation farms? The most intensive documentation in search of an answer was made in the midst of congressional deliberation on proposals to exempt the Central Valley Project in California from acreage limitation and residency provisions of federal reclamation law.

Two communities were compared—Arvin, founded upon large-scale farms, and Dinuba, founded upon smaller family-size farms.[54] The small farm community supported separate business establishments in a ratio of two to one; retail trade was greater by sixty-one percent; expenditures for household supplies and building equipment were three times greater. It was found further that the small farm community supported about twenty percent more people and that there was a higher average standard of living.

---

52. Forward to Ray, Corporate Invasion of Agriculture v (1968).
53. United Nations Food and Agricultural Organization, World Land Reform Conference, Country Paper: United States of America 3 (1966).
54. Senate Special Comm. to Study the Problems of American Small Business, Small Business and the Community, 79th Cong., 2d Sess. (Comm. Print 1946) [hereinafter cited as Arvin-Dinuba Study], *reprinted in 1968 Hearings, supra* note 43, at 295-441 (1968) *and reprinted in Hearings Before the Subcomm. on Monopoly of the Senate Select Comm. on Small Business on the Role of Giant Corporations in the American and World Economies*, 92d Cong., 1st, 2d Sess. pt. 3A, at 4465-4590 [hereinafter cited as *Senate Hearings*]. *See also* Kirkendall, *Social Science in the Central Valley of California: An Episode*, 43 Calif. Hist. Soc'y Q. 195-218 (1964), *reprinted in Senate Hearings, supra*, pt. 3, at 3897-920.

The occupational composition of the two communities contrasted sharply:

> Over one-half the breadwinners in the small-farm community are independently employed businessmen, persons in white-collar employment, or farmers; in the large-farm community the proportion is less than one-fifth. . . . Less than one-third of the breadwinners in the small-farm community are agricultural wage laborers (characteristically landless, and with low and insecure income) while the proportion of persons in this position reaches the astonishing figure of nearly two-thirds of all persons gainfully employed in the large-farm community.[55]

In the small-farm community schools, parks, churches and civic organizations were more plentiful; there were two newspapers with many times the news space, compared to the single newspaper in the large-farm community.

Notwithstanding the finding that small farm communities are substantially healthier, *i.e.*, culturally richer and better balanced economically and socially, than large farm communities, opposition to legislative controls over landownership favoring family farms remains strong on both state and federal levels. In 1968 the Task Force on the Acreage Limitation Problem appointed by Governor Ronald Reagan of California recommended giving owners of lands exceeding 160 acres the option of avoiding the provisions of reclamation law by repaying a minor portion of the subsidy conferred on them by construction of the project.[56] Two years later the federal Public Land Law Review Commission recommended complete abandonment of legislative controls intended to check land monopoly and speculation:

> The allocation of public lands to agricultural use should not be burdened by artificial and obsolete restraints such as acreage limitations on individual holdings, farm residency requirements, and the exclusion of corporations as eligible applicants.[57]

A third government board, the National Water Commission, also examined the Reclamation Act of 1902 and dismissed the concept of the family farm as "Agrarian Myth." More specifically, in 1973 the Commission recommended that "Congress should abolish the 160-acre limitation in reclamation projects constructed

---

55. ARVIN-DINUBA STUDY, *supra* note 54, at 5; *1968 Hearings, supra* note 40, at 307; *Senate Hearings, supra* note 54, at 4476.
56. REPORT OF THE GOVERNOR'S TASK FORCE ON THE ACREAGE LIMITATION PROBLEM 23 (Calif. 1968). For a critical comment by the author, see Letter from Dr. Paul S. Taylor to California State Board of Agriculture, March 5, 1968, *reprinted in* 114 CONG. REC. 7420-21 (1968).
57. PUBLIC LAND LAW REVIEW COMMISSION, ONE THIRD OF THE NATION'S LAND 182 (1970). Representative Wayne N. Aspinall and Senator Henry M. Jackson, Chairmen of the House and Senate Interior Committees, were among the signers; Representative Aspinall was Chairman of the Commission. *Id.* at iii-iv.

in the future; provided, however, that direct project beneficiaries pay the full costs of the projects allocated to irrigation."[58] The Commission did not apply the same financial standard to existing reclamation projects. It suggested termination of acreage limitation upon either pay-out after forty years without interest or lump-sum prepayment, the alternatives to be at the option of either irrigation districts or individual owners of excess lands. It also proposed payment of an interest charge. These options have long been favored by large landowners and administrators cool toward the law.[59]

Mere payment of interest charges, however, does not assure elimination of subsidy. In the Small Reclamation Projects Act, for example, the interest rate is well below market rate.[60] Furthermore, interest-free money is only one among the subsidies. On the Central Valley Project in California receivers of water from the Friant-Kern Canal were asked to pay only twenty-five percent of the rate that "would be necessary if subsidies and special benefits under reclamation law were eliminated."[61] On the project as a whole, "Irrigation represents 63% of the reimbursable costs but will repay only 17%."[62]

In addition to placing a low estimate on the importance of subsidization of past projects, the Commission failed to recognize a meaningful relationship between acreage limitation and residency provisions and the quality of rural life. According to the Report, "the acreage limitation has little to do with the nature of rural life or the mode of farming."[63] Furthermore, its "effect on land tenure and corporate farming would seem to be miniscule."[64] The Commission thus made no mention that administrators over a half-century ago had construed the residency requirement out of existence, and that only in 1971 had a federal district judge, as discussed above, declared it to be nevertheless valid.[65]

The Commission also noted that the "average size of the American farm has been on the increase as economies of scale are achieved with improved technology,"[66] and expressed the view that enforce-

---

58. NATIONAL WATER COMM'N, WATER POLICIES FOR THE FUTURE 149 (1973) [hereinafter cited as NATIONAL WATER COMM'N].
59. *E.g.*, correspondence between Senator Paul H. Douglas of Illinois and Secretary of Interior Fred A. Seaton, *reprinted in S. 1425 Hearings, supra* note 37, at 20-25.
60. Taylor, *Excess Land Law: Legislative Erosion of Public Policy*, 30 ROCKY MT. L. REV. 1, 20-29 (1958).
61. *Hearings Before a Subcomm. of the Senate Comm. on Public Lands on S. 912: Exemption of Certain Projects From Land-Limitation Provisions of Federal Reclamation Laws*, 80th Cong., 1st Sess. 869, at plate 8 (1947) (statement of Paul H. Johnstone, Regional Economist, Bureau of Reclamation) [hereinafter cited as *S. 912 Hearings*]. This estimate did not include the flood control subsidy. *Id.*
62. Page, *Acreage Limitation: Policy Considerations*, 38 CALIF. L. REV. 728, 730 n.13 (1950).
63. NATIONAL WATER COMM'N, *supra* note 58, at 147.
64. *Id.* at 148.
65. Yellen v. Hickel, 335 F. Supp. 200 (S.D. Cal. 1971).
66. NATIONAL WATER COMM'N, *supra* note 58, at 147.

ment of acreage limitation might be "at the cost of a less efficient irrigation industry."[67] The Commission ignored contemporary testimony before Congress that

> [i]n this structure of large and small farms, the large farm appears to be efficient, cost-conscious, and the source of much of our efficiency in agricultural production. But this could well be a transitional phase. If there are only large farms, the potentials for collusion, market sharing, restrictions on entry of new firms, and outright supply control are enormously increased. It is part of our mythology of large firms that they are efficient. For very large farms, the answer is clear: At the exercise of market power.[68]

Neither did the Commission take note of the observations of the *California Farmer* on efficiency and the quality of life on lands recently developed under the 160 acreage limitation law in Central Valley, California.[69] Posing the question of whether the 160 acre limitation helps or hinders, the *Farmer* answered:

> Short term financing has become almost routine. Methods to make agriculture profitable are working. Economies of big production are in evidence. Also, the economies of the small producer are there. Farm planning has been brought to engineering perfection. Production costs have been held if not actually reduced.
>
> In short, farming in southeast Tulare County has taken on a new glamor under the 160 acre limitation rule, or so it would seem. This has been done even in the face of the accusation that the limitation was throttling, rather than helping, agriculture.
> . . . .
>
> [Ray Cawelti] is a skilled mechanic and green thumb artist, as well as a beginning owner of 20 acres of producing trees. This, too, may be an advantage of many ownerships and cooperative farm management. Capable persons . . . can have ownership hopes and ambitions which large acreage owners deny their workers.
>
> The quality of living, too, in this new water area is good and has become available to many people. . . .
>
> [E]fficiencies usually attributed to large acreages can be met and perhaps surpassed for an owner of less than 160 acres, while the quality of country living is increased.[70]

Nevertheless, powerful forces within state and federal governments, exemplified by the Public Land Law Review and National Water Commissions, have been indifferent to preservation of the family farm and a balanced rural society.

---

67. *Id.*
68. *Senate Hearings*, *supra* note 54, pt. 3, at 3966 (statement of Philip M. Raup).
69. Porteous, *Is This a New Era in California Agriculture?*, CALIFORNIA FARMER, Sept. 18, 1971, *reprinted in Farmworkers in Rural America*, *supra* note 46, at 824.
70. *Id.* at 824-25.

Questions of the quality of rural life and stability of the place of individuals within it are not confined to the reclamation belt. Awareness of the relevance of the California Arvin-Dinuba study has spread eastward. In recent years, notably from the 1960's, spokesmen for family farmers on the fringes of the arid region and in the humid belt east of the hundredth meridian have voiced acute concern over their buffeting amid the forces of the marketplace and in the arena of politics. In 1968 the president of the South Dakota Farmers Union described the extreme impact on rural society:

> The exodus of our farm people . . . has produced economic and social decay in small towns and cities throughout the Nation. You can drive almost anywhere in the rural areas and see the results of our failure to weigh social consequences in determining our economic objectives: the weathered, abandoned farmhouse, a curtain flapping through a broken window; the soaped-up plate glass of the store front with the "closed" sign taped to the door; the weeds standing tall around the vacant service station, and the growing ratio of older people on our main streets in areas like South Dakota.[71]

At the same Senate hearing the economist of the Fond du Lac, Wisconsin Pure Milk Products Cooperative, pointed to the farmers' hard alternative in leaving the land:

> We cannot afford to force more of our farm population into urban slum areas as they are squeezed off farms. Many are trained, skilled, and experienced in agriculture with a lifetime on the farm, but would be qualified in the city only for the unskilled jobs at the bottom of the income ladder . . . and . . . will only add to the ranks of poverty.[72]

This concern for family farmers in both the humid and dry belts is a repetition of concerns for "actual settlers" stretching back for over a century. Expressed originally in federal policy-making legislation in the Homestead and Reclamation Acts, this concern has been evident more often in the deliberations of legislative or administrative committees than in enactment of supporting statutes to make the policy effective. Administrative initiative gave birth to the Resettlement Administration under the New Deal, but legislative attack from Farm Bureau opponents ultimately curbed its support of the family farm in the 1940's.[73] In the early fifties Congress, which had declined in the forties to exempt the big Central Valley Project from acreage limitation and residency requirements, approved giving owners of excess lands on "small" projects the op-

---

71. *Senate Hearings, supra* note 54, at 21 (statement of Ben H. Radcliffe); *1968 Hearings, supra* note 43.
72. *1968 Hearings, supra* note 43, at 275-76 (statement of Arthur Miller).
73. S. BALDWIN, POVERTY AND POLITICS 341-46 (1968) [hereinafter cited as BALDWIN].

tion of conforming to reclamation law or of paying a modest sum.[74] These are the cross-current winds of politics.

In perspective, it becomes clear that the survival of widespread family farming is as much a question of politics as of economics, if not more so. Some threats to family farming appear to have no relation to the issue, but do, *e.g.*, tax-loss loopholes that encourage investment of nonagricultural capital in land purchase and operation, and the search for monopoly market power through vertical integration raising antitrust questions. Therefore, the tactics relevant to family farm survival need to be broadly conceived.

REMEDIES

In the last half century those friendly to the family farm have produced numerous studies and proposed much legislation to shield it from the continuing trend towards industrialized or agribusiness farming. Most of this legislation, however, has not been enacted. For example, in 1939 and 1940 the LaFollette Committee carried out investigations focused on violations of free speech and rights of labor within western industrialized agriculture. A relationship between dependence on disadvantaged laborers in industrialized agriculture and disadvantaged working family farmers became evident. Senator Robert M. LaFollette, Jr., told Congress:

> This same disadvantaged [labor] status appeared to have spread to large numbers of family farms, affecting owner and tenant alike. They were persistently faced with the competition of cheap farm labor, mechanization, drought, debt, and the movement toward large-scale commercialized agriculture.
>
> I wish to point out . . . that the tendency toward commercialized or industrial farming is not confined to any one section of the country. It is manifesting itself all over the United States.[75]

The Senator then introduced five bills designed to raise standards of labor in industrialized agriculture to reduce industrialized agriculture's differential advantage over family farmers from the use of cheap labor. He made his committee report during the first year of World War II, and—whether because of that timing or other reasons—Congress took no action upon LaFollette's recommendations.[76]

Other congressional surveys related to family farming followed. Between studies of the acreage limitation provisions of reclamation law in 1947[77] and 1958[78] that produced no action, a House committee

---

74. Taylor, *Excess Land Law: Legislative Erosion of Public Policy*, 30 ROCKY MT. L. REV. 1, 20-29 (1958).
75. 88 CONG. REC. 8317 (1942).
76. *Id.* at 8317-38 (1942).
77. *S. 912 Hearings, supra* note 61.
78. *S. 1425 Hearings, supra* note 37.

reported on the family farm itself. This Report, too, despite its strongly expressed sentiments, and like other hearings from the forties through 1972, produced no family farm legislation:[79]

> The free-enterprise system grew out of an early dream of a nation sustained chiefly by and for devout, free, independent, and home-owning farmers. . . . Disturbing reports have come from the broad agricultural domain of America, telling of increasing numbers of farm families leaving the soil because of the deterioration of their competitive position, with their acreages becoming consolidated by purchase into larger holdings where hired labor supplants the family unit enterprise.[80]

Government purchase of farm lands also has been proposed nationally. In 1971 Congressman Robert W. Kastenmeier of Wisconsin introduced a Reclamation Lands Authority bill. It proposed government purchase of excess lands above the 160 acre limit of irrigated lands contained in the reclamation law; the administrators would resell or lease such lands. The present law requires the Secretary of the Interior to set the sale price of excess lands so as to relieve the purchaser of the burden of paying windfall profits to the dry land owner. The price is to be set "on the basis of its actual bona fide value . . . without reference to the proposed construction of the irrigation works."[81] Thus by adding government administration to present price controls, the prospect for effective and enduring achievement of policy goals would be substantially enhanced. The author of the bill has described its purposes as follows:

> One, to enact a long overdue, and long recommended, method for enforcing the public interest provisions of reclamation law effectively;
> Two, to finance public education by grants of revenues created from public water development, just as grants of 94 million acres of public lands financed public education at an earlier point in our history; and
> Three, to enable the public itself, through a newly established authority, to plan the environment that public water development creates.[82]

Although the bill is in the tradition of retention of national forest and grazing lands in public ownership, with government supervision of their use, no hearings were held.

Another proposal is the Nelson-Abourezk amendment to the Clayton Act which would limit participation in farming and farm-

---

79. The Small Reclamation Projects Act did emerge. Its concealed aim is to enable larger farmers to escape acreage limitation. *See* text accompanying note 74 *supra*.
80. SUBCOMM. ON FAMILY FARMS OF THE HOUSE AGRICULTURE COMM., THE FAMILY FARM, 84th Cong., 2d Sess. 1 (1956) (Comm. Print).
81. 43 U.S.C. 423e (1970).
82. 117 CONG. REC. 11201 (1971). Six California Congressmen co-authored the bill, and four Senators introduced identical bills.

land ownership by persons engaged "in a business other than farming, whose nonfarming business assets exceed $3,000,000 . . . ."[83] The proposal makes specific exemptions for farm cooperatives and charitable organizations. A land divestiture provision is also included in the proposal which would require sale of any farmland held by a violating corporation within five years of passage of the act. In the spirit of the Reclamation Lands Authority bill, the Nelson-Abourezk proposal would empower the Farmers Home Administration to purchase such land if the corporation could not divest by itself. The bill was introduced but not enacted in the ninety-third Congress; it was recently reintroduced.

The federal government is not lacking in expressions favoring family farming or in experience supporting it. The Farmers Home Administration and the Agricultural Extension Service were designed originally to make financial and educational assistance available to family farmers in need of them. These instruments, however, are presently wholly inadequate to meet the spread of industrialized agriculture.[84] Thus neither Congress nor federal administrators have been effective so far in checking the decline of the family farm.

A wide variety of measures more directly aimed at discouraging absorption of family farms has been passed or proposed on the state level. Some of these seek to limit or to bar corporate ownership or operation, in general only if beyond family membership in the corporation.[85] They vary widely in detail. For example, the South Dakota Family Farm Act of 1974 prohibits the use of the corporate form but allows exceptions when members of a family are a majority of the stockholders, own a majority of the stock, and one of the family members resides on the farm.[86] In contrast, North Dakota law prohibits any corporation from entering into farming and excepts only farmer owned cooperatives.[87] The effectiveness of these statutes is in dispute.[88] Another approach was proposed by California Assemblyman (now Congressman) John Burton. In 1972 he introduced a graduated land tax bill in the California Legislature. No action was taken.[89]

---

83. S. 1458, 94th Cong., 1st Sess. (1975). See Abourezk, *Agriculture, Antitrust, and Agribusiness: A Proposal for Federal Action*, 20 S.D.L. REV. 499 (1975).
84. *1968 Hearings, supra* note 43, at 91-101 (statement of Howard Bertsch, Administrator, Farmers Home Administration). See also BALDWIN, *supra* note 73.
85. WISCONSIN LEGISLATIVE COUNCIL, CORPORATE FARMING AND STATE LEGISLATION (Staff Brief 73-4, July 5, 1973).
86. S.D. COMPILED LAWS ANN. § 47-9A-14 (Supp. 1974).
87. N.D. CENT. CODE § 10-06-01, 04 (1960).
88. For a critical analysis of this matter and an analysis of the South Dakota Family Farm Act, *see*, Comment, *The South Dakota Family Farm Act of 1974: Salvation or Frustration for the Family Farmer?*, 20 S.D.L. REV. 575 (1975).
89. Oakland Tribune, April 17, 1972. *See also* California Legislative Assembly, S.B. No. 679 (1973) (introduced by Mr. Roberti), the intent of which is "to promote possessory interest in small farms." The bill proposes state purchase at fair market value of farms of less than 160 acres,

The search for remedies is not limited to securing the passage of laws. In California, for example, landless persons are actively seeking remedies through action on their own part. This is done sometimes by operating modest plots of land to raise labor intensive crops, seeking outside financial help to accomplish it. Sometimes the remedy sought is by initiating litigation in the courts to secure observance of acreage limitation and residency law by its administrators.

In the San Joaquin Valley a pilot community development program with public and private financing was initiated in 1973. It reports:

> One group of six families was loaned $5,000 to cover out-of-pocket crop expenses for growing cherry tomatoes on six rented acres, a labor intensive, low energy consuming operation. They grossed $65,000, enough to repay their loan, buy 40 acres, level the land and sink a well. They owed about $4,000 on the 40 acres at the end of their first year. WSPG provided, in addition to the loan, legal and accounting services and consultation on supply sources and marketing outlets.[90]

In Imperial Valley, California, 123 landless persons, inspired by a physician, have brought suit to enforce reclamation law's acreage limitation and residency provisions. Final outcome doubtless awaits decision by the Supreme Court, since neither side is likely to accept an adverse decision by a lower court.[91]

So far, persons in other states—farmers and would-be farmers—have shown little awareness that success in these endeavors in California could open access to farm lands for themselves as well as for Californians.

Conclusion

Since the earliest settlements in the seventeenth century, America has experienced both the stabilizing and the divisive influences of differing relationships of man to the land. The small family farms of New England contrasted greatly with the vast Southern plantations. The farms of the Middle West and Far West had elements of both systems, the former leaning strongly towards the New England pattern and the latter towards the Southern. In

---

to be rented back to the farmer for annual fee of one dollar per acre, the fee to go to the local school district. Should the lessor die or cease to lease, the option is to be given, in order of priority, to the spouse, to children of the lessor in descending order of their age, and finally to another qualified farmer. The land, once acquired by the state, is not to be sold without specific legislative enactment.

90. Westside Planning Group, Inc., Farms for Families. A strawberry cooperative organized among landless pickers near Watsonville, California, reports similar success. *Farmworkers in Rural America, supra* note 46, at 158.

91. Kinsley, *Ben Yellen's Fine Madness*, 2 Washington Monthly 38 (Feb. 1971).

the middle of the nineteenth century Congress declared in favor of the farm worked by the actual settler by adopting the Homestead Act of 1862, and later by reaffirming its choice in the Reclamation Act of 1902.

These declarations of national policy, however, often are at odds with other congressional actions. It has turned out, for example, that apparently neutral tax and agricultural subsidy laws have seriously undermined the declared policy and the position of the smaller farmer.

Furthermore, even when the congressional intent to favor family farmers is clear from the legislative history, administrators all too often have failed to carry out that intent. Perversion of the 160 acre limitation and residency requirements of the reclamation law is a prime example.

A result of these inconsistencies between announced policy and actuality is that the small farmer has suffered greatly. As noted above, 2,000,000 farms were eliminated through consolidation in the 1950's and 1960's.

The human and social costs have been tremendous. The Arvin-Dinuba study of 1946 demonstrated that residents of rural communities based on the family farm have a higher average standard of living than those of a community based on large-scale farming, and that the small farm community is much more socially balanced and less class-divided. Further, there is little hard evidence that, in the long run, the conglomerate corporate farm will be more productive, efficient and advantageous to the consumer than the smaller family farm; indeed, some suspect that the contrary might well be true.

The question posed at the beginning was whether a declaration of public policy towards rural society and its effective implementation were necessary, or whether the fate of that society could safely be left to the forces of technology and the marketplace. The political and economic realities discussed herein demand that Congress declare and administrators consistently enforce a policy favorable to the working farmer. In the past, failure to do so has led to the accelerating destruction of the small farm community by corporate conglomerates, with concomitant social disruption and narrowing control over the food supply. An internally consistent program supporting the family farm system is necessary to its survival as a way of life and as a foundation of a democratic society.

CALIFORNIA WATER PROJECT

Ecology Law Quarterly

VOL. 5   1975   No. 1

California Water Project: Law and Politics

*Paul S. Taylor**

    The California Water Project of 1960 represents a major effort on the part of large landowning interests within the State to circumvent national water policy. As expressed by the United States Supreme Court, that policy is to prevent private monopolization and speculation in the increased land values created by public reclamation projects. The tactic is to use a state, rather than a federal project, to avoid application of national reclamation law and policy. As administered by both state and federal agencies, circumvention has been successful so far.

    Viewed historically and nationally, distribution of landownership was the essence of the issue until westward settlement reached the hundredth meridian. Thereafter it centered on the joining of water to arid land. The California Water Project is but a relatively recent phase of this century-old issue.

    The pervasive influence upon society of the distribution or concentration of landownership was early understood. As Daniel Webster said on the 200th anniversary of the landing of the Pilgrims:

> Our New England ancestors . . . were themselves, either from their original condition, or from the necessity of their common interest, nearly on a general level, in respect to property. Their situation demanded a parcelling out and division of the lands; and it may be said fairly, that this necessary act *fixed the future frame and form of their Government* . . . . The consequence . . . has been a great

---

    * Professor of Economics Emeritus, University of California, Berkeley; consultant to the Office of the Secretary of the Interior and to the Bureau of Reclamation, successively, between 1943 and 1952. Martha M. Chase and Stefan Jovanovich assisted in the preparation of this paper. The Committee on Research and Institute of Business and Economic Research, University of California, Berkeley, gave support.

subdivision of the soil, and a great equality of condition; the true basis, most certainly of popular government.[1]

I

MAN IN HIS ENVIRONMENT

Let's ask ourselves "what is the environment?" In short, it is everything—everything that was here before man—plus all the changes man has wrought, both directly and indirectly. In addition, and not to be overlooked, it must include man himself.

—Secretary of Interior Rogers C.B. Morton, 1971[2]

[N]o one would believe that shrewd, calculating business men would invest their money on the strength of land rising in value while unimproved, for even the farmer himself has to abandon it who endeavors to add to its value without water. At the same time, purchasers are not lacking who would add it to their already extensive dry domain and the people, in the next legislature, will find themselves confronted by an array of force and talent to secure to capital the ownership of the water as well as of the land, and the people will at last have it to pay for . . . .

—Visalia (California) Delta, 1877[3]

"Environment" and "ecology" are words used currently to reflect concern about undesired effects of economic development left to uncontrolled market forces. But the issue of socially acceptable development of natural resources is not new. Two generations ago this public concern bore the name "conservation."

A generation ago a government study in California's Central Valley compared two rural communities: one, Arvin, was surrounded by large-scale farms and the other, Dinuba, was surrounded by smaller family-size farms. Proportionately, Dinuba had twice as many business, professional, and white collar workers; three times as many farm operators; slightly more skilled, semi-skilled, and service laborers; and fewer than half as many agricultural laborers. Per dollar of agricultural production, the family-size farms of Dinuba supported a larger number of persons in the local community at a higher average living standard than did the large-scale farms of Arvin. Similar contrasts were found between

---

1. D. WEBSTER, *Discourse, Delivered at Plymouth, December 22, 1820,* in COMMEMORATION OF THE FIRST SETTLEMENT OF NEW ENGLAND 53-54 (3d ed. 1825). (emphasis in original).
2. USDI News Release (April 22, 1971), Excerpts from Remarks by Secretary of the Interior Rogers C.B. Morton Before the Great Issues Forum of the University of Southern California, Los Angeles, California, April 22, 1971.
3. Visalia Delta, May 5, 1877, at 2, col. 3.

the two communities in the quality of civic life—Dinuba had more parks, schools, churches, recreational opportunities, local newspapers, etc.[4]

More recently, in 1969, another study found that Imperial County, California, was a "two-class" polarized community consisting of 4.4 percent "upper class" farm persons and 87.3 percent "mass of laborers."[5] More than half of the farmed land was in holdings in excess of 160 acres, the ceiling on individual water deliveries set by federal reclamation law.[6] By contrast, Livingston County, Illinois, was found to be an overwhelmingly "middle class" community, where only 1.3 percent of "farm personnel" was "upper class" and only 11.7 percent "lower class."[7]

Today, ownership of California agricultural land is heavily concentrated.[8] This concentration is largely an inheritance from early eras of railroad land grants, Spanish and Mexican land grants, and speculative acquisition of large blocks of public lands.[9] In the 1880's, British observer James Bryce recorded this description of the emerging environmental pattern in California's Central Valley:

> Some of these speculators, by holding their lands for a rise, made it difficult for immigrants to acquire small freeholds, and in some cases checked the growth of farms. Others let their land on short leases to farmers, who thus came into a comparatively precarious and often necessitous condition; others established enormous farms, in which the soil is cultivated by hired labourers, many of whom are discharged after the harvest—a phenomenon rare in the United States, which is elsewhere a country of moderately sized farms, owned by persons who do most of their labour by their own and their children's hands. Thus the land system of California presents features both peculiar and dangerous, a contrast between great properties, often appearing to conflict with the general weal, and the sometimes hard pressed

---

4. STAFF OF SENATE SPECIAL COMM. TO STUDY PROBLEMS OF AMERICAN SMALL BUSINESS, 79TH CONG., 2D SESS., SMALL BUSINESS AND THE COMMUNITY, A STUDY IN CENTRAL VALLEY OF CALIFORNIA ON EFFECTS OF SCALE OF FARM OPERATIONS, S. REP. No. 13 (Comm. Print 1946). *See also* W. GOLDSCHMIDT, AS YOU SOW (1947).

5. T. Smith, *A Study of Social Stratification in the Agricultural Sections of the U.S.*, 34 RURAL SOCIOLOGY 496, 508-09 (1969) [hereinafter cited as T. Smith].

6. *See* United States v. Imperial Irrig. Dist., 322 F. Supp. 11, 12 (1971) (233,000 acres owned by excess landowners in 1965); Yellen v. Hickel, 352 F. Supp. 1300, 1317 (1972) (437,000 irrigated acres in 1966).

7. T. Smith, *supra* note 5, at 508.

8. P. Taylor, *Water, Land, and People in the Great Valley* . . . , 5:2 AMERICAN WEST 24, 28 *et seq.* (1968) [hereinafter cited as *Water, Land, and People in the Great Valley*].

9. P. Gates, *Homestead Law in an Incongruous Land System*, 41 AM. HIST. REV. 668 (1936).

small farmer, together with a mass of unsettled labour, thrown without work into the towns at certain times of the year.[10]

As it was emerging, this pattern of concentrated landownership was sharply contested. Debate came to a particularly sharp focus at the State's 1879 Constitutional Convention. Ultimately, it was decided that future grants of state lands should be limited to 320 acres per individual.[11] In the same year, Major John Wesley Powell, explorer of the Colorado River, wrote that in the water-short West, "The question for legislators to solve is to devise some practical means by which water rights may be distributed among individual farmers and water monopolies prevented."[12]

This issue was not confined within the boundaries of any one state. It spread steadily throughout the West and arrived eventually at the national Capitol. A popular movement sprang up in the 1890's seeking development of Western waters. The minutes of the nearly annual sessions of the National Irrigation Congress reflect two principal concerns: (1) to find a public source of financing Western water development and (2) to prevent the building of water monopoly upon the foundations of existing land monopoly.

Both these purposes were embodied in a bill introduced in Congress in 1902. Congressman Francis G. Newlands of Nevada, author of the bill, explained that President Theodore Roosevelt

> was somewhat in doubt as to whether the bill was sufficiently guarded in the interest of homeseekers. It was a question simply of construction . . . . We all wanted to prevent monopoly and concentration of ownership, and the result was that certain changes were made absolutely satisfactory both to the Executive and to the Irrigation Committee . . . .[13]

Congressman Frank Mondell of Wyoming contributed his assurance that the bill would guard "against the possibility of speculative land

---

10. 2 J. BRYCE, AMERICAN COMMONWEALTH 427 (1913).
11. DEBATES AND PROCEEDINGS OF THE CONSTITUTIONAL CONVENTION OF THE STATE OF CALIFORNIA IN 1878, at 1136-1155, 1486 (1880). CAL. CONST. art. 17, § 3.
12. J. POWELL, REPORT ON THE LANDS OF THE ARID REGION OF THE UNITED STATES 41 (2d ed. 1879). The enduring and pervasive nature of the problem is suggested in a generalization by Solomon Blum:
> I find two forces at work in our economic life. They are antagonistic in principle. The first is private enterprise, in some of its aspects terribly wasteful, disorderly and reckless. Its valuations are simply the prices of the market. It is mechanistic. Individual and social responsibility can develop only when it is modified. For all this, possibly because of this, it is productive and it generates energy. Profits are the source of this energy. But individualistic competition has never had the field entirely to itself. It has always been too harsh to bear. Therefore society has always protected itself in some measure from the blind forces of the market. S. BLUM, LABOR ECONOMICS vii (1925).

13. 35 CONG. REC. 6674 (1902).

holdings . . . on the public land, while it will also compel the division into small holdings of any large areas . . . in private ownership which may be irrigated under its provisions."[14] The bill, which became the National Reclamation Act of 1902, stipulated that:

> No right to the use of water for land in private ownership shall be sold for a tract exceeding 160 acres to any one landowner, and no such sale shall be made to any landowner unless he be an actual bona fide resident on such land, or occupant thereof residing in the neighborhood of said land . . . .[15]

Although the words "ecology" and "environment" were not used during Congressional debate on the Reclamation Bill, it is clear that the relevance of environmental considerations to the issue of concentrated versus dispersed landownership was understood. During debate, Congressman Newlands pointed out that:

> Lord Macauley said we never would experience the test of our institutions until our public domain was exhausted and an increased population engaged in a contest for the ownership of land. That will be the test of the future, and the very purpose of this bill is to guard against land monopoly and to hold this land in small tracts . . . .[16]

In 1907, President Theodore Roosevelt invited similar recognition of the importance of husbanding and of using natural resources generally for the public benefit when he convened the first Governors Conference and chose "conservation" as its theme. Assembled in 1908, the Governors resolved:

> We declare our firm conviction that this conservation of our natural resources is a subject of transcendent importance, which should engage unremittingly the attention of the Nation, the States, and the People in earnest co-operation . . . . We agree that the sources of national wealth exist for the benefit of the People, and that monopoly thereof should not be tolerated.[17]

Thus the principles of the homestead tradition of giving actual settlers access to land, enacted six years earlier in the acreage and residency provisions of reclamation law, were recognized officially by the governors of the states as being vital to the nation's conservation of natural resources. A half century later, in the form of acreage limitation, this policy was challenged in the courts. The U.S. Supreme Court rejected the challenge in a unanimous decision declaring that reclamation projects were "designed to benefit people, not land," and to distrib-

---

14. *Id.* at 6677. *See also* statements by Sen. W.A. Clark of Wyoming, *id.* at 2222-24.
15. National Reclamation Act, 43 U.S.C. § 431 (1902).
16. 35 CONG. REC. 6734 (1902).
17. G. PINCHOT, BREAKING NEW GROUND 351 (1947).

ute benefits "in accordance with the greatest good to the greatest number of individuals."[18]

II

PRIVATE INTEREST VS. PUBLIC POLICY

In California much of the best land . . . is in huge private holdings. . . . Already owners of more than seventy huge tracts of land have signified their willingness to subdivide their lands for the benefit of intending settlers. This shows which way the wind blows and may be taken as an indication that when the Government is ready to go ahead our patriotic landed proprietors will be willing and ready to cooperate.

John W. Ferris, 1905[19]

The conclusion is inescapable: the DiGiorgio Fruit Corporation, like the Kern County Land Company, is not susceptible to the kind of land reform the Bureau [of Reclamation] seems interested in introducing via the back-door. Its 160-acre limitation clause is a wholly inadequate club with which to coerce the big landowners into dividing their baronies among the serfs.

Senator Sheridan Downey of California, 1947[20]

Private landowners, the Federal Government, and the California State Government all showed early interest in irrigating the arid and semi-arid lands of the Central Valley. Privately-financed stream diversions for this purpose were begun immediately following the Gold Rush. Because of the cost, these efforts spread slowly, reaching their peak on the Kern River in the 1880's.[21] In 1887 the California Legislature passed the Wright Irrigation Act, which authorized local financing of local water projects.[22] With hardly an exception, little financing of construction followed.[23]

In 1874 a federal commission reported to the President that irrigation of Central Valley was technically feasible, and that if undertaken the value of the land "could be increased many fold." It recommended that "[t]he rights of water which have given so much trouble in other

---

18. Ivanhoe Irrig. Dist. v. McCracken, 357 U.S. 275, 297 (1958).
19. J. FERRIS, *The Reclamation of Swamp Lands*, 2 FOR CALIFORNIA 14 (1905).
20. S. DOWNEY, THEY WOULD RULE THE VALLEY 180 (1947) [hereinafter cited as DOWNEY].
21. E. TREADWELL, THE CATTLE KING 78-94 (1931); P. Taylor, *Excess Land Law on the Kern*, 46 CALIF. L. REV. 153, 163-64 (1958) [hereinafter cited as *Excess Land Law on the Kern*].
22. Ch. 34, [1887] Cal. Stat. 29 (repealed 1943).
23. P. Taylor, *Central Valley Project: Water and Land*, 2 WESTERN POL. Q. 228, 234-35 (1949) [hereinafter cited as *Central Valley Project: Water and Land*].

countries . . . be established . . . on the principle of 'the greatest good for the greatest number.' "[24] In this spirit, landowners in the Sacramento Valley voluntarily accepted a 40-acre limit on water deliveries to encourage construction of a federal reclamation project at Orland in 1907.[25]

In 1920 the Irrigation Association of California published a report urging development of Central Valley waters.[26] Intensive studies followed, culminating in 1930 in a report to the State Legislature on a "State Water Plan" to be directed by Engineer Edward Hyatt.[27]

Three years later, in the depths of depression when unemployment was at its peak, the people of California authorized, by referendum vote, the issuance of $170 million in revenue bonds to construct a Central Valley project. The voters understood that federal aid of $43 million could be anticipated.[28] The measure authorized construction by the State and permitted the State to seek federal construction in compliance with terms prescribed by federal law.[29] The State Water Authority created by the referendum was

> expressly authorized and empowered, to accept cooperation from the United States of America, its instrumentalities and agencies in the construction, maintenance and operation . . . of said Central Valley Project, and . . . shall have full power to do any and all things

---

24. COMM'RS ON IRRIGATION OF THE SAN JOAQUIN, TULARE, AND SACRAMENTO VALLEYS, CALIFORNIA, H.R. EXEC. DOC. No. 290, 43d Cong., 1st Sess. 77, 78 (1874). For an historical review of the origins of Reclamation's role in Central Valley, *see* C. ENGLE, CENTRAL VALLEY PROJECT DOCUMENTS, PART II, H.R. DOC. NO. 246, 85th CONG., 1st SESS. 757-92 (1957).

25. USDI, BUR. OF RECLAMATION PROJECT FEASIBILITIES AND AUTHORIZATIONS 388-90 (1949).

26. R. MARSHALL, IRRIGATION OF TWELVE MILLION ACRES IN THE VALLEY OF CALIFORNIA, November 1920 (distributed by California State Irrigation Association, Sacramento, California).

27. CAL. DEP'T OF PUB. WORKS, DIV. OF WATER RESOURCES, REPORT TO THE LEGISLATURE OF 1931 ON THE STATE WATER PLAN (1930) (prepared pursuant to ch. 832, Stats. of 1929, Bull. No. 25 (1930)).

28. Cal. State Dept., Referendum Measure to be Submitted to the Electors of the State of California at the Special Election to be Held . . . December 19, 1933, at 3.
The measure carried by a vote of 459,712 YES; 426,109 NO.

29. The Warren Act of 1911 authorized the Secretary of the Interior to contract with "irrigation districts, . . . associations, corporations . . ." for construction and joint use of reclamation facilities, and applied the acreage limitation to land irrigated by these joint projects. 43 U.S.C. § 524 (1911). The 1926 Act authorized the Secretary to contract with irrigation districts for federal construction of projects and repayment by the districts. 43 U.S.C. § 423e (1926). Nothing in the language or in the legislative history of this later Act suggested that acreage or residency limitations were not to be applied before and after repayment. For an analysis of the effect of the 1926 provisions on the acreage and residency requirements, *see* Yellen v. Hickel, 335 F. Supp. 200 (S.D. Cal. 1971), *Supp.* 352 F. Supp. 1300 (S.D. Cal. 1972). Both of J. Murray's opinions are discussed in P. Taylor, *Water, Land and Environment, Imperial Valley: Law Caught in the Winds of Politics*, 13 NATURAL RESOURCES J. 22-30 (1973).

necessary in order to avail itself of such aid, assistance and cooperation under Federal legislation now or hereafter enacted by Congress.[30]

Thus, the measure extended to the authorized State Central Valley Project the authority previously given to state irrigation districts "[t]o cooperate and contract with the United States under the Federal Reclamation Act of June 17, 1902, and all acts amendatory thereof or supplementary thereto. . . ."[31]

The State Water Authority was unable to sell the revenue bonds because of the depression, so it sought federal aid. At Congressional hearings in February, 1935, the Chairman of the House Flood Control Committee questioned Edward Hyatt concerning California views on the nature of possible federal-state cooperation:

> THE CHAIRMAN. Is it your view that this project should be undertaken as a Federal project with State assistance or as a State project with assistance of the Federal Government?
>
> MR. HYATT. That is a matter of secondary interest in California. California wants the project constructed, and if the Federal Government desires to take charge of it I am sure that the people of California will say well and good. They are desperate. Our view is that it should be done by the State, and we have filed this application with the Public Works Administration and are proceeding under the State water authority. . . . However, the great desire is to get the project constructed and to safeguard this country; and the Government's desires in that matter will come first.[32]

The reaction of the Public Works Administration, under Secretary of the Interior Harold L. Ickes, was to take federal responsibility for Central Valley Project, allocating $20 million to begin construction. Two years later, Congress reauthorized the project under "the provisions of the reclamation law" in the 1937 Rivers and Harbors Act.[33]

---

30. Ch. 1042, § 15, [1933] Cal. Stat. 2654. The California Water Development Resources Bond Act, approved by referendum in 1960, adopted the 1933 "provisions of the code governing the Central Valley Project. . . ." Ch. 1762, § 1, [1959] Cal. Stat. 4235 (now CAL. WATER CODE § 12931 (West 1971).

31. Ch. 615, § 1, [1935] Cal. Stat. 1741, *amending* Ch. 160, § 1, [1917] Cal. Stat. 244.

32. *Hearings on H.R. 4122 & 4128 Before the House Comm. on Flood Control*, 74th Cong., 1st Sess. 60 (1935).

33. Act of Aug. 26, 1937, ch. 392, § 2, 50 Stat. 850. The President, by Executive Order of September 10, 1935, had authorized transfer of Emergency Relief Appropriation Act of 1935 funds to the Interior Department to commence construction of Central Valley Project, to be "reimbursable in accordance with the reclamation laws." In C. ENGLE, CENTRAL VALLEY PROJECT DOCUMENTS, H.R. DOC. NO. 416, 84th Cong., 2d Sess., pt. 1, 559 (1956). *See also* L. Graham, Some Aspects of Federal-State Relationships in California Water Resources Development, 1961 (unpublished mimeographed material in author's library).

Once the flow of federal funds started, a move was made to remove from Central Valley Project the reclamation law's acreage limitation and residency protections against monopoly and speculation. The original draft of the 1937 bill contained such a removal proviso that the "transfer of authority from the Secretary of War to the Secretary of the Interior shall not render the expenditure of this fund reimbursable under the reclamation law."[34] The House report on the bill, however, recommended repayment "under the Reclamation Law."[35] Without floor debate, the House agreed to the latter.[36]

Interests opposed to acreage limitation did not press their case at the jeopardy of obstructing initiation of the flow of funds. Large landholding interests, however, were acutely aware of the implications of the current phase of a longstanding California issue known from its nineteenth century beginnings as "land monopoly." Roland Curran, a spokesman for their point of view, related in retrospect the concerns over acreage limitation law as water development became an issue in the 1930's:

> In 1937, I was serving as secretary of the Kern County Water Development Commission, an agency of the county of Kern. We were requested by responsible officials of the Bureau of Reclamation to take the lead in organizing . . . districts . . . able to contract for project water. The question was raised about the application of acreage limitations, at that time, as a considerable percentage of the lands to be brought into a district organization were in holdings exceeding 160 acres. We were assured by officials of the Bureau of Reclamation that, as there were no public lands in the area and that at least half of the project water would be used, of necessity, for recharging the ground-water table and as there was no legal or physical way in which any land owner could be prevented from pumping what waters underlay his surface lands, that we could count with certainty that before the project was completed, the acreage limitations would be removed.
>
> Until 1944, this was the general understanding. In February of 1944, the Commissioner of Reclamation advised that, if any correction was made in the law or remedial legislation asked for, it was up to the people of the project area to bring it about, or to use his exact words: "I am handcuffed on this matter."[37]

In April of 1944, Russell Giffen, a large land operator on the west side of the San Joaquin Valley, similarly advised Congress of a change

---

34. 81 CONG. REC. 6716-17 (1937).
35. H.R. REP. No. 885, 75th Cong., 1st Sess. 60 (1935).
36. 81 CONG. REC. 6718 (1937).
37. *Hearings on S. 912 Before the Subcomm. of the Senate Public Lands Comm.*, 80th Cong., 1st Sess., 1310 (1947) [hereinafter cited as *Hearings on S. 912*].

in the attitude of Bureau of Reclamation officials. At first some officials forecast that the Central Valley Project would be exempted from acreage limitation, but later spokesmen affirmed that acreage limitation law was to be supported and enforced. Giffen testified:

> Two members of our committee went to Denver and talked to Mr. Harper of the Bureau. It was indicated to them there that the 160-acre provision was not to be taken seriously. It was their suggestion. We went there with the plea that they put in a district on the west side. They came back and said that there would have to be surveys there. It was their suggestion that we put up half of the money, half of $50,000. We put up $25,000 and they put up $25,000 . . . . It seems to me that the Bureau was completely in bad faith in taking that $25,000, knowing that they were going to support as vigorously as they have the 160-acre limitation knowing that our district could not accept that.[38]

The alleged bad faith on the part of Bureau officials was, in fact, as Commissioner Bashore implied, a response to directions from their superior, Secretary of the Interior Harold L. Ickes, to support acreage limitation against the attack upon it just begun in the House.[39] On March 22, 1944, a complete exemption had been passed by the House after brief floor debate and rejection of a compromise. This result was achieved in part by a tactic of surprise. The exemption was proposed as a committee amendment, without public hearings.[40]

The Senate, however, held public hearings and then killed the amendment. In conference committee, the exemption was restored. Supporters of acreage limitation, nevertheless, succeeded in holding up passage of the entire rivers and harbors bill, which would have authorized projects throughout the country.[41] Early in the next session, without the exemption of Central Valley Project from acreage limitation, the bill passed easily.[42]

---

38. *Hearing on the Central Valley Project Before a Subcomm. of the Senate Comm. on Military Affairs*, 93 (April 7, 1944) (unpublished mimeographed material in Graham's Library, Univ. Calif., Berkeley).

39. On May 4, 1944, for example, testimony from Secretary of Interior Ickes supported "traditional anti-land-monopoly and anti-speculation policies which the Congress has developed in the Federal reclamation laws for the protection of working farmers . . . ." *Hearings on H.R. 3961 Before a Subcomm. of the Senate Comm. on Commerce*, 78th Cong., 2d Sess. 534 (1944) [hereinafter cited as *Hearings on H.R. 3961*].

40. About six weeks earlier, Commissioner of Reclamation Harry W. Bashore had testified, "I think that in the Central Valley of California there will have to be a modification of that [acreage limitation] requirement . . . because you have a developed economy in that region." *Hearings on H.R. 4485 Before the House Comm. on Flood Control*, 78th Cong., 2d Sess. 642 (1944).

41. *Central Valley Project: Water and Land*, supra note 23, at 243-44.

42. P. Taylor, *Excess Land Law: Legislative Erosion of Public Policy*, 30 ROCKY MT. L. REV. 480, 492 note 71 (1958).

Three years later, a bill to exempt projects in California, Colorado, and Texas was the subject of hearings at which the Senate Public Lands Subcommittee received 1329 pages of testimony. That bill died in committee.[43]

The intensity of the battle was long remembered. A quarter of a century later, Senator Clinton P. Anderson, Chairman of the Subcommittee on Water and Power Resources, cautioned that further attempts at legislative exemption from acreage limitation "would engender great controversy. When such an attempt was made back in the middle '40's . . . it was rejected by the Congress but the turmoil that ensued plagued the reclamation program for many years."[44]

III

PLANNING TO CIRCUMVENT PUBLIC POLICY

If the big landowners in the valley lose out in this particular fight [for exemption of federal CVP from acreage limitation] they have several other proposals to accomplish their end. One of them is a House bill which would authorize the Army to add irrigation and power development to its present navigation and flood control powers. The legislation also would call for construction of a series of irrigation and power projects throughout the country, especially in Central Valley. This would circumvent the 160-acre rule, since the Army is not bound by that restriction.

Another proposal, said to have originated among the big landowners of Fresno County, is for the state of California to take over the Central Valley project, paying the entire bill. This, too, would sidestep the 160-acre limitation. Still other landowners are sinking wells around their holdings in order to be prepared to pump irrigation water from the raised water table, thus getting a free ride on the Central Valley project.

—Business Week, May 13, 1944[45]

---

43. *Hearings on S. 912, supra* note 37.

44. Letter from Sen. Clinton P. Anderson to Mitchell Melich, Solicitor of Interior, March 26, 1971.

45. *Valley Divided*, Bus. Week, May 13, 1944, at 24. The magnitude and concentration of economic incentives for large landowners in Central Valley to avoid acreage limitation is suggested by these data:

(1) Subsidy unrepaid by irrigators on CVP averaged $577 per acre ($92,320 on 160 acres and $577,000 on 1,000 acres). Letter from Congressmen Engle, Miller, Moss, Hagen, Sisk, and McFall to Gov. Edmund G. Brown, Feb. 4, 1957.

(2) Receivers of Class I water from Friant-Kern Canal (CVP) year after year pay one-fourth of what its price would be ". . . if subsidies and special benefits were eliminated." *Hearings on S. 912, supra* note 37, at 869.

(3) Measured by experience on reclamation projects begun prior to August 1913, the value of unimproved land rose by an average of 759 percent. *Id.* at 204.

(4) In 1947, thirty-four landowners "in probable, present, and future San Joaquin Valley service area," with 5,000 or more acres each, owned 748,490 acres, an average of 22,014 acres each. *Id.* at 864 (italics omitted).

Outright Congressional exemption was only one of the tactics employed by large landowners who sought to escape from national reclamation policy limiting water deliveries to the Central Valley Project. The tactic of substituting the Army Engineers for the Bureau of Reclamation as construction agent on Kings and Kern Rivers within the Central Valley was approved by Congress in 1944. Under Executive pressure, however, the bill was rewritten so that administration of irrigation use of water from Army projects was transferred from the Secretary of War to the Secretary of the Interior, and was placed under reclamation law.[46]

Reliance upon pumping from groundwaters, as a tactic to avoid acreage limitation, also encountered obstacles. Central Valley groundwaters have been long overdrawn. As a result, greater and more costly pumping lifts have become necessary. Mineral content of the water has increased and crop productivity has declined. Early suggestions that use of groundwater might free large landowners from repayment obligations generally have not materialized. A result of overdrafted groundwaters on the west side of the San Joaquin Valley is "subsidence of the surface of the ground . . . at the rate of only slightly less than one foot per year throughout the some 80 miles of the San Luis Canal right-of-way."[47]

Another tactic used by large landowners to avoid acreage limitation was to get the State to take over the Central Valley Project. While California several times had authorized its water districts to comply with federal reclamation law in return for federal assistance, and while the people, in a 1933 referendum, had conferred similar authority on the State Water Authority, the State had not attached equivalent controls over water distribution and speculation as conditions for receiving state financial assistance. This lack of controls opened the door to considering California, rather than the Federal Government, as the agency to construct and operate the Central Valley Project. At the Governor's Water Conference in December, 1945, State Engineer Edward Hyatt

---

Figures on the magnitude of subsidy for the Central Valley Project are not available, but the rise in land values attributable to subsidy is unlikely to be less than on other federal projects, and values may be much more as urbanization increases.

46. 43 U.S.C. § 390 (1944); *Excess Land Law on the Kern?, supra* note 21, at 169. *Cf.* United States v. Tulare Lake Canal Co., 340 F. Supp. 1185 (E.D. Cal. 1972), which held that even though section 8 of the Flood Control Act of 1944 (58 Stat. 877) provides that reclamation laws apply to irrigation projects, the flood control project at Pine Flat Dam was not subject to the 160-acre limitation on water released for irrigation purposes. The case (No. 72-2322) is currently on appeal to the 9th Circuit Court of Appeals. It was argued Dec. 13, 1973, and awaits decision.

47. *Hearings on H.R. 17787 Before a Subcomm. of the Senate Comm. on Appropriations*, 89th Cong., 2d Sess., pt. 3, at 841 (1967) (remarks by Ralph M. Brody, Manager-Chief Counsel, Westlands Water District).

discussed these related roles of financing and policy. Referring to federal plans for full development of Central Valley basin waters,[48] he said:

> This enlarged Federal activity, although advantageous to the State from a financial viewpoint, carries with it the threatened imposition of Federal laws and policies in the control and utilization of our water resources and the substitution of Federal control for State control of water and its development. This poses a whole series of new problems with regard to State rights matters. We have as an example the very serious problems facing potential users of Central Valley Project water brought into focus by the excess land provisions of the reclamation laws.[49]

At the same conference, George Sehlmeyer, Master of the California State Grange, stated the grounds for his opposition to the removal of acreage limitation:

> A man came to my office in Sacramento saying, "You are opposing the 160-acre limitation being taken off." He said, "A farmer can farm 10,000 acres today as easily as he could 160 acres 20 years ago."
>
> I replied in this way: "If you allow that large land operation, which is not farming"—don't call that 42,000 acre farm in Fresno County a farm; it is an industrial operation . . . .
>
> If you want to see the effect of nonresident corporate farming, just . . . drive west of Stockton in the most fertile section of California, and you can drive miles and miles and you will never see a farm home. You will see plenty of barracks for labor.
>
> And if we go to the point where we let land get into too large operations and the young men and young women . . . want to get married and we say to them, "You can't buy a home," then you destroy that community life that has built America, then you have pulled up one of the great anchors of our Democracy.
>
> The California State Grange fought the Elliott Amendment to take the 160-acre limitation off . . . speculators are . . . buying that land—one tract sold for $27.50 an acre. That land when the Central Valley water gets there will be worth $150 an acre without any more improvements. And we think it is fundamentally wrong that young men returning from the service of the country should be compelled to pay that difference to speculators who don't live there.[50]

---

48. USDI, Bur. Reclamation, Central Valley Basin Comprehensive Report on Development of Water and Related Resources, S. Doc. No. 113, 81st Cong., 1st Sess. (1949) (previously approved by Sec'y of Interior Ickes on Nov. 16, 1945, *id.* at 52).

49. Proceedings of the California Water Conference Called by Earl Warren, Governor 32 (Dec. 6 & 7, 1945).

50. *Id.* at 462-63.

In the preceding months, in light of the incipient agitation within California for return of Central Valley Project to the State, Secretary of Interior Ickes had expressed the federal view on the critical questions of finance and policy. Noting that the Federal Government had assumed responsibility for the Project when the State was unable to market its bonds, already had invested $157 million, and had plans to spend an additional $200 million, he asked Governor Earl Warren, "Do you think that the State is now prepared to assume full responsibility for the project?"[51] Eight months later, commenting on recommendations by the State Chamber of Commerce that the functions of irrigation and power be returned to the State, the Secretary said:

> . . . their principal objective is to avoid application to the Central Valley of California of the long-established reclamation policy of the Congress which provides for the distribution of the benefits of great irrigation projects among the many and which prevents speculation in lands by the few.[52]

For the time being, the question of turning the Central Valley Project over to the State of California rested there, pending outcome of a second attempt to persuade the 80th Congress (Republican) to grant the exemption from acreage limitation that the 78th Congress (Democratic) had refused.[53] The second attempt failed, as had the first.

---

51. Letter from Sec'y of Interior Harold L. Ickes to Gov. Earl Warren of California, March 7, 1945.

52. Open letter from Sec'y Ickes to Frank Clarvoe, Editor, San Francisco News, October 31, 1945. The Secretary further commented:
> I well know the State Chamber of Commerce's record on the Central Valley project. Originally it opposed the project outright in the early water and power act campaigns in California, but suddenly climbed on the band wagon after the people of California voted their approval of the project at the special election in December 1933. In the years that followed almost everyone in California, including even the State Chamber, paid vocal tribute to the Central Valley project when it was a matter of interesting the Federal Government in it and obtaining Federal money for its development. In recent year[s], however, with the Federal Government now committed to the program and the two main dams completed by the Bureau of Reclamation, the attitude of the State Chamber and some other special interests in California has changed from one of acclaim of the project's merits to claiming the project's benefits for their own exclusive profit. It is the age-old battle over who is to cash in on the unearned increment in land values created by a public investment.

Id.
Seven years later, Secretary of the Interior Oscar Chapman repeated Secretary Ickes' analysis when the prospect of State acquisition of Central Valley Project resurfaced:
> . . . the Department of the Interior would look with favor on acquisition of the Central Valley Project by the State of California, subject to consideration by the Congress, under terms and conditions . . . that will assure the same widespread availability of project benefits under State operation as is provided under existing Federal Reclamation laws.

Letter from Sec'y of the Interior Oscar L. Chapman to Congressman Samuel Wm. Yorty, July 10, 1952.

53. Cf. text accompanying note 37 supra.

The political alignment of groups supporting and opposing the federal law during these two attempts is revealing:[54]

Supporters of Excess Land Provisions

Farm Organizations
  State Grange
  Farmers' Union
  Western Cooperative Dairymen's Union
  California Farm Research and Legislative Committee
  Some local irrigation districts
Veterans' Organizations
  Veterans of Foreign Wars
  American Veterans' Committee
  American Legion
  Disabled American Veterans

Labor Organizations
  American Federation of Labor
  Congress of Industrial Organizations
Religious Groups
  Federal Council of Churches
  Catholic Rural Life Service
  Council for Social Action of the Congregational-Christian Churches
  Protestant Home Missions Council
  National Catholic Rural Life Conference
Other
  League of Women Voters
  Some local Chambers of Commerce

Opponents of Excess Land Provisions

Farm Organizations
  California Farm Bureau Federation and a number of local Farm Bureaus
  Irrigation Districts Association and a number of local irrigation and similar districts
  California Central Valleys Flood Control Association
  Agricultural Council for California
  Central Valley Project Association
  San Joaquin Valley Water Protective Association

Business Organizations
  California State Chambers of Commerce
  Many (but not all) local Chambers of Commerce
  Kern County Land Company
  Miller and Lux, Inc.
  DiGiorgio Fruit Corporation
California State Agencies
  Water Project Authority
  Agricultural Extension Service, University of California

IV

INSTRUMENT FOR CIRCUMVENTION: THE STATE. I

For some time we have had proposals . . . to transfer ownership of the project from the United States to the State of California. I have vigorously opposed these suggestions . . . on the ground that we need Federal assistance . . . such an action would not add a single drop of water or one kilowatt of additional power . . . . It seems to me that the State Engineer . . . and representatives approving this proposal should step forward and tell the people who it is that wants California's limited funds used in this manner and why they support California ownership of a great project that has been made possible by money from the taxpayers of the other 47 states.

—Congressman Clair Engle, 1954[55]

The excess land provisions are not now a part of state law, and have been opposed by the leading organizations seeking state purchase of the CVP and by the California Water Project Authority.

Calif. Assembly Interim Comm. Report, 1955[56]

---

54. BUR. PUB. AD. UNIV. CALIF., BERKELEY, CENTRAL VALLEY PROJECT: FEDERAL OR STATE? REPORT FOR ASSEMBLY INTERIM COMM. ON CONSERVATION, PLANNING AND PUBLIC WORKS 13 CALIF. ASSEMBLY INTERIM COMM. REP. 1953-55, 212 (1953). [hereinafter cited as CENTRAL VALLEY PROJECT: FEDERAL OR STATE?].
55. 100 CONG. REC. App. 452 (1954) (remark by Congressman Engle).
56. CENTRAL VALLEY PROJECT: FEDERAL OR STATE?, *supra* note 54, at 215.

The second failure in three years to obtain Congressional exemption of acreage limitation for the Central Valley Project brought a shift in the tactics of those seeking escape from acreage limitation. Without public hearings, the Legislature took the preliminary steps toward state acquisition of the project,[57] as was forecast by *Business Week* in 1944.[58] In 1951, the California Senate adopted a concurrent resolution instructing the State Water Authority to report "on the legal and financial feasibility of the State assuming ownership and operation of the Central Valley Project. . . ."[59]

This action was followed in 1952 by a $10 million appropriation to the Authority "for use in connection with acquisition by the State of the Central Valley Project . . . and to pay the initial installments . . . for such purchase . . . ."[60]

However, state purchase of the existing federal project faced opposition on financial grounds as well as in defense of the acreage limitation principle. Federal construction had involved minimal state contributions and no bond issues. State purchase would cost huge sums of money in order to repay the federal investment. Alternately, it was possible to consider a compromise tactic that would cost the State less but still would offer a prospect of avoiding acreage limitation on vast holdings. Known as the Feather River Project, it envisioned construction by the state of a reservoir near Oroville on this tributary of the Sacramento, moving the water southward, partly for use in the San Joaquin Valley and partly to be hoisted over the Tehachapi Mountains and into southern California. The prospect that the state might some day build the Feather River Project was a powerful influence, thereby impeding federal construction to make use of those waters under reclamation law. In 1956, the year after disastrous Feather River floods caused immense property damage and loss of 36 lives, Senator Thomas H. Kuchel commented, "I would venture the guess that if the State had not indicated its interest in Oroville, we would have had long before last year's flood a Federal dam at Oroville."[61]

---

57. Public hearings had exposed the deep divisions in public opinion within the State when a Senate Subcommittee came to California in 1944. *Hearings on S.R. No. 295 Before the Subcomm. on the Central Valley Project, California, of the Senate Comm. on Irrigation and Reclamation*, 78th Cong., 2d Sess. 29 (1944). *See also* SPECIAL HOUSE SUBCOMM. REPORT, IRRIGATION AND RECLAMATION ON CENTRAL VALLEY PROJECT, CALIFORNIA, H.R. Doc. No. 416, 84th Cong., 2d Sess., pt. 1, at 673 (1952).
58. See epigraph accompanying note 45 *supra*.
59. Ch. 135 [1951] Cal. Stat. 4563. *See also* Ch. 1441, § 2, [1951] Cal. Stat. 3401.
60. California Budget Act of 1952, ch. 3, item 428.5. [1952] Cal Stat. 108, *as amended* ch. 110, [1953] Cal. Stat. 2601.
61. *Hearings on S. 178 Before the Subcomm. on Irrigation and Reclamation of the Senate Comm. on Interior and Insular Affairs*, 84th Cong., 2d Sess. 179 (1956) [hereinafter cited as *Hearings on S. 178*].

At this 1956 Congressional hearing on a bill proposing federal construction of the San Luis Unit as an addition to Central Valley Project to serve the San Joaquin Valley's westside, divergent interests among potential water-receiving groups surfaced, stopping all federal action for the time. Although the bill left the door open to possible federal-state cooperative use of project facilities, California large land and water interests did not agree upon it.

Speaking in support, Governor Goodwin J. Knight urged "immediate construction," adding, "I sincerely believe that Federal construction of the San Luis unit in such a way that it can be integrated with the State's plan, is an example of the highest type of Federal and State cooperation in solving California's water problem."[62] Reliance on pumped westside groundwaters was turning out to be undependable for agricultural production as an alternative to surface deliveries of irrigation water. Pressure from westside interests for construction, despite the prospect of federal acreage limitation, was a result.

This was not the priority of southern California interests which wanted to assure water for their lands free of reclamation law. Mayor Norris Poulson of Los Angles told the same Congressional committee:

> The San Luis Dam is a basic element of the Feather River Project [which] . . . would . . . eliminate the water shortage in the San Joaquin Valley [and] . . . also meet the needs of the southern portion of the State. We thus oppose violently . . . the contents of the legislation in S.178, which would authorize development of the San Luis Dam as a Federal project of limited value.[63]

Confronted with those conflicting interest groups, the Committee took no action.[64]

By the time the 85th Congress was again ready to consider authorization of the San Luis unit of Central Valley Project, differences among California interests had not disappeared, but they had moderated sufficiently to reach agreement on federal construction of the San Luis unit, with protections against acreage limitation on lands served by the prospective, integrating state project.

Harvey O. Banks, Director of the California Department of Water Resources, testified in favor of the bill authorizing federal construction with financial cooperation from the State, but without wholly rejecting an alternative "Kern County concept" calling for state construction with federal financial cooperation. He explained that:

---

62. *Id.* at 4.
63. *Id.* at 16.
64. "The water situation is so confused in California that no Federal action is indicated until local agreement is reached." MEMORANDUM OF CONGRESSMAN HAGEN, CHAIRMAN OF THE SUBCOMM. ON IRRIGATION AND RECLAMATION OF THE SENATE INTERIOR AND INSULAR AFFAIRS COMM., 85th Cong., 2d Sess. 4 (1958).

The primary difference between the Kern County concept and the approach in S.1887 is in the responsibility for the construction and operation of the project. Under S.1887 the Secretary of the Interior would construct all of the joint-use features and the State would pay to the United States its appropriate share of the construction costs, and, in exchange, would be entitled to proportionate right to the use of the joint-use facilities . . . On the other hand, under the Kern County concept, the State would build and operate the joint-use facilities and the United States would pay to the State its appropriate share of construction costs and be entitled to use a proportionate part of the jointly used project capacities . . . . My position on the Kern County concept is, in short, that it would be acceptable to the State if it is found acceptable by the Department of the Interior, by the affected water users in California, and by the Congress . . . . It is obvious that expenditures of this magnitude cannot be made solely by any one entity, and that the combined efforts of State, Federal, and local interests will be essential if California's water resources are to be developed in a proper and timely manner . . . the saving to the United States under an integrated plan of development at San Luis would be in excess of $30 million.[65]

As a condition of support of S.1887 by the State Water Resources Department, Director Banks stipulated that the bill be amended specifically to exempt the state service area of an integrated federal-state project from "provisions of the Federal reclamation laws," including, of course, their acreage limitation and residency requirements.[66]

Allen Bottorff of the Kern County Farm Bureau spoke for the "Kern County concept" and asked for an amendment exempting the state service area. "If these amendments are accepted as proposed," he said, "the bills would be substantially in line with the California Farm Bureau Federation policy and should be supported." If not, they "should be opposed."[67] As requested by the State Director and the Farm Bureau spokesman, S.1887 was amended to exempt the state service area.

Had the proposed state and federal projects been physically separated instead of dependent upon joint-use facilities, specific exemption would not have been necessary to avoid acreage limitation. However, the

---

65. *Hearings on S. 1887 Before the Subcomm. on Irrigation and Reclamation of the Senate Comm. on Interior and Insular Affairs*, 85th Cong., 2d Sess., 56 & 57 (1958) [hereinafter cited as *Hearings on S. 1887*]. *See also* testimony of Allen Bottorff, Kern County Farm Bureau, *id.* at 103. William S. Peterson, General Manager and Chief Engineer of the Los Angeles Department of Water and Power, expressed belief that the "use of common facilities"—dam, reservoir and canal—would save not only $30 million to the Federal Government, but also "an equal amount to the State or thereabouts . . . ." *Id.* at 180.

66. *Id.* at 53 & 54.

67. *Id.* at 103 & 104.

Warren Act of 1911 applies acreage limitation law to water stored or carried in any reservoir, canal, or ditch of a federal reclamation project constructed or used, as San Luis was to be, under contract with "individuals, corporations, associations, and irrigation districts . . . ."[68] The location of the lands to be served was irrelevant. In the judgment of spokesmen for large landowning interests, a specific Congressional declaration to that effect clearly was necessary if excess lands above 160 acres per individual owner were to be exempted from federal policy.

Faced with the problem of winning Congressional approval of the exemption, the tactic employed was to stress that the state and federal projects would water differently located lands. As Senator Kuchel explained, the requested exemption "applies to land which may be served by State operations only, under the State's water plan, upon which, of course, State law should apply."[69] Federal law would apply within the federal unit.

---

68. 43 U.S.C. §§ 523, 524 (1911). The situations the Warren Act and the California Water Project were designed to meet are closely parallel. In 1911, Congressman William H. Reeder of Kansas, in charge of the Warren bill, told Congress:
> In many of the irrigation projects there is a large amount of land which can be irrigated. There is generally but one right good place to impound the waters. . . . Then the Government, having the reservoir, when others furnish the money, may increase the size of the reservoir and increase the carrying capacity of the ditches and permit those who furnish the necessary funds to use the surplus water on their own land.

46 CONG. REC. 2109, 2781 (1911). In 1958 Senator Thomas H. Kuchel of California told Congress:
> One reservoir to serve 2 systems, 1 Federal and 1 State, is in the interests of efficiency and economy. Indeed, it may be that Mother Nature has precluded the possibility of 2 reservoirs, and thus herself has commanded that the governments of the Nation and the State should labor together, and at San Luis cooperate in the cost and in the use of a dam . . . .

104 CONG. REC. 17726 (1958). There the parallel ends. Senator Kuchel continued: "Federal law, by the bill, would govern the waters impounded at San Luis for the [federal] Central Valleys project, and State law [i.e., no 160-acre limitation] would govern the waters impounded there for use . . . as a part of the State water plan." *Id.* The Warren Act, on the contrary, preserves the 160-acre national policy.

In the legislative history of the Warren Act, the Idaho State Land Board alludes to "cooperation between state and government projects," while the law authorizes cooperation with "irrigation districts"—creatures of states, but without mentioning "states." 45 CONG. REC. 4323 (1910). Speaking to this point, Federal District Judge Oliver Carter stated in 1973 that
> [I]t would appear unreasonable to believe that the State can escape application of the reclamation laws simply because it, rather than the individual irrigation districts, does the direct contracting, for under such conditions the State would in reality be acting as a 'super' irrigation district rather than as a participating sovereign.

Bowker v. Morton, *infra* note 169, at 13-14.

Additionally, note that payment of money to obtain cooperation from the federal reclamation service does not relieve the payers of the obligation to comply with national 160-acre limitation policy. *See also* P. Taylor, *Excess Land Law: Execution of a Public Policy*, 64 YALE L. J. 477, 512 (1955).

69. 104 CONG. REC. 17727 (1958).

An additional prospect was that by federal authorization of the joint-use San Luis Unit, the national treasury stood to be relieved by the State of the burden of financing additional development of California waters. The magnitude of this relief, as represented to Congress, would have dwarfed the $30 million mentioned by Director Banks when he referred only to the San Luis Unit. Responding on the Senate floor, Senator Arthur V. Watkins of Utah said:

> I wish to congratulate the State of California and California's representatives in the Senate, Senator Knowland and Senator Kuchel, on the fact that the great State of California will build this project, and a still larger project which will cost in the neighborhood of $11 billion, and do it on its own.[70]

Unconvinced, Senators Paul Douglas of Illinois and Wayne Morse of Oregon sought to strike the proposed exemption of the state service area. After considerable debate on the Senate floor on August 15, 1958, the motion was defeated.[71] However, in the absence of House action, the entire San Luis authorization bill died with the expiration of the 85th Congress.

V

SENATE DENIES EXEMPTION

I grant you, you start kicking the 160-acre limitation and it is like inspecting the rear end of a mule: You want to do it from a safe distance because you might get kicked through the side of the barn. But it can be done with circumspection, and I hope we can exercise circumspection.

—Congressman Clair Engle of California, 1955[72]

SENATOR ENGLE: *[E]verything the State does in order to put a bucketful of water on a square foot of land will be paid for with State money. That is the reason why we have a provision in the bill that the reclamation law shall not apply . . . . All the Federal Government has done has been to build the first story of the structure . . . .*
SENATOR DOUGLAS: *It would be impossible to have a second story without the Federal expenditures on the foundation and the first story.*

—Senator Clair Engle of California and
Senator Paul Douglas of Illinois, 1959[73]

---

70. 104 CONG. REC. 17730-31 (1958). Minutes later, Senator Kuchel corroborated this estimate. See text accompanying note 104 *infra*.
71. *Id.* at 17735.
72. *Hearings on H.R. 104, H.R. 384, and H.R. 3817, Before the Subcomm. on Irrigation and Reclamation of the House Comm. on Interior and Insular Affairs*, 84th Cong., 1st Sess. (1955).
73. 105 CONG. REC. 7490 (1959).

> *I have always supported the 160-acre limitation. For 4 years I was chairman of the [House] Subcommittee on Irrigation and Reclamation. . . . Never have I deviated from my support for the 160-acre limitation. I do not deviate now.*
>
> —Senator Clair Engle, 1962[74]

Early in the 86th Congress, debate was resumed over application of federal acreage limitation on water deliveries to the state service area via San Luis joint-use reservoir, pumping, and canal facilities. Governor Edmund G. Brown of California told Congress that local interests within his state had met to "remove potential sources of conflict . . ." and agreed upon the pending bill with "minor amendments." He added, "I hope and expect that the State of California will commit itself to invest more than $11 billion in the next 25 years over and above the Federal programs . . . ."[75] The Governor and California's senators, together with the Senate Interior Committee and a majority of its House counterpart, approved the bill including provision for exemption.[76]

When the bill reached the Senate floor, California's senators began with presentation of the physical aspects of the need for water. On the west side of the San Joaquin Valley, about 500,000 acres were to be served as part of the Federal San Luis Unit under federal acreage limitation law. Senator Kuchel said, "Years of overdraft have caused the groundwater table to recede at an alarming rate. . . . The supplemental water from this project would halt the inevitable abandonment of land which otherwise is liable to revert to semidesert."[77] The projected State Unit would use "a portion of the winter run-off which each year flows into the Sacramento-San Joaquin Delta and is wasted into the Pacific Ocean."[78] After passing through the San Luis joint facilities the water would be used:

> ultimately for either delivery to agricultural lands of the surrounding area . . . or for transportation through huge new aqueducts to the residential, industrial, metropolitan and other areas of Los Angeles,

---

74. 108 CONG. REC. 5697 (1962). *See also* 105 CONG. REC. 7851 (1959).

75. *Hearings on S. 44 Before the Subcomm. on Irrigation and Reclamation of the Senate Comm. on Interior and Insular Affairs*, 86th Cong., 1st Sess., 11 & 12 (1959) [hereinafter cited as *Hearings on S. 44*]. "Let us resolve to prove that we are one State, one people, and that we can produce one good water program. Let us grow with the strength of unity, as we begin to fulfill our destiny of greatness." *Id.* at 16.

76. *Id.* at 1.

77. 105 CONG. REC. 7484 (1959). Apparently, Sheridan Downey was forecasting a state project not subject to the federal 160-acre limitation when he wrote in 1947: "There is plenty of water in the Central Valley for the DiGiorgio holdings as well as for all other project farms, excess and nonexcess alike." DOWNEY, *supra* note 20, at 180.

78. *Id.*

Orange, Riverside, San Bernardino, Ventura and San Diego Counties.[79]

The "estimated cost to California" of the State water plan would be "nearly $12 billion." Since the State had not yet authorized funds to commence construction of its part of the joint project, the cut-off date for a federal-state contract was to be extended until January 1, 1962. Failing agreement by that date, construction of the Federal San Luis Unit was to proceed.[80]

Senators Paul Douglas of Illinois and Wayne Morse and Richard Neuberger of Oregon responded by introducing an amendment to S.44 to eliminate the proposed exemption of the state service area of the joint project from application of federal reclamation law. Senator Douglas maximized the strength of their strategic position by explicitly conditioning support for authorization of the project upon passage of the amendment, stating:

> I regard that section, which waives the 160-acre limitation of reclamation law on the so-called State service land, as the crucial part of the bill. If we were to strike out section 6(a) from the bill, I personally would vote for the bill. . . . [I]f the section is not eliminated from the bill, I shall be compelled to vote against the bill. I regard the debate on section 6(a) as of equal importance with debate on the bill itself.[81]

California's senators insisted that Congress declare the exemption of the state service area from federal reclamation law. Their dilemma was twofold: (1) that water, whether serving state or federal service area lands, could be stored and pass through but a single site (the site upon which S.44 prescribed that the Federal Government should construct the facilities) and (2) that the Warren Act applies federal law to waters passing through federal facilities no matter where they are delivered ultimately.

Accordingly, Senator Kuchel argued that S.44 "should unequivocally provide that in one area served by the Federal project, Federal reclamation law will apply, while in the other area, served by the Feather River project, California law will apply."[82]

---

79. *Id.*
80. *Id.*
81. 105 CONG. REC. 7488 (1959); *see also id.* at 7491, 7496. Senator Morse declared himself in favor of the bill "subject to the protection of some historic criteria." *Id.* at 7488. Senator Neuberger favored the project, but pointed out "the necessity for improving the bill to assure continuity of national water policy." *Id.* at 7493. He said, "[I]f the 160-acre limitation is breached in California, such action will set a precedent . . . by means of which all the other Western States would be able to request a similar prerogative." *Id.* at 7494.

82. *Id.* at 7484. He asked Senator Douglas whether the latter believed "that the people of California should have the right, by State law, to determine how water is to

Senator Engle argued, in justification of exemption, that investment of state money should free lands in the state service area from federal policy:

> The State government will pay every nickel of its share. Not a penny of it will be charged to the Federal taxpayers. That is the reason for this [exemption] provision in the bill. The projects are completely severable. They do not overlap or intermix.[83]

As debate progressed, Senator Engle assumed a new position, *viz.*, that it made no difference whether the amendment to eliminate the proposed exemption of the state service area was passed by Congress or not; federal law would not apply to state service lands either way:

> MR. ENGLE. Does the Senator believe that if section 6(a) is stricken from the bill the reclamation law will apply to the State projects service area?
> MR. DOUGLAS. Yes, I do, and I want to make a record to show clearly that it would.
> MR. ENGLE. I want to make a record which is very plain indeed that . . . the section is surplusage. It is merely a statement of what the law is.
> MR. DOUGLAS. If it is surplusage, then eliminate it.
> MR. ENGLE. The people affected want this additional assurance.
> MR. DOUGLAS. Who are they? What people?[84]

As Senator Engle declined to stand on his legal opinion to the extent of abandoning his support of section 6(a), Senator Kuchel intervened in the dialogue:

> MR. KUCHEL. I will tell the Senator what people they are. They are the people of southern California.
> MR. DOUGLAS. Does the Senator mean the big landowners of the Central Valley?
> MR. KUCHEL. I do not mean the big landowners of the Central Valley . . . . I mean the city government of the city of Los Angeles. . . . They are interested in getting supplemental water, so that when the housewife turns on the water tap she can get water.
> MR. DOUGLAS . . . . Surely the Senator does not oppose the application of the 160-acre limitation if he is just considering water distributed in the city of Los Angeles. It is in the Central Valley that this issue arises.[85]

---

be used in California under the State system?" Senator Douglas responded: "I do not believe that large landowners should be able to come to Congress and obtain an exemption from the Federal law." *Id.* at 7497.

83. *Id.* at 7490.
84. *Id.* at 7496.
85. *Id.* at 7496-97. Before Senate debate concluded, Senator Engle produced a telegram from Governor Brown concurring in the position that section 6(a) was surplusage. *Id.* at 7857. Water for irrigation as well as for domestic use was included in plans for the state service area in both southern California and Central Val-

Senator Kuchel was not content to rely upon Senator Engle's contention that section 6(a) was "surplusage" and, consequently, that it made no difference whether or not Congress specifically exempted the state service area from federal reclamation law. On the contrary, on the last day of the four-day debate on the issue, he read a telegram from a Sacramento attorney reinforcing his own contention that section 6(a) must be retained to prevent application of federal law. That telegram stated:

> I strongly urge that section 6(a) remain in S.44. Its inclusion was agreed to by all interests in the State of California, including the State itself and the congressional representatives from the affected areas. The reasons were (1) that Federal law should not control water deliveries by the State from the joint Federal-State project, and (2) that this should be made so clear by the Congress that a contrary argument could not later be made . . . . *If section 6(a) is deleted now as a result of the insistence of those who state flatly that they want Federal law to apply to water deliveries by the State, this legislative history might be almost conclusive as to the intent of the Congress that Federal law is to apply to such deliveries. Logically, the only valid argument for deletion of section 6(a) is that Federal law should control water service by the State. To prevent that result it is now plainly imperative that section 6(a) remain in the bill.*[86]

The issue was clear. Those leading the move to delete section 6(a) wanted federal law to apply to the state service area. California's senators, sponsoring 6(a), wanted specific exemption from acreage limitation. The latter was true notwithstanding Senator Engle's assertion that federal law would not apply regardless of what Congress might decide about deletion of 6(a). After four days of prolonged debate, the Senate voted to delete section 6(a).[87]

VI

HOUSE DENIES EXEMPTION

The section [7] was included in the bill at the request of the State of California as a means of bringing into unanimous agreement the many diverse interests and points of view in the State.

—Congressman Wayne Aspinall of Colorado, Chairman, House Committee on Interior and Insular Affairs, 1960[88]

---

ley. Elected in 1958 on a party platform affirming support of federal acreage limitation law, Governor Brown opposed its application to the state service area in 1959. P. Taylor, *Excess Land Law: Secretary's Decision? A Study in Administration of Federal-State Relations*, 9 U.C.L.A. L. REV. 1, notes 24-25 (1962). See also note 105 *infra*.

86. 105 CONG. REC. 7987-88 (1959) (emphasis added).
87. *Id.* at 7995.
88. 106 CONG. REC. 10450 (1960).

Fourteen or fifteen years ago this was a hot issue. It defeated a Democratic Senator for reelection from our State . . . . You can tell me all you want to that there is not something to be gained by keeping section 7 in the bill. I do not believe it. The ones who are trying to retain it are the prototype of those who have been against the 160-acre limitation clause for the past 30 years.

—Congressman George P. Miller of California, 1960[89]

. . . of the 1.4 million acres in the San Luis Valley, including the proposed Federal service area and surrounding areas, over 64 percent of the land is held by owners with more than 1,000 acres each . . . A similar pattern is to be found in Kern County including possible areas of irrigation service south of the Federal service area. Here, of 1.1 million acres of land, we again find that 64 percent is accounted for by owners of more than 1,000 acres each. The largest owner, the Kern County Land Co., accounts for 16 percent of the total and the various oil companies with large holdings account for another 15 percent.

Congressman Al Ullman of Oregon, 1960[90]

Within two weeks of the Senate action striking the exemption of the state service area from federal reclamation law, the House Interior and Insular Affairs Committee issued a report on the San Luis project authorization bills before it. The majority report, with six members dissenting, took essentially the same position as Senator Engle and Governor Brown; that is, deletion of specific exemption of the state service area from federal reclamation law would not affect the application of state law there, but the exemption nevertheless should be retained in the bill authorizing the project. The majority explained at length:

The worst that can be said about section 7 [exempting the State service area] then, is that it is surplusage. Its rejection from the bill would have no substantive effect on the law applicable to the San Luis undertaking. Only an amendment affirmatively requiring adherence to the Federal acreage limitations notwithstanding the State's full payment of its share of the construction cost of the project would

---

89. *Id.* at 10556. Responding to Congressman Miller, Congressman Charles S. Gubser of California chose another way of stating the issue between them: "I am wholeheartedly in favor of the 160-acre limitation. But my opposition to the amendment . . . is not based upon the philosophy of the 160-acre limitation. . . . It is based purely upon the philosophy of States rights." *Id.* at 10559. Congressman Miller's reference was to Democratic Senator Sheridan Downey who, in 1950, decided not to run in the primary for reelection. He was opposed by Congresswoman Helen Gahagan Douglas, supporter of the 160-acre law.

90. *Id.* at 10455.

accomplish that which those who seek to delete section 7 mistakenly believe would be the effect of doing so.

The committee recognizes that the inclusions of surplusage is usually undesirable in a bill, but it also recognizes that the author of a bill, particularly when he is dealing with a subject that has involved bringing together as many diverse interests and points of view in his State and district as the San Luis project involves, should be given considerable latitude in the way he expresses the position that is arrived at, more latitude than the committee might give itself if it were to start drafting a bill ab initio.[91]

Overlooking the Warren Act's application of acreage limitation to any lands served by federal facilities, the Committee continued:

The committee concludes that section 7 of the bill in nowise changes established principles of reclamation law. It can well understand the possibility, however, that there might be difficulties in securing both statewide agreement and financing for the State project if there were doubt in anyone's mind concerning the relationship and the applicable laws under which each project would be constructed and operated. The committee therefore concludes that inclusion of section 7 in the bill will contribute to clarity and advance construction of the projects. The inclusion of this section, to put the matter otherwise, . . . is not to be interpreted as indicative of a belief on the committee's part that without it the excess land provisions of the Federal reclamation laws would be applicable to the State-served lands.

It was in the light of such considerations as these that have just been set forth that the committee rejected, by rollcall votes, amendments which would, in one case, have deleted section 7 from the bill and, in the other, replaced it with language requiring the State to agree not to serve lands which would be ineligible to receive water if they were being served by the Bureau of Reclamation.[92]

---

91. CONGRESSMAN W. ROGERS, SAN LUIS PROJECT, CALIFORNIA, H.R. REP. No. 399, 86th Cong., 1st Sess. 15-16 (1959).

92. *Id.* at 16. Congressman John P. Saylor of Pennsylvania sponsored the amendment in committee to oblige the State to observe federal 160-acre law, explaining later to the House that "I would have liked to see my amendment in the bill or I would not have offered it." 106 CONG. REC. 19464 (1960). However, when the House voted on the amendment to strike section 7, aimed likewise to assure state observance of the same law, he voted "nay." *Id.* at 10564. Ten years later, Congressmen Saylor and Aspinall and Senator Anderson signed the Public Land Law Review Commission report recommending elimination from public lands the requirements of "acreage limitation . . . residency . . . and exclusion of corporations as eligible applicants", as "artificial and obsolete restraints." PUB. LAND LAW REV. COMM'N, ONE-THIRD OF THE NATION'S LAND: A REPORT TO THE PRESIDENT iii & 181-4 (1970). The Interior Department had advised the House Interior Committee that

> this Department has never contended that the proposed delivery of water by the State to its service areas from and through the joint-use works would be subject to the provisions of the federal reclamation laws, on the assumption, of course, that the State's share of the costs of construction would be met concurrently with the construction period.

H.R. REP. No. 399, *supra* note 91, at 23.

Thus, the committee majority assumed the posture that federal acreage limitation was inapplicable to the state service area and that deletion of the exempting section 7, should that occur, would not provide evidence of Congressional intent to apply it. Furthermore, the majority, in order to satisfy unidentified California "diverse interests," allowed inclusion of section 7, although redundant and meaningless in its view.[93] The committee minority of six stated a contrary position that deletion of section 7 was necessary to "protect Federal interests and the basic concept of Federal reclamation law . . ." from the "real possibility of enhancement of huge private interests through interest-free Federal investment."[94]

After nearly a year, the San Luis bill reached the House floor for two days of extended debate. As in the Senate, deletion of the proposed exemption from federal law was the crucial issue. During the debate, the identity of the "diverse interests" that had insisted on inclusion of section 7 emerged. Congressman Al Ullman of Oregon, opposing section 7, and Congressman Craig Hosmer, supporting it, engaged in this illuminating colloquy:

> MR. ULLMAN: The gentleman said it was surplusage . . . . [I]f it is surplusage it would be little to give in return for getting a bill through this House and through the other body and making sure that you have a project.
> MR. HOSMER. It is surplusage insofar as this bill is concerned, but it is not surplusage insofar as its actual, practical effect upon my part of the country is concerned and in the financing, the operation and the speed with which we can carry out our State project.[95]

Congressman Jeffrey Cohelan of California threw additional light on the "diverse interests" unwilling to accept the view that section 7 was surplusage and, on the contrary, insisted upon its inclusion:

> On this question of whether it does or does not make any difference . . . I am wondering if the gentleman is aware that the Feather River Association on February 12 of this year passed a resolution demanding that if the Congress declined to delete section 7, the State of California should be asked to build San Luis in order to avoid the 160-acre limitation. Somebody obviously feels that this is important.[96]

As debate progressed, it became more wide-ranging and the reasons for insisting upon inclusion became clearer. Congressman Hosmer explained:

---

93. H.R. REP. No. 399, *supra* note 91, at 23.
94. *Id.* at 25.
95. 106 CONG. REC. 10458 (1960).
96. *Id.* at 10456.

I fully agree with the report of this committee, which says that section 7 is surplusage, that without it you could take a case to court and get a decision that says, "Of course, Federal reclamation law does not apply to the State project." The 160-acre limitation cannot apply to this project by any type of legal gymnastics even without section 7.

Then why am I up here saying that I want to keep section 7 in? For this reason: the State project is going to require better than a billion dollars for just this San Luis phase including distribution systems. The entire State-wide water plan is going to require $5 billion out of the taxpayers of the State of California before it is through. What section 7 does and why it is necessary is. . . . It assures the matter stay out of litigation which could last for 20 years . . . . While the cases are in court you cannot go out and get a bonding house to float bonds . . . . In California we cannot wait 20 years for the water while this thing is in court. Section 7 makes sure to begin with it never goes to court and allows us to proceed with our vitally needed State water project.[97]

Finally, section 7 came to a vote. On a division the amendment to delete was defeated 84 to 81. Ullman then demanded tellers to record each vote and the amendment passed, 139 to 122. Congressman Hosmer demanded a roll call vote and the amendment passed again, 215 to 179.[98]

As a matter of practical politics, neither side was willing to treat section 7 as surplusage. Opposed to each other in purpose, both sides—in the House as in the Senate—treated the extent of coverage of the federal 160-acre law as a vital issue. Both Houses voted to delete the requested exemption of the state service area from federal law.

Apparently unnoticed during debate was a portentious provision, in the House version of the bill that became law, for review of any federal-state agreement effectuating joint use of San Luis facilities. As described in the House report, it offered "another opportunity to review project . . .," specifying that "no funds shall be appropriated to commence construction . . . prior to 90 days after it has been submitted to the Congress *and then only if neither the House nor the Senate Interior and Insular Affairs Committee disapproves it.*"[99] The result, in about three years time, would be a complete reversal of power between committee and body of the whole.[100]

---

97. *Id.* at 10458.
98. *Id.* at 10560, 10563, 10564.
99. H.R. REP. No. 399, *supra* note 91, at 16 (emphasis added).
100. See text accompanying notes 151-161 *infra*.

VII

INSTRUMENT FOR CIRCUMVENTION: THE STATE. II

Certainly there is no conflict between the legislative branches of the two governments . . . . The federal Congress . . . has determined . . . that the 160-acre limitation is a basic part of federal policy. The state Legislature has adopted this concept as state policy by specifically authorizing irrigation districts to enter into contracts for project water that contain the 160-acre limitation.

—California Supreme Court, 1960[101]

As we understand, neither the Bureau of Reclamation nor the State Administration desires to apply the Federal excess land provisions to the State service area. We are informed that an agreement is now being negotiated which, as we understand, on one ground or another, will permit State law to apply.

—Opinion of Counsel, Chas. T. Main, Inc. Report to California Department of Water Resources, 1960[102]

With authorization of the federal San Luis Unit achieved, including approval of cooperation with a prospective state water project, the next step was to make the latter a reality. This step was accomplished in about six months when California voters, by a very narrow margin, approved a $1.75 billion general obligation bond issue to finance it. No mention was made of acreage limitation in the Secretary of State's election pamphlet, furnished to all voters. Likewise, the magnitude of the proposed financial obligation that the State would assume was minimized.[103]

California's spokesmen before Congress had emphasized the burdens that California was prepared to assume, thus suggesting relief of the national treasury by appeals for equivalent help. "The State project," said Senator Thomas H. Kuchel, ". . . will cost the people of California $11 billion when completed . . . ."[104]

The financial aspect of the State's contribution was presented to its

---

101. Ivanhoe Irrig. Dist. v. All Parties, 53 Cal. 2d 692, 714-15, 350 P.2d 69, 82, 3 Cal. Rptr. 317, 330 (1960).
102. CHAS. T. MAIN, INC., APPENDIX TO THE FINAL REPORT, GENERAL EVALUATION OF THE PROPOSED PROGRAM FOR FINANCING AND CONSTRUCTING THE STATE WATER RESOURCES DEVELOPMENT SYSTEM 29 (Calif. Dep't of Water Resources Pub. No. 2229-1-2A, October 1960) [hereinafter cited as MAIN REPORT].
103. CAL. STATE DEP'T PROPOSED AMENDMENTS TO THE CONSTITUTION, GENERAL ELECTION, . . . Nov. 8, 1960 [hereinafter cited as PROPOSED AMENDMENTS TO THE CONSTITUTION].
104. 104 CONG. REC. 17730-31 (1958).

voters in a very different light. The argument for the $1.75 billion bond issue in the election pamphlet assured voters that:

> The program will not be a burden on the taxpayer; no new state taxes are involved; the bonds are repaid through the sale of water and power. In other words, *it will pay for itself.*[105]

---

105. PROPOSED AMENDMENTS TO THE CONSTITUTION 3 (emphasis in original).
It has turned out since that one of the ways in which the project "pay[s] for itself" is by levying assessments against taxpayers of the Metropolitan Water District of Southern California regardless of whether they receive water. K. Roberts, *The Public Role of Engineering: The California State Water Project*, 99 ENGINEERING ISSUES, Jan. 1973, at 19, 24. The project consumes more power to pump water than it produces. Another source of revenue for the project has been royalties received from the State's tidelands oil leases. As ex-Governor Edmund G. Brown has observed:

> When I was governor, we earmarked the tidelands funds for education. The Reagan Administration, under pressure from the water interests of Southern California, repealed this statute and gave the funds to the water project. This . . . resulted in diminished education for the people of this state.

Hearings Before the Subcomm. on Migratory Labor of the Senate Comm. on Labor and Public Welfare on Land Ownership, Use, and Distribution, 92d Cong., 1st & 2d Sess. 819 (1972) (reprinted from the San Francisco Bay Guardian, Sept. 30, 1969, at 6, col. 3) [hereinafter cited as *Hearings Before the Subcomm. on Migratory Labor*].

In May, 1959, Governor Brown, supporting exemption of the State service area, informed Senator Engle:

> I am, and I believe that the California Legislature also is, opposed to any unjust enrichment or monopolization of benefits by owners of large land holdings as a result of either Federal or State operation. I intend . . . to take this matter up with the California Legislature in order to preclude . . . undesirable results . . . .

105 CONG. REC. 7857 (1959). In June, the California Senate rejected an acreage limitation bill.

> At one stage in the bitter debate, Assemblyman Jesse M. Unruh (Dem-Los Angeles) declared, 'At times we have to rise above principle.' He had been twitted by Assemblyman Lloyd W. Lowry (Dem-Rumsey) for opposing the latter's water acreage amendment which is part of both the State and national Democratic platforms.

E. Behrens, Legislature Passes Giant Water Bill, San Francisco Chronicle, June 18, 1959, at 1, 15, col. 1.

The California Department of Water Resources originally planned a surcharge on water delivered to excess lands, which it estimated would total 404,747 acres by 1973, or 78 percent of the total 521,088 acres to be served. SURCHARGE AND SURCHARGE CREDIT PROVISIONS. (Calif. Dep't Water Resources, Water Service Contractors Council Memo No. 556, March 25, 1970) [hereinafter cited as SURCHARGE AND SURCHARGE CREDIT PROVISIONS]. Legal Counsel in the Main Report had said in 1960:

> Apparently the Department's plan is a modification of a plan announced by Governor Edmund G. Brown in a television broadcast from Los Angeles . . . on January 20, 1960. This plan would have charged the owners of so-called excess lands the market value of the power used to transport water, while all other landowners would have paid only the actual cost of such power, less an amount equivalent to the benefit derived from the sale of System power outside the System. The present plan exacts a *surcharge* on water delivered to excess lands in an amount equivalent to the power credit that is derived from the operation of the System. . . .

MAIN REPORT, *supra* note 102, at 32-33, 34.

In 1972 the California Department of Water Resources abandoned the surcharge, explaining that it was too deficient in substance to justify its "administrative costs." SURCHARGE AND SURCHARGE CREDIT PROVISIONS, *supra*; Letter from W.R. Gianelli, DWR Director, to Donald Currlin, October 24, 1972. In retrospect, Governor Brown said,

By 1973 the estimate of final construction cost of the State Water Project was nearly $3 billion.[106] However, construction cost is only a portion of the total cost. Current reports of the Department of Water Resources reveal that the total "application of revenues . . . thru project repayment period . . ." is expected to exceed $11 billion.[107] This is the same figure California's spokesmen gave to Congress,[108] but not to the State's voters.[109] Governor Brown, who had led the successful effort to win the voters' approval of the $1.75 billion bond issue, conceded

> that it would have been much cheaper . . . if the Federal Government had built the project . . . [and] that large landowners would benefit from [construction by the State] but I saw no way of building the project if we had to fight the 160-acre Federal limitation.[110]

The role of the State as an instrument to avoid acreage limitation law received little publicity among California voters. The election guide furnished by the State failed to mention the issue in arguments on either side of the bond issue.[111] However, ways to avoid the limitation received careful attention from state water officials right up to the 1960 water bond election time. In the month before the election, the State Department of Water Resources received from its hired consultants a report evaluating the California program. Included was an appendix prepared by legal counsel, addressing the question of whether the acreage limitation provisions of federal reclamation law would apply to the state service area under the proposed state Act and the already-adopted federal San Luis Act. Counsel concluded that the Warren Act, although applying reclamation law to water ". . . impounded, stored, or carried . . ." to private lands ". . . in excess of the requirements of the lands to be irrigated under any project . . .," was applicable to waters of the State Water Project given joint use of San Luis federal facilities:

> To hold that the Warren Act of 1911, which dealt with a wholly different factual situation, requires their application seems to us far-fetched. The deletion of Sections 7 and 6(a) of the bills somewhat

---

> As a matter of fact, there are far more benefits to more people in a large corporation that distributes its earnings rather than the acreage limitation which benefits relatively few people. One hundred and sixty acres is not a small farm because these farms are worth on an average . . . about $160,000. This is not the small farmer of the reclamation days of 1902. . . . It is a long story and I don't think you have it all.

Hearings Before Subcomm. on Migratory Labor, supra.

106. CAL. DEP'T WATER RESOURCES, THE CALIFORNIA STATE WATER PROJECT IN 1973, app. C, at 7. (Cal. State Water Project Bull. No. 132-73, 1973.)

107. CAL. DEP'T WATER RESOURCES, THE CALIFORNIA STATE WATER PROJECT IN 1969, app. C, at 7. (Cal. State Water Project Bull. No. 132-69, 1969).

108. 105 CONG. REC. 7484, 7486, 7672 (1959).

109. See text at note 103 *supra*.

110. *Hearings Before Subcomm. on Migratory Labor, supra* note 105.

111. PROPOSED AMENDMENTS TO THE CONSTITUTION, *supra* note 103, at 2, 3.

clouds the foregoing conclusion, but, on balance, is insufficient to change the result.[112]

The report dismissed the view that Section 7 was "surplusage": "It seems clear that if Section 7 had been left in the San Luis bill, the excess land provisions would not apply to the State service area. Doubts arise because of the deletion."[113]

Counsel examined an argument by the House committee majority that final payment of financial charges against beneficiaries of reclamation projects terminates applicability of acreage limitation. He noted that although this view had some support in administrative practice, it had been "severely challenged" by this present author.[114] He concluded conditionally that

> California can "pay out" its share of the cost of the San Luis Reservoir before water is supplied from it to the State service area. Hence, if the pay-out provision applies, the operation of the Federal reclamation laws is academic. Even if they apply today, they will no longer apply when water is delivered.[115]

As described earlier, the legislative history of the San Luis bill was marked by four days of heated floor debate in the Senate and two days in the House. Each House had voted to reject the recommendation of its own committee to exempt the state service area from federal acreage limitation law. Faced with this Congressional precedent favorable to applying acreage limitation, counsel recommended that administrators drafting the federal-state contract include the content of the exempting sections that Congress had denied:

> At any rate, it would seem apparent that the State should strive to obtain as a part of its agreement with the Federal government a provision that none of the waters supplied from the San Luis Reservoir, or from any of the aqueducts constituting a part of that project, to State service areas should be subject to the excess land provisions.[116]

The reasoning upon which this recommended tactic rested clearly was political was well as legal. Counsel continued:

> It is true that if in fact the Bureau of Reclamation did not have the authority to enter into such a contract, the agreement might be open to challenge. However, as a practical matter, such a challenge in the courts need not be anticipated in the normal course of events.[117]

---

112. MAIN REPORT, *supra* note 102, at 29.
113. *Id.* at 28.
114. P. Taylor, *Excess Land Law: Execution of a public policy*, 64 Yale L.J. 477, 512-514 (1955).
115. MAIN REPORT, *supra* note 102, at 28.
116. *Id.* at 29.
117. *Id.*

Counsel pointed out that the recommended agreement was not of itself sufficient to assure escape from acreage limitation on the state service area "even if the Department of Justice and other potential litigants concurred."[118] There was yet another Congressional hurdle to take. The way had been prepared, however. During original consideration of the San Luis authorization bill, the House had substituted its own text for the Senate version, and the Senate had accepted it. The House version prescribed a 90-day period for review of the federal-state contract before it could take effect. The review was to be done by the respective Interior Committees in each House.[119]

Apparently with the committee majorities' opposition to acreage limitation on the state service area in mind, counsel commented:

> We do not attempt to forecast whether either committee might disapprove the agreement, but in the light of the past legislative history surrounding S. 44, this possibility may not be disregarded. In any event, the action of the committees on the actual agreement as drafted will likely be decisive. A prediction as to what will happen in Congress can scarcely be grounded solely on legal considerations. . . . The reaction of Congress and its relevant committees is more a political than a legal problem. If Congress in effect approves the agreement worked out between the Bureau of Reclamation and the State, it would seem likely that this will be the end of controversy as to this subject.[120]

VIII

EXECUTIVE EXEMPTION

It is too bad that we cannot spread on the official record the history of the opinions—note that I use the plural—that were written . . . by lawyers in the executive department before the final official opinion was rendered.

I am satisfied that the original opinion was against the final decision that was made. . . . [T]he contract . . . should be considered as a total abdication of the national Government to the land and water monopolies which so completely dominate California.

—Senator Wayne Morse of Oregon, 1962[121]

---

118. *Id.*
119. See text accompanying note 102 *supra*.
120. MAIN REPORT, *supra* note 87, at 29.
121. 108 CONG. REC. 5688, 7812 (1962). Testimony confirming Senator Morse's 1962 statement contrasting the original with the final draft of the San Luis opinion was given in federal court in 1971. The *Fresno Bee* reported:

> The federal government as late as November 1961, was going to apply the 160-acre limitation to the state service area of the San Luis Project . . . . Water Attorney Breckinridge Thomas testified . . . he read a draft opinion Nov. 2, 1961, prepared by Department of Interior officials, which held that the limita-

The course taken by the federal-state agreement deviated little from that recommended and predicted by counsel for the Main Report. The contract submitted to the Secretary of the Interior for his approval, however, did not follow the recommendation of the Main Report to repeat the language of sections 6(a) and 7 exempting the state service area from reclamation law in the federal-state contract. Instead, it omitted all reference to application of acreage limitation.

On December 26, 1961, Solicitor of Interior Frank J. Barry issued his opinion in support of the agreement as drafted, minus the acreage limitation. He began by closing immediately one potential loophole for escape from acreage limitations; namely, payment by the State of its assigned share of the cost of joint-use facilities concurrently with construction. He "concluded that accelerated repayment of the cost of construction cannot relieve excess landowners" of acreage limitation. Nevertheless, he relieved them of any obligation to comply with the limitation on other grounds.[122]

The Solicitor's first argument for rejection of the obligation to comply was to deny that Congress, in rejecting proposals to exempt the state service area from acreage limitation, intended to apply that very law. First, he stated the general rule:

> Normally, when an exemption is removed from a bill before enactment, the presumption is that the legislative body intended the law to apply in the situation described in the exemption. To apply the rule here would be to say that Congress expressed its intent that the excess-land laws should apply to State water deliveries.[123]

Then the Solicitor proceeded to hold it nevertheless inapplicable at San Luis. He rested his conclusion upon his own interpretation of the legislative history of debates over exemption, saying, "In my opinion the legislative history clearly indicates that Congress did not intend to require application of Federal acreage limitations by striking Sections 6(a) and 7."[124]

---

tion applied to . . . the state area served by the San Luis Project south of Kettleman City. Less than two months later, Solicitor Frank Barry issued an opinion which . . . exempted the state-served area. . . . Thomas said the draft opinion read, 'The San Luis Act does not exempt the State of California from the acreage limitation.'
Frank B. Horne, former regional solicitor of the Bureau of Reclamation testified similarly. "Horne also testified he understood 'that Gov. (Edmund) Brown had said in the event of an unfavorable opinion on the state contract, the state would bring suit immediately.' " *Pine Flat Case Bares San Luis Project Plan*, The Fresno Bee, May 12, 1971, at B1, col. 1.

122. Agreement with Calif. for Construction of San Luis Unit, Central Valley Project, 68 Interior Dec. 412, 413 (1961); *see also* 108 CONG. REC. 5712 (1962).
123. *Id.* at 416.
124. *Id.* at 417.

A senator who had led the original fight against exemption was quick to deny this interpretation of his successful battle. Senator Wayne Morse said:

> Now, I regret to say, some lawyers in the executive branch have concluded that when we struck out that exemption clause our "intent" was that it should apply. The House of Representatives will probably be amazed to learn that their "intent" also was misinterpreted.[125]
>
> . . . .
>
> It is a novel experience to find the executive branch undertaking to reinterpret quite erroneously the intent of the legislative branch which had already gone to some pains to spell out and positively act to establish its intent. If this sort of practice prevails, our time honored system of checks and balances with the legislative, judicial, and executive branches is in real jeopardy.[126]
>
> . . . .
>
> Existing reclamation law is not changed by debate on the floor of the Senate.[127]

Senator Thomas Kuchel of California, sponsor of the San Luis bill, also had thought it necessary in 1959 to retain the exemption in order to free the state service area from acreage limitation. He had said:

> The Senator from Illinois . . . has stated several times that if his amendment shall be adopted, it will mean that Federal reclamation law shall apply to all waters which flow from the joint use reservoir, whether they go into the State system . . . or not. I deny that contention. . . . But I must say there is merit in the position . . . that if at this late date section 6(a) were stricken from the bill it would constitute an intention on the part of the Senate to make Federal law apply . . . .[128]

Despite disagreement over the precise meaning of denial of exemption of the state service area from federal law, congressional leaders on both sides battled to the end. Congress denied exemption. The Solicitor's opinion, grasping at some differences in interpretation, stripped six days of congressional debate and decision of meaning. In effect, the Solicitor approved an exemption that Congress specifically had denied.

In support of his conclusion, the Solicitor found conflict between federal and state law over reclamation policy. He said:

> In the consideration of the San Luis Act the Congress was scrupulous to avoid conflict with legitimate State authority . . . . we should not

---

125. 108 Cong. Rec. 5688 (1962).
126. *Id.* at 5698.
127. 105 Cong. Rec. 7989 (1959).
128. *Id.* at 7988-89.

precipitate a conflict with a State which Congress was careful to avoid . . . .[129]

The Solicitor apparently overlooked a decision of the California Supreme Court, issued only the year before, denying the existence of conflict. The California Court had stated: "Certainly there is no conflict between the legislative branches of the two governments . . ." over the federal acreage limitation.[130] Neither was there a conflict between California voters and federal law. As noted earlier, in 1933 they approved a referendum measure authorizing the State Water Authority to contract with the federal government under reclamation law.[131] The California legislators and the voters, in 1959 and 1960, respectively, renewed this authorization by incorporating "the provisions of the [State] code governing the Central Valley Project."[132]

The real conflict was between large California landowning interests and federal acreage limitation law, not one between state and federal law. The former conflict illuminates the insistence of California's spokesmen upon Congressional exemption of the state service area; there was no other conflict.[133]

The Solicitor was faced with a difficult statutory problem. The federal Warren Act of 1911 specifically applies acreage limitation when a federal project cooperates with a non-federal entity, and makes no distinction as to where water is delivered, so long as the cooperation involves use of federal facilities.[134]

---

129. Agreement with Calif. for Construction of San Luis Unit, Central Valley Project, *supra* note 122, at 426. The Solicitor supported his argument by citing *Davies Warehouse Co. v. Bowles*, 321 U.S. 144 (1943). As the Solicitor said, seeking to establish a parallel between the *Davies* and San Luis situations, "There, as here, Congress had omitted to be specific . . . . Here as there 'relevant authorities and considerations are numerous and equivocal, and different plausible definitions result from a mere shift of emphasis.'" Agreement with Calif. for Construction of San Luis Unit, Central Valley Project, *supra* note 122, at 425. However, Congress was specific in the original acreage limitation Act of 1902, and in the Warren Act of 1911, the latter applying acreage limitation specifically to federal cooperation with other entities. *Davies* and the state service area situation are not parallel. See also note 29 *supra* and text accompanying notes 134-138 *infra*.

130. Ivanhoe Irrig. Dist. v. All Parties, *supra* note 101. See also epigraph accompanying note 101 *supra*.

131. Ch. 1042, § 15, [1933] Cal. Stat. 2654.

132. Ch. 1762, § 1, [1959] Cal. Stat. 4235 (now CAL. WATER CODE § 12931 (West 1971)).

133. In the House, California Congressmen were divided. California Congressman Jeffrey Cohelan and Oregon Congressman Al Ullman led the fight for exemption.

134. 43 U.S.C. § 524 (1911). Undersecretary of Agriculture True D. Morse stated ". . . the Warren Act of 1911 . . . provided that water could not be delivered to landowners *outside the reclamation project boundaries* in excess of that amount needed to irrigate 160 acres." *Hearings on S. 1425, S. 2541, and S. 3448 Before the Subcomm. on Irrigation and Reclamation of the Senate Comm. on Interior and Insular Af-

At first the Solicitor conceded the *prima facie* application of the Warren Act to the federal-state cooperation in the San Luis project. He said:

> Section 2 of the Warren Act standing alone requires the application of acreage limitations where the United States cooperates with an entity in the construction of irrigation facilities even where no federal subsidy is extended to the lands served by the entity.[135]

To counter this generalization the Solicitor offered two arguments. The first rested upon the legislative history of the San Luis Act. He said:

> . . . the legislative history of the San Luis Act exhibits a recognition by the Senate and the House that acreage limitation should apply where Federal investment is made and because of the Federal investment.[136]

In contrast to this view, in a second opinion barely three years later, the Solicitor rejected the sufficiency of legislative history as a method of altering established law and policy. He said then:

> So firmly established are the excess land provisions of the reclamation law that Congress suspends their operation only where extraordinary circumstances dictate. Where Congress has seen fit to waive or modify the excess land laws in certain projects, it has always found it appropriate to enact positive legislation setting forth the exemption or other modification in unmistakable terms. Where Congress deems a departure from its established policy to be in order it so provides by express terms, and not by implication.[137]

This latter opinion conforms to the reasoning in a unanimous United States Supreme Court decision:

> Significantly, when a particular project has been exempted [from acreage limitation] because of its peculiar circumstances, the Congress has always made such exemption by express enactment.[138]

Even if it were assumed that legislative history could modify the Warren Act to limit acreage limitation to federal investment, both the Governor of California and the Director of Water Resources testified

---

fairs, 85th Cong., 2d Sess., App. C, at 41 (1958) (remarks by Undersecretary of Agriculture Morse to Senator Clinton P. Anderson, Dec. 19, 1957) (emphasis added).

135. Agreement with Calif. for Construction of San Luis Unit, Central Valley Project, *supra* note 122, at 426.

136. *Id.* The Solicitor cited Senator Paul Douglas, *inter alia*, in support of this argument. He did not quote an explicit colloquy:

> MR. ENGLE. Does the Senator believe that if section 6(a) is stricken from the bill the reclamation law will apply to the State projects service area?
> MR. DOUGLAS. Yes, I do; and I want to make a record to show clearly that it would.

105 CONG. REC. 7496 (1959).

137. Applicability of the Excess Land Laws, Imperial Irrig. Dist. Lands, 71 Interior Dec. 496, 506-07 (1964).

138. Ivanhoe Irrig. Dist. v. McCracken, *supra* note 18, at 292.

to the State's dependence upon federal investment at San Luis.[139] Thus, regardless of whether or not the fact of federal investment is necessary to require federal law, the Warren Act applies acreage limitation on the San Luis state service area.

The Solicitor's 1961 opinion offered a second ground for avoiding the application of acreage limitation as admittedly prescribed by the Warren Act when "standing alone."[140] The opinion stated:

> The Warren Act was enacted in 1911, before the maturity of national reclamation policy and long before anyone could get water for more than 160 acres by agreeing to sell his excess lands.[141]

The significance of this reference to the 1926 Omnibus Adjustment Act[142] requiring agreement to sell excess lands as precondition of watering them was unexplained. The 1926 Act repealed neither the Warren Act of 1911 nor the original Reclamation Act of 1902.

In contrast to the vagueness of the Solicitor's 1961 reference to the timing of the Warren Act is the clarity of his 1964 opinion. In the latter he relied upon the United States Supreme Court for guidance in construing the general body of reclamation law. He said:

> The rules in such cases were stated . . . as follows:
>
> First, that effect shall be given to all the words of a statute, where this is possible without a conflict; and Second, that, as regards statutes *in pari materia* of different dates, the last shall repeal the first only when there are express terms of repeal, or where the implication of repeal is a necessary one. When repeal by implication is relied on it must be impossible for both provisions under consideration to stand, because one necessarily destroys the other. If both can stand by any reasonable construction, that construction must be adopted.[143]

In this same 1964 opinion the Solicitor indicated clearly his own belief that the 1926 Act did not destroy the 1911 Act. He said:

> The provisions of reclamation law of general application dealing with land limitations include section 5 of the 1902 Act, Sections

---

139. Governor Edmund G. Brown testified: "We know that we cannot and should not depend entirely on the Federal Government. . . . California recognizes . . . that it cannot do the job alone." *Hearings on S. 44, supra* note 75, at 12. Director Harvey O. Banks testifed: "It is clear that Federal assistance will be required, and the joint venture . . . would be of financial advantage to both the State and the United States . . . ." *Hearings on S. 1887, supra* note 65.

140. See text accompanying note 135 *supra*.

141. Agreement with Calif. for Construction of San Luis Unit, Central Valley Project, *supra* note 122, at 426.

142. 43 U.S.C. § 423e (1926).

143. Applicability of the Excess Land Laws, Imperial Irrig. Dist. Lands, *supra* note 137, at 506.

1 and 2 of the Warren Act, . . . and Section 46 of the 1926 Act . . . .[144]

Finally, the San Luis Act of 1960 had said that "the Secretary shall be governed by the Federal reclamation laws (Act of June 17, 1902 . . . and Acts amendatory thereof or supplementary thereto)."[145] Nevertheless, the Solicitor determined that

. . . the San Luis unit does not include any lands "outside the Federal San Luis unit service area" and that it does not include the State service area.

Therefore, when the Act states that "in constructing, operating, and maintaining the San Luis unit, the Secretary shall be governed by the Federal reclamation laws," it directs the Secretary to apply reclamation law, not to the State service area but to the Federal service area, which is the only area included in the unit.[146]

In support of this conclusion the Solicitor cited section 1 of the San Luis Act barring commencement of construction

. . . until the Secretary has . . . secured, or has satisfactory assurance of his ability to secure, all rights to the use of water which are necessary to carry out the purposes of the unit . . . .[147]

From this authority, the Solicitor argued that "If the Secretary cannot proceed until he has secured rights for the use of water for the State service area, it is plain that he cannot ever commence construction of the San Luis unit."[148]

In arriving at his conclusion the Solicitor ignored the admonition of the United States Supreme Court, in its 1958 decision validating acreage limitation, that "the acquisition of water rights must not be confused with the operation of federal projects."[149] The conclusion stands that the Warren Act's criterion of applicability of federal reclamation law is not the location of the lands served, but the use of federal facilities to serve them.[150]

Thus the executive branch of government took its initial stand exempting the state service area. This position presumably was to be subject to review by higher executive authority, then by the legislative and judicial branches.

---

144. *Id.* at 501.
145. Act of June 3, 1960, Pub. L. No. 86-488, 74 Stat. 156 (not codified; also in 3 U.S.D.I., FED. RECLAMATION AND RELATED LAWS ANN. 1524, 1531 (1972)).
146. Agreement with Calif. for Construction of San Luis Unit, Central Valley Project, *supra* note 122, at 419.
147. Act of June 3, 1960, Pub. L. No. 86-488, 74 Stat. 156.
148. Agreement with Calif. for Construction of San Luis Unit, Central Valley Project, *supra* note 122, at 417.
149. Ivanhoe Irrig. Dist. v. McCracken, *supra* note 18, at 291.
150. 43 U.S.C. § 524 (1911). See also text accompanying notes 134-144 *supra*.

IX

COMMITTEE EXEMPTION

> . . . the Committee on Interior and Insular Affairs of the Senate should have brought to the Senate a recommendation either for or against [the Federal-State contract]. It should have submitted the question to the Senate, and should not have decided to have the committee take care of the matter . . . . I do not think the Senate would approve of this contract because, in my judgment, it circumvents the Congressional action of 1959.
>
> —Senator Wayne Morse of Oregon, 1962[151]

> I thought, along with the Senator from Oregon, that we had won in 1959. With him, I have been deeply disappointed by the turn of events.
>
> —Senator Paul Douglas of Illinois, 1962[152]

Three days after Solicitor Barry issued his opinion holding acreage limitation inapplicable to the state service area, Attorney General Robert F. Kennedy gave it his qualified approval. The issue, he said, concerned a national policy "of long standing and one not lightly abandoned . . . ," one presenting "a most difficult problem."[153] The intent of Congress, he continued, "is not free from doubt. Strong arguments can be made to the effect that they did not intend to abandon the policy even within the area to be serviced by the State."[154] Having qualified his concurrence in the Solicitor's opinion, the Attorney General appealed to Congress to clarify its intent. Noting the provision in the San Luis Act for a 90-day review of the agreement by the House and Senate Interior Committees, he urged the Secretary of the Interior

> . . . to seek a congressional reexamination of this question. I think that the Congress itself should make a clear determination whether or not the acreage limitations should apply to the State service area. Fortunately, under the provisions of the San Luis Act they will have the opportunity to do so, and I sincerely hope that they will take positive action in this respect.[155]

The review procedure, upon which the Attorney General placed his hopes for Congressional action, did not result in broad reassessment by the House and Senate, but on the contrary impeded it. The procedure had been inserted in the law under the leadership of Congressman

---

151. 108 CONG. REC. 5693 (1962).
152. Id. at 5711.
153. Id. at 5711-12.
154. Id.
155. Id.

Wayne Aspinall, Chairman of the House Interior Committee, after the House had followed the Senate in rejecting proposed exemption of the state service area from acreage limitation law. At his request, the House struck out all but the enacting clause of the Senate-passed bill and substituted the text of the House-passed bill containing the procedure for review of the federal-state contract if and when administratively agreed upon.

When this House version came to the Senate, Senator William Proxmire of Wisconsin interrogated Senator Clinton P. Anderson, Chairman of the Senate Interior Committee, as to its possible effect on the acreage limitation issue. The following colloquy took place:

> MR. PROXMIRE. Can the Senator inform me whether this bill, as it comes from the House, makes any substasntial changes in the bill as it passed the Senate. . . .
>
> MR. ANDERSON. No. I will say to the Senator from Wisconsin that there are no substantial changes. There are a few changes in wording, which I think probably improve the bill. Many of them were suggested by Representative SAYLOR, of Pennsylvania, who is a staunch friend of those who wish to keep reclamation within reasonable bounds . . . .
>
> MR. PROXMIRE. As I recall, there was a lengthy Senate debate on the floor . . . on the . . . 160-acre limitation . . . . That has not been affected?
>
> MR. ANDERSON. The bill has been strengthened, if anything. . . . I am sure the bill has been strengthened rather than weakened.[156]

A very different analysis subsequently was given to the California Department of Water Resources by legal counsel for the Main Report. As noted earlier, counsel had forecast that

> . . . in the light of the past legislative history . . . the *action of the committees* on the actual agreement as drafted will likely be decisive . . . . The reaction of Congress and its relevant committees is more a political than a legal problem.[157]

Between the Congressional debates of 1959-60 over application of acreage limitation to the state service area and review in 1962 of the draft federal-state agreement, two critical elements in the political-legal situation had altered. First, with passage of the San Luis Act, friends of acreage limitation on the state service area no longer held their original power to threaten denial of authorization to finance and construct the

---

156. 106 CONG. REC. 10695-96 (1960). Presiding at initial House hearings to consider construction of the federal San Luis project, Senator Clinton Anderson asked a witness: "If this is coordinated or combined with some State project and the water comes down to Kern County, do you understand that the provisions of Federal reclamation law with respect to the 160 acres will apply?" *Hearings on S. 178, supra* note 61, at 132.

157. MAIN REPORT, *supra* note 102, at 29 (emphasis added).

project unless their demands were met. In 1959-60 this power had been essential to defeat of the attempted exemption. Second, substitution of the House version for the Senate bill in 1960 had conferred what was unrevealed in floor debate—virtually complete power of legislative review over administrative execution of Congressional intent upon the very committees whose recommendation against acreage limitation both Houses had rejected.

Omission of acreage limitation from the federal-state contract evoked extensive Senate floor debate on April 2, 1962, with substantial echoes on April 10 and May 4.[158] Much of the debate consisted in restatement of views by leading opponents and proponents of the orginally defeated state service area exemption from national policy. Senator Morse, whom Solicitor Barry had quoted as giving support for his decision against applying acreage limitation, was emphatic in restating his original position against exemption:

> Our Nation as a whole has in the Central Valley Federal reclamation project an immense stake. Not only is there a vast Federal investment involved, but more important, there are human values upon which a price may not be placed. Important in that connection is the struggle to prevent land and water monopolies in the area by insisting upon compliance with the 160-acre limitation . . . . It was the failure of the Secretary of the Interior and his Solicitor to insist upon the applicability of those excess land provisions in . . . the State service area of the San Luis project which gave rise to my attack . . . on the latter's opinion . . . .[159]

Senators Proxmire and Anderson exchanged views as to the substance of the policy issue:

> Mr. PROXMIRE. I ask . . . what our Latin American friends will think of us if we go to their countries preaching land reform and at the same time adopting legislation which would perpetuate agricultural feudalism in California? . . .
>
> Mr. ANDERSON. The Senator from Wisconsin referred to the project as feudalism. I do not see anything feudalistic in it, because the law provides that the people in the San Luis Valley shall not produce crops which are in surplus.[160]

The effectiveness of the attack on the contract, however, was blocked by the refusal of the Interior Committee to refer the matter to the Senate for decision by the Senate. As Senator Clinton P. Anderson, Chairman, explained:

> The Interior Committee said . . . we would not review the contract since the Secretary of the Interior had made certain findings and de-

---

158. 108 CONG. REC. 5687-5725, 6237-40, 7809-14 (1962).
159. *Id.* at 7810.
160. *Id.* at 5690.

cisions, based on the concurrence of the Attorney General as to the law. . . . The committee considered the matter and voted not to disapprove the contract by resolution. I believe the committee's action was compliance with the Attorney General's recommendation. Committee consideration and decision is congressional action. It is complete, final congressional action so far as the Senate is concerned.[161]

The House committee raised no questions and the issue was not brought to the floor.

X

EXEMPTION: JUDICIAL REVIEW

. . . [W]e ought to leave to the courts the determination of these legal questions. . . . We believe that both sides in the controversy stand on an equal footing before the courts if we let the application of the bill go to the courts with section 6(a) eliminated. . . .

We are called upon to preserve a fundamental congressional prerogative the Senate has seen fit to defend on many previous occasions—that of assuring that the executive branch of Government shall carry out the intention of the Congress in administering Federal law. . . .

I am accustomed, in my public service, to seeing public officials yield to the kind of pressure to which the executive branch of the Government and the California officials have yielded. That is an old, old game in American politics, but that does not make it right. Why did . . . California not . . . test this provision in the courts? Why did they use the political route, after the decision in 1959?

—Senator Wayne Morse of Oregon, 1959, 1962[162]

If anyone wishes to take the case to court he may do so.
—Senator Clair Engle of California, 1962[163]

By late Spring of 1962, both executive and legislative branches of government (the latter for the second time) had gone on record on the issue of whether national reclamation policy controlling water monopoly and speculation should apply to the state service area. The Attorney General was uneasy over his own and the Secretary of Interior's decision that the law did not apply.[164] The legislative branch was divided internally. Senators who had won a 1959 vote denying exemption from

---
161. *Id.* at 5692-93.
162. 105 Cong. Rec. 7683 (1959); 108 Cong. Rec. 5687, 5690-91 (1962).
163. 108 Cong. Rec. 5696 (1962).
164. See text accompanying notes 153-155 *supra.*

national policy were deeply disturbed when the Senate's own Interior Committee, siding with the executive, allowed a federal-state contract omitting national policy to stand and obstructed full Senate review of the executive decision. It remained to be seen who, if anyone, would take the issue to the courts and, if the contract was challenged, how the judicial branch would interpret the validity of omitting national policy.

During Senate debates, both those who favored and those who opposed application of national policy to the state service area had referred to the opportunity for court review. However, they were not in agreement as to who should find it necessary to go to court to protect his interests. This lack of agreement is implicit in an exchange between Senators Morse and Anderson:

> MR. MORSE. I say most respectfully that I think the Department of the Interior should have followed a handsoff policy. It should have said .... We are not going to approve this contract. We are merely going to say to the parties, "Go on to court." ....[165]
>
> MR. ANDERSON. The Senator has said that if we had wished, we could have adopted a handsoff policy. That is precisely what we did deliberately .... The Interior Committee took a completely noncontroversial, handsoff position. We said that we would not review the contract since the Secretary of the Interior had made certain findings and decisions, based on the concurrence of the Attorney General as to the law. If these findings were wrong, they should be tested in a court of law.[166]

Agreement between the two Senators on the meaning of keeping "handsoff" was more apparent than real. Senator Morse rebuked the executive branch for approving the contract lacking acreage limitation. Had the executive branch objected to the contract, the burden of taking the acreage limitation issue to court would have been left to the State of California or to large landowning interests. Responsibility for defense of its application then would have rested on the Government.

Senator Anderson responded that the Interior Committee had kept "handsoff" the contract; *i.e.*, allowed it to stand without acreage limitation, as had the executive branch. The result was that landless or other private parties were left with the burden of taking to court the case for implementing national policy, with the Government defending its omission.

---

165. He added, "I would have liked to have the great lawyers of the Department of the Interior who rendered this final opinion do so without being assisted by those on the Hill." 108 CONG. REC. 5692 (1962).

166. *Id.* In recommending the review procedure that became law, but was now waived, the original House Interior Committee majority report proposal said: "Congress would be given an opportunity to review the final provisions of any agreement for joint Federal-State development and use." H.R. REP. No. 399, *supra* note 91, at 16.

This prospect that private parties might challenge omission of national policy had been evaluated previously in 1960 by legal counsel for the Main Report to the California Department of Water Resources. Recommending the course that was actually taken, *viz.*, omission of national policy from the contract, counsel forecast that "as a practical matter, such a challenge in the courts need not be anticipated in the normal course of events."[167]

Commenting on the practical balance of political power in 1962, Senator Douglas told Congress:

> I think we all know the practical difficulties in such a situation as this. The land is owned at present by a relatively small number of persons and corporations, each one of which owns an enormous amount of land; not merely thousands of acres, but in many cases tens of thousands of acres, and in some cases hundreds of thousands of acres. They are organized. They are powerful. They do not wish to have their holdings broken up by the application of the 160-acre limitation, and they can marshal tremendous resources in support of their position and against anyone who tries to stand against them.
>
> On the other hand, those who might benefit from the acreage limitation, the small farmers who would come into being if the huge estates were broken up, are persons in the future. They do not exist at present. Since they exist only in the future and not in the present, they lack voices and are in a sense unrepresented.[168]

Eight and one-half years elapsed before executive interpretation of the San Luis Act as exempting the state service area from federal reclamation law was challenged in court. Suit was brought, not by wholly landless persons seeking land, but by four family-size farmers on adjacent lands within the federal Central Valley project.[169]

Three years later, Federal District Judge Oliver J. Carter ruled against the challengers. He recited the Supreme Court observation in *Ivanhoe v. McCracken* "that Congress, when exempting a particular project from acreage limitation because of its peculiar circumstances, had always done so by "express enactment."[170] Against that fact, however, he set "practical" considerations. Relying upon two earlier Supreme Court decisions, Judge Carter said:

> Nevertheless, an administrative practice has peculiar weight when it involves a contemporaneous construction of a statute by the men charged with the responsibility of setting the machinery in motion, of making the parts work efficiently and smoothly while they are yet

---

167. See text accompanying notes 116-118 *supra*.
168. 108 Cong. Rec. 5711 (1962).
169. Bowker v. Morton, No. C-70-1274 (N.D. Cal., filed Aug. 2, 1973).
170. *Id.* at 12, citing Ivanhoe Irrig. Dist. v. McCracken, *supra* note 18, at 292.

untried and new. *Norwegian Nitrogen Co. v. U.S.*, 288 U.S. 294, 315 (1933). [G]overnment is a practical affair intended for practical men. Both officers, law-makers and citizens naturally adjust themselves to any long-continued action of the Executive Department —on the presumption that unauthorized acts would not have been allowed to be so often repeated as to crystallize into a regular practice. That presumption is not reasoning in a circle but the basis of a wise and quieting rule that in determining the meaning of a statute or the existence of a power, weight shall be given to the usage itself— even when the validity of the practice is the subject of investigation. *United States v. Midwest Oil Co.*, 236 U.S. 459, 472-473 (1915).[171]

The Federal District Judge, like the Senate Interior Committee before him, declined to review the original executive decision at issue. The opinion continued:

> The Court feels itself bound by those principles in the instant situation. Here the Department of the Interior, through its Solicitor, made a contemporaneous construction of the San Luis Act in order to determine whether it was exempt from the reclamation laws. In a thorough and well-reasoned analysis, the Solicitor's Opinion found that there was such an exemption. In reliance on that Opinion, the Department and the State, both charged with execution of the Act, proceeded to act through the intervening years. In light of the foregoing authorities, the Court sees no good reason to now question the validity of the Solicitor's Opinion.[172]

Examination of the two Supreme Court decisions cited by Judge Carter[173] is illuminating for the substantive contrast with *Bowker v. Morton*. In *United States v. Midwest Oil Co.*, the Supreme Court upheld executive action, not at the expense of public policy, but to give Congress opportunity to enact a specific statute to preserve an exposed and specific public interest. The Court stated that

> . . . when it appeared that the public interest would be served by withdrawing or reserving parts of the public domain, nothing was more natural than to retain what the Government already owned. And in making such orders, which were thus useful to the public, no private interest was injured . . . . The President was in a position to know when the public interest required particular portions of the people's lands to be withdrawn from entry or location; his action inflicted no wrong upon any private citizen, and being subject to disaffirmance by Congress, could occasion no harm to the interest of the public at large. Congress did not repudiate the power claimed or the

---

171. *Id.* at 12-13. Following district court decisions adverse to plaintiffs, the Ninth Circuit granted leave to appeal. Bowker v. Morton, Civil No. 75-8126 (9th Cir., May 2, 1975).
172. *Id.*
173. See text accompanying note 171 *supra*.

withdrawal orders made. On the contrary it uniformly and repeatedly acquiesced in the practice and, as shown by these records, there had been, prior to 1910, at least 252 Executive Orders making reservations for useful, though non-statutory purposes.[174]

Thus, the *Midwest Oil* case supported repeated executive action protective of public policy. By contrast, the District Court in *Bowker v. Morton* approved executive action destructive of Congressional opportunity to preserve public interest in wide distribution of public waters on a public project as prescribed in a national policy dating from 1902 and reaffirmed repeatedly. The executive action, founded on a Solicitor's opinion, was challenged in court within a decade.[175]

The issue in *Norwegian Nitrogen Co. v. United States* was the validity of administratively determined "contemporaneous construction" procedures to be followed in hearings and investigations to carry out the purposes of the 1922 Tariff Act.[176] Applicability of the Act itself was not at issue. Before Judge Carter this was the central issue.

In *Bowker v. Morton*, the relations between the three branches of government were deeply involved. The District Court, in legalizing executive exemption of the state service area from federal law, attached little importance to (1) the vote by both Houses of Congress in 1959 and 1960 against exemption; (2) Congressional rejection of exemption in 1944 and 1947 of the Central Valley Project, of which the San Luis Unit is a part; and (3) the Supreme Court notice of a long-standing Congressional practice of exempting particular reclamation projects "because of . . . peculiar circumstances . . . [only] by express enactment."[177] The lower court thus allowed to stand the Solicitor's rejection of the rule of law that "when an exemption is removed from a bill before enactment, the presumption is that the legislative body intended the law to apply . . . ."[178]

---

174. 236 U.S. 459, 471 (1915).
175. Norwegian Nitrogen Co. v. United States, 288 U.S. 294 (1933).
176. *Id.*
177. Agreement with the State of Calif. for Constr. of San Luis Unit, Central Valley Project, 68 Interior Dec. 412, 417 (1961). Commenting to the Senate on the Solicitor's rejection, Senator Wayne Morse, previously Dean of the University of Oregon Law School, said:
> Mr. President, that opinion was written by a lawyer; but he needs to go back to law school and refresh his memory and knowledge on how the courts determine legislative intent. If he would do so, he would find that that paragraph in his memorandum opinion is plain silly, because legislative intent is not legally determined by some lawyer's supposition as to what some Members of the Senate might have thought, and others to the contrary might have thought, when they voted on a bill. Most of this memorandum opinion is a conglomeration of silliness from the standpoint of legal analysis.

108 CONG. REC. 5688 (1962).
178. *Id.*

XI

IN PERSPECTIVE

There exists and is spreading in the West a tenant or hired labor system which not only represents a relatively low industrial development, but whose further development carries with it a most serious threat. Politically, socially and economically the system is indefensible.

—Public Lands Commission, 1905[179]

The central question in the [Imperial Valley, California] suit [over acreage limitation] was whether reclamation law applied to the 1928 Boulder Canyon Project Act . . . . Imperial Resources Associates, a private group of landowners . . . . raised a $600,000 defense fund . . . for the growers, including many corporate operations.

—Fresno Bee, September 16, 1973[180]

We must make it so that the poor man will have as nearly as possible an equal opportunity in litigating as the rich man; and under present conditions, ashamed as we may be of it, this is not the fact.

—Ex-President William Howard Taft, 1915[181]

As culmination to a decade of agitation by Western citizens and large landholding interests, Congress enacted the National Reclamation Act of 1902.[182] This legislation created a Reclamation Service, now known as the Bureau of Reclamation, financed originally from sales of public lands and empowered to construct Western dams, reservoirs, and canals necessary to store and move water to arid and semi-arid lands. As a condition of extending this public assistance, Congress attached the requirement that no individual could receive water for more than 160 acres and that the receiver had to be an occupant of the land, resident upon it, or in the neighborhood. In 1944 Secretary of the Interior Harold

---

179. Quoted in FINAL REPORT OF THE U.S. COMM'N ON INDUS. RELATIONS 15 (1915) [hereinafter cited as FINAL REP.].
180. G. Baker, *Is White House Linked to Imperial Case*, Fresno Bee, Sept. 16, 1973, at A1, A4, col. 4. The growers' opponent, seeking standing for landless Imperial Valley persons to appeal the decision against the U.S., is described by M. Kinsley, *Ben Yellen's Fine Madness*, 2 WASH. MONTHLY, Jan. 1971, at 38.
181. FINAL REPORT, *supra* note 179, at 52. In 1973, Attorney General Elliot L. Richardson spoke similarly: ". . . our democratic system fundamentally cannot tolerate—cannot withstand—one law for the rich and another for the poor, one law for the strong and another for the weak . . . ." Address before House of Delegates, American Bar Association, in Washington, D.C., Aug. 8, 1973.
182. P. Taylor, *Reclamation: The Rise and Fall of an American Idea*, 7:4 AMER. WEST 27 (1970). *See generally* P. Taylor, *Water, Land, and People in the Great Valley, supra* note 8, at 24.

L. Ickes testified that in the intervening 42 years, Congress had endorsed this policy ten times.[183]

In 1917, the California Legislature authorizied state-created water districts to contract for water with the Bureau of Reclamation in accordance with the terms of federal reclamation law. In 1959 and 1960 the legislature and people both reapproved the 1933 and earlier authorizations to accept federal acreage limitation policy. In the Fall of 1958, a unanimous U.S. Supreme Court reversed a divided California Supreme Court opinion to hold acreage limitation provisions constitutional. Accordingly, the California Supreme Court then declared unanimously in February, 1960, that, "For many years the two governments have peacefully and wholeheartedly cooperated . . . . The federal Congress . . . has determined . . . that the 160-acre limitation is a basic part of federal policy. The state Legislature has adopted this concept as state policy. . . ."[184]

In the months between the U.S. Supreme Court's validation of acreage limitation and the State Supreme Court's 1960 recognition of the unity of federal and state policy, California's governor and spokesmen in the United States Senate pleaded, concurrently with support from the Federal Bureau of Reclamation, for Congressional exemption of the planned state service area from acreage limitation. As Senator Kuchel told the Senate in 1959:

> S.44 is authorized by my distinguished colleague from California [Mr. Engle] and by me. It is endorsed by the Bureau of Reclamation and the Secretary of the Interior. The Bureau of the Budget has interposed no objection. The bill is recommended by the government of California presided over by the Honorable Edmund G. Brown, a Democrat; and it was recommended by the government of California presided over by his predecessor, Hon. Goodwin Knight, a Republican. Thus, my colleague and I are in the happy position of being able to say that the bill comes to the Senate floor recommended by all those agencies, State and Federal, which have an official interest in the subject matter . . . . Accordingly, the bill should unequivocally provide that in one area served by the Federal project, Federal reclamation law will apply, while in the other area, served by the Feather River project, California law will apply.[185]

---

183. *Hearings on H.R. 3961, supra* note 39, at 537.

184. Ivanhoe Irrig. Dist. v. All Parties, *supra* note 101. This view apparently was not shared by all spokesmen for California. Notably, in May, 1959, Senator Kuchel, seeking Congressional exemption from acreage limitation, asked Senator Douglas of Illinois, "Does he believe that the people of California should have the right, by State law, to determine how water is to be used in California under the State system?" 105 CONG. REC. 7497 (1959).

185. *Id.* at 7483-84.

Senate and House Interior Committees endorsed the bill, including specifically the requested exemption of the state service area from federal acreage limitation law. Both Houses of Congress approved the project. After extended floor debate, however, both Houses voted to eliminate the proposed exemption. Nonetheless, elimination of the exemption by both Houses has not proved to be decisive that federal acreage limitation law will apply.

After Congressional authorization of the joint project, it became necessary for executive branches of state and federal governments to draft a contract defining their cooperation in detail. In anticipation, the House inserted in the project authorization bill a provision purporting to assure Congressional oversight of the contract terms before they could become effective. Before voting Senate acceptance of the House version, Senator Proxmire, an active supporter of acreage limitation, sought and received assurance that the changes would not impair the Senate's original decision denying exemption of the state service area. Senator Clinton Anderson, Chairman of the Interior Committee which originally had recommended exemption, responded that the House version "strengthened rather than weakened" the bill.[186]

The actual outcome of the provisions for review, however, has been to deny observance of acreage limitation, not to assure it. Congress conferred review authority upon the Senate and House Interior Committees, both of which were opposed to acreage limitation on the state service area from the beginning. Thus, drafters and reviewers of the contract alike shared the same view of the undesirability of acreage limitation.

Executives of the Interior Department and the California Department of Water Resources simply omitted acreage limitation from the contract drafted between them. Then the Congressional Interior Committees simply decided, in Senator Anderson's words, that they "would not review the contract . . . ."[187] Thus, the review procedure was used to avoid review by the Senate and House as whole bodies.

Judicial review remained as a possibility. In the 1960 Charles T. Main Report to the State Department of Water Resources, legal counsel had predicted that, "If Congress in effect approves the agreement worked out between the Bureau of Reclamation and the State, it would seem likely that this will be the end of controversy as to this subject."[188] His prophesy nearly came true. Review, if there was to be any, was left to the initiative of private citizens.

---

186. See text accompanying note 156 *supra*.
187. See text accompanying note 161 *supra*.
188. See text accompanying note 120 *supra*.

Within a decade after Congressional appropriation of funds for the project and the beginning of construction, four family-size farmers asked the federal district court to review the omission of acreage limitation by the executive. The court declined. It felt "bound" by "practical" considerations to which "officers, law-makers and citizens naturally adjust themselves" in time.[189] The court saw "no good reason to now question the validity of the Solicitor's Opinion."[190]

Judge Carter, in effect, declined to review the Solicitor's opinion of a decade earlier, as had the Attorney General and the Congressional Interior Committees before him. By so declining, he was condoning an executive action destructive of a national water policy of 68 years' duration, with roots in national land policy reaching back more than a century and a quarter.

Here is where three branches of federal and state governments, grappling with man's relation to his environment, rest for the time being.

The California Supreme Court holds that there is "no conflict between the legislative branches of the two governments." Each has given specific approval to the policy embodied in the 160-acre limitation.[191] Yet this policy is absent from the vital contract executed by administrators of the two governments.

An administrative officer's challenged opinion that omission of policy is proper passes formally in review through three branches of the federal government, yet remains without review. An Attorney General avoids review, hoping he can leave that to Congress. The Senate Interior Committee not only avoids review, but obstructs review by the Congress as a whole. With the issue formally before him, a federal district judge concludes that reviewing is not for him.[192]

In the meantime, the door of opportunity to reclaimed land in the West, opportunity that the law promised to open to the landless of the nation, remains closed. The tide of migration flows away from the land into the ghettoes of the cities, a tide that national policy professes to curb. Monopolization of land by large interests and speculation in the windfall profits from public investment in reclamation go unchecked.[193]

---

189. Bowker v. Morton, *supra* note 169, at 12.
190. *Id.* at 13.
191. Ivanhoe Irrig. Dist. v. All Parties, *supra* note 101.
192. On May 2, 1975, the Ninth Circuit Court of Appeals granted leave to appeal the applicability of federal reclamation law to the state service area. Bowker v. Morton, Civil No. 75-8126 (9th Cir., May 2, 1975).
193. The Senate Small Business and Interior and Insular Affairs Committees have jointly opened inquiry into whether national reclamation policy is being observed even on the San Luis federal service area. They held Washington hearings on July 17 and 22, 1975, and forecast further hearings in California. *'Paper Farmer' Abuses Claimed*, S.F. Chronicle, July 18, 1975, at 8, col. 1.

The burden of sustaining national policy falls on the shoulders of those in whose immediate interest it was adopted, yet those least able to bear it.

A polarized society is nourished while the wheels of review spin. An historic national policy favoring "actual settlers" and "people, not land,"[194] lies dormant.

---

194. Ivanhoe Irrig. Dist. v. McCracken, *supra* note 18, at 297. *See also* P. Taylor, *Mexican Migration and the 160-Acre Water Limitation*, 63 CALIF. L. REV. 732 (1975); P. Taylor, *Public Policy and the Shaping of Rural Society*, 20 S. DAK. L. REV. 475 (1975).

CENTRAL VALLEY PROJECT

CENTRAL VALLEY PROJECT: WATER AND LAND

PAUL S. TAYLOR

University of California

Thus, practically, all values inhere in the water, and an equitable division of the waters can be made only by a wise system of parceling the lands; ... In general, the lands greatly exceed the capacities of the streams ... The magnitude of the interest involved must not be overlooked. All the present and future agriculture of more than four-tenths of the area of the United States is dependent upon irrigation, and practically all values for agriculture inhere, not in the lands but in the water. Monopoly of land need not be feared. The question for legislators to solve is to devise some practical means by which water rights may be distributed among individual farmers and water monopolies prevented.

—J. W. Powell, Report on the lands of the arid region of the United States, 1878.

THE Great Central Valley of California resembles an old-fashioned baby's bath-tub with one side, the west, slit to the bottom in the middle for an outlet. Ringed about by the high Sierra on the east, the Tehachapi mountains on the south, the Siskiyous on the north, and the Coast Range on the west, the Valley is an oblong watershed stretching lengthwise through the interior of the state for a distance of nearly 500 miles. Its average width is 125 miles. The floor of the Valley is an alluvial plain about 400 miles long, with an average width of 45 miles. The Sacramento River and its tributaries drain the northern portion of the watershed; the San Joaquin River and its tributaries drain the southern portion. These two streams meet and meander westward through a low agricultural area known as the Delta, then out through the Carquinez straits into San Francisco Bay.

Reclamation has been going on for nearly a hundred years in Central Valley. It has been a long slow process made up of numerous separate and little-coordinated efforts. Irrigation began immediately following the Gold Rush, and ditches built for placer mining soon began to serve the uses of agriculture. But for twenty years irrigated agriculture spread slowly. Then in 1869 completion of the transcontinental railroad gave irrigation in the Central Valley its first great impetus, for it opened eastern markets to western produce. In irrigation as in transportation the golden spike driven at Promontory Point in Utah opened an era.

The next three decades saw steady expansion of irrigation in Central Valley, yet by 1900 it still had reached less than a million acres. The four following decades saw it increase to nearly two and three-quarters million acres in 1939. Then the pace became even faster. About one and three-quarters million acres were brought under during the single decade preceding 1943, nearly three quarters of a million acres of it during the last four years. The Second World War brought markets that were assured and unlimited, at least for its duration, and with these came a rate of expansion beyond precedent.

To level and prepare land to receive water is one thing; to develop the supply of water for its irrigation is another. In Central Valley, the very means by which so many areas obtain their water supply is such that the more land prepared for irrigation, the more serious the discrepancy becomes between demand and supply of water.

From the early 1900's irrigators began to sink wells and pump ground water to the surface. By 1940 approximately a million and a half acres received most of their irrigation supply from this source. The danger signs of this kind of irrigation appeared early. Ground water was being used faster than nature was restoring it. Water tables began to fall and have continued to fall, and pumping lifts to rise. Irrigators have had to deepen wells, install more powerful pumps, and use more power to lift water.

This was the water condition in 1935 when the federal government allocated funds to start construction in the Central Valley. Federal intervention began in a way, as a rescue operation.[1] It was none too soon, but even the first unit, or Central Valley Project, was not enough. In many areas water tables are not yet stabilized, while preparation of still more land for crops increases the over-drafts upon underground supplies. Hardly more than half of the lands it will ultimately be possible to irrigate have been prepared for crops.[2] Yet already in late 1948, dust storms raised from plowed fields had begun to trouble the southern San Joaquin Valley.

Efforts to put Central Valley waters to use for irrigation can be regarded as attempts to solve the problem of where, when, and how to store and to move water. This is the way it looks to an engineer: Roughly two-thirds of the precipitation falls on the northern, or Sacramento Valley watershed, but about two-thirds of the irrigable land lies southward in the San Joaquin Valley. Moving surplus water from the Sacramento Valley to thirsty lands of the San Joaquin, therefore, will provide more irrigation. The problem is how to redistribute water, taking it from where it is unneeded to where it is wanted.

---

[1] Testimony of Edward Hyatt, state engineer of California, Hearings before House Committee on Flood Control, 74th Cong., 1st Sess. (Washington: Government Printing Office, 1935), pp. 60-72; Governor James Rolph, Jr., "Central Valley Project of State Water Plan," *State Water Plan Association (comp.), Manual for Speakers in Support of Central Valley Project Act, special election, December 19, 1933* (mimeo. Dec. 1, 1933), sec. 14, p. 1.

[2] U. S. Bureau of Reclamation, *Comprehensive Plan for Water Resources Development Central Valley Basin California*, Region 2 Project Planning Report No. 2-4.03, November, 1945, pp. 125-6. Cf. statement by Edward Hyatt, California state engineer, that the State Water Plan "provided for the ultimate irrigation in the Central Valley of 8,000,000 acres of land as compared with 3,500,000 acres now irrigated." (*Proceedings of California Water Conference* called by Earl Warren, State Capitol, Sacramento, California, December 6 and 7, 1945, p. 30. Hereafter cited as *California Water Conference*.)

Besides redistributing water in *space,* another problem is to redistribute water in *time,* to save it from wasting when it is unneeded, so as to put it to use later when wanted. The natural flow of streams into the Valley is strong in the spring, fed by winter rains and melting snowpack. Much of this water is uncontrolled now, and wastes to the sea. A few weeks later it is gone when irrigation needs it most.

The problem is more than how to save water in wet seasons for release in dry ones. It also is how to save water in wet years for release in dry years. The same storage reservoirs, properly constructed and properly operated, can solve both problems.

If Central Valley were fed by a single river, control of water for irrigation would be relatively simple, but there are more than a score of streams, great and small. It is not enough to control the waters of each stream separately. That still would leave local surpluses of water that could be used elsewhere by exporting it, and local deficiencies that could be remedied by importing it. The task therefore is to unite these streams into a single great system, with water storage and water releases coordinated, so as to eliminate waste by delivering all water where and when it is needed.

Engineers gradually have evolved a plan to solve these problems. The main outlines of it have been stated for twenty years or more, and engineers of the Bureau of Reclamation have given it the latest and most complete reformulation.[3] The plan is to make the watershed into an efficient unit by tying it together by means of a series of canals that will cut across virtually every stream. This will give maximum control over water, with power to move it season by season and year by year, from wherever it is surplus to wherever it is deficient. The plan will require building thirty-eight major reservoirs, hundreds of miles of main canals, and thousands of miles of laterals and drains. Half a generation or more will be needed to complete construction.

So far the Central Valley Project has been described as a plan to irrigate land, but irrigation is only one part of what can be done by controlling water. In the years since Major Powell wrote his famous report[4] on the arid region, men have learned how to generate electric power from falling water. A first result of knowing how to do this, is to be able to lift water and thereby move it to places previously impossible to irrigate when dependence was entirely on the flow of water down hill. Once gravity itself is made available to press back the limitations imposed by gravity, then hydroelectric power plants become tools for redistributing

---

[3] *Comprehensive Plan,* loc. cit.

[4] J. W. Powell, *Report on the lands of the arid region of the United States, with a more detailed account of the lands of Utah. With maps.* (Second edition; Washington: Government Printing Office, 1879), pp. xv, 185.

water as indispensable as canals. Without power to elevate Sacramento River water into canals high enough to flow south by gravity into the San Joaquin Valley, the Central Valley Project would be doomed at the outset. It never could move enough water from one valley to the other to achieve its main irrigation objective.

Important as power is to the extension of irrigation, that is only the beginning of its use. The power plants at storage reservoirs and upstream in Central Valley can develop far more energy than can be used advantageously to promote irrigation. This surplus can be disposed of to serve industries, businesses, and homes. In this way power takes a place beside irrigation as a major purpose of western water development.

When great reservoirs are constructed, it is possible to serve numerous purposes besides those which may have prompted construction initially. In addition to irrigating land and generating power, the storage of water in Central Valley will make it possible to moderate or prevent floods, to improve navigation on portions of some rivers, and to check injurious incursions of salt water that back up from the Bay into the Delta. Lesser incidental benefits will also result such as creation of recreation areas at the reservoirs.

The requirements made upon the project for serving all these purposes are not entirely consistent, each with those of the others. Control of floods requires empty reservoirs when heavy floods are expected. Irrigation requires that reservoirs be filled with flood waters to be held for release months later. Power generation requires generally steady releases of water, with special attention to daily peaks at early evening, to seasonal needs of the project to lift irrigation water into canals, and perhaps to fit fluctuating special needs of the power market. At times when all purposes cannot be served, the priorities determining what releases of water shall be made probably will follow state law.[5]

The technical name given to a project of this type is "multiple-purpose," and within the scale of priorities of purpose established by statute, the aim is maximum total benefit. To achieve this aim requires complete integration of all the numerous features of this complex and far-flung project. In Central Valley this means that a master water dispatcher must know the future needs of crops for water for days and even weeks in advance, so he can release proper amounts of water that will arrive on time from one or more reservoirs situated perhaps hundreds of miles away. He must anticipate the melting of snowpacks and the run-off of

---

[5] The Federal Act of Aug. 26, 1937 (50 *Stat.* 850) provides that "reservoirs shall be used, first, for river regulation, improvement of navigation, and flood control; second, for irrigation and domestic uses; and, third, for power." State law provides "that the use of water for domestic purposes is the highest use of water and that the next highest use is for irrigation." (*Water Code*, sec. 106.5). See John R. Bennett, "Some uncertainties in the law of water rights," 21 *Southern California Law Review* 344 (July, 1948).

flash floods to keep them harmless and prevent waste of their waters. He must study irregularities of precipitation, to know in which ones among the two-score reservoirs he should retain water longest, and from which he ought to release it first. Only by such fine operation can a complex project serving many purposes produce the greatest possible benefit year in and year out. Only if a single agency has control over every part of the project is it possible to achieve fine operation. Two agencies, or three, cannot do it, no matter how competent each may be individually.[6]

At the present time the United States Bureau of Reclamation has prepared the only comprehensive program under a legal authorization which provides for developing the full uses of the waters of the basin.[7] The plan of the State Engineer made in 1930 is, outdated,[8] and the current plan of the Army Engineers for flood control is not prepared under a legal authorization to develop fullest possible use of the waters of the Valley.[9] If and when this comprehensive basin-wide plan of the Bureau is carried to completion, it will make of Central Valley the greatest and most complex reclamation project on the continent. In addition to the thirty-eight reservoirs, the canals and the laterals, it calls for construction of twenty-eight hydroelectric power plants, supplementary fuel-electric plants, and power transmission lines to carry surplus power. The estimated cost of this development at 1945 prices was nearly two billion dollars, exceeding the federal investment in the Tennessee Valley and approximating the cost of developing the first atomic bomb.

The immediate results to be expected from completion of the comprehensive plan are impressive. The project will supplement inadequate ground waters for nearly two million acres of presently-irrigated fertile California land, protect another 400,000 acres from occasional damaging shortages in dry years, and protect about 360,000 acres in the Delta from destructive intrusion of saline waters from the Bay. It will bring water to over 3,000,000 acres not irrigated now. In addition, comprehensive development can provide about 360,000 acre-feet of water annually for municipal and industrial uses, for game refuges, etc. It can generate annually from falling water more than 8 billion kilowatt hours of electricity.

---

[6] See, for instance, Morris Llewellyn Cooke, "Rivers and Prosperity," New Republic, Vol. III, No. 25 (December 18, 1944), pp. 825-7.

[7] Reclamation Project Act of 1939, Act of August 4, 1939. Ch. 418, 53 Stat. 1187.

[8] State of California Department of Public Works, Publications of the Division of Water Resources, Edward Hyatt, state engineer, reports on state water plan prepared pursuant to Ch. 832, Stat. 1929, Bulletin No. 25, Report to Legislature of 1931 on State Water Plan, 1930 (California: State Printing Office: Sacramento, 1930), p. 204. Bulletins in this series cited hereafter as State Water Plan.

[9] Flood Control Act of 1944, Pub. L. 534, 78th Cong., 2d Sess. The Army Engineers provide for fewer reservoirs, and omit construction of power plants, canals, and transmission lines to distribute water and power.

This comprehensive engineering plan points a way to develop Central Valley water fully, in a carefully integrated system. It has not yet been presented to Congress for its authorization. Nevertheless its existence as tangible embodiment of an idea how full development can be secured is itself a landmark in the history of the Valley.

Making plans to develop waters in Central Valley is not new. It began practically a hundred years ago when California became a state in the Union. Its characteristics have been these—that the plans generally were for partial, or piecemeal, rather than for comprehensive development; that they were made by both private interests and public agencies without very clear definition of their interrelationships; that the roles and responsibilities of public agencies within local, state, and federal governments have not been harmonized, stabilized, or very clearly defined; that planning irrigation development has involved public decisions on policy not to be left to engineers or other technicians.

At most times over the past century, someone has been on hand to point to the necessity for unity and public enterprise. At some times, men have recognized the necessity for clear decisions on public policy as to who shall pay for the undertaking and who shall receive its benefits. At other times they have not, or have disputed the terms. Conflicts have been sharp, and they continue.[10]

In the beginning, integration and unity did not seem very important to those who carried responsibility for development. Projects were simple and relatively inexpensive, and private interests worked out solutions of the questions: who is to pay? and who is to benefit? that at least had the appearance of being satisfactory. Men did not see themselves up against complex and costly last efforts to wring the ultimate measure of benefit from the watershed. Yet even in the beginning they sought public help. The very first session of the legislature after admission of California to the Union in 1850 enacted a law calling for preparation of a plan to furnish water for irrigation.[11] In 1866 the legislature appropriated funds to survey a canal location in the Sacramento Valley.[12] In 1874, after study, a federal commission reported that "the Great Valley of California is admirably adapted to irrigation," and outlined a system of canals. It emphasized that "the works should be properly planned and located in

---

[10] For a denial of unity, see testimony of Raymond Matthew, *Hearings before Subcommittee of Senate Committee on Appropriations*, 79th Cong. 1st Sess. (Washington: Government Printing Office, 1946), pp. 1050-51. For resistance to public enterprise, see Arthur D. Angell, "Political and Administrative Aspects of the Central Valley Project of California," [Doctoral dissertation at University of California at Los Angeles, 1944 (typescript)]; also Mary Montgomery and Marion Clawson, *History of Legislation and Policy Formation of the Central Valley Project* (United States Department of Agriculture, Bureau of Agricultural Economics, Berkeley, California, March, 1946), pp. 179 ff. Hereafter cited as *History of Legislation*. For conflict over public policy on costs and benefits see present article below.

[11] *History of Legislation*, p. 9.

[12] *Ibid*.

the beginning, so that whatever is done to meet the present requirements of a sparse population may form a part of those that will be necessary to meet the demands of a population of millions by simply enlarging them," that "the works required, even at the present time, will be extremely costly," and that "unity of action is absolutely necessary to their proper execution."[13]

In 1878 the first State Engineer of California launched investigations with a legislative appropriation authorizing him to prepare "a system of irrigation, promote rapid drainage, and improve navigation on the Sacramento and San Joaquin Rivers."[14] As a far-sighted public official he saw the desirability of having a comprehensive plan to eliminate haphazard development. His purpose was well-conceived, but his funds were limited and in 1889 his office was abolished.

In the meantime private interests not only were making plans of their own but were active in development as well, especially after 1869. Here and there, they diverted water by canals from the streams of the Sierra wherever it could be done cheaply. Individuals, partnerships, and corporations all took a hand. What plans there were, were made each for a separate and immediate enterprise.

Late in the 1880's at the insistence of irrigators, the state of California stepped in again to assist water development. In 1886 the state supreme court in *Lux v. Haggin* had approved for California the common law doctrine of riparian water rights which had originated in humid England.[15] Many people believed the doctrine of riparian rights was inappropriate to arid and semi-arid country, and an obstacle to irrigation, especially of lands removed at a distance from a river bank and without riparian rights. Therefore they demanded public assistance from the state and were given it by passage of the Wright Act of 1887.[16]

The Wright Act authorized the voters and landowners of an area to form irrigation districts. Districts formed of these lands that could be watered from a common source were endowed with public powers needed to bring them unappropriated water, and to levy assessments or charges to pay the costs. In this way the state increased the capacity of groups to finance their own irrigation by clothing them with public authority to assure common action.

Around the turn of the century a number of water investigations in Central Valley had been made, mainly by the federal Department of

---

[13] *Report of the Board of Commissioners on the Irrigation of the San Joaquin, Tulare, and Sacramento Valleys of the State of California*, 43 Cong., 1st Sess., House Exec. Doc. No. 290 (Washington: Government Printing Office, 1874), p. 8.

[14] *History of Legislation*, p. 10.

[15] 69 Cal. 255.

[16] *California Statutes*, 1887, p. 29.

Agriculture.[17] Beginnings also were made for an extensive and continuous series of stream-gauging records. These have yielded continuous data on stream flow into the Central Valley for more than forty years, and now provide the foundations upon which the computations and decisions necessary to construct dependable engineering plans rest.

About the time of World War I, the limitations of both private enterprise and public districts were becoming apparent to landholders within the Valley. With sources of cheap water already developed, the costs of developing additional supplies were higher. Therefore not much more development was in sight that looked sufficiently attractive to private landowning interests to persuade them to undertake it, either through corporations or public districts.

As described earlier, this difficulty did not stop landholders from bringing more land under irrigation; on the contrary they were levelling land and putting down deep wells in ever greater numbers, as they continue to do right to the present. But the sure signs of overdrafts upon nature's supply were making it plain that although landowners could still sink wells and level land, they could no longer pay the costs of developing new and permanent sources of water.

This inability of landowners to finance further development slowed piecemeal planning by private agencies or irrigation districts to a standstill. Public financial support had become a necessity, and so, therefore, had public planning. With responsibility for full development in public hands, comprehensive, integrated planning was becoming practicable for the first time.

Here is how it happened. Shortly after World War I, the Irrigation Association of California published an important personal report on Central Valley by Colonel Robert Bradford Marshall, chief geographer of the United States Geological Survey.[18] It consisted of a comprehensive plan for a chain of great reservoirs, and for transference of Sacramento River water to the San Joaquin Valley by means of a system of long canals. This report, anticipating essential portions of the plan ultimately undertaken, brought the long-simmering state and federal interest to a boil, and helped to precipitate serious engineering studies by the State of California.[19]

A series of dry years became a further factor in the Central Valley situation, building up pressure from its victims to have something important done. Acute failure of natural replenishment was being added

---

[17] *Report of Irrigation Investigations in California, under the direction of Elwood Mead*, Bull. No. 100 (Washington: Government Printing Office, 1901). Same, *Irrigation Resources of California and Their Utilization*, Bull. No. 254 (1912).

[18] Robert Bradford Marshall, *Irrigation of Twelve Million Acres in the Valley of California*, distributed by California State Irrigation Association (Sacramento, California, November, 1920), pp. 1-12.

[19] *History of Legislation*, p. 21.

to the growing overdrafts upon ground waters created by continuous expansion of the area to be irrigated. At the high cost margin, some lands were going out of cultivation altogether. In the Delta region at the same time, salt water from the Bay was backing up into the slackening flow of the river. River water was becoming too saline for safe use by irrigators or by industrial plants. Only new supplies of water could meet these growing needs. In 1921, the California legislature authorized the first of a number of water investigations under the re-established office of State Engineer.[20] Ten years and over a million dollars spent on these investigations produced the notable series of engineering reports that formulated the "State Water Plan."[21]

The State Water Plan was an engineer's solution to the physical problems of water redistribution in Central Valley. By adopting the principle that a single watershed is a unit, it was able to propose transference of surplus Sacramento River water into the deficient basin of the San Joaquin.

The State Engineer gave explicit as well as implicit recognition to the necessity for unity. The report on the San Joaquin River Basin prepared under his direction stated that

> The plans for water supply development in the Sacramento and San Joaquin River basins must be combined under a unified project for the entire Great Central Valley, with all units of the project operated coordinately to effect the greatest conservation, regulation and utilization of the available water supplies to meet the needs for all purposes in both basins.[22]

This principle is so fundamental to full development of any watershed that it is surprising how hard it is to get it accepted in practice. Central Valley's development would be in better shape today if it had been adhered to consistently.

The State Water Plan did not overlook the economic problems of who would pay the costs. The Report to the 1931 legislature declared:

> The works required for the solution of the State's water problem are of such great magnitude and of such a far reaching scope that proper solution calls for a coordination and unification of the interests of not only the entire state, but the federal government as well, in the planning and execution of a complete program of development.
> Many obstacles—financial, legal and political—lie in the path of a program of complete relief and development. Although the past development of the state's water resources for irrigation, municipal, hydroelectric power and other uses has been successfully carried out by private and public agencies under existing laws, the greater magnitude of the problems arising in the planning and execution of works for complete coordination and utilization of the state's water resources calls for an entity of wider scope and greater powers than has heretofore been necessary. The magnitude and cost of the works involved are so great that it is questionable whether local interests would have the financial capacity to carry out the development required.[23]

---

[20] *Statutes of 1921*, Chap. 889.
[21] *State Water Plan* lists by title the full series of reports, Bull. 25-36.
[22] *State Water Plan*, Bull. 29, p. 65. See also footnote 91.
[23] *Ibid.*, p. 23.

Turning to examine precedents for financial support by the federal government, the report continued:

> The precedent established by the . . . activities and participation of the federal government in the state's water problem together with established policies relating to navigation, flood control and reclamation, would appear to offer a logical basis for extension of federal participation in construction of works required for conservation and utilization of the state's water resources.[24]

The State Engineer omitted at least one major problem in preparing his great report. While inquiring who would pay the costs, he did not ask who is to receive the benefits. That question is as fundamental as any other. When it is solved, the problem of how unity is to be achieved can be answered also, for it is efforts to reap special benefits that are most destructive of unity.[25]

A full generation before the State Water Plan furnished an answer to the engineering problems of developing Central Valley waters, and raised the question, who will pay? the national Congress already had examined the two questions, who will pay? and who will benefit? After thorough deliberation it gave clear answers to each.

This action by Congress grew out of a movement to enlist aid of the federal government for western reclamation which had begun formally in 1891. In that year the National Irrigation Congress held its first annual meeting in Salt Lake City.[26] It was founded upon the recognition that landholders could not afford the full costs of water development, and carried the hope that the federal government would pay what private landholders could not.

The sessions of the National Irrigation Congress—held long before the legislature of California authorized the State Engineer to make his investigations of what to do—were marked by a feeling that the job of developing the semi-arid West was too big for the method that had worked east of the 20-inch rainfall line. The ox and the breaking plow, driven by a family each on its own acres, would not do. In 1849 on the floor of the Senate, Senator Jefferson Davis of Mississippi had said, "Till the canals are cut, ditches and dams made, no person can reclaim the soil from Nature; an individual pioneer cannot settle upon it with his family, and support them by the product of his own exertion, as in the old possessions of the United States, where rain and dew unite with a prolific soil to reward freely and readily the toil of man. It is only by associated labor that such a country can be reduced to cultivation." [27] But the exponents of western reclamation in the 1890's drew no such

---

[24] *Ibid.*, p. 29.
[25] See below, and especially footnote 91.
[26] *Official Report of the Irrigation Congress*, held in the Exposition Building, City of Salt Lake, Utah, September 15, 16, and 17, 1891. (In Crerar Library, Chicago.)
[27] *Cong. Globe*, 31st Cong., 1st Sess. (1849-50), Appendix Vol. 1, p. 154.

conclusion as did Senator Davis, who had thought that irrigation in California logically required "the domestic servitude of African slavery." While they agreed that families rushing to quarter sections confronted defeat, they believed also that private capital controlling "associated labor" was not big enough to make the more costly developments of water, or if it was, that it could not be trusted to do the job in a way compatible with the public interest. To allow private enterprise to hold land enough to recoup itself for the costs laid out for development, they felt, might answer satisfactorily the question, who will pay? But they objected that to do this inevitably would make "monopoly" and "speculation" the answers in practice to the question, who will receive the benefits? A House Committee report on the reclamation bill of 1902 records their rejection of this solution. It says:

> If we were willing to abandon our time-honored policy of inviting and encouraging small individual landholdings, and were prepared to turn over all of the public lands under a large irrigation system to the control of a single individual or a corporation, we could undoubtedly secure the construction of extensive works which cannot be profitably constructed by private enterprise under present conditions, but no one contemplates paying so stupendous a price as this for irrigation development.[28]

In other words, they believed that only public enterprise was able to pay the costs of developing western waters fully, and at the same time to make sure that the families of actual settlers would receive the benefits.

The Irrigation Congress was a genuine citizens' movement, animated less by special interests than by those of the whole community. Membership was inclusive, not exclusive. It included Mormon enthusiasts for creation of more communities of family farmers; railroad land agents and businessmen seeking more western population to create more traffic and business; politicians seeking a wagon to hitch their stars to, perhaps even a vehicle to ride to statesmanship. Its debates revealed sharp divisions of opinion and at times of interest, but the results of deliberations were unifying, not divisive. The movement rested upon local participation and developed close teamwork among many men. It was spontaneous and proved itself an effective agency of democratic planning. When Congress passed the National Reclamation Act in 1902, these citizens of the Irrigation Congress had achieved their main goal during ten years' work.[29]

In laying the plans for public development of the West the national Congress in Washington wrestled with two fundamental questions, who will pay the costs? and who will receive the benefits? It examined engineering plans sufficiently to satisfy itself that development was possible,

---

[28] Committee on arid lands, *Report on Reclamation of Arid Lands*, H. R. Rep. No. 1468, ser. 4404, 57th Cong., 1st Sess. (April 7, 1902), p. 3.

[29] See *Proceedings of the National Irrigation Congress, 1891-1905*; William E. Smythe, *Conquest of Arid America* (New York: Macmillan, 1905); George Wharton James, *Reclaiming the Arid West; The Story of the United States Reclamation Service* (New York, 1917).

established a Reclamation Service with provision for capable engineers, and made it responsible for details. Then it devoted itself to answering the primary economic questions. The answers which it wrote into law in 1902 became the economic plan for all federal western reclamation. In 1937 it became the economic plan for Central Valley Project by act of Congress.[30]

Congress concluded that private enterprise, unaided, could not develop the West fully; that it ought not be given power sufficient to enable it to do it; that the national interest dictated that the West ought to be developed; therefore that use of public funds for the purpose was proper. In answer to the question, who will pay the costs? Congress produced a practical formula: the public treasury should advance the capital costs of reclamation, using revenues from the sale of public lands; private beneficiaries receiving irrigated farms should repay these capital costs, but spread over forty years and without interest. The value of waiving interest charges to private beneficiaries was equivalent to more than half the cost of the project.[31]

The other primary question, the one omitted from consideration in the State Water Plan, was, who will receive the benefits?

Since heavy public expenditures were to be made to bring water, these had to be justified by the purpose for which the water was to be used. It was not enough that a portion of the nation would be developed. Congress found its justification in the principle of the historic American land policy. The House Committee on the reclamation bill said, "It has been our time-honored policy to provide for the settlement of our public lands in small tracts to actual home builders."[32] So Congress embodied the spirit of the nation's land policy in the reclamation law, by prescribing that the benefits were to be distributed widely, and not to be allowed to go to monopolists.

It was easy to carry out this decision when public expenditures were to be made to water public lands. The lands simply would be sold in tracts of a size suitable for family farms, and water rights would go with them. But to justify spending public money to water private lands for the benefit of private landholders was more difficult. It caused thoughtful concern.

---

[30] Act of August 20, 1937, 50 *Stat.* 850.

[31] Computed by assuming 3 per cent interest and 40 years for repayment, the "percentage subsidy" equals 57 per cent. If repayment were extended to 50 years the percentage would be 62. U. S. Bureau of Reclamation, "Acreage Limitation in the Central Valley, A Report on Problem 19," Central Valley Project Studies (Berkeley, California, September 25, 1944) (mimeo.), p. 29, Table 4, Percentage subsidy in federal reclamation program for varying repayment periods and interest rates.

[32] Committee on arid lands, *Report on Reclamation of Arid Lands*, H. R. Rep. No. 794, ser. 4402, 57th Cong., 1st Sess. (March 8, 1902), p. 3.

One of the facts which Congress and the original exponents of reclamation had to face was the widespread existence of monopoly of arid lands. Nowhere was this more conspicuous than in the Central Valley. The historian, Paul Wallace Gates, has described the condition. He wrote:

> Following 1848 there came a rapid influx of settlers which, together with the large profits realized from the grazing industry in the interior valleys, created a land boom and led to extensive purchases. With great areas of land in the San Joaquin and Sacramento Valleys open to cash purchase the opportunity for speculative profits was unparalleled elsewhere; nor was the opportunity neglected. From 1862 to 1880 land sales and warrant and scrip entries in California were on an enormous scale, surpassing all other states for the period and in some years comprising well over half of the sales for the entire country. In the single year, ending June 30, 1869, 1,726,794 acres were sold in this state by the Federal government and for the entire period from 1862 to 1880 well over 7,000,000 acres were entered with cash, warrants, or scrip. . . . The total amount purchased from the Federal government by Chapman, Miller and Lux, Friedlander, E. H. Miller, and Mitchell was one and a quarter million acres. Forty-three other large purchasers acquired 905,000 acres of land in the sixties in California. Buying in advance of settlement, those men were virtually thwarting the Homestead Law in California, where, because of the enormous monopolization above outlined, homesteaders later were able to find little good land.[33]

In recognition of these and similar well-known conditions in other parts of the West, the House Committee devised the "160-acre water limitation," or "excess-land provision," in order to distribute the limited supply of water fairly and widely. The Committee offered the provision to Congress as the special justification for extending the benefits of public reclamation to private landowners. The chairman, Congressman Mondell of Wyoming, told the House:

> Under nearly every project undertaken by the Government there will undoubtedly be some lands in private ownership; and it would be manifestly unjust and inequitable not to provide water for these lands, providing their owners are willing to comply with the conditions of the Act; and in order that no such lands may be held in large quantities or by non-resident owners, it is provided that *no water right for more than 160 acres shall be sold to any landowner,* who must also be a resident or occupant of his land. This provision was drawn with a view to breaking up any large land holdings which might exist in the vicinity of government works and to insure occupancy by the owner of the land reclaimed.[34]

Three years later, during an attempt by large landholding interests of Central Valley and elsewhere to start a movement in the National Irrigation Congress for repeal of the 160-acre provision, Judge Raker of California gave authoritative testimony on the same point. He said:

> The committee of seventeen that originally planned and arranged the adoption of the National Irrigation Law secured *its adoption and presentation to Congress solely and entirely upon the question that the great land monopolies* in the United States *would be prohibited from getting the benefit of it.*[35]

---

[33] Paul Wallace Gates, "Homestead law in an incongruous land system," *American Historical Review,* July, 1936, pp. 668-9.

[34] *Cong. Rec.,* 57th Cong., 1st Sess. (June 12, 1902), p. 6678. Italics supplied by author.

[35] *Proceedings of Thirteenth National Irrigation Congress held at Portland, Oregon (1905),* p. 61. Italics supplied by author.

Since the 160-acre, or excess-land, provision is the special justification for spending public money for reclamation of private lands, proposals to remove or escape the provision, like some to be described later, are proposals to spend the public funds while removing the justification for doing so.

In facing the question, who will receive the benefits? and framing the 160-acre water limitation as an answer, the Congress of 1902 was deliberating over something far greater than financial equities between government and some of its citizens. It was concerned with the relations between man and man, with the development of a sense of community, with the forms and institutions of American society. Senator Hansbrough of North Dakota, sponsor of the reclamation bill, said:

> It is argued by some that as wealth grows larger in a few hands the opportunities of the laboring classes to secure employment are multiplied. Doutbless this contention is based upon sound reasoning, but looking a little beyond immediate benefits, it appears that the tendency under such a condition is to dwarf self-reliance in the masses and to make the mere service of opulent employers by the great army of breadwinners the fulfillment of all human ambition. I think it is the duty of the legislator to pursue a policy under which the greatest possible number of people may be provided with the means of independent employment, by which the aspirations of the individual may be encouraged and developed. To this end I give my support to this bill. . . .[36]

Congressman Martin of South Dakota said:

> The policy of the Government is to build up communities of many settlers with small holdings, and not to encourage the prosecution of agriculture by large corporations.[37]

Congressman Newlands of Nevada, co-sponsor of the bill, said:

> We have not felt in this country the evils of land monopoly. Lord Macauley said we never would experience the test of our institutions until our public domain was exhausted and an increased population engaged in a contest for the ownership of land. That will be the test of the future, and the very purpose of this bill is to guard against land monopoly and to hold this land in small tracts for the people of the entire country, to give to each man only the amount of land that will be necessary for the support of a family. . . .[38]

The 57th Congress was impressed by these considerations, passed the reclamation bill, and sent it to President Theodore Roosevelt, who signed it.

Between 1902 and the 1930's, the great landholding interests of the Central Valley made no move to take advantage of the National Reclamation Act. Their opposition to the 160-acre clause may have deterred them. A small project at Orland[39] was constructed in compliance with the excess-lands provisions and another was undertaken at Klamath in northern California and southern Oregon, but no more. In the middle

---
[36] Cong. Rec., 57th Cong., 1st Sess. (1902), p. 1386.
[37] Ibid., p. 6758.
[38] Ibid., p. 6734.
[39] In the Sacramento Valley.

1930's, when water shortage and unemployment were combined, it was different. Then the voters of California took a hand. They were told when they went to the polls in special referendum on a Central Valley water and power project, that there would be cooperation with the Federal Government in constructing and financing the project.[40] They gave their approval.[41]

After the election the difficulties in state-financing and the advantages of federal-financing became even clearer. So California Congressmen, the State Engineer, and others gave their approval to proposals in Washington that the federal government should undertake the first great unit of development under reclamation law, which includes the 160-acre provision. In 1936 both houses of the state legislature, in a memorial citing the reclamation law, requested Congress to give its approval to the project and to make appropriations.[42]

Nevertheless, after first appropriations were made and construction was started, holders of excess-lands became uneasy over the prospect that the 160-acre limitation on publicly-financed water might be enforced. Directors of the Madera Irrigation District recorded their objections in resolutions;[43] and more recently witnesses have testified that when they raised the point with engineers of the Bureau, they received assurances that the limitation would be removed before completion of the project.[44] How the assurances of officials could be regarded as binding on Congress is difficult to understand, but the implication seems to be that Congress ought to so regard them.

The reasons for wishing to escape the acreage limitation under reclamation law—not the appropriations—are not difficult to understand. If operations are now conducted with insufficient water on a scale above 160 acres, the desire to continue them with sufficient water on the same scale is natural. Besides, the average increment in value to lands not previously watered that can be expected from construction of the project

---

[40] "California secretary of state and legislative counsel (comp.), referendum measure to be submitted to the electors of the state of California at special election to be held Tuesday, December 19, 1933 together with arguments respecting the same" (Sacramento: State Printing Office, 1933), p. 3. See also *History of Legislation*, pp. 51 ff, and Governor James Rolph, Jr., *op. cit.*

[41] The vote in Los Angeles was about 2 to 1 against the measure; in San Francisco nearly 2 to 1 in favor; in Sacramento Valley 3 to 1 in favor; in San Joaquin Valley 5 to 1 in favor; and in the state 459,712 to 426,109 in favor. *History of Legislation*, p. 61.

[42] Cong. Rec., 74th Cong., 2d Sess. (1936), p. 8413.

[43] Hearings before a Subcommittee of the Senate Committee on Irrigation and Reclamation on S. Res. 295, 78th Cong., 2d Sess. (1944), pp. 320-1.

[44] Testimony of Russell Giffin, *Hearings before Subcommittee of the U. S. Senate Military Affairs Committee on Central Valley Water Project*, held at room 276, U. S. courthouse and postoffice building. San Francisco, California, Friday, April 7, 1944 (mimeo. by U. S. Bureau of Reclamation, Sacramento), pp. 93-95. Testimony of Roland Curran, *Hearings before Senate Subcommittee on Commerce*, 78th Cong., 2d Sess., on H. R. 3961 (1944), pp. 665-6; testimony of Roland Curran, *Hearings before Subcommittee of Senate Committee on Public Lands*, 80th Cong., 1st Sess., on S. 912 (1947), p. 1310.

is estimated conservatively at above $200 an acre.[45] The incremental value of supplementing a water supply, now inadequate, may often be substantial, although less on the average than the increment from a full supply.

The extent of the excess-landowning interest in having acreage limitation removed is not known accurately. One study by the Bureau of Agricultural Economics[46] found that about 4 per cent of the landowners of valley floor lands in three San Joaquin Valley counties held 53 per cent of all the irrigable land. Undoubtedly the interests of owners of excess lands are substantial and are concentrated largely in the San Joaquin Valley, which stands to gain most from the full project.

The dispute over the question, who will receive the benefits? broke into the open in 1944. Alarmed by public statements implying or saying flatly that the law would be enforced—statements made by President Roosevelt,[47] Secretary of Interior Ickes,[48] and Bureau of Reclamation officials[49]—representatives of large landholders moved quickly. Without public hearings, Congressman Alfred J. Elliott (D., Calif.) brought to the floor of the House a "committee amendment" to the rivers and harbors bill exempting Central Valley from acreage limitation.[50] The element of surprise made the tactic effective. Within a few minutes of debate a scattering of objections was brushed aside, a compromise was rejected by supporters of the exemption, and the amendment was passed.[51]

In the Senate, however, public hearings before the Senate Commerce Committee could not be avoided, and these gave supporters of reclamation law their opportunity. Despite that Senator Hiram Johnson (R., Calif.) let it be known he favored exemption, and that Senator Sheridan Downey (D., Calif.) worked to the same end, the entire rivers and harbors bill failed of passage because a number of senators, among them Senators Robert M. LaFollette, Jr. (Prog., Wis.), Carl Hatch and Dennis Chavez (D., N. Mex.), announced their strong opposition to the Elliott amendment.[52]

In the 80th Congress another effort was made to break down acreage limitation. This time exemptions were proposed for three projects, one each in the states of California, Colorado, and Texas. All six Senators

---

[45] Testimony of Paul H. Johnstone, *Hearings on S. 912* (1947), pp. 852-55, 861.

[46] Edwin E. Wilson and Marion Clawson, "Agricultural Land Ownership and Operation in the Southern San Joaquin Valley," (U. S. Department of Agriculture, Berkeley, California, Bureau of Agricultural Economics, June, 1945 [mimeo.]), p. 28, table 5.

[47] National Reclamation Association, *Proceedings Irrigation War Food Conference and 12th Annual Meeting, Denver, Colorado* (October 27-28-29, 1943), pp. 202-3.

[48] *Ibid.*, pp. 201-2.

[49] *Ibid.*, p. 67.

[50] *Cong. Rec.*, 78th Cong., 2d Sess. (1944), p. 2921.

[51] *Ibid.*, pp. 2922-4.

[52] *Cong. Rec.*, 78th Cong., 2d Sess. (1946), pp. 9495-9500, 9746-47.

from the three states sponsored the bill, including Senator Downey, and the newly-elected Senator William F. Knowland (R., Calif.). More than 1300 pages of printed testimony were taken on the bill, but its supporters did not muster strength enough to have it reported out of committee.

Reasons for the inability to remove this fundamental principle of the economic plan for western reclamation appear when the alignment of groups is examined, for and against. The California Farm Bureau Federation,[53] California State Chamber of Commerce,[54] and California Irrigation Districts Association[55] have supported removal of acreage limitation. From within each of these groups, however, some members have made public statements accepting the limitation.[56] Groups insisting on maintenance of the law have included the California Grange,[57] AFL,[58] CIO,[59] Veterans of Foreign Wars,[60] American Veterans Committee,[61] Catholic Rural Life Conference,[62] and Congregational Christian,[63] Presbyterian,[64] and Jewish organizations.[65] During public hearings the national organizations of some of these groups gave active support to their respective state organizations. The National Farmers Union[66] and national convention of the American Legion both recorded their support of acreage limitation.[67]

The question whether the original economic plan for western reclamation is to be sustained or broken down appears to be of non-partisan character. Members of both major parties have been active on both sides. However, the issue is becoming regarded as more clearly partisan within California. Senator Knowland (R.) declared himself against

---

[53] Hearings on S. 912 (1947), pp. 157-8. The position of the Farm Bureau Federation, like that of other organizations mentioned immediately following, was presented publicly upon numerous occasions. In these footnotes one or two occasions only are cited as examples.

[54] California water conference, address by James Mussatti.

[55] Hearings on S. 912 (1947), p. 158.

[56] Testimony of Frank T. Swett, Hearings before Subcommittee of Senate Committee on Commerce on H. R. 3961, 78th Cong., 2d Sess. (1946), p. 618; testimony of C. A. Talbott, Hearings before a Subcommittee of the Senate Committee on Irrigation and Reclamation on S. Res. 295, 78th Cong., 2d Sess. (1946), p. 286. Address by Warren Fowler, Sacramento Valley Council State Chamber of Commerce, Senator Hotel, Sacramento, 12:00 noon, February 28, 1947 (mimeo), 2 p. Testimony of R. W. Pixley, chairman, board of directors, Shafter-Wasco Irrigation District, on S. Res. 295, p. 461.

[57] Hearings on S. 912 (1947), pp. 265, 355.

[58] Ibid., pp. 1184-1188.

[59] Hearings on H. R. 3961 (1944), p. 683.

[60] Hearings on S. 912 (1947), p. 143.

[61] Ibid., p. 483.

[62] Testimony of Father Charles Phillips, Hearing before Subcommittee of Senate Military Affairs Committee, op. cit., p. 24.

[63] Hearings before the House Committee on Public Lands, 80th Cong., 1st Sess. pursuant to H. Res. 93, Committee Hearing No. 27 (1947), p. 13.

[64] Ibid., p. 17.

[65] Hearings on S. 912 (1947), p. 529.

[66] Ibid., pp. 615, 623.

[67] Ibid., p. 495.

acreage limitation during his 1946 campaign and was elected over a Democratic candidate who favored it.[68] In 1948 the Republican state platform was silent on acreage limitation but the Democratic platform gave it support with emphasis.[69] Congressman Elliott (D.), who had come close to defeat in 1946, did not stand for re-election. His place was taken by a Republican who generally is believed to share his views on this issue.[70] In the adjoining district Congressman Gearhart (R.), who opposed acreage limitation, was defeated by Cecil F. White (D.), who favored it. In these ways the lines are being drawn. While Senator Downey (D.) remains opposed to acreage limitation, the weight of the Democratic Party in political contests for office all the way from assemblyman up, clearly is moving to its active support.[71]

It is proper that the answer to this question, who will receive the benefits? should be made finally by the voters. It is a fundamental of the economic plan. It is not primarily a technical question to be answered by technicians, but an issue of public policy.

The tactics of the effort to break down the original plan for reclamation are varied. While the Elliott amendment was before Congress in May, 1944, the periodical, *Business Week*, enumerated four of them:

> If the big landowners in the valley lose out in this particular fight [for direct exemption], they have several other proposals to accomplish their end. One of them is a House bill which would authorize the Army to add irrigation and power development to its present navigation and flood-control powers. The legislation also would call for construction of a series of irrigation and power projects throughout the country, especially in Central Valley. This would circumvent the 160-acre rule, since the Army is not bound by that restriction.
>
> Another proposal, said to have originated among the big landowners of Fresno County, is for the State of California to take over the Central Valley project, paying the entire bill. This, too, would sidestep the 160-acre limitation. Still other landowners are sinking wells around their holdings in order to be prepared to pump irrigation water from the raised water table, thus getting a free ride on the Central Valley project.[72]

Until now every effort to secure a direct exemption has failed. The results of the 1948 elections in both the state and nation make further attempts of this kind unlikely for the present.

---

[68] *Ibid.*, p. 408.

[69] The California Democratic party platform adopted at Sacramento August 7, 1948 said: "We endorse and support the principles incorporated in the Federal Reclamation Law of 1902, specifically, acreage limitation and protection against land speculation and monopoly."

[70] For example, Representative Werdel voted in February, 1949 against repeal of a limitation imposed on appropriations to the Bureau of Reclamation by the 80th Congress at the insistence of Representative Elliott. The limitation, which became known as the Straus-Boke rider, had been made an issue in the November election. San Francisco *News*, February 22, 1949, "How they voted in Congress."

[71] Dinuba (California) *Sentinel*, Nov. 4, 1948. Since 1944, when an unsuccessful attempt was made to obtain support of the Democratic party for exemption of Central Valley from acreage limitation, the declarations of the party favoring retention of the limitation have become progressively more explicit.

[72] *Business Week*, May 13, 1944, p. 24.

The proposal that California shall take over the Central Valley Project is receiving much publicity within the state, but the success of this as a tactic to escape acreage limitation seems at least as doubtful for the present as the prospects for securing a direct exemption. At the very point where legislation became necessary to accomplish a transfer to the state, undoubtedly acreage limitation would be made an issue at once in both Congress and the state legislature. Besides, since federal reclamation law confers great financial advantages on the localities which it assists, it might be very difficult to persuade California taxpayers to assume responsibility for providing capital free of interest and for giving other forms of assistance for the sake of enabling excess-land owners to have their way.[73]

The tactic of using pumps to secure project water from underground seems unlikely to achieve its professed aim of helping owners of excess lands to escape enforcement of the acreage limitation, but not because of unwillingness to use the pumps. Holders of excess lands would hardly be so insistent upon obtaining a legal exemption if they believed they could secure their aim by so simple a device as using pumps. And especially if they believed—as the argument holds—that by pumping they could escape repayment besides. The principal function of this tactic so far, as well as of the tactic of proposing that the state take over the project, seems to be to provide the public with confusing arguments.

The status of the tactic of using the Army Engineers instead of the Bureau of Reclamation is entirely different. It is effective, and has succeeded already in overcoming resistance sufficiently to install the Army Engineers on three rivers in Central Valley, the Kings, Kern, and American. The Army Engineers have shown by public statement[74] that it is not their intention to enforce acreage limitation, even though Congress wrote it into the Flood Control Act of 1944 which authorizes these Army civil projects.

The issue is not simply, which of two federal agencies will design a dam and pour the concrete? There are at least two issues: (1) shall unity of Central Valley watershed development and operation be maintained or destroyed? (2) shall the answers given by historic reclamation law to the questions, who will pay the costs and who will receive the benefits, be accepted or rejected on federal projects in Central Valley?

---

[73] Editorials in *Sentinel*, December 14, 1948; Sacramento *Bee*, December 14, 1948; San Francisco *News*, Feb. 29, 1949. For opposing view see Harrison S. Robinson, president California State Chamber of Commerce, "Why the State Should Administer the Central Valley Project," address delivered before the Sacramento Valley council of the California State Chamber of Commerce, Sacramento, California, September 14, 1945.

[74] Lt. Gen. R. A. Wheeler, Chief of Engineers, to the Secretary of War, December 2, 1946. *Report on Allocation of Costs of Kings River and Tulare Lake Project*, House Doc. No. 136, 80th Cong., 1st Sess., p. 46; Major Gen. Thomas M. Robins, "The 160-acre limitation does not apply" (on Kings River and Tulare Lake Project), Fresno (California) *Bee*, Aug. 17, 1945.

Perhaps it would be more accurate to rephrase the second issue to state, shall these answers be accepted on some federal projects and rejected on others depending on the successes or failures of local special interests in pitting one federal agency against another?

The same local interests which challenge acreage limitation, also challenge the repayment provisions of reclamation law. The expectations of advantage to local project beneficiaries from repayment for projects constructed by Army Engineers, as compared with repayment for projects constructed by the Bureau of Reclamation, were told to the California Water Conference in 1945 by President Ray Wiser of the California Farm Bureau Federation. He said:

> Congress has authorized the U. S. Corps of Engineers to construct 24 dams in California, most of which will be in the Central Valley. These dams are to be constructed by the Federal Government in fulfillment of its flood control responsibility and the present program calls for only $2,326,000 in State funds to match $125,000,000 in Federal moneys. In some cases, local interests will be required to contribute a share in the total cost of the dams which benefit them, but regardless of any such contributions, these water conservation facilities will be obtained through this program for the use and benefit of California farmers *at far less cost than would be the case by any other means.*
>
> It is our understanding that the Corps of Engineers is making additional studies at the present time so as to insure the complete fulfillment ultimately of *Federal responsibility for flood control in California.*
>
> In accordance with Congressional procedure, the next step is to secure from the Congress appropriations for the specific projects. That is the immediate task ahead of us. *Thereafter the use of the stored waters for irrigation purposes under the State program and under State laws could be achieved without any substantial conflicts between flood control and irrigation purposes.*[75]

The opportunity to obtain construction of works that can be turned to the uses of irrigation, under the legislative classification of "flood control" (which is not reimbursable), may appear in a more favorable light when seen by beneficiaries than when viewed by taxpayers.

Perhaps the tactic of making use of the Army Engineers to escape reclamation law can be understood better by citing, as an example, the Kings River and Tulare Lake project. This project will improve water controls for about one million acres. It is located in the heart of Central Valley; it will benefit from federal construction of works on the Kings, Kaweath, Tule, and Kern, and can benefit from several other federal projects in Central Valley, either works under construction now, or works to be undertaken in the future. It was included by the State Engineer "as a unit for ultimate development of the State Water Plan for the San Joaquin River Basin,"[76] and the Kings River is crossed by the Friant-Kern canal of the Central Valley Project. Nevertheless it has been separated out from the comprehensive plan for Central Valley development by authorization to the Army Engineers.

---

[75] *California Water Conference,* p. 323. Italics supplied by the author.
[76] *State Water Plan,* Bull. 29, "San Joaquin River Basin," pp. 261-2.

This is the way it was done. In 1940 the Bureau of Reclamation possessed legal authorization under reclamation law to construct the project, but was instructed by President Roosevelt to postpone requests for appropriation owing to tensions in the international situation. At the request of landed interests on the project, particularly the Tulare Lake Water Storage District,[77] Congressman B. W. Gearhart began efforts in the same year to secure a Congressional authorization to have the Army Engineers construct the project.

The Tulare Lake Water Storage District, in the lower end of the project area, consists of nearly 200,000 acres with deficient water supplies and is subject to occasional flooding. In 1947 about twenty-five corporations owned 55 per cent of the lands of the district, and one hundred and two individuals owned about 36 per cent. All were holders of excess-lands, and together owned about 90 per cent of the district. The remaining 10 per cent was owned by more than six hundred holders of less than 160 acres each. In the entire Tulare Lake bed nine landowners own 109,000 acres.[78] The local interest in escaping acreage limitation therefore is substantial. Use of the Army Engineers seemed to offer a means of doing it; until 1944 irrigation features of flood control projects were not covered by reclamation laws. Although reclamation law was inserted in the Flood Control Act of that year which authorizes the project, an assistant chief of engineers has been quoted publicly in a Central Valley newspaper as saying that "the 160-acre limitation does not apply. . . ."[79] The initiative to use the Army came mainly from Tulare Lake where most of the excess holdings on the project are concentrated.

The remainder of the project area, the upper area of Kings River consisting of around 800,000 acres, has a relatively small proportion of its lands in holdings of excess size.[80] It is heavily populated, and the predominant form of organization is the irrigation district. From the moment Congressman Gearhart began his efforts to secure an authorization for the Army in 1940, a vigorous protest was made by citizens of this part of the project area. Their protest, which began with a petition bearing probably 2500 signatures, has grown in strength.[81] It became organized mainly around elements of the Grange, Veterans of Foreign Wars, and labor unions.

---

[77] "Resolution of March 14, 1940 by board of directors of Tulare Lake Water Storage District," *Hearings before House Committee on Flood Control on H. R. 9640*, 76th Cong., 3d Sess., p. 554.

[78] *Hearings on S. 912* (1947) p. 1237.

[79] See footnote 74.

[80] Computations from private excess-holdings listed in a letter of assessor-collector, Fresno Irrigation District, indicate excess-holdings in that district of 240,000 acres equal about 14,000 acres, or 13 per cent. *Hearings before Senate Committtee on Interior Department Appropriations, on H. R. 3024*, 79th Cong., 1st Sess., pp. 1001-3.

[81] Testimony of Representative B. W. Gearhart, *Hearings before House Committee on Flood Control on H. R. 9640*, 76th Cong., 3d Sess., pp. 544-5.

CENTRAL VALLEY PROJECT: WATER AND LAND 249

Although Kings River and Tulare Lake project is financed by the federal government, local water users' districts play an essential role in repayment. Contracts expected to be entered into between these districts and the United States under reclamation law obligate them to raise the local funds for repayment to the federal government, and to obtain compliance with acreage limitation. At the present time the districts are putting up resistance to the acreage limitation,[82] and to the amount proposed by the United States for repayment, as well.

Two principal forms of district organization exist in the project area. Nearly all of Tulare Lake bed is organized in the form of a water storage district. Under California law the electorate of water storage districts consists of landholders only, who cast votes in proportion to the assessed value of their lands.[83] In Tulare Lake this places overwhelming control in the hands of holders of excess-lands. Twenty-five corporations with 55 per cent of the land probably can make every decision. The more than six hundred landowners with less than 160 acres each who own only 10 per cent of the land, could hardly be effective even if they should choose to oppose the holders of excess-lands. The Water Storage District is uninhabited now, but unless future inhabitants should own land they could not vote anyway. Public opinion has no legal channel to express itself in a water storage district.

In the remainder of the project area the principal form of water users' organization is the irrigation district. Although the electorate of an irrigation district includes all registered voters, the directors of Kings River so far have not reflected the strong popular objections to use of the Army Engineers that are known to exist within their boundaries. On the contrary, the irrigation districts have taken the side of Tulare Lake Water Storage District, and bound themselves into a joint negotiating arrangement. This arrangement is through the Kings River Water Association, a voluntary organization to supervise allocations of Kings River waters between districts, that is without legal power to make a contract for repayment under reclamation law.[84]

There may be a number of reasons for the solid appearance of this front despite the serious disaffection within their electorates. For one thing, irrigation district directors are chosen for staggered terms at special elections held at an odd date, a Wednesday in February. Few positions

---

[82] Cost-allocation considerations in re Pine Flat reservoir—*Report of Board of Engineers, Kings River Water Association and Tulare Lake Basin Water Storage District, House Doc. No. 136,* 80th Cong., 1st Sess., p. 42.

[83] California Water Storage District Act, Sec. 9, *Deerings Gen. Laws,* 1944, Act 9126.

[84] Testimony of Philip A. Gordon, Chairman of Kings River Water Association and Chairman of board of directors of Fresno Irrigation District, *Hearings on S. Res. 295,* p. 428. The effect of making reclamation law a serious issue between candidates for irrigation district director is reflected in the increased vote cast in Fresno district, from 82 in 1947 to 2052 in 1949. (*California Farm Reporter,* March, 1949, p. 4.) Also perhaps in Assembly Bill No. 2210, introduced into the 1949 California Legislature to limit the exercise of suffrage in irrigation districts to freeholders only.

are open at any single election, and it has been customary to regard the elections as choices between persons, not between sides of an issue. For some reason Fresno Irrigation District boundaries were drawn to exclude Fresno city, which naturally is bound closely to the welfare of surrounding water users. This fact may minimize expressions of disaffection at the polls of that district. At any rate, there has been little serious effort to thresh out well-known issues at irrigation district polls, and the number of ballots usually cast is extremely small. As months and years go by without signature of water contracts, the interest of voters in their district organizations may become aroused; there are a few signs of this. Or the lethargy of citizens which democracies know well may continue.

In the meantime this curious paradox in the project area remains: while numbers of citizens speak up in public hearings, sign petitions, and elect members of Congress and the legislature to voice their support of reclamation, the directors of the districts which possess real and immediate power to put the law into effect give their support to the strongest opponents of reclamation law, although legally they are chosen by the same electorate.

The State Engineer of California, whose studies affirm the necessity for unity of Central Valley basin development, threw his influence against reclamation law, and in favor of the Army Engineers' entry into the Valley on Kings River. He made no appearance in support of appropriations to the Bureau of Reclamation for the Kings River project when Congress was considering them in 1944 and 1945.[85] But in 1946 his representative, in the names of the State Engineer and the Governor, asked Congress to make an appropriation to the Army Engineers. This representative, despite non-appearances (or failure to give support) in two preceding years when construction might have been expedited, now protested further "delay in getting flood relief" because "the need is urgent."[86]

In this way the long-standing answers to the questions, who will pay the costs? and who will receive the benefits? have been subjected to attack indirectly, but effectively. Although the essentials of the economic plan made in 1902 have been endorsed by Congresses again and again—in 1910, 1911, 1912, 1914, 1924, 1926, 1927, 1937, 1940 and 1943[87]—they

---

[85] Hearings before Subcommittee of the House Committee on Appropriations, 78th Cong., 2d Sess., on the Interior Department appropriations bill for 1945, p. 1125; Hearings before a Subcommittee of the Senate Committee on Appropriations on H. R. 4679, 78th Cong., 2d Sess.; Hearings before Subcommittee of House Committee on Appropriations, 79th Cong., 1st Sess., on interior department appropriations for 1946, p. 1323; Hearings before Subcommittee of Senate Committee on Appropriations on H. R. 3024, 79th Cong., 1st Sess., pp. 1050-51.

[86] Testimony of Northcutt Ely, Hearings before Subcommittee of Senate Committee on Appropriations on H. R. 5400, 79th Cong., 2d Sess., p. 471.

[87] Testimony of Harold L. Ickes, Secretary of Interior, Hearings on H. R. 3961, p. 537.

face the discard on Kings River now. If they can be circumvented by indirect tactics there, they can be scrapped elsewhere in the same way. Attempts to do this already are in progress, not only in California but elsewhere.[88]

In explaining the alignment of forces on Kings River and in Central Valley, this study restricts itself arbitrarily to reasons that relate to irrigation and reclamation, and excludes those that relate to power. Here it is enough to say that reclamation law contains a clause providing that public agencies shall be given "priority and preference" in disposing of surplus project power. The purpose of this clause is comparable broadly to that of the 160-acre provision, and is intended likewise to answer the question, who will receive the benefits? For this and related reasons, opposition to reclamation law and to the agency which administers it appears to serve the purposes of private utilities and holders of excess lands alike.[89]

In this genetic study of how, by whom, and for what purposes the development of Central Valley has been planned, a search has been made for broad perspectives rather than for systematic detail. In this light, it has seemed less important to detail and balance the arguments over issues, pro and con, than to examine the forces behind the arguments, the patterns of conflict, the roles of agencies of government.[90]

Some evaluation is in order. The 57th Congress planned the foundations of western reclamation carefully. The right questions were asked, who shall bear the costs? and who shall receive the benefits? Answers defensible before the public were given. Principles and purposes were sound and in accord with the best American tradition. When it came to planning the reclamation of Central Valley, however, the Congress has never provided a forum, or committee hearing, for considering the legislative problems of developing the basin *as a whole*. Instead, it has held

---

[88] Roscoe Fleming, "'Sleeper' Threat to West," Denver *Post*, June 6, 1948.

[89] "Declaration of purposes of Central Valleys project conference," *California Grange News*, May 5, 1948; Ruth Finney, San Francisco *News*, October 16, 1948. A San Francisco trade journal characterized the intensity of the conflict by writing editorially that "this great (Pacific Gas & Electric) company [is] now engaged in a life and death struggle with the federal Bureau of Reclamation. . . ." (*Western Construction News*, March, 1948, p. 71.)

[90] Views expressed in this article toward reclamation law and its applicability to Central Valley are strongly opposed by others. The extent and variety of detail of this opposition view forbid complete or detailed cataloging here. The following selected items will be useful: Senator Sheridan Downey, "They would rule the valley," San Francisco 1947. Testimony of Roland Curran, Sheridan Downey, Northcutt Ely, *Hearings on H. R. 3961*, pp. 652, 768, 623. "California Water Project Authority, Application of excess land provisions of federal reclamation law to Central Valley project," 1945, (mimeo.). Testimony of Harry Barnes, Roland Curran, J. J. Deuel, Sheridan Downey, Northcutt Ely, S. T. Harding, Edward Hyatt, Milton Kidd, Ralph H. Taylor, on S. Res. 295, pp. 316, 46, 440, 1, 65, 356, 17, 57, 42. Papers or remarks by Harry Horton, James Musatti, Ray Wiser, at California Water Conference, pp. 426, 309, 322. Testimony by Roland Curran, Sheridan Downey, Northcutt Ely, S. T. Harding, Ronald Harris, Harry Horton, Edward Hyatt, Charles L. Kaupke, Boyd Stewart, *Hearings on S. 912*; (Curran) pp. 1310; (Downey) 128, 939, 1190; (Ely) 1243; (Harding) 59; (Harris) 674, 1261; (Horton) 1262; (Hyatt) 8; (Kaupke) 173; (Stewart) 1136. Examination of witnesses by Senator Downey throughout *Hearings on S. 912* will be found a useful source of opposing opinion.

separate hearings on this and on that portion of the Valley's development. Committees, by their composition and experience, have had greater interest in an agency than in the area, a fact which has not cultivated an understanding that maximum benefits of basin development cannot be attained without integration.[91]

If Congress deserves criticism for throwing one part of Central Valley's development to one agency operating under one law, and another part to another operating under a second law, it must be said that the executive branch of the federal government has not done conspicuously better. So far the Bureau of the Budget has made no decision whether to forward to Congress the comprehensive plan of the Bureau of Reclamation for full water resource development, or the comprehensive plan of the Army Engineers for flood control. By advancing to Congress a single plan—or even both plans—the executive could bring issues to a focus, and help to secure consideration of the Valley's legislative problems not in bits, but as a whole.

Failure to promote unity violates the first principle of giving single authority and responsibility for a job. It permits a sort of broken field running of agencies maneuvered by pressure groups. By agility and forms of deception that are within the rules, it is possible to undermine unity and fundamental plans and principles without seeming to do so. Evils of this kind produced the recommendations of the Hoover Commission

---

[91] Authorization and appropriations bills for projects to be constructed by the Army Engineers go through different legislative channels from those which are followed if the same projects were to be constructed by Bureau of Reclamation. The agency, not the project, determines under what committee auspices and by whom the problem will be considered.
  While this article was in galley proof the Hoover Commission published a study on the Kings River and Tulare Lake project. (Arthur A. Maass, "The Kings River project in the basin of the great Central Valley—a case study." Appendix 7 of *Task Force Report on Natural Resources* [Appendix L] prepared for the U. S. Commission on organization of the executive branch of the government [Washington: Government Printing Office, 1949], pp. 149-182.) This project is now under construction by the Army Engineers. The study reports that "two federal agencies were put into competition with one another to, obtain support of the California beneficiaries," and "the fact that two federal water-resource agencies are operating in the same river basin, each planning multiple-purpose water control projects" is "the basic cause of the continuing conflict." The Hoover Commission has followed this study with a recommendation that "Rivers and Harbors and Flood Control activities of the Corps of Engineers be transferred to the Department of the Interior. . . ." (*Reorganization of the Department of the Interior: A Report to the Congress by the Commission on Organization of the Executive Branch of the Government* [Washington: Government Printing Office, 1949], p. 35.) Among significant results of the existing situation on Kings River, the Maass study lists the following: "2. It is still questionable whether or not the water resources of the Kings River are being developed and will be utilized in accordance with the most economic and beneficial utilization of all water and related land resources of the San Joaquin Valley and the Central Valley Basin. 3. The Kings River Project will cost the Federal Government considerably more than it should. A significant portion of the irrigation benefits, as yet not subject to precise evaluation, will in all likelihood never be repaid to the Federal Treasury. 4. Some of the beneficiaries of the Kings River project may be able, for all time, to avoid the acreage, land speculation, and full repayment provisions of Federal law. 5. The easing of repayment and operating requirements of Federal reclamation law with respect to the Kings River project may result in considerable pressure on the Federal Government to make equivalent concessions on other existing and proposed projects. Such pressure, if it succeeds, will increase the cost to the Federal Government of water resource programs by hundreds of millions of dollars. 6. The outcome of the conflict will in all likelihood favor the owners of large quantities of irrigation water. Prospective and small landowners and water users will not benefit proportionately. This finding has greater application to the Kern River and other areas to the south than to the Kings River area, where there are a number of relatively small landholders." (*Ibid.*, pp. 180-81.)

for governmental reorganization. In the current drive to enable the Army Engineers to avoid the purposes of the reorganization bill, holders of excess lands in Central Valley apparently have seen further opportunity to undermine reclamation.[92]

The Central Valley Project was undertaken by the federal government more hastily than principles of good administration dictate. Acute unemployment and water shortage explain the haste, but they do not remove the prolonged effects of failure, before work commenced, to secure clear acceptance by local water users' organizations of obligations to repay under reclamation law. Having permitted this failure in the first instance, Congress allows the federal interest in the project to continue to suffer, by neglecting to write into appropriation bills clauses requiring execution of contracts by beneficiaries before funds are spent.[93]

The state of California made an outstanding contribution toward unified development of the Valley in preparing the State Water Plan. Some of its officials have been less than devoted to unity in recent years, using their influence to break it down, and the economic plan for reclamation with it. Citizens of the Valley have not learned the crucial importance to their own future of the work of their own local water districts.

Whether the vision of Major Powell and the plan of Theodore Roosevelt and the 57th Congress to make it a reality are to survive or to become mere episodes of the past, is one way to state today's issue. Whether the future is to see full development of Central Valley's water resources, with costs distributed equitably and benefits widely, is another way. The character of communities to be created is in the hands of the people of the Valley, and of the Congress.

---

[92] Ruth Finney, San Francisco *News*, February 18, 1949. Roscoe Fleming, Denver *Post*, February 13, 1949.

[93] Ralph B. Wertheimer states, "The Act of May 10, 1926 (ch. 277, 44 *Stat.* 453) and the Act of March 3, 1925 (ch. 467, 43 *Stat.* 1186) prohibited the expenditure of any money for construction prior to the execution of the necessary contract with the irrigation district, while Section 46 (Omnibus adjustment act of May 25, 1926, ch. 383, 44 *Stat.* 636) makes the execution of the contract a condition precedent to delivery of water and not construction. The former seems the better policy." "Legislative and administrative history of acreage limitations and control of speculation on federal reclamation projects," p. 27, in *Report on problem 19*, Central Valley project studies.

THE 160-ACRE WATER LIMITATION
AND THE
WATER RESOURCES COMMISSION

THE 160-ACRE WATER LIMITATION AND THE WATER RESOURCES COMMISSION

PAUL S. TAYLOR
University of California

WHEN the Eighty-first Congress passed a bill raising the 160-acre water limitation to 480 acres on the San Luis Valley, Colorado, project, President Truman vetoed it and asked his temporary Water Resources Policy Commission to examine the problem of making exceptions to the 160-acre water limitation in particular cases. When the commission undertakes this assignment, it may find it neither possible nor desirable to halt its inquiries into the limitation at this point. For the 160-acre limitation, as the solicitor of the Interior Department has said, is "the heart of the reclamation law," not a mere appendage to it.[1] The limitation embodies the nation's high policy on land and water resources, and the maintenance of its integrity—not merely the question whether, in a particular instance, the proper acreage figure is 80, 160, or 480—is at stake.

The 160-acre water limitation is the device that was enacted by Congress in 1902 to extend the historic American land policy to water in the arid and semi-arid west. The policy, stemming from the Pre-emption Act of 1841 and the Homestead Act of 1862, was designed to distribute the benefits of the public domain widely, by favoring actual settlers against monopolists and speculators of that day. In 1902, when Congress was persuaded that the public treasury ought to help develop western irrigation, it limited water rights for private landholding beneficiaries to an amount adequate for no more than 160 acres of each holding. Congress regarded such a limitation necessary to justify spending public funds for private benefit. Without the limitation, Congress was unwilling to extend public assistance to reclamation of private lands.[2] When the lands to be irrigated were publicly owned, these were to be distributed "subject to the homestead laws in tracts of not less than 40 nor more than 160 acres. . . ."[3]

The benefits to private landowners under reclamation law are substantial. The value of waiving interest charges to private irrigation beneficiaries is alone equivalent to more than half the cost of a project.[4] The Bureau of Reclamation has given Congress additional figures indicating, on the Central Valley Project in California, that average Class I water

---
[1] Applicability of the excess-land provisions of the federal reclamation law to the Boulder Canyon Project Act. (Opinion of Solicitor, May 31, 1945, M.33902.)
[2] See Paul S. Taylor, "Central Valley Project: Water and Land," *Western Political Quarterly*, Vol. II (June, 1949), pp. 240-242.
[3] Act of June 17, 1902, chap. 1093, 32 Stat. 338, 43 U.S.C. 391, sec. 3.
[4] U.S. Bureau of Reclamation, "Acreage Limitation in the Central Valley, A Report on Problem 19," *Central Valley Project Studies* (Berkeley, California, September 25, 1944, mimeo.), p. 29, table 4.

rates would have to be $10.80 per acre-foot instead of the proposed charge of $2.70 if subsidies and special benefits under reclamation were eliminated.[5]

Foreseeing at the very beginning of legislation that private landowners would benefit heavily from public reclamation expenditures, Congress wrote into the original law the provision that "No right to the use of water for land in private ownership shall be sold for a tract exceeding 160 acres to any one landowner. . . ."[6] It also declared in the same section that no water right was to be sold "to any landowner unless he be an actual bona fide resident on such land, or occupant thereof residing in the neighborhood of said land."[7]

In 1924 a special advisory committee to the secretary of the interior was charged with conducting a thorough re-examination of federal reclamation. Its report, known as the Fact-finders' Report, reiterated the original purpose of reclamation. It said:

> A main purpose of the reclamation act was to provide opportunities for homestead making for rural-minded people. Making a homestead, a place able to support a family and desirable for family life, must remain the central thought of every activity connected with Federal reclamation.
> It was hoped that the homesteader under the Federal irrigation works would settle upon the land with a strong determination to subdue the soil, to build a home, and to add another rural farmstead to the thousands which form the stable foundation of our Republic.[8]

After reviewing the financial difficulties encountered by settlers on reclamation projects the report emphasized the dangers of private speculation in federally developed water and expressed regret that some provisions of the reclamation law designed to control speculation were proving "fruitless" or were "disregarded." Under the title "Homesteader Versus Speculator" the report stated:

> A closely related type of speculation has influenced the financial condition of many farmers. Large holdings of private land which became part of the project lands, but without water, had very little value before the project was authorized. When water became available their value immediately rose. The public lands were soon exhausted and the later settler attempted to secure his homestead by purchase from the large land holder. These private lands were often held at a very high figure, and the settler, full of hope, frequently agreed to pay a high price for the land, in addition to the construction cost included in his water-right contract. This added greatly to the farmer's burdens. It should be remembered, however, that, although two-thirds of the lands now under water contract with the Government were in private ownership at the time water was ready for delivery, not all of these private lands were in large holdings and susceptible of this type of land speculation. Such private land, when held for speculative purposes, only added to the difficulties of the farmer who was engaged in winning a homestead from the desert.[9]

---

[5] Statement of Paul H. Johnstone, in *Hearings before a Subcommittee of the Senate Committee on Public Lands*, 80th Cong., 1st Sess., on S. 912, p. 869, plates 7 and 8, pp. 871-872, 887.

[6] Act of June 17, 1902, *supra*, sec. 5.

[7] The phrase "in the neighborhood" was inserted to be sure to include Mormon farmers, who customarily reside in adjacent villages rather than on their farms.

[8] *Federal Reclamation by Irrigation*. A report submitted to the secretary of the interior by the Committee of Special Advisers on Reclamation. Sen. Doc. No. 92, 68th Cong., 1st Sess., pp. 111-112.

[9] *Ibid.*, p. 114.

A distinguished member of the special committee, Dr. John A. Widtsoe, was so impressed with the difficulties arising in the relations of government with private landowning beneficiaries that he wrote:

> In future as in earlier irrigation enterprises, large holdings will give most vexation. ... In the future it will be even more necessary to insist that large holdings shall not receive water from government supplies, unless divided into farm units of proper size, and offered to intending purchasers at reasonable terms. Speculators must be rigidly excluded from the benefits that flow from the operation of the Reclamation Act. The man with large holdings must be required to offer his lands at the price that the lands would command if reclamation work were not to be undertaken. ... It should be a concern of the government to permit only bona fide homemakers to enter into contracts for the use of water.[10]

Because of such strong objections to existing practices, the Omnibus Adjustment Act of 1926, passed under influence of the fact-finders' work, was designed to tighten the anti-speculation controls of the original law. The device employed was a revision of the 160-acre water limitation.[11] The limitation was incorporated into the repayment contract between the United States and the irrigation districts to be served with project water. Under the new law, lands above 160 acres were to be denied project water unless they signed recordable contracts agreeing to sell the excess at a fair, appraised price. The new provision declared:

> Such contract or contracts with irrigation districts hereinbefore referred to shall further provide that all irrigable land held in private ownership by any one owner in excess of one hundred and sixty irrigable acres shall be appraised in a manner to be prescribed by the Secretary of the Interior and the sale prices thereof fixed by the Secretary on the basis of its actual bona fide value at the date of appraisal without reference to the proposed construction of the irrigation works; and that no such excess lands so held shall receive water from any project or division if the owners thereof shall refuse to execute valid recordable contracts for the sale of such lands under terms and conditions satisfactory to the Secretary of the Interior and at prices not to exceed those fixed by the Secretary of the Interior. ... [12]

The same section of the Act provided further that until one-half the construction charges were repaid, "no sale of any such lands shall carry the right to receive water," unless the sale price is approved by the secretary of the interior, whether excess landholders sign recordable contracts or not.

The desirability of the policy which places actual settlers on the land and controls water monopoly and speculation is not questioned in this article. Since its inauguration in 1902, that policy has been upheld by more than a dozen Congresses of both parties in 1906, 1910, 1911, 1912, 1914, 1916, 1924, 1926, 1927, 1937, 1938, 1940, and 1943. Besides, every attempt to secure an exemption from acreage limitation for particular

---

[10] John A. Widtsoe, *Success on Irrigation Projects* (New York: John Wiley and Sons, 1928), p. 113.

[11] For the legislative history of the act of 1926 see Ralph B. Wertheimer, "Legislative and Administrative History of Acreage Limitation and Control of Speculation on Federal Reclamation Projects," in "Acreage Limitation in the Central Valley: A Report on Problem 19," *Central Valley Project Studies* (Berkeley, California, September 25, 1944, mimeo.), pp. 22-31 (separately paginated).

[12] Act of May 25, 1926, chap. 383, 44 Stat. 636, sec. 46. This section is in effect today.

reclamation projects has ended in defeat if it was forced to run the gauntlet of public hearings.[13] Congressional support of the principle over a period of forty-eight years may be taken as evidence that it represents settled national policy, notwithstanding continuing intense hostility among excess landholders.

The purpose of this article, and of the Water Resources Policy Commission, it may be assumed, is to examine the adequacy of existing legislation to render the policy effective. If the commission should find in the negative, it would not be the first time in American history that land laws, including reclamation water law, have been found deficient in this respect. The sober complaint of Congressman George W. Julian, chairman of the House Public Lands Committee in 1871, against the loopholes in the Homestead Act that permitted the "preferred right of the speculator to seize and appropriate the choice lands in large tracts and thus drive the pioneer further into the wilderness and on to less desirable lands";[14] the verdict of historian Paul Wallace Gates that "farm tenancy developed in the frontier stage at least a generation before it would have appeared had the homestead system worked properly";[15] and the bitter charge of Land Commissioner Sparks in 1885 that "the public domain was being made the prey of unscrupulous speculations and the worst forms of land monopoly through systematic frauds carried on and consummated under the public land laws," [16] bear witness to the need for continual vigilance if legislation of this kind is to serve efficiently the policy on which it is founded.[17]

Some evidence shows that the administration of reclamation law, like the Homestead law before it, has fallen at times into the hands of persons unsympathetic with its purposes. This evidence has been presented by opponents of reclamation law who declare that during the 1930's, when the Bureau of Reclamation was administered by engineers, one of them at least—an engineer in high offiice—had asserted that the 160-acre provision "was not to be taken seriously."[18]

---

[13] Exemptions without benefit of public hearings were given as follows: Colorado-Big Thompson Project, Act of June 16, 1938, 52 Stat. 764; Nevada projects, Act of November 29, 1940, chap. 922, 54 Stat. 1219.

Attempts to secure exemptions failed after public hearings were held, as follows: Central Valley Project, sec. 4 (Elliott rider) of H. R. 3961, 78th Cong., 2d Sess., 1944; Central Valley Project, Valley Gravity Project (Texas), San Luis Valley Project (Colorado), S. 912, 80th Cong., 1st Sess., 1947.

[14] *Congressional Globe*, 41st Cong. 3d. Sess., January 21, 1871, p. 650.

[15] Paul Wallace Gates, "Homestead Law in an Incongruous Land System," *American Historical Review*, Vol. LXI (July, 1936), p. 670.

[16] *General Land Office Report*, 1885, p. 28, quoted by Gates, *op. cit.*, p. 680.

[17] The Bureau of Reclamation has published a statistical record of compliance with acreage limitation, which this article does not attempt to evaluate, and itemizes "known excess land in violation," project by project. (*Land Ownership Survey on Federal Reclamation Projects*, Washington, D. C.: Government Printing Office, 1946.)

[18] Statement by Russell Giffen in *Hearings on Central Valley Project before Subcommittee of U.S. Senate Military Affairs Committee*, San Francisco, April 7, 1944 (mimeo.), p. 93; statement by Roland Curran, in *Hearings on S. 912, supra*, p. 1310; Roland Curran, "The 160-acre Limitation Law:

The selection of qualified officials who are sympathetic to the law they are charged with enforcing is a matter of administration, not of legislation. Consequently, it is not within the scope of the authorization of the President's Water Resources Policy Commission. Analysis of the ability of the reclamation law to fulfill its purposes under administrative rulings and interpretations, however, is clearly part of the commission's responsibility. The remainder of this article is devoted to examination of some points that should be considered in determining the adequacy of water resources legislation and in making recommendations for its improvement.

Instances in which it is apparent that no effective effort to secure enforcement has been made—sometimes for long periods of time—can be cited. One example is the Salt River Valley Project in Arizona, where the 160-acre water limitation has been virtually ignored since construction of the Roosevelt Dam in 1912. "Enforcement" has consisted in the empty gesture of limiting voting rights within the water users association to a maximum of 160 acres per landowner.[19] Recently the Bureau of Reclamation took steps to bring the Salt River Project into compliance.

Application to Private Land Will Prove Futile," *Western Construction News*, Vol. XXIII (August, 1948), p. 107. The purpose in making the charge was not to tighten enforcement but to repeal the law.

Claiming that engineering experience was the necessary qualification of a high administrator, the opponents of acreage limitation went so far as to secure passage by the Eightieth Congress of a law requiring that the commissioner of reclamation, assistant commissioners and regional directors must be engineers. The committee of the House that recommended to the Eightieth Congress that engineering experience be made an indispensable qualification said: ". . . if the vision of those who have planned the development of the resources of our Western States is to become a reality, then drastic changes in personnel, planning, and ideologies must be effected in the Bureau of Reclamation and the Department of the Interior . . . to restore the original concept of reclamation. We shall not burden this report with the conception or history of reclamation." (Investigation of Bureau of Reclamation, Department of the Interior, nineteenth intermediate report of committee on expenditures in the executive departments. House Report No. 2458, 80th Cong., 2d Sess., p. 2.) The committee statement appears to be the reverse of the truth, and the real purpose, as shown by the legislative history of the rider to the appropriation bill carrying the committee's recommendation, was to unseat two officials specified by name, neither of them engineers and both of them distinguished by devotion to the "original concept of reclamation," especially to acreage limitation. (Letter of Representative Forest A. Harness to Representative Ben F. Jensen, May 14, 1948, in *Congressional Record*, 80th Cong., 1st Sess., May 21, 1948, p. 6630; remarks of Senator O'Mahoney, *Congressional Record*, 80th Cong., 1st Sess., June 14, 1948, pp. 8098-8099.) The President signed the bill only because he "had no choice," and added: "This rider is designed to effect the removal of two men now holding such positions who have supported the public power policy of the Government and the 160-acre law which assures that western lands reclaimed at public expense shall be used for the development of family size farms. No matter what may be the asserted reasons for wanting to remove these men from office, the result would be to serve the purposes of special interests desirous of monopolizing the rich farm lands of the West and intent upon stopping the construction of transmission lines for the delivery of power from Federal dams. These same interests tried first to get the law changed but failed, and having failed then sought to get the management changed. . . . This type of action subjects federal officials to the risk of being legislated out of office if they incur the wrath of special interests as a result of vigorous enforcement of the law." (H. R. 6705 carried this legislation as a rider to the Interior Department appropriation bill in the Eightieth Congress, 1st Session. The President signed it on June 30, 1948.) The two officials received no salary while performing their duties for five months, until the rider expired with the end of the appropriation year, and the Eighty-first Congress voted them back pay.

[19] This laxity was cited in 1944 by California opponents of acreage limitation as reason why the Central Valley Project ought to be exempted from the 160-acre water limitation, and in 1949 as reason why Congress should not authorize construction of the Central Arizona Project. (Statement by Northcutt Ely in *Hearings before Subcommittee of the Senate Committee on Commerce*, 78th Cong., 2d Sess., on H. R. 3961, p. 631.)

This effort undoubtedly has been aided by a desire of Arizona landowners to reduce their vulnerability to attack by opponents of the pending congressional authorization of the Central Arizona Project.[20]

Another example of non-enforcement over a large area is found in the Imperial Valley, California.[21] Congress made the Boulder Canyon Act "a supplement to reclamation law." Moreover, the Bureau of Reclamation, with overwhelming approval of local voters, is enforcing the 160-acre limitation in Coachella Valley, an area adjacent to Imperial Valley that likewise receives its water through the All-American Canal constructed under the Boulder Canyon Act.[22]

Failure to enforce acreage limitation on irrigation uses of water may result not only from administrative laxity in the Department of the Interior, but also from laxity or lack of sympathy with the limitation law on the part of the Army Engineers.[23] It is proving extraordinarily difficult to secure any repayment contracts under reclamation law where one agency, the Army Engineers, constructs the dam and another agency, the Bureau of Reclamation, tries to enforce reclamation law. The Kings River in California is an example.[24]

---

[20] Statement by S. T. Harding, in *Hearings on S. 912*, p. 75. The remarks of the witness, an opponent of acreage limitation, were discouraging, rather than encouraging of the effort to secure enforcement. Congressman Donald L. Jackson of California said: "True, the Bureau of Reclamation says that the 160-acre law will be enforced if the Arizona project is built. But we know that this law never has been enforced there. There is no reason to believe it will be enforced in the future. Rather, there is every reason to believe that it will not be enforced." (*Congressional Record*, 81st Cong., 1st Sess., July 26, 1949, pp. A-4987–A-4992.)

[21] Statement by Northcutt Ely, in *Hearings on H. R. 3961, loc. cit.* See also Roland Curran, "The 160-acre Limitation Law: Application to Private Land Will Prove Futile." (*Western Construction News*, Vol. XXIII, [August, 1948], p. 107.) Mr. Curran, who has criticised officials sharply when they endeavored to support acreage limitation (e.g., *Hearings on S. 912*, p. 1310), commended them for not enforcing it: "Bureau officials, possessed of a fund of common sense, have . . . by contract waived any right to attempt enforcement on the Imperial Valley Project of the All-American Canal." His statement is not accurate. (See note 22.)

Opponents of acreage limitation argue that neglect to enforce the law justifies its repeal as, for instance, Roland Curran, *loc. cit.*; Northcutt Ely, *loc. cit.*; S. T. Harding, *loc. cit.* Unless and until public water policy is changed by Congress, the proper conclusion is that more effective efforts ought to be made to enforce acreage limitation, which is the instrument of that policy.

[22] The solicitor of the Interior Department, in holding that the 160-acre limitation does apply to Coachella Valley, had this to say about the failure of earlier officials to apply the limitation to Imperial Valley: "Furthermore an examination of the files reveals that the letter of the former Secretary was written at the request of counsel of the Imperial District who wanted a ruling on the application of the excess-land provisions 'provided, that such ruling would be that the 160-acre limitation did not apply.' Purposely, the letter of Secretary Wilbur never took the form of a formal decision. It was written solely for the purpose of giving partisan help to the Imperial Water District. . . ." (Opinion, May 31, 1945, *supra*, pp. 16-17.)

[23] Laxity and/or lack of sympathy of the Army Engineers with enforcement of the 160-acre law are well known, and the destructive effects on Kings River and Tulare Lake Basin in California are the subject of a trenchant study made for the Hoover Commission. (Arthur A. Maass, "The Kings River Project in the Basin of the Great Central Valley — A Case Study," Commission on Organization of the Executive Branch of the Government, *Task Force Report on Natural Resources*, Appendix L, January, 1949, Appendix VII.)

[24] Failure of enforcement on this project has caused protest by the Veterans of Foreign Wars. (Statement by M. C. Hermann, quartermaster-adjutant, Department of California, in *Hearings before Subcommittee of the Senate Appropriations Committee*, 81st Cong., 2d Sess., pp. 745-749.) See also statements by Representative John F. Shelley, *op. cit.*, pp. 768-770, and opposing statement by Charles L. Kaupke, *op. cit.*, pp. 757-758. See also defeat of attempt by Senator Paul H. Douglas to secure enforcement in 1950. (*Congressional Record*, August 1, 1950, pp. 11644-11647; August 4, 1950, pp. 12011-12012.)

If Congress should decide to follow the recommendation of the Hoover Commission that a single agency be charged with natural resource development "to put an end to the chaotic administrative machinery," the kind of administrative difficulty just described could be solved by legislation.[25]

The Central Florida Project furnishes another example of failure of enforcement, where the agency constructing the irrigation works is not the agency responsible for enforcing reclamation law. The word "irrigation" appears nowhere in the Army Engineers' report on the project, and upon its recommendation Congress authorized the project for "flood control."

The Central Florida Project bears some interesting resemblances to the Kings River Project. Although no great dams are to be built, great "impounding levees" are to be constructed to "prevent overflow" and to create "storage" for "excess water in wet seasons" in order to "provide a supply for use in the east-coast agricultural lands when needed, raise the ground-water table, improve water supply and ameliorate salt-water intrusion in . . . well fields and streams . . . benefit fish and wildlife . . . result in flood protection and better drainage for . . . agricultural lands."[26] The chief of engineers described the "problems of flood protection, drainage, and water control . . . in a land where there is either too much or too little water according to variations of the seasons and changes from year to year."[27] The similarity to the functions performed by western multiple-purpose reclamation projects is plain.

Citizens of central Florida, perhaps less aware than Army Engineers of the importance of care in the use of words in water resource development, wrote more frankly of the nature of the project. "The region must be drained in flood time, and irrigated in drought," wrote a staff writer of the *Miami Herald*. Her report spoke of "rich soil parched in dry seasons" when the land has "become a dust bowl," and a four-year "drought" when rainfall was eighteen months short in four years.[28] In the western United States, bringing water to the parched soil is called "irrigation" and is covered by reclamation law.

Although the Central Florida Project is called a "flood control" project, the Army Engineers estimated average annual benefits as only 33.6 per cent from "prevention of flood damages," and only 1.9 per cent to "navigation" and "preservation of fish and wildlife."[29] They estimated

---

[25] *Commission on Organization of the Executive Branch of the Government. A Report to Congress* (Department of the Interior, March, 1949), pp. 56, 67.

[26] See the comprehensive report on central and southern Florida for flood control and other purposes, H. Doc. No. 643, 80th Cong., 2d Sess., pp. 2, 10.

[27] *Ibid.*, p. 1.

[28] Jeanne Bellamy, "Taming the Everglades: A Report on Water Control." *The Miami Herald*, pages 17, unnumbered, published approximately 1948.

[29] H. Doc. No. 643, *op. cit.*, p. 50.

benefits of 64.5 per cent from "increased use of land attributable to project," and although "irrigation" and "reclamation" are not mentioned, their reports spoke of "conservation" and "land improvement" to provide "net increases in production" that will "range from about $1 per acre annually due to more intensive use of pasture lands . . . to an increase of $200 per acre annually for new citrus land. . . ."[30] Notwithstanding their admission that "increased use of land" accounted for approximately two-thirds of the estimated benefits and flood prevention only approximately for one-third, the Army Engineers proposed to Congress, and Congress accepted the recommendation, that the project be authorized for "flood control."

Estimated construction cost of the project is around two hundred million dollars. The Engineers' report recommended that "in view of the large benefits from land improvement, estimated as $15,855,000 per year . . . local interests should be required to make a cash contribution of $29,152,000 toward the initial cost of the project,"[31] a sum equivalent to only about two years' annual benefits from the project.

So far as is known, no one has raised the question whether the Central Florida Project is in accordance with reclamation law.[32] At present, the Bureau of Reclamation is not undertaking negotiations for repayment contracts. If reclamation law should be found applicable to the Central Florida Project, it probably would apply also to a good many other projects authorized for the Army Engineers, and would partially close an escape route from acreage limitation that has been developing during recent years.[33]

Although congressional declarations, committee reports, pronouncements of secretaries of the interior, and planks of both major political parties have uniformly stood for "actual settlers" and the "family farm" and against monopoly and speculation, the language of legislation and administrative interpretation has not always been as strong in implementing these policies. Since 1902 certain interests have developed a distinc-

---

[30] *Ibid.*, pp. 10, 48. The word "irrigation" is employed in the report apparently but once (p. 53), by the district engineer who notes, appropriately, his recognition of "the established Federal practice with irrigation projects. . . ."

[31] *Ibid.*, p. 10.

[32] The Flood Control Act of 1944 (58 Stat. 887, sec. 8), provides that "Dams and reservoirs operated under the direction of the Secretary of War may be utilized hereafter for irrigation purposes only in conformity with the purposes of this section. . . ." The section places such "dam and reservoir" projects "under the provisions of the Federal reclamation laws. . . ." While the bill was under debate in the Senate, the senator in charge, Senator Overton, was interrogated as to its purposes. His reply was explicit and sweeping: "Section 8 of the bill clearly places reclamation uses of water from these projects under the Secretary of the Interior and under the applicable reclamation laws. No project in this bill which may include irrigation features is exempted from the reclamation laws." (*Congressional Record*, 78th Cong., 2d Sess., December 12, 1944, p. 9264.)

[33] See, e.g., the Grand Prairie Project in Arkansas. *Business Week*, May 13, 1944, said: "If the big landowners in the [Central] Valley lose out in this particular fight [for direct repeal], they have several other purposes to accomplish their end. One of them is a House bill which would authorize the Army to add irrigation and power development to its present navigation and flood control powers. . . . This would circumvent the 160-acre rule. . . ." (Quoted in *Hearings on S. 912*, p. 628.)

tion between what may be called "technical compliance" and "compliance with the spirit" of the law. This distinction could easily become a chasm wide enough to engulf the original purposes of reclamation.

For example, the 1926 revision of the law, was stimulated by the Fact-finders' Report which declared strongly for homesteading. Yet this revised law omitted the original requirement of residence by the landowner on, or in the neighborhood of the farm, as a qualification for water deliveries, thereby opening the door to granting of water rights to absentee owners and corporations.[34] This undebated but profound change in policy stands in striking contrast to a century and a half of public declarations on land policy that goes back to Thomas Jefferson's historic and successful battle to abolish entailed estates in Virginia in 1776. The reason for this attempted reversal of policy, permitted by a few words of legal text, is not known, nor is it known whether it was the result of oversight.[35]

The extent to which corporate devices may be used to circumvent reclamation has not been fully revealed. However, pressure to exploit them will undoubtedly continue to be exerted. Since their drives for special legislative exemptions have failed thus far, opponents of reclamation law already have shown that they intend to explore the use of corporate devices to secure their ends.[36]

How far the breakdown of the reclamation law could proceed if this kind of legal interpretation should be allowed can be suggested by some examples: Suppose landowners were to organize a tract of 8,000 acres owned as separate parcels by 50 individuals (or perhaps 25 husbands and wives or a dozen families with two minor children each. If legislation were to be interpreted to permit this, the likelihood of achieving the aims of reclamation would be slight indeed. Or suppose the corporation were to be composed of joint tenants or tenants in common, each with an undivided interest not exceeding 160 acres. Or suppose that joint owners, each with an interest not exceeding 160 acres should arrange through a trustee to employ a person or corporation to operate their properties as a unit for a reasonable compensation, the joint owners receiving the profits and bearing the losses. Or suppose that a corporate farm should sell its land in parcels to its stockholders and take these parcels back on lease for operations. No doubt, excess landowners have a good deal of incentive to escape acreage limitations, if only because of incremental land

---

[34] Omnibus Adjustment Act of May 25, 1926, chap. 383, 44 Stat. 636, sec. 46, uses the phrase "land held in private ownership by any one owner," i.e. natural person or juristic person (corporation).

[35] For an account of earlier Interior Department rulings in 1909 and 1913, respectively, that corporations were, and were not, entitled to apply for water rights, see *Landownership Survey, op. cit.*, p. 37. The secretary of the interior in the 1913 ruling said: "I am satisfied that Congress did not intend that those reclaimed lands, upon which the Government is expending the money of all the people, should be the subject of corporate control. These lands are to be the homes of families."

[36] *Hearings on S. 912*, pp. 104-109.

values. Between date of construction and 1913, the value of unimproved land on reclamation projects increased by 759 per cent.[37] Average gains in incremental value to lands in Central Valley receiving full water supply from the proposed project have been estimated at well above two hundred dollars an acre.[38] With such prosperous incentives it would be unreasonable to believe that all ways to avoid or evade acreage limitation have been used.

Maintaining a proper definition of "any one owner" is likewise essential to preservation of the original purposes of reclamation. The trend of administrative rulings and opinion is toward relaxation, helped perhaps by the omission in 1926 of residence requirements from the revised statute now in effect. In this fashion the 160-acre limitation, which began as an attempt to adjust size to the requirements of one family, was "doubled" to 320 acres if owned by husband and wife as joint tenants or tenants in common, by the terms of a ruling in 1916.[39] It was a short additional step to rule that in certain states the community property law accomplished the "doubling" automatically.[40]

As early as 1904 an Interior Department ruling permitted the owner of more than 160 irrigable acres to transfer ownership of the excess to his wife and minor children, and thus entitle them to receive project water within the limitations of reclamation law.[41] The possibilities of acquiring water rights for generous acreages within a family under this ruling can be computed readily by multiplying 160 by the number of persons in the family, including babes in arms.[42] In recognition of the absurdity of this ruling, Congress defined a "family" in the Columbia Basin Act of 1943 as "either or both husband and wife, together with their children under eighteen years of age, or all of such children if both parents are dead."[43]

The effectiveness of present legislation in controlling speculation through the acreage limitation is as open to doubt as its effectiveness in controlling water monopoly. Some reclamation contracts now in effect between water districts and the United States provide control of incremental values on all project lands, non-excess as well as excess. Others

---

[37] Statement by William E. Warne, in *Hearings on S. 912*, p. 204, table 1.
[38] Statement by Paul H. Johnstone, *Hearings on S. 912*, pp. 852-855, 661.
[39] *Landownership Survey*, *op. cit.*, p. 37.
[40] Solicitor's Opinion, August 21, 1945, M. 34172. During hearings on S. 912 (p. 886) the following colloquy took place. "Senator Watkins: . . . It has been interpreted that they could go in where these State community property laws are so they could have 320 acres." "Senator Ecton: With more in the family, you can still go on with it and you can get technical compliance under the law. One family might own a couple of thousand acres as far as that is concerned." "Senator Watkins: They are ingenious; if they are ingenious, they could create enough corporations to own all of it." "Senator Ecton: That is right. . . ."
[41] *Landownership Survey*, loc. cit.
[42] Of course, the transfers must be actual, to the extent that profits and losses must go to the child rather than to the parent. This would be inconvenient to the parent; if bona fide it would be a step in the direction of the purposes of reclamation law, but it would be very difficult to enforce.
[43] Pub. L. No. 8, 78th Cong., 1st Sess., sec. 1 (v).

cover only the area in excess of 160 acres per individual owner.⁴⁴ If the latter practice should be allowed to become coupled with evasion by corporate devices, as described above, then speculation control will be at an end.

A further source of weakness lies in making the appraisals of excess lands for sale. Present law requires the secretary of the interior to fix sale prices "on the basis of its actual bona fide value at the date of appraisal without reference to the proposed construction of the irrigation works." ⁴⁵ This principle is to be followed without exception, but the meaning given to it in practice is subject to the greatest variation. In the absence of a reclamation project, a financial institution determining the loan value of land with insufficient or failing water supplies, would probably estimate how much water would be available and how many years the supply would last. These findings would limit the value of the land and consequently the amount of the loan. This, it would seem, was the intent of the reclamation law. However, local appraisers accustomed to place market valuations upon land in a project area such as Central Valley where both sellers and purchasers have been accustomed since 1935 to rely upon the federal government to complete the project it began, find it extremely difficult to extract from existing market values the portion of value that arises from expectation of completion of the project.⁴⁶

Techniques of enforcing land sales at appraised prices as prescribed by law are not effective. For example, violation of the law requiring sale of excess land at a price approved by the secretary of the interior does not injure the seller who pockets more than he should, but it denies water to the actual settler who, as buyer, has paid more than he should have.⁴⁷ Present law requires that water districts shall execute repayment contracts under reclamation law as a condition precedent to receiving water deliveries from a completed project.⁴⁸ But great reservoirs have few outlets, and when filled there may be little choice in releasing the accumulated water except to project beneficiaries who, in order to evade

---

⁴⁴ Ralph B. Wertheimer, *op. cit.*, p. 28.

⁴⁵ Omnibus Adjustment Act, sec. 46.

⁴⁶ It is not technically difficult to determine values based upon the expected life of the remaining water supply which may be only twelve to fifteen years, in absence of a project. But the owners of excess lands operating on temporary water supplies are physically present as important members of the community. These owners are conscious of their interest in securing the full benefits of public expenditures for themselves. Potential buyers are seldom present. Yet, they are the "actual settlers" in whose names the land and water laws were passed. However, even if they are present, they are scattered and probably unaware of their interests or even of their rights under the law. Between these two unequal pressures, the actual settlers' interest as buyers becomes subordinated to the excess landowners' interest as sellers.

⁴⁷ Omnibus Adjustment Act, sec. 46. Control of speculation might be improved by giving to the purchaser who has paid above the appraised price and finds he can get no water under the law, a right to recover the excess above the appraised price, and by requiring an excess landowner to execute a recordable contract agreeing to sell at appraised prices as condition to receiving any water (he now can get water for 160 acres without signing a contract).

⁴⁸ *Loc. cit.*

acreage limitation, might withhold acceptance of a repayment contract while they invite appropriations and construction, relying on precisely this ultimate loss of bargaining power in the hands of the government.[49]

A procedure more likely to secure the aims of national water policy would be to require execution of repayment contracts by the potential beneficiaries under reclamation law prior to expending funds on the project. This precedure has ample legal precedent both in earlier versions of reclamation law and as conditions attached to appropriations, and it represents sound administrative practice besides.[50] If execution of the repayment contract had been required by law and adhered to on Kings and Kern Rivers in Central Valley, most of the difficulties and conflicts that continue to plague these developments could have been avoided.[51]

It may not always be feasible to require contracts covering the whole project prior to commencement of construction, although this is the preferred method. Sometimes it is not possible to determine exactly what lands will receive water until construction is well advanced. In some instances, the interest of the public may be preserved by requiring execution of contracts to dispose of, for instance, 70 per cent of project water, prior to beginning construction.

The legislative device most likely to be effective in promoting family farming on reclamation projects by actual settlers, and in preventing water monopoly and controlling speculation, is to authorize purchase of excess landholdings by the government for purposes of resale to actual settlers, as now provided for the Columbia Basin. The Veterans of Foreign Wars, sensing the importance to veterans of having more public lands available for farms, has taken a leading role in demanding stricter interpretation and enforcement of the 160-acre limitation and in proposing purchase of excess lands by the government as a means to accomplish this end.[52]

---

[49] The Hoover Commission study, describing the failure to secure repayment contracts while construction of the reservoir approaches completion and appropriation is added to appropriation, says: "With respect to repayment, the necessity for the completion of repayment negotiations before construction of the Kings River project has been emphasized . . . once the dam is constructed it will be difficult, if not impossible, for the Army to resist the pressure from local interests to release water in the most economical measures from the point of view of downstream water users." (Arthur A. Maass, "The Kings River Project in the Basin of the Great Central Valley—A Case Study," op. cit., p. 178.)

[50] Ralph B. Wertheimer, op. cit., p. 27.

[51] The Columbia Basin Act of 1943 prescribed that "no water shall be delivered for irrigation within the project until the State of Washington by appropriate legislation, shall have adopted, authorized, ratified, and consented to all the provisions of this Act . . ." (sec. 5). This requirement could well be made a condition in all states precedent to federal construction.

[52] Statements by M. C. Hermann, in Hearings on S. 912, p. 148. See also Hearings before House Committee on Public Lands, 80th Cong., 1st Sess., pursuant to H. Res. 93, pp. 46-49; extension of remarks of Representative Chet Holifield on a bill (H. R. 7113) to provide farms for veterans and others in the Central Valley of California, Congressional Record, August 4, 1948; The Homestead Act of 1950, letter from M. C. Hermann, quartermaster-adjutant, Veterans of Foreign Wars, Department of California, San Francisco, to Senator Paul H. Douglas, undated, ca. 1949 (mimeo.).

It might be desirable to supplement government purchase by using facilities that assist farmers to buy farms under existing tenant-purchase legislation. The proposal for purchase of excess landholdings by the government as a measure necessary to secure enforcement of reclamation probably was made first by Commissioner of Reclamation, Elwood Mead, to the Sixty-eighth Congress.[53] Unfortunately, the proposal was not adopted until 1943, and then only for the Columbia Basin.

Present law attaches acreage limitation solely to water services that are designated as "irrigation." When owners of agricultural land receive similar measurable benefits from "flood control" or "drainage," the question may be properly raised why a similar limitation should not apply. Present law makes only irrigation reimbursable to the government by private beneficiaries, just as it attaches the acreage limitation designed to implement public policy only to irrigation. It could be argued to the contrary that the less the direct reimbursement to the treasury for benefits, the greater the moral obligation to comply with acreage limitation. The manner in which the Kings River and the Central Florida projects, for example, have been made to appear as "flood control" projects, strengthens the argument.[54]

Another example of the necessity for separating the question of reimbursability from the question of acreage limitation — now tied together by the repayment contract device for enforcing both through the same legal instrument — is furnished by the original version of H.R. 1770 (81st Cong., 1st Sess., sec. 2), that declared "general salinity control" to be "nonreimbursable." To adopt such a provision automatically would remove acreage limitation from an area improved for agricultural purposes by salinity control. The effect of virtually exempting an irrigated area such as, for instance, the Sacramento-San Joaquin River Delta in the Central Valley of California, would be serious. For more than twenty years the California state water plan has included proposals to control salinity in that area, first by releases of Central Valley Project water, ultimately by erection of a salt water barrier. (Walker R. Young, "Report on Salt Water Barrier below Confluence of Sacramento and San Joaquin Rivers, California," California Department of Public Works, Division of Water Resources, Bulletin No. 22, 1929, pp. 26, 28, 30. See also U. S. Bureau of Reclamation, *Central Valley Project Studies*, Problem 10, September, 1944, pp. 4-7.) Delta lands to be benefited by salinity control are owned predominantly by great farming corporations. The cost to the federal taxpayer of a nonreimbursable salt water barrier would be far

---

[53] Ralph B. Wertheimer, *op. cit.*, p. 26.

[54] Arthur A. Maass, *op. cit.*, p. 179, shows that the Army Engineers claimed a benefit ratio of 1.19 to 1 for flood control in 1940 while seeking congressional authorization for the Kings River Project but dropped their estimate to .63 to 1 in 1948 after authorization was obtained and construction well started.

above the estimate of forty million dollars based on 1929 prices, and the national water policy embodied in acreage limitation would not be observed. Recent incursions of salt water into delta agricultural tracts aggregating over 4,000 acres are reviving talk of salinity control by construction of a barrier, perhaps as part of the costly Reber plan for a chain of fresh water lakes. (*California Farmer*, July 15, 1950.) The two issues of reimbursing the federal taxpayer and of requiring conformance to national antimonopoly, anti-speculation controls are separable and the decisions upon them should be made separately.

So long as the family-size farm remains the object of national policy, the Water Resources Commission should seriously consider any means by which the country's water policy can contribute to securing this public purpose. Under present legislation, enforcement of acreage limitation terminates when construction charges have been paid in full.[55] This fact can shorten greatly the period of the law's effectiveness, although it does not do so on projects that pay out slowly. There seems to be no reason grounded on public policy why this particular distinction between projects should exist. There are valid reasons for encouraging projects to pay out on schedule but none for holding out an escape from the public policy that motivated a project.

If legislation were enacted to provide that "at no time" shall excess lands receive deliveries of water unless their owners sign recordable contracts to dispose of the excess at an appraised price, the question may, perhaps, be raised whether maximum farm sizes might be "frozen" at an undesirably small figure. This need not occur, provided a proper size were set in the first instance. In any event, Congress can correct the figure in the future if a serious mistake proves to have been made, or if public opinion as to what constitutes a desirable size should change.

Review of the problem of adjusting the acreage limitation to practical conditions in order to make it effective brings into correct perspective the President's request to the Water Resources Policy Commission arising from the San Luis Valley bill. It is desirable to prescribe by legislation a means for setting acreage limitation at 80, 160, or 480, or whatever particular conditions may warrant in the light of the purposes of reclamation.[56] But unless loopholes in the present law are closed, it will be

---

[55] Administration letter No. 303, December 16, 1947, and supplements 1, 2, and 3. The alternative of paying up construction charges in lieu of executing a recordable contract to dispose of excess lands at an appraised price opens a wide loophole for evasion. Excess landholders are given great financial incentives to stave off enforcement until they can complete their payments. Entire projects are seeking now to use payment of an initial lump sum as means of avoiding acreage limitation entirely. See for instance the Werdel bill, H. R. 7915, 81st Cong., 2d Sess., which makes this proposal on the Kings River and Tulare Lake Project, California, where great landholdings, often corporate in form, are numerous.

[56] Excess landholders complain against the 160-acre figure only when they claim that it is too low to support a family. In most instances the figure probably is higher than necessary for this purpose. For example, the Fresno, California, Chamber of Commerce, in the Central Valley where it was argued that 160 acres was too low, circulated a folder in 1944 among prospective purchasers and

nearly useless to do so, and it could be harmful.[57] Besides, the bitterest opposition to acreage limitation does not come from owners with a few more acres than the limitation allows to be watered but from those with thousands of acres. Their opposition is directed against national water policy itself and will not be allayed by an equitable readjustment such as framers of the San Luis Valley bill professed to seek.

Legislation to establish a single agency for water resource development would prove one of the most effective steps toward securing the purposes of public water policy. It would remove the opportunity that private interests now have to pit one agency against the other, with lax enforcement (or non-enforcement) of acreage limitation as accepted coin in the bidding for authorization to construct.

Legislation to tighten enforcement along lines suggested above represents a second step.

Above all, an informed public is necessary. People need to hear freely the views of representatives of private interests and of their own public agencies alike. If they hear both, they can be trusted to sift the facts and conclude whether public laws are failing or succeeding in fulfilling the purposes for which they were designed.

The people amended the Constitution in 1913 to permit Congress to levy a progressive income tax. The amendment was founded on the principle that the greater the income of the citizen, the greater proportionately was his obligation to contribute to the support of the government. The drive to break down the national water policy as written into reclamation law—whether by repeal, exemption, evasion, or lax enforcement—is tantamount to a drive to reversing that principle. It is a proposal that

---

tenants, recommending not less than the specified acreages as "economic units . . . on the assumption that the grower intends to derive the total income necessary to support a home and family from the production of a single crop," as follows: figs, 60 to 80 acres; peaches, 30 to 40 acres; oranges, 20 to 30 acres; apricots, 30 to 40 acres; cotton, 120 to 160 acres; alfalfa, 80 to 120 acres; grapes and raisins, 30 to 60 acres; grain and flax (generally unirrigated when grown as the single crop), 320 acres. (Hearings on S. 912, pp. 149-152.) Francis G. Newlands, co-author of the National Reclamation Act of 1902, declared it was "intended to secure to every man of industry an area of land sufficient, according to the soil and climate or productiveness, for the support of a family, and sufficient for that alone (applause), it is also intended to break up existing land monopoly." (Address at Red Bluff, June, 1905. Sacramento Valley Development Association, Bulletin No. 23, p. 14.) Undoubtedly there are special instances where 160 acres is too low for the purposes of the Act.

[57] The problem of underground waters, which some persons feel is bound to defeat acreage limitation in Central Valley, likewise falls into proper perspective. As a staff memorandum of the Bureau of Reclamation (Region II, January, 1950), says: "Underground waters will behave in the future as they have in the past. The many existing irrigation districts in the valley, which limit water service to farmers located within the district's boundaries, have operated successfully for years under this area limitation, without appreciable loss of water to non-participant farmers located outside the boundaries. Non-participants under the CVP, whether they are excess landholders or small farmers, will have no better luck getting a 'free ride' in the future than farmers outside irrigation districts have in the past. The control and use of groundwater in the Central Valley to the extent that it is a problem, is one that exists today under present irrigation operations, was not caused by the Central Valley Project or the Reclamation Law, will not be solved by any change or repeal of Reclamation Law, and has nothing to do with the size of landholdings. It seems patent that if the large landowners concerned really believed the acreage limitation of Reclamation Law would enable them to get a 'free ride' on the Central Valley Project, they would not be striving so hard to have that provision of law repealed."

the government ought to contribute public waters to its citizens in proportion to the land that they hold. To permit this to succeed—by whatever means—would be to permit defeat of the purposes of national land and water legislation virtually from the beginning. To weigh this hazard should be one of the responsibilities of the President's Water Resources Policy Commission.

WHOSE DAM IS PINE FLAT?

WHOSE DAM IS PINE FLAT?*

by Paul S. Taylor

ON MAY 22, 1954, Pine Flat Dam on the Kings River in California was dedicated. The ceremonies marked completion of the first of a pair of great dams—the other on the Kern, called Isabella—that serve the southern portion of the Central Valley. "In a voice choked with emotion," records the *Fresno Bee*, Major General Sturgis, the chief of engineers, spoke these words: "On behalf of the people of the United States, I hereby dedicate Pine Flat Dam to the service of the San Joaquin Valley and of this great nation of ours."

All can admire the magnificent structures the engineers have built, can believe that they will control floods and serve irrigation, and can agree that a pause to symbolize the harmonious merging of diverse interests in the common good is appropriate to a ceremony of dedication. But informed persons, after the pause in which the chief engineer's words were uttered, will still face the fact that these rivers remain today, as for two generations, the scene of some of the bitterest water fights of our national history. Monopoly and speculation are central issues now, as always.

The Kings and Kern have been famous for a long time, not only for the beauty of their canyons in the Sierra, where hikers love to "pack in" during summer vacations, but for the energy that men have expended to acquire title to huge blocks of the fertile lands on the valley floor below. Here the public domain passed into private hands during the latter half of the nineteenth century under circumstances that historian Paul Wallace Gates describes as "enormous monopolization." This process of land acquisition long ago literally laid the groundwork for today's battles over water.

Newspapers of the time were outspoken. The *San Francisco*

---

* The editors of *The Pacific Spectator* recognize that this is a controversial article. Their columns are open to an article presenting the other side, given only that it is as carefully documented and as readable as is the one here presented.

WHOSE DAM IS PINE FLAT?

Chronicle said on May 31, 1877, "If those who call themselves statesmen and lawmakers continue much longer to disregard the rights and interests of the great body of the citizen class—to promote the absorption of the land of the nation by a few wealthy and unscrupulous capitalists, aided by corrupt officials and perjured locators at the Government Land Offices, depriving the poor men of small means of the opportunity of obtaining homes, and white laborers generally of all chance of securing work at fair wages the oppressed millions will be impelled to the last resort of revolution to redress their wrongs." The same year the *Tulare Times* declared, "The Desert Land swindle is causing some of the honest farmers on Kings river to be fearful lest it might sweep their rights to the four winds. Let them organize and fight for their rights. Poor men and laboring men must begin to protect themselves. Corruption held up and backed by capitalists will never benefit the tillers of the soil." The *Chronicle* talked about "The Grand Khan of Kern," and newspapers were filled with phrases like "land-grabbers," "dummy entries," "monstrous monopolies," and "dead to the welfare of the people, to the public good, to the honor and glory of the country, and to the preservation of its beneficent institutions."

The *Visalia Delta* prophesied that the monopolists of an "already extensive dry domain" would attempt later "by an array of force and talent to secure to capital the ownership of the water as well as of the land, and the people will at last have it to pay for. . . ." Land monopoly became the biggest single issue before the California Constitutional Convention of 1879, and filled the debate with its reverberations. The Convention declared the public intention (locking the barn after the horse was stolen) by writing a 320-acre land limitation into the State Constitution. The question of water monopoly was left for a later day—our day.

Late in the nineteenth century leading citizens of the West began searching for help to develop Western water resources. Their efforts culminated in the National Reclamation Act of 1902, passed with the encouragement of President Theodore Roosevelt. This law became the first pillar of his conservation movement and the epitome of the program he came to call "The Square Deal." His purpose was to use the federal government to develop water resources for the greatest good of the greatest number for the longest time. The legal devices within the reclamation law for assuring proper use of resources and prevention of monopoly were, respectively, a grant of interest-free money for constructing dams and the excess lands provision. This provision sets a maximum of water deliveries to any individual; no one may obtain more than enough to irrigate 160 acres. The excess lands provision curbs monopoly and speculation at a stroke. The reader should remember that one irrigated acre equals in production perhaps three acres in the humid parts of the nation. He should remember also that the reclamation law is generous to all private landowners and takes nothing from anybody except by consent.

Theodore Roosevelt and the Congress were following one of the pioneers' most dearly won and dearly held traditions. The first settlers beyond the Alleghenies had struggled against the twin evils of the land monopolists and the speculators, and had written their political victories into the language of the Pre-emption Law of 1841 and the Homestead Law of 1862. It is said to have been T.R. himself who insisted on perpetuating this tradition in the Reclamation Act; at any rate, Congress proclaimed the excess lands provision as one of the principal justifications for voting passage of the bill, and T.R. signed it with pride.

When Congress was debating whether to authorize construction of Pine Flat and Isabella dams, Overton of Louisiana, the senator in charge of the bill, gave emphatic assurance to Senator Lister Hill of Alabama, and to the Senate, that the reclamation law would be applied. Without this assurance the bill would certainly have failed. Congress was willing to authorize construction of these dams only under the established principles of the Square Deal.

Reasonable men would suppose that Congress had settled these issues of monopoly and speculation in 1944. But writing a law is one thing, and administering it sometimes turns out to be quite another. Complaisant administration by Secretary of the Interior Douglas McKay is in a fair way to make true the gloomy prophecy of water monopoly at public expense made by the *Visalia Delta* in 1877. In the language of the sports page, he is KO-ing the Square Deal on the Kings and Kern.

The cost of Pine Flat and Isabella dams is around $39 million and $21 million, respectively. Most of this outlay turns out to be a free gift from the taxpayer. If and when administrators get signatures from beneficiaries on a contract of repayment, the amount returned to the Treasury will be only about 36 percent of the cost of Pine Flat Dam. The public will be left holding the bag, paying for the other 64 percent. McKay, it is true, did not set this low repayment figure, but he could review it if he chose to do so, or ask the Army Engineers to review it. Evidently, as the *Delta* said, "the people will at last have it to pay for."

Loss of a few million dollars to the Treasury to build a dam is by no means the worst prospect. Far more disturbing is McKay's willingness to validate the rest of the forecast, viz., that the large landholders would secure "the ownership of the water as well as of the land." He has chosen to open the door to complete and permanent nullification of the excess lands law.

Secretary McKay is now negotiating a repayment contract with Kings River water users that should have been signed before the dam was begun. Reclamation officials tried, but failed mainly because excess landholding interests were able to persuade Congress year after year to appropriate money to build the dams, while their spokesmen went through the motions of negotiation but never signed. Probably they hoped that by stalling long enough a way might turn up to let them out of compliance with the excess lands law. McKay now shows them the way. He offers to accept lump sum prepayment for the dam, and as soon as the cash is laid on the barrelhead, to relieve all excess lands of the obligation to comply with the law now and forever.

How does the Secretary arrive at this curious position that would strike most observers as a complete inversion of the intention of the law? By building a house of cards, with a joker in the deck. In 1944, at the very time Congress was making certain that the excess lands law would be enforced at Pine Flat, it gave the executive an option in procedure, to accept either lump sum or annual installments in payment, at discretion. Three years later, in 1947, subordinates in Interior expressed the opinion that making the final repayment of construction charges relieves excess lands of the law. No statute says this. Other subordinates then said that lump sum prepayment relieves excess lands of the law entirely. No statute says this. McKay is willing to regard both as the law.

Now comes the joker. Unsound as these subordinates' opinions are, and unknown to a determined Congress in 1944, they do not require McKay to act as he does. No opinions, rulings, or statutes bind him to accept prepayment. To offer to let the excess landholders on Kings River escape the law by buying their way out is his own personal choice and responsibility.

The excess landholders, representing great power and influence, are massed heavily behind McKay's offer. They have been battling the excess lands provision for fifteen years. They are often men of energy and ability; some of them have farmed their lands skillfully with meager and uncertain water supplies. They feel they are entitled to whatever gains they can get. But the stark fact remains that they sought help from the federal government to develop their water supply, and the excess lands provision is the standard condition under which public aid is given.

Landownerships on Kings River are very large. In one water district alone, known as Tulare Lake Basin, 25 corporations own around 165 square miles, or 105,000 acres. Single holdings reach 12,000 and 19,000 acres each. There is virtually no farm home on the entire fertile 300-square mile district. There could be many when reclamation is completed, but probably there will be few if the great landholders of Tulare Lake Basin can press their way through the door that McKay is now holding open for them.

The financial stake of excess landholders is roughly measurable. The incremental value of a full water supply to nonirrigated but cultivated land is around $460 an acre. The value of adding a half-supply, which comes closer to actual conditions on much of the Kings River and Tulare Lake project, is around half that, say, a couple of hundred dollars an acre, more or less. A 10,000-acre landowner might stand to gain as much as a couple of million dollars. These bounteous incremental values serve to explain why large landholding individuals and corporations are so insistent on circumventing national reclamation law. They explain the pressures put upon officials who administer the law. They are of generous enough proportions to justify description as a "giveaway."

It is curious how persistently people will misrepresent the facts about a law they do not like. The record of false description by opponents of the excess lands provision is impressive, too long to recite here. Repeated exposure of errors of fact seems not to affect greatly either the repetition of errors or the ardor with which the law is opposed. The latest example is from no less a public figure than former President Herbert Hoover. Perhaps following in the footsteps of newspapers that called the excess lands provision communistic in 1944 while it was under unsuccessful attack in Congress, he interrupted his address on "Federal Socialization of Electric Power" at Case Institute last year to advise his nation-wide radio audience that "apparently," in the view of the excess lands provision, holders of excess lands seeking water from public sources are "Kulaks." Kulaks, as everybody knows, were Russia's expropriated large landowners.

How differently his Republican predecessor President Theodore Roosevelt described the same law! At the Commonwealth Club of California in 1912, T.R. said in debate, "Now I have struck the crux of my appeal. I wish to save the very wealthy men of this country and their advocates and upholders from the ruin that they would bring upon themselves if they were permitted to have their way. It is because I am against revolution; it is because I am against the doctrines of the Extremists, of the Socialists; it is because I wish to see this country of ours continued as a genuine democracy; it is because I distrust violence and disbelieve in it; it is because I wish to secure this country against ever seeing a time when the 'have-nots' shall rise against the 'haves'; it is because I wish to secure for our children and our grandchildren and for their children's children the same freedom of opportunity, the same peace and order and justice that we have had in the past."

PAUL S. TAYLOR

It is nothing new for Presidents, Republican or Democratic, to turn against the principles of their predecessors. It need not have surprised anyone when Herbert Hoover joined with President Eisenhower in dedicating Sagamore Hill as a national shrine to Theodore Roosevelt's memory while, together, they were engaged in undermining one of the greatest monuments of statute and principle that T.R. had himself set up.

If the excess landholders can breach the reclamation dike on Kings River the day when all excess landowners can escape the law will be brought closer. The prospect can be spelled out. In the southern San Joaquin Valley alone, within the Central Valley of California, some 30-odd corporations and individuals own about three-quarters of a million irrigable acres in the present or prospective service area of the Central Valley project and its extensions. The smallest of these holdings is 5,000 acres. In a single west side water district of about 400,000 acres, a single owner holds 65,000 acres. Unless McKay interprets the law correctly, and/or changes his own policy, it is likely that any of these excess landholders who can first persuade the public to construct projects to bring them water will buy their way out of the law. Why not? It will pay them well.

As the gains to excess landholders from defeat of the excess lands law are measurable in dollars, so also are a part of the losses to the public. Aside from loss to the federal Treasury under the prospective repayment contract, the merchants of the new local communities in the southern San Joaquin will have to make out with an annual dollar volume of trade smaller by about 40 percent, if the large landholders are allowed to have their way. This estimate rests on the famous comparative study of Arvin and Dinuba, two towns between the Kings and Kern, founded respectively on large-scale agriculture and on working farmers. Opportunity for professional men in law and medicine, for dealers in real estate, and for members of service trades will be reduced correspondingly. If new farmers ever do buy their way into the area, they will begin their operations saddled with the weight of indebtedness for incremental values that the reclamation law was specifically intended to

WHOSE DAM IS PINE FLAT?

spare them. And they will be poorer customers because of the load they will have to bear.

The price paid by local communities will be even greater and more pervasive than dollar figures can measure. They will have a more floating population, fewer and less stable churches, higher annual turnover of schoolteachers, fewer civic associations, such as clubs, PTA's, and veterans' organizations that enrich daily living and bind citizens together. The Biblical admonition, as you sow so also shall you reap, applies not only to individuals and crops but also to communities.

Americans have always known the dangers of a highly stratified society, and have sought to avoid it. Perhaps Secretary McKay forgets this, now that he has it in his hands to preserve or to destroy. If so, he ought to be reminded. The tradition is bipartisan, and has the names of the greatest Democrats and Republicans alike associated with it.

In the year 1776 Thomas Jefferson secured passage in the colonial legislature of Virginia of his famous bill to abolish entailed estates. His language bears repeating. "In the earlier times of the colony," he said, "when lands were to be had for little or nothing, some provident individuals procured large grants: . . . desirous of founding great families. . . . The transmission of this property from generation to generation, in the same name, raised up a distinct set of families . . . privileged by law in the perpetuation of their wealth (and) thus formed into a patrician order. . . . To annul this privilege, and instead of an aristocracy of wealth, more harm and danger than benefit to society, to make an opening for the aristocracy of virtue and talent, which nature has wisely provided for in the direction of the interests of society, and scattered with equal hand through all its conditions, was deemed essential to a well-ordered republic." Primogeniture went out the same way, and Americans of a former day felt secure that monopoly of the land and of the power over the lives of other men which it confers never would survive in America. In 1820, in an address commemorating the two hundredth anniversary of the landing of the Pilgrims, Daniel Webster told how the New England ancestors had left behind them "the whole feudal policy of the other continent." "They were themselves," he declared, "either from their original condition or from the necessity of their common interest, nearly on a level in respect to property. Their situation demanded a parceling out and division of the land, and it may fairly be said that this necessary act fixed the future frame and form of their Government. . . . The consequence of all these causes has been a great subdivision of the soil and a great equality of condition; the true basis, most certainly, of popular government." In the spirit of this tradition Abraham Lincoln signed the Homestead Act in 1862, and Theodore Roosevelt approved the excess lands law, to give families an opportunity to own the land they tilled.

Handing out huge water deliveries to a few will not add a cubit to our claims to moral leadership of the free world, nor enhance our reputation for knowing how to relieve agrarian distress. It will not elevate our prestige with the masses toiling on Asian lands, whose confidence we need so urgently.

The issue whether an administrator is to be permitted to scuttle the historic excess lands provision is not of concern to Californians alone, nor to the present generation in Central Valley only. The same, and similar, devices will be used to destroy national water policy and turn its benefits to the few in almost every part of the United States. Arkansas has prospect of irrigating several million acres, and faces first on Grand Prairie project and later elsewhere, the question whether a plantation form of agriculture is to be perpetuated and strengthened. Will its farm youth, recently driven by drought from the hills to California or Arizona, be limited to similar dubious refuges in the future, or will they be provided farming opportunities at home? Through the Missouri Valley, the East, and the Southeast, the harnessing of water for irrigation in the future raises the same question in places where it has not been thought of before. The issue is truly national now. The spotlight is on California today, but it will move back and forth over the nation as first one locality then another seeks federal support for its project.

There are several bills in Congress to lift the excess lands provision here and there, by one device or another. The Administration itself is now publicly on the side of evasion rather than enforcement, and favors legislative as well as administrative devices to get around reclamation law. On April 9, 1954, the Bureau of the Budget gave the green light to an Interior Department proposal in support of H.R. 5301, to extend federal financial aid for irrigation to local districts, with the excess lands provision severed from the transaction. This splits the Square Deal concept of reclamation in two, and tosses the antimonopoly, antispeculation half of it into the discard. It turns a half century of national effort to use water to provide opportunity for poor men who need it, into a program for the rich. We are being pushed to the brink of the end of the reclamation era.

The Undersecretary of Interior sought to minimize the evasion proposed in April; he said, as reported in the press, that it would not be widespread. His remark resembles the defense of the young woman whose child was born without benefit of clergy, "But it's such a *little* baby!"

Of course Secretary McKay gives reasons for his emasculation of the excess lands law, but these, as indicated earlier, are no more than a succession of recent shabby administrative opinions and interpretations that have not been subjected either to the sharp challenge from without, or the scrutiny from within, that their momentous public importance requires.

Except that McKay may be easily impressed by powerful people, or his staff may not have informed him very well of the facts, it is not easy to explain his clear preference for excess landholders. He is Republican, but so was T.R., who signed the law restraining their monopolization of water and limiting their speculative gains. He identifies himself as Presbyterian, but his national church organization supports the excess lands law. More than that, the California-Nevada Presbyterian Synod, after restudying the Kings River thoroughly for a year at request of Kings River spokesmen, refused to withdraw its staunch support of the law. The Secretary is a member of four national veterans organizations, all of them on public record favoring the excess lands provision. One of them, the Veterans of Foreign Wars, through its California Department, has attacked prepayment on Kings River publicly as an injury to the interests of veterans. A veteran of proved physical courage, McKay is not moved to brush away the weak and unsound counsel of subordinates, and like a courageous predecessor in 1913 to declare: "I am satisfied that Congress did not intend those reclaimed lands, upon which the Government is expending the money of all the people, should be the subject of corporate control. These lands are to be the homes of families."

If McKay was more in sympathy with the purposes of the reclamation law, i.e., if he was interested in the heart of the problem, he would withdraw his offer to accept lump sum prepayment while ordering a thorough review of his subordinates' opinions. He would take a serious look at the real issues on which he has chosen to line up beside large and powerful interests. He would give thought to the long and close relationships between large landholdings and landless people, heavy rural relief loads, hordes of migratory laborers, labor conflict, and wetbacks. Then he could make up his mind whether to use the powers of high office to strengthen and perpetuate this situation.

Citizens who know American history and the struggle to achieve a society not dominated by the privileged few will have deep concern over the "to the rear, march" maneuver now being executed by the national administration in an effort to bypass Theodore Roosevelt's most farsighted and principled legislation, as inconspicuously but effectively as possible. While our eyes are glued to TV, watching to see if Congress can usurp the functions of the Executive, shall we overlook it when the Executive invades the domain of the Congress?

California newspapers said in advance that 15,000 persons were expected to join the dedication ceremonies at Pine Flat Dam on May 22. The weather was fine and the day was Saturday. The papers reported afterward that only about 3,000 came. Perhaps more citizens would have been present if they had felt that it was really their dam, that they had more to celebrate.

RECLAMATION AND EXPLOITATION

The People's Land
The People's Water
The People's Money
The People's Lives

RECLAMATION & EXPLOITATION

PAUL S. TAYLOR

EVER HEAR OF RECLAMATION law's 160-acre limitation on water deliveries to irrigators? Have you been told that this is "petty political tyranny," inefficient and uneconomic? That because of it the housewife pays more for food in the market? That it is an outmoded myth from bygone times? That it should be eliminated, as the Public Land Law Review Commission, under former Congressman Wayne Aspinall, recommended? (More recently, Senator Lee Metcalf of Montana called this body the "National Watered-Down Commission" because the Nixon Administration replaced members friendly to "the 160.")

Or have you heard that the 160 is a true conservation instrument, essential if properly used, for achieving a decent environment, even for preserving a decent rural society from self-destruction? Ever hear that in Imperial Valley, where the law goes unenforced, almost nine out of ten farm workers (87.3 percent) belong to the economic lower class, compared to, say, Iowa, just outside the reclamation belt, where the proportion is less than one in seven (13.6 percent)? Ever hear that the Sierra Club, joined by Friends of the Earth, National Wildlife Federation, and other civic and labor organizations, sees opportunity for using the 160 to check reclamation's current diseconomies, and through public planning to preserve open spaces and a decent physical and social environment?

Each generation defines "conservation" for itself. Today we are witnessing a great revival of public concern for conservation, and an expanding definition of its meaning. The word itself entered popular usage in the early 20th century, but action came earlier. Preservation of rare and scenic sites came first, notably Yellowstone Park. At that time, when men talked of water they spoke of "reclamation"—"irrigation" if too little, or "flood control" if too much. Only later was the word "conservation" used to cover alike preservation of sites and proper use of resources. Today, "environment" and "ecology" are added to "conservation," and Secretary of the Interior Rogers C. B. Morton reminds us that the meaning of environment "must include man himself." In so doing he opens doors and raises more questions than his department answers.

By whatever name you call it, national reclamation policy is a conservation perennial. It could not be otherwise. It seeks to govern the use and misuse of natural resources—millions of irrigated acres of land, more millions of acre-feet of water, and billions of public

Paul S. Taylor, Professor Emeritus of Economics at the University of California, Berkeley, is co-author (with photographer Dorothea Lange) of American Exodus: A Study in Human Erosion, *which was originally published in 1943 and reissued in 1969 by Yale University Press.*

7

dollars to store the water and—at a right time and place—to move it to thirsty land. Who decides how much water is to be taken from where, and moved to where? Who pays? Who benefits?

The search for answers began in 1902, when Congress enacted the Reclamation Law. Particular attention was given to the last question: who benefits? Congressman Francis G. Newlands of Nevada explained as the bill was pending that President Theodore Roosevelt had invited members of the House Irrigation Committee of both parties to the White House for consultation. Personally familiar with the extent of large private landholdings in the West, Roosevelt, in Newland's words, ". . . was somewhat in doubt as to whether the bill was sufficiently guarded in the interest of homeseekers. . . . We all wanted to preserve that domain in small tracts for actual settlers. . . . We all wanted to prevent monopoly and concentration of ownership, and the result was that certain changes were made absolutely satisfactory both to the Executive and to the Irrigation Committee. . . ." With these changes, he said, the reclamation law would assure "above all, holding that vast [western] area for the unborn generations . . . in your States of the East . . . the Middle West, and . . . the South, to be held as a heritage for the entire people . . . dedicated forever to American home building, the true foundation of the Republic." These concluding words were greeted with "applause" and the bill became law, reciting that "No right to the use of water for land in private ownership shall be sold for a tract exceeding 160 acres to any one landowner, and no such sale shall be made to any landowner unless he be an actual bona fide resident on such land, or occupant thereof residing in the neighborhood. . . ."

Building on this foundation President Roosevelt in 1908 assembled the first Conference of Governors of the States. Natural resources was its subject, and its title was "Conference on Conservation." In the spirit of the Reclamation Act, the Declaration of the Governors states: "We declare our firm conviction that this conservation of our natural resources is a subject of transcendent importance, which should engage unremittingly the attention of the Nation, the States, and the People in earnest cooperation. We agree that the sources of national wealth exist for the benefit of the People, and that monopoly thereof should not be tolerated."

However, neither a governors' declaration nor even a statutory enactment suffices to ensure adherence to principle and law. Only the other day, 71 years after passage of the Reclamation Act, with its prohibition of water monopoly, the *San Francisco Chronicle* appropriately headlined a story on the law with these words: "The Endless Water War of the 160." To anyone familiar with western history this need be no surprise. As long ago as 1877, the "war" was forecast by the *Visalia* (California) *Delta*, and the questions raised: Who pays? and, Who benefits? In words that serve as text for this phase of a century of western history the *Delta* reported: "No one would believe that shrewd, calculating business men would invest their money on the strength of land rising in value while unimproved, for even the farmer himself has to abandon it who endeavors to add to its value without water. At the same time, purchasers are not lacking who would add it to their already extensive dry domain and the people . . . will find themselves confronted by an array of force and talent to secure capital ownership of the water as well as of the land, and the people will at last have it to pay for. . . ."

The forecast came true. In 1947, a Bureau of Reclamation economist testified that the subsidy to water users along the Friant-Kern Canal in California's Central Valley was 75 percent or more of the cost of providing the water. In 1957, six California Congressmen estimated that the *unrepaid* federal subsidy to landowners for watering Central Valley Project lands amounted to $577 an acre, or $92,320 for 160 acres, exclusive of flood-control subsidy. On the entire project, irrigation was allocated 63 percent of cost, but irrigators were asked to repay only 17 percent. On western projects generally, recent estimates place the unrepaid subsidy to irrigators at from $400 to $2,000 an acre, varying from project to project. These subsidies tell who pays, and give half the answer to who benefits. Interior Secretary Harold Ickes rounded out the answer in 1945, corroborating the 1877 forecast of the *Visalia Delta*. The drive to avoid application of "the 160" designed to distribute reclamation benefits among "the many" instead of among "the few," he explained, is simply "the age-old battle over who is to cash in on the unearned increment in land values created by a public investment."

That is how sympathetic administrators up to a generation ago de-

> ". . . in Imperial Valley, almost nine out of ten farm workers belong to the economic lower class."

scribed the issue and pointed the direction in which solution lay. They did not say they wanted public planning of the environment in the reclamation belt, but clearly they were unwilling to leave the outcome to self serving, large landholding interests. Yet no one has described more realistically how decisions have been made than William E. Warne, former Assistant Commissioner of Reclamation. In 1973 he wrote: "Since June 17, 1902 . . . projects have been undertaken where a sufficient number of representatives and senators desired them and when congressmen who wanted the work done were strategically placed on committees in which authorizations or appropriations were originating in order to get the necessary action." Aside from engineering considerations, that describes past land use planning only too well.

Five years ago the Sierra Club took fresh look at the problem and sought ways of doing something about it. To begin with, the law says that in order to receive water, the owners of "excess lands" above 160 acres must agree to sell the excess at the pre-water price literally "without reference to the proposed construction of the irrigation works. . . ."

The Sierra Club, concerned to preserve the environment, has proposed taking full advantage of this opportunity. It proposed in 1968 the "federal purchase of excess lands . . . with the understanding that lands so purchased would be sold or leased under open space regulations."

The idea caught on. Congressman Robert W. Kastenmeier of Wisconsin introduced a Reclamation Land Authority Bill to fulfill unrealized potentials of the historic 1902 statute that marked the dawn of the nation's conservation movement. Suppo came quickly. Identical bills were introduced in the 92nd Congress by six California Congressmen: George Danielson, Ron Dellums, Don Edwards, John McFall, Edward Roybal, and Jerome Waldie. Four Senators did likewise: Birch Bayh, Alan Cranston, Fred Harris, and Philip Hart. The Interior Committees, then chaired by Congressman Wayne Aspinall and Senator Henry M. Jackson, have so far held no hearings on the bill.

Congressman Kastenmeier sees the public stake in his bill in the broadest terms inviting coalition support. Its purposes he described as three-fold: "One, to enact a long overdue, and long recommended, method for enforcing the public interest provisions of reclamation law; two, to finance public education by grants of revenues created from public water development, just as grants of 94 million acres of public lands financed public education at an earlier point in our history; and three, to enable the public itself, through a newly established authority, to plan the environment that public water development creates." The proposal has drawn support from other conservation, civic, and labor organizations, including the National Education Association, and awaits hearings.

The bill's potential for preserving rural open space has been estimated at 900,000 acres in California alone, provided "the 160" is fully enforced. It could curb the inroads being made on prime agricultural land by urban sprawl in critical areas, notably in California and Arizona, where the opportunity for conserving agricultural land is confronted by considerable resistance. Enforcement of "the 160" would also discourage large corporate farm combines from continuing to push for further water reclamation projects, which, for the most part, have proven uneconomical for everyone but them. Finally, by encouraging smaller family farms, enforcement of "the 160" would give us a better chance to get away from our present dependence on pesticides and inorganic fertilizers, the use of which seems closely tied to large-farm economies.

In 1962, Senator Paul Douglas, of Illinois, threw light on the paralysis of reclamation policy that nominally, but not actually, governs water development in this country. Commenting on the circumvention of reclamation policy on the California Water Project, he told the Congress: "I think we all know the practical difficulties in such a situation as this. The land is owned at present by a relatively small number of persons and corporations, each one of which owns an enormous amount of land....They are organized, powerful . . . do not wish to have their holdings broken up . . . and . . . can marshal tremendous resources in support of their position and against anyone who tries to stand against them. . . . Those who might benefit from the acreage limitation . . . the small farmers who would come into being . . . if the huge holdings were broken up are persons in the future . . . they lack voices and in a sense are unrepresented."

Republican California Congressman Donald L. Jackson spelled out in 1949 what this means on the Salt River in Arizona, a project initiated a half-century ago and on the boards for expansion. "It is true that under reclamation law," he said, "each individual ownership is entitled to 160 acres of irrigated land. However, in the Salt River area alone, which contains more than two-thirds of the proposed Arizona project, there are 995 ownerships in excess of reclamation law. About 32 percent of the irrigable land in this one area is held in excess ownership.

"True, the Bureau of Reclamation says that the 160-acre law will be enforced. . . . But we know that this law has never been enforced there. There is no reason to believe it will be enforced in the future. Rather, there is every reason to believe that it will not be enforced. . . . If the . . . project should be authorized . . . the idle land now held by the big landowner will immediately increase in value six to ten times. If . . . the large landowner should be forced to sell all but 160 acres, he would, of course, sell at tremendous profit."

Opportunity for public environmental planning was likewise circumscribed by bureaucratic circumvention of the law in the Sacramento Valley. In 1964, the *Sacramento Union* reported "an historic compromise" after endless negotiations. The settlement allows excess land owners, by various devices, to "get the water without having to break up their farms. . . . Thus a battle which has been waged since 1944 when Shasta Dam was built, ended." The *Union* forecast this ricochet: "Similar contracts are also being prepared for use in San Luis Project water." As part of the so-called compromise, the Bureau of Reclamation abandoned all attempts to collect repayment for 19 years' use of project water by the Sacramento diverters.

In 1933, a Secretary of the Interior ruled that the excess-land law does not apply to Imperial Valley, California, although the valley is saved from inundation and served in other ways by the Boulder Canyon Project. There, as noted earlier, nearly nine of ten "farm personnel" belong to the "lower class," and 4.4 percent belong to the "upper class." Half of the irrigated lands of the valley are owned in parcels larger than 160 acres. The secretary's executive assistant, a distinguished water attorney, recorded his opinion contrary to the secretary's ruling previous to its issuance, and subsequently testified before Congress that the law simply "has been ignored." Today the issue is before the Ninth Circuit Court of Appeals. It got

"We all wanted to preserve that domain for actual settlers. We all wanted to prevent monopoly..."

there, not through the insistence of the Departments of Interior and Justice, but through the persistence of 123 landless Imperial Valley residents alerted and guided by a Brooklyn physician who had come to the valley to practice medicine.

One could go on and on. The devices destructive of public control over water and land monopoly are infinite, and thoroughly exploited. With their success and spread, opportunity for public planning of open space and the environment recedes.

Why is it so hard to obtain enforcement of the reclamation law at the hands of officials who administer it? Why is law observance relegated as a last resort to the courts, with the initiative and the costs of preserving what the law promised them left so largely to farm families and the landless? Can it be that bureaucrats perceive more clearly than others that "the 160" is indeed—as alleged—no more than "petty political tyranny," and inefficient and uneconomic besides? That it is a burden on consumers? That it is an outmoded myth from long ago? And that wisely in the public interest they relax enforcement to a bare gesture? This is the burden of unending public-relations attacks upon national reclamation policy and law. Can it be true? The questions call for specific answer.

Is "the 160" really "petty political tyranny" imposed upon landowners of more than 160 acres? In 1958, the U.S. Supreme Court listened to argument calling the law formally "a taking of vested property rights both in land and ... water," and charging that it "discriminate[s] between the non-excess and the excess landowner." The Court's immediate response was that "We cannot agree. . . . In short, the project is a subsidy, the cost of which will never be recovered in full." The 160-acre law, continued the Court, does not deprive owners of excess lands "of any rights to property or water." In other words, the claim of "petty political tyranny" seeks unsuccessfully to turn the truth bottom-side up.

Does "the 160" render agricultural production inefficient and uneconomical? On September 18, 1971, the *California Farmer* undertook to evaluate the charge that it does. In carefully chosen words it said: "What happens when irrigation water is introduced into the arid area? Does the 160-acre limitation help or hinder? What does farming become under imposed conditions? Southern Tulare County may not give a final answer, but it is old enough so there is a pattern of farming emerging. . .'. Short-term financing has become almost routine. Methods to make agriculture profitable are working. Economies of big production are in evidence. Also, the economies of the small producer are there. Farm planning has been brought to engineering perfection. Production costs have been held if not actually reduced. . . . This has been done even in the face of the accusation that the limitation was throttling, rather than helping agriculture. The limitation rule actually appears to be solving long-term financing for many owners. . . . In this operation, efficiencies usually attributed to large acreages can be met and perhaps surpassed by an owner of less than 160 acres. . . . The barren land of southeast Tulare County is fast becoming a profitable garden with high-quality country living." Here it may be noted that the average irrigated farm in California is 142 acres.

Is "the 160" a burden on consumers, who might fare better with products from much larger producing units? Comparing the market impact of larger with smaller farms, Philip M. Raup, Professor of Agricultural Economics at the University of Minnesota, testified in 1972: "The large farm appears to be efficient, cost-conscious, and the source of much of our efficiency in agricultural production. But ... if there are only large farms, the potentials for collusion, market sharing, restrictions on entry of new firms, and outright supply control are enormously increased. It is a part of our mythology of large farms that they are efficient. But the key question is: efficient at what? For very large farms, the answer is clear: At the exercise of market power ... the effects of concentration in agriculture are quite likely to drive up the relative price of food in the long run." And Raup pointed out that "What is now needed is a research effort that will alert communities to the potential environmental costs of large-scale agri-business firms."

With these diversionary allegations examined—tyranny, inefficiency, high production costs, and high market prices—we return to the fundamentals of conservation and wholesome environment. The admonition of the original Governors' Conference on Conservation not to tolerate resource monopoly is not out of date, although in practice it remains in jeopardy. The same is true of the 1902 statute's preference for public planning of water and land use over private speculation. The Supreme Court's reassurance that the meaning of the 160-acre limitation is that reclamation projects are "designed to benefit people, not land," has a very modern ring. The fate of this principle is uncertain, however, notwithstanding approval by the highest court. As remarked earlier, administrators relax enforcement under pressure.

A conspicuous example is the State Water Project of California. Faced with the prospect that Congress would refuse to exempt Federal Central Valley Project from acreage limitation, *Business Week* reported on March 13, 1944, that "If the big landowners in the valley lose out in this particular fight they have several other proposals to accomplish their end. One of them . . . said to have originated among the big landowners of Fresno County, is for the State of California to take over the Central Valley project, paying the entire bill." Years elapsed, but finally the idea took hold.

In 1960 the voters of California, assured that the project "will pay for itself," approved a $1.75-billion bond issue by a small margin. They were ill-informed that motivation for the state project was to escape acreage limitation; likewise that three of the State's senators and Governor Brown had publicly assured Congress, in Brown's words, that "the State of California will commit itself to invest more than $11 billion . . . over and above the Federal program." Outlay on the state project already has reached $2.8 billion, not including the huge interest payments this commits the state to make to retire construction costs. In water-receiving districts such as Metropolitan Water District in Southern California, property owners pay for project water whether they receive any or not, and the state's taxpayers, north and south, underwrite the entire bill:

Notwithstanding that Congress—besought to exempt the state project from acreage limitation while allowing joint use of reservoir, pumping, and canal facilities—had debated for six days and refused exemption, administrators signed a federal-state contract minus any provision for acreage limitation.

A decade has elapsed awaiting challenge of the administrators' omission of acreage-limitation law from the contract. It has been left to private citizens to undertake this. Now four Central Valley family farmers have brought suit in San Francisco Federal District Court. Two conservation organizations—the Sierra Club and the North Coast Rivers Association—have asked to intervene in the case on the side of the farmers seeking observance of the law. On August 2, 1973, the presiding judge granted their motion. This is a great step to assure full airing of the conservation and environmental essence of a law that too many, for too long, have assumed was little more than an economic technicality. The Sierra Club, with others, is moving into a key role in two branches of government, to represent the public interest in preservation of a decent environment, practically and effectively.

WALTER GOLDSCHMIDT'S
BAPTISM BY FIRE

WALTER GOLDSCHMIDT'S BAPTISM BY FIRE: CENTRAL VALLEY WATER POLITICS

PAUL S. TAYLOR[1]
Department of Economics
University of California, Berkeley

> A social scientist employed by the government frequently finds himself in the midst of a political battle, the object of harsh criticism by some groups and warm praise by others. . . . People with a point of view that conflicts with his own treat him in a rough fasion, while other groups, who evaluate the situation as he does, see him as an ally. And, try as he might to escape by assuming a neutral pose and insisting that as a scientist he is above the battle, the conflicting groups bar the door. His values determine his relations with other people, draw him into the fight and keep him there.
>
> —Richard S. Kirkendall[2]

The best way to describe the entry of Walter R. Goldschmidt into the profession of social scientists is to call it "baptism by fire." Of course it wasn't called that at the time. When first published in 1946, the title of his research was couched in sober academic language, reading: "Small Business and the Community: A Study in Central Valley of California on Effects of Scale of Farm Operations."[3]

The author was careful to state his "methods of research," from which the following is an excerpt:

> A variety of techniques were used to gather the data upon which this study is based. Fundamental were the schedules which afford data on population, composition, social participation, and level of living They were obtained by two field enumerations, over a period of four weeks in each community (spring 1944) based upon a 10-percent sample of the houses in the town and surrounding country. The information from this source was enriched by interviews with community leaders taken by the author. The area surrounding each community was determined by a well-established technique of

community delineation long used by rural sociologists and executed by a person trained in its application.[4]

And so on. This was the academic spirit and climate in which the comparison was made of two communities, the one, Arvin, based upon large-scale farms and the other, Dinuba, based upon smaller family-size farms.

The published study spelled out its findings in specific factual comparisons of the two communities, measured in numbers where feasible:

> The small farm supports in the local community a larger number of people per dollar volume of agricultural production . . . a difference in its favor of about 20 percent . . . people in the small-farm community have a better average standard of living than those living in the community of large-scale farms. . . .
> Over one-half the breadwinners in the small-farm community are independently employed businessmen, persons in white-collar employment, or farmers; in the large-farm community the proportion is less than one-fifth. . . . Less than one-third of the breadwinners in the small-farm community are agricultural wage laborers (characteristically landless, and with low and insecure income) while the proportion of persons in this position reaches the astonishing figure of nearly two-thirds of all persons gainfully employed in the large-farm community. . . .
> Physical facilities for community living—paved streets, sidewalks, garbage disposal, sewage disposal, and other public services—are far greater in the small-farm community; indeed, in the industrial-farm community some of these facilities are entirely wanting. . . . Schools are more plentiful and offer broader services in the small-farm community . . . the large-farm community has but a single elementary school. . . . The small-farm community is provided with three parks for recreation; the large-farm community has a single playground, loaned by a corporation. . . .
> The small-farm community has more than twice the number of organizations for civic improvement and social recreation . . . Boy Scout troops, and similar facilities for enriching the lives of the inhabitants . . . two newspapers, each with many times the news space carried in the single paper of the industrialized-farm community. . . . Churches bear the ratio of 2:1. . . .
> Facilities for making decisions on community welfare through local popular elections are available to people in the small-farm community; in the large-farm community such decisions are in the hands of officials of the county.[5]

This was the academic tone of the study's conclusions when finally they appeared in print. But their impact did not await their publication, nor even their tentative formulation. Their probable nature was surmised and the study itself exposed to slashing attack in the national political arena before the staff completed gathering the field data.

Evidently Congressman Alfred J. Elliott of California felt pretty sure of what the conclusions would be; they would favor Dinuba, and this would interfere with his political interests. Although both Arvin and Dinuba were within his district, his immediate aim was to persuade Congress to exempt large landowners from the historic reclamation law limiting deliveries of irrigation water to holdings not larger than 160 acres and requiring the recipient to be resident upon the land or in the neighborhood.[6] According to tabulation by the Bureau of Reclamation, in an area largely within the congressman's district, thirty-four landowners together owned nearly three-quarters of a million acres, much of it potentially irrigable.[7]

Secretary of the Interior Harold L. Ickes described the issue as "the age-old battle over who is to cash in on the unearned increment in land values created by a public investment."[8] Confirming this later in its own words, the United States Supreme Court was to say that the purpose of reclamation is to distribute benefits "in accordance with the greatest good to the greatest number of individuals" and to prevent "the use of the federal reclamation service for speculative purposes."[9]

On March 22, 1944, Elliott's attack upon this law and policy broke out into the open. Although the House Flood Control Committee had held extensive hearings on proposed projects, none were held on the Elliott rider to the rivers and harbors bill to which the exemption was attached as a committee amendment. Thus it came to the floor for a vote virtually without notice. Although opposed on the floor by spokesmen for the Interior Department, the exemption rode through to victory in about twenty minutes of floor debate.

But now the issue was in the open, and headed for hot debate in the Senate. Hardly twenty-four hours after his exemption victory in the House, Congressman Elliott took his issue to the floor again, this time to attack the Arvin-Dinuba study. He inserted in the Record a letter signed by Walter R. Goldschmidt inviting help from the University of California Bureau of Occupations in recruiting qualified recent graduates from the San Joaquin Valley for six to eight weeks' employment taking questionnaire schedules in the valley communities of Arvin and Dinuba.

Then Elliott began his attack on the study:

> I am wondering at this particular time just where we are heading. Here are the taxpayers of the Nation, and you are asking them to produce food in great quantities. You are asking their cooperation, and then we turn around with the Department of Agriculture, right out of our own Federal bureau here, setting up one of the silliest things I ever heard of.
>
> In my State we do not have to have somebody running around asking people how they can live. We are living all right out there. If some of these bureau heads would just tend to their own business and let the farmers operate their own business once in a while, we would get along a whole lot better. Some silly professor, some dreamer, some man who knows nothing about agriculture, knows nothing about the living conditions of the farmers and the people

who work there, is doing this. I venture to say there is not a State in the Union that has better facilities for the farmers than they have in the State of California or for the laborers who work on the farm. But here we are going to take the taxpayer's money, gasoline we do not have, tires we do not have, and money that we do not have to support some childish dream.[10]

The terrain was different when the Elliott rider reached the Senate. Now the supporters of acreage limitation were forewarned, and they had a public forum in which to voice their objections to exempting Central Valley Project from national reclamation law. Given this opportunity to be heard, spokesmen from organized labor, Grange, and National Catholic Rural Life Conference, among others, appeared as witnesses before the Senate Commerce Subcommittee urging retention of law and policy favoring family-size farms. Advocates of exemption also spoke up in the same forum. Neither side overlooked the relevance of the study in progress comparing the Arvin and Dinuba communities.

The Senate Commerce Subcommittee hearings had barely begun when Congressman Elliott let drive again. This time he spread upon the pages of the Congressional Record the text of the questionnaire currently in use as the basis of interviewing for the Arvin-Dinuba study. He said on April 27:[11]

> ... several weeks ago my attention was called to a situation in my State where the Department of Agriculture was sending people about to secure from the farmers answers to certain questions ... listen to this silly stuff. ... These investigators are going out into the agricultural communities with a lot of these silly, asinine questions, when the farmers are trying to produce foodstuffs despite the shortage in manpower, when part of their help has been taken away from them.

Another California congressman, John Phillips, joined in by attacking the investigator:

> I think the gentleman should say that the snooper that did that is being paid $212 a month and $5.60 a day for the expenses of his car, and he is promised that the bureau of the Department of Agriculture will see that he gets the necessary gasoline, in spite of the fact that the farmers cannot get gasoline.

Resuming his remarks about the questionnaire, and after thanking his California colleague for his "contribution," Congressman Elliott said:

> ... in all seriousness now, this country is at war. We hear talk about the shortage of paper, about the shortage of manpower, about the shortage of tires and gasoline; yet many people are on the pay roll, going around and taking up the time of people who have something else to do besides giving answers to these silly questions. The taxpayers are paying for all this. I just do not like it, and I wonder how long Congress is going to sit around here without putting a stop to this foolishness.

At the Senate hearings Marion Clawson, Goldschmidt's superior in the Berkeley Regional Office of the Bureau of Agricultural Economics, summarized the study's preliminary findings and pointed out that these related to the issue raised by Elliott rider, viz., distribution versus concentration of landownership in Central Valley:

> In every important respect these two communities bear out . . . that where you have family-sized farms you have far better business communities, better communities in which to live and bring up families. We think this is important because ofttimes this relationship of one farming area and the little towns that lie in it is overlooked; so that we have emphasized that point . . . We feel quite strongly if section 4 [the Elliott rider exempting Central Valley Project from acreage limitations] remained in the act, that with the control over size of holding or size of land ownership would go any control over speculation in those lands. . . . That would not only mean a very substantial gain to the owners of these lands, but, more important, as . . . [the spokesman for the Bureau of Reclamation] pointed out this morning, it would mean a very heavy burden on the settlers, a very heavy burden which they might have difficulty in meeting and in succeeding on the project.[12]

Under questioning by Congressman Elliott, Clawson submitted the names of four landholders with over 20,000 acres each, a large portion of it in the congressman's district.

Two farmers presented diametrically opposed views on the Elliott rider to exempt Central Valley Project from acreage limitation. The first was Frank. T. Swett, a 170-acre Contra Costa County farmer:

> Congressman Elliott's own district has for generations been looked upon as a satrapy of "haciendados muy grande" with owners more or less nonresident, astutely managing vast estates, and in coalition with other corporate interests overwhelmingly dominating politics much of the time, perhaps temporarily, but we hope not forever. Vast haciendas, great plantations, land baronies, latifundia, may provide caviar and champagne for the barons, their associates, and their knights in legal armor, but their men who do the work on the acres, in the past, have had rather meager fare and rather meager wages. Vast plantations tend to create irregular employment, to multiply migrant workers, to break down cooperation, and to multiply labor troubles and class antagonisms.
> We are hoping that more of our representatives at Sacramento and our Senators at Washington may decide to give consideration to the agriculture of the family farm, and to consider the welfare of farmers, including the workers on the farms. . . . When our boys return from the war, some will have to become farmers or farm workers. Should they be forced to bow down to the domination of caviar and champagne landowners and to live in barracks, to be deprived of family life, and perhaps to toil alongside great gangs of alien laborers . . .
> Speculators would have a fertile field. . . .[13]

A second view, one favoring the Elliott rider, was expressed by Russell Giffen:

> I operate a family-size farm. It is operated by my wife, my four children, and myself. It is composed of about 42,000 acres . . . we think any boy engaged in agriculture should have the right to go out and achieve all he can if he wants to work hard. . . . I have no quarrel at all with the statement made yesterday by Mr. Clawson and Mr. Tolley that the community in that kind of country they referred to is more satisfactory and sound as a community than a community such as I come from. . . . We do not differ with you in our views that this country ought to be broken up and settled. We differ only that we do not want it done under the threat of some future Secretary of the Interior with that much power in his hands.[14]

Not specifically mentioned, but implicit, was the Secretary's responsibility to deny windfall profits from public investment to owners of lands in access of 160 acres. In words of the Supreme Court, acreage limitation "prevents the use of the federal reclamation service for speculative purposes" and "sets a ceiling, imposed equally upon all participants, on the federal subsidy that is being bestowed."[15]

The Senate Committee killed the Elliot rider, the conference between Senate and House restored it, but the rivers and harbors bill died. Although it carried projects for many districts and was known as the "gravy train," it was held up finally by the threat of Senator Robert M. LaFollette, Jr. of Wisconsin to deliver a three-hour speech against it on the floor of the Senate. Minus the rider, Congress passed the bill when the next session opened.

Two years passed before the completed Arvin-Dinuba study appeared in print. This time the initiative to publicize came from its friends. These were new friends, while old institutional friends whose personnel had made the study in the first place either dragged their feet, or stood silently aside.

The Senate Small Business Committee, not the Bureau of Agricultural Economics whose personnel had made the study, nor the Bureau of Reclamation which had financed it, now took the lead and published the study. Its chairman, Senator James A. Murray of Montana, describes the study in these words:

> . . . here is a detailed analysis, following the approved techniques of social and economic research, of two "case studies." Such careful, unbiased, and impartial scientific collections of facts permit of conclusions having considerable validity and reliability. . . . The data suggest many questions concerning the relative desirability of different types of farm organization as their size and the character of their operations influence the cities which are their trading and cultural centers. . . . The conclusion drawn, and which impresses itself on any unbiased readers as in reality emerging from these

numerous facts, is that the size and character of the farm holdings and operations is responsible in no small degree for the conditions in these cities. On the one hand, in the community surrounded by big farms the social, cultural, and economic attributes of life are developed to a lesser degree than in the other community which is in the midst of an area made up primarily of smaller farms independently operated where the community welfare is of a higher order and more wholesome in every particular.[16]

This language does not reveal the substantial differences of interest within the national bureaucracy that came to the fore. O. V. Wells had replaced Howard Tolley as chief of the Bureau of Agricultural Economics. About the same time appropriations for the Bureau had come under congressional attack. The Arvin-Dinuba study and the acreage limitation issue to which it was related were not the only targets but they were involved. As historian Richard S. Kirkendall has observed,

> Wells and Secretary Clinton Anderson were in no mood to publish such a controversial document [as the Arvin-Dinuba story], for the BAE had just suffered a series of attacks that had produced new restrictions on its activities. One commentator (Business Week) saw the Arvin-Dinuba study as the work that 'brought down the killing blow.'[17]

In retrospect nearly thirty years later, Goldschmidt pointed to the possible effect of such pressures upon the ability of a vulnerable bureaucracy to conduct objective research upon highly controversial issues. He said:

> It was a part of the original research design to engage in a second phase of the study in which we would investigate all the rural communities in the San Joaquin Valley. . . . But a powerful pressure against the study developed, spearheaded by the Associated Farmers and picked up by the national press. Pressure was brought to bear on the BAE, so that its director ordered me to discontinue the investigation after I had completed the work on Arvin and Dinuba. I doubt [that an Arvin-Dinuba type study] could be done within the framework of U.S. Department of Agriculture as it is presently set up. . . . No one really knew how my study was done because of the Secretary's insistence that there be no mention of the Department of Agriculture. . . . It looked as if the Senate Small Business Committee had commissioned the study, which it had done no such a thing.[18]

This helps to explain why nowhere in the published study is there information that it was conducted by staff from the Bureau of Agricultural Economics. Responsibility is attributed solely to "Dr. Walter R. Goldschmidt, Assistant Professor of Anthropology and Sociology, University of California at Los Angeles."

An open battle to exempt Central Valley Project from acreage limitation broke out again in 1947. Sponsors numbered six western Senators and the printed record of the hearings ran to 1326 printed pages.

Naturally the Arvin-Dinuba study surfaced again. A witness for the International Longshoremen's and Warehousemen's Union, for example, reminded the Senate Public Lands Subcommittee that:

> The ideal and purpose of acreage limitation has been stated again and again to be to promote sound communities of independent farmers who will make homes on the land. . . . Dinuba is a good place to live in. Arvin is not.[19]

While the battle was on in Congress to remove acreage limitation law from Central Valley Project the Arvin-Dinuba study remained a football kicked back and forth between the sides. Hardly six months after the end of these 1947 exemption hearings which he dominated, the name of Senator Sheridan Downey of California appeared as author of a book entitled *They Would Rule the Valley*. As evidence of the political effectiveness of the Arvin-Dinuba issue, Downey devoted a chapter of his book to "Two Towns," closing with these words:

> That Arvin will soon pull up beside, and pass, Dinuba is the confident expectation of most Arvinite "boosters." . . . When that day comes, it may be that the people of Arvin, taking second thought, will erect a statue in the city square in grateful memory of Dr. Goldschmidt and his little band. For it is obvious to any visitor that Arvin has now set its heart on proving that Dr. Goldschmidt is as crazy as a jaybird. Already, the town has built up a fair brief for its viewpoint. By the time Arvin has clinched its case, it may realize that one of the most potent stimuli galvanizing it toward great glories will have been the town's most assiduous detractor, and it will honor him accordingly. Arvin may be pardoned, however, if its sculptor depicts Dr. Goldschmidt standing on his head.[20]

Downey argued seriously that the age difference between the two towns was the determining factor of their difference in character, not the predominant size of surrounding farms:

> In reality, of course, Dr. Goldschmidt's determinism is a fake. . . . The factor which Dr. Goldschmidt has conveniently left out of the equation is the really vital one: the difference in ages of the two towns . . . the key to the whole muddled debate.[21]

Thereafter for a score of years the Arvin-Dinuba study lay dormant in the political arena. Those interests demanding removal of acreage limitation law from the Central Valley Project had changed tactics, as the study as a weapon had not helped either Congressman Elliott or Senator Downey even to retain their seats in Congress; by the end of the forties both had lost them. Not until the close of the sixties did congressional interest in the Arvin-Dinuba study revive.

When it did revive, it was friends of the family-size farm, not its opponents, who took the initiative. Aroused by the intrusion of large corporations east of the hundredth meridian dividing the humid and the reclamation belts, they saw the usefulness of the Arvin-Dinuba study as a weapon of resistance, stressing the advantages of the homogenous small-farm community over the divided large-farm community. The Senate Small Business Committee, which had first printed the study in 1946, now reprinted it in 1968. Reprinting was not the occasion for extended discussion, but committee chairman Senator Gaylord Nelson of Wisconsin explained the reason for reviving the study:

> There have been a few individual studies of corporation farming made, including one by this committee some 20 years ago. But, there has not yet been an in-depth, comprehensive investigation of this expanding trend in American agriculture and its implications. There is mounting evidence supplied by private sources and reported by the public news media that more and more corporations are turning to agriculture as a means to diversify their corporate activities.[22]

Four years later, in 1972, the same subcommittee again reprinted the original Arvin-Dinuba Study as part of its hearings on the role of giant corporations and agribusiness.[23] The committee also heard Goldschmidt as an invited witness speaking on his Arvin-Dinuba study.[24] Likewise he testified in Los Angeles at a 1972 hearing conducted by Senator Fred R. Harris.[25]

The public arena was again political, and the subject the same as when the study was attacked by Congressman Elliott and Senator Downey in the mid-forties, but the climate was totally different. This time it was the author of the study testifying at the invitation of two friendly senators. Both favored the study's implications so adverse to large-scale corporate agriculture.

A few excerpts from Goldschmidt's testimony illustrates its scope and temper. He responded in these words to fellow academician Kirkendall who had referred to the author's "eagerness" and "passion":

> There was passion in my response to the actions to suppress the Arvin-Dinuba findings, but it was not the passion to propagandize . . . it was the passionate belief in the right to make the investigation and the right to report its results.[26]

Further, Goldschmidt spoke of the importance of the auspices under which such studies are made, and the need to keep them free from bureaucratic, political pressures.

> It is . . . of the greatest importance, not only that the study be updated, expanded, and brought to bear on areas such as your own State of Wisconsin and elsewhere in the farming heartland, but that it be done with the sponsorship and support of this vital Committee of the United States Senate.[27]

Then Goldschmidt spoke of the "matter of values":

> There is a great confusion about the relationship between science and values. It is generally recognized that the reality of values is not amenable to scientific proof. This is clearly the case, for values are sentiments we hold and share. It is also said that science is value-free, by which it is properly meant that the scientist must set aside his own values in examining the reality of cause and effect. But these two points have led some to assert that science cannot deal with values at all. This is manifestly false, for values regularly enter into scientific study. For example, the President's current all-out effort to analyze the causes of cancer operates on the assumption that cancer is bad and that therefore a cure for cancer is good. These are values that all of us accept. Again, when an economist analyzes the profitability of an enterprise, he takes for granted that it is good to make a profit. Nothing the scientist does validates the assumption that cancer is bad and profits are good; what the scientist does is to determine the causes and conditions under which good or evil will prevail.[28]

Goldschmidt was fully aware of the length and breadth of his issue, and he knew on which side he stood, and why. In 1972 he testified:

> ... there are few who doubt that the nature of rural land tenure is intimately related to the character of the social order. Since the dawn of civilization, when intensive agriculture became the means by which man supplied his basic wants, the control of land has been a basic element in forming the character of society. By and large, where democratic conditions prevail, the man who tilled the soil was a free holder and in control of his enterprise. Where, on the other hand, the farming lands are owned and controlled in the urban centers, and the men engaged in production are merely peasants, serfs, or hired laborers, democratic institutions do not prevail. Those who framed our constitution and set the course of American history believed that this relationship was paramount. It lay behind Jeffersonian democracy; it lay behind the homestead act, and it lay behind the extension of the homestead principles in the development of irrigation under the Reclamation Act as formulated at the beginning of this century.[29]

Walter Goldschmidt's professional research at the beginning of his career produced conclusions favorable to wide distribution rather than concentration of landownership as a determining influence on the quality of life in rural communities. These conclusions gave support to legal provisions of existing federal reclamation law limiting individual deliveries of irrigation water to 160 acre tracts. At the time, that law was under attack by large landed interests, so Goldschmidt's research was caught in the crossfire. Foes of the law led the attack, but were held in check by the law's friends. This was Goldschmidt's baptism by fire.

After two decades, friends of family-sized farms, concerned for their survival across the country, revived and reprinted Goldschmidt's original research. His confirmation, so to speak, came two decades after his baptism.

Notes

1. Martha Chase assisted in preparation of this paper.
2. Richard S. Kirkendall, *Social Science in the Central Valley of California, An Episode*. XLIII California Historical Society Quarterly 195.
3. Small Business and the Community: A Study in Central Valley of California on Effects of Scale of Farm Operations. Report of the Senate special committee to study problems of American small business 79 Cong., 2 sess., pursuant to S. Res. 28, No. 13, 1946. Cited hereafter as Arvin-Dinuba study.
4. Ibid., 7.
5. Ibid., 5, 6.
6. 32 Stat. 389. 1902.
7. Exemption of certain projects from land limitation provisions of federal reclamation laws. Hearings before subcommittee of Senate public lands committee, 80 Con., 1 sess., on S. 912, 864. 1947.
8. *San Francisco News*, December 18, 1946.
9. Ivanhoe v. McCracken, 357 U.S. 275 at 297. 1958.
10. 90 Cong. Rec. 3003. March 23, 1944.
11. 90 Cong. Rec. 3753 ff.
12. Rivers and harbors omnibus bill. Hearings before subcommittee of Senate commerce committee, 78 Cong. 2 sess. on H.F. 3961, 616. 1944.
13. Ibid., 617.
14. Ibid., 698.
15. Ivanhoe v. McCracken, 357 U.S. 275 at 297. 1958.
16. Arvin-Dinuba Study, viii.
17. Kirkendall, *Social Science in the Central Valley*, 206.
18. 118 Cong. Rec. 17947. May 17, 1972.
19. Exemption of certain projects from land limitation provisions of federal reclamation laws. Hearings before subcommittee of Senate public lands committee, 80 Cong., 1 Sess. on S.912, 332-3. 1947.
20. Downey, S. *They Would Rule the Valley*, 192, 1947. Responding to Downey's 1947 claim that in time Arvin would pass Dinuba, Goldschmidt commented to a Senate Committee in 1972:

> Arvin has changed its character. . . . And whereas Arvin and Dinuba had exactly the same economic base in '44 when I was there, I'm sure Arvin's base now has doubled, or tripled, or quadrupled. And I'm also quite sure that if that had been done with 160-acre homestead-like farms, that you would have not had one Arvin almost as good as Dinuba but you would have had two or three or four Dinubas. . . . the nature of the way things went wouldn't have been exactly like Dinuba . . . but they would have been communities.

21. Op. cit., 184. Twenty-five years later, as witness before Senator Fred R. Harris, Goldschmidt gave a professional answer to Senator Downey:

> It is reasonable to ask whether in fact the size of farm differential was the essential determinant of these differences—and needless to say, this question was raised. Research under natural conditions cannot produce those perfect controls that a laboratory will provide, and we examined with great care the alternate hypotheses that were put forward by the critics of this study. The alternate explanation most frequently argued was that Arvin was much younger than Dinuba. When we plotted the

growth of the towns, we found that Arvin was between 20 and 25 years younger, but that the facilities that differentiated the two communities were, in all instances, much older than this differential in age. We also made some comparisons with neighboring towns of Arvin's age where the farms were smaller and these, too, showed a richer local social life than the larger-farm community. We examined also differentials in the cost of production, such as water charges, and found that these were so nearly alike that they could not have had a differentiating effect on the local economy and community life.

118 Cong. Rec. 17948. 1972.

22. Hearings before subcommittee on monopoly of Senate select committee on small business, 90 Cong., 2nd sess., on effects of corporation farming on small business, 1, 2, 295-441. 1968.

23. Role of giant corporations, Hearings before subcommittee on monopoly of Senate select committee on small business, 92 Cong., 1 and 2 sess., 4465-4609. 1972.

24. Statement before Small Business Committee printed in Farmworkers in Rural America 1971-1972, Hearings before subcommittee on migratory labor of Senate committee on labor and public welfare, 92 Cong., 1 and 2 sess., 3306-3328, 3363-3364. 1972.

25. 118 Cong. Rec 17946-17948. 1972.
26. See footnote 24 at 3319.
27. Ibid., 3321-3322.
28. Ibid., 3323-3324.
29. 188 Cong. Rec. 17946. 1972.

THE DEVELOPMENT OF PUBLIC LAND IN THE UNITED STATES

An Arno Press Collection

Bartley, Ernest R. **The Tidelands Oil Controversy.** 1953

Bayard, Charles J. **The Development of the Public Land Policy, 1783-1820, With Special Reference to Indiana** (Doctoral Dissertation, Indiana University, 1956). 1979

Bledsoe, S[amuel] T[homas]. **Indian Land Laws.** 1909

Copp, Henry N[orris]. **Manual for the Use of Prospectors on the Mineral Lands of the United States.** 1897

Copp, Henry N[orris]. **Public Land Laws.** 1875

Copp, Henry N[orris]. **United States Mineral Lands.** 1882

Dana, Samuel Trask and Myron Krueger. **California Lands.** 1958

Davison, Stanley R. **The Leadership of the Reclamation Movement, 1875-1902** (Doctoral Dissertation, University of California, Berkeley, 1952). 1979

Gould, Clarence P. **The Land System in Maryland, 1720-1765.** 1913

Ise, John. **Our National Park Policy.** 1961

Johnson, V. Webster and Raleigh Barlowe. **Land Problems and Policies.** 1954

Martz, Clyde O. **Cases and Materials on the Law of Natural Resources.** 1951

Malone, Joseph J. **Pine Trees and Politics.** 1964

Montgomery, Mary and Marion Clawson. **History of Legislation and Policy Formation of the Central Valley Project.** 1946

O'Callaghan, Jerry A. **The Disposition of the Public Domain in Oregon.** 1960

Peters, William E. **Ohio Lands and Their History.** 1930

Rae, John B. **The Development of Railway Land Subsidy Policy in the United States** (Doctoral Dissertation, Brown University, 1936). 1979

Shambaugh, Benjamin F[ranklin]. **Constitution and Records of the Claim Association of Johnson County, Iowa.** 1894

Smathers, George H. **The History of Land Titles in Western North Carolina.** 1938

Stewart, Lowell O. **Public Land Surveys.** 1935

Tatter, Henry W. **The Preferential Treatment of the Actual Settler in the Primary Disposition of the Vacant Lands in the United States** (Doctoral Dissertation, Northwestern University, 1933). 1979

Taylor, Paul S. **Essays on Land, Water, and the Law in California.** 1979

U.S. House of Representatives. **The Existing Laws of the United States of a General and Permanent Character, and Relating to the Survey and Disposition of the Public Domain, December 1, 1880.** 1884

U.S. House of Representatives. **Laws of the United States:** Of a Temporary Character, and Exhibiting the Entire Legislation of Congress Upon Which the Public Land Titles Have Depended. Two vols. 1881

U.S. Senate. **A National Plan for American Forestry.** Two vols. 1933

U.S. Senate. **The Western Range.** 1936

Wiel, Samuel C. **Water Rights in the Western States.** Two vols. 1911

Winter, Charles E. **Four Hundred Million Acres.** 1932

Wirth, Fremont P. **The Discovery and Exploitation of the Minnesota Iron Lands.** 1937

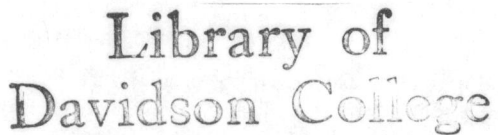